# THE COURT OF JUSTICE
# OF THE
# EUROPEAN COMMUNITIES

WITHDRAWN

AUSTRALIA
LBC Information Services
*Sydney*


CANADA and USA
Carswell
*Toronto*


NEW ZEALAND
Brooker's
*Auckland*


SINGAPORE and MALAYSIA
Sweet & Maxwell (Asia)
*Singapore and Kuala Lumpur*

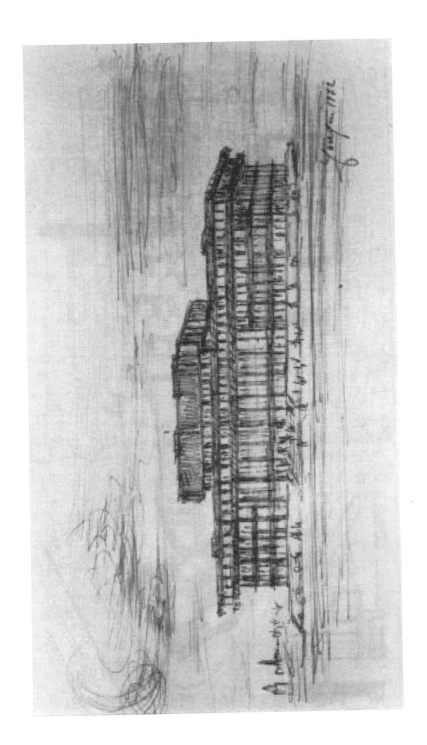

Individual applications for judicial review before the European Court of Justice face many barriers (see Chapter 7). Illustration by Nik Baker published in the *Financial Times*, March 31, 1995.

# THE COURT OF JUSTICE
# OF THE
# EUROPEAN COMMUNITIES

By

## L. NEVILLE BROWN, SOLICITOR

*Emeritus Professor of Comparative Law, University of Birmingham*

## TOM KENNEDY, BARRISTER

*Chief, Press and Public Affairs Unit,*
*International Criminal Tribunal for Rwanda*

FIFTH EDITION

LONDON · SWEET & MAXWELL · 2000

Published in 2000 by
Sweet & Maxwell Limited of
100 Avenue Road, Swiss Cottage, London NW3 3PF
(http://www.sweetandmaxwell.co.uk)
Typeset by LBJ Typesetting Ltd of Kingsclere
Printed in England by Clays Ltd, St Ives Plc.


No natural forests were destroyed to make this product;
only farmed timber was used and replanted


ISBN 0 421 68120 9


A CIP catalogue record for this book
is available from the British Library

# Preface

We completed the last edition of this book in December 1993, just one year before the last enlargement of the European Union by the accession of Austria, Finland and Sweden. In May 1995 an Update in the form of an addendum to that fourth edition took account of the changes made in the judicial architecture of the Union necessitated by those accessions. The incorporation of those changes into the main text, the entry into force of the Treaty of Amsterdam on May 1, 1999 and continuing developments in the case-law of the Court of Justice and the Court of First Instance have made a complete revision of the work somewhat overdue.

Other commitments on both our parts, but especially the departure of half of our partnership to Africa has, inevitably, further delayed the preparation of this new edition. This has, on the one hand, meant that some of the earlier work of revision overtaken by events, required reworking, and that some matters presented as predictions for the future have already come to pass. On the other hand it has given us the opportunity to take account of developments up to the end of June 2000.

The risk of instant obsolescence of printed materials is once again demonstrated by the opening in February 2000 of a new intergovernmental conference among the Member States mandated to bring changes to the Union's decision-making processes. There is also an increasing likelihood that, during the currency of this edition, at least six, and possibly as many as ten, more States will join the Union.

The Treaty of Paris of April 18, 1951 establishing the European Coal and Steel Community (ECSC) set up an institutional structure, including a Court of Justice, which has proved remarkably durable. That Treaty was the only one of the founding instruments of the European Union expressed to be of limited duration and its fifty-year lifespan will expire on July 25, 2002. We have nonetheless kept all of our references to cases dealing with provisions of the ECSC Treaty which will remain good authority on the interpretation of equivalent provisions in the remaining treaties.

A new edition of any book inevitably entails the drafting of new material, trimming and revision of old and compromises to avoid expanding the size of the volume more than necessary. All of these processes have been involved in the preparation of this edition of "Brown and Jacobs". Undoubtedly however the most fastidious and unwelcome part of the work has been that of taking account of the renumbering of the Treaties effected by Article 12 of the Treaty of Amsterdam. The problems caused by this *"fausse bonne idée"*, as it has been aptly called, are well illustrated by the elaborate Note on citation of Treaty provisions after May 1, 1999 published by the Court of Justice and the Court of First Instance. The Note is reproduced at the end of the Table of Community Treaties.

Without wishing to add to the difficulties caused to students and practitioners of Community Law by the changes, we have not followed the form of citation used by the Courts in their judgments. Thus articles of the Coal and Steel Treaty are referred to as "Article 88 ECSC" and provisions of the Atomic Energy Community Treaty are referred to as "Article 153 Euratom". We have also preferred (with a few exceptions) to give both the old and new numbering upon each mention of a Treaty provision citing, for example, "Article 234 (ex Article 177) EC" or "Article 85 (now Article 81) EC" as appropriate.

We would like to express our gratitude to Advocate General Jacobs and his Legal Secretary, Vanessa Edwards, for their assistance in keeping us up to date with developments at the Court and to Gillian Byrne and Nadine Cavanihac for providing documents and creating the statistical tables respectively. The slow gestation of this edition has tried the patience of our publisher and we are grateful for both the forbearance of the Editor and the skill of Sweet and Maxwell's technical staff in producing the work in its final form from a complex blend of annotated photocopies, e-mails, faxes and courriered copy.

As mentioned above, a part of that slowness is attributable to Tom Kennedy's removal from Luxembourg to a new and challenging job in Tanzania. Communication between us has not always been easy and we must thank numerous friends, relatives and neighbours for facilitating e-mail links without which this joint venture would not have been possible at all. While this modus operandi has spared our wives their forced participation in sometimes arcane discussions, both Mary and Liv-Ellen have given us their unfailing support and encouragement.

Even the miracle of e-mail is no substitute for the face-to-face discussions over dinners and dog walks which characterised the preparation of the fourth edition; nevertheless we take joint responsibility for the result and for any deficiencies which may remain. Even this Preface must, alas, be signed in Cyperspace by

L. NEVILLE BROWN                              TOM KENNEDY
Compton,                                         Arusha,
Wolverhampton.                                Tanzania.

# Acknowledgments

*Grateful acknowledgment is made for permission to reproduce the following:*

Cover illustration of the model of the extension to the Court of Justice of the European Communities is reproduced courtesy of Dominique Perrault (Architect) and Georges Fessy (Photographer).

Drawing of original Court building, *the Palais de Justice*, by Edmund Goergen.

Drawing by Nik Baker, published in the *Financial Times*, March 31, 1995.

Drawing by Domenico Roas on page 116, published in *Il Sole 24 Ore* October 28, 1991.

Commemorative postage stamp of Natasha on page 203, by Frederic Waithery issued by the Belgian Post Office.

Drawing by Les Gibbard on page 240, published in *The Guardian*, July 26, 1991.

Drawing by Peter Bensch on page 252, published in *Handelsblatt*, December 17, 1992.

Drawing by Nik Baker on page 383, published in the *Financial Times*.

# Contents

# Table of Cases before the Court of Justice (in alphabetical order)

# Table of Cases before the Court of Justice (in numerical order)

# Table of Cases before the Court of First Instance (in numerical order)

# Table of Cases before National Courts

## Belgium

## France

## Germany

# International Treaties and Conventions

# Community Treaties

OFFICIAL NOTE ON THE CITATION OF ARTICLES OF THE TREATIES IN THE PUBLICATIONS OF THE COURT OF JUSTICE AND THE COURT OF FIRST INSTANCE

Pursuant to the renumbering of the articles of the Treaty on European Union (EU) and of the Treaty establishing the European Community (EC), brought about by the Treaty of Amsterdam, the Court of Justice and the Court of First Instance have introduced, with effect from May 1, 1999, a new method of citation of the articles of the EU, EC, ECSC and Euratom Treaties.

That new method is primarily designed to avoid all risk of confusion between the version of an article as it stood prior to May 1, 1999 and the version applying after that date. The principles on which that method operates are as follows:

- Where reference is made to an article of a Treaty **as it stands after** May 1, 1999, the number of the article is immediately followed by two letters indicating the Treaty concerned:

  EU for the Treaty on European Union
  EC for the EC Treaty
  CS for the ECSC Treaty
  EA for the Euratom Treaty.

  Thus, "Article 234 E.C." denotes the article of that Treaty as it stands **after** May 1, 1999.

- Where, on the other hand, reference is made to an article of a Treaty **as it stood before** May 1, 1999, the number of the article is followed by the words "of the Treaty on European Union", "of the EC (or EEC) Treaty", "of the ECSC Treaty", or "of the EAEC Treaty", as the case may be.

  Thus, "Article 85 **of the EC Treaty**" refers to Article 85 of that Treaty **before** May 1, 1999.

- In addition, as regards the EC Treaty and the Treaty on European Union, again where reference is made to an article of a Treaty **as it stood before** May 1, 1999, the initial citation of the article in a text is followed by a reference in brackets to the corresponding provision of the same Treaty as it stands **after** May 1, 1999, as follows:

  - "*Article 85 of the EC Treaty (now Article 81 EC)*", where the article has not been amended by the Treaty of Amsterdam;
  - "*Article 51 of the EC Treaty (now, after amendment, Article 42 EC,*" where the article has been amended by the Treaty of Amsterdam:
  - "*Article 53 of the EC Treaty (repealed by the Treaty of Amsterdam*", where the article has been repealed by the Treaty of Amsterdam.

- By way of exception to the latter rule, the initial citation of (the former) Articles 117 to 120 of the EC Treaty, which have been replaced *en bloc* by the Treaty of Amsterdam, is followed by the following wording in brackets." (*Articles 117 to 120 of the EC Treaty have been replaced by Articles 136 EC to 143 EC*)".

For example:

- *"Article 119 of the EC Treaty (Articles 117 to 120 of the EC Treaty have been replaced by Articles 136 EC to 143 EC)"*.

The same applies to Articles J to J.11 and K to K.9 of the Treaty on European Union.

For example:

- *"Article J.2 of the Treaty on European Union (Articles J to J.11 of the Treaty on European Union have been replaced by Articles 11 EU to 28 EU)"*;

  *"Article K.2 of the Treaty on European Union (Articles K to K.9 of the Treaty on European Union have been replaced by Articles 29 EU to 42 EU)"*.

# Community Legislation

# Rules of Procedure of the Court of Justice and Court of First Instance

# Chapter One

# General Introduction

When on May 9, 1950, the French Foreign Minister, Robert Schuman, announced his proposal to place the whole of French and German coal and steel production under a common High Authority, in an organisation open to the participation of other European countries, he took care to include in the proposal the establishment of a court of justice which would subject the new Authority to judicial control.

Less than one year later, on April 18, 1951, the Treaty establishing the European Coal and Steel Community (the ECSC) was signed in Paris, creating, among other institutions, the Court of Justice. The elaborate institutional apparatus, including, as well as the High Authority and the Court, a Special Council of Ministers and a Common Assembly, was no doubt intended to ensure that the new Community should be based on democratic principles and the rule of law. The judicial structure was strongly influenced by ideas derived from continental, especially French, administrative law. But there was also a hint, in the Preamble to the Treaty, of a wider function for the institutions; the Preamble recalled that the six founding Member States – Belgium, France, Germany, Italy, Luxembourg and the Netherlands – were resolved "to lay the foundations for institutions which will give direction to a destiny henceforward shared".

When the same States signed the two Treaties of Rome, on March 25, 1957, establishing the European Economic Community (the EEC) and the European Atomic Energy Community (Euratom) respectively, the institutions were indeed given a wider task. Each of the new Communities was endowed with a Court of Justice, as well as a Commission (rather than a High Authority), a Council of Ministers, and an Assembly. At the same time it was provided that there should be only a single Court (and a single Assembly) to serve all three Communities; this was effected by the Convention on Certain Institutions Common to the European

Communities. Thus the Court of Justice of the ECSC became the Court of Justice of the European Communities.[1]

Later, the "Merger Treaty" of 1965 provided that there should be a single Council and a single Commission for all three Communities. But the functions and powers of all four institutions – Council, Commission, Court and Assembly (now the European Parliament) – are separately assigned in the three founding Treaties. In practice the EC Treaty is by far the most important, although due account must be taken of the amendments made by the Single European Act (SEA) of 1986,[2] the Maastricht Treaty on European Union (TEU) of February 7, 1992 and the Treaty of Amsterdam of October 2, 1997.

In nomenclature, the TEU replaced the term "European Economic Community" by the term "European Community". It introduced the term "European Union" to designate a new constitutional structure consisting of three elements or "pillars": the first pillar being the European Communities,[3] the second the provisions on a common foreign and security policy (CFSP) and the third the provisions on co-operation in the areas of justice and home affairs.

The SEA made provision (implemented in 1989) for a Court of First Instance to be attached to the Court of Justice in Luxembourg. Notwithstanding that change the Court of Justice remains the single institution exercising judicial authority within the Communities although the specific tasks assigned to it are, as we shall see, divided between the two Courts which together make up the institution as a whole. It is with the working of both Courts in that framework under the EC Treaty that this book is primarily concerned.

The provisions governing the Court with the amendments made by the Maastricht and Amsterdam Treaties are substantially identical in the EC and Euratom Treaties; however they differ in some important respects from those in the earlier ECSC Treaty.

The Treaty of Amsterdam, less ambitious than the Maastricht Treaty, introduced mostly minor changes which will be discussed, where relevant, in later chapters. One change, with important practical consequences for users of the Treaties (and for readers of this book), was to introduce a renumbering of the Articles of the

---

[1] Notwithstanding the Council decision of November 9, 1993 to change its own title to Council of the European Union, the title of the judicial institution remains unchanged.

[2] Despite its name the SEA is, in both form and substance, a treaty.

[3] "Communities" (plural) as denoting, not only the European (Economic) Community, but also the European Coal and Steel Community and the European Atomic Energy Community (Euratom).

EC and Maastricht Treaties. While this change was needed to clarify a numbering system grown unwieldy as a result of multiple amendments, the method chosen has created pitfalls for the unwary. In this edition we will usually give the new number first but add in brackets the old number, for example, "Article 234 (ex Article 177) EC". An appendix at the end of our book sets out tables of equivalence.

Frequently, where the provisions of the EC Treaty are cited in this book, there are corresponding provisions in the other founding Treaties. The composition of the institutions is the same under all three Treaties. When, on January 1, 1973, the three Communities were enlarged to include Denmark, Ireland and the United Kingdom, the institutions were correspondingly enlarged under the Treaty of Accession, but their jurisdiction was not affected except in its territorial extent. The same can be said of the further enlargements by the accessions of Greece on January 1, 1981, and of Spain and Portugal on January 1, 1986.

By the Maastricht Treaty, the Court of Auditors, created in 1977 under the terms of the Financial Provisions Treaty of 1975, has been raised to the status of the fifth Community institution. The Court of Auditors replaced the ECSC Auditor and the Audit Board under the EC and Euratom Treaties. Its task is to ensure closer control and audit of all Community income and expenditure and to pass judgment, where appropriate, on the financial management of the Communities. Members of the Court of Auditors are appointed by the Council but in consultation with the European Parliament, and a member may only be removed if the Court of Justice finds the conditions and obligations of office are no longer being met.

Politically, the Maastricht Treaty marks a major step forward in the evolution of the European Communities. In the first place, it prepares the way for Economic and Monetary Union to be achieved except for those Member States not able to meet the strict economic convergence conditions and for Denmark and the United Kingdom if they elect to exercise their options under the Treaty not to take part in that process. Secondly, it provides for a "cohesion fund" intended to increase the financial help given by the richer northern to the poorer southern Member States and Ireland. Thirdly, it introduced, as we have seen above, a system of co-operation and common action in two new areas, (a) foreign and security policy, and (b) justice and home affairs, but these so-called "second and third pillars" were expressly excluded from the jurisdiction of the Court of Justice. However, the Amsterdam Treaty will now allow the Court of Justice to exercise its jurisdiction on limited issues relating to the third pillar.

Fourthly, the Maastricht Treaty enhanced the powers of the European Parliament to help meet the so-called "democratic deficit" within the Community. Finally, it demarcated more clearly the boundary between the powers of the Community and those of the Member States, using for this purpose the principles of specific attribution (the Community has only such powers as are expressly attributed to it), subsidiarity (the Community shall only use its powers where action by the Member States cannot achieve the Treaty objectives equally well) and proportionality (Community action should not exceed what is necessary to achieve its objectives).

Overall, the Maastricht Treaty, as further glossed at the Birmingham and Edinburgh Summits of October and December 1992, steered a middle course. On the one hand, limitations on national sovereignty will be increased by the move to EMU, by the increased powers of the Parliament in Community decision-making and by the new jurisdiction of the Court to impose fines on Member States who fail to fulfil their Community obligations.[3a] On the other hand, common action in the areas of foreign and home affairs is to be by intergovernmental agreement: it will require unanimity and so respect sovereignty in these areas. Significantly, the Birmingham Declaration of October 16, 1992 reaffirmed respect for the identity and diversity of the Member States. This balances the opening words of the Treaty itself as marking:

> "A new stage in the process of creating an ever closer union among the peoples of Europe, in which decisions are taken as openly as possible and as closely as possible to the citizen."[4]

The balancing act has been continued by the Amsterdam Treaty, whose impact on our subject, the Court of Justice, is relatively slight.

In addition to their specific functions, the five institutions are required, by Article 7 (ex Article 4(1)) of the EC Treaty, to carry out the tasks entrusted to the Community; each institution is to act within the limits of the powers conferred upon it by the Treaty, as amended by the SEA and the Maastricht and Amsterdam Treaties. Both the Council, composed of government ministers from the Member States, and the Commission, an entirely independent body, are given legislative and decision-making powers. The SEA recognised that the Assembly should officially be known as the European Parliament, a style which the Assembly had assumed for itself since 1962. In this respect the SEA reflected the enhanced role of the Parliament in the legislative process through the

---

[3a] A power wielded for the first time on July 4, 2000 in case C–387/97 *Commission v. Greece* (not yet reported), see Chapter Six, below.
[4] Art. 1 (ex Art. A) TEU.

so-called "co-operation procedure" introduced by that Treaty (see p. 8). The role of the Court, in the pregnant formula of Article 220 (ex Article 164) EC, is to "ensure that in the interpretation and application of the Treaty the law is observed". It is thus required to ensure that the other bodies act within the limits of their respective powers. Subsequent Articles of the Treaty spell out the Court's wide-ranging and multifarious jurisdiction, the main aspects of which will be discussed in Part Two of this book.

All five institutions are in principle equal under the Treaties; but, inevitably in the real world of politics as in the world of George Orwell, some are more equal than others. The formal equality of the institutions is symbolised by the fact that the members of the Courts and of the Commission are appointed not by the Council – for that might be taken to imply the superiority of the Council – but "by common accord of the Governments of the Member States".[5] On the other hand, the Commission may be collectively dismissed by the Parliament[6]; and individual members of the Commission may be compulsorily retired by the Court if they no longer fulfil the conditions for performance of their duties or have been guilty of serious misconduct.[7]

In early 1999, a serious crisis arose in relation to the Commission. At the instigation of the Parliament, a Committee of Experts completed an investigation of the Commission's affairs, including the Commission's finances. The report of the Committee was a devastating indictment of incompetence, mismanagement, corruption and nepotism within the Commission. Threatened by the Parliament with the impeachment of some of its members before the Court of Justice, the whole Commission resigned, including its President, Jacques Santer, only remaining in being on a caretaker basis pending the selection of a new Commission. The leading Italian statesman, Romano Prodi was appointed as its new President. Only four members of the outgoing Santer Commission retained their posts and, of the departing members, Hans Bangeman faced criticism and the threat of action before the Court of Justice in respect of a lucrative private sector appointment.

After hearings in September 1999 before the European Parliament, the Parliament approved the new Commission and the President, enabling it to take office on September 16, 1999 after being sworn in at the Court.

We shall see that the relationship between the Council and the Commission is by no means that between political superior and inferior, even though the Council is undoubtedly the supreme

---

[5] Art. 223 (ex Art. 167) and Art. 214(2) (ex Art. 158) EC.
[6] Art. 201 (ex Art. 144) EC.
[7] Art. 216 (ex Art. 160).

expression, subject only to summit meetings of heads of government (below, p. 9), of political will (or lack of it) in the Community. The relationship between the Council and the Court is also very different from that between government (or legislature) and judiciary, at least as it is known in the United Kingdom. While a decision of even the highest court in the United Kingdom can be reversed by Act of Parliament, even with retroactive effect, the decisions of the Court of Justice cannot be reversed by an act of the Council; on the contrary, any measure of the Council having legal effect can be annulled by the Court if contrary to the Treaties or other provisions of Community law. This has not infrequently happened.[8] In fact a ruling of the Court could be reversed only by the Court itself in a subsequent case, or by an amendment of the Treaties which, since it requires the unanimous approval of the Member States, each acting through its own constitutional processes for treaty ratification, is not normally a practical possibility. Conversely, the political obstacles to amending the Treaties lend added significance to the Court's rulings on their interpretation, especially as the Court (as we shall see in Chapter 14) has been ready to interpret boldly in the face of political deadlock between the Council and the Commission. This boldness has at times led to a hostile reaction from national supreme courts; thus, the French *Conseil d'Etat* rebelled against the well-settled case law of the Court of Justice on the direct effect of directives, partly on the ground that law-making by the Court was less to be tolerated once there was a directly elected European Parliament to take political initiatives.[9] In Germany, both the Federal Constitutional Court and the Federal Finance Court had expressed reservations about the case law of the Court of Justice, although those reservations have now been overcome.[10] The Spanish Constitutional Court has also found it difficult to bow to the supremacy of Community law.[11]

---

[8] See for example Case 81/72 *Commission v. Council* [1973] ECR 575; [1973] C.M.L.R. 639 the first *Staff Salaries* case (see below, p. 142); Case 45/86 *Commission v. Council* [1987] ECR 1493; [1988] 2 C.M.L.R. 131 (the *Generalised Tariff Preference* case (see below, p. 159) and Case C–70/88 *European Parliament v. Council* [1990] ECR I–2041 (admissibility) and [1991] ECR I–4529, 1 C.M.L.R. 91 (substance) (known as *the Chernobyl case* – see below, p. 144).

[9] *Cohn-Bendit*, C.E., *conclusions* Genevois [1980] 1 C.M.L.R. 543, has now, in effect, been reversed by *Nicolo*, C.E. October 20, 1989, *conclusions* Frydman [1990] 1 C.M.L.R. 173, and *S. A. Philip Morris*, C.E. February 1992, *conclusions* Laroque [1993] C.M.L.R. 253.

[10] See T.C. Hartley, *Foundations of European Community Law* (3rd ed., 1994), p. 243.

[11] See cases discussed in Chap. 17 below, pp. 400 *et seq.*

## Sources of Community Law

We shall have occasion to revert to the novel character of Community law which it is the Court's business to interpret and apply; here we must say a word about the sources of that law. In addition to, and derived from, the founding Treaties which make up the Constitutional Charter of the Communities, it includes the regulations, directives and decisions of the European Parliament acting jointly with the Council, of the Council acting alone and of the Commission, mentioned in Article 249 (ex Article 189) EC. These instruments are officially styled "acts" of the institutions. The acts of general application – regulations and directives – are sometimes referred to as "secondary legislation", the implication being that the Treaties are in some sense "primary legislation". This classification is misleading since, although the implementing regulations of the Commission are often akin to subordinate or delegated legislation, there is nothing secondary, in character or in scope, about the basic regulations of the Council in such fields as agriculture, the free movement of workers, social security, and competition. That legislation is both as fundamental in character and as broad in scope as any national legislation, and its relationship to the founding Treaties is comparable to that which national legislation has to a national constitution, with the Court of Justice fulfilling the role of a constitutional court.[12] Consequently we shall refer to regulations and directives as Community legislation, and for convenience we shall include in that term all general enactments of the Council (whether acting alone or jointly with the Parliament) and of the Commission.

The European Parliament has no autonomous legislative powers. Under numerous provisions of the founding Treaties, its opinion must be sought by the Council before legislation can be enacted, but this opinion need not be followed. The Parliament's own Draft Treaty (1984) for establishing the European Union suggested a two-chamber system for legislation. But these proposals were not fully adopted in the Single European Act (1986), which introduced instead a new "co-operation procedure" involving the Council, the Commission and the Parliament acting together. The procedure is complex but involves the proposed legislation receiving both a first and a second reading in the Council and also in the Parliament.[13]

---

[12] See generally D. Curtin and D. O'Keeffe (eds.) *Constitutional Adjudication in European Community and National Law* (Dublin, 1992).
[13] For further details of this procedure and that of "co-decision", see T.C. Hartley, *Foundations of European Community Law* (3rd ed., 1994), pp. 41–48 and D. Wyatt and A. Dashwood, *European Community Law* (3rd ed., 1993), Chap. 3, pp. 37 *et seq.*

Although the scope of the new procedure is limited, it has given the Parliament more influence in the legislative process.

By the Maastricht Treaty, the Parliament was granted for the first time a power of "co-decision" with the Council. This power was extended by the Amsterdam Treaty. It seeks to give it an equal voice with the Council in shaping Community legislation in such key areas as free movement, freedom of establishment, the internal market and environment. Nevertheless, in the event of disagreement persisting despite a procedure of conciliation, the Parliament can only reject the Council's proposal, not replace it with its own. Used skilfully, this power of veto must result in the Parliament having greater political influence than it has had in the past.

Parliament also has the power, in certain circumstances, to take part in proceedings before the Court: we revert to this in Chapter 7, below. In other respects the European Parliament is more like a national parliament. It has been given gradually increasing control over the Community budget; historically, budgetary powers have been of much importance to national parliaments in their struggles with the executive. The European Parliament also exercises supervisory functions over the Community executive: its members can put questions to the Commission (and to the Council), and, as mentioned above, it can even dismiss the Commission. Until 1979, its effectiveness had been limited by many factors, not least by the fact that its members had to combine their duties with serving in their respective national parliaments, from which they had been appointed. With direct elections, although such a "dual mandate" remains possible (see Article 5 of the Act concerning the election of representatives of the European Parliament) most MEPs are able to give more time to their duties, and their increased authority as a result of direct election led them to reject the Community budget in 1979 and subsequently to exercise their budgetary powers up to (and even beyond) their limits.[14] Clearly, the European Parliament is destined in future to play a greater role, and to develop for itself a more active part in the legislative process. The Maastricht Treaty fell far short of meeting all of the Parliament's aspirations in this respect so, for the present, the supreme Community legislature remains the Council representing the governments of the Member States.

The founding Treaties conceived of the Council as a Community institution rather than as an inter-governmental body. Thus, although the Council consists of representatives of the Member States (Article 2 of the Merger Treaty), each State being

---

[14] See, for example, Case 34/86, *Council v. European Parliament* [1986] ECR 2155, 3 C.M.L.R. 94.

represented either by the foreign minister or by the minister responsible for the subject in question (agriculture, education, finance, transport, etc.), nevertheless the Treaties provide for majority voting on most matters, in contrast with the unanimity rule often found in inter-governmental organisations. Again, in contrast with the normal rule (in inter-governmental organisations) of one State, one vote, the Treaties provide for weighted voting (Article 205 (ex Article 148) EC) in certain important areas of Community activity. But in practice, under the so-called "Luxembourg Accords" of 1966, unanimity became the rule in cases where vital national interests were claimed to be at stake.

The legality of those accords was never tested before the Court of Justice. Subsequently, under the SEA, the increased use of majority voting in the Council, which reflected the new political will to achieve the Single Market by the end of 1992, meant that those accords became a dead letter.[15] On the other hand, the SEA prompted a series of cases before the Court where the Member State or States outvoted in the Council challenged the legal basis of the decision claiming that it should have been adopted on the basis of unanimity and not a majority vote. Conversely the Commission and the Parliament questioned the legal basis why the Member States have decided to act on a basis requiring unanimity resulting in the use of procedure that either reduces the influence of the European Parliament or substantially changes the substance of the legislation concerned.[16] In the past, the obstacles to legislative progress caused by disagreements at the political level have been partially overcome, as we shall see, by the creative use of its powers by the Court of Justice and by the development there of judicial law-making.

Bagehot remarked that "nations touch at their summits". In this connection, apart from the institutions set up under the founding Treaties, mention must be made of the "summit" meetings of heads of Governments together with the President of the Commission, formerly arranged *ad hoc* when the occasion arose – a famous occasion being the Hague Summit of 1969 which opened the way to the first enlargement of the Communities – but regularised at the Paris Summit of 1974 under the name of "European Council",

---

[15] Nonetheless, in Spring 1994, in the debate over the number of votes needed to form a blocking minority following enlargement of the Community, the continued existence of the accords was asserted from both sides of the House of Commons; on the Luxembourg Accords See T.C. Hartley, *Foundations of European Community Law* (3rd ed., 1994), pp. 20–23. In January 1995 the Council agreed that the blocking minority should be 26 out of a total of 87 votes (the so-called "Ioannina compromise").

[16] See K. Bradley, "The European Court and the Legal Basis of Community Legislation" (1988) 13 E.L.Rev. 379 and the cases there discussed.

to which the SEA gave Treaty recognition in Article 2, recognition confirmed by Article 4 (ex Article D) of the Maastricht Treaty. The European Council has become *de jure* the supreme organ of the Communities in matters of high policy but it is still not an institution of the Communities according to the letter of the Treaties, a term restricted to the four original Treaty bodies (the European Parliament, the Council, the Commission and the Court of Justice) to which, as already mentioned, the Maastricht Treaty has added the Court of Auditors.

The Council and the Commission are sometimes contrasted as the legislature and executive respectively of the Community. This contrast accords well with the traditional doctrine of the separation of powers, distinguishing legislature, executive and judiciary. The Commission, however, should not be regarded as a mere administration, for it has important political and legislative responsibilities which it exercises in its own right.

Of greatest importance in this respect is the crucial role of the Commission in the legislative process. In almost every area of major policy under the EC Treaty, the Council can legislate only on a proposal made by the Commission. This exclusive "right of initiative" is vested in the Commission to ensure that legislation respects the Community interest; for "The members of the Commission shall, in the general interest of the Communities, be completely independent in the performance of their duties . . . they shall neither seek nor take instructions from any Government or from any other body."[17]

Moreover, under Article 250 (ex Article 189a) EC, a proposal of the Commission can be amended only by a unanimous vote of the Council; so that if there is disagreement among the ministers, no decision at all can be taken until the Commission puts forward a different proposal. This has important consequences: not only is the Council unable to legislate unilaterally; the Commission is also actively involved in the law-making process within the Council. In practice, the Commission will have discussed its proposals with the Committee of Permanent Representatives of the Member States, which prepares the work of the Council (Article 4 of the Merger Treaty); the proposals will have been considered, in collaboration with the Commission, by the European Parliament, and by the Economic and Social Committee (Article 262 (ex Article 198) EC) if the Treaty so requires; the Commissioner most closely concerned with the proposal will attend the meetings of the Council at which the proposal is discussed, and may take part in the discussion. The Commission thus has, in a sense, its own seat at

---

[17] Art. 213(2) (ex Art. 157(2), formerly Art. 10(2) of the Merger Treaty).

the Council table, although it has no vote in the Council. To describe the Commission, therefore, as the Community executive, or merely as a "bureaucracy", is misleading unless the notion of executive is understood as including responsibility for policy and for implementing the aims and general programme of the Community.

The Court of Justice has no direct part to play in this formal legislative process. No doubt it will be consulted informally if the proposals affect its jurisdiction. Exceptionally it may suggest legislation; the power to establish a Court of First Instance was included in the Single European Act on the basis of a suggestion from the Court. However, the only area where the Court is truly involved in the legislative process is in the drafting and adoption of its own Rules of Procedure and those of the Court of First Instance, although even those rules require the unanimous approval of the Council before they can be adopted by the Courts. Generally however, its concern is only with the end product of the legislative process – the Law. This distancing of the Court is essential to avoid prejudicing the Court's approach to any future judicial proceedings which might arise.

Here, as has been mentioned, the Court may have to adjudicate on the limits of the powers of the other institutions. In this way it has a constitutional role in determining the balance of power between the Community on the one hand and the Member States on the other, as well as the institutional balance between the Council, the Commission and the European Parliament. In exploring the jurisdiction of the Court in Part Two we shall have frequent occasion to illustrate this constitutional role of the Court.

The description of the Commission as the Community executive is also misleading about the nature of the Communities themselves, for it conceals the fact that, except to some extent under the ECSC Treaty, and in the field of competition under the EC Treaty, the Community does not have an "executive" at all. Generally, Community policies are carried out, and Community legislation applied, by the national authorities of the Member States. Thus it is the national customs administrations which are responsible for applying the common customs tariff[18]; it is the national intervention agencies which implement the common agricultural policy[19]; it is the national social security offices which apply the regulations on the social security of migrant workers.[20]

---

[18] See for example Case 26/62 *Van Gend en Loos v. Nederlandse Administratie der Belastingen* [1963] ECR 1; [1963] C.M.L.R. 105.

[19] See for example Case 146/77 *British Beef Co. v. Intervention Board for Agricultural Produce* [1978] ECR 1347; [1978] 3 C.M.L.R. 47.

[20] See for example Case 17/76 *Brack v. Insurance Officer* [1976] ECR 1429; [1976] 2 C.M.L.R. 592.

The Community is not, therefore, a State writ large; or at least not a centralised State, like France, Spain or the United Kingdom. Nor does it have a federal or quasi-federal structure like those of Germany or Belgium. Community policies are made in Brussels and the legislation is enacted there, but the regulations, directives and decisions of the Council and Commission are implemented and applied by the Member States themselves. In this sense the Community's administration is decentralised.

So too with the judicial organisation of the Community: litigation involving questions of Community law is normally for the national courts. A dispute between individuals, or between an individual and the national authorities, falls within the jurisdiction of the appropriate national court or tribunal. It may come before the Court of Justice on a reference from the national court, as will be seen in Chapter 10, but it cannot be brought directly before that Court.

Thus a person claiming the right to enter a Member State, under the Treaty provisions on the free movement of workers and the implementing Community legislation, must seek his remedy before the courts of that State against the immigration authorities who have refused the right he claims.[21] Or if the defendant, in an action for breach of contract, alleges that the contract was void under Article 81 (ex Article 85) of the Treaty, that defence must be decided upon by the national court, subject again to the possibility of a reference to the Court of Justice on the interpretation, or validity, of Community law.

Only if the individual litigant seeks to challenge directly some Community measure affecting his interests may he go directly to the Court of Justice or to the Court of First Instance; and even then, his right to do so, as will be seen in Chapters 5 and 7, is limited. In most cases, the appropriate forum is the national court.

It follows that, although the Court in Luxembourg is often described as the Community Court (in company now with the Court of First Instance), an essential role in the application of Community law is played by the whole range of national courts and tribunals. In civil and commercial matters, in administrative and industrial disputes, and even in criminal cases, all these courts may have to apply Community law, and they too are therefore, in a real sense, Community courts. In this capacity they are to be guided and assisted by the Court of Justice, and to adopt the principles of interpretation developed by the Court – principles which, as we shall see, have had a far-reaching effect on the evolution of Community law.

---

[21] See Case 41/74 *Van Duyn v. Secretary of State for Home Affairs* [1974] ECR 1337; [1975] 1 C.M.L.R. 1, and see further p. 326, below.

## LINGUISTIC REGIME

Linguistic regime is "Euro-speak" for the bundle of rules which regulate how the Community applies the fundamental principle of the equality of all the 11 official languages of the 15 Member States. These are, in English alphabetical order[22]: Danish, Dutch, English, Finnish, French, German, Greek, Italian, Portuguese, Spanish and Swedish.[23] Not accepted for this purpose are Catalan, Letzebuergisch, Sami (spoken in parts of Finland and Sweden), Scottish Gaelic or Welsh, but Irish has a special status as we shall see.

The principle of linguistic equality means that Community law is plurilingual and differs therefore in this important respect from the (mostly) monolingual national laws in the European Union – monolingual in the sense that the law exists only in a single language. The difference is as dramatic as that, in the medium of film, between colour and black-and-white, yet this is easily over-looked by those studying, being taught or applying Community law wholly in their own language.

The basic Treaties (other than the ECSC Treaty)[24] have texts which are authentic, that is they have equal validity, in all the official languages and in Irish. On the other hand, Community legislation is authentic only in the 11 official languages.

Parties before the Court of Justice, however, are in a privileged situation in being permitted to use as the language of procedure for a particular case not only any of the 11 official languages but also Irish. Likewise the Court of First Instance. Which language of procedure is to be chosen is discussed below in Chapter 12.

In the Court of Justice the principle of linguistic equality has especially serious financial consequences for the provision of translation and interpreting services, but the principle has been doggedly maintained despite the growth in the number of languages from only four in the original Community of the Six to 11 in the present European Union. For interpretation and translation this means 110 possible combinations. With the projected expansion eastwards of the Union to add Poland, Hungary, the Czech Republic, Slovenia and Estonia, the language combinations would

---

[22] The official order of these languages is to list them according to the way they are spelled each in their own language. Thus: *Castellano* (Spanish), *Dansk, Deutsch, Ελληνικοζ*; English, *Français, Italiano, Nederlands, Português, Suomi, Svenska*. This is the order in which the name of the Court is given on the letterhead both of the Court of Justice and the Court of First Instance. Irish (*Gaelige*) is added between *Français* and *Italiano* for reasons mentioned in the text.

[23] Regulation No. 1 of 1957, as amended.

[24] Only the French text of the ECSC Treaty is authentic (Art. 100).

increase exponentially to 240.[25] The problem is common to all of the institutions but the Court of Justice has specific difficulties which it has drawn to the attention of Member States and to which we will return in the concluding chapter of this book.

## LOCATION OF THE INSTITUTIONS

This introduction would be incomplete without mention of a matter of geography. Article 289 (ex Article 216) EC provides that the seat of the institutions of the Community shall be determined by common accord of the governments of the Member States. Under a decision of the representatives of the Member States of April 8, 1965[26] it was decided that Luxembourg, Brussels and Strasbourg were to remain the provisional places of work of the institutions of the Communities. Article 3 of that decision provided that the Court of Justice was to remain in Luxembourg and that any future judicial or quasi-judicial bodies should also be located there. While workable arrangements were made for most of the institutions, this situation proved highly unsatisfactory for the European Parliament whose secretariat was based in Luxembourg, while the monthly, week-long plenary sessions were held in Strasbourg and committee meetings took place in Brussels where the MEPs could maintain close contact with the members and officials of the Council and the Commission responsible for drafting legislation and formulating policy.

The clear wish of the Parliament to move all of its activities to Brussels and the tensions which this caused between the Parliament, France and Luxembourg led to a series of cases before the Court at which the respective powers of the Institutions and Member States to define their working methods were at issue.[27] The Gordian knot was finally cut by the European Council Meeting at the Edinburgh Summit on December 23, 1992 where, after reciting the decision of April 8, 1965 and stating that the

---

[25] See R. Barents, "Law and Language in the European Union" E.C. Tax Review 1997/1, 49, at 51. The formula is $C = L \times (L-1)$ where C is the number of combinations and L the number of languages.

[26] Decision of the representatives of the Governments of the Member States on the provisional location of certain institutions and departments of the Communities, J.O. 152/67, July 13, 1967 (English Special Edition).

[27] See Case 230/81 *Luxembourg v. European Parliament* [1983] ECR 255; [1983] 2 C.M.L.R. 726 below, p. 139; Case 358/85 *France v. European Parliament* [1988] ECR 4821; [1988] 3 C.M.L.R. 786; [1990] 1 C.M.L.R. 309, (noted at 13 E.L.Rev. 293). For further discussion on the seat of the European Parliament see L. Neville Brown, "The Grand Duchy Fights Again: Comment on Joined Cases C–213/88 and C–39/89" (1993) 30 C.M.L.Rev. 599–611.

present decision was without prejudice to the provisions in the 1965 decision concerning the seats of future institutions, the Council essentially confirmed the status quo, making the previously provisional places of work definitive.

Thus the Court of Justice, the Court of First Instance, the Court of Auditors and the European Investment Bank have their seats in Luxembourg while the Council and the Commission have theirs in Brussels although, during the months of April, June and October, the Council will continue to hold its meetings in Luxembourg and certain specific departments of the Commission will also be established there.

The European Parliament's peripatetic existence continues since, under Article 1 of the 1992 decision, its seat is to be in Strasbourg where the 12 periods of monthly plenary sessions, including the Budget session, are to be held, whereas meetings of any additional plenary sessions and committees of the Parliament are to be held in Brussels. The General Secretariat of the Parliament and its departments remain in Luxembourg. The decision also provided that the seats of other bodies and departments set up or to be set up would be decided by common agreement between the governments of the Member States at the forthcoming European Council and, at the Brussels Summit of November 1993, a number of new agencies and bodies were distributed among the Member States, giving some priority to those who did not at present provide the sites for any Community institutions.[28]

The Court of Justice has its seat in Luxembourg, where it is in permanent session. Luxembourg is also the seat of the Court of First Instance: this is not only an obvious convenience but also a legal requirement. For, by Article 225 (ex Article 168a) EC, the new jurisdiction is "attached" to the Court; and it has no separate administration or organisation (see the organigramme at p. 45, below).

That Luxembourg, the mini-State among the Twelve, should have become the judicial centre of the Communities, has consequences that may escape the notice of anyone unfamiliar with the Grand Duchy and its capital. The City of Luxembourg, where the Court has sat since its inception, numbers barely 90,000 inhabitants[29] and has very much the atmosphere of a pleasant provincial town. There is neither the bustle of Brussels nor the

---

[28] These bodies included the European Central Bank (Frankfurt), the European Environment Agency (Copenhagen), the European Agency for the Evaluation of Medicinal Products (London), Europol (The Hague), the Office for Veterinary and Plant Health Inspection and Control (Dublin) and the Community Trade Mark Office (Alicante).

[29] The population of the whole Grand Duchy in 1999 was 429,000.

sophistication of Strasbourg. Letzebuergers (as the natives of Luxembourg call themselves) are serious and hardworking people. There are no frivolities and few distractions, apart from the quiet charm of the surrounding countryside. Expatriates who work at the Court tend to entertain each other in their homes and to restrict their social life to a small circle of colleagues. This helps to produce a sense of camaraderie and of loyalty to the Court that transcends national differences. On the other hand, narrowness of outlook is prevented by the constant stream of visitors to the Court and by the great diversity of backgrounds from which the members and personnel of the Court are drawn: this aspect is returned to in Chapter 3.

# PART ONE: ORGANISATION AND COMPOSITION

## Introductory

This part will be devoted to what may be termed the judicial administration of the Court. Chapter 2 will examine the administrative organisation of the Court and of its non-judicial staff, of which the head is the Registrar. Chapters 3 and 4 concern the two categories of members of the Court, the judges and advocates general. Considerable descriptive and biographical information is included in this part, the better to convey to those who have not visited it the atmosphere of the Court and the character of the men and women who operate there the central machinery of Community justice. Chapter 5 gives the background leading to the setting up of the Court of First Instance and outlines its organisation, composition, jurisdiction and the relationship between this new court and the Court of Justice.

# Chapter Two

# Court Organisation

## INTRODUCTION

The Court shares certain organisational features generally found in most courts, but it has also many particular features of its own.

Among features generally present in any court, one may mention the Registry under its administrative head, the Registrar, which carries out the normal administrative functions associated with a court Registry. There is also at Luxembourg the dichotomy made in several continental legal systems between, on the one hand, those who sit in judgment – the Bench, as we would say in England, or *la magistrature assise* as the French jargon puts it, and, on the other, "the standing judiciary" (*la magistrature debout*), by which are meant the nine advocates general. The latter do not themselves sit in judgment but rather stand to proffer advice to the Bench on how it should decide the cases before the Court: their distinctive function will be examined further in Chapter 4.

At Luxembourg both judges and advocates general together constitute the judicial personnel of the Court and as such are to be contrasted with the members of the Bar who represent the parties and plead before the Court. But "the Bar" entitled to practise in the Court of Justice is very different from any single national Bar: its potential membership includes every member of the national Bars of the 15 Member States, and in the case of the United Kingdom and Ireland this includes solicitors as well as members of the Bar (see Chapter 13, below).

Again, like any court, the Court of Justice has a certain defined jurisdiction. This jurisdiction however is not open-ended in character, in the way, for example, that the English High Court has a certain inherent jurisdiction. Rather, as the French would say, the Court has only a *compétence d'attribution*, that is, only such jurisdiction as is expressly conferred upon it by the Treaties or by a convention.[1] In Part Two we shall see how extensive that attribution is; nevertheless its limits are precise.

Finally, the Court is sub-divided into Chambers.[2] This common device to enable a greater work-load to be handled is being extensively resorted to at Luxembourg, there now being six Chambers which, under the latest revision of the rules, deal severally with the greater part of the cases before the Court. The most important cases, however, are still reserved to the full Court.

Features peculiar to the Court of Justice arise from its multi-national and multi-lingual character.

Thus, its judges are of 15 different nationalities – one from each of the Member States. When, as has happened in the past and may well recur in the future, there is an even number of Member States, an extra judge is appointed to avoid a deadlocked court. For example, in the Community of the Twelve consequent upon the accession of Spain and Portugal, an additional judge was drawn in rotation from France, Germany, Italy, Spain and the United Kingdom (although the United Kingdom's "turn" never arrived).

The Act of Accession of Norway, Austria, Finland and Sweden provided, in Article 17, for the Court to be composed of 17 judges, thus allowing each of the four new Member States to nominate one judge and maintaining the principle of an additional judge in order to ensure that there was an uneven total. The failure of Norway to ratify the Accession Treaty made it necessary to amend the Act of Accession in several respects and raised the awkward question of the composition of the Court. Since the number of Member States was now uneven (15), it was not strictly necessary to have an additional judge (the Italian Antonio La Pergola) whose presence would result in their being an even number of judges (16). However, a 15-judge Court, including two Italian judges,[3] would mean that only two out of three of the new Member States would be able to nominate a judge. This too would have been unacceptable. Finally, to leave Article 17 unchanged and thus maintain a 17-judge Court would have required an additional appointment to be made. This was regarded as both unwieldy and unnecessary.

The solution adopted was therefore to amend Article 20 of the Act of Accession, which provided for the Court of Justice to be

---

[1] But for a contrary view see: A. Arnull, "Does the Court of Justice have Inherent Jurisdiction?" (1992) 27 C.M.L.Rev. 683.

[2] On a point of nomenclature the term "Chamber" is used in the texts to translate the French "*Chambre*" as indicating a division or section of the court. It does not, of course, carry the connotation of the English term "Chambers" as suggesting a hearing in camera or in the private room of the judge or judges.

[3] An Italian, Antonio La Pergola then held the "odd" judge position.

assisted by eight advocates general, so that a ninth advocate general would be appointed as from the date of accession until October 6, 2000. Antonio La Pergola accepted appointment to that ninth post: thus, after tenure as a judge for little over three months, he became the third Italian judge to migrate from the *Magistrature assise* to the *Magistrature debout*. In the result the Court was composed of 15 judges and nine advocates general.

The increase in the strength of the corps of advocates general from six to nine also raised the question of the national distribution of the three new posts. One, which will exist only until October 6, 2000, was to be occupied by Mr La Pergola; the second was to be a post permanently reserved for a Spanish advocate general; while the third was to be filled by an advocate general from the smaller Member States in rotation, including all three of the new Member States.[4] But for changes of December 1999, see p. 72, below.

The above arrangement is nowhere prescribed by Treaty but is the inevitable consequence of the principle under Article 167 EC that appointments to the Court require a unanimous decision of the 15 Governments (see p. 48, below). The judges (like the advocates general) do not of course in any sense represent their governments or their countries but must, and do, reach their decisions (or deliver their opinions) with complete independence and impartiality.

Nevertheless, the fact that each nationality of the Fifteen has its place on the bench of the Court does bring to its decisions a special authority transcending national viewpoints. It also has the practical advantage that at least one member of the Court is conversant with each of the national legal systems and languages with which the Court may come into contact. However a party may not apply for a change in the composition of the Court or of one of its Chambers on the grounds of either the nationality of a judge or the absence from the Court or from the Chamber of a judgeofthenationalityofthatparty.[5] The authority of the Court is also enhanced by the requirement that it frame its decision as a single collegiate judgment: the oracles of Community law thus speak with one voice.

The Court may work in any of the 11 official languages and, potentially, in Irish too. We have referred to this characteristic of the Court's work in Chapter 1. Rules have been framed to

---

[4] Belgium, Denmark, Greece, Ireland, Luxembourg, Netherlands, Austria, Portugal, Finland, Sweden.
[5] See Art. 16 of the Statute of the Court of Justice. The Statute is contained in a Protocol to each of the three founding Treaties and provides the basic framework governing the composition, organisation and procedure of the Court.

determine the language of a particular case: these will be discussed later. For practical convenience, however, as we shall see, French has been adopted as the internal working language of the Court—at least up to the present time. But the variety of languages available and the inevitable need for assistance from translators and interpreters have determined, to some extent, the procedures which the Court follows in handling its case-load. This will become apparent in the discussion of these procedures; but one general influence of the problem of language diversity has been to emphasise written procedure at the expense of orality and to diminish the impact of counsel when pleading in the less familiar languages. The administrative structure of the Court is shown clearly in the organigramme of the Court below (p. 45).

## CABINETS

Each judge or advocate general has a *cabinet*, translated into English as "chambers", although the French word refers ambiguously both to the suite of rooms and to the staff working there, for the judge or advocate general has a small team of personal assistants and secretaries working exclusively for him. *Cabinet* in this sense is also used for "the private office" of each Commissioner in Brussels and of the President of the European Parliament. At Luxembourg the *cabinet* also houses the archives and personal library of the judge or advocate general. The entrance door to the cabinet bears his name and designation in his national language (or two languages in the case of the Belgian, Irish and Finnish judges). These cabinets were grouped on the second and third floors of the Court building, those of the members of the Court of First Instance are grouped together in the new annexes to the Courthouse, known as the Erasmus and Thomas More Buildings.[6]

The *cabinets* (or chambers) should not, of course, be confused with the use of the word "Chamber" for a subdivision of the Court.[7]

## ASSISTANT RAPPORTEURS

The Statute provides for the appointment of assistant rapporteurs to co-operate with the judge-rapporteur (whose function is described in Chapter 12): no such appointments have yet been made.

---

[6] But from August 1999 new locations will be needed due to the vacation of the main Courthouse.

[7] See above, p. 20, n. 2 and below, p. 39.

## LEGAL SECRETARIES

Key figures in the work of the Court are the "legal secretaries". Three lawyers are attached to each judge and each advocate general of the Court of Justice and two to each member of the Court of First Instance as personal assistants. The Court of First Instance has also appointed a small group of legal secretaries, not attached to any individual judge, as a "task force" to help any judge rapporteur or an entire chamber with especially burdensome cases. Commonly, they undertake the preliminary research on a case and help draft essential documents required by the procedure. They work in the closest association with the judge or advocate general to whom they are attached. This personal relationship is reinforced by physical proximity: the legal secretary will occupy an office as close as possible to the judge's or advocate general's "chambers", usually within the same suite of offices.

"Legal secretary" is the term in English which has come to be preferred since British members joined the Court. The previous term employed was either, in French, *Attaché* or the more imposing title *Référendaire*. *Conseiller-référendaire* is used in the French *Cour de Cassation* to describe a class of career judges who are attached to that Court to assist its senior members. In Germany, *Referendar* is used to denote a legal apprentice, and to avoid this confusion the word *Referent* has been adopted to designate the German legal secretaries.

The closest analogy in the common law world is the law clerk of the American judicial system.[7a] In the United States, an outstanding law graduate may be invited upon graduation to serve for a year or, at most, two years as personal assistant to a senior judge. Such law clerks often rise to high distinction in their subsequent careers, as may also the Court's own legal secretaries, four of whom (Jacobs, Gulmann, Ruiz-Jarabo Colomer and Saggio) now serve as members of the Court and no fewer than six serve or have served as members of the Court of First Instance (Biancarelli, Kalogeropoulos, Lenaerts, Saggio, Jaeger and Jung). The American analogy breaks down in that, at Luxembourg, a legal secretary has usually had other legal experience after qualifying, commonly serves a longer term, and some used to serve in that rank for a considerable period of years. Nevertheless, "law clerk" is the term officially used for legal secretary in the Staff Regulations. Usually but by no means invariably the legal secretary is of the same nationality as the judge or advocate general to whom he (or she) is attached.

---

[7a] For a detailed comparison of U.S. Supreme Court law clerks and the referendaires of the Court of Justice see Sally J. Kennedy, 'Beyond Principles and Agents' Seeing courts as organisations by comparing Referendaires at the European Court of Justice and Law Clerks at the U.S. Supreme Court, Comparative Political Studies, Vol. 33, No. 5, June 2000, p. 593.

In the earliest days of the Court, a single legal secretary sufficed for each member. Now that a team is needed, inevitably the closeness of the relationship to his or her judge or advocate general may have diminished somewhat, although that will be more than compensated for by the advantage of having close colleagues in the team (sometimes of different nationality) with whom to discuss ideas and cases. Moreover the increase in the sheer pressure of work means that each bears a heavier professional responsibility: more must be delegated to the legal secretary. The danger which some critics have associated with American law clerks is that the clerk's draft of a judgment may be merely rubber-stamped by the judge. This situation could not arise at Luxembourg because (as we shall see) a single collegiate judgment has to emerge from the secret deliberations of the Court (from which legal secretaries are excluded). And, while it is true that the advocate-general's opinion might be much influenced by the ideas of a legal secretary (indeed, it should be so influenced if the ideas are sound), each advocate general develops his own style which indelibly stamps his opinion as his own.

## READERS OF JUDGMENTS

Since 1980 there has been attached to the Chambers of the President of the Court a "Reader of Judgments", a somewhat portentous translation of the French term "*lecteur d'arrêts*" whose job it is to peruse the French drafting of the judgments of the Court and its Chambers in order to ensure consistency of style, correctness of citations and clarity of drafting. In cases where neither the judge-rapporteur nor any of his legal secretaries is francophone she may also give advice on tricky points of French legal drafting.

The first "*lecteur d'arrêts*", Roger Grass, now Registrar of the Court of Justice, was a French judge seconded from the Ministry of Justice in Paris. He was succeeded by a former legal secretary to one of the French members of the Court and, since 1989, she has had the assistance of a second "*lecteur*", also drawn from the French *magistrature*, in order to cope with the growing workload.

## THE REGISTRY

The duties of the Registrar are set out in the Protocol on the Statute of the Court and the Rules of Procedure[8] and the

---

[8] A consolidated version of the Rules of Procedure incorporating amendments up to December 1997 was published in OJ [Amendments for new languages and Member States [1997] O.J. L103/1 and 3 and corrigenda L351 of December 23, 1997]. The Instructions to the Registrar have hardly been altered since December 4, 1974: [1974] O.J. L350/33, December 28, 1974. Minor amendments were made in 1986: [1986] O.J. C286/4, November 13, 1986.

Instructions to the Registrar adopted pursuant to those rules. The Treaties merely require that "the Court shall appoint its Registrar and lay down the rules governing his service": Article 224 (ex Article 168) EC. Like the Registrar of the International Court of Justice in The Hague or that of the European Court of Human Rights in Strasbourg, the Registrar in Luxembourg is dignified with an importance and status quite unlike that normally associated with the officer of the same name in the English court system or the French *greffier*. This difference is evident from his being seated at the bench of the Court, to one side of but at the same level as the judges; he wears formal robes of the same colour as the members of the Court though of less sumptuous design, and accompanies the members of the Court upon ceremonial visits; his photograph and curriculum vitae are given equal prominence with those of the judges and advocate general in the Court's Annual Report; and like them he is mentioned in the founding Treaties.

According to the Protocol the Registrar must reside in Luxembourg as the seat of the Court. The Rules of Procedure require that he be appointed by secret ballot by the judges and advocates general for a term of six years. He is eligible for re-appointment, and the first holder of the office, Mr Albert Van Houtte, had the remarkable distinction of having served as Registrar for 29 years from 1953 when the Court began its existence as the Court of the Coal and Steel Community. Previously, Mr Van Houtte, a doctor of laws and *avocat*, had held academic and governmental posts in his native Belgium; from 1945 to 1952 he was attached to the Food and Agriculture Organisation of the United Nations. Mr Paul Heim, who succeeded Mr Van Houtte in February 1982, is British and a member of the English Bar; he had previously served as Registrar of the Supreme Court of Kenya and as a senior official in the Council of Europe and the European Parliament. He was succeeded in February 1988 by a Frenchman, M. Jean-Guy Giraud, an official for many years in the European Parliament – latterly, in the *cabinet* of its British President, Lord Plumb. His previous career, after law studies in Paris and Washington, included a period as legal and economic adviser at the French Embassy in Canberra. From February 1994 the Registrar has been another Frenchman, Mr Roger Grass, the first *lecteur d'arrets* (see above, p. 24).

Upon appointment the Registrar swears an oath to perform his duties impartially and conscientiously and, somewhat superfluously, to preserve the secrecy of the Court's deliberations, since, in contrast to the Registrar of the European Court of Human Rights, he does not accompany the Court when it withdraws to deliberate, nor does he take part in the drawing up of the judgment. He performs all his duties under the authority of the President. These duties are two-fold.

In the first place, he is responsible, under the President of the Court, for the conduct, at all stages, of proceedings before the Court. The Registry serves all documents upon the parties, verifies that the documents comply with the Rules of Procedure, especially with regard to time limits, and gives the parties the notices and communications required under the Rules. It also distributes copies of the documents in all cases to each member of the Court. The emphasis on the written procedure, which will be considered in Part Three, results in a considerable volume of documents being distributed in the Court; in the corridors of the Court the visitor is very likely to be met by the sight of trolleys laden with piles of documents, being circulated by a small army of messengers (known as *huissiers*). There is also a system of miniature lift-cum-railways specially installed for the transport of documents and books within the Court's complex of buildings. The Registry is responsible also for publishing the Court's decisions.

Secondly, the Registrar holds a position analogous to that of the Secretary General of other international institutions as the head of the administration of the Court. When the Court is convened for a general meeting (as distinct from its judicial deliberations) the Registrar is always present, although, unlike the judges and advocates general (all of whom attend) he has no vote. In general, he has a heavier responsibility than the Registrar of a national court whose administration and finances would be the ultimate responsibility of a Minister of Justice.

There are two Assistant Registrars, one of whom deals with the judicial side of the Registrar's duties and is responsible for the day to day management of the Registry itself, while the other works on the administrative side, ensuring co-ordination of the Courts' administrative departments.

## REPORTS AND CITATIONS

The official series of reports of judgments and other decisions is called "Reports of Cases before the Court of Justice and the Court of First Instance", abbreviated (in English) to European Court Reports (ECR). As the reports are published in all 11 official languages[9] – but not in Irish – the different versions are distinguished by the colour used for binding them, thus the English

---

[9] Spanish, Danish, German, Greek, English, French, Italian, Dutch, Portuguese, Finnish and Swedish.

series is bound in purple (like this book).[10] That series represents the only authentic source for the judgments of the two Courts and the opinions of the advocates general[11] and so citations to that series should be used wherever possible. The correct mode of citation in English[12] is first the number of the case, the names of the parties, then the year of publication of the judgment in square brackets, the abbreviation ECR and the page reference. The case, or docket number as it is sometimes called, is simply the consecutive number attributed to the case upon its arrival in the relevant registry accompanied by the year concerned. Thus the *Brown Boveri* case (see below) was the seventy-ninth case registered in the Court of Justice in 1989. Since the establishment of the Court of First Instance the case number of cases before that Court has been preceded by a capital letter "T"[13] and those of the Court of Justice by a "C". From 1990 onwards the volumes of reports have also been divided into two sections so that the page number is preceded by the numeral "I" for cases before the Court of Justice and by the numeral "II" for cases before the Court of First Instance. Where reports of cases are especially voluminous, Parts I and II are bound separately.[14]

Thus cases before 1990 will be referred to as, for example, Case 283/84 *Trans Tirreno Express SpA v. Ufficio Provinciale IVA.*[15] From 1990 onwards the correct mode of citation is as follows: Case C-79/89 *Brown Boveri v. Hauptzollamt Mannheim.*[16]

Special forms of procedure are indicated by a capital letter or letters added after the case number. The letters are all derived from the French term for the procedure concerned. Thus the most common such suffix is a capital "R", from the French *référé* in

---

[10] Curiously the various ducts, valves and other equipment for the ventilation and air-conditioning system in the old courthouse employ the same colour scheme as the law reports. We are convinced however that this does not mean that different parts of the building are supplied with respectively Dutch, French or Portuguese air as the case may be.

[11] It should be noted that in legal terms authenticity only attaches to the version of the judgment in the language of the case (mentioned in a footnote on the first page of each report) and the opinion of the advocate general in the language in which he delivered it (likewise mentioned in a footnote): see Art. 31 of the Rules of Procedure of the Court. For the choice of the language of procedure see p. 275, below.

[12] Methods of citation vary according to the differing legal traditions of the Member States.

[13] From the French *"Tribunal de première instance"*.

[14] See for example [1991] ECR I–3359–4326 and [1991] ECR II–467–678.

[15] Case 283/84 *Trans Tirreno Express SpA v. Ufficio Provinciale IVA* [1986] ECR 231; [1986] 2 C.M.L.R. 100.

[16] Case C–79/89 *Brown Boveri v. Hauptzollamt Mannheim* [1991] ECR I–1853; [1993] 1 C.M.L.R. 814.

interim measures proceedings.[17] Increasingly frequent is "P" for *pourvoi* in the case of appeals to the Court of Justice against judgments of the Court of First Instance[18] and, since an appeal to the Court of Justice may be accompanied by a request for interim measures ordering the stay of execution of the disputed judgment, those letters may be combined as in Case C–372/90P–R *Samenwerkende Elektriciteits-Produktiebedrijven NV v. Commission.*[19] Other suffixes which may be met with from time to time include "REV" in applications for revision,[20] "Imm" in applications for the lifting of immunity of Community institutions[21]; "TO" for third party proceedings, from the French *tierce opposition*,[22] "OPPO" for an application to set aside a judgment given in default from the French *opposition*[23] and "AJ" for legal aid applications from *"assistance judiciaire"*.[24] For its part the Court of First Instance has adopted the style of using the number of the relevant Article in the Rules of Procedure instead of letters, in some cases at least. Thus in cases concerning taxation of costs formerly indicated by the suffix "DEP" or "DEPE", the case number is now followed by (92).[25]

Prior to the publication of a judgment in the ECR, offset printed copies of the text of the judgment are made available first by the Registry which, immediately after delivery of the judgment concerned, places a number of copies in the language of the case, in the Court's working language, French, and, since January 1994, in all of the other official languages outside the door of the courtroom from where they may be collected free of charge. On the same day, and for at least 12 months after the judgment concerned the full text of the judgment is available on the Court's website

---

[17] For example Case C–313/90R *Comite International de la Rayonne et des Fibres Synthetiques and Others v. Commission of the European Communities* [1991] ECR I–2557.

[18] For example Case C–115/90P *Turner v. Commission* [1991] ECR I–1423.

[19] Case C–372/90 P-R *Samenwerkende Elektriciteits-Produktiebedrijven NV v. Commission* [1991] ECR I–2043.

[20] See for example Case T–4/89 REV *BASF AG v. Commission* [1992] ECR II–1591.

[21] This is one for aficionados since the only known example is Case C–2/88Imm *Zwartveld and Others* [1990] ECR I–4405.

[22] See for example Case C–147/86 TO1 *Panhellinia Omospondia Idioktiton Frontistirion Xenon Glosson and Others v. Hellenic Republic and Commission of the European Communities* [1989] ECR 4103. This was one of a series of three cases which are numbered accordingly.

[23] See for example Case T–42/89 OPPO *European Parliament v. Wolfdieter Graf Yorsk von Wartenburg* [1990] ECR II–299.

[24] See for example the Order of the President of the Court of First Instance in Case T–149/97 AJ *Helmers* (order of July 10, 1997 not published).

[25] See for example Joined Cases T–177/94 (92) and T–377/94 (92) *Altmann and Others v. Commission* [1996] ECR II–1245.

free of charge. Subsequently, and until publication of the bound volumes, offset copies may be obtained on application from the Internal Services Division of the Court for 330 Belgian francs each. Alternatively, provided that a subscription is already held to the ECR, the offset copies too may be sent by subscription.

Since the judgments are always drafted in French,[26] as are all of the summaries and indexing material prepared by the Research Division, the bound volume in French is always the first to appear. It is usually published approximately five to six months following the end of the month to which it relates. Including the index there are usually 11 monthly paperback volumes or *fascicules* per year (since no judgments are delivered during the month of August) which are subsequently bound up into several hardback volumes.

At present all judgments are translated into all of the other Community languages for publication in the Reports. The Reports thus provide the only *complete* record of the Courts' judicial activities. However this policy is under severe strain as a result of the sheer volume of material being produced by the two Courts and an insufficient capacity to carry out the translations rapidly in the Court's Translation Directorate. In the Directorate priority must be given to translating judgments and advocate-generals' opinions into the language of the case, preliminary rulings for transmission to the governments of the Member States and other procedural documents which may be required. This has had the effect that, until 1994, there was a delay of up to two years between the publication of the French volume and publication of the equivalent volume in English, since the cases to be included in that volume in which the language of the case was other than English had to await their turn for translation.

The Court is acutely aware of the difficulties which this situation has caused for practitioners and academic lawyers and, given that it is unlikely that the Community's budgetary authorities will allow the recruitment of a sufficient number of additional translators, the Court is anxiously examining ways of either reducing the volume of translations demanded or of changing working methods in order to speed up the process. However none of the possible solutions is without substantial drawbacks as is illustrated by the fact that two previous attempts to reduce the volume of demand for translations failed.

Thus for about 18 months from the end of 1984 the Court decided to omit the part entitled "Facts and issues" from the version of the judgment published in the ECR This was to reduce

---

[26] See p. 283, below.

the burden on the Translation Directorate. That change met with some dissatisfaction amongst practitioners, law teachers and national government departments in response to which the Court decided to restore the published report of the facts and issues by simply reproducing the Report for the Hearing with each judgment.[27] That practice was introduced at the beginning of the new judicial year in September 1986[28] and since then the full report has consisted of the title of the case, including keywords as to its subject matter, the summary of the judgment or headnote prepared by the Research and Documentation Division; the Report for the Hearing (giving the facts and issues); the advocate-general's opinion and finally the judgment itself. That arrangement has the merit of reflecting the actual sequence of events.

In another attempt to reduce the volume of translations and hence to expedite publication of the Reports, it was decided that from 1989 judgments in uncontested actions for non-implementation of directives brought by the Commission, certain staff cases and cases of purely technical interest would be published in summary form only.[29] In cases selected for publication in that fashion the report consists only of the title as before, the summary of the judgment prepared by the research division, the conclusion of the advocate-general's opinion in which he makes his recommendation to the Court, and under the heading "Judgment of the Court" the full title of the case, the composition of the formation which decided it and the operative part of the judgment. Instead, the full text of the judgment including the grounds upon which it was based could be consulted in the Court's Registry and copies obtained at the usual fee, but only in the language of the case. Likewise the full text of the advocate-general's opinion would only be made available in the language in which he delivered it. That approach too gave rise to serious objections, particularly on the part of some Member States, and therefore had to be abandoned for cases published after 1991.

From January 1994 the Court decided once again to cease publishing the Report for the Hearing in all languages. It will however remain a public document in the language of the case (see p. 275, below) made available to the public on the day of the hearing and thereafter obtainable from the Registry. The time thus

---

[27] For a recent example see the report of Case C–213/89 *The Queen v. Secretary of State for Transport, ex p. Factortame Ltd and Others* [1990] ECR I–2433 at 2434; [1990] 3 C.M.L.R. 1.

[28] See the report of Case 116/82 *Commission v. Germany* [1986] ECR 2519.

[29] The first such case appears to have been Case 259/88 *Godfroy v. Court of Justice* [1989] ECR 123; see also the Reports on Case 233/87 *Merkur Aussenhandel GmbH & Co. KG v. Hauptzollamt Hamburg-Jonas* [1989] ECR 569; [1988] 2 C.M.L.R. 620 and the three following cases in the same volume of the Reports.

saved in translation has enabled judgments to be made available in all languages on the day of delivery, or very shortly thereafter, and the printed volumes to be published in all languages within one month after the French version.

For its part the Court of First Instance has contributed to relieving the burden on the Translation Directorate by publishing its judgments in staff cases[30] in the ECR only where they raise points of general interest or of principle. All other staff cases are now published in a separate series[31] with the full text only in the language of the case accompanied by a summary in the language chosen by the subscriber. That series will also include summaries of staff cases decided on appeal by the Court of Justice, the full text of such appeal judgments being published in the normal way in the ECR.

Partially in recognition of the problems caused by such delays and partly also to enable lawyers to approach the almost impossible task of keeping abreast of developments across the whole field of Community law, the Court has, through its Information Office, for many years published an invaluable weekly summary of all of the judgments delivered by the Court during the week concerned. The weekly "Proceedings" as they are called in English[32] are distributed free of charge by simply sending a written request to the Court's Information Office. The French version is completed and printed in the week immediately following the week to which it relates and so reaches its subscribers in Europe within a week to 10 days. The other language versions of course have to be translated and are therefore distributed, normally, about two to three weeks later. The Proceedings too are available on the Court's website.

An alternative means of access to the Court's case law[33] is provided by the Celex legal database. This is a vast and invaluable inter-institutional computerised documentation system for Community law containing both bibliographic information and the full texts of the various documents. The database covers Community legislation including the Treaties establishing the Communities, various amending Treaties, Acts of Accession, the Single European Act and the Maastricht and Amsterdam Treaties, Agreements and other Acts relating to the Community's external relations and

---

[30] See Chap. 9, below.
[31] Known as "Reports of European Community Staff Cases", abbreviated to ECR–S.C.
[32] The full title is "Proceedings of the Court of Justice and the Court of First Instance of the European Communities".
[33] Including judgments of the Court of First Instance and advocate-generals' opinions.

secondary legislation (regulations and directives). It also contains ancillary material such as preparatory acts for the preparation of legislation including Commission proposals and opinions of the European Parliament, the Economic and Social Committee and the Court of Auditors. Questions addressed by Members of the European Parliament to the Commission or the Council are also included as are the answers to those questions. Following the legislative process references are added to the database to national provisions adopted by each Member State to comply with Community directives.

So far as the Court of Justice is concerned Celex includes the case law of the Court of Justice and of the Court of First Instance including judgments, orders and the opinions of the advocate general (the latter only for opinions delivered after 1987).

The information provided consists of bibliographical data such as the case number, a reference to the field of activity concerned, the year, subject-matter, descriptors and, in the matter of text, the full title of any document, the full text except for the "Facts and Issues" (or latterly the Report for the Hearing) and for advocate-generals' opinions published prior to 1987. Those earlier opinions are being progressively incorporated. The database is fully cross-referenced to all legislation and other cases cited in the case being read · and it is even possible to consult the different language versions of the same document. At present the database exists in Danish, Dutch, English, French, German, Greek and Italian, although the state of completeness of the database in each language depends upon the availability of translations. It contains some 150,000 entries and is updated at a rate of about 5,000 entries per year. The database is managed and distributed by the Commission of the European Communities through the Office for Official Publications of the European Communities[34] to whom enquiries may be addressed. It is available throughout the world via various host databases subject to different conditions and differing availability in terms of sectors and languages covered and services offered. Some of the hosts have made parts of the database available on CD-ROM and research is continuing with a view to making this medium more widely available.

It should also be mentioned that several independent publishers produce reports of the Court's activities. These are generally selective as to the cases reported and even those judgments reported are frequently not accompanied by the relevant advocate-general's opinion and rarely by the Report for the Hearing. So far as reports in English are concerned chief among these unofficial

---

[34] OPOCE, 2 rue Mercier, L–2985 Luxembourg.

reports is the Common Market Law Reports (cited as C.M.L.R.). They commenced publication in 1962, prior to the accession of the United Kingdom, and their main advantage has been the more rapid publication of a selection of the most important cases dealt with by the two Courts, particularly where the language of the case is not English. This is possible because C.M.L.R. commissions its own translations but, although these are carried out with care, they do not necessarily reach the exacting standards required of translators in the Court's own Translation Directorate whose translators have available to them a vast range of documentary materials as well as, crucially, the originals of all procedural documents and direct access to the authors of the judgments and opinions.

The C.M.L.R. has the additional advantage of including English translations of cases decided by national courts within the Member States relating to important points of Community law.[35] The original C.M.L.R. has spawned a number of offspring such as the Antitrust Supplement and the European Law Digest providing a more specialised service to lawyers in those fields.

The Weekly Law Reports and the All England Law Reports also include occasional reports of cases before the Court of Justice[36] and although these are based upon the Court's own style of presentation the selection is principally of cases with specific interest to English lawyers such as cases referred by English courts or Article 169 proceedings brought against the United Kingdom. Simon's Tax Cases similarly contains occasional reports on judgments of the Court of Justice within its specialised field, although these are less focussed on United Kingdom courts.

Finally, it should be recalled that law reports prepared by a barrister (as is the case for all of the above-mentioned series) are to be distinguished from reports made by journalists of Court decisions. In the case of journalists' reports of such cases these are likely to be, at best, based upon the helpful, but necessarily highly compressed, press summaries issued by the Court's Information Office of the highest profile cases, and examples of the worst are

---

[35] See for example *Minister for Economic Affairs v. St. Fromagerie Franco-Suisse "Le Ski"* [1972] C.M.L.R. 330 or the judgment of the French *Conseil d'Etat* in *Nicolo* [1990] C.M.L.R. 173.

[36] See for example Case C–31/90 *Johnson v. Chief Adjudication Office* [1993] 2 W.L.R. 192; [1991] 3 C.M.L.R. 917; *Webb v. Emo Air Cargo Ltd* [1993] 1 W.L.R. 49, a report of the House of Lords' decision to refer the case to the Court of Justice where it was registered as Case C–32/93: Case C–169/91, *Stoke on Trent City Council v. B&Q plc* [1993] 1 All E.R. 481; [1993] 1 C.M.L.R. 426.

almost too painful to contemplate.[37] However the regular European Law Reports published in *The Times* are generally reliable, if highly condensed, as are those occasionally published in the *Financial Times* and *The Independent*.

## LIBRARY AND DOCUMENTATION SERVICE

In addition to the Registry, there are five other departments which make up the administration of the Court.

The first of these is "the Library, Research and Documentation Directorate" which is, in turn, divided into a Library Division and Research and Documentation Division. The library has a very extensive collection of legal materials, especially those published in the 15 Member States. As well as a complete collection in the field of Community law, it maintains comprehensive collections of the laws of all the Member States, selections from some non-Member States, in particular the United States, public and private international law and comparative law. Total holdings are in excess of 135,000 volumes (65,000 titles). The library is open to any lawyer of a Member State as well as to bona fide research scholars. It is in the charge of the librarian, whose staff includes several lawyers who review each of over 750 periodicals to which the Court subscribes and enter references to decisions of the Court and all aspects of Community law into the library's computerised catalogue. This not only facilitates research but also enables the invaluable "*Bibliographie juridique de l'intégration européenne*" to be published annually.

## THE RESEARCH AND DOCUMENTATION DIVISION

The Research and Documentation Division is staffed by some 20 lawyers representing all of the legal systems of the Member States. The main task of the Division is to assist the members of the Court of Justice and the Court of First Instance with research on the legal background to cases when so requested by one of the members (usually the judge-rapporteur). That assistance takes the form of

---

[37] See for example the report of Case 142/84 *BAT v. Commission* [1987] ECR 4487; [1987] 2 C.M.L.R. 55; [1988] 4 C.M.L.R. 24 contained in the *Financial Times* of November 17, 1987 which was headed "Rogue elephant at The Hague" and, more recently the report of the judgment of the Court of First Instance in Case T–66/89 *Publishers' Association v. Commission* [1992] ECR II–1995; [1989] 4 C.M.L.R. 825, contained in *The Times* of July 10, 1992 which committed the same solecism.

research notes on particular aspects of Community law or comparative law notes surveying the relevant provisions of the law of the Member States or countries further afield in particular areas. In addition the Division contributes to the publication of the ECR by preparing the summaries of judgments which appear at the beginning of each report and the indices which are published at the end of each year. The Division is also responsible for the preparation and publication of the digest of case law relating to the European Communities in four series of which the A series covers the general case law of the Court and the D series, covers the case law of the Court of Justice and national courts on the Brussels Convention on jurisdiction and the enforcement of judgments in civil and commercial matters: both series are available to the public and are regularly brought up to date. The B series, covering decisions of national courts in matters of Community law other than the Brussels Convention, is kept in the form of a computerised database which may be consulted by interested researchers, while the C series, covering the staff law of the European Communities, is still in preparation.

The Division also includes a legal data processing department which supplies the case law section of the Celex legal database, described above.

The department also manages other internal databases based on software which it has developed specially for specific internal information requirements. These databases may be used for rapid research by members of the Courts, the Research and Documentation Division, the Press and Information Division and others who may need them. They have also facilitated and accelerated the publication of the indices to the ECR and enable lists to be published such as the A–Z Index of all cases brought before the Court since 1954.

## TRANSLATION DIRECTORATE

As will already be apparent the Translation Directorate is a vital branch of the Court's administration. A team of some 225 legally qualified linguists have to cope with the heavy demand for translations which the multi-lingual character of the Court entails. Pleadings may need to be translated into French as the working language as well as into whatever language is prescribed for the particular case and requests for preliminary rulings from national courts must be translated into the other 10 official languages for notification to all of the Member States. For publication the opinions of the advocates general and the Court's judgments have to be in all 11 languages.

The four enlargements of the Community produced a need for the pre-1973, pre-1981, pre-1986 and pre-1995 decisions of the

Court to be translated into English and Danish, Greek, Portuguese and Spanish, and Finnish and Swedish respectively. All of the Court's decisions between 1953 and 1972 are now available in English. Only the principal decisions prior to 1973 have been translated into Danish: they extend to six volumes as compared with the 20 volumes of the complete reports. A similar abridgement in Greek of the principal decisions prior to 1981 (17 volumes) has now been completed.

With regard to Portuguese and Spanish, a similar solution was initially adopted. The most important cases have been translated into Portuguese by the Courts' own translators, others have been contracted out to freelance translators but revised in the Court. The aim was to complete the work by the end of 1996. However, the Spanish Government decided that a complete set should also be prepared in that language. Such a task was beyond the resources of the Court to complete within a reasonable time so the Translation Department has undertaken to translate a selection of about 500 of the most important cases prior to 1986. These will act as a guide and a benchmark for a group of translators engaged by the Ministry of Foreign Affairs in Madrid to complete the remainder of the set. The Finnish and Swedish governments have taken similar measures for the translation of about 450 essential cases.

The Directorate is divided into 11 language divisions, to correspond with the official languages, and a terminology branch.

Irish is a special case. Although it is accepted as a procedural language (below, p. 251), in practice, all cases emanating from Ireland have been conducted so far in English. There are no official versions in Irish of the Court's decisions. Indeed, the Translation Directorate has no translators for the Irish language, nor does the Interpretation Division (below) have interpreters competent in that language. If it should be necessary for a case to be conducted in Irish, linguists would need to be specially hired for the purpose. Hitherto, however, the Irish Government has adopted English when faced with the choice of the language of the case. If it should happen, as one day it may, that a reference is made for a preliminary ruling (see Chapter 10) from an Irish court or tribunal where the proceedings have been conducted in Irish, or a disgruntled Community official exercised his or her option to use Irish in a staff case, Irish would become the procedural language of the case, the judgment would be authentic only in that language, and presumably the Court would publish an official report in Irish of the opinion and judgment. By way of analogy, there have been occasional publications of the Official Journal in Irish in order to provide official texts in Irish of certain Community acts or conventions.[38]

---

[38] See, *e.g.* Final Act of Single European Act in O.J. L169, p. 28; Decision of October 24, establishing a Court of First Instance in [1988] O.J. L319/1.

However, a court in Wales could not rely upon the Welsh Courts Act in order to submit a preliminary reference in Welsh: unlike Irish, Welsh is not accepted under the rules as a procedural language.

## INTERPRETATION SERVICE

Besides its team of translators, the Court has need of interpreters to provide simultaneous translations during the oral proceedings or at other meetings organised by the Court (such as judicial conferences). Before 1980 the Court did not have these scarce specialists in its exclusive employ but used to hire a number of freelance interpreters who also served the European Parliament (which frequently met in Luxembourg where it has its administrative headquarters, although it now generally meets in Strasbourg). Since then, the Court has recruited its own specialists in legal interpretation. This Interpretation Division, as it is termed, falls under the direct control of the Registrar. By 1993 it included 34 interpreters but is being expanded so as to provide, eventually, interpretation from and into all the official languages. The possible combinations amount, in theory, to an horrendous total of 110. In practice, the burden may be lessened by using an interpreter in one of the principal languages (usually English or French) to act as a link in a relay, so that, for example, in proceedings conducted in Danish, an English interpreter will translate from Danish into English while a Spanish interpreter will listen to the English interpretation and interpret this into Spanish. Although this procedure works quite well, it inevitably entails a slight delay and a risk of a "Chinese whispers" effect.

## PRESS AND INFORMATION DIVISION

This department provides information for the press, for the professional and academic worlds and for the general public. It also organises study conferences for judges from national courts and programmes for groups of visitors since, like other Community institutions, the Court is inundated by requests from interested individuals and groups to visit the Court. Over 10,000 national judges, professors and law students flock to Luxembourg each year to study its working.

This service also issues press statements on important new judgments. It publishes weekly summaries of proceedings, which are very widely distributed (see p. 31, above). Since 1996 it has managed the Courts internet site (www.curia.eu.int) which, in addition to the texts of judgments and the weekly proceedings already mentioned, includes all press releases, the main legal instruments (such as Treaty provisions, Rules of Procedure), the A–Z Index of cases and official statistics of the Court's work.

## ADMINISTRATION, PERSONNEL AND FINANCE

The staff of the Court numbered [765] permanent and [241] temporary posts in February 2000 and, because the Court has to be administered as a self-contained institution, it requires the services of a personnel department. This department, together with a Finance Department and an Internal Services Department, constitutes the Directorate of Administration. Internal Services is the "house-keeping" branch, responsible for the Court building, furnishings, equipment, security and such like.

While it is invidious to place a price on the administration of justice, salaries and rents must be paid, and books, furniture and office materials bought. Although the Court of Justice is one of the five Community institutions, it is, necessarily, wholly autonomous. In financial terms this means that the money to enable it to function is allocated to it each year as part of the general Community budget.[39] However, once the budgetary authority (the Council and the European Parliament) has adopted the general budget of the Communities, the Court itself is responsible for managing its own finances. At the end of each financial year the accounts are scrutinised by the Court of Auditors which may make comments either on specific items of expenditure or on matters of financial management by the institution concerned.

In the 2000 general budget the Court's total expenditure is estimated at 131,256,645 Euro. From this total the projected amount of the Court's own income is deducted. Such income derives principally from the tax, pension and social security deductions from the salaries of the Members and staff of the institution. This is supplemented by small amounts from the sale of publications, interest on bank accounts and occasional sales of vehicles and equipment due to be replaced.

The contribution to the Court's running expenses which remains to be met from the general Community budget is estimated at 97,725,695 Euro for 2000. This represents approximately 2.44 per cent of the overall budget for administering the Community

---

[39] For a general analysis of the problems faced in managing European Community finances see "Financing the European Community" M. Shackleton, Chatham House Papers, Royal Institute of International Affairs, 1990. The full Community budget including that of the Court is published in the *Official Journal* each year.

institutions but barely 0.13 per cent of the total general budget of the Communities.

Of this sum some 97,725,695 Euros is required to pay the salaries of the Members of the institution and its staff while nearly 21,100,000 Euros are payable for the rental of the Court's buildings, which are owned by the Luxembourg Government.

## CHAMBERS

As mentioned above, in order to facilitate its work the Court has been divided into six Chambers, two consisting of six judges each and four of three judges. One judge in each Chamber is designated as President of that Chamber. The advocates general, by contrast, are not attached to particular Chambers.

Power to set up Chambers was included in the Treaties (see, for example, Article 32(1) ECSC, Article 221(2)(ex Article 165(2)) EC), and the Rules of the Court now provide that "the Court shall set up Chambers" in accordance with the Treaty provisions "and shall decide which judges shall be attached to them" (Article 9, r. 1). The Rules further provide that "the Court shall lay down general principles governing the assignment of cases to Chambers".

The use of Chambers has evolved considerably. Originally, a Chamber of three was used in lieu of the full Court only for the hearing of "staff cases", that is, cases where the Community civil servants or officials are in dispute with the Community institution which employs them: here the Court, under jurisdiction conferred by Article 236 (ex Article 179) EC, sat in effect as an industrial tribunal of first and last resort. Staff cases are more fully considered in Chapter 9; they have formed in the past a significant part of the business of the Court but have now been transferred to the Court of First Instance and will only reach the Court upon appeal on a point of law.

A modest extension of the use of Chambers took place in 1974 by an amendment of the Rules so as to provide that a reference for a preliminary ruling under Article 177 EC (or Article 41 ECSC, Article 150 Euratom) could be assigned to a Chamber if it was "of an essentially technical nature" or concerned "matters for which there was already an established body of case law". The first such assignment took place in 1976.

Following the further enlargement of the Court by the accession of Greece in 1981, the three existing Chambers of three judges were supplemented by the establishment of two further Chambers of five judges. And upon the accession of Spain and Portugal in 1986, the two larger Chambers were expanded to include six judges each, although continuing to sit as Chambers of five. After the Court's enlargement to 15 judges in 1995 and given the fact that the President of the Court is not assigned to any of the Chambers, two of the four smaller Chambers now have four judges attached to them, and the two large chambers (the fifth and sixth Chambers) have seven judges attached to them. Since in cases assigned to a small chamber, only three judges will in practice sit and in the large Chambers only five judges will sit, a somewhat Byzantine system has been adopted in order to determine the judge who will actually sit in a given case.[40] These larger Chambers, representing as they do a broader cross-section of legal systems than the Chambers of three, have been entrusted with cases which it was formerly thought necessary to reserve for the full Court.

Further, more drastic amendments of the rules were made in 1979 and again in 1991 as a part of a strategy to deal with the substantial increase in the Court's workload.[41] The present text of Article 95 of the Rules extends not only to references for preliminary rulings but also to appeals brought against decisions of the Court of First Instance and any other case other than those instituted by a Member State or a Community institution. Under the new provisions, the Court may assign to a Chamber any such case "as the difficulty or importance of the case or particular circumstances are not such as to require that the Court decide it in plenary session".

Finally Article 221 (ex Article 165) EC was amended by the Maastricht Treaty so as to enable the Court to refer any case to a Chamber, including actions brought by or against Member States, unless a Member State or an institution requests a plenary hearing. This change gives the Court much greater flexibility in arranging its workload. Article 95 of the Rules of Procedure was amended to take account of this development.

The decision whether to assign to a Chamber and, if so, whether to a three-judge or five-judge Chamber, is taken by the Court at the end of the written procedure upon consideration of the preliminary report of the judge-rapporteur and after the advocate general has been heard (Article 95(2)). A case may not, however,

---

[40] In Case C–7/94 *Landesamt fur Ausbildungsföderung Nordrhein-Westfalen v. Lubor Gaal* [1995] ECR I–1031, before the Sixth Chamber the representative of the German Government opened his argument by complaining about the composition of the Chamber, pointing out that, as it then stood, Article 165 EC enabled the Court to form Chambers consisting of three or five judges but that, in the *Official Journal*, six judges were named as being attached to that Chamber, despite there being no legal basis for such a number. Despite this objection, the Court proceeded to judgment.

[41] The 1997 amendments were only those necessary to accommodate the revised composition of the Court and the new languages after the fourth round of accessions.

be assigned to a Chamber if trial by the full Court is requested by a Member State or a Community institution taking part in the proceedings whether as a party, or as intervener in a direct action, or by submitting written observations on a reference for a preliminary ruling.[42]

The revised formulation of Article 95 and the use made of it by the Court in practice has meant that since October 1979 cases have been commonly heard by a Chamber rather than by the full Court; and this has become more markedly so since the establishment of the larger Chambers.

The device of subdividing a court to enable it to handle a heavier caseload is a familiar one in the Member States. Thus the French *Conseil d'Etat* has 10 *sous-sections* of its *Section du Contentieux*. Subdivision of a court may also be a means for ensuring specialisation, as with the Divisions of the English High Court, but there has not yet developed any such specialisation at Luxembourg, although it has long been mooted as a development for the new Court of First Instance (see Chapter 5, below).

## THE COURT BUILDING

Pericles expressed the view that it was not walls that made a city great but the men within them. Physical environment however does have important influences, both practical and psychological, upon human activity. Some description therefore is appropriate here of the actual premises and location in which the Court operates.

In January 1973 the enlargement of the Community was the occasion of the addition to the Court of three new judges and an advocate general. On the same day as they swore their judicial oaths, the Luxembourg Government handed over to the President of the Court the new Courthouse (if we may so translate *Palais de Justice*). Previously the Court had enjoyed no permanent home. From 1953, as the Court of Justice of the Coal and Steel Community, it had occupied the Villa Vauban, a large mansion in a park in the centre of Luxembourg, now used as an art gallery.[43] In 1959 it became the Court of Justice of the European Communities and moved to a more modern building, also in the city centre.

---

[42] These detailed matters of procedure are more fully explained in Chap. 12, as is the function of a Chamber in undertaking the instruction, or preparatory inquiry, which may be an important phase of the procedure in rare instances (below, pp. 276 *et seq.*).

[43] And temporarily as the town residence of H.R.H. the Grand Duke of Luxembourg while the Royal Palace was undergoing a major restoration.

The present building, opened upon the accession of Denmark, Ireland and the United Kingdom, is situated on the Kirchberg Plateau, a magnificent, elevated site on the further bank of one of the deep ravines which encircle the ancient fortified City of Luxembourg. The Plateau was mostly woodland and fields until acquired in 1961 by the Luxembourg Government to provide a special precinct for the various European institutions based in the Grand Duchy. As well as the Court, the Plateau contains the two buildings providing the administrative headquarters of the European Parliament, a "Hemi-cycle" where the Parliament occasionally sat before 1981 (see p. 14, above), a conference centre where the Council holds its meeting during the months of April, June and October,[44] and the Commission Building (which houses three of the Commission's Directorates-General), the Statistical Office for the Communities, the Court of Auditors and the European Investment Bank.

The complex of buildings also includes a large European School to provide schooling in the Community languages for the children of the international community, and, inevitably, that commercial enterprise found at every international crossroads – a Holiday Inn, subsequently re-named the "Pullman Hotel" and now "Sofitel".

The Courthouse is a remarkable building on many counts. Despite its five storeys it appears squat because of its large dimensions. Its exterior structure is predominantly of glass and special rustproof steel, left unpainted and now with a natural brown patina. The interior is functional but elegant with much use of granite, marble and plain carpeting. The library has extensive stack-space and staff offices but a painfully small reading-room.

By 1981 the Courthouse had already proved too small for the needs of the enlarged Community. The large Translation Directorate had to move out first into the Commission Building and later into a temporary, prefabricated building, and the third floor is no longer adequate to provide separate cabinets for the increased number of judges and advocates general. To help relieve the congestion, an extensive annexe adjoining the Courthouse was opened in 1988. That annexe was christened the "Erasmus" building and houses the Members and Registry of the Court of First Instance, two Courtrooms and the administrative services of the institution as a whole. It was joined in 1992 by a second annexe containing two further Courtrooms as well as administrative offices which has been called the "Thomas More" building.

---

[44] As it is required to do by Art. 1(b) of the Decision taken by common agreement between the Representations of Governments of the Member States on the location of Seats of the Institutions and of certain bodies and Departments of the European Communities, at the Edinburgh Summit on December 12, 1992.

A third annexe in the form of a tower, contiguous with and in the same style as the Thomas More and Erasmus buildings, was completed in 1994 and inaugurated by M. Jacques Santer, then Prime Minister of Luxembourg, just three weeks before the swearing in of the new members of the Court of Justice and Court of First Instance on October 6, 1994.

The main feature of the original Courthouse, indeed its *raison d'être*, was the set of three Courtrooms, a main Courtroom for plenary sittings of the Court and two for use by the Chambers. Each Courtroom had a striking and distinctive colour scheme and they are decorated with modern tapestries or mural paintings; the public accommodation is spacious and consists of comfortable tip-up seats, each equipped with ear-phones for simultaneous interpretation.

Across the head of each courtroom, both in the *Palais* and in the new annexes which follow the same layout, is the raised bench for the judges and at each end of the bench a separate seat for the advocate general (from the public seats, on the left) and the Registrar (on the right).

The judges, advocate general and Registrar wear dignified robes of deep crimson; their French-style caps of the same colour have been discarded (alas) even for ceremonial occasions. Lawyers appearing before them wear the gowns of their own national profession: the wig made its appearance with British and Irish entry.

Public judicial sittings are generally held on Tuesdays, Wednesdays and Thursdays. The overall impression upon most visitors is one of a dignified and orderly procedure. No time is wasted but there is no feeling of haste: the mills of Community justice grind smoothly. There is none of the drama, the cut and thrust and impromptu repartee of an English trial. The advocates deliver their set speeches: the rhetoric is subdued and often misunderstood, and humour intervenes rarely, and then lightly.

Having been designed in the late 1960s and completed in 1972 it was well known that the construction of the Courthouse included the use of the then state of the art insulating material, asbestos. Although no actual contamination had occurred a report in 1995 required certain precautionary measures to be taken and gave the building a usable life of only three to four years. The precautionary measures were implemented at once, but entailed the closure and sealing of all three of the Courtrooms. The whole courthouse was evacuated in summer 1999 to enable the asbestos to be safely removed and it will be closed for some six years while refurbishment is carried out. Both the Court and the Court of First Instance must of course continue to function, so an immense and logistically complex process of "musical chambers" has been implemented.

First, in order to provide the flexibility for the other moves, the huge Translation Directorate was moved into a purpose built, "temporary" building (dubbed the "Portacourt" but officially "*Bâtiment T*"), said to be the largest prefabricated building of its kind in Europe. The Court of First Instance then returned to its original premises in the Erasmus building while the Court of Justice now occupies the tower.

This state of affairs will last until about 2006 when the new construction programme is due to be completed resulting in spectacular extensions to the complex. The two towers will each be 25 storeys high, the second and third skyscrapers in Luxembourg. They and the "halo" which will surround (and sadly partially obscure) the elegant old *Palais* were designed by Jean-Louis Perrault, architect of the *Très Grande Bibliothèque* in Paris.

## Abridged organigramme of the Court of Justice and the Court of First Instance

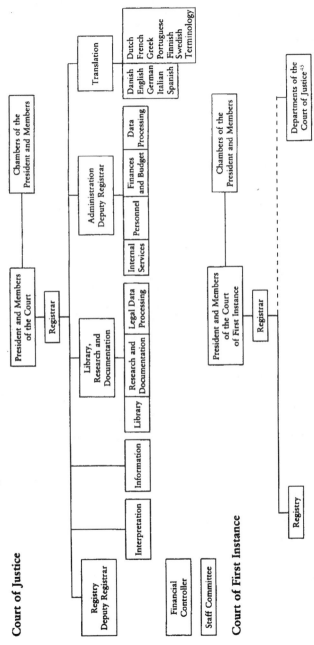

**Court of Justice**

**Court of First Instance**

President and Members of the Court

[45] Pursuant to the new Article 45 of the Protocol on the Statute of the Court of Justice, "officials and other servants attached to the Court of Justice shall render their services to the Court of First Instance to enable it to function."

# Chapter Three

# Judges

## INTRODUCTION

The reputation of a court depends upon the quality of its judges. Judicial quality is itself dependent upon the ability of an institution to attract outstanding lawyers into its service. Long-established institutions like the English High Court or the French *Conseil d'Etat* exert this attraction by the prestige accumulated over generations or even centuries. A relatively new institution such as the Court of Justice lacks this power in its formative years: those called to serve it have been attracted rather by a sense of mission or vocation. But within the 48 years of its existence the Court has built up, by bold and imaginative judgments, its own tradition that should ensure the highest level of recruits to its ranks.[1]

In this chapter, we will examine the Treaty provisions governing the appointment of members of the Court and their conditions of service. Much of what is said will apply both to the judges and the advocates general, although the distinctive function of the latter warrants their being made the subject of a separate chapter. Some account will be given of the backgrounds from which the past and present judges of the Court have been drawn. In order to show the end-product of their labours, the judgments of the Court will be considered, especially from the point of view of their form and style. Judgments are further considered in later parts, but we think it desirable to provide this early introduction to their form and to the way in which they should be read.

---

[1] We may date the start of the Court as December 4, 1952 when the Court of Justice of the ECSC was installed in the Villa Vauban (see "XXXV ANN. 1952–1987" p. 70) and 7 judges took their Oaths of Office.

# APPOINTMENT

## Number

The Court of Justice now consists of 15 judges, assisted by nine advocates general. The Act of Accession of 1994, in anticipation of ratification of entry by Austria, Finland, Norway and Sweden, provided for the Court to be composed of 17 judges and enabled it to set up Chambers of seven judges in addition to the existing Chambers of three and five judges already constituted. The Court however did not avail itself of this possibility when the amendments made to the Accession Treaty following Norway's non-ratification reduced the number of judges to 15, one of each Member State. The Court therefore continues to sit (without its President) in two Chambers of five or four Chambers of three. The use of these Chambers, which has now become the rule rather than the exception (see p. 39, above), has already been discussed in the previous chapter.

The number of judges is mainly a reflection of the number of the Member States.[2] The principle, however, of collegiality, whereby the Court, when sitting *in pleno* or as a Chamber, must reach a single judgment, if necessary by a majority, means that an uneven number of judges is required. Thus, in the original Community of the Six the Court was composed of seven judges; at one time, two of these were Dutch, and at the moment of the Six becoming the Nine, two were Italian. For the same reason, the Accession Treaty of 1972, in anticipation of Norway's entry, raised the required number of judges to 11 and so had to be amended later to nine when the Norwegian people decided, by referendum, against entry.

After the accession of Greece in 1981, and the consequent raising of the Member States to an even number, there had been an additional judge who served a single term and was drawn in turn from the five larger Member States, France, Germany, Italy, Spain and the United Kingdom (although the United Kingdom's turn has not yet arrived and the Italian tenure was truncated). The accession of Spain and Portugal in 1986 maintained the need for this additional (then thirteenth) judge, but the latest accession in 1995 of the three new Member States, Austria, Finland and Sweden, has removed the need for such an additional judge. When an additional judge is needed, entitlement to nominate the judge has been determined, in the absence of agreement, by drawing lots. To date, there have been four additional judges; Grévisse (France),

---

[2] For a detailed consideration of this issue see T. Kennedy "Thirteen Russians! The Composition of the Court of Justice" in *Legal Reasoning and Judicial Interpretation of European Law: Essays in honour of Lord Mackenzie Stuart* (1996) at p. 69.

Bahlmann (Germany), Diez de Valesco Vallejo (Spain) and La Pergola (Italy). The ECSC Court had one additional judge, the Dutchman Van Kleffens.

In contrast with the membership of the Commission, it is nowhere stipulated that each Member State shall provide a judge for the Court. It is therefore misleading to refer to "the British place" on the Court as announcements of new appointments have sometimes done. Nor is it a requirement that the judges or advocates general be Community citizens. Indeed in an interview with *The Times* (August 18, 1988), the then President of the Court, Lord Mackenzie Stuart, remarked that, so far as the Treaties were concerned, the Court could be made up "entirely of Russians". Inevitably, in practice, the members are all drawn from the Member States. For every appointment of a judge (or advocate general) requires the common accord of the Governments of the Member States (Article 223 (ex Article 167) EC): no State is likely to forego its "representation" on the Court, nor has this happened. But political considerations make it almost inconceivable that someone who is not a national of a Member State would be appointed. The general acceptability of each State's candidate is a matter of prior informal consultations between the 15 Governments.

Appointment of the members of the Court by common accord of the Member States has not escaped criticism. In a resolution of July 6, 1982, the European Parliament expressed the view that it should be involved in the appointment of the members of the Court. Various possibilities might be considered: nominations might be subject to ratification by the Parliament, a solution similar to that in the United States where the appointment by the President of Supreme Court judges is subject to ratification by the Senate, after exhaustive and sometimes unseemly public hearings. In the European Court of Human Rights, the judges are elected by the Council of Europe's Parliamentary Assembly from lists drawn up by the Governments. The European Parliament proposed in its Draft Treaty establishing the European Union (1984), that half the members of the Court of Justice should be appointed by the Parliament and half by the Council: *i.e.* there would be no requirement that the Court should include at least one citizen from each Member State. In 1993, adopting the Rothley Report[3] the

---

[3] Report of the Committee on Institutional Affairs on the role of the Court of Justice in the development of the European Community's constitutional system Rapporteur: Mr Willi Rothley. European Session Document A3-0228/93. On February 9, 1994 a resolution put forward by the German MEP (now Advocate General), Siegbert Alber, requiring the Parliament to be consulted upon judicial appointments was adopted. The President in office of the Council, Theodoros Pangalos suggested that the question might be examined by the working group preparing for the 1996 Intergovernmental conference.

European Parliament endorsed the proposal that judges (and presumably advocates general) at the Court should be elected (*sic*) by the European Parliament and the Council for a non-renewable period of nine years. Details of the procedure for such elections were left unspecified, but in the explanatory statement accompanying the motion for a resolution the view is expressed that there should be no public hearings involved. In the event the Treaty of Amsterdam left the procedure for appointments to the Courts unchanged.

### Qualifications

The Treaties require that judges and advocates general "shall be chosen from persons whose independence is beyond doubt and who possess the qualifications required for appointment to the highest judicial offices in their respective countries or who are jurisconsults of recognised competence". This formulation follows closely that for appointment to the International Court of Justice at The Hague which also provided the model for judicial appointments to the European Court of Human Rights. It has been retained in a modified form for judicial appointments to the Court of First Instance.

It is significant that the independence of candidates is made a first and paramount consideration. This moral requirement counters any notion that a judge is representing his Member State or the Government which has nominated him. Nevertheless, the criticism has been made that political considerations have entered into the selection of judges from some Member States where party affiliation is an important consideration in domestic judicial appointments. Once so appointed, a judge who failed "to please" his Government might then be in danger of not being re-appointed; but the principle of collegiality and the secrecy of the Court's deliberations would appear adequate safeguards against this risk.

The professional qualifications for appointment are expressed in the alternative. In some countries of the common law tradition, such as England or Ireland, the alternative is a real one, inasmuch as legal scholarship as such is not in itself a qualification for appointment to the highest judicial office. In most civil law countries, on the other hand, the second alternative is subsumed in the first. Thus, in all the original six Member States the holder of a University chair of law may be translated to the bench, sometimes at the highest levels.

So far as the United Kingdom is concerned, up to 1988, only the first alternative was used, although there were not lacking precedents for academic appointments by the British Government to international courts and tribunals. The first two British appointments to the Court in 1972 involved, respectively, a judge of the

Scottish Court of Session and a leading English barrister who held the post of Junior Counsel to the Treasury, the third most senior Government lawyer. The eligibility of a Treasury Junior to be appointed to the English High Court was properly regarded as fulfilling the first alternative. The third British appointment, in 1981, was that of an English High Court judge, at the time of his translation President of the Employment Appeal Tribunal. The fourth appointment, in 1988, was that of a professor of law, although, as a Q.C., he also qualified for appointment under the first alternative. Likewise the fifth United Kingdom appointment, in March 1992, was an elevation from the Court of First Instance of a judge who, before being appointed to that Court, had practised as a Q.C. at the Scottish Bar, a practice he maintained after his appointment as Salvesen Professor of European Institutions at Edinburgh University.

Under the ECSC Treaty a prior legal qualification was not necessary: Article 32 ECSC, as originally drafted, merely stipulated that candidates should be "persons of recognised independence and competence". Two of the original judges of the Coal and Steel Court were not possessed of formal professional qualifications in law. The Dutchman Joseph Serrarens was a parliamentarian and a leading figure in the international labour movement, and the Frenchman Jacques Rueff was an expert in finance and banking who had distinguished himself in administrative and ministerial posts in France.[4] The former was replaced in 1958 when the Court became the Court of the three Communities but the latter continued as a judge until 1962 when he was succeeded by Robert Lecourt.

## Oath

On taking up their appointment, the judges take an oath in the following terms: "I swear that I will perform my duties impartially and conscientiously; I swear that I will preserve the secrecy of the deliberations of the Court". They also sign a written undertaking that, both during and after their term of office they will respect the obligations arising therefrom, in particular the duty to behave with integrity and discretion as regards the acceptance, after they have ceased to hold office, of certain appointments or benefits.[5]

## Term of Appointment

Appointment is for a term of six years, but a judge (or advocate general) is eligible for re-appointment for a further term or terms.

---

[4] Including steering the introduction of the "heavy" franc in 1960.
[5] See Art. 4 of the Statute.

Appointments are staggered in such a way that seven or eight of the 15 judges (and four of the eight advocates general[6]) come up for renewal at triennial intervals: Article 223 (ex Article 167) EC. This guarantees a measure of continuity of membership even if new appointments were always made. In practice, most of the members of the Court (the additional judge apart) have had their terms of office renewed at least once, and some twice or thrice. There is no prescribed age for retirement. Indeed, at least one judge was a septuagenarian when appointed.

Nevertheless, despite the practice of renewal, the term of six years can be objected to as too short and in conflict with that security of tenure which is the hallmark of judicial independence in all the legal systems of the Member States. Such relatively short terms of appointments are commonly adopted for international courts or tribunals (for example, nine years in the case of a judge of the International Court of Justice), but they seem undesirable in what is held out to be, and is, a distinct legal order of a novel kind, neither international nor national but more akin to an embryonic federation. Even with a quasi-federal judiciary the impression should not be created that those appointed may be looking over their shoulders every six years towards their political masters, the Governments of the Member States. In practice such decisions are no doubt rarely taken on political grounds, but appearances are also of importance on so sensitive a matter. Moreover, too rapid a turnover – in 1988, on the triennial renewal of half the judges and advocates general, six members were replaced – may be extremely disruptive.[7]

## DISMISSAL

As we have seen, the opportunity for Member States to replace a judge or advocate general occurs every six years. During the term of appointment dismissal can only take place by the unanimous decision of the other judges and advocates general that their colleague no longer fulfils the requisite conditions or no longer meets the obligations arising from his office. This procedure of trial by one's peers (copied from the International Court of Justice) provides a very effective safeguard against dismissal and applies in like terms to advocates general. The procedure has never

---

[6] The ninth is a "one-off" appointment until October 6, 2000 only: see Art. 222 (ex Art. 166) EC.

[7] See Lord Mackenzie Stuart's farewell address in "Synopsis of the work of the Court of Justice, 1988 and 1989", p. 201 at p. 202, and see the Rothley report, note 3, p. 48, above.

yet been invoked. A judge may, however, submit his resignation at any time, and this has happened on several occasions. Thus, Judge O'Dalaigh resigned in 1975 in order to become the President of Ireland and Judge Slynn did so in 1992 upon his appointment to the House of Lords. The Irish judge, John Murray, resigned in July 1999 to take up a seat on the Irish Supreme Court and Christopher Bellamy, British judge on the Court of First Instance, resigned to become President of the newly formed Competition Commission in the United Kingdom.

## President of the Court and Presidents of Chambers

The judges (but not the advocates general) choose one of their number to serve as President of the Court for a term of three years. This appointment is renewable. Thus, President Robert Lecourt, who retired in October 1976, served three terms as President (1967–76); his immediate predecessor was Charles Hammes of Luxembourg. The President from 1958 to 1964 was a Dutchman, Professor A.M. Donner, who remained a judge of the Court until his retirement in 1979. The German judge, Hans Kutscher, succeeded Robert Lecourt as President in October 1976, and upon his resignation in October 1980 was in turn succeeded as President by the Belgian judge, J. Mertens de Wilmars. From 1984 to 1988 the British judge, Lord Mackenzie Stuart, was President. His successor, the Danish judge, Ole Due, served two terms as President (1988–94), then retiring as judge of the Court. His successor as President is the Spanish judge Gil Carlos Rodrigues Iglesias, elected to serve from 1994 to 1997 and now re-elected for a second term expiring in 2000. The President's functions, in the words of the Rules of the Court, are to direct the judicial business and the administration of the Court and to preside at hearings and deliberations.

The choice of President is made by secret ballot, being determined by a simple majority. The same process is used to elect annually a President for each of the Chambers of the Court, the composition of which is also determined annually. In practice the composition of each Chamber remains constant, but its presidency rotates annually.

After the President of the Court, the Presidents of the Chambers and the First Advocate General, the members of the Court (both judges and advocates general) rank equally in precedence according to their seniority in office. Where there is equal seniority in office, by reason of appointments having been made on the same date, precedence is determined by age. When the Court sits *in pleno* the President will be flanked to right and left by his fellow judges seated in order of seniority, a right-hand seat being superior to the equivalent position on the left, a practice which is carefully observed.

## IMMUNITIES, PRIVILEGES AND SALARY

The judges (and advocates general) enjoy, as might be expected, immunity from suit or legal process. This immunity is retained after they vacate office in respect of acts performed by them in their official capacity. This is provided by the respective Protocols of the Statute of the Court of Justice annexed to the three founding Treaties.

Under the Protocol on the privileges and immunities of the Communities annexed to the Merger Treaty, the judges have the benefit of certain privileges, for example, as to tax and customs duties. In particular, they are exempt from national taxes on their Community salaries; but they are liable to Community income tax, the rates for which rise to 45 per cent. In addition to their other privileges, each judge (and advocate general) has the use of a car and chauffeur.

Judicial salaries (and those of the advocates general, which are identical) are fixed by a Council Regulation.[8] A judge's salary is the same as that of an ordinary member of the Commission and is very substantial. It would however be very misleading to compare it to the salary of a senior English judge, for, with the exception of the Luxembourg judge, the members of the Court of Justice naturally have to maintain two homes; they also find themselves called upon to fulfil a semi-diplomatic function and to foster links with judges and lawyers in their own countries.

## INCOMPATIBILITIES

It is incompatible with his appointment for a judge to hold any political or "administrative" (that is, governmental) office (Article 4 of the Statute of the Court). Nor may he be engaged in any occupation, whether gainful or not, unless exemption is exceptionally granted by the Council (*ibid.*). In practice, several members of the Court have been permitted to undertake teaching engagements in University faculties and institutes.

---

[8] Regulation (ECSC, EEC, Euratom) 1546/73 [1973] O.J. L155/8, determining the emoluments of the President and Members of the Commission and of the President, Judges, Advocate General and Registrar of the Court of Justice. For judges (other than the President) and advocates general this amounts to 112.5% of the basic salary of the most senior community official on the last step of his or her salary scale.

In addition, when taking up their duties, the judges undertake that they will behave with integrity and discretion as regards the acceptance, even after they have ceased to hold office, of certain appointments or benefits. Not to canvas more extravagant possibilities, this would, it was thought, prevent a former judge from appearing as counsel at the bar of the Court: this has, however, occurred.

## COMPOSITION OF THE COURT

When the Court sits as a full court, a quorum of nine judges is required. A relatively low quorum is felt desirable to allow for illness or other unavoidable absences. So, normally, 11 judges sit on a hearing of the full Court, thus freeing four for other work (including perhaps a hearing of a three-judge Chamber) and ensuring that a quorum will not be broken by the absence of one or even two judges through sickness or for other reasons. Only for the most exceptional cases will all 15 judges take part: such a Court is, by usage, referred to as a "*Grand Plenum*" as opposed to the "*Petit Plenum*" of nine or 11 judges.[9]

As the President has no casting vote, an uneven number must sit for decisions to be valid. If a judge is prevented from attending the hearing (for example, through illness), the most junior judge present abstains from taking part (*i.e.* voting) in the deliberations unless he is the judge-rapporteur, in which case the judge immediately senior to him abstains.

The Statute of the Court provides expressly that a party may not apply for a change in the composition of the Court (or of a Chamber) on the grounds of either the nationality of a judge or the absence from the Court (or Chamber) of a judge of the nationality of that party. This is in contrast with the Statute of the International Court of Justice which allows an *ad hoc* judge in certain circumstances.

## FORM OF JUDGMENT

The Court follows the general continental practice in delivering judgment as a collegiate body. In contrast to the International Court of Justice at The Hague and the European Court of Human Rights in Strasbourg, no separate or dissenting judgments are

---

[9] See further Chap. 12, p. 277, below.

permitted. The strict secrecy which surrounds the Court's deliberations, as underlined by the members' oath of office, means that
only the judges themselves know whether their decision was
reached unanimously or by a majority. The natural desire to
achieve unanimity will lead to compromises which may then be
reflected in the somewhat equivocal language of some of the
judgments, criticised by one English practitioner as "simply oracu-
lar and almost apocryphal".[10]

Help in understanding a judgment can be derived from the
opinion of the advocate general in the case. Usually, it is better to
start by reading this opinion and then to turn to the judgment.
Often, the Court follows the path urged upon it by the advocate
general, but as mentioned in the next chapter (below, p. 71), there
have been notable instances where the Court has gone its own
way.

The form of the judgment is very different from that of an
English or Scottish judgment. In the formative years of the Court's
history, after essaying other styles, it decided to adopt the practice
of the higher French courts in framing the whole judgment as,
grammatically, a single *Ciceronian* sentence, with the facts of the
case, the steps in the procedure and the legal reasons all recited in
a long series of subordinate clauses leading eventually to the main
sentence: "the Court hereby rules".

As is apparent, the English version of the judgment has departed
from the French model by the conversion of the subordinate
clauses from ablative absolutes into separate sentences. Nevertheless, as judgments are normally drafted first in French, even the
English version retains the succinct, even sybilline, quality of the
original; notionally, it remains if not a single sentence, at least a
single coherent whole. The influence which this style of drafting
judgments has upon the law which they contain is not to be
underestimated, even though it be intangible.

In 1979 the Court decided, even for its judgments in French, to
move away from the original model and no longer to confine its
reasoning within the grammatical strait-jacket of a single sentence.
The increased linguistic diversity of the Court has also led, on rare
occasions to a judgment being drafted first in English and then
translated into French, especially where English has been the
language of the case.

As a typical example, in Case 22/76 *Import Gadgets*[11] (a
judgment set out in full in the first and second editions of this
book), the judgment starts "In Case 22/76" and after mentioning
the parties, the subject-matter of the case, and the composition of

---

[10] L. Melville in (1978) 75 L.S. Gaz. 567.
[11] Case 22/76 *Import Gadgets S.a r.l. v. L.A.M.P., SpA* [1976] ECR 1371.

the Court, the main body of the judgment is in two parts, facts and law, ending with the ruling of the Court.

The first part is entitled "Facts" in *Import Gadgets*. Originally, in the French text (before the relaxation introduced in 1979) each paragraph in this part was introduced by the conjunction "*attendu que*" which might be rendered in English "whereas," although the conjunction was omitted in the English text. The part summarises, first, the facts of the case and the procedure before the Court, secondly the submissions made to the Court. As the case was a reference from a national court for a preliminary ruling, observations in writing were invited from the parties, the Member States and the Commission. In the actual case the defendant in the main action (*i.e.* the action before the national court) and the Commission put in observations which are summarised. This part of the judgment is based on the "report for the hearing"[12] which is described in Chapter 12. Then the oral hearing and the delivery of the advocate-general's opinion are mentioned.

The second part of the judgment contains the law and is so entitled in *Import Gadgets*; but since 1978 the title "Decision" is preferred. After an introduction explaining how the question or questions for decision have arisen, this part sets out the *motifs* or reasons for the Court's ruling, followed by the ruling itself. This part is set out in a series of propositions, formerly linked in the French version by the conjunction "*cousidivout que*", omitted in the English text. The paragraphs are numbered for ease of reference. The ruling, introduced by the phrase "On those grounds" (*pour ces motifs*), is usually quite short, as in the example chosen, which reads:

> "The Court, in answer to the question referred to it by the *Tribunale di Pavia* by order of January 22, 1976, hereby rules:
> Laughing devices suitable for use principally in dolls that are representations of human beings come within heading 97.02 B of the Common Customs Tariff."

The original copy of the judgment bears the signatures of all the participating judges whether or not they agree with the outcome or the reasoning and is authenticated as having been so delivered in open court by the President and the Registrar.

## JUDICIAL STYLE

The collegiate nature of the Court's judgments lends them a certain flatness such as we associate with the language of a

---

[12] As we have seen in Chap. 2 (p. 30, above), the Report for the Hearing was, from 1994, no longer published in the ECR.

Government report. The tone is measured; there is neither excitement nor humour. One must not expect the often elegant, sometimes idiosyncratic, prose of an English judgment, upon which the individual judge will have imprinted his own personality and particular style. At Luxembourg the individual voices are muted; they blend in unison; there is a single refrain. The only solo will have been that of the advocate general.

On the other hand, collegiality has in no way inhibited the development of Community law through judicial decisions. The Court's judgments have become an important, if secondary source of that law, as this book will demonstrate. Here mention may be made of one particular technique which law-making in committee, Luxembourg-style, appears to encourage.

Study of the case law of the Court reveals certain *leitmotifs* that recur through whole sequences of its decisions. Phrases or passages will be repeated in case after case, sometimes in identical terms, sometimes with subtle variations. By constant rehearsal the Court, like a Welsh choir, finds the exact note it wants to sound. Examples abound of this technique whereby phrase-building becomes law-making: elsewhere in these pages we refer to the Court's classic definition of the nature of the Community legal order (below, p. 238, Case 6/64 *Costa v. ENEL*,[13] which refined the definition in Case 26/62 *Van Gend en Loos*[14]); to the *Zuckerfabrik Schoppenstedt* formula as a yardstick for certain actions for damages under Article 215(2) EC[15] (now Article 288(2)); and to the *Plaumann* test for *locus standi* of "non-privileged" applicants under Article 173 EC[16] (now Article 230). The same technique has defined, and is still refining, the key concept of the direct effect of Community law, in a sequence of cases extending from Case 26/62 *Van Gend en Loos* to Case 148/78 *Ratti*,[17] Case 8/81 *Becker v. Finanzamt Munster*,[18] Case 152/84 *Marshall v. Southampton etc. Area Health Authority*[19] and *Foster v. British Gas*.[20]

---

[13] Case 6/64 *Costa v. ENEL* [1964] ECR 585 at 593; [1964] C M L.R 425.

[14] Case 26/62 *Van Gend en Loos* [1963] ECR 1 at 12; [1963] C.M.L.R. 105.

[15] p. 178, below, Case 5/71 *Aktien-Zuckerfabrik Schoppenstedt v. Council* [1971] ECR 975 at 984.

[16] p. 148, below, Case 25/62 *Plaumann & Co. v. EEC Commission* [1963] ECR 95 at 107; [1964] C.M.L.R. 29.

[17] Case 198/78 *Pubblico Ministero v. Ratti* [1979] ECR 1629; [1980] 1 C.M.L.R. 96.

[18] Case 8/81 *Becker v. Finanzamt Munster* [1982] ECR 53; [1982] 1 C.M.L.R. 499.

[19] Case 152/84 *Marshall v. Southampton, etc., Area Health Authority* [1986] ECR 737; [1986] 1 C.M.L.R. 688; see also Case C–271/91 *Marshall v. Southampton etc., A.H.A.*: judgment of August 2, 1993 [1993] 3 C.M.L.R. 293, *The Times*, August 4, 1993.

[20] Case C–188/89 *Foster v. British Gas* [1990] ECR I–3313; [1990] All E.R. 897.

## Biographical Background of the Judges

During the almost half-century of its existence (the original seven judges of the Coal and Steel Court took their oaths of office on December 4, 1952) the Court has had some 80 members, if we include for this purpose both judges and advocates general. Some account is given in the next chapter of the background of the past and present advocates general. Here it is proposed to give brief biographical details of some of those (all men) who have served, or are serving, as judges of the Court. Fidelma Machen of Ireland became the first woman judge on the Court of Justice when she was appointed in 1999 to succeed John Murray upon the latter's nomination to the Irish Supreme Court, although (as we shall see) the French, with true republican "*égalité*", chose a woman in 1981 for appointment as advocate general. In the Court of First Instance both the Finnish and Swedish judges are women.

Our attention will be directed mainly to the present membership, but some knowledge of the previous careers of the past as well as present judges will give an idea of the variety of expertise and professional experience on which the Court has been, and is, able to draw.

Of the past judges of the Court (some 40 in number),[21] mention has already been made of Serrarens and Rueff as exemplifying appointees to the Coal and Steel Court without formal legal qualifications. With those two exceptions all the others had a variety of legal backgrounds. Many had judicial experience in their own countries.[22] Thus, Galmot and Grévisse had been senior members of France's highest administrative court, the *Conseil d'Etat*. Pilotti, van Kleffens and Strauss also began their careers as judges, but Pilotti turned to international law (he was Assistant Secretary General of the League of Nations from 1932 to 1937), van Kleffens moved into legal practice and then held important posts in the Dutch Ministry of Economics, and Strauss served in high administrative and governmental posts in post-war Germany as well as being politically active in the Christian Democratic Party.

Several judges had held ministerial posts in their own countries. Delvaux was Belgian Minister of Agriculture in 1945–46. Lecourt had been French Minister of Justice for several periods between

---

[21] The counting is complicated by the fact that (to date) six Judges have also served the Court as advocates general, namely Trabucchi, Capotorti, Mancini, Gulmann, Slynn, and La Pergola.

[22] Bahlmann, Hammes, Galmot, Grévisse, Koopmans, Kutscher, Mackenzie Stuart, O'Higgins, O'Caoimh, Riese, Rossi, Slynn, Touffait, Sevón, Puissochet, Kapteyn, Hirsch, O'Higgins, Kakouris, Diez de Velasco Vallejo, Jann, Ragnemalm.

1948 and 1958 and was Minister for Overseas Departments shortly before his appointment to the Court in 1962. Strauss was Secretary of State in the Federal Ministry of Justice from 1949 up to his appointment to the Court in 1963; Bahlmann had held important posts in the same Ministry after serving as a judge in Cologne. Rueff had been French Minister of Finance in Poincaré's Government as long ago as 1926. Catalano also held senior governmental posts in Italy. O'Dalaigh was the Irish Attorney-General (like his successors O'Caoiush and Murray) before being appointed to the Supreme Court: he resigned from the Court in Luxembourg in order to become President of the Irish Republic. Pescatore, who served the Court as Luxembourg judge for 18 years, had previously held high office in the Luxembourg Ministry of Foreign Affairs and helped to found the Institute of European Legal Studies at the University of Liège. Schockweiler had a long career in the Luxembourg Ministry of Justice. Due had served in the Danish Ministry of Justice as well as directing courses on Community law for practitioners and civil servants. Wathelet (Belgium) held posts of Minister of Defence, Minister of Justice and Deputy Prime Minister. At some stages of their earlier careers, Catalano, Delvaux, Lecourt and van Kleffens all practised law or acted as legal counsel to commercial or public institutions.

Also significant as a group are those who had an academic career: Monaco and Trabucchi occupied Chairs of Law in the Universities of Rome and Padua, Sorensen a Chair of Law in the University of Aarhus, and Donner a Chair of Constitutional and Administrative Law in the Free University of Amsterdam, and Joliet a Chair of European Community Law at the University of Liège. Riese taught in the University of Lausanne from 1932 to 1951 before returning to Germany as judge of the Federal Supreme Court. The Italian judge, Bosco, combined a long career in Italian universities with political service in the Italian Senate from 1948, rising to hold office successively as Minister of Education, Finance, Justice, Employment and Foreign Affairs; Catalano and Hammes too combined professorial appointments with their other functions. Chloros, the first Greek judge, who died in office in 1982, held the Chair of Comparative Law at King's College in the University of London at the time of his appointment: he had been actively involved for his country in the negotiations leading to the Greek accession in 1981; Ioannou, who also died in office in 1999, had a Chair of International and Community Law at the University of Thrace and had been a member of the Greek delegation to the General Assembly of the United Nations. Everling, the German judge until 1988, held various governmental posts in the Federal Ministry of Economics in Bonn as well as acting as Honorary Professor at Munster University where he taught and wrote extensively on Community law.

As already mentioned, several past judges had been active in politics. Strauss was a prominent Christian Democrat and ran (unsuccessfully) for election to the *Bundestag*. Lecourt was *Deputé* for Paris from 1945 to 1958 and was a leading member of the *MRP*. Delvaux and Serrarens were both elected to their respective Parliaments. O'Dalaigh was a prominent lawyer in the Irish Fianna Fail party, before accepting judicial office. O'Coaimh, his successor, became Senior Counsel in Dublin in 1951; subsequently he was Attorney-General of Ireland (in the Fianna Fail Government), Judge of the Supreme Court and President of the High Court. Kakouris, who succeeded Chloros as Greek judge in 1983, was previously a senior member of the Greek Council of State and had been an outspoken critic of the dictatorial regime of "the Colonels", spending time in prison for his conscience.

Mertens de Wilmars, the Belgian President of the Court from 1979 to 1984, had practised in Antwerp as an advocate from 1935, specialising in administrative law and later in European law, and had appeared as an advocate before the Court. He had also been active in political life in Belgium. Mackenzie Stuart, his successor as President of the Court, was appointed judge in 1973 upon the accession of the United Kingdom. After war service he graduated in law from Cambridge and Edinburgh and practised as an advocate at the Scots Bar. His first judicial appointment was as Sheriff Principal in 1971, and in the following year he was elevated to the Court of Session in Edinburgh.

This varied background, ranging far beyond the narrowly legal, is well designed to serve the needs of the Court, whose jurisdiction, as we shall see, touches economic, social, fiscal, administrative and even political issues lying beneath the surface of Community law. The American commentator, Werner Feld, has perceptively remarked:

> "The broad knowledge possessed by some of the justices in the field of economics, finance, and administration may be a significant factor in arriving at decisions which transcend narrow judicial considerations and which reflect an application of the Treaties with a keen eye on the purpose of the Communities and with an appreciation for the future. The assumption is justified that the diversity of interests, experiences, and values represented in the deliberating sessions of the Court may have stimulated a fertile interchange of concepts and ideas and thus broadened the views of the participants."[23]

---

[23] In Werner Feld, *The Court of the European Communities: New Dimension in International Adjudication* (Martinus Nijhoff, The Hague, 1964), p. 32.

When we turn to the present judges, a similar diversity is evident. Paul Kapteyn, the Dutch judge, had held chairs at Utrecht and Leyden Universities and was Director of the Europa Institute in Leyden before being appointed in 1976 to the Dutch *Raad van State* (Council of State) where he became President of its Chamber for the administration of justice in 1984. With VerLoren van Themaat (a former advocate general) he is co-author of a leading treatise, in both English and Dutch, on Community law. John Murray, the recently departed Irish judge, was called to the Irish Bar in 1967 and practised as Senior Counsel in Dublin. He served on two occasions as Attorney-General of Ireland, an office which he held in the Fianna Fail Government immediately prior to his appointment to the Court in 1992. His successor is Mrs Fidelma Macken, member of both the Irish and English Bar and a judge of the High Court in Ireland; she is the first woman to be appointed a judge at the Court of Justice, but will be followed on July 14, 2000 by Frau Ninon Colneric as successor to the German judge Günther Hirsch. Puissochet, like his predecessor Jean-Pierre Grévisse, had been a senior member of the *Conseil d'Etat* from which he had been detached to serve as Director of Legal Affairs in the French Foreign Ministry. The *Conseil d'Etat*, France's supreme administrative court, has supplied several members of the Court, whether as judges or advocates general. For the French pattern of appointments to the Court strives to maintain a balanced representation from the "administrative" and "judicial" hierarchies of the dual system of courts in France. Thus, Puissochet's colleague at Luxembourg, Advocate General Philippe Léger, was previously a member of the *magistrature*, moving between service in the Ministry of Justice and various judicial appointments, including serving both as judge and advocate general in the *Paris Cour d'appel*. Likewise their immediate predecessor as judge and advocate general at the Court were, respectively, Grévisse of the *Conseil d'Etat* and Marco Darmon, a former President of Chamber of the *Paris Cour d'appel*.

The British judge, David Edward, is the first judge of the Court to arrive by way of the Court of First Instance, to which he was appointed at its inception in 1989. He had previously practised as a silk at the Scottish Bar before becoming Salvesen Professor and Director of the Europa Institute at Edinburgh University. Like Edward, the Luxembourg judge, Romain Schintgen, was translated to the Court in 1996 from his judgeship on the Court of First Instance. A member of the Luxembourg Bar and an expert on labour law, he had been appointed to the Luxembourg Ministry of Employment and Social Security and subsequently held a number of important positions, frequently representing his country before international bodies.

After the death in office of the Belgian judge, René Joliet, he was replaced by Melchior Wathelet in September 1995. A law graduate of Liège and Harvard, he had held senior post in various Government ministries, including the Belgian Ministry of Justice.

Claus Gulmann is another example of the transmogrification of an advocate general into judge of the Court, when in 1994 he was appointed to succeed the retiring President Ole Due in his capacity as the Danish judge. His previous career had included some nine years service in the Danish Ministry of Justice before taking up a chair at the University of Copenhagen and becoming Dean of the Law School. From 1973 to 1976 he had worked at the Court, serving as legal secretary to the first Danish judge. After being *référendaire* to Sørensen he wrote the first ever Danish doctoral thesis on Community law.

The late Federico Mancini (who died on July 27, 1999), formerly the Italian advocate general, also switched roles to become judge in succession to Giacinto Bosco in October 1988. Before his appointment as advocate general in 1982, he had spent most of his previous career as an academic lawyer in Bologna and Rome. His place as Italian judge was taken by Advocate General La Pergola.

Rodriguez Iglesias, the Spanish judge and now President of the Court, studied law at the Universities of Oviedo and Freiburg; he taught at various Spanish Universities before being appointed to the Chair of Public International Law at the University of Granada in 1983. Prior to his elevation to the Court he occupied the Chairs of European Law at both Granada and Madrid Universities. Moitinho de Almeida, the Portugeuese judge, entered the career judiciary after graduating in law at Lisbon University; following service as Assistant Public Prosecutor at the Lisbon Court of Appeal he became a senior official in the Ministry of Justice, with special responsibility for Community law.

With the death in office in 1999 of Krateros Ioannou, the new Greek judge is Vassilios Skovris. After a doctorate at the University of Hamburg, he pursued an academic career, holding the Chair of Public Law at Thessalonika from 1982 and directing there the Centre of International and European Economic Law. He had also been active in government service and administration. He has published widely, especially on issues of constitutional and administrative law.

Günther Hirsch, appointed to succeed Manfred Zuleeg as the German judge, was a Director at the Bavarian Ministry of Justice from 1973 to 1999 and had served as judge and President of *Verfassungagerichtshof des Freistaats Saachsen* (Constitutional Court of Saxony) and the *Oberlandesgericht* (Court of Appeal, Saxony) and the *Oberlandesgericht* (Court of Appeal, Dresden) following the reunification of Germany. He retires July 2000.

The judges from the three new Member States all have considerable judicial experience. Peter Jann of Austria holds a doctorate of the University of Vienna and his career as a judge culminated in membership of the *Bundesverfassungsgerichtshof* (Austrian Constitutional Court). Hans Ragnemalm had been a Professor of Public Law and Dean of the Faculty of Law at the University of Stockholm. He served as Parliamentary Ombudsman from 1978 to 1992 when he became a judge on the Supreme Administrative Court. Leif Sevón was a senior official in the Finnish Ministry of Justice and counsellor to the Commercial Section of the Ministry of Foreign Affairs. Subsequently, he was a judge of the Finnish Supreme Court until his appointment in January 1994 as President of the EFTA Court.[24] As the above biographical sketches show, the criticism sometimes made in the United Kingdom that the Court consists manly of academics is belied by the facts: the Court has always had a majority of judges with previous judicial experience. It is also a Court with peculiar linguistic competence, as it will include at least one judge whose mother tongue is one of the 13 official languages, other than Irish – the Irish judge will not necessarily be an Irish speaker.

---

[24] On this Court, see Appendix 2 of the previous edition of this book (4th ed., 1994) and 1995 Update to that edition, at p. 23. The Court's life has now been extended. For a recent commentary, see Per Christiansen, "The EFTA Court" (1997) 22 E.L.Rev. 539–553.

# Chapter Four

# Advocates General

While the functions of a judge are generally understood, the role of the advocate general in the Court is less easily grasped, especially in countries where the legal system has no precise equivalent. His title, too, is something of a misnomer, since he is really no more an advocate than he is a general.[1] On the contrary, he is a member of the Court. But that term is itself ambiguous, being sometimes restricted to the judges alone, as in the first paragraph of Article 222 (ex Article 166), which provides (as amended) that "The Court of Justice shall be *assisted* [italic added] by eight Advocates-General". This ambiguity may reflect a certain ambivalence, in the minds of the authors of the Treaties, about the role of the advocate general: although a member of the Court, he acts as its independent adviser. Unlike however his counterpart in the French *Conseil d'Etat*, the *commissaire du gouvernement*, he does not attend the judges' deliberations (see p. 283, below), even in a consultative capacity. On the other hand, the advocates general do join the judges and vote in parity with them on all procedural issues and matters of administration of the Court, for example, to appoint a new Registrar: Article 224 (ex Article 168) EC; but, in accordance with the final paragraph of Article 223 (ex Article 167) EC, only the judges[2] elect the President of the Court "from among their number".

In 1982 the Court assumed the practice (despite the English spelling adopted in the Treaties) of omitting the hyphen in written references to the advocate general, thus complying with the English usage commended by the great Fowler, although a hyphen

---

[1] A quip first made by the first advocate general from the United Kingdom, J.-P. Warner in *Some Aspects of the European Court of Justice* (1976) 14 S.P.T.L. 16.
[2] At the signing of the Treaty of Amsterdam the Member States declined to include the advocates general in this electorate despite the Court's entreaty for them to do so.

should still be used in the possessive case.[3] For ease of expression, the advocate general is referred to in this chapter in the masculine gender; the authors intend no disrespect to the first woman advocate general, M. Simone Rozes, or the other Portias who will follow her on the Kirchberg.

As each case arrives at the Court, it is assigned to one of the advocates general by the First Advocate General, a role which each of them assumes in turn for one judicial year. While the President of the Court designates the "judge-rapporteur" (below, p. 277), it is the First Advocate General who allocates the cases among the corps of advocates general (including himself). Judge-rapporteur and advocate general are designated on similar principles, the aim being to achieve a balanced workload but not to produce any particular specialisation by way of subject-matter. There is however one difference in the designation of the advocate general: the unwritten rule that the judge-rapporteur should not be a judge from a Member State concerned in the case does not apply to the advocate general, no doubt because the latter performs his function in public so that there can be no suspicion of his opinion being influenced by national political considerations.

It is the main task of the advocate general, again according to Article 222 (ex Article 166), "acting with complete impartiality and independence, to make, in open court, reasoned submissions on cases brought before the Court of justice, in order to assist the Court in the performance of the task assigned to it in Article 164". This he does by delivering what is termed an "opinion", (in French, "*conclusions*"), after the case has been heard and normally at a later hearing, in which he gives the judges his view of the case and seeks to help them to reach their judgment. Usually in his opinion he will review the facts of the case, deal with the submissions of the parties and of any others who have taken part in the proceedings, review the law, and finally express his own opinion on how the judges should decide the case. Since 1991, however, he no longer reads his whole text in open court, but only the recommendations at the end of his opinion. Indeed, even that formality may be carried out by one of the other advocates general sitting in the case to be heard that day. The full text will be made available to members of the Court, the parties and any interested members of the public, such as journalists. The advocate general takes no further part in the case and does not attend the private meetings at which the judges deliberate. He also advises the Court,

---

[3] Although this linguistic rigour has not been followed in the latest consolidation of the Court's own Rules of Procedure. In this book, as in previous editions, the style "advocate general" has been adopted except where reference is made to a named advocate general, when capital initial letters will be used.

in "General Meetings"[4] on questions of procedure before the case comes up for hearing; more will be said of this in Chapter 12.

The position of the advocate general is symbolised by his physical position at Court hearings: he sits on the Bench, together with the judges, but apart from them, to the side of the Court, and opposite the Registrar. After the case has been argued by the parties, and almost invariably after an adjournment of a few weeks to enable him to consider and prepare his opinion, his recommendations are read to the judges, to whom his opinion is addressed, in open court: Article 222 (ex Article 166) EC requires that "his reasoned submissions" be made in open court.

To the English lawyer the closest analogy to the advocate general might be an institutionalised *amicus curiae* or Queen's Proctor, who intervened in every case, but as will be apparent neither analogy is exact. The advocate general may also see himself as in effect delivering a reserved first instance judgment in a case being automatically taken to appeal, but his opinion, while it may have authority in future cases, does not of course decide the instant case, even provisionally.

The parties may not comment on his opinion, which closes the oral procedure. In continental legal systems, such as the French, the institution of a legal representative for the public interest is well established before the higher courts. Thus, in France the *ministère public* may interpose its view ("*conclusions*"), distinct from that of the parties, in civil cases before the *Cour de Cassation*, *Cours d'appel* and *Tribunaux de grande instance*. In the *Conseil d'Etat*, the *commissaire du gouvernement* is often regarded as having provided the model for the advocates general, although the former (unlike the latter) retires with the judges and may participate in their deliberations, whilst having no vote in the ultimate decision.

The status of the advocate general as a member of the Court is illustrated by the fact that his appointment, and the terms and conditions of his office, including dismissal, are governed (as we saw in the previous chapter) by the same provisions as those of the judges. Likewise, according to the Rules of Procedure, judges and advocates general rank equally in precedence according to their seniority in office. On three occasions, a judge has changed roles to become advocate general, Trabucchi taking this step in 1973 and Capotorti, another Italian judge, in 1976; and in 1995 La Pergola, who held the post of additional judge which was necessary in the Community of Twelve Member States, moved in the enlarged

---

[4] For General Meetings, see p. 270, below. Until recently, the preferred term was "Administrative Meetings".

Community of the Fifteen to assume the role of a second Italian advocate general.[5] The reverse has also occurred, Advocates General Mancini and Sir Gordon Slynn becoming judges in 1988 and Advocate General Gulmann succeeding Ole Due as the Danish judge in 1994. The First Advocate General ranks equally with the Presidents of Chambers, the others taking precedence between themselves and among the judges according to their respective personal seniority.

An advocate general enjoys, in a sense, a greater independence than a judge since he is free, and indeed obliged, to speak his mind in public and in his own language.[6] Nor is he bound by the collegiate character of the Court's judgments. He may range beyond the questions for immediate decision. In addition to presenting his own view on those questions, he can also comment on the circumstances in which the case has arisen, on the way in which it has been presented, on any irregularities or special features of the procedure, and can deal generally with other matters beyond the purview of the Court's judgment with its more formal style.[7] As Lord Mackenzie Stuart once observed in a tribute to Maurice Lagrange, it is as if the advocate general held a professorial Chair of Community Law.

The advocate general, as well as setting out the facts, expounding the law, and (in a reference under Article 234 (ex Article 177) EC) proposing the reply which the Court in his view should give to the question referred, may also comment on other matters, such as the compatibility with Community law of the actions of the national authorities, matters which are outside the scope of the Court's judgment.

---

[5] This transformation was necessitated by Norway's failure to ratify the 1994 Accession Treaty.

[6] This naturally allows an occasional flash of humour to relieve the pages of the Court reports. See for example Case 115/73 *Serio v. Commission* [1974] ECR 341 at 352, in which Advocate General Warner expressed his surprise at the requirement that candidates for a particular competition should "have knowledge of Anglo-Saxon law" and if possible practical experience of it, since he had understood that system to have become defunct about 900 years previously; in Case 407/85 *3 Glocken and Another v. USL Centre-Sud and Another* [1988] ECR 4233 at 4269, Advocate General Mancini brandished packets of pasta bought in a supermarket in Luxembourg (a translator's note sardonically records that "the four packets for technical reasons, cannot be reproduced here") and compared the Commission to Santiago the fisherman in Hemingway's *The Old Man and the Sea* who had fallen asleep, dreaming of lions. In Case C–168/91 *Konstantinidis v. Stadt Altensteig* [1993] ECR I–1191, Advocate General Jacobs amusingly points out the problems of transliterating names into different languages and has a jibe at the inability of the Court's own word-processing equipment to reproduce the diacritical marks which are indispensable to some languages.

[7] See Dashwood (1982) Legal Studies 202 at 208.

Similarly, the opinion often ranges more widely in setting out the sources of law, referring for example in some detail to relevant previous decisions of the Court, to decisions under national law from the courts of the Member States where national law is relevant, and also occasionally to the opinions of legal writers ("*la doctrine*"). The Court's judgment, by contrast, is less free and less full, usually setting out only those propositions which are necessary to its decision, and often not seeking to justify or substantiate them.

The advocate-general's opinion is normally written in advance of delivery and translated as necessary into the language of the case and into the working language of the Court, but he is free to deliver it in his own language and invariably does.[8] Thus the version in the advocate-general's own language should be looked to in case of doubt on any point. Subsequently it will be translated into the other official languages for publication in the European Court Reports (see p. 26, above), where it now appears immediately before the judgment to which it relates, thereby facilitating citation from it as persuasive, and sometimes even binding, authority (see Chapter 16). Up to 1984 in the European Court Reports the opinion followed the judgment. Since then however the Court has adopted the layout of the Common Market Law Reports in which it has always appeared before the judgment, thus according with the actual sequence of events.

Although the advocate general may have started work in preparing a case before the oral hearing of the parties, he will normally write his opinion in the week or fortnight following that hearing. He will work closely with his legal secretaries, whose role has been mentioned in Chapter 2. In some respects, his relationship with his legal secretaries may be closer than that of the judges with theirs, since the judges will be able to discuss the case among themselves, while the advocate general is on his own. Usually he will not want to know too much of the minds of the judges, so that he can preserve his independent viewpoint.

About four to six weeks after the oral hearing, when the opinion has been prepared and translated as necessary, it will be delivered in open court. This is something of a formality,[9] since the judges

---

[8] If the advocate general is in court to read the concluding recommendation of his own opinion he will equally do so in his own language. Where another advocate general notifies the Court of one of his colleagues' opinions he will use the author's language if it be known to him, otherwise he will read the French version. Thus one could have a situation where (for example) a Greek advocate general might read out, in French, an opinion drafted in German in a Swedish case.

[9] All the more so since the new practice adopted in 1991 of a mere oral communication to the Court of Justice of the recommendation at the end of each opinion. For further details, see Chap. 12, p. 282.

will have the written text (at least in its French translation), and the parties, as has been mentioned, have no right to comment on the opinion, so that there is no need for them to attend. The reading by the advocate general of his opinion closes the oral procedure, although there is a rarely used provision, in Article 61 of the Rules of Procedure, for the oral procedure to be re-opened before the Court gives judgment (see p. 283, below). Judgment itself is always reserved, so that there is a full opportunity for the judges to consider the advocate-general's opinion.

The judges are of course in no way bound to follow that opinion and indeed they not infrequently depart from it. Until recently judgments made no reference to the opinion at all. Now, occasionally, a judgment may refer to specific points made by the advocate general, or even adopt his reasoning wholesale (see pp. 67 and 373 below).

It has often been asked why there is any need for an advocate-general's opinion. Yet even when the judges disagree with him, they may derive much assistance from his opinion, if only because it provides a single coherent picture of the complexities of the whole case and a starting-point for their own deliberations. Its value may be greater the larger the Court, and especially with one whose judges come from different legal systems and speak, at least metaphorically, no common language.

In some respects, the assistance which the Court is given by the advocate general may be compared with that which an English or Scottish court obtains from the Bar. The standard of counsel appearing before the Court of Justice is extremely varied, the right of audience being very wide, as will be seen in Chapter 13, and forensic traditions and advocacy styles varying considerably among the Member States. To take one illustration only, there is no general convention, as in the United Kingdom and Ireland, requiring counsel before the Court to cite authorities which are against him. Thus the advocate general may fill a considerable gap.

Apart from the immediate practical utility of their opinions, the advocates general have contributed over the years to the development of Community law, and are frequently cited on questions which the judges have not found it necessary to decide. This part of the advocate-general's role was referred to by the Court when, in its proposals for the establishment of the Court of First Instance, it suggested that the latter should not be assisted by advocates general on the ground that their role in assisting in the development of Community law would not be necessary before that court.[10]

---

[10] See Chap. 5 below and Kennedy, "The Essential Minimum" (1989) 14 E.L. Rev. 7 at 17.

The authority of such pronouncements is a question to which we shall return when we come to the subject of precedent in the Court. But in developing the law, and in guiding the Court in its early years over the uncharted terrain of the Community Treaties, the first advocates general, Maurice Lagrange of France and Karl Roemer of Germany, made a remarkable impact which can still be seen in the reports of the latest cases. For illustrations of their respective contributions one need look only at the opinion of Maurice Lagrange in the first reference to the Court under Article 177 EC,[11] or his *dicta* on the subject of interpretation of Community law[12]; or, in the case of Karl Roemer, at many of the early cases on judicial review under the ECSC Treaty.[13]

An incidental advantage of the institution of advocate general, as was pointed out in the previous chapter, is that the opinion, which is printed in full as part of the report of the case, often provides a clearer introduction to a case than the judgment itself, and so may be best read first. Moreover, the short-lived practice of the Court, in certain straightforward cases,[14] of simply adopting the reasoning of the advocate general by direct reference: "For the reasons given by the advocate general . . ." means that, in those cases the opinion, rather like the *conclusions* of the *commissaire du gouvernement* in the French *Conseil d'Etat*, become the only source for the reasoning of the Court. To that extent the opinion transcends the role of mere advice, intended to "assist" the Court and assumes, *ex post facto*, the authority of a judgment.

Although this development has undoubted advantages in terms of procedural economy, it must inevitably blur the distinction between the respective roles of judge and advocate general, possibly to the detriment of the authority of the Court itself.

Comments are sometimes made on the proportion of cases in which an advocate general is or is not followed by the Court. But it seems doubtful whether any reliable statistics could be assembled on this question. Frequently the Court will agree with the advocate general on some aspects of the case but disagree on others; or it may arrive at the same result but on grounds which diverge to a greater or lesser extent from his reasoning. Some suggestions of

---

[11] Case 13/61 *Bosch* [1962] ECR 45; [1962] C.M.L.R. 1.

[12] See for example Case 8/55 *Fédéchar v. High Authority* [1954–56] ECR 245.

[13] See for example Cases 7 and 9/54 *Groupement des Industries Sidérurgiques Luxembourgeoises v. High Authority* [1954–56] ECR 175.

[14] See for example the judgments in Case C–284/91 *Suiker Export v. Belgium* (Opinion of Advocate General Gulmann) [1992] ECR I–5473; Case C–59/92 *Ebbe Soennischen GmbH v. Hauptzollamt Hamburg St. Annen* [1993] ECR I–2193 (Advocate General Darmon) and Case C–377/92 *Felix Koch Offenbach Couleur und Karamel GmbH v. Oberfinanzdirektion Munchen* [1993] ECR I–4795 (Advocate General Jacobs).

the advocate general may be passed over in silence, so that it is not possible to state with certainty whether the Court accepts them or not.

It is true, however, that in some of the cases which represent the most striking advances in its jurisprudence, the Court has gone against the views of the advocate general. Examples of such landmarks can be found in cases like *Van Gend en Loos* (p. 219), *Continental Can* (p. 340), and the *ERTA* case (p. 138), of which more will be said in later chapters. The explanation of this phenomenon may lie partly in the fact that the advocates general often regard it as one of their principal functions to remind the Court of its previous case law and to emphasise the virtue of a consistent and harmonious development of the law; it may also simply be easier for the judges collectively to advance further than an individual advocate general.

Although it may only be a matter of impression, it does not seem that the advocates general, despite their more exposed position, are more influenced by their national background or are any less "Community-minded" than the judges. Indeed, Rasmussen asserts that the opinions of the advocates general over the years "have provided a powerful and steady pro-Community input into the Court's process".[15] This tendency was cited as a negative factor in the House of Commons debate on the Maastricht Treaty.[16]

The number and national origins of the advocates general have been determined by somewhat arbitrary factors. In the original Community of the Six there had to be seven judges in order to ensure that there was an uneven number of judges and not less than one from each Member State. As the larger Member States were considered entitled to a second member of the Court, there were from 1952 to 1972 a French and a German advocate general, with Italy, towards the end of that period, having two judges. (Earlier, there had been two Dutch judges.) After the first enlargement of the Communities to nine, there was one judge from each Member of State and an advocate general from each of the "big four", France, Germany, Italy and the United Kingdom. Following the second enlargement, a Greek judge was added, as well as a second French judge in order to preserve an uneven number; by way of concession to the smaller Member States, a fifth advocate general was added, drawn initially from the Netherlands. Upon the accession of Spain and Portugal in 1986 a sixth advocate general was added; it was apparently agreed that both the fifth and sixth advocates general should be drawn from the eight smaller Member

---

[15] In *On Law and Policy in the European Court of Justice* (1986), p. 273.
[16] See Hansard, col. 934 (March 24, 1993), Iain Duncan-Smith M.P. cited the third edition of this book in support of his contention.

States (*i.e.* including Spain) by rotation. Under that system advocates general have been appointed from Belgium, Denmark, Greece, Ireland, Luxembourg (twice), the Netherlands and Portugal.

Upon the enlargement of the Community in 1995 by the accession of Austria, Finland and Sweden, the number of posts of advocate general was raised from six to eight. A ninth advocate general was also provided for, but only from January 1, 1995 until October 6, 2000 (Article 222 (ex Article 166) EC). By the Act of Accession Spain, in future, was to have its own advocate general, being treated because of the size of its population like France, Germany, Italy and the United Kingdom: Ruiz-Jarabo Colomer, a former legal secretary to Judge Rodrígues Iglesias, was nominated as the Spanish advocate general. The second of the three additional posts was filled by Antonia La Pergola, being translated from his existing post as thirteenth judge, required in the Community of the Twelve but no longer needed in the Community of the Fifteen. Then, on the untimely death in office of Judge Marcini in July 1999 he took office as Italian judge on December 15, 1999.

The remaining post of advocate general was added to the two existing posts for filling by rotation from the 10 smaller Members States, Austria, Finland and Sweden now having been added to the seven listed above. In the event, this third post was filled by Nial Fennelly, a Senior Counsel of the Irish Bar since 1978, who had been President of the Irish Bar Council and of the Legal Aid Board.

Under the system of rotation, Advocate General van Gerven of Belgium was replaced by Georgios Cosmas of Greece; the latter had been a member of the Greek Council of State since 1963.

Jean Mischo of Luxembourg has the unique distinction of returning to serve a second time as an advocate general. This was in December 1997 when Luxembourg became entitled to the post by rotation. He had been similarly called to serve as advocate general in 1986. After postgraduate studies in international law at the Universities of Paris and Cambridge, he spent five years in the Legal Service of the Commission in Brussels; later, he returned to the Grand Duchy to play a prominent part in the Luxembourg Ministry of Foreign Affairs.

If we turn to the past and present advocates general, drawn from the four larger States, France, Germany, Italy and the United Kingdom, pride of place belongs to the Frenchman Maurice Lagrange who, with the German Karl Roemer, filled the only two posts of advocate general which the Court had from its inception in 1952 until the first enlargement in 1972. Lagrange was detached to Luxembourg from the *Conseil d'Etat*, and, with Roemer, made notable contributions by their opinions to the early landmark decisions of the Court. He was followed by a succession of French advocates general drawn from the *Conseil d'Etat*, appropriately enough since the *commissaire du gouvernement* in that institution is probably the closest model for the Court's advocates general. Indeed one has the impression, in reading the opinions of a French advocate general, that he sees his function in Luxembourg as equivalent to that of his counterpart in Paris.

However, with the appointment of Simone Rozès that pattern was broken although, as we have seen (p. 59 above), the second French judge was drawn from the *Conseil d'Etat*. For, before being appointed to the Court, M. Rozès had risen through the career judiciary to the presidency of the *Tribunal de Grande instance de Paris*, the most important court of first instance in all France. She left Luxembourg to become First President of the *Cour de Cassation*, France's supreme court in civil and criminal cases. Her successor, Marco Darmon, had also risen to senior judicial office in the Paris *Cour d'appel*. The present French advocate general in succession to Darmon is Phillippe Léger. He too is a member of the French judiciary having served also at the Ministry of Justice from 1966 to 1970 and in the private office of the *Garde des Sceaux* (Minister of Justice) from 1976 to 1978. He sat as judge in the Paris *Cour d'appel* between 1983 and 1986 and served as *Chef de Cabinet* of the Minister of Justice and as advocate general at the Paris *Cour d'appel* since 1993.

The first German advocate general, Karl Roemer, who served from 1952 to 1973, was succeeded by Gerhard Reischl, who had combined judicial and political experience in Germany and had been a member of the European Parliament. In 1984 he in turn was succeeded by Carl Otto Lenz, a German constitutional lawyer and practising notary, who had had a long parliamentary career, holding several senior posts in the *Bundestag*. From October 1997 Lenz was followed by Siegbert Alber. Following law studies at several universities, including Tubingen, Paris and Cambridge, Alber sat as a member of the *Bundestag* from 1969 to 1980. He was elected to the European Parliament in 1977 and served as its Vice President from 1984 to 1992.

Of previous Italian advocates general, Francesco Capotorti achieved eminence in his own country as a professor of international law; both he and his immediate predecessor as advocate general, Trabucchi, had previously been judges of the Court, a change of role which we have already referred to. His successor as advocate general was Giuseppe Tesauro, who combined appointments as Professor and Director of the International Law Institute at Rome University with practice as an *avvocato* in the Italian *Corte di Cassazione*. Tesauro had been joined in 1994 by La Pergola as a second Italian advocate general, La Pergola no longer being required as an additional judge on the enlarged Court of Fifteen. Thus, after tenure as a judge for little over three months he became the third Italian judge to migrate from the *Magistrature assise* to the *Magistrature debout*. He has had a distinguished academic, judicial and political career. Professor of constitutional law and general and comparative public law at the Universities of Padua, Bologna and Rome he was a member of the constitutional court and served as its president from 1986 to 1987. He was Minister of Community Policy from 1987 to 1989 and in that capacity was instrumental in introducing the law which bears his name[17] and which facilitates the implementation of Community directives in the Italian legal system. That law has already had a marked effect in diminishing the number of Article 226 (ex Article 169) EC proceedings against Italy for simply failing to implement directives within the prescribed time-limit.

In March 1998 Tesauro was succeeded as Italian advocate general by Antonio Saggio who had had judicial and administrative experience in Italy before becoming, successively, legal secretary at Luxembourg to Capotorti (then the Italian judge on the Court) a judge on the Court of First Instance and then, from 1995, President of the latter court.[18]

The first British advocate general, Jean-Pierre Warner, had been junior Counsel to the Treasury in Chancery matters from 1964 to 1972. After distinguished service in Luxembourg from 1973 to 1981, he became a judge in the Chancery Division of the High Court. He was succeeded as advocate general by Sir Gordon Slynn, who had previously been junior Counsel to the Treasury in common law, Senior Counsel to the Crown, High Court Judge, and President of the Employment Appeal Tribunal. His successor as advocate general is Francis Jacobs who was co-author of the first two editions of this book. A legal secretary at the Court from 1972 to 1974 (for this function, see p. 23, above), he was then appointed to the Chair of European Law at King's College in the University of London. A member of the Bar (Middle Temple) he took silk in 1984 and frequently appeared as an advocate before the Court.

The diverse backgrounds of the advocates general seem to have influenced the style rather than the substance of their opinions. One may read more like the reserved judgment of an English court; another may read more like the *conclusions* of a *commissaire du gouvernement*; another may be more clearly marked by a particular national legal system; but taken together the opinions are as much the product of a Community view, and of the *esprit de corps* which characterises the Court as a whole, as are the judgments themselves.

---

[17] Law No. 86 of March 9, 1989 on the procedure for implementing Community rules (known as the "*Legge la Pergola*") *G.U.R.I. 10 Mazo, 1989, no. 58*.

[18] For a penetrating recent analysis by the Court of the role of the advocate general, see C–17/98 *Aruba, The Times*, February 29, 2000 (see below, p. 403, n. 48).

# Chapter Five

# The Court of First Instance

On October 31, 1989 a major change occurred in the judicial system of the European Communities for, from that date, the new Court of First Instance became empowered to hear cases falling within its jurisdiction. For those categories of cases the Community's system of judicial review was thereby transformed from a "one-stop shop", with a unique Court of Justice ruling at both first and last instance, to a two-tiered system of judicial review closer in nature to the systems of the Member States. The Court of Justice itself also took on a new role for the first time, that of an appellate court. As we shall see, that development was intended to deal with problems inherent in the existing scheme of legal protection provided by the Treaties. In addition however it has also paved the way for certain future developments which will be examined more closely in Chapter 17.

## BACKGROUND TO THE ESTABLISHMENT OF THE COURT OF FIRST INSTANCE[1]

As long ago as 1974 the Court of Justice had suggested that a specialised court or tribunal be established to deal with staff cases, that is disputes between officials of the various Community institutions and those institutions themselves in their capacity as employers.[2] Worries had also been expressed by legal practitioners and academics[3] that the increasing complexity of cases before the

---

[1] The establishment of the Court of First Instance created a veritable cottage industry of publications on the subject. References to some of the main publications in English will be found in the bibliography, Appendix I, p. 413.

[2] See further Chap. 9.

[3] See, for example, the evidence given to the Select Committee on the European Communities of the House of Lords in their report, "A European Court of First Instance", Session 1978–88, 5th Report, H.L. Paper 20 and A. Tizzano "La Cour de Justice et L'Acte Unique Europeen" in "Du droit international au droit de l'integration" (Baden-Baden, 1987).

Court and in particular cases requiring the examination of voluminous documents and complex factual situations (especially in the economically sensitive areas of anti-dumping, competition and state aids cases) had revealed the inadequacy of the fact-finding capacity of the Court of Justice.

Those concerns were not acted upon as long as the Court was seen to be dealing, however imperfectly, with the cases that were submitted to it, but they were given increasing scrutiny as the workload of the Court of Justice grew during the late 1970s and early 1980s. That growth led to an increasing backlog of cases[4] and, which was more worrying, to a general increase in the average time the Court was taking to complete the cases submitted to it.[5] That increase is clearly shown in table 4 in the Appendix of judicial statistics. In brief, whereas in 1978, 268 cases had been brought and 97 judgments delivered within an average time of nine months for direct actions and six months for references for a preliminary ruling, leaving only 265 cases pending at the end of the year, by 1984, 312 cases had been brought, 165 judgments delivered in average times of 17 months for direct actions and 14 months for preliminary rulings, leaving 465 cases pending on 31 December.

Those times still compared fairly favourably with the time taken to deal with cases before the superior courts of almost any of the Member States. Nevertheless, it was a matter of general concern to the Court that any unnecessary delay was unacceptable. It was especially worried that any substantial delay, whether real or perceived, in its treatment of cases submitted by national courts for preliminary rulings might have adverse repercussions and, in particular, might make national courts reluctant to submit questions in appropriate cases, thus undermining the role of the Court as guarantor of the uniform interpretation of Community law.

The first of those problems was addressed both by the Council and the Commission during the 1970s and indeed the Commission put forward a proposal for a Council regulation amending the Staff Regulations so as to establish an administrative tribunal in order to deal with staff cases,[6] although that proposal was never acted upon. Certain other changes were made to the Court's structure, staff and procedures which were designed to accelerate its disposal of cases. For example, on the successive accessions of Greece, then of Spain and Portugal, the numbers of judges were increased first to 11 and then 13 and the numbers of advocate general to five and then six while the numbers of legal secretaries[7]

---

[4] *i.e.* cases pending before the Court.
[5] See table 3, Appendix II.
[6] See [1978] O.J. C255/6.
[7] See Chap. 2, p. 23.

assisting each member of the Court was increased from two to three. The Rules of Procedure were also amended so as to allow an increasing proportion of cases to be dealt with by Chambers of three or five judges.

It was clear to the Court that, the reform of the procedure for dealing with staff cases having fallen by the wayside, a more radical approach was required, including amendment of the Treaties themselves, and it realised that the inter-governmental conference, convened for other reasons in 1985, presented an opportunity not to be missed.

The Court therefore submitted to the Member States drafts of proposed provisions to be added to the three founding Treaties, and for certain other adjustments to be made, so as to empower the Council to create a new Court of First Instance. Subject to slight modifications those drafts became Articles 4, 11 and 26 of the SEA which added identically worded provisions respectively to the ECSC Treaty, the EC Treaty, and Euratom Treaty. The Council was thereby empowered at the request of the Court of Justice and after consulting the Commission and the European Parliament, to attach to the Court of Justice a Court with jurisdiction to hear and determine at first instance certain classes of action or proceeding brought by natural or legal persons. Upon ratification of the SEA those provisions entered into force as Article 168a EEC Treaty (now, after amendment, Article 225 EC), Article 32d ECSC and Article 140a EAEC.

## ESTABLISHMENT OF THE COURT OF FIRST INSTANCE

Article 168a EEC (now, after amendment, Article 225 EC) laid down the procedure by which the Council was to establish the Court of First Instance. The Council was also to determine the composition of the new Court and to adopt the necessary adjustments and additional provisions to the Statute. As far as those changes were concerned a new paragraph added to Article 188 EEC[8] (now, after amendment, Article 245 EC) enabled the Council, acting unanimously, at the request of the Court of Justice and after consulting the Commission and the Parliament, to amend the provisions of Title 3 of the Statute, the title which lays down the main elements of the Court's procedure. The new Article made it clear that the Statute also applied to the Court of First Instance. Finally it defined the qualifications for Members of the new Court and required it to draw up its Rules of Procedure in agreement

---

[8] Art. 45 ECSC and Art. 160 Euratom.

with the Court of Justice and subject to the unanimous approval of the Council.

Much work remained to be carried out in order to make the Court of First Instance a reality. In view of the urgency which it felt, the Court of Justice, even prior to ratification of the SEA, had circulated its draft proposals for a decision of the Council establishing the Court of First Instance and for certain amendments to its own Rules of Procedure necessitated by the arrival of the new Court.[9] Thus very rapidly after ratification of the SEA the Court was able to initiate the procedure laid down in Article 168a EC (now, after amendment, Article 225 EC) by making a formal request for the establishment of the Court of First Instance supported by a draft decision which already reflected many of the concerns of interested parties. As a result within little more than a year the decision establishing the Court of First Instance was adopted.[10]

The decision itself bears the hallmark of long and difficult negotiations resulting in a series of compromises in many important areas. As one commentator has pointed out the drafting of certain aspects *"révèle une propension pour l'ambiguïté"*.[11] Those compromises related to all of the most important aspects of the new body such as the precise scope of its jurisdiction, its composition, the nature of its relationship with the Court of Justice itself and its Rules of Procedure. As will be seen consideration of some of the thornier problems was deferred until the adoption of the Rules of Procedure.

## JURISDICTION

In its proposals for the transfer of jurisdiction to the Court of First Instance the Court of Justice did not exploit the full potential of Article 168a EC as it then stood, a broad interpretation of which would have enabled the Court to suggest the transfer of *all* cases brought by natural or legal persons.[12] Instead the Court of Justice

---

[9] The English text of those draft proposals was published unofficially in [1988] 1 C.M.L.R. 185.

[10] Decision 88/591 (ECSC, EEC, Euratom) establishing a Court of First Instance of the European Communities [1988] O.J. L319/1. A consolidated version of the decision with minor linguistic corrections was published in the *Official Journal* [1989] O.J. C215/1.

[11] Van Ginderachter, *"Le tribunal de premiere instance des Communautes Europeennes"* (1989) C.D.E. 63.

[12] The second sentence of Art. 168a(1) EC (before amendment by the TEU) which provided that the Court of First Instance "shall not be competent to hear and determine actions brought by Member States or by Community institutions or questions referred for preliminary ruling under Art. 177 (now Art. 234)" appears to state the obvious.

proposed a transfer of jurisdiction in only four categories of cases. Those were competition cases, anti-dumping cases, cases arising from the application of the Coal and Steel Treaty and staff cases. At the same time the Court indicated that it would have no objection in principle if it were decided to transfer a wider range of cases and to include, in particular, actions for damages.

The transfer of staff cases, a matter which had been under discussion for more than a decade, was uncontroversial. The ECSC Treaty cases were included because during the 1970s and early 1980s the implementation of the so-called Davignon plan for restructuring the Community's steel industry had resulted in a very large number of cases relating to the application of rules for fixing production and delivery quotas for different categories of steel products and the imposition of fines in cases where steel undertakings exceeded those quotas. By the time the Court of First Instance was established the Davignon plan had been completed and the flood of cases had dwindled to a mere trickle so that when the Court of First Instance started its work in late 1989 only two such cases were transferred to it.

Competition cases, under Articles 85 and 86 EC (now Articles 81 and 82 EC), were more sensitive both because of the scale of the economic interests which were frequently involved and because of the important political role of those Articles in maintaining the "level playing field" for trade within the common market. Nonetheless it was accepted that, for the reasons already mentioned and because such cases often required complex assessments of fact, it was appropriate that they should be transferred. The proposal to transfer anti-dumping cases, one of the central elements in the Court's plan, encountered greater difficulty and negotiations reached an impasse.

The first of the compromises referred to above was therefore included in Article 3 of the Decision establishing the Court of First Instance. That Article conferred on the Court of First Instance the jurisdiction hitherto exercised by the Court of Justice in respect of the other three categories of cases but it effectively deferred consideration of the transfer of dumping cases. In paragraph (3) it provided that the Council would, in the light of experience, "including the development of jurisprudence" and after two years of operation of the Court of First Instance, re-examine the proposal by the Court of Justice to give the Court of First Instance competence in cases of dumping and subsidies. Paragraph (2) of that Article provided that where the same party brought an action in one of the three categories in which the Court of First Instance had jurisdiction and at the same time included a claim for compensation for damage caused by a Community institution, the Court of First Instance would also have jurisdiction to deal with the claim for compensation.

In order to effect the transfer of jurisdiction Article 14 provided that, on entry into force of the Decision, not only would the Court of First Instance deal with cases lodged after that date but also with cases falling within those three categories of which the Court of Justice was seised on that date but in which the preliminary report had not yet been presented. Thus, following the entry into force of Article 3 on October 31, 1989 the Court of Justice by an order of November 15, 1989[13] transferred 153 cases to the Court of First Instance. Apart from the two steel cases already mentioned that list included 78 staff cases and 73 competition cases including 54 cases falling within four large groups of actions for the annulment of Commission decisions in the PVC, Low-density Polyethylene, Polypropylene and Welded Steel Trellis industries.

On June 8, 1993[14] the Council, in response to a request made by the Court of Justice in October 1991, decided to transfer to the Court of First Instance all cases brought by natural or legal persons with the exception of cases involving anti-dumping measures. That category was finally transferred by a Council Decision of March 7, 1994[15] so that the Court of First Instance now enjoys the maximum scope of jurisdiction allowed to it under Article 168a EC (now Article 225 EC) as it stood prior to amendment by the Maastricht Treaty. The transfer of cases took effect in the same manner as provided for by Article 14 of the 1988 Decision described above. Thus, from August 2, 1993 new cases brought by natural or legal persons have been lodged before the Court of First Instance. On September 27, 1993, 451 such cases were transferred from the Registry of the Court of Justice to that of the Court of First Instance, although that figure included no less than 380 claims against the Community for damages arising out of the annulment of milk quota regulations.[16] Finally on April 18, 1994 the 14 anti-dumping cases then pending before the Court of Justice were transferred to the Court of First Instance.[17] Article 225 (ex Article 168a) EC as now amended enables the Council, by unanimous decision to transfer any category of direct action to the Court of First Instance, including actions against Member States. The express exclusion of preliminary rulings from the jurisdiction of the Court of First Instance is retained.

To summarise, the Court's jurisdiction now extends to the following:

---

[13] [1989] O.J. C317.

[14] [1993] O.J. L144/21.

[15] [1994] O.J. L66/29.

[16] See Chap. 8 on Plenary Jurisdiction, below at pp. 170 *et seq.* For a full list of cases transferred see the weekly "Bulletin of Proceedings of the Court of Justice and the Court of First Instance" No. 26/93, week of September 20–27, 1993.

[17] Weekly Proceedings 13/94.

- challenges by individuals or undertakings to Commission decisions under the Community competition regulations, including challenges by undertakings to decisions concerning the award of aid by Member States (the Member States concerned may only challenge such decisions before the Court of Justice);
- cases brought under the ECSC Treaty;
- challenges to anti-dumping regulations adopted by the Commission or the Council;
- claims for compensation for damage caused by the Community institutions or their servants in the course of their duties;
- cases brought by Community officials against the institutions acting in their capacity as employers; and
- challenges to the decisions of the appeal boards of the European Community Trademark Office[18] and of the Plant Variety Rights Office.

## COMPOSITION

Further compromise is evident in the composition of the Court of First Instance. The original wording of Article 168a(2) (now Article 225(2)) EC left it open to the Council to determine the composition of the new Court although paragraph (3) requires that its members[19] shall be chosen from "persons whose independence is beyond doubt and who possess the ability required for appointment to judicial office". That wording contrasts somewhat with that of Article 223 (ex Article 167) EC which also provides that the judges and advocate general of the Court of Justice are to be chosen from persons whose independence is beyond doubt but which then adds that they must "possess the qualifications required for appointment to the highest judicial offices in their respective countries or who are jurisconsults of recognized competence." That difference in wording suggests that the members of the new Court should possess the practical skills and experience necessary for taking part in the judicial process, in particular for

---

[18] In a splendid piece of obfuscation the official title for this body is the "Office for Harmonization of the Internal Market (trade marks and designs)". It was established, and jurisdiction for its interpretation conferred on the CFI, by Council Regulation 40/94/EC of December 20, 1993 on the Community Trade Mark [1994] O.J. LII/1. See now Case T–163/98 *Proctor & Gamble v. OHIM* [1999] 2 C.M.L.R. 1442.

[19] Art. 2 of those Rules make it clear that those who are referred to as "Members" in both Art. 168a and in the decision of October 24, 1988 perform the function of judge and are to be referred to as "Judges".

the fact-finding role for which the Court of First Instance was, at least in part, conceived. In order to ensure that appointees to the new Court were of sufficient calibre despite the apparently less rigorous (but narrower) qualifications required, the preamble to the Decision reinforces the fact that the new Court is to exercise "important judicial functions".

So far as the composition of the new Court is concerned, none of the Court of Justice's proposals were followed. Taking into account both the number and nature of the cases which the new Court would be called upon to determine the Court of Justice proposed that seven judges would suffice. It also proposed that there should be no advocates general since it would not be the role of the new Court to assist in the development of Community law and that it would not be necessary for the new Court to sit in plenary session but that it would work exclusively in Chambers of three judges each. During the negotiations leading to the establishing decision various permutations were put forward. Some suggested that there should be 12 members of whom three would be advocates general, while the European Parliament mooted 12 judges plus three advocates general, a total of 15 members. The compromise which emerged in Article 2(1) of the decision was that the Court of First Instance should consist of 12 "members".

That was perhaps inevitable given that any other solution would have raised the problem of which Member States were to forego the privilege of having one of their nationals sitting on the new body or alternatively which would enjoy the greater privilege of having more than one of their nationals sitting.[20] So far as advocates general were concerned it was agreed that, in the majority of cases to be dealt with at first instance, decisions could be reached without the assistance of an advocate general. However, recognising that it might be useful in certain cases, Article 2(3) provides that the members of the Court of First Instance may be called upon to perform the task of an advocate general. That task is defined in the second paragraph of Article 2(3) in identical terms to those used in the second paragraph of Article 222 (ex Article 166) EC save that the advocate general is required to make reasoned submissions only "on certain cases . . . in order to assist the Court of First Instance in the performance of its task". The problems of defining the criteria for the selection of such cases and the procedure for designating an advocate general where necessary were deferred to the Decision on the Rules of Procedure.

---

[20] In this regard see also Chaps 3 and 4 relating to the number of judges and advocates general on the Court of Justice.

Article 2(4) of the Decision provides that the Court of First Instance shall sit in chambers of three or five judges but again, in certain cases to be defined by the Rules of Procedure, the Court of First Instance was authorised to sit in plenary session. The criteria adopted in the Rules of Procedure for selecting cases both for plenary sessions and for the designation of an advocate general are similar and are both broad and flexible. Article 14 of the Rules of Procedure provides that "whenever the legal difficulty or the importance of the case or special circumstances so justify, a case may be referred to the Court of First Instance sitting in plenary session . . ." whereas Article 18 provides that "a Chamber of the Court of First Instance may be assisted by an advocate general if it is considered that the legal difficulty or the factual complexity of the case so requires." It is thus only logical that Article 17 should provide that "when the Court of First Instance sits in plenary session, it shall be assisted by an Advocate General", a rule which provides the additional benefit that the remaining judges will be uneven in number, thus avoiding the possibility of a hung court in an important case. However, out of some 400 cases brought before the Court of First Instance prior to the enlargement of its jurisdiction in 1993, only two cases were heard by the Court sitting in plenary session.[21] In addition the assistance of an advocate general has been called upon in two non-plenary cases.[22]

Finally, Article 11 of the Decision, dealing with the appointment of the first President of the Court of First Instance, reveals most clearly the propensity for ambiguity to which reference has already been made, for it provides that the first President of the Court of First Instance is to be appointed for three years in the same manner as its members, that is to say the appointment would be made directly by the Member States. Article 11 however goes on to add that the Governments of the Member States may decide that the procedure laid down in Article 2(2) whereby the President may be elected by the members from among their number shall be applied.

In the event the Member States chose the first of those options and appointed José Luis da Cruz Vilaça of Portugal to be the first

---

[21] Case T–51/89 *Tetra Pak Rausing S.A. v. Commission* [1990] ECR II–309; [1991] 4 C.M.L.R. 334 (the German judge, Judge Kirschner, acting as advocate general delivered his opinion on February 21, 1990, reported at [1990] ECR II–312) and two related cases dealt with together but not joined, T–24/90 *Automec v. Commission* [1992] ECR II–2223; [1991] 4 C.M.L.R. 177 and T–28/90 *Asia Motor France and Others v. Commission* [1992] ECR II–2285; [1992] 5 C.M.L.R. 484 in which the advocate general was Judge Edward.

[22] The group of *Polypropylene Cartel* cases (see below p. 100 and note 76), in which Judge Vesterdorf acted as advocate general and Case T–120/89 *Stahlwerke Peine-Salzgitter AG v. Commission* [1991] ECR II–279, in which Judge Biancarelli acted as advocate general.

President of the Court of First Instance. Prior to his appointment to the Court of First Instance he had served as advocate general in the Court of Justice from January 1986 until October 1988 and had previously held a number of important political and academic positions including that of Secretary of State for European Integration during the negotiations leading to Portuguese accession to the Communities. Upon the expiry of his term as a judge, he was succeeded as President of the Court by the election of the serving Italian judge, Antonio Saggio. Upon the latter's appointment as Advocate General to the Court of Justice, he was succeeded by his Danish colleague, Bo Vesterdorf, the current President.

Of the other initial appointments to the Court, these are listed with some bibliographical details in the previous editions of this book.[23] The present members of the Court are given in Appendix IV in order of precedence and with a brief note of their backgrounds. As will be seen, several former legal secretaries[24] from the Court of Justice are now serving (or have served) on the Court of First Instance. Albeit a minority of the membership, such a group must bring to the Court of First Instance considerable experience of the ways of the Court of Justice; this may bring advantages, such as continuity of judicial approach and practice, but also possible disadvantages, such as a reluctance to depart from established ways and even some deference to the Court "upstairs".[25]

Finally, the Court of First Instance appointed as its Registrar Hans Jung, yet another former legal secretary in the Court of Justice. Jung had also worked as a lawyer-linguist, was legal secretary to two successive German members of the Court of Justice including its late President Hans Kutscher and, as Deputy Registrar of the Court of Justice, had been closely involved with the preparation of the Court of Justice's proposals for establishing the Court of First Instance and had represented the Court during the negotiations leading to its establishment.

The accession in 1994 of the three new Member States brought the first appointment of women as judges of the Court of First Instance, although it must be remembered that the Court of Justice

---

[23] 4th ed., 1994, pp. 79–81.

[24] See p. 23 above.

[25] Literally upstairs as the Courthouse of the Court of Justice on the Kirchberg plateau is immediately above the Erasmus and Thomas More buildings which house the Court of First Instance. A moving staircase links the two levels. See the artist's impression (reproduced on the cover of the 4th ed., 1994, n. 23, above) of what the Prime Minister of Luxembourg Jacques Santer, has pertinently called *"une cité judiciaire monumentale"* (in his address on the occasion of the 40th anniversary of the Court of Justice on December 4, 1992). But from July 1999 the whole complex is undergoing change, due to the closure of the courthouse of the Court of Justice for removal of asbestos.

had a woman member in the person of Simone Rozès who served as advocate general from 1980 to 1984. Both Finland and Sweden appointed women as their judges to the Court of First Instance. The first Finnish judge is Mrs Virpi Tiili, a Doctor of Law at the University of Helsinki and formerly Director of Commercial Affairs in the Finnish Chamber of Commerce; she had been Director-General of the National Consumers Administration of Finland since 1990. Mrs Pernilla Lindh, the Swedish judge, was a judge of the Court of Appeal in Stockholm and since 1989 had been Director of the legal service in the commercial division of the Ministry of Foreign Affairs in Stockholm.

## STRUCTURE

The Court of First Instance is not a separate institution but rather a new judicial body, in the words of Article 225 (ex Article 168a) EC, "attached" to the Court of Justice. Thus all of the administrative departments of the Court of Justice are at the disposal of both Courts for such practical matters as interpretation, translation, research, information, finance and general services. In addition to the personal staff of each Member, two legal secretaries and clerical staff, the only department which is exclusive to the Court of First Instance is, logically enough, its Registry. Although smaller than the Registry of the Court it operates in like manner and, like its counterpart in the Court of Justice, is responsible for ensuring that the various procedural steps are carried out correctly and in due time, for keeping the archives of the Court of First Instance and, generally, acting as the interface between the Court of First Instance and the parties for the cases before it.[26]

## PROCEDURE BEFORE THE COURT OF FIRST INSTANCE

It is unsurprising that the procedure in cases brought before the Court of First Instance should be similar in its general outline and identical in many of its details to that applicable in direct actions brought before the Court of Justice itself. Indeed the similarity between the two sets of rules is underlined in the preamble to the Court of First Instance rules which notes that it is "desirable that the rules applicable to the procedure before the Court of First Instance should not differ more than is necessary from the rules applicable to the procedure before the Court of Justice". This is

---

[26] See also Chap. 2, pp. 24 *et seq.*, above.

firstly because the Court of First Instance exercises jurisdiction in areas previously dealt with by the Court of Justice and, on a formal level, because Article 225 (ex Article 168a) EC provides that the provisions of the Protocol on the Statute of the Court of Justice are also to apply to the Court of First Instance and that the rules of the latter Court are to be established in agreement with the former. Finally, although Article 11 of the establishing Decision required the Court of First Instance to adopt its Rules of Procedure immediately upon its constitution, the third indent of that Article provided that until the entry in force of its own Rules of Procedure the Court of First Instance was to apply the Rules of Procedure of the Court of Justice *mutatis mutandis.*

That provision[27] was clearly included so as to enable the new Court to relieve the Court of Justice of the cases falling within its jurisdiction as soon as possible and also because the parties to proceedings which had been started before the Court of Justice were entitled to assume that their cases would be dealt with in accordance with the rules as they stood at the time their cases were lodged. As a result of that provision the Court of First Instance was in the apparently anomalous position of having matters brought before it prior to the adoption and publication of its Rules of Procedure. For the reasons already mentioned however that situation was not as surprising as it might appear at first sight.

Nonetheless the rules of the Court of First Instance do present certain special features stemming essentially from the specific role it is to fulfil and from the particularities of its composition outlined above. We therefore discuss at this stage only the special features of the procedure before the Court of First Instance and it may be assumed that in other respects the procedure before that Court follows that of the Court of Justice in direct actions,[28] as described in Chapter 12 below.

The preamble to the Rules states that it is "necessary to lay down for the Court of First Instance procedures adapted to the duties of such a Court and to the task entrusted to the Court of First Instance of ensuring effective judicial protection of individual interests in cases requiring close examination of complex facts". The peculiar features of the Rules of Procedure of the Court of First Instance therefore arise from one of three reasons. First, the

---

[27] Which may be contrasted with Art. 244 EC (now repealed) which provided that "no matter may be brought before the Court of Justice until its Rules of Procedure have been published."

[28] The Court of First Instance has at present no jurisdiction in cases referred for preliminary rulings (but see Chap. 17, p. 386, for proposals to confer a limited jurisdiction in such cases). The special rules on costs in staff cases, both before the Court of First Instance and on appeal to the Court of Justice, are dealt with in Chap. 9 "Staff Cases", below at p. 200.

rules relating to the assignment of cases to Chambers or plenary sessions of the Court of First Instance and for the designation of advocates general. These rules have already been mentioned.[29] Secondly, the organisation of the fact-finding stage of the procedure, in particular what are described as "measures of organization of procedure". Thirdly, matters arising out of the relationship between the two Courts covering, on the one hand, cases in which one Court or the other declines jurisdiction or suspends its proceedings pending a decision by the other and, on the other hand, the rules for dealing with cases referred back to the Court of First Instance in the event of one of its earlier decisions having been set aside on appeal.

## MEASURES OF ORGANISATION OF PROCEDURE

This slightly cumbersome term is introduced into the rules by Article 49 and expanded upon in Article 64. Article 49 enables the Court of First Instance, at any stage of the proceedings, to prescribe any measure of organisation of procedure or any measure of inquiry or order that a previous inquiry be repeated or expanded. Article 64 makes it clear that the purpose of measures of organisation of procedure is to ensure that cases are prepared for hearing, procedures carried out and disputes resolved under the best possible conditions. Article 64(2) explains that such measures shall, in particular, have as their purpose:

(a) to ensure efficient conduct of the written and oral procedure and to facilitate the taking of evidence;

(b) to determine the points on which the parties must present further argument or which call for measures of inquiry;

(c) to clarify the forms of order sought by the parties, their pleas in law and arguments, and the points at issue between them; and

(d) to facilitate the amicable settlement of proceedings.

A selection of the type of measures which may be prescribed for one or more of those purposes is listed in Article 64(3) which mentions that measures of organisation may include putting questions to the parties, inviting the parties to make written or oral submissions on certain aspects of the proceedings, asking the parties or third parties for information or particulars, asking for documents or any papers relating to the case to be produced, or summoning the parties' agents or parties themselves to meetings.

---

[29] At pp. 82–83, above.

It may be noted that neither paragraph (2) nor (3) of Article 64 is exhaustive and that the wording of those two paragraphs clearly implies that, where appropriate, other measures may be taken for other purposes in connection with the proceedings. Although the measures specifically mentioned in Article 64(3) do not appear to add substantially to the measures of inquiry which may be ordered pursuant to Article 65[30] there is clearly an emphasis on the active participation and co-operation of the parties. This is reinforced by Article 64(4) which gives the parties the opportunity, at any stage of the procedure, to propose the adoption or modification of measures of organisation of procedure, and although the second subparagraph of Article 64(4) requires the Registrar to inform the parties of measures envisaged by the Court of First Instance and to give them an opportunity to submit comments, it seems that need only be done "where the procedural circumstances so require." This contrasts with measures of inquiry for which Article 66(1) provides that before the Court of First Instance decides on the measures of the inquiry the parties shall be heard. The novelty of those provisions then seems to lie in the fact that measures which are slightly less formal than those previously available to the Court of Justice (but which might have been thought to be within the discretion of either Court in any event) have been expressly mentioned in the Rules of Procedure. Their main utility may therefore be that they signal to the parties the intention of the Court of First Instance to adopt a flexible approach with a view to assembling all the elements necessary for its decision.[31]

One curious feature of the Court of First Instance's procedure in respect of staff cases may be mentioned in this context, that is that, under Article 46(2) of the Rules of Procedure, it is for the defendant (*i.e.* the Community institution concerned in its capacity as employer) to produce in its defence the complaint submitted by the applicant official under the Community's internal dispute resolution procedure[32] and the decision rejecting that complaint

---

[30] Precisely the same measures of inquiry have always been available to the Court of Justice under Art. 45(2) of its Rules of Procedure.

[31] For an example of measures of organisation of procedure see the judgment of the Court of First Instance of April 22, 1993 in Case T–9/92 *Automobile Peugeot S.A. v. Commission* (supported by Eco System) in which para. 12 makes it clear that, having heard the report of the judge-rapporteur the Court of First Instance decided to open the oral procedure without carrying out any measures of inquiry although, by way of measures of organisation of procedure, it invited the intervener, Eco System, to provide a copy of the standard order form which it used for its clients. The nature of the contract entered into by that form was central to the outcome of the case, which turned on the question of whether or not Eco System's activities amounted to those of simply an independent intermediary or, as Peugeot contended, of a re-seller thus infringing its rights under a block exemption.

[32] Art. 90(2) of the Staff Regulations of Officials, see below, p. 199.

together with the dates on which the complaint was submitted and the decision notified. This reverses, in those respects, the usual position in civil proceedings whereby it is for the applicant to prove all of the elements of his case. It is clearly a provision intended to avoid conflict over pure formalities from dominating the substance of any given case. This partial reversal of the burden of proof in staff cases may also have the effect of reducing, if not eliminating entirely, the frequent practice of institutions of avoiding giving a direct answer to an official's complaint and allowing it simply to be implicitly rejected by effluxion of time as is allowed for by the Staff Regulations. It may be noted, by contrast, that in the event of an appeal the appellant must annex to his application to the Court the decision of the Court of First Instance which he is challenging and the date upon which that decision was notified to him.[33]

## THE INTERACTION BETWEEN THE TWO COURTS

As the heading to this section suggests there is more to the relationship between the Court of Justice and the Court of First Instance than the mere subordination of an inferior court to an appellate one as in a normal judicial hierarchy. There may in fact be a two-way traffic between the Registries of the two Courts in four sets of circumstances, each of which may give rise to complex situations, not all of which are expressly dealt with by the Rules of Procedure. The four circumstances are:

(a) a document might be mistakenly lodged at the Registry of the wrong Court;

(b) upon examination of the case the Court seised discovers that it does not have jurisdiction to deal with it;

(c) different cases falling within the jurisdiction of each of the two Courts raise connected issues; and

(d) appeals are brought against judgments or other decisions of the Court of First Instance.

The procedural framework for dealing with the first three of these situations is provided by Article 47 of the Protocol on the Statute of the Court.[34] That Article is complemented by special provisions in the Rules of Procedure of each Court, in separate chapters dealing respectively with stay of proceedings[35] and with

---

[33] See Art. 112(2) of the Rules of Procedure of the Court.
[34] Added to the Statute by Art. 7 of the 1988 Decision establishing the Court of First Instance.
[35] Chap. 4 of Title II of the CFI Rules, covering Arts 77 to 80 and Chapter 10 of the CJ Rules, consisting of a single Art. 82(a).

preliminary objections.[36] The rules governing appeals are contained in Articles 49 to 51 of the Statute which are in turn given more detail in the Rules of Procedure.[37]

## 1. Mistake

A simple error in lodging an application or other procedural document addressed to the Court of First Instance with the Registrar of the Court of Justice, or vice versa, is a forgivable mistake given that, as already mentioned, the two Courts are housed in contiguous buildings and share common services including those of the post-room and the messengers. Therefore where such a mistake arises the first indent of Article 47 of the Protocol provides that the mistakenly lodged document shall be transmitted immediately by the Registrar concerned to his opposite number. Neither that provision nor the Rules of Procedure of either of the two Courts mentions the consequences of such a mistake for the running of time limits. However it has been suggested[38] that, taking account of the purpose of that provision, namely to avoid any unnecessary formalism in the interests of the parties, the lodging of a document in good time with one of the Registries should be regarded as sufficient to satisfy any time limit which might be running before the other.

## 2. Lack of Jurisdiction

The remaining three circumstances dealt with in Article 47 of the Protocol are more complex.

The second indent of Article 47 provides that, where the Court of First Instance finds that it does not have jurisdiction to hear and determine an action in respect of which the Court of Justice has jurisdiction, it shall refer that action to the Court of Justice. The Court of Justice has a reciprocal obligation and therefore, to avoid the situation where both Courts might decline jurisdiction leaving the parties deprived of judicial review, it is provided that the

---

[36] Chap. 2 of Title III of the CFI Rules, covering Arts 111 to 114, and Chap. 2 of Title III of the CJ Rules, covering Arts 91 and 92; those provisions lay down the procedure enabling the Court to deal with preliminary objections as to admissibility, other preliminary pleas not going to the substance of the case or situations where the Court concerned has no jurisdiction to deal with an action or it is manifestly inadmissible.

[37] Chap. 4 of Title II of the CFI Rules (Arts 117 to 121 on Judgments of the Court of First Instance delivered after its decision has been set aside and the case referred back to it); and Title IV of the CJ Rules (Arts 110 to 123).

[38] By F. Hubeau in *"Changement des règles de procédure devant les juridictions communautaires de Luxembourg"* [1991] C.D.E. 499.

Court of First Instance may not itself decline jurisdiction where a case has been referred to it by the Court of Justice.

## 3. Connected Issues

The third and final paragraph of Article 47 of the Protocol provides for the situation where the Court of Justice and the Court of First Instance are seised of cases in which the same relief is sought, the same issue of interpretation is raised or the validity of the same act is called in question. In such circumstances, if both Courts were to continue to hear and decide the cases a difficult and embarrassing situation could arise that the two Courts might arrive at different or even contradictory results. At the very least there would be likely to be a considerable duplication and therefore waste of work and effort.

To avoid such difficulties the Court of First Instance may stay the proceedings before it until the Court of Justice has delivered its judgment. Where applications are made for the same act to be declared void the Court of First Instance may also decline jurisdiction in order that the Court of Justice may rule on the application.

However it is possible that the parallel proceedings before the Court of Justice may have been lodged some time later than those before the Court of First Instance which may have reached an advanced stage and possibly already be approaching judgment. For maximum flexibility the final sentence of Article 47 therefore provides that the Court of Justice may also decide to stay the proceedings before it, in which event the proceedings before the Court of First Instance shall continue. Thus, as where a case is lodged before the wrong Court the decision of the Court of Justice is to be given priority in order to avoid a so-called negative conflict of jurisdiction or a situation where both Courts stay their proceedings, thereby creating a form of judicial paralysis.

That such circumstances are not merely figments of the imagination of the fertile mind of a legislative draughtsman may be illustrated by reference to a number of specific cases. For example Joined Cases C–48/90 *Netherlands v. Commission* and C–66/90 *PTT Nederland v. Commission*[39] were actions for annulment against a Commission Decision relating to the provision of courier services in the Netherlands. The first case was an action brought by a Member State and therefore fell within the exclusive competence of the Court of Justice[40] whereas the second, being a case brought

---

[39] Joined Cases C–48/90 *Netherlands v. Commission* and C–66/90 *PTT Nederland v. Commission* [1992] ECR I–565.
[40] See the last sentence of Art. 168a(1) (now, as amended, Art. 225), in its original wording.

by a legal person, fell within the jurisdiction of the Court of First Instance. The Court of Justice therefore made an order[41] referring Case C–66/90 to the Court of First Instance without hearing the parties. Given that in both cases the applicants sought the annulment of the same act, the Court of First Instance (now seised of Case C–66/90 registered in the Court of First Instance as Case T–42/91) in the interests of good administration of justice and so as to enable the Court of Justice to have before it the arguments of the companies (who could not intervene in the action brought by the Netherlands by virtue of Article 37 of the Statute) made an order declining jurisdiction so that the Court of Justice could determine both applications.[42]

In Case T–65/91 *White and Another v. Commission*, White, a member of the Commission's staff and the union to which he belonged[43] jointly brought proceedings in which they raised various issues concerning the appointment of officials to consultative committees; they also claimed damages. The Commission raised a preliminary objection to the admissibility of the case. However, the Court of First Instance,[44] applying the second indent of Article 47 of the Protocol and Article 112 of the Court of First Instance rules, referred the case, so far as the trade union was concerned, to the Court of Justice on the basis that its claim was a direct action based upon Article 173 of the EC Treaty (now Article 230 EC) which, at that time, did not fall within the scope of Article 3 of the Decision establishing the Court of First Instance. Shortly afterwards,[45] in accordance with the third indent of Article 47 of the Protocol and Article 77a of the Rules of Procedure, the Court of First Instance decided to stay the proceedings in Case T–65/91 until the Court of Justice had ruled on the objection as to admissibility in the union's case, now case C–44/92 *TAO/AFI v. Commission*. Following procedural developments in Case C–44/92 the Court of First Instance decided[46] to resume dealing with White's case and joined the objection relating to its admissibility to the substance. The Court of Justice found[47] that the TAO/AFI case was manifestly inadmissible under Article 92(1) of the Rules of Procedure of the Court of Justice, so White's case then continued before the Court of First Instance.

---

[41] Order of June 4, 1991; [1991] ECR I–2723.
[42] Order of the Court of First Instance in Case T–42/91 *PTT v. The Netherlands* [1991] ECR II–273.
[43] The Association of Independent Officials for the Defence of the European Civil Service/*L'Association des fonctionnaires indepéndents pour la défense de la fonction publique*, known as TAO/AFI.
[44] By an order of January 27, 1992.
[45] By an order of March 10, 1992.
[46] By an order of April 6, 1992.
[47] By an order of December 3, 1992.

Finally it should be noted that it is not only in the context of direct actions that these problems may occur. The French rules relating to the payment of royalties for the use of sound recordings by discotheque owners to the French Copyright Management Society SACEM[48] have been referred to the Court on several occasions[49] in cases in which discotheque owners have claimed that SACEM's fees are arbitrary, unfair and constitute an abuse of a dominant position. Four further cases came before the two Courts. In the first two cases applications were made to the Court of First Instance for the annulment of decisions contained in letters of the Commission in which the applicants were informed of the Commission's decision not to pursue an investigation in the matter and referring the applicants to the jurisdiction of the national courts by virtue of the principle of subsidiarity.[50] Subsequently the *Tribunaux de Commerce* of Troyes and of Avesnes-sur-Helpe each referred a case to the Court of Justice[51] for preliminary rulings under Article 177 EC. Pursuant to Article 47 of the Protocol as to which court should stay its proceedings or whether the Court of First Instance should defer its cases to the Court of Justice, the Court of First Instance decided to defer its cases to the Court of Justice.

Although the possibility for the Court of First Instance to defer cases to the Court of Justice in such circumstances makes obvious sense from the point of view of economy of procedure, such a measure does have the side effect of removing, for the cases concerned, the benefits of two-tier judicial review.

## 4. Appeals[52]

It is inherent in the change to a two-tier system of courts that decisions of the Court of First Instance shall be subject to appeal to the Court of Justice. This is made clear in Article 225(1) (ex Article 168a(1)) EC which provides that the Court of First Instance exercises its jurisdiction subject to a right of appeal to the

---

[48] *Société des Auteurs, Compositeurs et Editeurs de Musique* (Association of Authors, Composers and Music Publishers).

[49] See in particular Case 402/85 *Basset v. SACEM* [1987] ECR 1747; [1987] 3 C.M.L.R. 173; Case 395/87 *Ministère Public v. Tournier and Club Whisky a Go-Go* [1989] ECR 2521; [1991] 4 C.M.L.R. 248 and Case 110/88 *Ministère Public v. Lucazeau* [1989] ECR 2811; [1991] 4 C.M.L.R. 248.

[50] Cases T–114/92 *BEMIM v. Commission* [1993] O.J. C43/25 and Case T–5/93 *Tremblay and Others v. Commission* [1993] O.J. C43/26.

[51] Case C–53/93, *Sàrl BAB le Club 7* [1993] O.J. C88/10 of March 13, 1993, and Case C–104/93 *Le Dryat* [1993] O.J. C114/15 of April 24, 1993.

[52] This section deals only with cases referred back to the Court of First Instance following a successful appeal to the Court of Justice. The procedure followed by that Court in dealing with an appeal to it is dealt with in Chap. 12, below.

Court of Justice on points of law only and in accordance with the conditions laid down by the Statute. The use of the word "right" makes it clear that appeals are not subject to any process of filtering or leave to be given by either Court. However it is evident that if all cases decided by the Court of First Instance, or even a large proportion of them, were subject to systematic appeals, one of the purposes of the establishment of the Court of First Instance, namely that of relieving the Court of Justice of part of its workload, would be frustrated. Article 51 of the Protocol therefore reinforces the point that appeals may be on a point of law only. Article 51 further restricts the scope for appeals by stating that an appeal may lie only on the grounds of lack of competence of the Court of First Instance, a breach of procedure before it which adversely affects the interests of the appellant or the infringement of Community law by the Court of First Instance. The precise scope of the right to appeal has yet to be clarified by the Court of Justice. However, in its own interest, the Court is likely to construe those criteria both strictly and narrowly. Article 113 of the Court of Justice's rules adds that "the subject matter of the proceedings before the Court of First Instance may not be changed in the appeal".

The Protocol also provides for the effects of an appeal with a view to giving the two Courts maximum flexibility in the interests of justice and of the parties. In the first place it is provided[53] that the lodging of an appeal does not have the effect of suspending the operation of the judgment of the Court of First Instance. This is subject to the appellant's right to apply to the Court of Justice for interim measures (see p. 287, below) for example so as to suspend the application of a Commission decision imposing a fine which had been upheld by the Court of First Instance. A similarly flexible solution is provided with regard to the effect of a judgment on an appeal. Thus, although the Court of Justice may of course quash the decision of the Court of First Instance, it has the option of either itself giving final judgment in the matter, where the state of the proceedings so permits, or of referring the case back to the Court of First Instance for judgment.[54] A distinction may therefore be made between the Court of Justice, in its appellate capacity, acting as a Court of révision substituting its own judgment as the final one in the matter,[55] or as a Court of *cassation* in which the

---

[53] By Art. 53 of the Protocol.
[54] See Art. 54 of the Protocol.
[55] See for example Case C–345/90P *Hanning v. European Parliament* [1992] ECR I–949 in which the Court of Justice quashed the judgment of the Court of First Instance in Case T–37/89 *Hanning v. Parliament* [1990] ECR II–463, the effect of which was to restore the disputed decision of the Parliament which the Court of First Instance had annulled.

judgment of the lower court is quashed and referred back to that Court for rehearing in the light of findings by the Court of Justice on the points of law on appeal. In the latter case the Rules of Procedure of the Court of First Instance provide that where the judgment concerned was a judgment of the Court of First Instance sitting in plenary session the case must be assigned to that Court as so constituted[56] but where the Court of Justice has set aside a judgment or an order of a Chamber, the President of the Court of First Instance may assign the case to another Chamber composed of the same number of judges as the one which gave the original decision against which the appeal had been lodged.

Since appeals may be lodged not only against final decisions of the Court of First Instance but also against its decisions on interlocutory matters (such as decisions disposing of substantive issues in part only or disposing of a procedural issue concerning a plea of lack of competence, or of inadmissibility or decisions dismissing applications to intervene or for interim measures[57]) the procedure to be followed by the Court of First Instance in a case referred back to it by the Court of Justice will depend upon the stage the proceedings had reached before the Court of First Instance when the appeal was lodged and when the judgment of the Court of Justice referring the case back to the Court of First Instance was delivered.[58] Where the written procedure before the Court of First Instance had been completed by the time of delivery of the judgment referring the case back, the appellant may lodge a statement of written observations and, in the month following the communication to him of that statement, the defendant may lodge a statement of written observations.[59] Where the written procedure before the Court of First Instance had not been completed it is to be resumed at the stage which it had reached, the Court of First Instance adopting any measures of organisation of procedure (see above, p. 87) which may be necessary for the purpose.[60] If it is justified in the circumstances of the particular case the Court of First Instance may allow supplementary statements of written observations to be lodged by any of the parties.[61]

---

[56] Art. 118(2) of the CFI Rules.
[57] See Arts 49 and 50 of the Protocol.
[58] In the case of an appeal against an order of the Court of First Instance refusing a party leave to intervene, the main proceedings before the Court of First Instance would continue unless the Court of First Instance were to make use of its power to stay the proceedings pursuant to Art. 77(b) of its Rules of Procedure.
[59] See Art. 119(1) of the CFI Rules.
[60] Art. 119(2) of the CFI Rules.
[61] Art. 119(3) of the CFI Rules.

THE IMPACT OF THE COURT OF FIRST INSTANCE

Now after a decade of its existence it is possible to draw some conclusions[62] about the extent to which the Court of First Instance has succeeded in discharging the dual task placed upon it by the 1988 decision, namely: (a) to improve the legal protection of individual interests in cases requiring the examination of complex facts; and (b) to relieve the Court of Justice of part of its caseload.

WORKLOAD

Some caution must be exercised in drawing conclusions from the statistics relating to the workload of the two Courts as presented in the statistical appendix. The total volume of litigation at the Community level appears to be increasing inexorably and even exponentially when cases brought before the two Courts are aggregated. This burden is now to some extent shared between two Courts. Furthermore, the figures for the Court of Justice from 1990 onwards include not only cases relating to its original jurisdiction but also appeals lodged against decisions of the Court of First Instance. While these of course represent cases which the Court of Justice must decide and are therefore rightly included in that Court's case-load they do not represent new Community litigation, indeed, in some cases, they will be included in the figures for cases brought before the Court prior to 1989 in matters which were subsequently transferred to the Court of First Instance. Nonetheless, despite those caveats, it is clear that the tendency of Community litigation is to increase and it must be remembered that, had the Court of First Instance not been established, *all* of the cases lodged since November 1989[63] would have had to be dealt with by the one court. It is therefore safe to conclude that,

---

[62] The Court of First Instance celebrated its tenth birthday on September 25, 1999, the anniversary of the date upon which its first members were sworn in. To mark the occasion a colloquium was held in which senior legal advisers of the institutions and practitioners before the Court of First Instance gave their assessments of the Tribunal's record. The papers presented at that colloquium will be published by the Court of Justice shortly. The authors are grateful to have had access to the manuscripts of those papers. Another interesting reflection on this theme from the point of view of one of the judges of the Court of First Instance was provided by Judge Lenaerts at a meeting of the UKAEL in November 1999. An edited version of his paper, entitled "The European Court of First Instance: ten years of interaction with the Court of Justice" will be published shortly by Kluwer Law International in *Essays in Honour of Lord Slynn of Hadley*.

[63] Over 3,000 cases were brought before the Court of First Instance between 1990 and the end of 1999.

while it may not be possible yet to discern a significant beneficial effect resulting from the establishment of the new Court, without that development the pressure on the Court of Justice would certainly have increased to the point of becoming intolerable.

The statistics for 1999 show that staff cases completed during that year took upon average 17 months to conclude, intellectual property cases 8.2 months and, somewhat surprisingly, all other direct actions only 12.6 months. Here is another case for caution with statistics for the chart which accompanies those figures shows that, of all cases completed by judgment or order, some 365 took six months or less, substantially reducing the average. The majority of these were presumably repetitive cases such as those concerned with milk quotas or customs agents which could be disposed of by order after a reasoned decision in a leading case. However, 90 cases, presumably concerning competition or anti-dumping proceedings, took over 24 months to deal with.

It may be noted that the two large groups of cartel cases relating to the polypropylene and PVC industries (see further below) were decided within about two years of being transferred to the Court of First Instance. Nonetheless, in a recent judgment[64] the Court of Justice criticised the slowness of disposal of a case[65] by the Court of First Instance. In that case Advocate General Leger even suggested that such delay might be open to challenge as an infringement of Article 6 of the European Convention on Human Rights, although the Court did not follow him on that point.

## SINGLE JUDGE

In a written submission to the Council of Ministers in February 1997, the Court of First Instance, supported by the Court of Justice, proposed that certain cases before it should be heard by a single judge.[66] In the Court's view this would maximise productivity and procedural efficiency. As a safeguard against inappropriate cases being dealt with by a single judge it was suggested, first that cases would be delegated to a single judge by the chamber of three judges before whom the case was pending, and secondly that the single judge would have the power to refer the case back to the Chamber if it subsequently became clear that it raised a point or points of particular importance. Moreover certain categories of cases were expressly precluded from delegation to a single judge.

---

[64] See Case C–185/95 P *Baustahlgewebe v. Commission* [1998] ECR I–8417.
[65] See Case T–145/89 *Baustahlgewebe* v. *Commission* [1995] ECR II–987.
[66] A proposal first publicly mooted by Judge Donal Barrington, the first Irish judge, when he left the Tribunal to take up a seat on the Supreme Court of Ireland.

In the result the judge designated as Judge-Rapporteur may be delegated by the Chamber to which he or she belongs to decide cases which do not raise any difficult questions of law or fact, which are of limited importance and which do not involve any other special circumstances in the following cases:

- cases concerning officials of the Communities ("staff cases" – see Chapter 9 below);
- direct actions brought by natural or legal persons contesting decisions of the European Parliament, the Council, the Commission or the European Central Bank and cases concerning the non-contractual liability of the Community, provided that those cases raise only questions already clarified by established case law or form part of a series of cases in which the same relief is sought and of which one has already been finally decided; and
- cases in which the Court of First Instance has jurisdiction to give judgment pursuant to an arbitration clause contained in a contract concluded by the Community.

Cases may not be delegated to a single judge where they concern the implementation of the rules:

- on competition or merger control;
- on State aid to industry;
- on anti-dumping measures; and
- where a Member State or a Community Institution party to such a case objects.

The proposal found support from many practitioners and other interested bodies although some, including the Community Staff Unions, expressed reservations that the move would diminish the collegiality of the Community judicial system and its "European" character. In a report in June 1998, the Select Committee of the House of Lords[67] considered that the proposal was "likely to have a modest but significant impact in improving the efficiency of the CFI" and gave it support. The Committee felt that staff cases were particularly suitable for determination by a single judge. They also felt that an application for the annulment of an act of general application should be excluded from the categories of cases subject to delegation. Far from being a threat to the collegiality of the Court the Committee took the view that the single judge proposal could reinforce the independence of the judges in exercising a European jurisdiction in which nationality is irrelevant. This may be a particularly British view.

The 1988 Decision establishing the Court of First Instance was therefore amended by a Decision of April 26, 1999[68] which came

---

[67] House of Lords, Session 1997–98, 25th Report "The Court of First Instance: Single Judge" (HL Paper 114), June 9, 1998.
[68] See [1999] O.J. L114/52 of May 1, 1999.

into effect on July 1, 1999. The first decision[69] has now been given by a single judge under the new procedure; it remains to be seen to what extent the measure will ease the Tribunal's workload problems.

The judicial statistics in the Annual Report for the year 1998 show that on average the Court of First Instance takes 20 months to decide cases, other than staff cases, which take 16–17 months. The overload on the Court may be much increased by its new jurisdiction over challenges against decisions of the appeal boards of the European Community Trademarks Office.

It is a truism that justice delayed may mean justice denied. This issue arose in the case of *Baustahlgewebe*.[70] This was a complex competition case where an appeal was brought to the Court of First Instance against a fine imposed by the Commission. It then took the Court five years to decide in favour of the Commission. That decision was appealed to the Court of Justice. The Court of Justice took another three-and-a-half years to allow the appeal, on the ground that there had been excessive delay in the lower court, a delay tantamount to a denial of the complainant's fundamental rights. The Court reduced the amount of the fine but awarded no costs to the complainant on the appeal.

## Judicial Approach

A number of interesting decisions demonstrates the willingness of the Court of First Instance to grasp the nettles presented to it and, where appropriate, to adopt a bold and sometimes radical approach which has occasionally startled litigants and observers.

This robust approach was demonstrated from almost the first case which the Court of First Instance was called upon to decide. Thus in Case T–51/89 *Tetra Pak Rausing v. Commission*[71] the Court was required to determine a novel point of competition law, the importance of which, it decided, necessitated both that the Court of First Instance sit in plenary session and that it should have the assistance of an advocate-general's opinion. Those two procedural features, while commonplace before the Court of Justice, are exceptional before the Court of First Instance and Article 2 of the establishing Decision provided that the criteria for

---

[69] Judgment in Case T–180/98 *Cotrim v. CEDEFOP*, October 28, 1999. The judgment was delivered just six weeks after the hearing and less than one year after the case was lodged.

[70] Case T–145/89 [1995] ECR II–987; Case C–185/95 P [1999] 4 C.M.L.R. 1203.

[71] Case T–51/89 *Tetra Pak Rausing v. Commission* [1990] ECR II–309; [1991] 4 C.M.L.R. 334.

selecting either cases in which an advocate-general's opinion was required or cases in which the Court might sit in plenary session were to be governed by the Rules of Procedure of the Court of First Instance. Those rules having not yet been adopted at the time, the Court of First Instance was applying the Rules of Procedure of the Court of Justice (which made no provision for such arrangements) *mutatis mutandis*.[72]

In 1986 Tetra Pak, which held a dominant position in the market for packaging of liquid foodstuffs, had acquired control of another undertaking which also produced and marketed machines for filling such cartons. Tetra Pak had thereby acquired use of a patent licence and know-how relating to an advanced packaging procedure. The licensing agreement qualified for a block exemption under Article 85(3) EC and the relevant Commission regulation.[73] The Commission had found[74] that that acquisition constituted an infringement of Article 86 EC. The applicants argued that Article 86 could not be applied to an agreement which was covered by a block exemption under Article 85(3) since conduct could not be expressly allowed under the one Article and at the same time prohibited under the other. The Commission maintained that it was the acquisition of the exclusive license which constituted the infringement of Article 86. In its judgment, against which no appeal was lodged and which therefore represents the law as it stands at least until the Court of Justice says otherwise,[75] the Court of First Instance following the opinion of Judge Kirschner, acting as advocate general, held that the fact that an agreement was covered by Article 85(3) did not exclude the application of Article 86.

In the *Polypropylene Cartel* cases[76] 14 of the largest petrochemical companies in Western Europe brought proceedings

---

[72] Art. 11 of the establishing decision. See the judgment in *Tetra Pak* at para. 9, p. 352.

[73] Commission Regulation (EC) No. 2349/84 of July 23, 1984 on the application of Art. 85(3) of the Treaty to certain categories of patent licensing agreements.

[74] By Commission Decision 88/501/EC of July 26, 1988 [1984] O.J. L219/15. [1988] O.J. L272/27 relating to a proceeding under Arts 85 and 86 of the EC Treaty (IV/31.043 – *Tetra Pak I* (BTG license)).

[75] As to precedence between the decisions of the two courts see Chap. 16, below.

[76] These cases were not joined because of significant differences in the arguments put by the applicants although in his opinion Judge Vesterdorf, designated as advocate general in the case, dealt with all 14 cases together. The Report of the first case, T–1/89 *Rhône-Poulenc SA v. Commission* [1991] ECR II–867 also includes Judge Vesterdorf's Opinion (at p. 869) and the judgments in Cases T–2/89 *Petrofina*, Case T–3/89 *Atochem* are reported in [1989] ECR II–1087 and [1989] ECR II–1117 respectively. The Reports of the next batch of cases to be decided (Case T–4/89 *BASF AG*, Case T–6/89 *Enichem Anic SpA*, Case T–7/89 *Hercules Chemicals NV-SA* and Case T–8/89 *DSM NV*) are in [1991] ECR II–1523 *et seq.*

against the Commission seeking the annulment of a decision adopted in 1986[77] by which it had found that the companies concerned had operated an agreement under concerted practice between 1977 and 1983 creating a price cartel by various means including market sharing arrangements. The decision had imposed fines totalling 56.8 million ECUs and ranging from 500,000 ECUs to 11 million ECUs. Apart from detailed arguments relating to the administrative procedure in relation to each of them the applicants raised the question of the definition of a "concerted practice" for the purposes of Article 85. The question was whether a concerted practice arises at the time when the alleged concertation occurs or whether there must also be an application of the alleged concertation in order to constitute a "practice", for example by implementing the agreement in the context of negotiations with customers of the undertakings concerned. Given the importance of the case and in particular of that point[78] the Court decided to appoint an advocate general for the whole series of cases. The Court held that attendance by representatives of the companies at meetings (during which information was exchanged between competitors relating to prices on the market for the product, profit margins or restrictions on volume of sales) could be regarded by the Commission as concerted practices since the participants at such meetings not only pursued the aim of eliminating in advance any uncertainty about the future conduct of their competitors but also because, in their activity on the market, they would inevitably take account, directly or indirectly, of the information which they had obtained at those meetings.

The decision of the Court of First Instance in the *PVC Cartel* case[79] caused a great stir when it was misguidedly claimed that the effect of the decision would be that Jacques Delors would have personally to sign every one of the 8,000 or more decisions adopted by the Commission each year![80] In its judgment the Court concluded that the Commission had in several respects infringed its own internal Rules of Procedure for the adoption of decisions

---

[77] Commission Decision of April 23, 1986 relating to a procedure in application of Art. 85 of the EC Treaty (IV/31.149 – Polypropylene) [1986] O.J. L230/1.

[78] Which also arose in the *PVC* and *Low-Density Polyethylene* cases which involved essentially the same parties and raised similar questions of law.

[79] Joined Cases T–79/89, T–84–86/89, T–89/89, T–91/89, T–92/89, T–94/89, T–96/89, T–98/89, T–102/89 and T–104/89 *BASF AG and Others v. Commission* [1982] ECR II–315; [1992] 4 C.M.L.R. 357; *The Times*, March 25, 1992.

[80] *Financial Times*, February 28, 1992. A few days later on March 2, discussing the judgment under the heading "When bureaucrats are brought to book" the same newspaper gleefully began: "As a headline 'Brussels slammed for lack of bureaucracy' is from the same school as 'Man Bites Dog'—unexpected, unbelievable and eminently newsworthy."

and that Commission officials, following the adoption of the decision by the Commission at its weekly meeting, had made several important modifications to the text of the decision as it had been adopted. As a result the Commission had been unable to produce to the Court an authenticated copy of the original measures which it purported to have adopted and the Court found that it was unable to ascertain the precise content of the measures adopted owing to the amendments which had been made to them. The Court could neither determine with sufficient certainty the precise date from which the measure was capable of producing legal effects nor, owing to the amendments made to it, ascertain with certainty the precise terms of the statement of reasons which it had to contain pursuant to Article 190 of the Treaty nor could it define and verify clearly the extent of the obligations which it imposed on its addressees or the description of those addressees. It therefore held that the decision was vitiated by particularly serious and manifest defects rendering it non-existent in law.[81] Since they were attacking a non-existent act the applicants' cases were declared inadmissible.

Further complications arose because the Commission, in the course of the oral hearing before the Court of First Instance, had stated that the procedure which had been followed by the Commission in the PVC cases was the procedure which it had followed in all cases for many years. Two of the applicants in the Polypropylene cases referred to above (in which judgment had already been delivered) therefore applied to the Court of Justice for revision of their judgments while four other applicants applied for their cases to be reopened. Those applications were rejected by the Court of First Instance, holding that the mere fact that these breaches of procedure had been established in the PVC cases could not in itself constitute a reason to allow the applicants to raise new issues since they had failed to demonstrate on the balance of probabilities that the same breaches had been committed in their cases.

Mention should also be made of some cases in the other areas of the jurisdiction of the Court of First Instance. In Case T–120/89 *Stahlwerke Peine-Salzgitter AG v. Commission*[82] the Court of First Instance also designated an advocate general (Judge Biancarelli)

---

[81] On appeal the Court of Justice, while substantially upholding the reasoning of the Court of First Instance, held that the irregularities which the latter had found were not of such obvious gravity that the decision had to be treated as legally non-existent, Case C–137/92P *Commission v. BASF and Others*, *The Times*, July 6, 1994.

[82] Case T–120/89 *Stahlwerke Peine-Salzgitter AG v. Commission* [1991] ECR II–279.

even though the case was dealt with by a five-judge Chamber of the Court of First Instance. The applicant, a German steel company, had previously successfully brought actions in the Court of Justice for annulment against various Commission decisions imposing steel quotas on it and now claimed damages against the Commission of over DM77,600,000 as income lost as a result of the annulled decisions. Despite the large number of cases brought before the Court of Justice during the operation of the steel quota regime there was no previous case law relating to the Commission's obligation under Article 34 of the ECSC Treaty, on which the claim was based, to provide compensation for harm caused by a decision which was subsequently declared void. The question which therefore arose was whether Article 34 of the ECSC Treaty was to be interpreted in like manner and in accordance with the case law of the Court of Justice on compensation for liability under the second paragraph of Article 215 of the EC Treaty. The Court of First Instance answered that question in the affirmative and the Court of Justice, dismissing the appeal lodged by the Commission,[83] essentially upheld that approach.

The impact of the Court of First Instance in staff cases (see Chapter 9, below) has already been significant, the Court demonstrating a willingness to deal in a forthright manner with difficult situations and insisting that cases be correctly and carefully handled by the institutions, both at the administrative level and before the Court itself. To cite only a few examples, in Case T–58/91 *Booss and Fischer v. Commission*,[84] the Court of First Instance annulled two Commission decisions which made appointments to vacant posts of Director in Directorate-General for Fisheries on the basis that the Commission had reserved the posts for candidates of a predetermined nationality and that it had therefore not carried out a proper examination of the qualifications and experience of the applicants.

In Case T–45/90 *Speybrouck*[85] the Court upheld the principle that an employee of the European Parliament could not be dismissed on the sole ground of her being pregnant, but it found in the instant case that there were other reasons, not linked to her pregnancy, which did justify the dismissal.

In Case T–43/90 *Diaz Garcia*[86] an official of the Parliament challenged the refusal of that institution to treat as his children the offspring by his concubine: the Court rejected his application holding that, despite the changes in moral attitudes since the Staff

---

[83] Case C–220/91-P *Commission v. Peine-Salzgitter AG* [1993] ECR I–2393.
[84] Judgment of March 3, 1993 [1993] ECR II–147.
[85] Case T–45/90 *Speybrouck v. European Parliament* [1992] ECR II–33.
[86] Case T–43/90 *Diaz Garcia v. European Parliament* [1992] ECR II–2619.

Regulations were adopted in 1962, the Court was not competent to enlarge the legal interpretation of those regulations in the way proposed.

In Cases T–121/89 and T–13/90 *X v. Commission*[87] a candidate for a temporary post with the Commission was rejected on medical grounds. He alleged that the Commission's medical service had, without his knowledge, carried out a blood test upon him for AIDS. The Court rejected his application as it did not find the allegation proved, but it declared that such a test could only be carried out on candidates with their full consent.

In a further case in this most difficult and sensitive field the Court of First Instance has held that although a person who was HIV positive, but did not show any symptoms of AIDS was to be treated as a normal employee, fit for work, that principle did not apply to a person who showed symptoms of AIDS and associated infections.[88]

## TRANSPARENCY

In a more recent series of cases the Court of First Instance has made a decisive contribution to the development of European Community law by putting flesh on the bones of the Community's policy of transparency and openness. It has helped to ensure that that policy amounted to more than merely political rhetoric and that it created enforceable legal rights and obligations.[89]

The policy was developed in the wake of the difficulties encountered in implementing the Maastricht Treaty, following the negative referendum result in Denmark and the very narrow positive vote in France. These setbacks made the Community institutions and the Member States aware of a widespread perception of the Communities as a secretive organisation. To counter that view the Council and the Commission adopted a Code of Conduct on public access to their documents.[90] Such a code of conduct might have remained mere "soft law", but the two

---

[87] Joined Cases T–121/81 and 13/90 *X v. Commission* [1992] ECR II–2195, an appeal is pending in this case.

[88] Case T–10/93 *A v. Commission* [1994] ECR II–179.

[89] See further B. Vesterdorf, "Transparency, More than just a buzzword", (1999) 22 Fordham Int. L. J. The subject of transparency in the Community Institutions is also addressed in several of the contributions to the Court of First Instance Tenth Anniversary Colloquium.

[90] Adopted on December 6, 1993, see O.J. L340/41.

institutions each implemented the Code by adopting decisions to give it effect.[91]

Both institutions provided that requests for documents were to be made in writing identifying the documents concerned. If the request was refused or was left unanswered within 30 days a confirmatory request could be submitted to the Secretary-General of the institution concerned and if that was refused the applicant's right to challenge the decision before the Court of First Instance or to submit a complaint to the Ombudsman were to be notified to him.

The first legal action relating to the two decisions was a case brought by the Netherlands government against the Council Decision.[92] While not challenging the substance of Decision 93/731, the Government argued that the measure should have been adopted through the regular legislative procedure including consultation with the European Parliament. The latter institution intervened in support of this argument. However, the Court held that, in the absence of general rules on public access to documents applicable to all of the institutions, it was for each institution to adopt the measures it deemed necessary to handle such requests. Importantly however the Court added that such internal measures were capable of having legal effects *vis-à-vis* third parties.

Even before that decision was delivered a British journalist, John Carvel of *The Guardian*, had been refused access to the minutes of Council meetings on immigration policy, police co-operation and social policy. He and the newspaper lodged proceedings in the Court of First Instance[93] in which they were supported by the Danish and Dutch Governments and by the European Parliament. The Court held that Article 4(2) of the Council's own decision required the institution to carry out a genuine appraisal, balancing the interest of the individual in obtaining access to a particular document against the institution's interest in keeping it confidential. A blanket refusal of access to a whole category of documents was not consistent with such a duty.

As for the Commission, the environmental NGO, Worldwide Fund for Nature (WWF U.K.), requested information on the Commission's investigation of the use of structural funds for the construction of a visitors' centre at the sensitive Mullaghmore

---

[91] Council Decision 93/731/EC of December 20, 1993 on public access to Council Documents (O.J. L340/43); and Commission Decision 94/90/ECSC, EC, Euratom of February 8, 1994 on public access to Commission Documents (O.J. L46/58).

[92] Case C–58/94 *Netherlands v. Council* [1996] ECR I–2169.

[93] Case T–194/94 *Carvel and Guardian Newspapers Ltd v. Council* [1995] ECR II–2765.

prehistoric site in Ireland. When this was refused WWF U.K. brought an action[94] challenging the refusal which had been justified on the ground of "protection of the public interest" since the investigation had been carried out with a view to the possible opening of infringement proceedings. Although this was one of the grounds for refusal of access to documents allowed by Decision 94/90 the Court pointed to the distinction between mandatory grounds for refusal (protection of the public interest) and discretionary grounds (protection of the confidentiality of the Commission's proceedings).

In the latter case the Commission had to carry out the genuine balancing of interests test as the Court had previously held in *Carvel*. Furthermore even if the institution relied upon both mandatory and discretionary exceptions to the principle of access, it had to indicate explicitly why it considered that a particular document might be relevant to the opening of infringement proceedings. Moreover the reasons given were subject to the requirement in Article 190 EC (now Article 253 EC) to state the reasons on which they are based.

In *Interporc*[95] the Court of First Instance quashed a decision refusing access to documents based upon the public interest exception in respect of judicial proceedings. The documents concerned were said to relate to a decision whose annulment was at issue in other proceedings before the Court. The decision refusing access gave no explanation which would enable the Court to check whether all of the documents concerned were covered by the exception relied upon.

*In Van der Wal*[96] on the other hand the Court of First Instance dismissed a challenge to the refusal to grant access to letters sent by the Commission to a national court. The Commission had been correct to rely on the public interest exception, despite the fact that it was not a party to the proceedings concerned.[97] The Court stated that that exception to the general principle of open access to documents was intended to ensure the respect of the right of any person to be heard fairly by an independent court and was not limited to the protection of the parties to a specific case.

---

[94] Case T–105/95 *WWF U.K. v. Commission* [1997] ECR II–313, Case C–135/97 [2000] 1 C.M.L.R. 149.
[95] Case T–124–96 *Interporc v. Commission* [1998] ECR II–231.
[96] Case T–83/96 *Van der Wal v. Commission* [1998] ECR II–545.
[97] This judgment is subject to two appeals lodged before the Court of Justice by the Netherlands (Case C–174/98-P) and by Van der Wal (Case C–189/98). See now Joined Cases C–174/98 P and C–189/98, judgment of January 11, 2000.

In the *Swedish Journalists*[98] case the Court of First Instance was asked to assess the legality of the Council's refusal to divulge certain documents relating to Europol to the journalists' professional association. In fact the association had already obtained many of the documents from the Swedish Government through the latter's long-standing (since 1766) constitutional principle of openness. The Council's refusal had been based upon the mandatory exception based on protection of public security as well as upon the discretionary one based on the need to maintain the confidentiality of the Council's deliberations.

The Council first objected to the admissibility of the application, arguing that Europol questions were covered by the Third Pillar and therefore outwith the Court's jurisdiction. Here the Court found that although it did not have jurisdiction to review the legality of measures adopted under Title VI of the TEU, it was competent to review the legality of decisions taken pursuant to Decision 93/731. On the substance of the case the Court found that, in the absence of any reasons for which the release of the documents might in fact have been likely to compromise some aspect of public security, the Court was unable to establish whether the refusal fell within one of the permitted exceptions.

Moreover, in so far as the decision was based upon the exception for the protection of the Council's deliberations, neither the journalists' association nor the Court were able to establish whether or not the Council had carried out the genuine balancing of interests which it was required to do.

The *Swedish Journalists* case was remarkable for another reason. During the proceedings the applicant association had published an edited version of the Council's defence on its Internet site and invited members of the public to send their comments to the Council's legal representatives. The Tribunal suspended the case to examine the implications of this act and, in the judgment, penalised the association in costs for what was considered an abuse of process. This was based upon the principle that the good administration of justice required all parties to be able to defend their interests before the courts without outside pressure, especially from the public.

Finally, in *Hautala*[99] the Court of First Instance took the view that confidentiality, where applicable, did not apply to a document as such, but to the information which it contained. The important

---

[98] Case T-174/95 *Svenska Journalistöbundet v. Council* [1998] ECR II-2289; this case is also known as the *Journalisttidningen* case.
[99] Case T-14/98 *Hautala v. Council* [1999], judgment of July 16, 1999, not yet reported.

consequence of that ruling is that institutions may be obliged to disclose non-confidential parts of a document even though other parts may fall within one of the exceptions.

## EVALUATION

It is clear from the foregoing examples that the Court of First Instance has developed for itself a strong and distinctive voice in the first decade of its existence. While it has not escaped criticism, in particular for the length of its judgments and the time taken, in some cases, to deliver them, on the whole the main users have been satisfied with its performance.

As Julian Currall[1] has said:

> "It is I think accepted on all sides that . . . the CFI has to a very large extent fulfilled the hopes placed in it 10 years ago, not least by the Court of Justice itself. One need only glance at the detail in reports of such cases as the *Polypropylene* cartel and the most recent judgments in similar cases, such as *Cartonboard, Steel beams* and *PVC II.* There are many other examples. All of these cases involved deciding extremely complex issues of fact, economics and law. The comparison between the first cartel judgments and the most recent also shows that the standard has been maintained over the years. Further proof of the reliability of the findings in such cases can be found in the case law of the Court, which has upheld in all essentials all of the CFI's substantive judgments in such cases."

That final assertion is borne out by an examination of the statistics concerning appeals.[2] During the ten years to the end of 1999, 317 appeals were lodged compared with the total of 1170 decisions of the Court of First Instance open to appeal during that period. Of the 57 appeals decided by the Court of Justice during 1999, only eight, or 14 per cent, were successful wholly or in part. 22 were unfounded and 24 manifestly inadmissible, or manifestly unfounded, or both.

---

[1] Legal Adviser to the European Commission and frequently its representative in proceedings before the Court of First Instance in his contribution to the Tenth Anniversary Colloquium entitled "Measures of organisation of procedure, Measures of inquiry and some thoughts on the appeal system".

[2] For a review of the approach of the Court of Justice to dealing with appeals see Sylvia Sonelli "Appeal on points of Law in the Community system—a Review" (1998) 35 CML Rev. 871.

Further evidence of the success of the Court of First Instance and of the confidence placed in it is the steadily increasing scope of its jurisdiction.[3] This process seems to be continuing since, at the time of writing, the Council has before it a proposal to include certain cases brought by Member States within its jurisdiction.

[3] The Court of First Instance delivered its first decision on the Community Trade Mark Regulation on July 8, 1999: Case T–163/98 *The Proctor and Gamble Company v. Office for Harmonization in the Internal Market (trade marks and designs)*.

# PART TWO: JURISDICTION

## Introductory

In the Community legal order the Court of Justice has a crucial role. It has to see that the Council and the Commission, as the decision-taking and policy-making organs of the Community, keep within their powers under the Treaties. It has to restrain Member States who act in breach of the Treaties. It has also a legislative function, inasmuch as it often falls to the Court to fill gaps in the legal system arising from the political impotence of the Council – impotence which the SEA and the Maastricht Treaty have attempted to correct.

For these important and varied tasks the Court is armed by the Treaties with an extremely wide jurisdiction. Indeed, the Court is vested with powers which in most continental countries lawyers would expect to find shared between a number of specialised courts. But in the Community legal order the Court of Justice has had to serve as a judicial maid of all work, at least until the creation in 1989 of the Court of First Instance.

Thus, the Court acts as an administrative court to impose judicial control on the other institutions of the Community. Again, in certain circumstances, an individual may bring before the Court[1] an action for annulment of a Community act or a suit for damages against an institution of the Communities. Until 1989 it also acted as would a continental administrative court by providing a tribunal to which the public servants of the Communities might appeal in disputes relating to their terms of service; but since 1989, as we saw in the last chapter, this head of jurisdiction, which used to constitute about one third of the Court's business, has now passed to the Court of First Instance and may only reach the Court on appeal on a point of law (Chapter 9).

The Court exercises powers of judicial review not only over administrative acts but also over Community legislation, such as

---

[1] Since Monday August 2, 1993 such cases are initiated before the Court of First Instance (see Chap. 5, above) and only reach the Court of Justice on appeal, if at all.

regulations or directives of the Council or Commission. The Court may also rule upon the conformity with the Treaties of any international agreement entered into by the Communities. In this respect, the Court resembles a constitutional court such as that of the German Federal Republic or the Supreme Court of the United States.

If the Court in these respects resembles the administrative or constitutional courts familiar to continental lawyers, it also serves, in a sense, as an international court by hearing suits brought against a Member State for an alleged violation of the Treaties. Such suits may be brought by another Member State but are usually instituted by the Commission in the exercise of its watch-dog function.

Among the Court's functions, of the highest importance is its jurisdiction to give preliminary rulings when requested to do so by a court of a Member State. Preliminary rulings may be given upon a question of the interpretation of Community law or of the validity of Community legislation. This head of the Court's jurisdiction has proved in the event to be much the most influential for the development of Community law and will be fully discussed in Chapter 10. From a procedural point of view preliminary rulings may be contrasted with the other heads of the Court's jurisdiction. For, whereas a reference for a preliminary ruling can only be made by the national court and not by the parties themselves, all other cases are brought directly before the Court by the party initiating the proceedings, whether this be a Member State, a Community institution, a legal person such as a firm or company, or a private individual.

In Appendix II are included various Judicial Statistics concerning the work of the Court from its inception up to December 31, 1999.

There (Table 1, pp. 420–421) the term "Direct actions" is used in contrast to "Preliminary Rulings" on the other. Direct actions may conveniently be divided into (A) actions against Member States (which will be the subject of Chapter 6) and (B) actions against Community institutions including staff cases which will be the subject of Chapters 7, 8 and 9. Category (B) corresponds to what we have termed above the administrative and constitutional jurisdiction of the Court; category (A) to its international jurisdiction.

This last expression must be treated with caution. To receive and decide suits against States is the characteristic function of an international tribunal; contemporary examples are the International Court of Justice at The Hague or the European Court of Human Rights at Strasbourg. In this sense one may speak of the Luxembourg Court's international jurisdiction, for under various provisions of the Treaties the Court may be seised of complaints that a Member State is failing to fulfil its treaty obligations, including the failure to implement obligations arising under regulations or directives.

Nevertheless, this jurisdiction of the Court differs in significant respects from that of a traditional international tribunal. Thus, it differs from the Hague Court in that the breaches by Member States with which it is concerned are breaches primarily of Community law, not of international law (except in so far as they stem from a Treaty infringement). The concern here of the Luxembourg Court is with upholding and enforcing the Community legal order, whereas that of the Hague Court is the settlement of international disputes. Again, suits against Member States are usually brought to Luxembourg not by another State but by the Community's own policeman or watchdog, the Commission. Moreover the Court's jurisdiction in these cases is compulsory, as opposed to the consensual jurisdiction before the International Court of Justice.

A somewhat similar relationship existed until recently at Strasbourg between the European Court and the European Commission of Human Rights, but such a filtering device is not characteristic of international tribunals. Furthermore, preliminary references to Luxembourg from courts in Member States have, as we shall see later, the same effect as certain direct actions in putting a particular Member State in the dock there for a Treaty infringement with the watchdog role of the Commission being played by the individual plaintiff; but such references are not normally thought of as falling within the international jurisdiction of the Court.

The last head of jurisdiction to be considered in this part does have an international aspect. Under Article 300(6) EC (ex Article 228(6)) the Court may be asked its opinion on whether an international agreement which the Community is contemplating entering into is compatible with the provisions of the Treaty. This jurisdiction was exercised for the first time in 1975 and, although exercised infrequently, has now sufficient significance to warrant a separate chapter: Chapter 11.

The six chapters which form this part will cover then the main categories of cases falling within the Court's jurisdiction. But this manifold jurisdiction also extends to a few exceptional types of case not dealt with below, such as the power of the Court under Article 13 of the Merger Treaty compulsorily to retire a member of the Commission who no longer fulfils the conditions required for the performance of his duties or if he has been guilty of serious misconduct: this power has been used only once, in 1976, when a Commissioner was permanently incapacitated by a stroke.

Potentially more significant, but rarely exercised, is the jurisdiction of the Court under Article 95 ECSC to give an opinion if it is found necessary to amend, subject to certain limitations, the provisions of the ECSC Treaty. This power is analogous to but not identical with the Court's jurisdiction under Article 300 EC mentioned above. Other heads of jurisdiction can be found in Articles 237 to 239 (ex Articles 180 to 182) EC. Frequently contracts concluded by the Community with outside bodies include an arbitration clause conferring jurisdiction on the Court pursuant to Article 181 EC (or Article 153 Euratom: an instance of this jurisdiction is mentioned below, p. 172).

Article 239 (ex Article 181) confers upon the Court jurisdiction in any dispute between Member States which relates to the subject matter of the Treaty, if the parties agree to submit their dispute to the Court. Moreover, Member States whose disputes concern the interpretation or application of the Treaty are bound by Article 292 (ex Article 219) EC not to submit their dispute to any other method of settlement than those provided by the Treaty.

From 1989 a further task now falls to the Court by virtue of the creation of the Court of First Instance. This is to act as an appellate jurisdiction from the latter. In this capacity, it will also have to resolve any conflicts of jurisdiction arising between itself and the lower court. The interaction between the two Courts was examined in Chapter 5, above.

# Chapter Six

# Actions Against Member States

## INTRODUCTION

Proceedings may be brought before the Court of Justice against Member States to establish that they have infringed their Community obligations. Under the EC Treaty such direct actions against Member States arise, principally, under Articles 226 and 227 (ex Articles 169 and 170) EC. They may also be brought under Article 93 in the special context of "State aids", and, since the SEA under Article 95(9) (ex Article 100a(4)) EC if the Commission or any Member State considers that another is making improper use of the possibility of opting out of a measure of harmonisation as provided by that Article. In the ECSC Treaty, as we shall see, it is the Commission which acts, in effect, as a jurisdiction of first instance to determine the infringement and issue a decision addressed to the Member State in breach of the Treaty.[1] Such a decision may then reach the Court for judicial review under Article 88(2) ECSC.

Articles 226 and 227 (ex Articles 169 and 170) EC provide two distinct but inter-related procedures. Under the former Article it is the Commission which brings the action against the Member State, whereas under the latter the action is brought by another Member State.

While actions under Article 170 (now Article 227) have been very rare (only one to date taken to judgment),[2] enforcement actions by the Commission under Article 226 (ex Article 169) have become increasingly frequent; for instance, directives to harmonise VAT have led to many such actions. There was a total of 166 actions for the 28 years 1953–81, an average of barely six cases

---

[1] Art. 88(1) ECSC.
[2] Case 141/78 *France v. United Kingdom* [1979] ECR 2923; [1980] 1 C.M.L.R. 6 and Case C–388/95 *Spain v. Belgium* (concerning Rioja Wine), judgment of May 16, 2000 (not yet reported).

*More infringement proceedings under Article 169 of the EEC Treaty have been brought against Italy than any other Member State (see Table 4 in the statistical appendix)**

per year for the whole period. In the early 1980s around 50 cases per year were brought by the Commission and, in the second half of the decade, an average of over 80 applications per year was reached with a sudden jump to 114 cases in 1985 and 99 cases in 1989. During the period up to mid-1993 the average settled down to about 60 cases per year but then rose to well over 100.[3]

---

* Drawing by Domenico Rosa published in *Il Sole 24 Ore* October 28, 1991.
[3] For greater detail see Table 4 in Appendix II below. The Cautionary Note at the beginning of Appendix II is particularly important in this context.

Criticism has been expressed that the Commission should be more selective in its resort to the big stick: not every peccadillo by a Member State warrants the diversion of precious time and manpower which Commission proceedings entail; it should exercise sparingly the discretion to "prosecute" which, as we will see, Article 226 (ex Article 169) EC allows it.[4] Excessive use of the procedure might risk diluting its dissuasive effect and even undermining the authority of the Court's judgments. Since the amendment of Article 221 (ex Article 165) by the Maastricht Treaty, infringement proceedings against Member States are most often heard by a Chamber of five judges. This too may give the impression that such infringements are, in some sense, regarded as not of the highest importance so as to justify a Full Court. Moreover, as will be seen below (p. 133), infringements of Community law may be the subject of proceedings before a national court in the Member States by virtue of the doctrine of direct effect; and, even where that doctrine does not apply, an action may lie in the national court for damages to compensate individuals for loss caused by the Member State's failure to fulfil its Community obligations; in some sense, regarded as not of the highest importance so as to justify a Full Court.[5]

## Procedure under Article 226 (ex Article 169)

An action by the Commission under Article 226 (ex Article 169) involves three phases. The formal procedure however is invariably preceded in practice by the Commission writing a letter to the Member State warning it of its breach and inviting its comments. If this does not settle the matter, and in two cases out of three it does so, then the first formal step is for the Commission to invite the State formally to submit its observations on the alleged breach, after which, if it is not satisfied by the explanations or undertakings given by the State, the Commission will deliver a reasoned opinion. This pre-contentious phase may well result in a settlement of the matter by the State recognising its breach and correcting it. In practice, a high percentage of the cases terminate at this stage.[6]

If the State is recalcitrant, the second phase in the procedure is for the Commission to bring the matter before the Court. Settle-

---

[4] See Audretsch, *Supervision in European Community Law* (2nd ed., 1986); also Evans, "The Enforcement Procedure of Art. 169 EEC: Commission Discretion" (1979) 4 E.L.Rev. 442.

[5] See Joined Cases C–6 and C–9/90 *Francovich and Bonifaci v. Italy* [1991] ECR I–5357; [1993] 2 C.M.L.R. 66 and Chap. 15 below, p. 363.

[6] See Table 4 in Appendix II below.

ments are also sometimes reached at this stage. The third phase is for the Court to give judgment.

Under Article 228 (ex Article 171) this judgment is only declaratory and, until the entry into force of the Maastricht Treaty, there were no sanctions for non-compliance. Article 171 (now, after amendment, Article 228) simply declared that the State shall be required to take the necessary measures to comply with the judgment of the Court. A failure to do so would itself be a failure to fulfil an obligation under the Treaty which might give rise to further proceedings under Article 226 (ex Article 169). Although this scheme implies a theoretical possibility of an infinite series of cases, in practice the Commission has only had to bring such follow-up proceedings relatively rarely.[7]

Yet the violation of a treaty obligation by a Member State is a serious matter which must carry political consequences in its relations with other Member States and a systematic refusal to comply with the Courts' judgments would be in flagrant contravention of the principle of the rule of law and might even amount to a repudiation of the Treaty as a whole. To date, almost every judgment against a Member State has been complied with, although in a few instances only after considerable delay.

The two notorious instances of reluctance to conform concern, respectively, Italy and France. The Italian Government imposed a tax, pursuant to a Law of 1939, on the export of art treasures, which it was only prevailed upon to repeal as a tax on exports contrary to Article 16 EC, after having been declared in breach in three different proceedings before the Court.[8]

In the so-called Lamb War between France and the United Kingdom (1978–80), a French ban on the import of mutton and lamb from the United Kingdom was declared by the Court, in proceedings under Article 169 (now Article 226) EC, to be an infringement of Articles 12 and 30 EC[9] (now, after amendment Articles 25 and 28 EC). When France did not comply with this judgment, the Commission began a second action under Article 169 (Case 24/80, lodged in January 1980), based upon France's infringement of Article 171 (now, after amendment, Article 228),

---

[7] A total of 45 times up to 1999. Of these, 22 cases were brought against Italy, ten against Belgium and France. However, 16 cases were settled and withdrawn before judgment. See, generally, European Commission's Annual Reports on Monitoring the Application of Community Law, especially Fifteenth Annual Report, COM (98) 317 final, discussed Anne Bonnie (1998) 23 E.L. Rev. 537. And see Table 5, Appendix II.

[8] Case 7/68 *Commission v. Italy* [1968] ECR 423; [1969] C.M.L.R. 1; Case 18/71 *Eunomia v. Italian Ministry of Education* [1971] ECR 811, Case 48/71 [1972] C.M.L.R. 4, *Commission v. Italy* [1972] ECR 527; [1972] C.M.L.R. 699.

[9] Case 232/78 *Commission v. France* [1979] ECR 2729; [1980] 1 C.M.L.R. 418.

which requires a State to take the necessary measures to comply with any judgment of the Court. Before this case was heard, the Commission, in March 1980, lodged a further action (Case 97/80) against France under Article 169 (now Article 226) EC in respect of an illegal charge upon mutton and lamb imports and of the continuing defiance of the first judgment. Cases 24/80 and 97/80 then proceeded as joined cases, in the course of which the Commission, pursuant to Article 186 (now Article 243) EC and Article 83 of the Rules of Procedure, made an application for the adoption of "interim measures" in which it invited the Court "to order the French Republic to desist forthwith from applying any restriction and/or levying any charge on imports of mutton and lamb from the United Kingdom". For reasons which will be discussed below (p. 287) when interim measures are explained, the Court refused the order requested. Nevertheless, in September 1980 a compromise was reached in the Council of Agricultural Ministers by the adoption of a sheepmeat regime (long demanded by France) which induced the latter to remove the charge on imports.

By contrast with the earlier dispute with Italy over the art treasures tax (above) or the later dispute with the United Kingdom over an import ban on potatoes,[10] in the Lamb War no challenge to the French action was brought in the French courts, though this might have proved more effective. Other important proceedings in recent years have included infringement actions by the Commission against Germany for its strict application to beer imports of the national criteria for the ingredients of beer and against France for impeding the import from Spain of agricultural produce (see above) and for non-compliance with a Community directive for the protection of wild birds.[11]

Because of such occasional reluctance to comply with the Court's judgments, whether real or perceived, the Member States, at the instigation of the United Kingdom, decided to reinforce the Court's powers in this respect. Thus the Treaty on European Union[12] (TEU) added a new paragraph (2) to Article 228 (ex Article 171) which empowers the Court, in the last resort to impose a lump sum or penalty payment on a Member State which has not complied with its previous judgment.

---

[10] Case 231/78 *Commission v. United Kingdom* [1979] ECR 1447; [1979] 2 C.M.L.R. 427, and Case 118/78 *Meijer v. Department of Trade* [1979] ECR 1387; [1972] 2 C.M.L.R. 398.
[11] Case 178/84 *Commission v. Germany* [1987] ECR 1227; Case C–265/95 *Commission v. France* [1997] ECR I–6959; Case 252/85 *Commission v. France* [1988] ECR 2243.
[12] [1992] O.J. C224, August 31, 1992, generally known as the Maastricht Treaty.

While this measure may give the appearance of reinforcing the Community legal order it may be doubted whether it will have any significant practical consequences. As already indicated[13] the problem of non-compliance, although serious, is neither widespread nor frequent and arises generally in certain Member States which suffer from serious internal political problems (especially Belgium and Italy). Any dissuasive effect of the imposition of such a penalty is likely to arise from the adverse publicity which it would entail as it is difficult to envisage the Court imposing (even if the Commission were to recommend) a fine sufficiently large to deflect one of the Member States from a course which it was bent upon taking. In the final analysis the authority of the Courts' judgments and hence their effectiveness must depend upon the quality of their legal reasoning and the genuine independence of the institution.

Nonetheless, the Commission has given notice of its intent to use the new weapon at its disposal to secure effective compliance by the Member States with their treaty obligations. First, in August 1996 it released a "Memorandum on applying Article 171 of the EC Treaty".[14] In the memorandum the Commission points that it has a discretion in deciding whether to refer a case to the Court for a second time but that, if it does decide to do so, it is required to give its view as to the penalty and the amount thereof when lodging its application. In those circumstances it felt that it should publicly state the criteria which it would apply in inviting the Court to impose monetary penalties.

The three fundamental criteria would be the seriousness of the infringement, its duration and the need to ensure that the penalty itself was a deterrent to further infringements. As regards seriousness the Commission states that a failure to comply with a Court judgment (it should not be forgotten that *this*, rather than the original infringement is what is at issue in Article 228 proceedings) is always quite serious. However, for the specific purposes of fixing the penalty, the Commission will take account of two factors closely linked to the established infringement which gave rise to the original judgment, namely the importance of the Community interests which have been infringed and the effects of the infringement on general and particular interests.

The memorandum was amplified and extended in early 1997 by a note on the method of calculating the penalty payments.[15] The Commission stated that the method used had "to comply with the

---

[13] See p. 118 above and table 5 in the statistical appendix, p. 425.

[14] "Memorandum on applying Art. 171 of the EC Treaty" [1996] O.J. C242/6. Art. 171 should now be read as Art. 228.

[15] "Method of calculating the penalty payments provided for pursuant to Art. 171 of the EC Treaty" [1997] O.J. C63/2.

principles of proportionality and equal treatment for all the Member States". To that end the amount of the daily penalty is calculated by multiplying a uniform flat-rate by two coefficients, one reflecting the seriousness of the infringement and the other its duration. The flat-rate was set at ECU 500 (now 500 Euro) per day and the result of the sum is multiplied by a special factor (n) reflecting the ability to pay of the Member State concerned, as measured by its GDP, and the number of votes it has in Council. Thus for example the "n" factor for Luxembourg is 1, for the United Kingdom it is 17.8 and for Germany 26.4. The resulting amount would be payable for each day of delay in implementing the Court's judgment, starting from the day on which the Court's second judgment was brought to the attention of the Member State concerned and ending when it finally complies with the judgment.

Within a few weeks of announcing the method of calculation the Commission lodged its first applications under the revised Article 171 (now Article 228). These were three cases against Germany and two against Italy in respect of earlier judgments establishing failure to implement environmental Directives. In one case the Commission proposed a fine of ECU 26,400 per day for Germany's failure to implement the Directive on the protection of wild birds and in another ECU 158,400 per day for failure to implement the Directive on the protection of surface water intended for drinking water.

At the time of writing those cases had been withdrawn, the Member States having satisfied the Commission of their compliance with the earlier judgments. Three further cases are currently pending, one against France and two against Greece. Of the latter, one, Case C–387/97,[16] was heard by the Court on June 26, 1999 and seems likely to proceed to judgment. The Commission has proposed a penalty of ECU 24,600 per day.[16a]

In some Member States it has been accepted that it may be possible for an individual with a sufficient interest to sue the Government for damages in respect of its breach of Community law.[17] In English and Scots law the question is moot and straddles

---

[16] An application for a declaration that, by failing to comply with the judgment of the Court in Case C–45/91 *Commission v. Hellenic Republic* [1992] ECR I–2509, Greece had failed to fulfil its obligations under Art. 223 (ex Art. 171).

[16a] On July 4, 2000 the Court gave judgment imposing a penalty of (in sterling equivalent) £13,000 a day against Greece.

[17] See, for example, in France *Avilar* (*Conseil d'Etat* March 23, 1984) and *Steinhauser v. City of Biarritz* (*Tribunal Administratif de Pau*, November 12, 1985), and in the Netherlands *Roussel Laboratories* (Hague District Court, July 18, 1984): these and other cases are discussed by Green and Barav in *Yearbook of European Law* (1986), pp. 54 *et seq.*

the uncertain boundary between public and private law. In *Garden Cottage Foods v. Milk Marketing Board*[18] there were dicta in the House of Lords in favour of a remedy in damages against the Board for breach of statutory duty. But in *Bourgoin v. Ministry of Agriculture, Fisheries and Food*[19] the Court of Appeal (Oliver L.J. dissenting) reversed the decision of Mann J. at first instance who had awarded damages in tort to a French producer of turkeys whose imports to the United Kingdom had been illegally embargoed by the Ministry in breach of Article 30 EEC Before a further appeal could come before the House of Lords, the case was settled by the parties.[20]

In respect of Community provisions which have direct effect national courts are, in any event, required to provide an effective remedy for infringement of the rights which the provision sought to bestow.[21] In Marshall II[22] the Court emphasised that an award of compensation, where this was the means adopted to guarantee real and effective judicial protection, could not be arbitrarily limited and had to be sufficient fully to make good the loss. Even if provisions do not have direct effect, a claim for compensation may lie against a Member State if the conditions prescribed in *Francovich* are fulfilled.[23]

Under Article 88 ECSC the procedure is different. Thus, under the first phase the Commission reaches a decision whether the State is in breach: it does not merely deliver an opinion. In the second place it is therefore the State which must bring the matter before the Court by way of a challenge to the Commission's decision. Finally, in the third phase, if the State does not challenge the decision or if the Court upholds it, then the Commission is empowered to impose certain sanctions, provided the Council supports this by a two-thirds majority. The sanctions include the

---

[18] [1983] 2 All E.R. 770.

[19] [1985] 3 All E.R. 585.

[20] See Steiner, "How to Make the Action Suit the Case: Domestic Remedies for Breach of E.C. Law" (1987) 12 E.L.Rev. 102. Following the House of Lords decision in *Kirklees Borough Council v. Wickes Building Supplies Ltd* [1992] 3 All E.R. 717; [1992] 3 W.L.R. 170; [1992] 2 C.M.L.R. 765 there is serious doubt as to the correctness of the Court of Appeal's decision in *Bourgoin*

[21] See Case 14/83 *Von Colson and Kamann v. Land Nordrbein-Westfalen* [1984] ECR 1891; [1986] 2 C.M.L.R. 430 where the Court had held that even if a directive did not prescribe a specific measure to be taken in the event of its breach but left Member States free to choose between the different solutions for achieving its objective (namely the prohibition of discrimination), the measure adopted had to be such as to guarantee real and effective judicial protection.

[22] Judgment of August 2, 1993 in case C–271/91 *Marshall v. Southampton and South West Hampshire Area Health Authority* [1993] ECR I–4367; [1993] 3 C.M.L.R. 293, *The Times*, August 4, 1993.

[23] See note 5, above.

suspension of payments otherwise due to be paid by the Commission to the State in default or the taking of discriminatory measures which would normally be proscribed under Article 4 ECSC (for example, a ban on imports from the State in question). It remains to be seen whether these special procedures will be retained when the ECSC treaty expires in 2002.

Member States have shown much ingenuity in defending themselves against the Commission's claims of having failed to fulfil their Treaty obligations. However the Court has generally had little difficulty in exposing specious arguments. Thus in Cases 2 and 3/62 *Commission v. Luxembourg and Belgium*[24] the Court reaffirmed its view[25] that a subsequent request for special authorisation does not operate to suspend Article 169 (now Article 226) proceedings; to decide otherwise would deprive the Article of its effectiveness.

A different line of defence to Article 169 (now Article 226) proceedings was attempted in Cases 90 and 91/63 *Commission v. Luxembourg and Belgium.*[26] Here the two Governments argued that the actions against them were inadmissible because the Council was itself in default in having delayed the setting up of a common organisation for dairy products, although it had resolved that it would do so by regulation before July 31, 1962. The Governments therefore argued that their own protective import duties would have been unnecessary if the Council had done its job by the date it had itself proposed and made a regulation governing dairy products generally. They argued that under the theory of interdependence of obligations in international law a party which is affected by the failure of another party to fulfil its obligations has the right not to fulfil its own obligations.

The Court roundly rejected this plea as having no place in Community law: the Treaty created a new legal order whose structure, except for cases expressly covered by the Treaty, involved the prohibition of Member States taking justice into their own hands. Hence, the Council's failure to fulfil its obligations could not excuse the defendant Governments from carrying out their own obligations. Furthermore, self-help was not an appropriate remedy where an agency (namely, the Commission) existed for law enforcement. Accordingly, the import duties were declared contrary to Community law.

Although the Belgian Government then abolished the duties, the recovery of duties already paid was prohibited by statute. This led

---

[24] [1962] ECR 425; [1963] C.M.L.R. 199 (the *Gingerbread* case).
[25] First stated in the very first action brought under Art. 169, the *Italian Pigmeat* case, Case 7/61 *Commission v. Italy* [1961] ECR 315.
[26] [1964] ECR 625; [1965] C.M.L.R. 58 (the *Dairy Products* case).

to further proceedings in the Belgian courts, culminating in the landmark decision of the *Cour de Cassation* upholding in Belgium the supremacy of Community law over conflicting national law: *Minister for Economic Affairs v. Fromagerie Franco-Suisse "Le Ski"*.[27]

It is well established that a Member State may not rely upon provisions, practices or situations in its internal legal system in order to justify a failure to fulfil obligations arising under Community law. Thus, in Case 58/81 *Commission v. Luxembourg*[28] the Grand Duchy was held in breach of a Directive on equal pay despite its plea that it needed time to enact implementing legislation and to study the budgetary consequences of the Directive. The date by which a Directive must be implemented is, after all, set by the Member States themselves when they adopt a Directive and takes into account the time needed to adopt legislation.

In Case 167/73 *Commission v. French Republic*[29] the longstanding rule of French law was challenged under which a certain proportion of the crew of French merchant ships had to consist of French nationals. The Commission argued that this was contrary to Community law, in particular Article 48 EC enshrining the principle of free movement of workers. The French Government did not agree that this principle automatically applied to transport, especially transport by sea in view of the terms of Article 84(2) EC; but it did indicate its intention to amend the offending provision of the *Code du Travail Maritime*, although not accepting that it was under any treaty obligation to do so. The Court held that the basic principle of free movement of workers was not subject to any qualifications in relation to sea transport and that consequently France was in breach of Article 48, nor had France in any way atoned for this breach by its declared intention to amend its ways. Moreover, the principle of legal certainty required the removal from the French statute book of a provision contrary to Community law.

---

[27] [1972] C.M.L.R. 330. Consistent with the *Dairy Products* case is the later Case 63/83 *R. v. Kirk* [1984] ECR 2689; [1984] 3 C.M.L.R. 522, where the United Kingdom Government took unilateral action to impose a ban on fishing in British waters, arguing that this was justified by the failure of the Council to agree a new Common Fisheries Policy. A Danish skipper defied the ban, was caught and fined £30,000 by North Shields Magistrates; he appealed to the Crown Court, which sought a preliminary ruling under Art. 177 (now Art. 234) EC. The Court of Justice declared the British ban to be contrary to Community law; consequently, the fine was quashed.

[28] Case 58/81 *Commission v. Luxembourg* [1982] ECR 2175; [1982] 3 C.M.L.R. 482.

[29] Case 167/73 *Commission v. French Republic* [1974] ECR 359; [1974] 2 C.M.L.R. 216.

Some recent, high profile actions under Article 226 (ex Article 169) have been the actions brought by the Commission against Germany in connection with its beer purity legislation (*Reinheitsgebot*)[30] and proposed motorway tolls,[31] Denmark for failing to observe the Community's rules on public procurement in connection with the Great Belt (*Storebaelt*) bridge construction project,[32] the United Kingdom for failure properly to implement the directive on purity of bathing water at Blackpool, Formby and Southport,[33] and France for failure of its police to curb attacks by angry farmers on lorries carrying agricultural products from neighbouring countries.[34]

## PROCEDURE UNDER ARTICLE 227 (EX ARTICLE 170)

The alternative procedure to Article 226 (ex Article 169) is that under Article 227 (ex Article 170) which permits any Member State to bring another Member State before the Court if it considers the latter has failed to fulfil an obligation under the Treaty. This form of action has rarely been used. Like the procedure under Article 226 (ex Article 169) the Article 227 (ex Article 170) procedure is in successive phases. The first phase requires the complaining State to bring the alleged infringement before the Commission. The Commission must then deliver a reasoned opinion, as under Article 169, after allowing the States concerned to submit their observations. Only if the Commission has not delivered an opinion after three months may the complaining State bring the defaulting State before the Court.

That the procedure under Article 226 (ex Article 169) is preferred to that under Article 227 (ex Article 170) is readily understandable. Direct confrontation between Member States as litigants at Luxembourg is better avoided by leaving it to the Commission to initiate any suit. In any event, the Commission has still to be involved whichever of the two procedures is used, although under Article 227 (ex Article 170) a Member State could commence an action in the Court even if the Commission's opinion was that no treaty infringement had occurred. Under the

---

[30] Case 178/84 *Commission v. Germany* [1987] ECR 1227; [1988] 1 C.M.L.R. 780.

[31] Case C–195/90 *Commission v. Germany* [1992] ECR I–314. See also the interim measures proceedings in this case reported at [1990] ECR I–2715 and [1990] ECR I–3351.

[32] Case C–243/89 *Commission v. Denmark* [1993] ECR I–3385.

[33] Case C–56/90 *Commission v. United Kingdom* [1993] ECR I–4109; *The Times*, July 15, 1993.

[34] Case C–265/95 [1997] ECR I–695; (1998) 23 E.L.Rev. 467.

corresponding provision of the ECSC Treaty (Article 89) only one action was begun, by Belgium against France, but it was not pursued. Under the EC Treaty actions have occasionally been threatened but only rarely pursued. Thus, Italy threatened to proceed against France during the "Wine War" of 1975–76 and Spain dropped the action which it had initiated against the United Kingdom relating to alleged discriminatory taxation of imported (primarily Spanish) sherry.[35] Only two cases to date have proceeded to judgment: Case 141/78 *France v. United Kingdom*,[36] where the United Kingdom was adjudged in breach of its obligations under the EC Treaty by adopting a national measure governing the minimum size of mesh for fishing nets used in British territorial waters. As required by Article 170(3), the Commission gave a reasoned opinion, which was in support of the French application; it also intervened in the proceedings (for such interventions, see p. 289 below).

Case C–388/95 *Belgium v. Spain*[36a] concerning the rebottling of Rioja wine. Belgium's action against Spain was discussed on the basis that the maintenance of the quality and reputation of Rioja wine justified the requirement that the wine be bottled in the region of production.


## Procedure under Articles 88 (ex Article 93) and 95(9) (ex Article 100a(4))

In addition to the general enforcement procedure available to the Commission under Article 226 (ex Article 169 EC), certain categories of infringements by Member States may be the subject of a more expeditious procedure which dispenses with the requirement of the Commission delivering a reasoned opinion. Instead, the Commission may proceed directly to the taking of a binding decision or bring the matter directly before the Court of Justice. Such derogations from the general procedure under Article 226 (ex Article 169) EC are permitted by Articles 88 (ex 93), 95(9) (ex 100a(4)) and 298 (ex 225). The last mentioned Article concerns improper use by a Member State of the powers given it by Articles 296 and 297 (ex Articles 223 and 224) to disregard the provisions of the EC Treaty in the essential interests of its security, where these involve arms production or the withholding of information.

---

[35] Case C–349/92 *Kingdom of Spain v. United Kingdom* [1992] O.J. C256/14 removed from the register November 27, 1992 [1992] O.J. C340/6.

[36] [1979] ECR 2923; [1980] 1 C.M.L.R. 6.

[36a] Judgment of May 16, 2000 (not yet reported), see Court Press Release No. 36/2000.

Article 88 (ex Article 93) concerns State aids to industry and has proved most important in practice and Article 95(9) (ex Article 100a(4))[37] applies where Member States seek to opt out of a harmonising measure adopted, for the purposes of the establishment or functioning of the internal market, by the Council acting by a qualified majority.

Under Article 88 (ex Article 93), where a State aid distorts or threatens to distort competition within the common market, the Commission, after giving notice to the parties concerned to submit their comments, may proceed to decide that the State concerned shall abolish (or alter) such aid within a prescribed time. If the State does not comply with this decision within the time prescribed the Commission (or any other interested State) may refer the matter to the Court of Justice direct. Of course, the decision (unlike the reasoned opinion under Article 226 (ex Article 169) EC) is open to challenge by the State as a binding act under Article 230 (ex Article 173) (see Chapter 7, below).

The special procedure under Article 88 (ex Article 93) EC resembles therefore the enforcement procedure under Article 88 ECSC in that, under the latter provision, the Commission takes a decision that the State is in breach of the ECSC Treaty; as we have seen (p. 122, above), it does not merely deliver an opinion. It differs, however, from that Article in that under Article 88 (ex Article 93) EC it is the Commission which must seise the Court of the fact that the offending State has not complied with the decision, whereas Article 88 ECSC leaves it to the State to challenge the decision before the Court. For, if not challenged, or if challenged but upheld, the decision under Article 88 ECSC carries with it certain sanctions for non-compliance, though none have ever in fact been imposed. No such (theoretical) sanctions attach to a decision under Article 88 (ex Article 93) EC, although, as we shall see, when brought before the Court, it may be the subject of interim measures, and although not enforceable in the national courts, such provisional measures may in practice ensure compliance by the Member State concerned.

An example of the special procedure under Article 93 EC (now Article 88 EC) is provided by the *Pig Producers* case.[38] The British Government introduced a subsidy for United Kingdom pig producers to help them compete with Dutch and Danish imports subsidised by the Community. The Government had informed the Commission of its intention to introduce the subsidy, but before

---

[37] Art. 100a EC was added to the Treaty by the SEA in order to facilitate the adoption of single market legislation.
[38] Cases 31/77 and 53/77R *Commission v. United Kingdom* [1977] ECR 92 1; [1977] 2 C.M.L.R. 359.

the Commission had decided whether the subsidy was compatible with the common market within the terms of Articles 92 and 93 EC (now Articles 87 and 88 EC), it brought the subsidy into operation, thereby infringing the clear prohibition in Article 93(3) EC (Now Article 88(3) EC).

The Commission thereupon took a decision on February 17, 1977 which required the United Kingdom to terminate the pig subsidy "forthwith". As the British Government did not comply, the Commission began an enforcement action under Article 93(2) EC (now Article 88(2) EC) on March 11, 1977. And it went further, for on May 12, 1977 it asked the Court to make an interim order requiring the United Kingdom to stop paying the subsidy. As we will see later, the power for the Court to grant what are, in effect, interlocutory injunctions is contained in Article 243 (ex Article 186) EC, which states:

> "The Court of Justice may in any cases before it prescribe any necessary interim measures."

Despite advice to the contrary by Advocate General Mayras in his opinion, the Court in a laconic order on May 21 directed the United Kingdom to end the subsidy, again "forthwith". In fact, payment of the subsidy did cease towards the end of June, so that the enforcement action was not pressed to judgment.

The procedure under Article 95(9) (ex Article 100a(4)) EC is similar to that under Article 88 (ex Article 93) EC[39] whereas the test for bringing proceedings directly, before the Court – that a Member State is making "improper use" of the powers provided for – is drawn from Article 298 (ex Article 225) EC. In the present context it is not necessary to examine in detail the role of Article 95(9) (ex Article 100a(4)) EC in the establishment of the internal market or the controversy which has surrounded it.[40] Suffice it to mention that, in order to enable the internal market to be completed by January 1, 1993, the SEA added a new Article 100a (now, after amendment, Article 95) to the Treaty, providing for qualified majority voting in the Council on "measures" (*sic*) whose object was the establishment or functioning of the internal market. Certain Member States (notably Denmark), being anxious to maintain their high standards in matters such as environmental protection, food hygiene and animal health, could only accept such a derogation

---

[39] The similarities (and important differences) between Arts 100a(4) and 93 (now Arts 95(9) and 88 EC) are discussed by J. Flynn in "How will Art. 100a(4) work? A comparison with Art. 93" (1987) 24 C.M.L. Rev. 689.

[40] For such an examination see Wyatt and Dashwood, *European Community Law* (London, 1993), Chap. 12 "Completing the Internal Market" (especially pp. 363–368); and J. Flynn *op. cit.* n. 39, above.

from the principle of unanimity (Article 94 (ex Article 100) EC) if it were accompanied by such an "escape" clause.

Thus if, after the adoption of a harmonising measure by a qualified majority, a Member State deems it necessary to apply national provisions on grounds of major needs referred to in Article 30 (ex Article 36) EC, or relating to the protection of the environment or working environment, it must first notify the Commission of those provisions. A failure to notify such provisions could give rise to proceedings under Article 226 (ex Article 169) EC in the normal way, without recourse to the derogation in Article 95(9) (ex Article 100a(4) EC. Following notification the Commission must verify that the measures concerned are not a means of arbitrary discrimination or a disguised restriction on trade between Member States. The Commission's decision in this regard may be the subject of annulment proceedings under Article 230 (ex Article 173) EC brought either by the Member State concerned (in the event of a negative decision) or by another Member State (in the event of a favourable decision).[41]

It would seem then that direct recourse to the Court would only be taken *in extremis* and, given the Member States' reluctance to bring proceedings against each other under Article 227 (ex Article 170) EC, as noted above, it seems likely that they will be equally reluctant to bandy about allegations of "improper use" being made of this possibility of opting-out. No ruling has yet been made under Article 298 (ex Article 225) so there is no definitive guidance as to what might constitute such improper use. One may speculate that a unilateral widening of a category in respect of which an opt-out had been duly granted might lead to action by the Commission under the fourth paragraph of this Article.[42]

## EFFECT OF JUDGMENTS AGAINST MEMBER STATES

It may be helpful to summarise the effects of a judgment delivered in proceedings brought under Articles 226, 227, 88 or 95(9) (ex

---

[41] Judgment in the first case involving the application of Art. 100a(4) was given on June 18, 1994 in Case C–41/93 *France v. Commission* [1994] ECR I–1829.

[42] In Case C–120/94 *Commission v. Greece* lodged at the Court on April 22, 1994 the Commission brought proceedings under Art. 225 arising out of the Greek prohibition on exports into or through its territory from the Former Yugoslav Republic of Macedonia. It should be noted that Art. 225 requires the Court to give its ruling in camera. By an order of June 29, 1994 the Court rejected the Commission's application for interim measures. Although Advocate General Jacobs delivered his Opinion in the case on April 6, 1995, the Commission withdrew its application before judgment could be delivered, Mr Jacobs' Opinion is published at [1996] ECR I–1457. He concluded that the existence of a sufficiently serious threat to invoke the exception was a subjective matter for the Member State concerned and was not therefore a justiciable issue.

Articles 169, 170, 93 or 100a(4)) EC. Such judgments, unlike those to be discussed in the next chapter, are not made against a Community institution, but against a Member State. They touch, therefore, the tender nerve of national sovereignty.

In contrast with Article 88 ECSC, a judgment under any of these four Articles is only declaratory: it has no executory force, no sanctions may be imposed except after further proceedings pursuant to Article 228(2) (ex Article 171(2)) EC nor are any national measures thereby annulled. Essentially, it is left to the defaulting Member State to recognise the error of its ways and to comply with its treaty obligations.

Nevertheless, it is in the nature of the proceedings under these Articles that the Commission will have specified the acts which have given rise to the breach. If the Court finds the charges made by the Commission proved, then the Member State is left in no doubt as to what it must do, and, as the Court pointed out in Case 314/81 *Procureur de la Republique v. Waterkeyn*,[43] the courts also of the Member States are bound, by virtue of Article 171 (now Article 228) EC, "to draw the necessary inferences from the judgment of the Court". Thus, in Case 70/72 *Commission v. Germany*[44] Germany had provided State aids for certain mining regions which, the Commission alleged, was an infringement of Article 92 (now Article 87) EC. In an enforcement action under Article 93 (now Article 88) EC the Commission invited the Court to declare not only that Germany had infringed the Treaty but also that it should be required to obtain repayment of the aids from the recipients. For the German Government it was submitted that such a ruling for repayment could be neither requested by the Commission nor made by the Court. The Court did not accept this submission, although, on the merits of the case, it dismissed the action: had it found against Germany, it could not formally have ordered the repayment of the aids, but it could have achieved the same result, in substance, by an appropriate wording of its declaratory judgment. Moreover, the Court made clear that its approach would be no different in proceedings brought under Articles 226 and 227 (ex Articles 169 and 170) EC: under these Articles as under Article 88 (ex Article 93) EC, the Commission may specify what measures must be taken by the Member State concerned to meet its treaty obligations, and, in the event of non-compliance, the Court may grant a declaration in no less specific terms.

Likewise, where the breach consists of the enactment (or retention) of legislation contrary to Community law, the Court has

---

[43] [1982] ECR 4337; [1983] 2 C.M.L.R. 145.
[44] [1973] ECR 813; [1973] C.M.L.R. 741.

no power to annul the offending national measures. It will confine itself to condemning such measures as conflicting with Community law. The Member State concerned should then he in no doubt how it must amend its own law. Thus, in Case 167/73 *Commission v. France*,[45] as we have seen (above, p. 124) the successful action under Article 169 (now Article 226) EC induced the French Government, albeit reluctantly, to amend its *Code du Travail Maritime*. The Court brushed aside the Government's plea that, even if its own law did conflict with Community law, it would therefore be inapplicable and so not require to be repealed: the Court made clear that the unamended Code would leave Community seamen uncertain of their rights to seek employment on French ships; nor was it a sufficient answer that the French Government no longer applied the offending provision of the Code.

In enforcement actions under Articles 88, 95(9), 226, 227 or 298 (ex Articles 93, 100a(4), 169, 170 or 225) EC the Court of Justice has no power to award damages against Member State in favour of those who may have been prejudice by the infringement: this follows from the declaratory nature of the judgment. Moreover, such actions are normally brought, not by the parties prejudiced, but by the Commission acting in the Community interest. Nevertheless, an ingenious attempt may have been made in the *Lamb War* cases[46] to achieve indirectly what could not be done directly. Thus, the British Government is reported to have proposed to the Commission that it should invite the Court to make a declaration that France was in further breach of the Treaty by reason of its failure to pay compensation to British meat exporters prejudiced by the import ban which the Court had already declared illegal in the previous proceedings.[47] The British Government considered, presumably, that the language of Article 171 (now Article 228) was wide enough to permit the Court to do this. The Commission, however, did not adopt the British proposal, and the claim for compensation was dropped once the dispute over lamb was settled. Accordingly, it remains a moot question whether an appropriately worded declaration could be issued by the Court if the Commission (or another Member State) proved that the particular breach consisted in the State's failure to pay compensation or damages to an injured party. Since *Francovich* however the question is unlikely to arise.[48]

As we have seen above (for example, in the *Lamb War* cases) proceedings under Articles 226, 227, 88 or 95(9) (ex Articles 169,

---

[45] [1974] ECR 359; [1974] 2 C.M.L.R. 216.
[46] Cases 24/80 and 97/80 R [1980] ECR 1319; [1981] 3 C.M.L.R. 25.
[47] Case 232/78 [1979] ECR 2729; [1980] 1 C.M.L.R. 418.
[48] See n. 5 above.

170, 93 or 100a(4)) EC culminate in a judgment under Article 171. Under this Article the State is required by the Treaty to take the necessary measures to comply with the judgment: it is not ordered to do so by the Court. However, as we have seen above,[49] the Court has been empowered under the Treaty on European Union to impose financial penalties for non-compliance. To initiate this power is at the discretion of the Commission, which also decides whether to ask the Court for a lump sum or a penalty payment. By the end of 1999 several cases had been referred by the Commission to the Court, but only one has yet come to judgement.[50] We have also seen that the failure to comply with the judgment may constitute a further Treaty infringement by the Member State, this time of Article 228 (ex Article 171) EC, for which a new enforcement action may be brought under Articles 226 or 227 (ex Articles 169 and 170) EC. We shall see later how to such proceedings under Articles 226 and 227 (ex Articles 169 and 170) EC may be attached a request for interim measures to be prescribed by the Court under Article 243 (ex Article 186) EC; we shall see too that an interim measure may be couched as an actual order by the Court to the offending State that it shall desist from certain conduct on its part, pending judgment in the principal action.[51]

We have already noted in the previous section how the general enforcement procedure available to the Commission under Article 226 (ex Article 169) EC is replaced, for certain categories of treaty infringement by a Member State, by a more expeditious procedure, notably under Article 88 (ex Article 93) EC relating to impermissible State aids. Where the offending State fails to comply with the Commission's decision requiring the abolition or alteration of the aid, the Commission may refer the matter to the Court, which may then prescribe any necessary interim measures pursuant to Article 243 (ex Article 186) EC.[52]

It will now be appreciated that in some respects the Court enjoys wider powers in interim proceedings under Article 243 (ex Article 186) EC than it has when giving final judgment in

---

[49] See p. 119, above.

[50] See Anne Bonnie, "Commission Discretion under Art. 171(2) EC" (1998) 33 Euro. L.R. 537, at p. 540. And see now judgment of July 4, 2000 in Case C–387/97 *Commission v. Greece*, note 16a above, p. 121.

[51] See Case 45/87R *Commission v. Ireland* [1987] ECR 783, 1369; [1987] 2 C.M.L.R. 197, 536, application for interim measures relating to a water supply scheme for the town of Dundalk; and Case C–195/90 *Commission v. Germany* [1992] ECR I–314 and interim measures applications [1990] ECR I–2715 and 3351.

[52] See *Pig Producers* case: Cases 31/77R and 53/77R *Commission v. United Kingdom* [1977] ECR 921; [1977] 2 C.M.L.R. 359.

enforcement actions (an anomaly justifiable by the interim or interlocutory nature of the relief), although it may be most reluctant to use these powers, where it has already given judgment against a Member State, to seek to compel the State to comply. The Court dislikes merely beating the air, so that when it has a discretion (as it has under Article 243 (ex Article 186) EC), it may well refuse the interim measures sought for fear of further undermining respect for the authority of the Court by provoking disobedience of its specific order: a recalcitrant child who disobeys its parent's first request is just as likely to disobey the second or third. Nor will it award interim measures where, to do so, would produce a fait accompli making the main action devoid of purpose.

In the last resort, a Member State complies only when it has the political will to do so. Defiance, however, puts in jeopardy the whole future of the Community.

In recent years the European Parliament has followed closely the issue of enforcement of Community law against Member States; the Commission now submits to the Parliament an annual report on "monitoring of the application of Community law".[53]

Even if there is no completely effective remedy in the Court of Justice, a remedy may lie in the national courts of the Member State in breach. For, as the Court ruled in its landmark decision in Case 26/62 *Van Gend en Loos*,[54] "The vigilance of individuals concerned to protect their rights amounts to an effective super-vision in addition to the supervision entrusted by Articles 169 and 170 to the diligence of the Commission and of the Member States." Furthermore, the individual will have such a right of action in the national court whenever either the Community provision in question is categorised by the Court of Justice as having direct effect or the conditions in *Francovich* are met.[55] However, the remedies available to the individual will vary according to the way in which the issue comes before the national court. Thus, in Case 88/77 *Minister for Fisheries v. Schoenenberg*[56] a Dutch fisherman was acquitted by an Irish court on a charge of illegal fishing in Irish waters because he established, as his defence, that the Irish Government had imposed restrictions which were contrary to Community law. Community law may afford not only, as here, a shield, but also a sword. Thus, a Dutch potato exporter

---

[53] See, most recently the Sixteenth Annual Report to the European Parliament on Commission monitoring of the application of Community law [1999] O.J. C.
[54] Case 26/62 *Van Gend en Loos* [1963] ECR 1 at 13 (see p. 162); [1963] C.M.L.R. 105.
[55] See n. 5, above.
[56] Case 88/77 *Minister for Fisheries v. Schoenenberg* [1978] ECR 473; [1978] 2 C.M.L.R. 519.

successfully sought a declaration in the English High Court that the United Kingdom's ban on potato imports infringed Community law and was, therefore, invalid.[57]

In both of those cases Community law was effectively upheld in the national courts of the Member State concerned in its breach. Both cases involved references to the Court of Justice for preliminary rulings to establish whether Community law was being infringed. Parallel actions under Article 169 (now Article 226) EC were brought by the Commission against the infringing State in both cases[58] but such enforcement at Community level should not conceal the important function of the national judiciary in sanctioning breaches of Community law by their own Governments. While the Article 226 (ex Article 169) EC procedure is an effective method of bringing Member States into line for the future, an action in the national courts coupled if necessary with a reference for a preliminary ruling under Article 234 (ex Article 177) EC may provide, as we shall see in Chapter 10, an immediate remedy for the individual in the instant case.

---

[57] Case 118/78 *Meijer v. Department of Trade* [1979] ECR 1387; [1979] 2 C.M.L.R. 398.

[58] Case 61/77 *Commission v. Ireland* [1978] ECR 417; [1978] 2 C.M.L.R. 466, Case 231/78 *Commission v. United Kingdom* [1979] ECR 1447; [1979] 2 C.M.L.R. 427.

# Chapter Seven

# Judicial Review of Community Acts

## INTRODUCTION

In democratic constitutions, limits are normally set to the power exercisable by the agencies of government. Thus, in the United Kingdom there are legal limits upon the powers of the central government and local authorities; these limits are one of the main topics falling within the subject of English administrative law and are found under such headings as "the doctrine of *ultra vires*" "the judicial review of administrative action" or "the judicial control of public authorities". In all the Member States of the European Communities the powers of governmental bodies are confined within prescribed limits and so, in Dicey's sense, subject to the rule of law. In some, the policing of these limits is the task of a separate system of administrative courts. This is the case, for instance, in France where there is now a three-tier system, comprising the *tribunaux administratifs* of first instance, six regional *Cours administratives d'appel* and the *Conseil d'Etat* as the supreme administrative court.[1]

Again, in some countries the constitution sets limits upon the permissible extent of legislation, and the legislature may then be subject to control by a constitutional court exercising judicial review of the constitutionality of its enactments. The United States and the Federal German Republic provide examples of such courts. In the United Kingdom, on the other hand, the doctrine of Parliamentary sovereignty prevailed absolutely, at least south of the Scottish border, until British accession to the Community.

In the Community legal order, the administrative (or executive) agencies are the Commission and, to some extent, the Council, although the function of the latter is, first and foremost, that of the legislature, a function now exercised mainly in conjunction with

---

[1] See Brown and Bell, *French Administrative Law* (5th ed., 1998) for a general account.

the Parliament. As in the Member States, so in the Communities the administrative agencies have only limited powers of rulemaking and individual decision. The Treaties serve as constitutional documents to define those powers, including those of the Council when acting as a legislature whether alone or in partnership with the Parliament. The Treaties also vest in the Court the necessary jurisdiction to control the lawful exercise of such power. Hence, Valentine referred to the Court, neatly, as a *"Conseil d'Etats"*.[2] Hence also we might adopt the heading "administrative jurisdiction" under which to describe this part of the Court's jurisdiction. Nevertheless, the jurisdiction may also be regarded as "constitutional" in so far as the Court reviews the legality of legislation by the Council or Commission.[3] For, as we have seen in Chapter 1, many regulations and directives of these institutions are better regarded as Community legislation than likened to delegated or subordinate legislation as that term is used in English law.

In this Chapter we deal with Article 230 (ex Article 173) and Article 232 (ex Article 175) EC and their ECSC counterparts as amended by the Maastricht Treaty. The amendments essentially embody the results of certain judgments of the Court discussed in the following pages.

As amended by the Maastricht Treaty, Article 230 (ex Article 173) EC states:

> "The Court of Justice shall review the legality of acts adopted jointly by the European Parliament and the Council, of acts of the Council, of the Commission and of the European Central Bank, other than recommendations and opinions, and of acts of the European Parliament intended to produce legal effects *vis-à-vis* third parties."

And Article 232 (ex Article 175) EC, as amended, deals with actions for inactivity, or the failure to act, on the part of the European Parliament, the Council, the Commission or the European Central Bank.

But it must be borne in mind that, in addition to the action for annulment, there are various ways in which the legality of Community measures may be the subject of indirect challenge. First, there is the "plea of illegality", considered later in this chapter (p. 164). Secondly, an action for damages (Chapter 8) may put in issue the legality of a measure alleged to have injured the applicant: and in practice actions for damages have frequently led the Court to examine the legality of Community legislation.

---

[2] Valentine, *The Court of Justice of the European Communities* (1965), Vol. 1.
[3] For general comparisons see D. Curtin and D. O'Keeffe (eds), *Constitutional Adjudication in European Community and National Law* (1992).

Thirdly, a reference from a national court to the Court of Justice for a preliminary ruling (Chapter 10) may be directed to the validity of any measure adopted by a Community institution, so that an aggrieved person may be able to obtain, not by a direct action in the Court of Justice but by proceedings originating in a national court, a ruling by the Court of Justice that a Community measure is invalid.

## A. ACTIONS TO ANNUL (ARTICLE 230 (EX ARTICLE 173))

Our discussion will consider in sequence the following questions:

1. What acts can be attacked?
2. Who can attack?
3. Within what time limit?
4. On what grounds?
5. What effect has annulment?

### 1. What acts can be attacked?

Article 230 (ex Article 173), as we have seen above, refers to "acts" of the designated institutions "other than recommendations or opinions".

Having regard to the terms of Article 249 (ex Article 189) (as amended) which lists acts of the Parliament, the Council and the Commission as "regulations, directives, decisions, recommendations or opinions", one might expect that only the first three were subject to review under Article 230(1) (ex Article 173(1)). The Court however has adopted a more liberal interpretation. What is required is an act binding in law, and the Court has always been prepared to look behind the label of an act to its substance. Thus, under the ECSC Treaty, in *Saar Tubes*,[4] it was argued by the applicants that what was in form an opinion did in fact impose binding obligations, and the Court accepted that it had a duty to consider whether the act complained of, though in form and name an opinion, did constitute a disguised decision. In the event, it held that it was only an opinion and that consequently the action to annul was inadmissible (under Article 33 ECSC).

However, in the first group of *Cement-Cartel* cases[5] a "communication" issued by the Commission under Regulation 17,

---

[4] Joined Cases 1 and 14/57 *Societe des Usines a Tubes de la Sarre v. High Authority* [1957 and 1958] ECR 105.
[5] Joined Cases 8 to 11/66 *Cimenteries v. Commission* [1967] ECR 75; [1967] C.M.L.R. 77.

Article 15, to remove protection from certain cartels was held by the Court to constitute not a mere opinion but a decision (and consequently to be binding in law); the plea of inadmissibility under Article 173(1) raised by the Commission was accordingly rejected, and the Court proceeded to review the legality of the communication in issue.

On the other hand, the Court has not accepted as a reviewable act the "statement of objections" which, under the regulation governing competition proceedings, the Commission is required to send to a firm whose marketing practices are under investigation.[6] Similarly, in Case 7/61 *Pigmeat*,[7] the Court made clear that the reasoned opinion which is required under Article 169 (now Article 226) proceedings (discussed at p. 117, above) cannot be the subject of review for illegality under Article 173.

The *ERTA* case[8] well illustrates the bold approach of the Court to the interpretation of the term "acts" in Article 230 (ex Article 173(1)). In this case the Commission challenged the action of the Council in laying down guidelines for Member States to follow in the negotiations to revise the European Road Transport Agreement, such action being allegedly a usurpation by the Council of a function reserved to the Commission by the EC Treaty. The Court, although deciding against the Commission on the merits, held the action to be admissible: the Commission had *locus standi* (see below), and the Council's action in laying down guidelines did amount to an act having legally binding consequences for the Member States and one therefore reviewable under Article 173 (now Article 230). On this last point the Court disagreed with Advocate General Dutheillet de Lamothe in whose view the Council's discussion of the guidelines could not constitute an act of the Council open to review under Article 173(1) (now Article 230(1)). The Court did not accept that the Article was confined to the category of acts (regulations, directives and decisions) enumerated as legally binding in Article 249 (ex Article 189). It held that "an action for annulment must . . . be available in the case of all measures adopted by the institutions, whatever their nature or form, which are intended to have legal effects."

Was there significance in the words "measures adopted by the institutions", when Article 173 (in its then unamended version) referred only to "acts of the Council and the Commission" and not to acts of the European Parliament? The question was raised 10 years later whether acts of the Parliament could be challenged under the original version of Article 173. The fact that the

---

[6] Case 60/81 *IBM v. Commission* [1981] ECR 2639; [1981] 3 C.M.L.R. 635.
[7] Case 7/61 *Commission v. Italy* [1961] ECR 317; [1962] C.M.L.R. 39.
[8] Case 22/70 *Commission v. Council* [1971] ECR 263; [1971] C.M.L.R. 335.

question could arise may surprise the English lawyer, since the question seems excluded by the clear terms of Article 173, as originally framed. The answer which the Court of Justice gave to this question deserves examination, despite the amendment of Article 173 by the Maastricht Treaty, as illustrating the very different approach of Community law to constitutional texts. The first in a series of cases, Case 230/81 *Luxembourg v. European Parliament*[9] was inconclusive. Here the Government of Luxembourg challenged a resolution of the European Parliament purporting to decide that future sessions of the Parliament should be held in Strasbourg (and not, as previously, in either Strasbourg or Luxembourg). The Government argued that, under the Treaties, it was for the Member States to fix the seat of the Community institutions. The action was based in part on Article 38 ECSC which does provide for annulment (at the suit of a Member State or the Commission) of a measure adopted by the Parliament, but there is no corresponding provision in the EC and Euratom Treaties and it was open to question whether a provision in the ECSC Treaty can confer jurisdiction in respect of acts common to the three Communities. It was easier to contend that the EC Treaty governs such common acts. The difficulty then was that Article 173 (now Article 230) did not refer to the Parliament. The action was also based on Article 173 (now Article 230): it was argued that, by analogy with the ERTA decision, that Article provided a remedy against any measure of any institution having legal effects. The Court was content (typically) to allow the action under Article 38 ECSC.

The example set by Luxembourg was followed by the Council itself, which in 1982 brought proceedings under Article 173 (now Article 230) (the Council having no standing under Article 38 ECSC) against the Parliament (Case 72/82) for annulment of the act of the President of the European Parliament declaring that the general budget of the European Communities for the financial year 1982 had been finally adopted. Here it could he argued that, although the gap in the original text of Article 173 (now Article 230) could be explained historically by the fact that the Parliament had no legally binding powers when the EC Treaty was drawn up, nevertheless with the development of the Parliament's budgetary powers the Treaty should be interpreted dynamically to avoid the development of a hiatus in the system of judicial protection. However the budgetary dispute was settled on the political level and the Council's action withdrawn.

---

[9] [1983] ECR 255; [1983] 2 C.M.L.R. 726; see Brown: "Judicial Control of Acts of the European Parliament" (1983) L.I.E.1. 75.

Another case was brought by the Council (and by several Member States) against the Parliament in 1986 over the budget for that year. Here it was alleged that the Parliament, which is empowered to increase, within certain limits, some heads of Community expenditure, had exceeded those limits and that the entire budget adopted by the declaration of the President was consequently void. The Council's action was expedited by the Court because of its urgency but before the action was heard and before the issue of admissibility under Article 173 (now Article 230) was decided the United Kingdom obtained an interim order[10] from the President of the Court suspending the implementation of the budget, the United Kingdom having convinced the President that it would otherwise suffer irreparable damage: Case 23/86R *United Kingdom v. European Parliament*.[11]

The Council's action against the Parliament was successful: Case 34/86[12], but by the time the Court gave judgment it had already resolved the issue of admissibility in yet another case brought against the Parliament; Case 294/83 *Partie Ecologiste 'Les Verts' v. European Parliament*.[13] The Parliament had allocated funds from its own budget to the political parties for an "information campaign" leading up to the direct elections to the Parliament to be held in 1984. The new French environmentalist or "green" party complained that by reserving only a limited proportion of funds to parties putting up candidates for the first time in 1984 the Parliament was discriminating in favour of parties already represented in Parliament.

The Court held, in a judgment of great constitutional significance, and in which it clearly had the budget case in mind, that proceedings could be brought against the Parliament under Article 173 (now Article 230). The Court emphasised that "the European Economic Community is a Community based on the rule of law, inasmuch as neither its Member States nor its institutions can avoid a review of the question whether the measures adopted by them are in conformity with the basic constitutional charter, the Treaty." Although Article 173 as originally worded referred only to acts of the Council and the Commission, the "general scheme" of the Treaty was to make a direct action available against "all measures adopted by the institutions . . . which are intended to have legal effects" (the *ERTA* case). The Parliament was not expressly mentioned, according to the Court, because, in its original version, the Treaty merely granted it powers of consulta-

---

[10] See on interim measures below, p. 287.
[11] [1986] ECR 1085.
[12] [1986] ECR 2155.
[13] [1986] ECR 1339.

tion and political control rather than the power to adopt measures intended to have legal effect *vis-à-vis* third parties. An interpretation of Article 173 (now Article 230) which excluded measures adopted by the Parliament from those which could he contested would lead to a result contrary both to the spirit of the Treaty as expressed in Article 164 (now Article 220) and to its system:

> "Measures adopted by the European Parliament in the context of the EC Treaty could encroach on the powers of the Member States or of the other institutions, or exceed the limits which have been set to the Parliament's powers, without its being possible to refer them for review by the Court. It must therefore be concluded that an action for annulment may lie against measures adopted by the European Parliament intended to have legal effects *vis-à-vis* third parties."

The Court went on to find that the measures challenged by the Green Party in this case did have such effects and to declare them void. The judgment is of interest on other points to which we shall return below. Here may be noted that the amendment to Article 173 (now Article 230) effected by the Maastricht Treaty closely follows the reasoning (and wording) of the Court. The original version of Article 173 EEC referred only to acts of the Council and the Commission Even though the version as amended by the Maastricht Treaty now includes an extended list of institutions whose acts may be challenged in this way, the Court has refused to extend the list to acts of the representatives of the Member States.[14]

## 2. Who can attack?

### (i) Member States, the Council and the Commission

In the first place Article 173 enumerates a Member State, the Council or the Commission as competent to bring an action to annul: they are accepted as having a sufficient legal interest to give them locus stands for such an action, and for this reason they are sometimes referred to as "privileged applicants". It does not matter that the Member State is attacking some act of a Community institution which relates to another Member State. Thus, in

---

[14] Joined Cases C–181 and C–248/91 *European Parliament v. Council* [1993] ECR I–3685. In a somewhat metaphysical judgment, concerning a decision on aid to be granted to Bangladesh, the Court held that the decisions in issue had been adopted by representatives of the Member States acting not as members of the Council but as representatives of their Government, collectively exercising the competence of the Member States.

Case 6/54 *Netherlands v. High Authority*[15] (a case under the ECSC Treaty) the Court permitted the Netherlands to seek annulment of a decision of the High Authority relating to German coal companies: not only Germany but the other Member States had a sufficient interest in the legality (or otherwise) of that decision. And in Case 41/83 *Italy* v. *Commission*[16] the Italian Government challenged a competition decision of the Commission addressed to British Telecom. In recent years Member States have frequently challenged measures of the Council and Commission, and often with success.

Again, the Council has *locus standi* in relation to the acts of the Commission, and vice versa. Suits of this kind are not infrequent: one example is the *ERTA* case (Case 22/70, discussed above).

Another is the pair of *Staff Salaries* cases.[17] These cases concerned the Staff Regulations governing Community civil servants, which provide for an annual review of salaries by the Council after a report by the Commission. The Council is required to take into account various factors, including inflation, changes in the purchasing power of salaries of civil servants in the Member States, etc. How to quantify these factors had led to disagreement with the staff associations, to resolve which a scheme was eventually negotiated and embodied in a Council decision. The decision was expressed to be applicable for three years, but at the next annual review the Council made a salaries regulation which the Commission alleged to be in breach of the scheme. Accordingly, it sought to annul the regulation. The main issue before the Court was whether the decision of the Council was legally binding or a mere statement of policy, a "policy decision". The Court, declining to follow the view of Advocate General Warner, held the policy decision to be binding on the ground, first, that it laid down basic principles for reviewing salaries and, secondly, that it was announced as applicable for three years and consequently the Community staff were entitled to rely upon it. It followed that the salaries regulation was invalid in that it conflicted with the policy decision; the Council had therefore to devise new arrangements. These were in turn the subject of proceedings to annul brought by the Commission (Case 70/74, above). Staff salaries came before the Court again in Case 59/81 *Commission v. Council*,[18] where the Council's measures were again declared unlawful.

---

[15] Case 6/54 *The Netherlands v. High Authority* [1954–56] ECR 103.

[16] Case 41/83 *Italy v. Commission* [1985] ECR 873; [1985] 2 C.M.L.R. 368. The case was dismissed on the substance but, as Advocate General Darmon pointed out, the admissibility of the claim was uncontested.

[17] Case 81/72 *Commission v. Council* [1973] ECR 575; [1973] C.M.L.R. 639, and Case 70/74 *Commission v. Council* [1975] ECR 795; [1975] 2 C.M.L.R. 287.

[18] [1982] ECR 3329.

Other examples are cases brought by the Commission against the Council where the Commission has challenged the legal basis of the measure adopted by the Council: *e.g.* Case 45/86 *Commission v. Council*[19] (the *Tariff preferences* case discussed below, p. 159).

Particularly, the Commission has sought to uphold the Treaty where it provides a legal basis for a decision of the Council to be taken by a majority vote without the need for unanimity. The advantage of a majority decision is to reduce the chance of a Commission proposal being watered down to secure unanimity; also, the Articles requiring a majority decision bring the Parliament into the process of decision-making through the co-operation and co-decision procedures,[20] and the Parliament is usually the natural ally of the Commission. An instance of the Commission successfully attacking a Council directive as taken on the wrong basis is C–300/89 *Commission v. Council*,[21] where a Directive concerning disposal of certain toxic waste was taken by unanimity under Article 130s (now Article 175), whereas the Court agreed with the Commission and the Parliament that the correct legal basis was Article 100a (now Article 95) EC, requiring only a qualified majority: accordingly, the Directive was annulled.

A Member State too may be concerned to secure the correct legal basis in order to preserve its veto where that base requires unanimity. It may then bring Article 230 (ex Article 173) proceedings itself or intervene in proceedings brought by the Commission.[22]

### (ii) The European Parliament and the European Central Bank

The amended third paragraph of Article 230 (ex Article 173) (see above) now expressly gives standing to sue to the Parliament and the European Central Bank. As regards the Parliament, Article 173, as originally drafted, did not name the Parliament as a potential plaintiff and appeared to exclude that possibility. But the Court had accepted, in 1980, that the Parliament could intervene in proceedings before the Court (on such interventions, see below,

---

[19] Case 45/86 *Commission v. Council* [1987] ECR 1493; [1988] 2 C.M.L.R. 131.
[20] The term "co-operation procedure" was introduced into the EC Treaty by the Single European Act, but then replaced by the Maastricht Treaty, which refers rather to "the procedure referred to in Art. 189c". The "co-decision procedure" is not an expression to be found in any Treaty: its precise designation is "the procedure referred to under Art. 251 (ex Art. 189b)".
[21] C–300/89 *Commission v. Council* [1991] ECR 2867; [1993] 3 C.M.L.R. 359.
[22] See Case 68/86 *United Kingdom v. Council* [1988] ECR 857; [1988] 2 C.M.L.R. 543 and Cases C–51, 90 and 94/89 *United Kingdom, France and Germany v. Council* [1991] ECR I–2757; [1992] 1 C.M.L.R. 40.

p. 289); and in 1985 the Parliament's entitlement to bring actions under the more widely drafted Article 175 (now Article 232) was upheld (below, p. 163). Once the Court had accepted, in 1986, as described above, that the Parliament could be sued although not named as a defendant under Article 173 (now Article 230), the Parliament seemed to consider that justice or even symmetry required that it should equally be able to sue.

Accordingly, the Parliament launched its first proceedings under Article 173 against the Council in 1987.[23] It contended that Article 173 (now Article 230) must be interpreted extensively in favour of the Parliament, as it had been against the Parliament in *Les Verts* (Case 294/83, above) and in the 1986 budget case (Case 34/86, above). But the analogy was not exact. The Parliament could be sued because that was necessary to complete the availability of judicial review of all Community acts and so secure the rule of law. There was no corresponding justification for giving the Parliament an unqualified right to sue.

The Court, in a carefully reasoned judgment, firmly rejected any right of the Parliament to sue under Article 173. It was not impressed by the argument either of symmetry or justice: Parliament had its own political machinery for making its voice heard. Advocate General Darmon, however, in his opinion, proposed a compromise: while not contending that the Parliament had an unqualified right of action under Article 173, he argued that it could be entitled to sue where its interests or prerogatives were directly affected by a measure of the Council or the Commission, for otherwise it would be in an uniquely unfavourable position compared not only with other institutions and Member States but even with private parties.

This compromise, while rejected in the *Comitology* case, found favour with the Court soon afterwards in Case C-70/88, the so-called *Chernobyl* case.[24] This concerned a decision taken by the Council, allegedly in breach of its obligation to consult the Parliament. The Court modified its view in Comitology by holding that the Parliament did have standing to challenge acts of the Council or Commission under Article 173 (now Article 230) where this was necessary to protect its prerogatives. This has now

---

[23] Case 302/87 *European Parliament v. Council* [1988] ECR 5615 (the so-called "*Comitology*" case).

[24] Case C-70/88 *European Parliament v. Council* [1990] ECR I-2041; [1992] 1 C.M.L.R. 91, known as "the *Chernobyl* case" because the Parliament was seeking the annulment of Council Regulation (Euratom) No. 3954/87 of December 22, 1987 laying down maximum permitted levels of radio-active contamination of foodstuffs and of feeding stuffs following a nuclear accident or any other case of radiological emergency [1987] O.J. L371/11, adopted following the accident at Chernobyl in April 1985.

been put beyond peradventure by the new wording of paragraph (3) of Article 230 (ex Article 173) which states:

"The Court shall have jurisdiction under the same conditions in actions brought by the European Parliament, by the Court of Auditors and by the European Central Bank for the purpose of protecting their prerogatives."

Here then we have another example of the case law of the Court anticipating, and preparing the way for, an amendment of the Treaty.

The Parliament's protection of its prerogatives was the main issue in the post-Maastricht case of Case C–316/91 *European Parliament v. Council.*[25]

Although the Parliament's application for the annulment of a Council financial regulation relating to expenditure by way of development was dismissed on the merits, the Court did hold the application to be admissible. On this aspect, the Court first rejected the Council's submission of inadmissibility on the ground that the regulation was not an act which might be challenged under Article 173 (now Article 230) since it had been adopted not pursuant to the Treaty but pursuant to a power conferred upon the Council by agreement between the Member States. Here the Court simply noted that judicial review had to be available in the case of all measures adopted by the institutions, whatever their nature or form, which were intended to have legal consequences.

With regard to the Parliament's claim that its prerogatives had been infringed, in that the regulation should have been adopted on the basis of Article 209 (now Article 279) EC (requiring the Parliament to be consulted), the Court held that the right to be consulted in accordance with a Treaty provision was a prerogative of the Parliament and that adopting an act on a legal basis which did not provide for such consultation was liable to infringe that prerogative, even if, as in the present case, there had been optional consultation. It seems therefore that a mere claim by the Parliament that a given measure should have been adopted on the basis of a Treaty provision *requiring* that it be consulted suffices to make such a claim admissible.

### (iii) Natural and legal persons

If the Parliament's standing to sue under Article 230 (ex Article 173) has been a vexed question now finally resolved, the most troublesome question has certainly been the defining of the

---

[25] Case C–316/91 *European Parliament v. Council* [1994] ECR I–653. For a commentary on this case, see R. Barents (1995) 32 C.M.L.Rev. 249.

sufficiency of interest requisite for natural and legal persons to sue under Article 230 (ex Article 173), where the original text has not been changed by the Maastricht Treaty. The fourth paragraph of Article 230 (ex Article 173) states:

> "Any natural or legal person may, under the same conditions, institute proceedings against a decision addressed to that person or against a decision which, although in the form of a regulation or a decision addressed to another person, is of direct and individual concern to the former."

As the Article makes clear, no problem arises where the measure sought to be challenged is addressed to the applicant. But the second limb of the Article introduces for the "non-addressee" a requirement to show "direct and individual concern". Here the Court has not pursued a consistent line, being anxious, on the one hand, to allow individuals or companies an opportunity to seek annulment of acts of the Council or the Commission in the interest of justice, yet on the other hand fearful of finding itself overwhelmed by a flood of such suits. Accordingly, it is difficult to reconcile the conflicting cases. One conclusion is clear: it is now exceedingly difficult for an individual or company to satisfy the test of "direct and individual concern" as prescribed under the second limb of the second paragraph of Article 230 (ex Article 173).

That limb allows only a decision to be attacked, not a (true) regulation: Case 789/79 *Calpak*.[26] If the decision is addressed to the applicant, no problem arises. A common instance is where the Commission has issued a decision declaring the applicant to be infringing the competition law of the Community.[27] If however the decision is in the form of a regulation or is addressed to some other person, the applicant has then to establish that it is of direct and individual concern to him.

Anti-dumping regulations, inevitably, present special problems under the second paragraph of Article 230 (ex Article 173), since they involve elements of both regulation and decision. Dumping, typically, is where an exporter in a third country sells goods into the Community at a lower price than he charges on his home market. To protect the Community against this form of unfair

---

[26] Joined Cases 789 and 790/79 *Calpak v. Commission* [1980] ECR 1949; [1981] 1 C.M.L.R. 26.

[27] Landmark cases in which the applicants have then challenged such decisions include Cases 56 and 58/64 *Consten and Grundig v. Commission* [1966] ECR 299; [1966] C.M.L.R. 418; Case 6/72 *Continental Can v. Commission* [1973] ECR 215; [1973] C.M.L.R. 199, Case 17/74 *Transocean Marine Paint Association v. Commission* [1974] ECR 1063; [1974] C.M.L.R. 459.

competition, the Council has adopted legislation under Article 133 (ex Article 113) EC which enables duties to be imposed on such imports to counter the effects of dumping. After an investigation conducted by the Commission, provisional duty may be imposed by regulation of the Commission and definitive duty by regulation of the Council. The procedure has elements of a decision since the Commission will investigate individual exporters and importers and base its finding of dumping on those investigations. But the regulations will be general in nature, will often extend to all imports of the product from the third country in question, and will affect importers generally, all of whom are liable to pay the duty.

In the first anti-dumping case, *Japanese Ball-Bearings*[28] the Court accepted that the Japanese exporters could challenge the Council regulation, but that was a somewhat unusual regulation which named the exporters concerned. In Joined Cases 239 & 275/82 *Allied Corporation v. Commission*[29] the Court accepted that exporters could challenge the regulations regardless of whether they were named provided that they were "concerned by the preliminary investigations", *i.e.* took part in the Commission investigation. A similar test is applied, as we shall see, to complainants, *i.e.* the Community industry seeking protection against dumping. As for importers, if they are independent of the exporter and are members of an open class, they cannot challenge the regulation directly in the Court under Article 230 (ex Article 173): their only remedy will be in the national court, with the less satisfactory avenue of a reference under Article 234 (ex Article 177) on the validity of the regulation.[30] It seems that only an importer who is commercially related with an exporter, and whose resale price is used as a basis for determining the export price, can bring proceedings under Article 230 (ex Article 173): see the Order in Case 279/86R *Sermes v. Commission*.[31] However, in Case C–358/89 *Extramet Industrie v. Council*[32] the Court has now accepted that a dumping measure may, without losing its character as a regulation, be of individual concern to certain importers (even

---

[28] Case 113/77 NTN *Toyo Ball-Bearing Co. Ltd v. Council and Commission* [1979] ECR 1185; [1979] 2 C.M.L.R. 257.

[29] Joined Cases 239 and 275/82 *Allied Corporation v. Commission* [1984] ECR 1005; [1985] 3 C.M.L.R. 572.

[30] See the *Royal Scholten-Honig* cases (p. 156, below) for an example of proceedings being brought under national law leading to a reference under Art. 177 on the validity of a regulation.

[31] Case 279/86R *Sermes v. Commission* [1987] ECR 3110.

[32] Case C–358/89 *Extramet Industrie v. Council* [1991] ECR I–2501; [1993] 2 C.M.L.R. 619, see the Opinion of Advocate General Jacobs for an analysis of the case law.

though not associated with any exporter), who will, as a result, have standing to seek its annulment.[33]

By this complex series of decisions, the Court has sought to reconcile, within the terms of what is now the fourth paragraph of Article 230 (ex Article 173), the need to avoid opening its doors to an unlimited category of applicants with the requirement to afford the possibility of direct judicial review to those most immediately affected by anti-dumping measures.

Dumping apart, in relatively few cases have applicants succeeded in satisfying the Court of their direct and individual concern. In Cases 106 & 107/63 *Toepfer v. Commission*,[34] the Commission addressed to the German Government a decision authorising it to impose a levy on the import of maize. The applicants were two of the largest maize importers and sought to have the decision annulled. On the question of admissibility the Court held that the applicants were *directly affected* by the decision addressed to their Government, since a decision authorising protective measures of this kind was to be regarded as directly applicable. The applicants were also *individually concerned* because at the time of the decision the Commission knew that there were only 27 importers (of which the applicants were two) whose import applications could be affected by the decision in issue.

The Court here applied a formula which it had first propounded in the *Clementines* case[35] where it stated:

> "Persons other than those to whom a decision is addressed may only claim to be individually concerned if that decision affects them by reason of certain attributes which are peculiar to them or by reason of circumstances in which they are differentiated from all other persons and by virtue of these factors distinguishes them individually just as in the case of the person addressed."

Plaumann, an importer of clementines, was held not to satisfy this test.

The *Plaumann* formula was again applied by the Court in Case 62/70 *Bock v. Commission*,[36] where the applicant was one of a limited category of importers of Chinese mushrooms who would

---

[33] For a discussion of this case see Castillo de la Torre, "Anti-dumping policy and private interest" (1992) 17 E.L.Rev. 344 at p. 348 and Anthony Arnull "Challenging EC Anti-dumping regulations: the problem of admissibility" (1992) European Competition Law Review 73.

[34] [1965] ECR 405; [1966] C.M.L.R. 111.

[35] Case 25/62 *Plaumann v. Commission* [1963] ECR 95 at 107; [1964] C.M.L.R. 29.

[36] [1971] ECR 897; [1972] C.M.L.R. 160.

be affected by a decision of the Commission addressed to the German Government authorising it to prohibit such mushroom imports, a prohibition which that Government had already made clear it wished to impose. At the date of the decision the number and identity of the importers concerned was already fixed and ascertainable, and this factor differentiated them from all other persons in accordance with the *Plaumann* formula, distinguishing Bock and his fellow importers individually just as in the case of the person addressed. Accordingly, the application was held admissible.

The *International Fruit* case[37] concerned not a decision but a regulation. The Commission had introduced a system whereby it issued licences for import of dessert apples into the EC, on the basis of weekly data which Member States supplied setting out the licences applied for in each State; the Commission gave its decision by means of regulations. At the moment when the regulation was adopted, the number of applications was fixed and no new applications could be added. It was on the basis of the global amount applied for that the Commission decided what percentage of each individual application should be allowed. A Dutch apple importer objected to the reduction of its application and challenged the relevant regulation under Article 173. The Court held that the regulation had to be regarded as a bundle of individual decisions taken by the Commission, each of which, although in the form of a regulation, affected the legal position of one of the applicants. Thus, the decision was of individual concern to the Dutch importer within the terms of (what is now) Article 173(4). As the decision directly affected the applicant, it was also of "direct concern" to him.

The Court did not attempt to reconcile this decision with the earlier Case 64/69 *Compagnie Française Commerciale et Financière v. Commission*,[38] where it refused to accept Advocate General Roemer's view that the Regulation in question was really a decision since the persons affected by it were a closed category whose identity was ascertainable. But in the later case of *C.A.M., SA v. Council and Commission*[39] the Court disregarded (*sub silentio*) the *Compagnie Française* case and followed its approach in the *International Fruit* case: since the applicant was one of a fixed and identifiable category he was individually concerned; and the Court also found that he was also directly concerned. It followed that the application was admissible.

---

[37] Joined Cases 41 to 44/70 *International Fruit Co. v. Commission* [1971] ECR 411; [1975] 2 C.M.L.R. 515.
[38] [1970] ECR 221; [1970] C.M.L.R. 369.
[39] Case 100/74 [1975] ECR 1393.

The Court also seems to have felt driven to adopt a more liberal view of individual concern in the case of *Les Verts* (above, p. 140). There the decision in issue affected all political groupings which might decide to present candidates at the 1984 elections, a class whose members could not be identified at the date when the decision was taken. In its judgment the Court emphasised the uniqueness of the situation, in which those political groupings which were represented in the Parliament took part in the adoption of a decision dealing both with their own treatment and with that of rival groupings which were not represented. To regard only the former as individually concerned would give rise to unequal protection. The latter would be unable to prevent the allocation of funds before the beginning of the campaign: they would be able to challenge only the individual decisions refusing to reimburse sums greater than those provided for by the decision. The Court ultimately decided that the Parliament had no power to allocate funds for this purpose at all; and the Court seemed anxious to avoid a legal hiatus in which the Parliament could adopt a decision which the political groupings within Parliament would have no interest in challenging and which those outside Parliament would be debarred from challenging. Accordingly the Court did not insist on a strict definition of individual concern in this case. At bottom, the Court seems to have been guided in its decision by a sense of what Community public policy required.

A strict application of the *Plaumann* formula has recently been upheld in the face of a threatened flood of challenges by groups or individuals to Community decisions on environmental matters. In Case C–321/95 *Greenpeace v. Council*,[40] the Court set its face against adding a new category of environmental claimants provided for in Article 230 (ex Article 173) EC. In *Greenpeace* Advocate General Cosmas conducted a lengthy and detailed review of the development of the existing case law on *locus standi* under the fourth paragraph of Article 230 (ex Article 173) EC. The case concerned a Commission decision addressed to Spain granting financial assistance under the European Regional Development Fund for the building of two power stations in the Canary Islands. Greenpeace and other environmental associations as well as 16 private individuals challenged the legality of the decisions on various grounds, especially the non-compliance with Community provisions on environmental protection such as a prior environmental impact assessment.

The case reached the Court of Justice on appeal from the Court of First Instance,[41] which had accepted the plea of inadmissibility

---

[40] Case C–321/95P *Greenpeace v. Commission* [1998] ECR I–1651.
[41] Case T–585/93 *Greenpeace v. Commission* [1995] ECR II–2205.

raised by the Commission: neither the individual applicants nor the associations had established their *locus standi* under the fourth paragraph of Article 230 (ex Article 173) EC. The Court of Justice agreed and rejected the appeal. The individual applicants did not satisfy the *Plaumann* test: they were not affected by the contested decision other than in the same manner as any other local resident, fisherman, farmer or tourist who is, or might in the future be, in the same situation. As regards the *locus standi* of the applicant associations, the Court of First Instance (and the Court of Justice agreed) had followed settled case law according to which an association formed to further the collective interests of a category of persons does not have *locus standi* to challenge a measure adopted by a Community institution affecting the general interests of that category where the members of the association do not have standing to do so individually.[42] The Court of Justice was persuaded, it seems, by the floodgate argument forcefully put by Mr Cosmas:

> "If the Court were ultimately to follow the proposal of the appellant associations, in future every measure of a Community institution concerning the environment or having an impact on it could be expected, on each occasion, to form the subject-matter of proceedings brought by a plethora of environmental associations."

As we have seen, Article 173(4) refers to "a decision addressed to another person" being open to challenge if the claimant can show the necessary direct and individual concern. In most cases the decision has been addressed to a Member State government, but the Court from the first saw no difficulty in interpreting "person" to include a government (for example, *Toepfer* and *Greenpeace*, above). A further and novel point of interpretation arose in *Metro v. Commission*.[43]

Here the Commission had addressed a decision to SABA, a German producer of electronic equipment. The decision followed a complaint lodged with the Commission by Metro, who operated as self-service wholesalers of such goods. SABA had refused to recognise Metro as distributors of their products because Metro was unable (or unwilling) to comply with their usual conditions of sale. Metro then asked the Commission to strike down these conditions as in restraint of competition and so contrary to Article 85 EC; they invoked the procedure under Council Regulation 17

---

[42] Joined Cases 19/62 to 22/62 *Fédération Nationale de la Boucherie en Gros et du Commerce en Gros des Viandes and others* [1962] ECR 491.

[43] Case 26/76 *Metro SB-Grossmarkte GmbH & Co KG v. Commission* [1977] ECR 1875; [1978] 2 C.M.L.R. 1.

under which anyone with a "legitimate interest" may complain to the Commission of infringements of Articles 85 and 86.

The Commission, after an investigation, concluded that, subject to some minor modifications, the SABA conditions did not infringe Article 85 and it addressed to SABA a decision to this effect. It also informed Metro of its decision.

Metro challenged the decision addressed to SABA. The Court upheld the action as admissible under (what is now) the fourth paragraph of Article 230 (ex Article 173) EC. In a somewhat cryptic judgment, illuminated by the opinion of Advocate General Reischl, who invoked the *Plaumann* formula (above, p. 148), the Court simply ruled that it was in the interests of a satisfactory administration of justice that a person lodging a complaint with the Commission should be able to institute proceedings before the Court to protect its legitimate interests. Accordingly, Metro must be considered to be directly and individually concerned. Certainly, by complaining the applicants had "distinguished themselves individually" and "differentiated themselves" from self-service wholesalers generally (all of whom were affected by the conditions of sale in issue). As for directness, the judgment appears to endorse *sub silentio* the argument of the advocate general that, although the decision merely empowered SABA to maintain their sale conditions, it was a commercial certainty that they would embrace the decision in order to keep the system complained of by Metro.

The Court has adopted a similar approach in other proceedings analogous to competition proceedings. A complainant in anti-dumping proceedings can challenge a regulation it considers inadequate.[44] Similarly, where the Commission takes a decision under the Treaty provisions governing State aids or subsidies (ex Articles 92 to 94), Articles 87 to 89 EC, although there is no formal status for private complainants in the proceedings, and although an indefinite category of persons might be affected by an aid which distorted competition, the Court considered that a person who takes a part in the procedure comparable to that of a complainant was entitled to challenge the Commission's decision if that person's position in the market was significantly affected by the aid. Thus where the Commission decides that there is no aid incompatible with the common market and terminates the proceeding, the "complainant" can challenge that decision before the Court.[45]

As the above cases demonstrate the Court has laid more emphasis on the requirement of individual concern than that of

---

[44] Case 264/82 *Timex v. Council and Commission* [1985] ECR 849; [1985] 3 C.M.L.R. 550 or a refusal by the Commission to initiate a proceeding: Case 191/82 *FEDIOL v. Commission* [1983] ECR 2913; [1984] 3 C.M.L.R. 244.
[45] Case 169/84 *COFAZ v. Commission* [1986] ECR 391; [1986] 3 C.M.L.R. 385.

direct concern: if the more difficult obstacle of the former can be overcome, the latter seems almost at times to be assumed. Nevertheless, the Court has sought to define direct concern and has done so by analogy to the doctrine of direct effect. Thus, if the addressee of the decision is left no margin of discretion as to how the decision is to be applied, then that decision will be of direct concern to the applicant. As we saw above, in *Toepfer*, the Commission's decision addressed to the German Government was one falling within the doctrine of direct effect: since the applicant could have invoked that doctrine in relation to the decision, the latter was also of direct concern to him. Likewise, in the *Japanese Ball-Bearings* cases direct concern was accepted because the national measures implementing the Community provisions in question were purely automatic. On the other hand, in Case 69/69 *Alcan*,[46] the applicant was not directly concerned because the two Member States to whom the decision (refusing them a certain import quota) was addressed retained a complete discretion how (if at all) to allocate any quota granted to them. Moreover, quite apart from the question of direct effect, direct concern is established if it can be shown (as in *Bock* above, at p. 148) that the addressee has already tied his own hands in advance of the decision; for there is then a close causal connection between the eventual decision and the application of that decision by the addressee with regard to the applicant. The same reasoning was extended, as we have just seen, in the *Metro* case.

In a development causing some surprise in 1994, Case C–309/89 *Codorniu v. Council*,[47] the Court appeared to widen the scope for individuals to challenge the legality of regulations, over and beyond those which are, in reality, decisions in the form of a regulation and which are of direct and individual concern to them: we have seen (p. 146, above) such decisions can be challenged under the terms of Article 173(4).

Codorniu, a Spanish producer of sparkling wine, sought the annulment of a Council regulation in so far as it reserved the use of the term *crémant* exclusively for certain sparkling wines produced in France and Luxembourg. The Council objected that the application was inadmissible in that it was brought against a true regulation. Moreover, Codorniu was only one among many wine-

---

[46] Case 69/69 *Alcan v. Commission* [1970] ECR 385; [1970] C.M.L.R. 337.
[47] Case C–309/89 *Codornio v. Council* [1994] ECR I–1853. This was the last case to be dealt with at first (and last) instance by the Court of Justice under Art. 173 (now Art. 230) EC. By the date judgment was delivered jurisdiction in such cases brought by natural or legal persons had been transferred to the Court of First Instance. For commentaries on this case, see D. Waelbroeck and D. Fosselard (1995) 32 C.M.L.Rev. 257 and J. Usher, "Individual concern in general legislation – 10 years on" (1994) 19 E.L.Rev. 636.

makers using the term *crémant* and could not therefore be said to be individually concerned by the provision in issue.

In a somewhat laconic judgment the Court first reiterated the normal rules governing the admissibility of challenges to legislative measures, including reference to the *Plaumann* test (p. 148, above). It then found that, since Codorniu had registered the graphic trade mark *Gran Crémant de Codorniu* in 1924 and had traditionally used it even before that date, the contested provision prevented it from using its mark. Codorniu was therefore differentiated from all other traders. The objection of inadmissibility was therefore dismissed and the Court annulled the disputed provision on the ground that it was discriminatory.

The case, lodged prior to the establishment of the Court of First Instance and decided after the transfer to it of jurisdiction in all cases brought by natural or legal persons (a transfer delayed for some four-and-a-half years), appears to lower the standard necessary for a challenge to a regulation to be held admissible. Thus, at least in certain cases, it may no longer be necessary to demonstrate that the contested measure is in reality a decision and is merely masquerading as a regulation. It remains to be seen whether this development will give rise to an increase in the number of challenges to regulations before the Court of First Instance. Significantly, in his opinion in *Greenpeace,* Advocate General Cosmas appeared to regard *Codorniu* as an exceptional case where, just as in *Extramet* in relation to a dumping regulation (see p. 147 above), the Court of Justice was prepared to mitigate the rigour of its case law. But, by way of contrast, he refers to the later case of C–209/94P *Buralex v. Commission* as marking a reversion by the Court to the strict approach of that case law, intended to safeguard the legislative nature of a regulation as not open generally to challenge by individuals.[48]

On *locus standi*, Article 33 ECSC differs in several respects from Article 230 (ex Article 173) EC. In the first place, only undertakings (*entreprises*, in the French text) can sue and not individuals: and the right of action is further limited to undertakings engaged in production in the coal and steel industries (Article 80 ECSC). Secondly, the undertaking must show either that the challenged decision or recommendation (the term used in the earlier Treaty for a directive) is "individual in character" or that the decision or recommendation, although general in character, involves a misuse of power affecting that undertaking. Thirdly, there is no requirement under Article 33 ECSC of direct concern: no doubt because, under the scheme of the ECSC Treaty, the High Authority was the

---

[48] Case C–209/94P *Buralex v. Commission* [1996] ECR I–615.

hub of the Community, decisions radiating directly from the High Authority to the undertakings without the mediation of the national authorities.

In the early decisions on this Article the Court adopted a liberal interpretation: the floodgate which the Court has hesitated to open too wide under Article 173 EC (now Article 230 EC) could at most under Article 33 ECSC only admit the limited number of coal and steel undertakings. Thus, in the early *Luxembourg Steel* cases[49] the applicants brought proceedings under Article 33 ECSC against the implied refusal of the High Authority to declare illegal a Luxembourg levy on coal imports. The Luxembourg Government intervened in the proceedings to argue that the applicants had no *locus standi* as they were a steel-producing, not coal-producing, firm. The Court had little difficulty in rejecting this plea. The Court agreed with Advocate General Roemer that there was no provision in the Treaty which required that the particular product made by the producer should be connected with the subject-matter of the dispute and that the silence of the Treaty on this point could not be interpreted in any manner which would be detrimental to companies. The Court also appeared to accept that the act being challenged (namely, the implied refusal of the High Authority to declare the levy illegal) was a decision "individual in character", that is, that it did apply to the applicants individually. This was hardly surprising as the Group represented the main consumers of coal in the Grand Duchy.

The absence of any reference to direct, as distinct from individual, concern in Article 33 ECSC reflects the quite different system of the earlier Treaty, in which the High Authority, true to its name, was to be the real source of power rather than the Member States. Hence, its relationship with the coal and steel enterprises was necessarily assumed to be direct, being almost that of overlord to vassals. The ECSC is due to expire in 2002.

Under the EC Treaty, covering as it does the entire economy, the Community's functions are normally exercised through the Member States; and it was therefore considered appropriate that anyone seeking to challenge a Community measure directly before the Court should have to show both individual and direct concern. In its earlier decisions on Article 173 EC (now Article 230 EC), however, the Court of Justice, perhaps conditioned by its experience under the ECSC Treaty, laid more emphasis on the first of these two requirements, as we have seen.

The difficulty of establishing direct and individual concern under Article 230 (ex Article 173) EC and the non-availability of

---

[49] Cases 7 and 9/54, *Groupement des Industries Sidérurgiques Luxembourgeoises v. High Authority* [1954–56] ECR 175.

this Article where an individual wishes to challenge a regulation (not being one in form only) can sometimes be circumvented by challenging the measure in issue, even a regulation, by a reference for a preliminary ruling on the measure's validity under Article 234 (ex Article 177) EC. As we shall see in Chapter 10, a reference under Article 234 presupposes that proceedings relevant to the challenged measure have been commenced in a court or tribunal of a Member State.

An illustration of the interaction of Articles 173 and 177 (now Articles 230 and 234) EC is provided by the *Royal Scholten-Honig* cases.[50] The company challenged a measure of the Council under Article 173 (now Article 230) but failed to establish *locus standi* as the Court of Justice held that the measure was a true regulation. Some 18 months later the company obtained a declaration of the measure's invalidity on a reference under Article 177 (now Article 234). Such outflanking of Article 230 (ex Article 173) is only possible however where national law offers some basis for an action in which the validity of the Community measure can be called in question. Moreover, such a route will not be available to a party who would have had *locus standi* under Article 230 (ex Article 173) EC, had it not let the time-limit slip by. For a party in this position recourse to the preliminary ruling procedure will be regarded by the Court as an abuse of process.[51]

Another way to overcome the strict rules of *locus standi* as well as the very strict time limit under Article 230 (ex Article 173) is to invoke the plea of illegality under Article 184. This plea is discussed below.

### 3. Within what time limits?

The third paragraph of Article 230 (ex Article 173) EC lays down a time limit of two months for bringing proceedings to annul. This period is calculated from the publication of the measure in issue, or from its notification to the applicant, or, in the absence of publication or notification, from the date when it came to his knowledge. Under Article 33 ECSC the corresponding time limit is one month.

So short a time limit as one or two months, while desirable in the interests of legal certainty, can give rise to problems. As we

---

[50] The action under Art. 173 was Case 143177 *Koninklijke Scholten-Honig NV v. Council and Commission* [1979] ECR 3583; [1982] 2 C.M.L.R. 590, the ruling under Art. 177 was given on Cases 103 and 145/77 *Royal Scholten-Honig (Holdings) Ltd v. Intervention Board for Agricultural Produce* [1978] ECR 2037; [1979] 1 C.M.L.R. 675.

[51] See Case C355/95 *Textilwerke Leggindorff (TWD) v. Commission* [1995] ECR I–2549.

shall see below (p. 164) Article 241 (ex Article 184) (Article 36 ECSC) may provide a partial solution, and, as we have already noted (p. 156), other forms of challenge to validity escape such stringent time limits. Moreover, in Cases 6 and 11/69 *Commission v. French Republic*[52] the Court was prepared to entertain a plea by the French Government that the Commission had reached a decision in a field reserved by the EC Treaty to the Member States, even though the time limits to challenge under Article 173 had expired, for in the Court's words, "if this allegation were valid, the above-mentioned decision would lack all legal basis in the Community legal system." It seems possible that the Court was here adopting from French administrative law the notion, well developed there, of the inexistence of an administrative act taken wholly without legal authority: such an act may be declared non-existent even outside the normal French time limit (of two months) for annulment proceedings.[53]

### 4. On what grounds?

Article 230 (ex Article 173) EC sets out four grounds for annulment. These are:

(a) lack of competence (or authority);
(b) infringement of an essential procedural requirement;
(c) infringement of the EC Treaty or of any rule of law relating to its application; and
(d) misuse of powers.

All four grounds appear to raise only questions of law, not of fact nor of the merits of the challenged act. But the Court may be led inevitably into a review of the facts as found by the Council or Commission if, for example, the issue is whether there is such a manifest error of fact as to constitute a violation of law. The lines between the four grounds are fluid and one or more may be pleaded in the alternative or in combination. The Court is always at pains to avoid undue formalism in proceedings brought before it.

Historically, the grounds are derived from French administrative law where the *Conseil d'Etat* has elaborated in its case law the

---

[52] [1969] ECR 523; [1970] C.M.L.R. 43.

[53] For another example of the application of this concept of "inexistence" see the judgment of the Court of First Instance in joined Cases T–79/89 etc., *BASF and others v. Commission* [1992] ECR II–315; [1992] 4 C.M.L.R. 357, appealed to the Court of Justice as Case C–137/92P *Commission v. BASF* [1994] ECR I–2555. See further Chap. 5, p. 101, above. On the concept of *inexistence* in French law, see Brown & Bell, *French Administrative Law* (5th ed., 1998), pp. 240–242.

precise meaning of the corresponding French terms: *incompétence, vice de forme, violation de la loi, détournement de pouvoir.* Community law, however, has a life of its own, and reference to French decisions would, at best, be only persuasive authority in the Court of Justice. Moreover, German and, since 1973, English administrative law have influenced the development of the grounds of review at Luxembourg; as now no doubt will the legal systems of the newer Member States.

The grounds in Article 230 (ex Article 173) EC, with certain limited exceptions, correspond to those in Article 33 ECSC. Some of the illustrative cases now to be discussed derive from the ECSC Treaty.

Thus, Case 9/56 *Meroni v. High Authority*[54] is a useful example of both lack of competence and an infringement of the ECSC Treaty. The High Authority imposed certain levies on scrap iron on the basis of decisions taken by a subordinate body (the Scrap Bureau) to which the Authority had purported to delegate its powers. The Court quashed the levies on the grounds, first, that the Treaty had been infringed inasmuch as it did not permit the Authority to delegate its decision-making powers (*delegatus non potest delegare*), and secondly, that there was a lack of competence on the part of the Authority to proceed as it had.

Procedural infringements are commonly invoked, and it is then for the Court to assess whether the infringement is of an essential requirement. Thus, in the *First Cement Cartel* case,[55] it was pleaded that the failure to give sufficient reasons for the decisions in question constituted the infringement of an essential procedural requirement, namely, the general rule in Article 253 (ex Article 190) EC that decisions of the Commission shall state the reasons on which they are based. The same Article was successfully invoked in Case 24/62 *Germany v. Commission*,[56] when the Commission partially rejected Germany's application to import a large quantity of wine from outside the Community for distillation for domestic consumption. By way of reasons the Commission simply stated that its decision was based on "information that has been gathered indicating that the production of wines of this nature within the Community is amply sufficient".

The Court explained the purposes of the requirement of reasoning as follows:

> "In imposing upon the Commission the obligation to state reasons for its decision, Article 190[57] is not taking mere

---

[54] [1958] ECR 133.
[55] Joined Cases 8 to 11/66 *Cimenteries CBR SA v. Commission* [1967] ECR 75; [1967] C.M.L.R. 77.
[56] [1963] ECR 63.
[57] Now Art. 253 EC.

formal considerations into account but seeks to give an opportunity to the parties of defending their rights, to the Court of exercising its supervisory functions and to Member States and to all interested nationals of ascertaining the circumstances in which the Commission has applied the Treaty."

To attain these objectives a decision must set out, in a concise but clear and relevant manner, the principal issues of law and of fact upon which it is based.

In the *Tariff Preferences* case[58] the Commission challenged two Council regulations which, under the Generalised System of Preferences (GSP), granted favourable tariffs to developing countries. The Commission had no objection to the substance of the regulations but complained that the regulations did not specify their treaty basis, as Article 190 (now Article 253) EC required. The Commission had taken the view that such regulations could be based on Article 113 (now Article 133) EC (and could therefore be adopted by majority vote) while the Council's position was that such regulations went beyond the scope of Article 113 and could be adopted only by the use of Article 235 (now Article 308) EC (and therefore unanimously). The Court held that it was essential in such a case to specify the legal basis of the measures, that the failure to do so infringed the requirement of a statement of reasons, and that the regulations should have been adopted on the basis of Article 113 (now Article 133) EC.

Another instance of an "essential procedural requirement" is the requirement that the Council should consult the European Parliament on proposals for legislation when the Treaty so prescribes. Thus in the *Isoglucose cases*[59] producers of isoglucose sought the annulment of a Council regulation imposing a levy on isoglucose, contending that the requirement of consultation of the European Parliament had not been observed as the Parliament, although asked for its opinion, had not given its opinion when the regulation was adopted by the Council. The Parliament intervened to support the applicants (see p. 289) and the Court annulled the regulation.

The third ground of annulment includes, as we have seen, both treaty infringements and an infringement of any rule of law relating to the application of the relevant Treaty. This last expression has been liberally construed by the Court. Thus, it includes all legislation made pursuant to the Treaties (for example,

---

[58] Case 45/86 *Commission v. Council* [1987] ECR 1493; [1988] 2 C.M.L.R. 131.
[59] Cases 138 and 139/79 *Roquette and Maizena v. Council* [1980] ECR 3333 and 3393.

regulations or directives) and such general principles as are recognised in international law, or such "general principles common to the laws of the Member States" as the Court deems to be applicable in the particular case.

The expression "general principles common to the laws of the Member States" is only expressly referred to in Article 288 (ex Article 215) EC where these principles are declared the basis of the non-contractual liability of the Community (below, p. 174). The principles, however, have been extended beyond this narrow but important context and may be invoked under other Articles, such as Article 230 (ex Article 173) EC. Moreover, despite the absence of any reference to such general principles in the ECSC Treaty, the Court has in several ECSC cases (some prior to the EC Treaty) invoked these principles. Examples include the principle of proportionality of administrative acts,[60] and the principles of legal certainty and of due process.[61] Subsequently there has been an important extension of this doctrine of general principles to embody fundamental rights, as in *Stauder v. Ulm*,[62] *Internationale Handelsgesellschaft*,[63] and the second *Nold* case[64] in which the Court roundly declared that "fundamental rights form an integral part of the general principles of law, the observance of which it ensures" (below, p. 359). But whereas, in the cases mentioned, the Court finally concluded that there had been no breach of the principles invoked, more than lip service was paid to the principles in the *Transocean Marine Paint Association*[65] case, in which the Court decided, at the prompting of Advocate General Warner, that the Commission had acted in breach of the principle of natural justice as embodied in the maxim *audi alteram partem*.

General principles of law have proved of great importance in the review by the Court of legislation and decisions, both under Article 230 (ex Article 173) EC and in references on validity (below, p. 234) under Article 234 (ex Article 177) EC. They also provide a striking example of the creative development of the law. For these reasons they warrant treatment in a separate chapter (Chapter 15), where the Court's role as lawmaker is explored, and which illustrates the use of general principles to challenge Community measures.

The remaining ground for review under Article 230 (ex Article 173) EC is misuse of powers. This is a well developed notion in

---

[60] Case 8/55 *Fédéchar v. High Authority* [1954–56] ECR 245.
[61] Cases 42 and 49/59 *SNUPAT v. High Authority* [1961] ECR 53.
[62] Case 29/69 *Stauder v. Ulm* [1969] ECR 419; [1970] C.M.L.R. 112.
[63] Case 11/70 [1970] ECR 1125; [1972] C.M.L.R. 255.
[64] Case 4/73 [1974] ECR 491; [1974] 2 C.M.L.R. 338.
[65] Case 17/74 [1974] ECR 1063; [1974] 2 C.M.L.R. 459.

some continental systems of administrative law: the French text speaks of *détournement de pouvoir*, a notion familiar in French administrative law. English law variously acknowledges the same notion under such labels as "abuse of power", "misuse of power" or "bad faith". As interpreted by the Court, the term includes not only the use of a power for an unlawful purpose but also its use for a purpose, itself lawful, but not the one contemplated in conferring the power in question. An early decision to explore this ground under Article 33 ECSC was Case 1/54 *French Republic v. High Authority*[66] the Court's first judgment.

In this case the High Authority had taken three decisions purportedly on the basis of Article 60 ECSC so as to prevent discrimination in prices. The French Government argued that the real object of the Authority had been to secure a general reduction in prices and the prevention of price agreements: for these objects the Authority should have exercised the powers conferred upon it by Articles 61 and 65. Accordingly, it was argued, there had been a misuse of powers. The Court held that there was no misuse of powers where (as in the case) the act complained of has as its dominant or primary object the purpose for which that power is conferred, even though the act achieves incidentally some other object which is not properly the object of the power in question. By contrast with the EC Treaty, under Article 33 ECSC only misuse of powers may be invoked by undertakings to challenge general, as distinct from individual, decisions or recommendations. This point arose in *Fédéchar v. High Authority*.[67] The applicant was an association of Belgian collieries. They challenged the validity of a decision of the Authority fixing lower prices for coal as a result of which three collieries within the Association would receive lower compensation payments. The Authority contested the argument of the Association that the decision was on that account individual in character and so open to review on any of the four grounds. The Authority maintained that the fact that a decision might have different effects for different collieries was not relevant in determining the nature of the decision: a decision was general or individual according to the scope of its application, and the decision in question had a general character as it was intended to be general in effect and to apply to all the firms falling within its scope. The Court accepted this argument, with the consequence that the applicants were limited to establishing a misuse of powers as the only ground for annulling the decision, and this they failed to show on the facts.

---

[66] [1954–56] ECR 1.
[67] Case 8/55 *Fédération Charbonnière de Belgique v. High Authority* [1954–56] ECR 245.

## 5. What effect has annulment?

Article 233 (ex Article 176) states that the institution whose act has been declared void shall be required to take the necessary measures to comply with the Court's judgment. Article 34 ECSC is in similar terms.

The Court has accepted the principle that a challenged act, like the curate's egg, may be bad in part only. Thus, in Cases 56 and 58/64 *Consten and Grundig v. Commission*,[68] Consten and Grundig had entered into an agreement whereby Consten was to be sole agent for Grundig in France. Competitors wishing to sell Grundig's products in France complained to the Commission that the agreement infringed Article 85 EC. The Commission agreed with the complainants and issued a decision declaring an infringement of Article 85. This decision was challenged by Consten and Grundig under Article 173 (now Article 230) EC. The Court held that the decision was partly valid and partly invalid inasmuch as the agreement in part infringed Article 85 but in part did not. The Court followed in this respect its earlier decision in Case 6/54 *The Netherlands v. High Authority*,[69] under the ECSC Treaty, where part only of a decision was annulled for lack of adequate reasons. Not all the national laws of the Member States permit such severability of the good from the bad.

Where a regulation is annulled, the second paragraph of Article 231 (ex Article 174) EC expressly provides that the Court may, if it considers this necessary, state which of the effects of the void regulation shall be considered as definitive. Thus, as we have seen above in Case 81/72 *Commission v. Council*, a Council regulation laying down a scale for staff salaries within the Community institutions was declared void, but in order that salaries could continue to be paid the Court ordered that the regulation should continue in operation until the Council could pass a new (and valid) regulation. Similarly in the *Tariff Preferences* case the Court ruled that, having regard to the circumstances of the case and the requirements of legal certainty, the effects of the annulled regulations must be treated as definitive.

## B. Actions For Inactivity (Article 232 (ex Article 175) EC)

The authors of both the ECSC and the EC Treaties recognised that a remedy should be available not only where an institution had

---

[68] [1966] ECR 299; [1966] C.M.L.R. 418.
[69] [1954–56] ECR 103.

acted illegally but also where it had failed to act. Article 232 (ex Article 175) EC and Article 35 ECSC seek to fill this gap.

The first paragraph of Article 232 states:

> "Should the European Parliament, the Council or the Commission, in infringement of this Treaty, fail to act, the Member States and the other institutions of the Community may bring an action before the Court of Justice to have the infringement established."[70]

The third paragraph of Article 232 (ex Article 175) EC confers upon individuals and companies the right to complain to the Court that an institution has failed to address to the complainant any act other than a recommendation or an opinion. Finally, the new fourth paragraph of Article 232 (ex Article 175) EC, added by the TEU, enables the ECB to sue or be sued.

It should be noted that Article 232 (ex Article 175) EC permits the European Parliament, as one of "the other institutions of the Community", to bring the Council or Commission before the Court for a failure to act. The Parliament, having threatened to do so on several previous occasions, exercised this right for the first time in proceedings which it introduced against the Council in 1983 complaining of the latter's failure to adopt an adequate transport policy as required by the EC Treaty (Articles 74 (now Articles 70) *et seq.*).[71] The Court rejected various objections by the Council to the admissibility of the action and upheld the action in part.

An action under Article 232 (ex Article 175) EC is only admissible if the institution in default has first been called upon to act. If then, within two months of being so called upon, the institution has not defined its position, the action may be brought within a further period of two months. This procedure is prescribed by the second paragraph of Article 232 (ex Article 175) EC.

There are two further obstacles to success in proceedings under Article 232 (ex Article 175) EC which are more difficult to overcome. The first arises from the requirement that the applicant (if not a Member State or a Community institution) must apparently show that the desired act would have been addressed to him, when it will often be the case that he wanted the defendant (normally the Commission) to take a decision in respect of someone else: for example against another undertaking which he alleges is infringing the EC competition rules. It would be more

---

[70] The European Parliament was added to the Art. by the Maastricht Treaty.
[71] Case 13/83 *European Parliament v. Council* [1985] ECR 1513; [1986] 1 C.M.L.R. 138.

consistent with the purpose of Article 232 (ex Article 175) EC if the same test of *locus standi* were applied as under Article 173, namely that the desired act would have been of direct and individual concern to him.[72]

Secondly, the defendant will be able to meet the complaint of failure to act if it has "defined its position." As the cases show,[73] the Commission may be able to "define its position" without adopting a measure which can be challenged under Article 230 (ex Article 173) EC. In contrast, under the ECSC Treaty, the decisions of the Court establish that a complaint of inactivity (under Article 35 ECSC) can be met only by a binding act, which will itself be liable to challenge under Article 33. There is therefore an apparent gap in the protection afforded under the EC Treaty, although the existence of such a gap has been ingeniously disputed.[74] The fact remains that, with the exception of the Transport case brought by the European Parliament, no action brought under Article 175 EC has to date succeeded, and the remedy has proved ineffective for private litigants. On the other hand two successful actions were brought under Article 35 ECSC[75] and, more recently a Portuguese company successfully brought proceedings against the Commission under Article 148 Euratom.[76] Those Articles provide the equivalent remedy for inactivity to that provided by Article 232 (ex Article 175) EC.

## C. Plea of Illegality (Article 241 (ex Article 184) EC)

This (to English ears) curiously named remedy is derived from French administrative law where it is known as *l'exception d'illégalité*. A close parallel in English procedure is where a challenge is raised collaterally to the validity of a statutory instrument or bye-law in a prosecution for its infringement. In Community law it is a means of challenging an illegal act, even after the lapse of the strict time limit imposed by Article 230 (ex

---

[72] See Advocate General Dutheillet de Lamothe's opinion in Case 15/71 *Mackprang v. Commission* [1971] ECR 797 at 807–808; [1972] C.M.L.R. 52.

[73] See for example Case 48/65 *Lutticke v. Commission* [1966] ECR 19; [1966] C.M.L.R. 378 and Case 125/78 *GEMA v. Commission* [1979] ECR 3173; [1980] 2 C.M.L.R. 177.

[74] See T. C. Hartley, *The Foundations of European Community Law* (2nd ed., 1988), pp. 406–409.

[75] Joined Cases 42 and 49/59, *SNUPAT v. High Authority* [1961] ECR 53 and Joined Cases 167 and 212/85 *ASSIDER and Another v. Commission* [1987] ECR 1701; [1988] 2 C.M.L.R. 783.

[76] Case C–107/91 *Empresa Nacional de Uranio SA v. Commission* [1993] ECR I-599.

Article 173) EC. The plea, if successful, renders the act, not void, but "inapplicable". This is made clear by the language of Article 241 (ex Article 184) EC[77]:

> "Notwithstanding the expiry of the period laid down in the fifth paragraph of Article 230, any party may, in proceedings in which a regulation adopted jointly by the European Parliament and the Council, or a regulation of the Council, of the Commission, or of the European Central Bank is at issue, plead the grounds specified in the second paragraph of Article 230, in order to invoke before the Court of Justice the inapplicability of that regulation."

The remedy under Article 241 (ex Article 184) EC is an important supplement to that given under Article 230 (ex Article 173). In the first place it mitigates the effect of the very short time limit under the latter Article. For, although the regulation in issue may now have become immune from annulment by lapse of time, a decision based upon that regulation may he challenged by the person affected through the plea of illegality. This will permit a party to have the decision set aside upon satisfying the Court that the "parent" regulation is tainted with illegality on one or more of the grounds set out in Article 230 (ex Article 173) EC. The Court will then hold the regulation "inapplicable" in the particular case, so that the decision becomes without legal foundation.

Whereas Article 230 (ex Article 173) EC may be invoked, as we have seen, against a wide category of acts, the plea of illegality only lies, on a strict reading of Article 184, against a regulation. But in Case 92/78 *Simmenthal v. Commission*,[78] the Court of Justice interpreted Article 184 (now Article 241) EC as giving expression to a general principle conferring upon any party to proceedings the right to challenge, for the purpose of obtaining the annulment of a decision of direct and individual concern to that party, the validity of previous acts of the institutions which form the legal basis of the decision that is being attacked, but which that party lacked *locus standi* to challenge under Article 173 (now Article 230) EC.

Thus, in *Simmenthal*, the applicant was allowed to bring the plea against a general notice of tender issued by the Commission for the purchase, by importers such as Simmenthal, of meat held by an intervention agency. The general notice, though not in form a regulation, was held to be analogous in effect and normative in character: it could therefore be challenged by way of the plea of

---

[77] As amended by the Maastricht Treaty.
[78] [1979] ECR 777; [1980] 1 C.M.L.R. 25.

illegality although the applicant was directly and individually affected only by the consequent decision of the Commission which fixed the price for tenders from Italian importers at a price above that offered by Simmenthal, thereby leading to the rejection of the tender.

The plea of illegality reconciles two otherwise conflicting policies of Community law. On the one hand, there is the policy, in the interest of legal certainty (*sécurité juridique*), of making the acts of Community institutions unimpeachable after short time limits; on the other, there is the countervailing policy, exemplified in Article 241 (ex Article 184) EC (Article 36 ECSC), of not allowing an illegal act, although perfected by lapse of time, to "father" further illegal acts: a party affected thereby may challenge the offspring as illegal because of the original illegality of the parent regulation. If the challenge succeeds, the regulation is rendered inapplicable in the particular case. To that extent, one may speak of the "relative nullity" of the regulation, that is, relative to the particular party who has invoked the plea. But the regulation is not thereby rendered absolutely null and void: in the unlikely event of it being invoked again to found a further decision, a party affected by that decision will be obliged, in turn, to invoke the plea: otherwise the decision will be valid.

The plea is also important in another respect. We have seen that the rules of *locus standi* under Article 230 (ex Article 173) EC are very restrictive so far as actions by individuals or companies are concerned. In particular, a private party cannot challenge a regulation, unless it is in substance a decision of direct and individual concern to him. The plea, however, permits the private party to plead the illegality of any regulation (or a general decision or recommendation under the ECSC Treaty) which is now being applied in a specific decision affecting him.

It should be emphasised that the plea does not provide an independent cause of action but can only be invoked where proceedings are already properly before the Court under some other Article of the Treaties. The Court has made this clear in the *Wohrmann* and *Dalmas* cases relating to Article 184 (now Article 241) EC and Article 36(3) ECSC respectively.[79] Commonly, the plea is made in conjunction with an action to annul under Article 230 (ex Article 173) EC (or Article 33 ECSC). But in the *SNUPAT* case (see above, p. 164), it was invoked in an action for inactivity under Article 35 ECSC. It could also arise in a staff case under Article 234 (ex Article 179) EC.[80]

---

[79] Joined Cases 31 and 33/62 *Wohrmann v. Commission* [1962] ECR 501; [1963] C.M.L.R. 152 and Case 21/64 *Macchiorlati Dalmas & Figli v. Commission* [1965] ECR 175; [1966] C.M.L.R. 46.

[80] See Case 20/71 *Sabbatini v. European Parliament*, p. 197, below.

An illustration of the plea is provided by Case 9/56 *Meroni v. High Authority*[81] a case arising under the ECSC Treaty and involving, *inter alia*, Article 36(3) which states:

> "In support of its appeal, a party may, under the same conditions as in the first paragraph of Article 33 of this Treaty, contest the legality of the decision or recommendation which that party is alleged not to have observed."

Meroni was appealing against a decision of the High Authority of October 24, 1956 which imposed a pecuniary obligation and was accordingly enforceable pursuant to Article 92 ECSC. By the decision the Authority requested Meroni to pay a levy on scrap bought by Meroni for its steel production. This decision was based upon two general decisions (No. 22 of 1954 and No. 14 of 1955) which founded the general system of levies on scrap imports, a system administered by a special "Scrap Bureau". To support its action (under Article 33 ECSC) challenging the decision of October 24, 1956, Meroni alleged (under Article 36(3) ECSC) the illegality of decisions Nos 22/54 and 14/55 on grounds which we have previously discussed above (p. 158). The Authority argued that Meroni's case should be dismissed as the time limit of one month under Article 33 had long expired so that the question of the illegality of decisions Nos 22/54 and 14/55 was out of time and statute-barred.

The Court held that the plea of illegality could be raised by Meroni under Article 36(3). For, although the language of Article 36 is limited to appeals against pecuniary penalties, the Article is the application of a general principle, namely, the plea of illegality, and this can be raised at any time to challenge the irregularity of general decisions or recommendations upon which the individual decision is based. The plea, however, cannot lead to the annulment of the general decision but only to the annulment of the individual decision based upon it.

The Court went still further in its bold interpretation of Article 36(3). For it proceeded to hold that, notwithstanding the words "under the same conditions as in the first paragraph of Article 33", the scope of the plea was not limited to misuse of powers, despite this being the sole ground upon which a private party could challenge a general decision under Article 33: rather, all the four grounds could be invoked in support of the plea. As we saw in the previous discussion of this case, Meroni successfully pleaded the grounds of both lack of competence and infringement of the Treaty.

---

[81] [1958] ECR 133.

Having considered the nature of the plea, we must now examine by whom it may be made. The plea may not be invoked by a Community institution, for the apparent purpose of this remedy is to protect the interests of a private party against the threatened application of an illegal general act, such as a regulation. Moreover, Community institutions are not subject to the restrictive rules of *locus standi* applicable to private parties in annulment proceedings: the Council or Commission have an unrestricted opportunity to challenge general acts under Article 230 (ex Article 173) EC, subject only to the two months time limit.

So far as concerns private parties, an individual or a company can rely upon Article 241 (ex Article 184) EC, but under Article 36(3) ECSC the plea of illegality may be invoked only by the limited class of undertakings having *locus standi* under Article 33 ECSC (above, p. 154).

Under Article 241 (ex Article 184) EC the extent to which a Member State may invoke the plea is not entirely settled. In Case 32/65 *Italy v. Council and Commission*[82] the Court impliedly accepted that a Member State could do so when challenging a regulation under Article 173 (now Article 230) EC: Italy there invoked Article 241 (ex Article 184) EC to extend its challenge to earlier (and related) regulations. The justification for this is questioned by some authors on the ground that a Member State has the same opportunity as the Council or Commission to challenge any act, including regulations, directly under Article 230 (ex Article 173) EC. The Court went some way to recognise the logic of the objection in Case 156/77 *Commission v. Belgium*[83] where, in the course of enforcement proceedings brought against Belgium by the Commission under Article 88 (ex Article 93) EC in respect of a prohibited State aid (above, p. 126), the Belgian Government sought to invoke the plea against a specific decision addressed to it which it had failed to challenge directly and timeously by an action under Article 173. The Court ruled that the plea "can in no case be invoked by a Member State to whom an individual decision has been addressed: in effect, Belgium was seeking to challenge the decision, out of time, by resort to the plea". If, then, a Member State may invoke the plea against a regulation, but not against an individual decision addressed to it,

---

[82] [1966] ECR 389; [1969] C.M.L.R. 39.

[83] Case 156/77 *Commission v. Belgium* [1978] ECR 1881. Noted by Usher (1979) 4 E.L.Rev. 36, see also Case 226/87 *Commission v. Greece* [1988] ECR 36/1, where the Court held that a Member State could only plead the unlawfulness of a decision addressed to it as a defence in an action under Art. 169 (now Art. 226) where the measure concerned contained such particularly serious and manifest defects that it could be deemed non-existent.

the question remains open whether it may do so against a directive, which may not be individual in character but may be addressed to it.

For the comparative lawyer the plea is a particular illustration of the insertion into the Treaties by the founding Member States of a concept well known in civil law systems but one which the common lawyer of the United Kingdom or the Irish Republic hardly recognises as a form of judicial review, although in practice it is common enough for the substantive or procedural validity of bye-laws, regulations or executive action to be raised as a defence in proceedings taken to enforce administrative decisions.

# Chapter Eight

# Plenary Jurisdiction

## INTRODUCTION

The title of this chapter calls for explanation, especially for common lawyers. In French administrative law a broad division is made, in suits brought to the administrative courts, between actions to annul and *recours de pleine juridiction*, that is, actions where the court is asked to exercise its fullest powers, for example by awarding damages against the administration or by itself revising (as distinct from merely quashing) the administrative act submitted to it. This notion of plenary jurisdiction was carried over into the EC Treaty as one familiar to French and other continental systems of administrative law. It appears, for instance, in Article 172 (now 229) EC where, in the English text, the Court may be given "unlimited jurisdiction" in regard to penalties provided for in the regulations made by the Council pursuant to the Treaty. This means that the Court can not only cancel such a penalty but also alter its amount. This is made explicit in Article 17 of Regulation 17/62 of the Council (relating to competition) which states:

> "The Court shall have unlimited jurisdiction within the meaning of Article 172 of the Treaty to review decisions whereby the Commission has fixed a fine or periodic penalty payment; it may cancel, reduce or increase the fine or periodic penalty payment imposed."

The Court's plenary jurisdiction in the above sense includes, or used to include, the following categories of actions:

(a) Actions to review penalties (Article 172 (now 229) EC, Article 36(2) ECSC);
(b) So-called "staff cases" involving disputes between the Communities and their staff in relation to their terms of service (Article 179 (now 236) EC);

(c) Actions for damages based upon the non-contractual liability of the Communities (Article 178 (now 235) EC, Article 40 ECSC).

Category (b) has now been transferred into the jurisdiction of the Court of First Instance and may only reach the Court of Justice on appeal (see Chapter 5, above); and is the subject of a separate chapter below (Chapter 9). Category (a) has already been briefly referred to above. The present chapter will be concerned with category (c): although actions for damages by natural or legal persons have now been transferred to the Court of First Instance (see p. 80, above), the Court of Justice has shaped the principles of non-contractual liability and will still control their development on appeal. But first reference must be made to the contractual (as distinct from the non-contractual) liability of the Communities.

## CONTRACTUAL LIABILITY OF THE COMMUNITIES

Liability on the part of the Communities may obviously arise in contract as well as in tort: such is the wide range of their activities and functions. In the EC Treaty, Article 215 (now 288) EC draws a distinction, in the terminology more familiar to continental lawyers, between contractual and non-contractual liability, although the latter term, because of its residuary character, could extend beyond tort into the field, for example, of restitution. Under the first paragraph of Article 215 (now 288) contractual liability is governed by the law applicable to the contract in question. The law referred to will be whichever national law governs that contract as its proper law, and any litigation arising on the contract will come before the relevant national court.

The jurisdiction of the national courts is exclusive; for the jurisdiction of the Court of Justice arises only where it is expressly conferred by the Treaties, and there is no provision conferring jurisdiction on the Court in these cases, as there is (under Article 178 (now 235) EC) in cases of non-contractual liability. Only where the contract contains an arbitration clause conferring jurisdiction in any dispute upon the Court of Justice (as Article 181 (now 238) EC and Article 153 Euratom permit) will a question of contractual liability come directly before the Communities' own Court: for example, Euratom research contracts usually contain such clauses. Indirectly, however, a claim in contract against the Community may be the subject of a reference to Luxembourg by a national court under Article 177 (now 234) EC.

Articles 181 (now 238) EC and 153 Euratom are applicable whether the contract in question be categorised as "public" or "private" – a distinction derived from French administrative law and embodied in the terms of the Articles.

For a case involving such a contract with Euratom, see Case 23/76 *Pellegrini*,[1] where the contract included an arbitration clause conferring jurisdiction upon the Court; it also provided that the contract was to be governed by Italian law: the Court accepted jurisdiction and resolved the dispute in accordance with Italian law. Similarly, contracts made between the Commission and universities in the Member States for the provision of various technical or research services usually embody an arbitration clause and provide for the contract to be governed by the national law of the university in question or of the seat of the Community institution concerned (in the case of the Commission, Belgium). In such cases the Court may find itself determining substantive questions of national law and treating such questions as ones of law (of which it has judicial notice) and not of fact (for which it would require expert evidence). Lord Slynn would discourage such arbitration clauses, which require the Court to decide disputes by reference to national law, not Community law.[2] Moreover, such cases in contract are the only instances in which a private individual may find himself the defendant before the Court in a direct action brought by the Community: in Case 426/85, *Commission v. Zoubek*[3] the Commission invoked Article 181 (now 238) EC to recover, under an arbitration clause, an advance paid to a journalist who had failed to produce a report which it had commissioned.

For the avoidance of doubt, Article 183 (now 240) EC makes explicit that the Communities may be a party to a dispute brought before a court or tribunal of a Member State. Thus, "should the Court of Justice purchase some stationery in Luxembourg from a Luxembourg supplier and then, to imagine the unimaginable, default on the purchase price, the supplier would have his remedy in the Luxembourg courts according to Luxembourg law".[4]

Special considerations apply to contracts of employment entered into by Community institutions with their officials and other servants. As we shall see in the next chapter, such staff disputes were previously a separate head of the Court's jurisdiction under Article 179 (now 236) EC and so fell outside the sphere of application of Articles 178 and 215 (now 235 and 288) EC[5]: they now come within the jurisdiction of the Court of First Instance. The law applicable to these contracts will be that laid down in the

---

[1] Case 23/76 *Pellegrini v. Commission* [1976] ECR 1807; [1977] 2 C.M.L.R. 77.
[2] Gordon Slynn, *Introducing a Community Legal Order* (43rd Hamlyn Lectures, 1992), p. 33.
[3] Case 426/85 *Commission v. Zoubek* [1986] ECR 4057; [1988] 1 C.M.L.R. 257.
[4] Lord Mackenzie Stuart, "The Non-Contractual Liability of the European Economic Community" (Maccabaean Lecture in Jurisprudence, 1975), 4.
[5] Case 9/75 *Meyer-Burckhardt* [1975] ECR 1171.

official Staff Regulations or Conditions of Employment or, in default, "the general rules of administrative law."[6]

## NON-CONTRACTUAL ACTIONS AGAINST THE COMMUNITY

This relatively clear-cut pattern in contract contrasts with the Communities' non-contractual liability. Here Article 178 (now 235) EC confers exclusive jurisdiction on the Court (now exercised by the Court of First Instance), by virtue of Article 183 (now 240) EC.

Why there should be this fundamental divergence in the treatment of contractual and non-contractual liability of the Communities is an interesting question. Maurice Lagrange, a former advocate general of the Court, suggests an historical explanation.[7] The framers of the ECSC Treaty saw that an independent legal order required special provision to be made for the legal liabilities of the Community arising from contract or of a non-contractual character. Contractual liability could be left to be governed by the more or less uniform principles found in the national laws of the original Member States. But non-contractual liability raised questions of delicacy and importance involving the activities of the Community as a "public authority": the rules governing the liability of public authorities differed considerably in the national laws of the various Member States, nor might they have been wholly appropriate to apply unchanged to the liability of the Community. Accordingly, a conscious choice was made to vest in the Court of Justice exclusive jurisdiction over the non-contractual liability of the Community and to entrust the Court with the fashioning of an independent Community law to govern such liability, guided only by the broad terms of Article 40 ECSC (and later Article 215(2) (now 288) EC, Article 188(2) Euratom).

Lagrange points out that the terms of Article 40 ECSC were borrowed directly from French administrative law. For that system was felt the most appropriate, since, unlike the systems prevailing in the other five Member States, France had entrusted jurisdiction over the tortious liability of public authorities exclusively to its administrative courts (in particular the *Conseil d'Etat*); moreover, that liability was governed by its own public law principles, elaborated in praetorian fashion by the *Conseil d'Etat* in complete independence of the private law principles enshrined in the Civil Code: see the landmark decision of *Blanco* in the *Tribunal des Conflits* February 1, 1873.[8]

---

[6] See, for this phrase, Cases 43, 45, 48/59 *Von Lachmuller v. Commission* [1960] ECR. 463; also Case 1/55 *Kergall v. Common Assembly* [1954–56] ECR 151.

[7] M. Lagrange in [1965–66] 3 C.M.L Rev. 32.

[8] See further Brown and Bell, *French Administrative Law* (4th ed., 1993), Chap. 3.

The ECSC Treaty therefore adopted the French solution of vesting in one and the same jurisdiction actions for the annulment of official acts and suits for damages arising from the tortious liability of public authorities. In this way, the Court of Justice would be fully equipped to exercise the most effective judicial control over Community institutions. This solution had the added advantage of excluding the national courts from sitting in judgment upon the administrative activities of Community institutions. To have permitted this would have threatened, it was thought, the Community's independence. Subsequently, the principles in this respect embodied in the ECSC Treaty were carried over without substantial modification into the EC and Euratom Treaties.

In the result, Article 178 (now Article 235) EC and the second paragraph of Article 215 (now Article 288) EC, read together, render unnecessary any recourse to the principles of private international law so far as the Communities' non-contractual liability is concerned. For Article 178 (now Article 235) settles categorically the question of which court shall have jurisdiction, and Article 215(2) (now Article 288(2)) determines what principles of substantive law shall govern that liability. In effect, for such liability the *lex causae* is to be the *lex fori*: the Community Court is to apply Community law. What, however, the second paragraph of Article 215 (now Article 288) offers as the Community law governing non-contractual liability is a mere reference to "the general principles common to the laws of the Member States." This vague formula has been left for the Court itself to elaborate in a series of cases. Dependent on the accidents of litigation, the working out of a consistent body of principles is still far from complete. Moreover, the Court has shown itself properly cautious in not wishing to expose the Communities to a flood of speculative claims in damages. The account which follows is therefore necessarily tentative, but the dearth of clear principle does not mean that the subject is not of vital importance as completing the armoury of remedies which the individual needs for his legal protection within the Communities.

Parenthetically, we may observe that the Court has also invoked the same concept of general principles, by way of analogy, in cases not involving liability under Article 215 (now Article 288) EC. This wider development of the concept, outside the context of non-contractual liability, calls for separate consideration (Chapter 15).[9]

So far as non-contractual liability is concerned, "the general principles common to the laws of the Member States," to which

---

[9] A valuable study is A. Arnull, The General Principles of EEC Law and the Individual (1990).

Article 215(2) (now Article 288(2)) refers, provide no certain guide in this matter. There does not exist within the 12 countries of the Communities a common corpus of legal principles governing State liability in tort. Comparative study of the 15 national laws (or rather 16, as the Scottish law of reparation is distinct from the English law of tort) is a regular exercise of the Court in the preparation of cases and of the advocates general in their opinions; but, as Professors Kapteyn and VerLoren van Themaat well remark:[10]

> "This use of the comparative technique is not governed by a prior intent to find the greatest common denominator; rather is it governed by an intent to trace elements from which such legal principles and rules can be built up for the Community as will offer an adequate, fair, and fruitful solution for the questions with which the Court is confronted."

In this free-ranging enquiry the Court has established certain essential elements for Community liability: there must be damage, an illegal act on the part of the Community, and a causal link between the damage and the act complained of. A number of leading cases illustrate these elements.

In Cases 5, 7 and 13–24/66 *Kampffmeyer v. Commission* [1967] ECR 245, a group of cereal importers, Kampffmeyer and others, sued the Commission for damages in respect of its decision to authorise the German Government to take certain "safeguard measures" in the cereal market. Such measures could only be taken legally if there was a threat of "serious disturbances" in the market. In the earlier case of *Toepfer*,[11] (p. 148, above) the Court had held that this particular decision of the Commission must be annulled as the Commission had had no grounds to expect serious disturbances. Kampffmeyer and the other importers proved that they had been prejudiced by the illegal decision and claimed damages accordingly. The Court found there was liability in principle on the part of the Commission arising from what it categorised as a *faute de service*. But the Court deferred a decision on the amount of damages until the plaintiffs had exhausted any remedy they might have against the German Government in the German courts (this latter aspect of the case is returned to later).

As this case shows, although the second paragraph of Article 215 (now Article 288) EC refers simply to the Community making good any damage caused by its institutions or by its servants in the course of their duties, the practice of the Court appears to require a finding of fault on the part of the Community. The importation

---

[10] Introduction to the Law of the European Communities (1973), p. 94.
[11] Joined Cases 106 and 107/63 *Toepfer v. Commission* [1965] ECR 405.

of the concept of *faute* into the interpretation of the second paragraph of Article 215 (now Article 288) was no doubt influenced by the fact that the corresponding Article in the earlier ECSC Treaty (Article 40) specifically based liability upon fault. The Court has usually adopted the distinction known to French administrative law between a *faute de service* and a *faute personnelle*, that is a fault in the functioning of the system as distinct from a purely personal fault by the individual Community servant. A further distinction is then made in the French case-law between a purely personal fault (what an English lawyer might term "a frolic of his own" by the official) wholly unconnected with his duties and for which no liability attaches to the administration, and a personal fault which is nevertheless so linked with the public service that the service becomes vicariously liable as well as the official himself: this is the French doctrine of so-called *cumul*. The former concept of French law is wide enough to overlap with what an English lawyer would regard simply as maladministration, to be redressed, if at all, through the Parliamentary Commissioner for Administration: the more narrow English rules which curtail the scope of actions for damages against administrative authorities are therefore little guide to the French-inspired principles governing Community liability.

What constitutes a *faute de service* so as to impose liability on the Community was further examined in Case 4/69 *Lütticke v. Commission* [1971] ECR 325. There the Court held that under the general principles referred to in Article 215(2) (now Article 288(2)) the liability of the Community presupposed the combination of a number of conditions relating to (a) the reality of the damage, (b) the existence of a causal link between the injury relied upon and the behaviour of the institution complained of, and (c) the illegality of this behaviour. Lütticke complained that they were being required by the German Government to pay a tax on imports of powdered milk at too high a rate. After recourse to various remedies without success, they sued the Commission for damages under Article 215(2) on the ground that it had a duty to intervene with a Member State who (allegedly) was imposing a tax offending Community law; accordingly, the Commission had defaulted in its duty. On the facts, the Court held that the Commission had done all that could be expected of it in its extensive negotiations with the German Government: there had been no failure in its duty. Accordingly, the action was dismissed on the merits, no *faute de service* being established.

By contrast, a *faute de service* was established by the applicants in Cases 19, 20, 25, 30/69 *Richez-Parise v. Commission*.[12] The

---

[12] Cases 19, 20, 25, 30/69 *Richez-Parise v. Commission* [1970] ECR 325.

applicants were Community officials who, on the basis of incorrect information given by the Commission concerning their pensions, had resigned from the service and elected to take their pensions in a certain form; subsequently, the Commission discovered that their advice was misleading but did not immediately inform the applicants to this effect. The Court held that, while the initial information supplied did not constitute a wrongful act, the failure to correct it as soon as the Commission discovered their mistake was a *faute de service*.

The series of misfortunes which befell Stanley Adams provided the grounds for a successful action for damages against the Commission, based in this case on a breach of the duty of confidentiality which it owed him: Case 145/83 *Adams v. Commission*.[13] Adams was employed by the pharmaceutical company Hoffmann-La Roche in Switzerland and supplied the Commission with information which led to the company being fined in competition proceedings for breaches of Article 86 (now Article 82) EC. Due to the carelessness of the Commission, the company identified Adams as the informant. He had now left the company and set up his own business in Italy. On a later visit to Switzerland he was arrested for economic espionage, an offence under the Swiss Penal Code, and held in solitary confinement. His wife was interrogated by the Swiss Police and committed suicide. He was released on bail and returned to Italy. In his absence he was convicted under Swiss law and given a one year's suspended prison sentence. This conviction destroyed his creditworthiness so that his business failed. Not surprisingly, the Court held the Commission liable in damages both for the breach of confidentiality and for failing to warn Adams of the risk of prosecution in Switzerland, a threat of such prosecution having been made by the company's lawyer on a visit to the Commission. But if the Commission had been at fault, so also, in the Court's view, had Adams, who had been careless of his own interests: the agreed damages had therefore to be reduced by half. In the event, for this public-spirited act, Adams received £200,000 as compensation, with a further £200,000 as costs.[14]

## LIABILITY ARISING FROM LEGISLATION

Liability under the terms of Article 215(2) (now Article 288(2)) EC can extend to liability in respect of legislation – what has been

---

[13] Case 145/83 *Adams v. Commission* [1985] ECR 3539; [1986] 1 C.M.L.R. 506.
[14] See March Hunnings (1987) 24 C.M.L.Rev. 65. For his own, inevitably partial, account of his tribulations see Stanley Adams *Roche v. Adams*.

referred to in the context of Community law as "normative injustice." Normative is here used to describe an act such as a regulation, laying down a rule, as opposed to an individual decision. The notion that administrative rule-making may give rise to an action for damages is a novelty in English law, but Lord Wilberforce did canvass the possible need for such a remedy in *Hoffmann-La Roche & Co. v. Secretary of State for Trade and Industry.*[15] Case 5/71 the *Zuckerfabrik Schöppenstedt* case[16] explored the nature of this normative injustice in Community law. It arises where a Community institution (in this case the Council) has taken a measure of a legislative or normative character, such as a regulation, which measure is subsequently proved to be in breach of the Treaties or other provisions of Community law. But the Court requires, as it stated in the case, "a sufficiently flagrant breach of a superior rule of law protecting individuals." This stringent test was held not to be satisfied in this case. It is enough however that the provision allegedly violated was for the protection of individuals generally rather than for the protection of the particular plaintiffs: there is no equivalent under Article 215 (now Article 288) of the requirement of "direct and individual concern" under Article 173 (now Article 230). At least the balance of cases appears so to decide.[17]

The Schöppenstedt formula cited above was applied by the Court in Joined Cases 83, 94/76, 4, 15, 40/77 *Bayerische HNL v. Council and Commission*[18] (part of a series of *Skimmed-Milk Powder* cases).

Over-production of milk in the Community had led to the creation of a skimmed-milk powder "mountain," to reduce which the Council made a regulation requiring animal feed producers to buy skimmed-milk powder from the intervention agencies; the powder would be mixed with the feed to supply protein in place of soya. But as the powder was more expensive than soya, livestock farmers had to pay more for their animal feed.

The farmers brought various actions to challenge the legality of the Council regulation. One group of actions was brought in the national courts, and the question of the validity of the regulation was referred to the Court of Justice under Article 177 (now Article

---

[15] [1975] A.C. 295 (H.L.) at 359.

[16] Case 5/71 *Zuckerfabrik Schöppenstedt v. Council* [1971] ECR 975.

[17] Compare Joined Cases 9 and 12/60 *Vloeberghs v. High Authority* [1961] ECR 195 (see p. 185 below); Case 9/56 *Meroni v. High Authority* [1958] ECR 133 (see p. 158 above); Joined Cases 5, 7 and 13 to 24/66 *Kampffmeyer v. Commission* [1967] ECR 245 (see p. 175 above); Case 5/71 *Schöppenstedt* (note 16 above) and Cases 9 and 11/71 *Compagnie d'Approvisionnement v. Commission* [1972] ECR 391 (see p. 184 below).

[18] [1978] ECR 1209; [1977] 1 C.M.L.R. 566.

234) EC.[19] Another group was actions for damages brought directly before the Court of Justice under the second paragraph of Article 215 (now Article 288) EC: the *HNL* case was in this category.

Judgment was given first in the cases under Article 177 (now Article 234). The Court ruled the regulation to be invalid as offending the principle of proportionality and as producing discrimination between the different agricultural sectors contrary to Article 40(3) (now Article 34) EC.

In the action by HNL under Article 215(2) (now Article 288(2)) the Court had no difficulty in finding that there had been an infringement of a superior rule of law: the previous ruling under Article 177 (now Article 234) EC had established that the regulation infringed the principles both of proportionality and non-discrimination. The principles were also intended for the protection of individuals. But had there been a sufficiently flagrant breach to justify an award of damages? In the circumstances, the Court held that there had not: where the Community institution was charged, as here, with wide discretionary power to legislate on matters involving choices of economic policy, it would not be liable unless it had manifestly and gravely disregarded the limits on the exercise of its powers. In the Court's view the Council had not shown such disregard, nor was the effect of the invalid regulation upon HNL sufficiently serious.

Subsequent cases falling on either side of the line are exemplified by the so-called *Quellmehl*, *Gritz* and *Isoglucose* cases, all involving Council regulations ruled invalid as discriminatory. In the *Quellmehl* and *Gritz* cases the Court found the Council's violation sufficiently flagrant and awarded damages under the second paragraph of Article 215 (now Article 288) EC[20]; on the other hand, this test was held not to be satisfied in the *Isoglucose* cases,[21] in which a gloss appeared to be added to the Schöppenstedt formula, the Court stating that liability thereunder could only arise "in exceptional cases where the institution concerned has manifestly

---

[19] *e.g.* Case 114/76 *Bergmann v. Grows-Farm* [1977] ECR 1211; [1979] 2 C.M.L.R. 83; Case 116/76 *Granaria v. Hoofdproduktschap voor Akkerbouwprodukten* [1977] ECR 1247; [1979] 2 C.M.L.R. 83.

[20] Cases 64, 113/76, 167, 239/78, 27, 28, 45/79 *Dumortier v. Council* [1979] ECR 3091; Case 238/78, *Ireks-Arkady v. Council and Commission* [1979] ECR 2955; Cases 241, 242, 245-250/78 *DGV v. Council and Commission* [1979] ECR 3017; Cases 261, 262/78 *Interquell Starke Chiminie v. Council and Commission* [1979] ECR 3045. Other Successful actions were brought in case C–152/88 *Sofrimport v. Commission* [1990] ECR I–2477 and Cases C–104/89 and C–37/90 *Mulder and Others v. Minister van Landbouw en Visserij* [1992] ECR I–3061. For details of the latter case and its consequences see below.

[21] Cases 116, 124/77 *Amylum and Tunnel Refineries* [1979] ECR 3497; [1982] 2 C.M.L.R. 590; Case 143/77 *KSH v. Council and Commission* [1979] ECR 3583; [1982] 2 C.M.L.R. 590.

and gravely disregarded the limits on the exercise of its powers"; and grave meant "conduct verging on the arbitrary."

A striking example of liability arising from Community legislation is provided by the lengthy saga of the "SLOM" cases.[22]

As part of the Community's continuing effort to reduce over-production of dairy products a regulation was adopted by the Council introducing a system of premiums (*sic*) for the non-marketing of milk and milk products and for the conversion of dairy herds.[23]

Mulder and other dairy farmers in the Netherlands and Germany gave undertakings pursuant to that regulation not to deliver milk or dairy products from their farms for a five year period including 1983. Subsequently that year was adopted by the Netherlands and Germany as the "reference year" for the purposes of allocating milk production quotas.

Those quotas were used for calculating the additional levy on milk payable on amounts produced in excess of the quota. Since Mulder and the other farmers who had accepted a "SLOM" premium had produced no milk in the reference year, their production quotas were fixed at nil by the national intervention agencies.

Mulder challenged that decision before a Dutch court which referred the matter to the Court of Justice for a preliminary ruling. In its judgment[24] the Court declared the rules upon which that decision had been based invalid on the ground that they were in breach of the principle of the protection of legitimate expectations in so far as they did not provide for the allocation of such a quota.

Following that judgment the regulation was amended so as to enable milk producers who had not delivered any milk during the reference year, because of a non-marketing undertaking, to be awarded a special reference quantity of 60 per cent. of the quantity of milk delivered during the year prior to that in which the undertaking was given. That 60 per cent. rule was in turn declared invalid by the Court for being in breach of the principle of legitimate expectations.[25]

Mulder and three other affected farmers then brought claims for damages under Article 178 (now Article 235) EC and the second paragraph of Article 215 (now Article 288) EC for compensation

---

[22] This rather unpleasant acronym is derived from the Dutch "Rageling voor *sl*achting en *om*shakeling" (Regulations on slaughter and removal from production of dairy cows). Conveniently but misleadingly it also stands for "supplementary *l*evy on *m*ilk".

[23] [1977] O.J. L131/1.

[24] Case C–120/86 *Mulder v. Minister van Landbouw en Visserij* [1988] ECR 2321; [1989] 2 C.M.L.R. 1.

[25] Case C–189/89 *Spagl v. Hauptzollamt Rosenheim* [1990] ECR I–4539.

for the damage they had suffered as a result of the application to them of those regulations. In a judgment of May 19, 1992[26] the Court ordered the Community institutions to make good the damage sustained by the applicants as a result of the application of the first regulation. However, although the 60 per cent. rule had itself been declared invalid the Court held that, in fixing that proportion, the Council had made an economic policy choice with regard to the means by which it chose to implement the earlier judgments and in doing so, it had taken account of a higher public interest, without gravely and manifestly disregarding the limits of its discretionary power in the area concerned.

Rather than fixing the amount of damages payable the Court ordered the parties to inform it within 12 months from the date of the judgment of the amount of damages payable, arrived at by agreement, or in the absence of agreement that they should submit to the Court their own assessments, with supporting figures, by the same deadline.

Subsequently some 400 other farmers have submitted similar claims for compensation to the Court of Justice. As a result of the Decision of the Member States of June 8, 1993[27] all those claims as well as those introduced in the future, with effect from August 1, 1993, fell to be decided by the Court of First Instance.

## LIMITATION PERIOD

As well as being more generous in matters of locus standi, actions under Article 215 (now 288) EC (or its equivalent in the other Treaties) are subject to a limitation period of five years (Article 43 of the Statute of the Court). This may be compared with the very short period of two months allowed for actions to annul under Article 173 (now Article 230) EC. Article 43 of the Statute makes the period of five years run from the occurrence of the event giving rise to the alleged liability; the period is interrupted if an application for relief is made to the Community institution concerned, in which case, if the institution has not defined its position (for example, by accepting liability) the applicant will have two further months in which to commence proceedings.[28]

Case 51/81, *De Franceschi SpA Monfalcone v. Council and Commission*[29] concerned these provisions. The applicant suffered

---

[26] Joined Cases C–104/89 and C–37/90 *Mulder and Others v. Council and Commission* [1992] ECR I–3061.

[27] O.J. L144/21, see p. 80 above.

[28] See Article 175 (now Article 232), p. 162, above.

[29] Case 51/81 *De Franceschi S.p.A. Monfalcone v. Council and Commission* [1982] ECR 117.

loss through the operation of a Council regulation, published on March 4, 1975 and abolishing certain refunds, which was held invalid by the Court on October 19, 1977 in Joined Cases 124/76 and 20/77. The present action was commenced on March 9, 1981. The defendants argued that proceedings were time-barred, the five-years limitation period having begun to run on March 4, 1975. The Court, however, agreed with the applicant that the period only began to run from the moment when the damage became known: the injurious effects of the regulation were produced only with effect from October 19, 1977, on which date the measure was adjudged unlawful. Similarly, in Case 145/83 *Adams v. Commission* (above, p. 177), the limitation period did not begin to run until the injured party became aware of the event giving rise to his claim, namely the visit of the company's lawyer to the Commission; he only learnt of this visit when it was disclosed in the Commission's pleadings.

## DISTINCTIVE NATURE OF THE REMEDY

The distinctive nature of the remedy under Article 215 (now 288) EC was blurred in the earlier decision of Case 25/62 *Plaumann v. Commission*.[30] There the Court pronounced that an administrative act which had not been annulled could not amount to a wrong founding liability in damages. This view has been rejected in several more recent cases: the Court now acknowledges that the two Articles have different objectives; Article 173 (now Article 230) seeking to annul a particular act *erga omnes*; Article 215 (now Article 288) providing compensation to the individual who has sustained damage through the faulty exercise of its functions by a Community institution. Thus, in *Zuckerfabrik Schöppenstedt* the plaintiffs sought damages for the loss they had suffered in consequence of a regulation of the Council fixing sugar prices. The Court was prepared to entertain the claim under Article 215 (now 288) EC without action also being brought under Article 173 (now 230) EC, observing (at p. 984) that "in the present case, the non-contractual liability of the Community presupposes at the very least the unlawful nature of the act alleged to be the cause of the damage."

Subsequently, in Case 43/72 *Merkur*,[31] the Court made explicit its readiness to rule on the illegality of an act in an action brought for damages. Thus, the two-months limitation period in Article

---

[30] Case 25/62 *Plaumann v. Commission* [1963] ECR 95; [1964] C.M.L.R. 29.
[31] Case 43/72 *Merkur v. Commission* [1973] ECR 1055.

173 (now Article 230) EC may be circumvented either by way of an action under the second paragraph of Article 215 (now Article 288) (subject to a five-years limitation period), or by resort to the plea of illegality under Article 184 (now Article 241), or by a reference for a preliminary ruling as to validity made by a national court under Article 177 (now Article 234) EC (neither Article 184 (now Article 241) nor Article 177 (now Article 234) being subject to any period of limitation).

Nevertheless, in several staff cases, claims for damages have been rejected on the ground that the plaintiffs could, by timely proceedings, have sought annulment of the allegedly illegal regulations; having failed to do so, they could not then complain of the damage caused them by such illegality.[32] The cases seem to illustrate a wider principle: the Court will not usually entertain a claim for damages by a plaintiff who could have sought annulment of the normative act in issue – *vigilantibus non dormientibus iura subveniunt.*

## DAMAGE, CAUSATION AND LIABILITY WITHOUT FAULT

The Court has avoided laying down firm principles as to the categories of damage which may be claimed or on what basis the actual damages will be calculated. Thus, it has admitted claims for such financial damage as loss of profit or loss due to currency fluctuations[33]; and in staff cases, damages may be claimed for anxiety and injured feelings by Community employees wrongfully dismissed or unfairly treated.[34]

Actual damage must be proved, or at least imminent damage which is foreseeable with sufficient certainty.[35] A mere expectation or likelihood of damage in the future will not suffice. Nor must the damage be too remote: the Court speaks of the need for there to be a causal link between the damage and the act complained of.[36]

This causal link was present in Case 74/74 *CNTA v. Commission,*[37] where an exporter relied, as he claimed that he was entitled to do, on the fact that a payment from Community resources to offset the effects of the devaluation of the dollar would not be

---

[32] Case 4/67 *Müller-Collignon v. Commission* [1967] ECR 365; Joined Cases 15-33, etc.,/73 *Schots-Kortner and Others v. Council, Commission and Parliament* [1974] ECR 177.
[33] See Cases 5, 7 and 13-24/66, *Kampffmeyer*, above, Case 74/74 *CNTA*, below.
[34] e.g. Case 7/56, 3–7/57 *Algera v. Common Assembly* [1957 and 1958] ECR 39.
[35] Cases 56–60/74 *Kampffmeyer* [1976] ECR 711.
[36] Case 4/69 *Lütticke*, above.
[37] [1975] ECR 533; [1977] 1 C.M.L.R. 171.

discontinued without due notice and, in such reliance, entered into certain binding contracts; the Commission suddenly suppressed the payments, thereby causing the exporter to sustain a quantifiable loss. The Court held him entitled to recover: in the absence of an overriding public interest, the Commission could not abolish the right to these payments without notice but must either provide transitional measures to cushion the effects of suppression or render itself liable in damages. In later proceedings, however, he failed to establish any damage.

Damage may be adjudged to be non-existent where the plaintiff is able to pass on the loss sustained to his customers: the Court so held in the *Quellmehl* and *Gritz* cases.[38] Lord Mackenzie Stuart, speaking extra-judicially, has expressed the view that in the Court's more recent decisions "there can be detected a change of emphasis from the culpability of the administration to the protection of the legitimate interests of the administered," and he raises the question whether Community liability can arise without fault and without illegality. "Can a normative act competently made under the powers contained in the Treaties and justifiable in the Community interest form the basis of a claim for damages if injury has been sustained as its consequence?"[39] Two cases touch on this important question.

In Cases 9 and 11/71 *Compagnie d'Approvisionnement v. Commission*,[40] certain French importers alleged not only fault on the part of the Commission in that it had acted illegally in fixing certain payments at too low a level, but also that, even in the absence of any illegality on its part, the Commission was liable to them in damages as they had suffered "abnormal and special loss" in comparison with Dutch and German importers. The Court rejected their argument on the ground that the measures in question had been taken in the general economic interest to reduce the consequence of devaluation for the whole body of French importers. Nevertheless, Advocate General Dutheillet de Lamothe left open the possibility that the principle of "equality in the face of public burdens," to which, in effect, the plaintiffs were appealing, might be applied in Community law, as it undoubtedly has in French administrative law, to cover an appropriate case (which this was not).

It should be pointed out, however, that if the French analogy were adopted, breach of the principle would constitute the violation of a general principle of law and, as such, amount in French eyes to an illegality. The *Compagnie d'Approvisionnement* case

---

[38] See above n. 20, but for criticism of this view, see Rudden and Bishop (1981) 6 E.L.Rev. 243.

[39] Maccabaean Lecture in Jurisprudence 1975, 20.

[40] [1972] ECR 391; [1973] C.M.L.R. 529.

therefore does not resolve the problem whether the Community can be liable without fault and without illegality.

No less ambiguous in this respect is Case 169/73 *Compagnie Continentale France v. Council*.[41] The applicants were exporters of wheat who, in September 1972, had contracted to sell wheat to British customers for delivery in early 1973. They did so in the expectation of being entitled to certain compensatory payments for which the Treaty of Accession made provision. The amount of these payments had been fixed in advance by a draft regulation approved by the Council in July 1972; the regulation would be formally adopted after the Treaty of Accession came into force. This unusual step, as the Council explained, was taken so that dealers in the products covered by the proposed regulation should know with certainty what payments to expect from the beginning of 1973. However, the actual regulation which was adopted in January 1973 contained a modification permitted by the Treaty but having the effect of substantially reducing the value of the compensatory payments due to the applicants, a reduction made all the more substantial by the general rise in the price of wheat on the world market.

The advocate general advised the Court that, in his view, the Council's resolution of July 1972 which approved the regulation amounted to a promise to all interested parties that the text would be applied. It therefore had the consequence in law of imposing liability on the Community, because "the protection of confidence is a principle recognised in the Community legal system."

The Court rejected the applicants' claim for want of the necessary causal link between the acts of the Community and the damage suffered. It differed from the advocate general by holding that Community liability might have arisen, not because of reliance upon the Council's promise, but rather because of the Council's failure to give warning that it must act in accordance with the Treaty of Accession and that the application of the Treaty depended upon prevailing world prices for wheat. On either view, liability would have been based upon fault, that is, a *faute de service*.

In the Coal and Steel Treaty, Article 34 provides specifically that, where a decision or recommendation of the High Authority is annulled in circumstances involving a *faute de service* on the part of the Community, undertakings which have suffered direct and special harm in consequence have the right to damages. As the Article is not limited to individual decisions, liability extends to normative injustice, provided that the legislative measure has been annulled. This has been made clear in Case T–120/89 *Stahlwerke*

---

[41] [1975] ECR 117; [1975] 1 C.M.L.R. 578.

*Peine-Salzgitter v. Commission* by the Court of First Instance whose judgment has been upheld on appeal.[42]

The undertakings referred to in Article 34 ECSC are the limited category of coal and steel producers defined in Article 80 ECSC. In Case 9, 12/60 *Vloeberghs v. High Authority*,[43] the applicant was a Belgium firm of coal distributors. It claimed damages from the High Authority on the ground that the latter had refused to bring an enforcement action against France under Article 88 ECSC, although the French Government had banned Vloeberghs from bringing into France coal which it had imported into Belgium from outside the Community, thereby causing it loss. The Court rejected the High Authority's argument that Article 34 was an exhaustive statement of the right to damages in these circumstances, and that Vloeberghs, as a distributor, could sue neither under that Article nor under Article 40. The Court allowed the action under Article 40, although it rejected as inadmissible the parallel action brought by Vloeberghs under Article 35 for the High Authority's failure to act (Article 35 being only available to coal and steel *producers*).

## ACTS OF COMMUNITY SERVANTS

Often the wrongful or illegal act of a Community institution is anonymous in that it cannot be ascribed to any particular civil servant of the Communities. Sometimes, however, the fault can be laid at the door of an individual servant. In this event, the second paragraph of Article 215 (now Article 288) EC, like Article 40 ECSC, limits the non-contractual liability of the Community to acts of servants in the performance of their duties. For such acts the party injured can claim damages against the Communities in the Court of Justice. If he attempted to sue the civil servant in the servant's personal capacity in the appropriate national court, he could expect to be met by a plea of immunity. For the Treaties confer upon Community servants immunity from legal proceedings "in respect of acts performed by them in their official capacity." Such official acts, however, may give rise to internal disciplinary action, which in turn may be challenged by the civil servant before the Court of First Instance (or, previously, the Court of Justice under Article 179 (now Article 236) EC). Only where the civil servant was acting completely outside the scope of his duties ("on a frolic of his own," as English law might express it), would he lose his immunity, and in such a case only he and not the Communities could be sued.

---

[42] Case C–220/91–P *Commission v. Stahlwerke Peine-Salzgitter*, judgment of May 18, 1993, [1993] ECR I–2393.
[43] [1961] ECR 197.

The exact nature of the Communities' vicarious liability (as an English lawyer would regard it) for the acts of civil servants depends upon the interpretation to be given to the phrase "in the performance of their duties."

In the two *Sayag* cases[44] the Court had to consider this question when Sayag, an engineer employed by Euratom, was driving in his private car to a destination in Belgium to visit an atomic plant in connection with his work. He caused an accident on the way and was the subject of both criminal and civil proceedings in the Belgian courts. The Belgian Court of Cassation referred to the Court of Justice the question of possible immunity and of the meaning of the phrase "in the performance of their duties." The Court ruled that the use of a private car by a Community servant could only be considered as constituting the performance of his duties in the case of *force majeure* or exceptional circumstances of such compelling nature that the Community could not otherwise perform its functions. In the event, therefore, the Belgian courts had jurisdiction. It would have been otherwise, it seems, if a serious emergency at the atomic plant had required the immediate presence of the engineer at a time when neither official transport nor public transport was available.

The *Sayag* cases indicate a conservative attitude on the part of the Court of Justice. The vicarious liability of the Communities should not be extended so as to make the Community purse an insurance fund for the victims of every wrongful act of a Community servant. In the event, as Josephine Steiner points out, the Court adopted a slightly narrower view of vicarious liability than that applied in English law.[45]

The present state of the law, however, is open to several criticisms. In the first place, there is the risk of the civil servant invoking immunity for acts which are not committed in the performance of his duties. This risk is partly removed by the power of the Community institution which employs him to waive the immunity. If the immunity is not waived, then the Community would be impliedly admitting the official nature of the act in question. This would invite an action against it. But in such an action the Court of Justice might hold that the act fell outside the performance of the servant's duties. The aggrieved plaintiff would be left without further remedy, unless the immunity was at this stage withdrawn, which would mean the plaintiff having to recommence an action in the national court against the civil servant personally.

A second criticism is that the Community might improperly waive immunity in order to leave the civil servant, rather than

---

[44] Case 5/68 *Sayag v. Leduc* [1968] ECR 395; [1969] C.M.L.R. 12 and Case 9/69 *Sayag v. Leduc* [1969] ECR 329.

[45] J. Steiner, *Textbook on EEC Law* (3rd ed., 1992), p. 347.

itself, exposed to the action for damages. In the first *Sayag* case (above) the Court made clear that the mere waiver of immunity could not affect any possible liability on the part of the Community itself. Moreover, the civil servant would be able to seek judicial review of the waiver in proceedings before the Court of First Instance.

A third criticism arises from the lack of uniformity of the principles governing non-contractual liability in the laws of the Member States. Thus, assuming immunity has been properly waived, a plaintiff who sued the civil servant in State A might succeed in his suit, whereas in State B he might fail because of a difference, for example, in the principles of limitation of actions or remoteness of damage or contributory negligence.

## CONCURRENT FAULT ON PART OF MEMBER STATES

The nature of the European Communities requires that Member States may be called upon to collaborate with Community institutions in certain tasks. Indeed, Article 5 (now 10) EC requires them to "facilitate the achievement of the Community's task." In the result, the execution of Community law may be entrusted to the Member States. Without this help from national administrations the relatively small Community civil service would be overwhelmed by its work-load. Moreover, members of the public may feel themselves better served by the more accessible, more familiar officials of their own governments.

In carrying out a function on behalf of the Communities, a Member State (that is, its government, officials or civil servants) may itself commit a wrongful or illegal act. Occasionally this may be deliberate; more often it will be a case of simple error – for example, a mistaken application of Community law.

Does then the principle of vicarious liability apply where a Member State is cast in the role of an agent, so as to attach liability to the Communities? An English lawyer might well see the State's relationship as analogous to that of an independent contractor, since the Communities exercise no real control over the Member States even when they perform Community functions; in which case, vicarious liability could not arise, although State and Communities might be joint tortfeasors. On such questions, the Treaties are silent. The problem, however, has arisen before the Court of Justice on several occasions. Thus, in a typical case, the plaintiff complains that his own government, acting on behalf of the Communities, is refusing to pay him money allegedly due under Community law, but he elects to bring his suit against the Communities in the Court of Justice rather than to sue his own government in the national court, prompted perhaps by the likelihood of a more speedy decision from Luxembourg.

Faced with this kind of problem the Court has proceeded by way of the following analysis. First, is there joint liability on the part both of the Community and the Member State? If there is, then, secondly, is the Member State to be considered primarily liable so that it would be reasonable for it rather than the Communities to pay compensation? If so, then, thirdly, the plaintiff must pursue his remedy in the national courts, before the Court of Justice can further entertain his claim. If, of course, he succeeds in his national court, the Member State may be entitled to recoup itself, wholly or in part, against the Communities in separate proceedings before the Court.

Thus, in *Kampffmeyer v. Commission*,[46] as we have seen, the Court found liability established against the Community on account of the Commission's decision, held illegal, authorising the German Government to take safeguard measures. But the Court refused to settle the amount of damages until the plaintiffs had completed proceedings against their government in the German courts: "final judgment cannot be given before the applicants have produced the decision of the national court."

CRITIQUE

The principle that normally the plaintiff should first pursue his remedy in the national courts has been upheld by the Court in a series of cases beginning with Case 96/71, *Haegeman v. Commission*.[47] Behind the very complicated facts of the three later cases was the common basic feature that, as the plaintiffs alleged, their national government was refusing them certain payments to which they believed themselves entitled under Community regulations (relating in the instant cases to cereals, cattle and meat, and colza seeds, respectively). In each case the Court decided there was a concurrent remedy in the national courts which had therefore to be pursued first before any action would be admissible against the Community.

This approach by the Court is open to criticism. In the first place, as Professor Hartley has pointed out,[48] the Court's own

---

[46] Cases 5, 7 and 13–24/66 *Kampffmeyer v. Commission* [1967] ECR 245 (above, p. 161).

[47] [1972] ECR 1005, [1973] C.M.L.R. 365. More recent cases have been Case 99/74 *Societe des Grands Moulins des Antilles v. Commission* [1975] ECR 1531; Case 46/75 *Importazione Bestiame Carni v. Commission* [1976] ECR 65, and Cases 67–85/75 *Lesieur Cotelle S.A. v. Commission* [1976] ECR 391; [1976] 2 C.M.L.R. 185.

[48] T. Hartley in [1976] 1 E.L.Rev. 299–304, 396–399.

jurisdiction is made to turn on the presence or absence of a remedy under national law, and this is not a question on which the Court can give an authoritative ruling, should the parties disagree on the point. Presumably, if the Court did take the view that a remedy existed in the national court, and then, in subsequent proceedings, the national court decided otherwise, the matter would have to come back to the Court at Luxembourg – a process both dilatory and expensive. Contrariwise, where it is established there is no remedy in the national courts, the plaintiff may bring his claim before the Court.[49]

A second criticism arises from the considerable variations in the scope of the remedy which the national laws provide to recover damages against public authorities. Differences exist on such matters as the choice of remedy,[50] the heads of damages, the modes of assessing these, the periods of limitation, and the recovery of money paid under a mistake of law. Because of such differences an applicant in one Member State might well fare better than one in another, although both applicants were complaining, in effect, of the same fault on the part of the Community. Such lack of uniformity within the Community seems intolerable.

Again, the remedy in the Court of Justice may be more generous than that available in the national court, as, for instance, in Case 96/71 *Haegeman* (see above), where Belgian law did not permit recovery of loss of profit although this was recoverable under Community law (as held by the Court of Justice): hence the applicant was told by the Court that he could come back to the Court to obtain compensation under this head after he had sued in the Belgian court for the refund which he was claiming from the Belgian authorities (in respect of customs duties paid on imported Greek wine). This kind of circuity of actions seems also quite intolerable.

A procedure so dilatory and circuitous is hard to justify. A partial justification for it may be found in the fact that, if the Community is sued, rather than the Member State, and is then adjudged liable for the whole damages, no provision exists in the Treaties whereby the Community may recoup itself against the Member State, even though the latter bears joint liability for the plaintiff's loss. Professor Schermers suggests however that such a right of action might be deduced from the general principles referred to in the second paragraph of Article 215 (now Article 288) EC.[51]

---

[49] Cases 197–200, 243, 245, 247/80 *Ludwigshafener Walzmuhle Erling v. Council and Commission* [1981] ECR 3211.
[50] Especially in English law since the House of Lords, in *O'Reilly v. Mackman* [1983] 2 A.C. 237 resurrected the importance of the plaintiff's "form of action."
[51] Henry G. Schermers in *Legal Issues of European Integration* (1975/1), p. 113.

A subsequent case suggests that the Court may be ready to relax its restrictive approach of requiring the prior exhaustion of the national remedy, at least where the action under Article 215(2) (now Article 288(2)) is for damages in tort rather than a claim in quasi-contract for money (such as levies) unlawfully exacted (as is alleged) by the national authorities on behalf of the Community. Thus, in Case 126/76 *Dietz v. Commission*[52]: the applicant was a German exporter who contracted to export certain goods from Germany to Italy. After the contract was made, certain charges were introduced by the Community on the imported goods, which resulted in Dietz making an unexpected loss on the transaction. He sued the Commission under the second paragraph of Article 215 (now Article 288) for his actual loss on the ground that the sudden imposition of the charges was a violation of the principle of the protection of legitimate expectations. The Commission argued that the claim was inadmissible since Dietz should first be required to proceed in his national court against the national authority imposing the charges. In fact such an action by Dietz was pending. But the Court of Justice held the action before it to be admissible; for the alleged loss stemmed from the act of the Community itself rather than from the measures adopted by the national authorities in applying Community law. In the event, however, the action failed on the merits.

Again, in Case 175/84 *Krohn v. Commission*,[53] Krohn applied to the German Intervention Agency for an import licence (for manioc from Thailand) but this was refused by the Agency acting on mandatory instructions from the Commission. When Krohn sued the Commission for damages under the second paragraph of Article 215 (now Article 288) EC, the Court rejected the argument of the Commission that Krohn should first sue the Agency, holding that the Commission was responsible, by its instructions, for the Agency's alleged unlawful conduct. Thus, the admissibility of the action before the Court was not dependent upon the prior exhaustion of the national remedies; nor was the action under the second paragraph of Article 215 (now Article 288) barred by the fact that Krohn had not challenged the instructions by proceedings to annul under the second paragraph of Article 173 (now Article 230).

Whether the Court can work out solutions to these (and other) problems simply by way of its case-law – hanging its decisions on the peg of "general principles" provided by the second paragraph of Article 215 (now Article 288) EC – is an intriguing question.

---

[52] Case 126/76 *Dietz v. Commission* [1977] ECR 2431; [1978] 2 C.M.L.R. 608.
[53] Case 175/84 *Krohn v. Commission* [1986] ECR 753; [1987] ECR 97; [1987] 1 C.M.L.R. 745.

The drastic alternative would be a revision of the Treaties so as to confer jurisdiction upon the Court of Justice in respect of actions against Member States for non-contractual liability arising out of the administration of Community law by national authorities. The Communities and the Member States could then be sued jointly in the one Community Court, which could allocate liability between them as it thought fit. If the Communities alone were sued (and the plaintiff might often prefer to proceed thus) then the Communities would be able to join the Member State as a party and claim a contribution or even a complete indemnity from it, as appropriate.

## METHODS TO CHALLENGE THE VALIDITY OF A REGULATION

In the light of the discussion in this and the preceding chapter, it may be helpful to gather together, in summary form, the various methods by which, directly or indirectly, the validity of a Community regulation may be called in question before the Court (or, where appropriate, the Court of First Instance) at the suit of the individual. These are:

(a) Action to annul the regulation as a disguised decision (Article 173 (now Article 230) EC);

(b) Action for damages for "normative injustice" where the regulation constitutes a sufficiently flagrant breach of a superior rule of law protecting individuals (the second paragraph of Article 215 (now Article 288) EC);

(c) Plea of illegality in respect of the regulation (Article 184 (now Article 241) EC);

(d) Reference from a national court or tribunal for a preliminary ruling on the validity of the regulation (Article 177 (now Article 234) EC: see Chapter 10, below).

The consequences of the challenge to the validity of the regulation, even if it be successful, will vary according to which method is adopted. Thus, a successful action under Article 173 (now Article 230) EC ((a), above) will result in the quashing of the regulation: it is annulled *erga omnes* and (unless the Court rules otherwise) retrospectively. The award of damages under the second paragraph of Article 215 (now Article 288) EC necessarily imports a decision on the invalidity of the regulation in issue: although not formally annulled by the Court, *erga omnes*, the regulation will, in practice, cease prospectively to be applied until such time as it is revoked or replaced by its authors. As we shall see (in Chapter 10 below, p. 234), the Court has treated a ruling of invalidity under Article 177 ((d), above) as rendering the regulation void *erga omnes*; but a successful plea of illegality under Article 184 ((c), above) merely declares the regulation inapplicable in the present case.

# Chapter Nine

# Staff Cases

## INTRODUCTION

"Staff cases," *i.e.* actions by employees of the Community institutions who have complaints concerning their employment, are usually omitted from general works on Community law as being too specialised a topic. Dealing with such matters as recruitment procedures, pensions, allowances, promotions and disciplinary measures, they may seem of limited interest and perhaps even unworthy of the august attention of the Court.[1] Yet, although transferred since 1989 to the Court of First Instance, with appeals to the Court of Justice on points of law, they have constituted, as we shall see, an important aspect of the Courts' jurisdiction and continue to do so both quantitatively and jurisprudentially.

Staff cases also have a special human interest and importance, since they are virtually the only cases where a private individual (as distinct from a legal person) goes directly to the Court. In all other cases, the only access of the individual to the Court in practice is the indirect route by way of a reference for a preliminary ruling from a national court as described in the next chapter.[2]

The fact that the Court should have been given jurisdiction in such cases is once again a reflection of the influence of French administrative law, since the French *Conseil d'Etat* has a similar

---

[1] In this Chapter "the Court" refers to the institution as a whole since both the Court of Justice and the Court of First Instance have a specific role in this context. It should of course be remembered that prior to 1990, all staff cases were decided by the Court of Justice sitting at first and last instance.

[2] National courts have occasionally been required to refer cases involving Community employees to the Court of Justice for a preliminary ruling: see for example Case 44/84 *Hurd v. Jones* [1986] ECR 29; [1986] 2 C.M.L.R. 1; (1986) 23 C.M.L.Rev. 895 (note, Brown) on the taxation of part of the salary of a teacher at the European School, and Case C–37/89 *Weiser v. Caisse Nationale des Barreaux Francais* [1990] ECR I–2395 on the transfer of pension rights from a private scheme to the Community.

jurisdiction in respect of the higher ranks of the French civil service. The British tradition, by contrast, has been to deny civil servants access to the courts and to favour non-judicial arbitration, through Whitley Councils, of staff disputes over pay, promotion and conditions of service, although a civil servant may now sue for wrongful dismissal.

However international organisations have generally adopted the French conception of the status and conditions of service of public servants being regulated by detailed statutory provisions and subject to judicial control; thus, within the United Nations an Administrative Tribunal was set up in 1949 for the purpose of hearing staff disputes, and the Administrative Tribunal of the International Labour Organisation, set up in 1946, has jurisdiction not only over the International Labour Office but also over various specialised agencies of the United Nations[3] and other international organisations. In yet other organisations, special internal tribunals have been established.

## THE COURT'S JURISDICTION

Within the European Community it was appropriate, in accordance with the principle of unity of jurisdiction, that the Court (rather than a special tribunal, or still less, the national courts of the various Member States in which officials carried out their duties) should be the forum for staff disputes. Accordingly, Article 179 (now Article 236) EC gives the Court jurisdiction in any dispute between the Community and its servants within the limits and under the conditions laid down in the Staff Regulations or the Conditions of Employment. Thus the staff of the Community institutions, including for this purpose not only the five "institutions" so described in Article 4 (now Article 7) EC[4] but also the Economic and Social Committee and the European Investment Bank,[5] can bring their complaints against their employing institutions before the Court.

---

[3] Including the World Health Organisation, the Food and Agriculture Organisation and UNESCO.

[4] As amended by Art. G(6) of the Maastricht Treaty.

[5] In Case 110/75 *Mills v. European Investment Bank* [1976] ECR 955 the Court held that by using the words "any dispute between the Community and its servants," Article 179 EEC was not restricted exclusively to the institutions of the Community but also included the Bank as a Community body established and with legal personality conferred by the Treaty. The Court therefore had jurisdiction under that Article in any dispute between the Bank and its servants. No doubt the same principle applies to servants of the newly created European Central Bank.

Contrary to the popular myth of a vast bureaucracy the staff of the Community institutions is very small, compared with a national civil service. Thus the total number of officials at February 2000, taking all of the institutions together is only 30,777. Of this total some 17,087[6] work for the Commission, the largest institution, but this apparently large number is comparable with the administration of only a single government department or County Council in the United Kingdom.[7] As we have seen in Chapter 2 the Court now has over 1000 officials.[8] In all of the institutions moreover around one third of the total staff is devoted to the translation of documents into and from the eleven official languages.

There are two main categories of employee, the established "officials" of the European Communities, whose status and conditions of service are laid down in the Staff Regulations, and "other servants," often engaged under contract for a limited period of time, who are subject to the "Conditions of employment of other servants of the Communities." Both these Conditions and the Staff Regulations are enacted by regulation of the Council on a proposal from the Commission, and the provisions in the Staff Regulations conferring jurisdiction on the Court apply to all employees alike. This is one case, therefore, where the jurisdiction of the Court can be altered, without amendment of the Treaties, by a decision of the Council acting by a qualified majority. Another unusual feature of staff cases is that the Court can adjudicate in cases brought by its own employees against the Court itself; such cases, apparent exceptions to the principle *nemo iudex in causa sua*, are relatively rare but do arise from time to time.[9]

As Professor O'Keeffe has pointed out[10] the creation of the Court of First Instance has not resolved this problem in the way

---

[6] Although this figure rises to nearly 21,703 when the staff of bodies such as the Office for Official Publications of the European Communities, Joint Research Centres and the Foundation for the Improvement of Living and Working Conditions in Dublin are included.

[7] In answer to a question in Parliament, the Earl of Caithness compared the staff of the Commission with the 14,400 staff of the Department of Transport 12,800 employed by the London Borough of Croydon, 15,000 by Gloucestershire County Council, 17,600 by the Fife region in Scotland and 14,800 by the Gwent County Council in Wales. *Hansard* July 23, 1993, col. 895.

[8] The other institutions and bodies have the following numbers of staff: Parliament: 4,126; Council: 2,648; Court of Auditors: 552; European Investment Bank: 1,011; Economic and Social Committee: 742.

[9] See *e.g.* Case 15/60 *Simon v. Court of Justice* [1961] ECR 115 and Case 2/80 *Dautzenberg v. Court of Justice* [1980] ECR 3107. In the latter case the Court, sitting judicially, annulled its own administrative act refusing a promotion to a librarian at the Court.

[10] D. O'Keeffe, "The Court of First Instance of the European Communities" in C. de Cooker (ed.), International Administration V.5/1-20.

the establishment of a wholly separate administrative tribunal for staff affairs might have done. First of course either an official of the Court or the Court's own administration may appeal to the Court of Justice against an adverse decision of the Court of First Instance. Secondly officials assigned to the Court of First Instance may themselves bring proceedings.[11]

The Court has interpreted its jurisdiction more broadly than is suggested by the reference in Article 179 (now Article 236) EC to disputes "between the Community and its servants."

Thus the Court of Justice has held that decisions of selection boards in recruitment procedures (for example to exclude a candidate, or not to take into consideration certain diplomas or professional experience) may be submitted directly to the Court.[12] Moreover the Court has held that Articles 90 and 91 of the Staff Regulations (which govern complaints by officials) apply not only to those who are officials or agents but also to candidates for a post.[13] The recourse to an action under Article 179 (now Article 236) is also open to persons claiming rights under the Staff Regulations even though they are not themselves officials[14] or to retired officials and other servants.[15]

In terms of numbers alone staff cases, until transferred to the Court of First Instance in 1989, contributed substantially to the Court's case-load,[16] and in the first years after the establishment of the Court, when other business was sometimes slack, they furnished grist for the judicial mill. These early cases provided the Court with the opportunity to start its work of building up a body of case-law where the texts gave little guidance. In particular, they enabled the Court to develop the principles of Community law on the nature and scope of judicial review of administrative action. Those principles were subsequently applied to full-scale actions under Article 173 (now Article 230) EC, and despite the specialised nature of the disputes, despite the apparent lack of merit of some complaints which have been entertained, and despite the

---

[11] See for example Case T–38/90 *Andersen and Others v. Court of Justice,* a case subsequently withdrawn following a settlement [1991] O.J. C56/14.

[12] See Case 44/71 *Marcato v. Commission* [1972] ECR 427.

[13] See Joined Cases 81 to 88/74 *Marenco and Others v. Commission* [1975] ECR 1247; Case 130/75 *Prais v. Council* [1976] ECR 1589. For an application "*a contrario*" of this principle see Case C–126/90P *Bocos Viciano v. Commission* [1991] ECR I–781, where, on appeal, the appellant's case was dismissed since his application (to the Court of First Instance) was governed by Art. 179 and hence, to be admissible, required the pre-contentious procedure laid down in Arts. 90 and 91 of the Staff Regulations.

[14] See for example Joined Cases 75 and 117/82 *Razzouk and Beydoun v. Commission* [1984] ECR 1509; [1984] 3 C.M.L.R. 470 discussed below.

[15] See Case T–54/90 *Lacroix v. Commission* [1991] ECR II–750.

[16] See Table 1 in Annex II.

fact that staff cases were (and on appeal still are) normally heard by a Chamber of three judges, rather than by the full Court,[17] the judgments in these cases remain authoritative and, where appropriate, can be cited equally with decisions given by the full Court in cases of less parochial concern.

Thus one of the earliest staff cases, which occupies no less than one-third of the volume of reports for 1957, raised the constitutional issue of the balance of power between the authorities set up under the ECSC Treaty.[18] Legislative authority in staff matters was originally conferred under the ECSC Treaty on a Commission composed of the Presidents of the then four Institutions (the Court, the High Authority, the Assembly and the Council) in order to maintain a balance of power among the institutions. The ECSC Assembly, the precursor of the European Parliament, had taken certain decisions admitting the applicants to the protection of the Staff Regulations, and appointing them at certain grades and at certain levels of seniority. Subsequently those decisions were revoked, and the applicants challenged that revocation as being unlawful. The Court's judgment laid down important principles governing the circumstances in which an administrative act can lawfully be revoked, referring, in the absence of express provisions of Community law, to the laws of the Member States as a source of general principles of law: this aspect of the case is returned to below, p. 338. The case was the first authority for the principle that compensation could be given, under Community law, for non-material damage (*dommage moral*); and also, although with less precision, for the degree of negligence required to establish liability for damages. Staff cases have also given the Court the opportunity to interpret and clarify its own rules of procedure in areas such as legal aid[19] and the computation of time limits.[20]

The jurisdiction of the Court in staff cases is wider than that of many staff tribunals in international organisations, since it can pronounce on the legality of the Staff Regulations themselves as well as on particular decisions taken in application of those Regulations. This may arise on a plea of illegality under Article 184 (now Article 241) EC (p. 164, above), whereby any party challenging a particular decision before the Court may plead the inapplicability of the parent regulation. An example is a case considered more fully in Chapter 15, *Sabbatini v. European Parliament*.[21] Signora Sabbatini complained of discrimination on

---

[17] But see p. 200, below.
[18] Cases 7/56 and 3–7/57 *Algera and Others v. Assembly* [1957 and 1958] ECR 39.
[19] See Chap. 13, below and T. Kennedy, "Paying the Piper: Legal Aid in proceedings before the Court of Justice" (1988) C.M.L.Rev. 599.
[20] See Case 152/85 *Misset v. Council* [1987] ECR 223.
[21] Case 20/71 [1972] ECR 345; [1972] C.M.L.R. 945.

grounds of sex, since she lost her expatriation allowance on marriage, while men in the same circumstances did not. Although the decision was taken in conformity with the Staff Regulations, it was annulled by the Court, which held that the relevant provisions of the Regulations were discriminatory and therefore unlawful. The Regulations were subsequently amended on this point by the Council so as to apply equally to men and women. Henceforth they were entitled to the allowance under the same conditions, but subsequent attempts by other women to claim arrears of payment of the allowances were unsuccessful, the applications being rejected as out of time.[22]

It is sometimes overlooked that men, as well as women, can be victims of discrimination on grounds of sex. The point is illustrated by Joined Cases 75 and 117/82, *Razzouk and Beydoun v. Commission*.[23] The Staff Regulations provided that the widow of an official was normally entitled to a survivor's pension, while the widower of a deceased female official could receive a survivor's pension only if he had no income of his own and was permanently incapacitated. A widower's claim that he was entitled to a pension on the same terms as a widow was upheld by the Court, which held that the legislation infringed the fundamental right of equal treatment. The legislation has accordingly been amended to establish equality between the sexes. In the meantime, the Commission was to re-examine the widower's claim, which it had rejected, and must apply to it the provisions dealing with widows' pensions. If he would have received a pension had those provisions been applicable to men, he was to receive that pension, together with arrears and interest.

As well as the jurisdiction to rule on the validity of the Staff Regulations, it will be recalled that in staff cases the Court has plenary jurisdiction in the sense described in Chapter 8 (above, p. 170). The effect of this may be illustrated by Case 32/62, *Alvis v. Council*,[24] where the applicant claimed wrongful dismissal. The facts of the case were unusual and, it may be added, uncharacteristic of the behaviour both of Community servants and of the administration. The applicant was not an established official but had been engaged under contract. He had been dismissed for alleged misconduct; among other incidents, it was said that on one occasion he had reported for duty in a state of intoxication and that on another occasion, when he was also intoxicated, glasses

---

[22] Joined Cases 15-33, 52, 53, 57-109, 116, 117, 123, 132 and 135-137/73 *Schots-Kortner and Others v. Council, Commission and Parliament* [1974] ECR 177.
[23] Joined Cases 75 and 117/82 *Razzouk and Beydoun v. Commission* [1984] ECR 1509; [1984] 3 C.M.L.R. 470.
[24] Case 32/62 *Alvis v. Council* [1963] ECR 49; [1963] C.M.L.R. 396.

were thrown from the ninth floor of his office block into the street below. He claimed that he had been dismissed without being given any opportunity of submitting his defence, and had not been informed of the incidents on which his dismissal was based. The Court, applying a generally accepted principle of administrative law in force in the Member States, held that the administration must allow its servants the opportunity of replying to allegations before any disciplinary decision is taken. That had not been done. However, the Court exercised its plenary jurisdiction, and ruled that, in this case, the failure to observe this principle was not such as to render the dismissal void. Nor did the failure justify the award of damages to the applicant; but it did justify ordering the Council to pay a substantial proportion of the applicant's costs.

The Court's plenary jurisdiction thus enabled it to substitute, in effect, its own judgment for that of the administration. Although the decision to dismiss the applicant was technically vitiated by the denial of his right to be heard, it was considered that the decision should stand on its merits. Indeed the Court went on, in its judgment, to review the decision on its merits and held that the facts which had been established, with the assistance of witnesses summoned by the Court,[25] justified the dismissal, revealing "an attitude and conduct incompatible with the functioning of the European institutions."

## Procedure in Staff Cases

In most respects the procedure in staff cases is similar to that described in Chapter 12, below for any other direct action; but staff cases do have a number of special features.

The complaint must first be brought before the appropriate authority[26] in the institution concerned; in other words, domestic remedies must be exhausted. If the complainant is not satisfied by the response, or if there is no response within four months (in which case there is deemed to be an implied decision rejecting the complaint),[27] then he can appeal to the Court of First Instance

---

[25] *i.e.* in the exercise of its inquisitorial powers.

[26] Article 90 (2) of the Staff Regulations. The term used in the English text of the Staff Regulations is "appointing authority," a term which recurs frequently in reports of staff cases. Although it is derived from the grandiloquent French expression *autorité investie du pouvoir de nomination*, usually abbreviated to A.I.P.N., the term covers any authority responsible for adopting a decision in relation to an official. Thus, depending on the subject matter at issue, and the grade of the official concerned, the relevant appointing authority may be the official's immediate superior, a disciplinary board or a complaints committee of directors or members of the institution.

[27] Art. 90(2) of the Staff Regulations.

against the decision of rejection. The time limit for the appeal is three months, as compared with two months under Article 173 (now 230).

By way of derogation from that procedure the person concerned may, immediately after filing a complaint, bring the matter directly before the Court of First Instance provided that such an appeal is accompanied by an application either for a stay of execution of the contested act or for the adoption of interim measures,[28] see p. 287, below.

Staff cases are normally heard by a Chamber of the Court of First Instance[29] or, on appeal, of the Court of Justice,[30] although the Chamber concerned may, at any stage in the proceedings, refer a case to the full Court[31] or, in proceedings before the Court of First Instance, to a Chamber composed of a different (*i.e.* larger) number of judges. Since the introduction of the possibility of certain cases being heard by a single judge (see p. 97 above) staff cases too may be heard in this forum.

Such a transfer has not yet occurred in a case before the Court of First Instance; however on several occasions where the case in question raised an issue of general importance or difficulty a Chamber of the Court of Justice has exercised its power to transfer.[32] The full Court of Justice also heard some of the early appeals in staff cases, even though the legal issues did not seem to be of general importance.[33] This was presumably in order to establish a common practice and approach with regard to such appeals so as to avoid disparities between different Chambers.

Staff cases also differ from other types of case in that, under Article 88 of the Rules of Procedure of the Court of First Instance,

---

[28] Art. 91(4) of the Staff Regulations. For an example of this procedure see Case 176/88 R *Hanning v. Parliament* [1988] ECR 3915.

[29] Art. 12 of the CFI Rules. Contrary to the situation in the Court of Justice, the normal formation of the Court of First Instance is a chamber of three or five judges. See Art. 2(4) of the Council decision establishing a Court of First Instance of the European Community [1988] O.J. L319.

[30] Art. 95(1) of the CJ Rules. Since the Amendments to the CJ Rules of May 15, 1991: [1991] O.J. L176, staff cases are no longer automatically assigned to a chamber, a decision so to assign a case is taken on a case by case basis at the Courts administrative meeting.

[31] Art. 95(3) of the CJ Rules and Art. 14 of the CFI Rules.

[32] See for example the *Mills, Razzouk and Beydoun, Misset and Maurissen* cases mentioned elsewhere in this Chapter. In Joined Cases 271/83, 15, 36, 113, 158 and 203/84 and 13/85 *Ainsworth and Others v. Commission and Council* [1987] ECR 167 the Third Chamber, having heard Advocate General VerLoren van Themaat's opinion, referred the case to the full Court, which having heard fresh argument and a substantially similar Opinion from Advocate General Mischo, delivered one of its least creditable judgments.

[33] See for example Case C–283/90P *Vidranyi v. Commission* and Case C–132/90P *Schwedler v. Commission* [1991] O.J. C331/9.

the defendant institution normally has to pay its own costs, even if the action is unsuccessful. However, on appeal to the Court of Justice, that rule applies only to an appeal brought by an institution[34]; thus where an official appeals unsuccessfully, he or she will normally be liable for the institution's costs also unless the Court of Justice makes use of its power to order the parties to share the costs "where equity so requires." The rationale of these provisions is to discourage officials from bringing hopeless appeals against adverse decisions of the Court of First Instance while giving the Court of Justice a discretion to attenuate the effects of the rule in the event of a reasonable but unfounded appeal.

If the action succeeds, the decision complained of is annulled and the applicant may also be awarded damages. Thus, in the *Algera* case mentioned above, the Court awarded damages for non-material harm (*dommage moral*) although only at the modest rate of 100 units of account[35] (approximately £50) per applicant. In other cases, more substantial damages have been awarded; in one such case the Commission was ordered to pay the applicant some 77,000 Belgian Francs (approximately £1,500), as compensation for leave which he had been unable to take "owing to the requirements of the service."[36] In general, the amounts awarded for mental distress or injured feelings have been small.

A special feature of staff cases is that, as will already be apparent, the Court has frequently been confronted with disputes concerning the facts of the case. Accordingly preparatory inquiries and the calling of witnesses were more frequent here than in other cases and the burden on the Court has been correspondingly greater, especially perhaps because the procedures available to it for the establishment of the facts of a case are not entirely satisfactory – a matter to which we return in the chapter on procedure. It was therefore appropriate to transfer staff cases to the Court of First Instance, so enabling the Court of Justice "to concentrate its activities on its fundamental task of ensuring uniform interpretation of Community law" and "relieving it of responsibility for examining questions of fact."[37] As pointed out in Chapter Five, changes have been made to the burden of proof in staff cases to facilitate the establishing of the facts; it is also in this context that the greatest use of the Court of First Instance's express power to seek an amicable settlement is likely to be most frequently used.

---

[34] Art. 122 of the CJ Rules. See *Bocos Viciano* (cited above at note 13) at p. 196.

[35] The ancestor of the Euro.

[36] Case 39/69 *Fournier v. Commission* [1970] ECR 267.

[37] See preamble to the Decision establishing the Court of First Instance and see generally Chap. 5, above.

The problem of case-load is aggravated by the fact that very large numbers of officials may be affected by Staff Regulations, such as the provisions on pensions and related matters which were challenged by large groups of officials in 1979 and 1980.[38]

The civil service unions have no power to bring such actions on behalf of their members under Article 91 of the Staff Regulations since the remedy provided by that Article is available only to officials and other servants themselves.[39] The possibility for a union to bring an action for annulment under Article 173 (now Article 230) is also severely limited. Thus in Case 72/74, *Union Syndicale v. Council*[40] the Court, applying the *Plaumann* test,[41] held that an organisation formed for the protection of the collective interests of a number of persons could not be considered as being directly and individually concerned by a measure affecting the general interests of that category. The fact that the organisation had taken part in the discussions which preceded the disputed measure made no difference in that regard.

By contrast in Joined Cases 193 and 194/87, *Maurissen and Others v. Court of Auditors*[42] the action of the European Public Service Union in challenging a decision addressed to it was held admissible under the second paragraph of Article 173 (now Article 230) EC. The decision, refusing to grant time off to trade union representatives in order to take part in meetings concerning salaries and related issues, was subsequently annulled by the Court.[43]

Occasionally, moreover, Council Regulations adversely affecting the Community civil service have been challenged by the Commission, acting as the guardian of the Community interest; examples have been seen in the *Staff Salaries*[44] cases (above, p. 142). Such actions are based on the Commission's general power to challenge Council measures under Article 173.

---

[38] See, *e.g.* the Opinion of Advocate General Capotorti in Case 167/80 *Dunstan Curtis v. Commission and Parliament* [1981] ECR 1499 at 1512.

[39] See Cases 175/73 *Union Syndicale and Others v. Council* [1974] ECR 917; [1975] 1 C.M.L.R. 131 and 18/75 *Syndicat général du personnel v. Commission*; [1974] ECR 933; [1975] 1 C.M.L.R. 144.

[40] Case 72/74 *Union Syndicale v. Council* [1975] ECR 401; [1975] 2 C.M.L.R. 181.

[41] Case 25/62 *Plaumann v. Commission* [1963] ECR 95 at p. 107; [1964] C.M.L.R. 29, see p. 148, above.

[42] Joined cases 193 and 194/87 *Maurissen and Others v. Court of Auditors* [1989] ECR 1045, the judgment of May 11, 1989 deals only with the question of admissibility.

[43] See Joined Cases C–193 and C–194/87 *Maurissen and European Public Service Union v. Court of Auditors* [1990] ECR I–95.

[44] Case 81/72 *Commission v. Council* [1973] ECR 575; [1973] C.M.L.R. 639 and Case 70/74 *Commission v. Council* [1975] ECR 795; [1975] 2 C.M.L.R. 287.

*In* Defrenne v. Sabena *the Court ruled that a Belgian air hostess could rely directly upon Article 119 of the EEC Treaty in proceedings against the airline which employed her.*\*

---

\* Postage stamp issued on October 18, 1993. The drawing by François Walthéry is of Natasha, the heroine of a popular Belgian comic strip.

# Chapter Ten

# Preliminary Rulings

## INTRODUCTION

In many ways the most important aspect of the work of the Court is its jurisdiction to give "preliminary rulings" under Article 177 (now Article 234) EC and corresponding provisions of the other Treaties (Article 41 ECSC, Article 150 Euratom). As a Belgian expert has pointed out, most of the *"grands arrêts"* of the Court have been under this head of its jurisdiction.[1]

As we have seen, disputes involving Community law, whether between individuals or companies, or between private parties and the national authorities of the Member States, never come directly before the Court of Justice, but begin before the courts and tribunals of the Member States. Most of them are concluded in the national courts as well, those courts simply applying the relevant Community law rules or domestic implementing legislation to the case in hand. However the Treaty provisions enable the Court of Justice, at the request of the national court, to rule on questions of Community law which arise in such litigation. This jurisdiction is exclusive to the Court of Justice: the Court of First Instance cannot give preliminary rulings.

The preliminary ruling has proved a particularly effective means of securing rights claimed under Community law: Signora Leonesio claimed a premium for the slaughter of her cows which had been refused her under Italian law; Mme Defrenne claimed arrears of salary from the Belgian airline SABENA on the ground that air hostesses and male members of the cabin crew performing identical duties did not receive equal pay; Signor Bonsignore

---

[1] Paul Demaret, Jean-Monnet Professor at the College of Europe, Bruges, *Le juge et le jugement dans les traditions juridiques européenns* (Paris, 1996), 311. *"Grands arrêts"* are landmark judgments.

challenged a deportation order made by the German authorities; Dr Klopp, a Dutch lawyer who had also qualified for admission in France, asserted his right to practise as an *avocat* at the Paris Bar, whilst retaining his Dutch chambers, despite a rule of the Paris Bar prohibiting a second office outside Paris; Mrs Drake could not be refused invalid care allowance simply because she was a married woman; Mr Cowan, an English tourist mugged in the Paris Metro, could benefit from the French scheme for criminal injuries compensation despite the objection that he was not a French citizen; Mrs Rosie Hughes, an Irish woman residing with her family in the Republic, was entitled, by virtue of her husband working in Northern Ireland, to family credit under British social security law; Mr Newton, an Englishman rendered tetraplegic by a car accident in France where he was self-employed, returned to England and was awarded mobility allowance; that allowance could not be withdrawn merely because he returned to live in France.[2] The type of claim varies considerably, as does the nature of the procedure before the national court; but in essence, in all these cases, the mechanism is the same.

The right is claimed under Community law, despite the absence of any provision of national law, or even in opposition to national law. The remedy is before the national court, but the scope of the right is determined by the Court of Justice.

Conversely, Community law may be invoked by the defendant, whether in civil or in criminal proceedings. In an action for infringement of patent or trade mark rights, or in a prosecution for importing medicinal drugs without complying with requirements laid down by national law, the defendant may rely on the Treaty provisions on the free movement of goods, Articles 28 to 30 (ex Articles 30, 34 and 36) EC.[3] The defence is raised in the proceedings before the national court; its scope is determined by the Court of Justice by means of a preliminary ruling. The Court will of course have regard to the exceptions set out in Article 30 (ex Article 36) EC, for example, public morality, as where on a

---

[2] Case 93/71 *Leonesio v. Italian Ministry for Agriculture and Forestry* [1972] ECR 287; [1973] C.M.L.R. 343, Case 43/75 *Defrenne v. SABENA* [1976] ECR 455; [1976] 2 C.M.L.R. 98, Case 67/74 *Bonsignore v. Stadt Koln* [1975] ECR 297; [1975] 1 C.M.L.R. 472, Case 107/83 *Ordre des Avocats au Bureau de Paris v. Klopp* [1984] ECR 2971; Case 150/85 *Drake v. Chief Adjudication Officer* [1986] ECR 1995; Case C–186/87 *Cowan* [1989] ECR 195; Case C–78/91 *Hughes v. Chief Adjudication Officer* [1992] ECR I–4839; *The Independent*, July 23, 1992; [1992] 8 C.L. 541; Case C–356/89 *Newton v. Chief Adjudication Officer* [1992] 1 C.M.L.R. 149.

[3] Cases 15 and 16/74 *Centrafarin v. Winthrop* [1974] ECR 1147 and 1183; [1974] 2 C.M.L.R. 480, Case 104/75 *De Peijper* [1976] ECR 613; [1976] 2 C.M.L.R. 271.

reference from the House of Lords the English importers of Danish pornography from Holland, prosecuted before the Ipswich Crown Court, pleaded unavailingly the principle of free movement of goods.[4]

The term "preliminary ruling" is something of a misnomer. The ruling is requested and given, not before the case comes to the national court, but in the course of the proceedings before it. It is therefore an interlocutory ruling, a step in the proceedings before the national court. But it is a step which may be taken, and is frequently best taken, before the case comes to trial. Thus references are commonly made in the course of interlocutory proceedings.[5] The French *"renvoi prejudicial"* is clearer: that is, the submission of an issue for prior judgment before determining the principal issue.

It follows from the nature of a preliminary reference that it cannot be made once the principal issue has been decided; thus, in *S.A. Magnavision v. General Optical Council (No. 2)*,[6] the Queen's Bench Divisional Court refused to refer where the judgment had already been given (although the formal order of the Court had not yet been drawn up) and leave to appeal had been refused, for a reference at this stage could in no sense be interpreted as "preliminary".

Generally, the national proceedings stand adjourned pending the outcome of the reference. However, in *Portsmouth City Council v. Richards*,[7] the English Court of Appeal upheld the granting of an interlocutory injunction restraining deliberate and flagrant breaches of the criminal law, notwithstanding a reference in the case having been made to Luxembourg. Again, in Case C–213/89 *Factortame* (above) the House of Lords accepted the ruling of the Court of Justice and granted an interim injunction against the Crown suspending the offending statute.

The ECSC Treaty (Article 41), in its terms, confers upon the Court jurisdiction only to give preliminary rulings on the validity of Community acts, but the Court has boldly interpreted this as extending also to their interpretation.[8] Under the EC (and

---

[4] Case 34/79 *R. v. Henn and Darby* [1979] ECR 3795; [1980] 1 C.M.L.R. 246, *cf.* Case 121/85 *Conegate v. H.M. Customs and Excise* [1986] ECR 1007.

[5] See, for example, Cases 51, 86 and 96/75 *EMI v. CBS* [1976] ECR 811; [1976] 2 C.M.L.R. 235 *et seq.*, references from English, Danish and German courts also Case C–213/89 *The Queen v. Secretary of State for Transport, ex p. Factortame (Factortame I)* [1990] ECR I–2433 where the House of Lords referred the procedural question whether Community law required the interim suspension of a British statute.

[6] [1987] 2 C.M.L.R. 262.

[7] *The Times*, November 21, 1988 [1989] C.M.L.R. 673.

[8] Case C–221/88 *ECSC v. Busseni* [1990] ECR I–495; see also Opinion of Advocate General Van Gerven in Case C–128/92 *R.J. Banks and Co. Ltd v. British Coal* [1994] ECR I–1209, Opinion delivered on October 27, 1993.

Euratom) Treaty it has jurisdiction expressly on questions of interpretation as well as validity. While Article 41 ECSC has proved virtually a dead letter (because of the readier availability of the direct action under Article 33), it provided a model for expansion in the later Treaties, its principal architect, we are told,[9] being Nicola Catalano (later the Italian judge on the Court) who drew on the experience of the Italian Constitutional Court. Article 234 (ex Article 177) EC provides:

> "The Court of Justice shall have jurisdiction to give preliminary rulings concerning:
>
> (a) the interpretation of this Treaty;
> (b) the validity and interpretation of acts of the institutions of the Community and the ECB;
> (c) the interpretation of the statutes of bodies established by an act of the Council, where those statutes so provide.
>
> Where such a question is raised before any court or tribunal of a Member State, that court or tribunal may, if it considers that a decision on the question is necessary to enable it to give judgment, request the Court of Justice to give a ruling thereon.
>
> Where any such question is raised in a case pending before a court or tribunal of a Member State, against whose decisions there is no judicial remedy under national law, that court or tribunal shall bring the matter before the Court of Justice."[9a]

The effect of that Article is that any question of Community law in issue before a national court may be authoritatively determined by the Court of Justice if that question is referred to it; that a national court is in all cases entitled, and in some cases obliged, to make such a reference; and that the Court of Justice may thus be the final arbiter on matters of Community law although the case is heard and determined in the national forum. Moreover, a question of interpretation may also extend to the question of the direct applicability or direct effect of the Community provision in issue. Finally, it is important to note that a national court may also raise the question of the validity of a Community act by means of this procedure; indeed, as the Court of Justice has ruled, the national court has no power itself to rule such an act invalid (see below).

The Court however declined to accept a reference under Article 234 (ex Article 177) EC on the question of the validity of a

---

[9] See Address at the Court's Formal Sitting on October 18, 1984.
[9a] See new important amendment of CJ Rules of Procedure (p. 241, below).

Community act where the party challenging the act in the national court could have directly challenged the act in the Court of Justice under Article 230 (ex Article 173) EC, there being no doubt as to the party's legal standing to do so under Article 230 (ex Article 173) EC.[10] The case involved state aids, and it has been argued that this rule of "procedural exclusivity" should be confined to state aid cases.[11] Failure to challenge a state aid under Article 230 (ex Article 173) EC may cause genuine prejudice to third parties or to the public interest. Subsequently, the Court has held that challenges in the national court, with subsequent reference under Article 234 (ex Article 177) EC, are not precluded where it is not obvious that an action under Article 230 (ex Article 173) EC would lie.[12]

Article 234 (ex Article 177) EC, as originally drafted (see above), must now be read in the light of amendments made by the Maastricht and Amsterdam Treaties. These confer a new jurisdiction to make preliminary rulings in relation to matters still falling under the Third Pillar (Justice and Home Affairs) of the Maastricht Treaty. The Third Pillar however has now been reduced to include only provisions on police and criminal judicial co-operation. References under this truncated Third Pillar may be made to the Court of Justice on the validity and interpretation of framework decisions and decisions on the interpretation of measures implementing conventions. Moreover, this new jurisdiction is optional in the sense that a Member State must declare its acceptance of the Court's jurisdiction to hear references from its courts, and this declaration may limit the power to make references to its courts of last instance.[13]

## SCOPE OF THE PRELIMINARY RULING SYSTEM

The need for a system of preliminary rulings can be seen most clearly in relation to questions of validity. Plainly it would lead to intolerable confusion if national courts were to declare Community legislation invalid: for example, to hold that a Council regulation was *ultra vires*. Under Article 41 ECSC, indeed, the Court of Justice was expressly given "sole jurisdiction" to rule on

---

[10] Case C–188/92 *TWD Deggendorf v. Commission* [1994] ECR I–833.

[11] D. Wyatt, "The relationship between actions for annulment and references on validity after *TWD Deggendorf*: in J. Lonbay and A. Biondi, *Remedies for breach of EC Law* (Wiley, 1997), 55.

[12] Case C–408/95 *Eurotunnel SA v. SeaFrance* [1997] ECR I–6315.

[13] See further S. Langrish "The Treaty of Amsterdam: Selected Highlights" (1998) 23 E.L.Rev. 3, at pp. 10–11; also Editorial (1997) 22 E.L.Rev. 290.

the validity of acts of the High Authority and of the Council. Although the Court is not expressly given exclusive jurisdiction on questions of validity under Article 234 (ex Article 177) EC, it would clearly be improper for a national court to declare Community acts to be invalid, not least because a court in another Member State might come to a contrary conclusion. Thus any serious challenge in the national courts to the validity of such acts should be referred to the Court of Justice. That such self-denial is required on the part of the national judge was finally made clear beyond peradventure by the Court of Justice itself. In Case 314/85 *Foto-Frost*[14] the Court interpreted Article 177 (now Article 234) EC as depriving the national judge of the power to declare Community acts invalid, although he may grant an interim injunction where there are serious doubts as to the validity of the Community act and the applicant is at risk of serious and irreparable harm.[15] On the other hand, unlike Article 41 ECSC, Article 177 (now Article 234) EC did leave the national courts competent to pronounce a Community act to be valid where there were no grounds for doubt.

Illustrations of references on the validity of Community law, as opposed to its interpretation, may be found in the legislation on the social security of migrant workers. Article 42 (ex Article 51) EC requires the Council to "adopt such measures in the field of social security as are necessary to provide freedom of movement for workers." Hence regulations of the Council provide, for example, that periods spent in different Member States should qualify for the calculation of the worker's retirement pension. While the detailed provisions of the legislation are inevitably complex, the essential principle underlying it, derived from Article 42 (ex Article 51) EC, is that a person who has worked successively in different Member States should not be deprived of social security benefits that he would have secured if he had always worked in the same Member State. In some cases, a claimant has been faced with a calculation, purportedly based on the regulations, which would have the result of depriving him of the benefits to which he would have been entitled on the basis of national law taken alone. Here the Court has ruled that the provisions of the regulations, to the extent to which they lead to that result, are, in effect, *ultra vires* Article 42 (ex Article 51) EC and void.[16] Such decisions, invalidating Community legislation and

---

[14] Case 314/85 *Foto-Frost v. Hauptzollamt Lübeck-Ost* [1987] ECR 4199, (1988) 13 E.L.Rev. 125 (note, Arnull).

[15] Cases C–143/88 and C–92/89 *Zuckerfabrik Süderdithmarschen v. Hauptzollamt Itzehoe* [1991] ECR I–415.

[16] Case 191/73 *Niemann v. Bundesversicherungsanstalt für Angestellte* [1974] ECR 571; Case 24/75 *Petroni v. Office National des Pensions pour Travailleurs Salariés* [1975] ECR 1149.

so requiring the Council to enact amending provisions, could not properly have been taken by national courts; indeed, as the Court has now ruled (*Foto-Frost*, above), it would be contrary to Community law.

A moment's reflection will show, however, that a similar line of reasoning may apply equally to questions of interpretation as well as validity. The applicability of Community law in particular situations may depend as much upon its interpretation as upon its validity. A restrictive interpretation of legislation might be tantamount to holding it invalid; or the actual validity of a provision may depend upon its precise construction. Thus the uniform interpretation of the law is necessary to secure its uniform application. As the Court itself has stated:

> "Article 177 is essential for the preservation of the Community character of the law established by the Treaty and has the object of ensuring that in all circumstances this law is the same in all States of the Community.[17]"

Uniform application of the law is the basis of the common market and the famous "level playing field" of commerce. Without it Community law, applied by the national courts, would be liable to fragment and become overlaid by the national legal systems in all of their diversity.

In the absence of a federal structure or of any Community appellate court, the preliminary ruling is the only means by which uniform application of Community law can be attained. Moreover, the provisions of the Treaty and the measures taken by the Community institutions cannot readily be interpreted by national courts without assistance. They have to be interpreted in the light of the purposes for which they were drafted, they are often broad and general in scope, and texts in the different official languages may have to be compared. These problems of interpretation are examined in Chapter 14.

In *Customs and Excise v. Samex*,[18] Bingham J., as he then was, explained why the Court of Justice is better equipped than any national court to decide questions of Community law:

> "Sitting as a judge in a national court, asked to decide questions of Community law, I am very conscious of the advantages enjoyed by the Court of Justice. It has a panoramic view of the Community and its institutions, a detailed knowledge of the treaties and of much subordinate legisla-

---

[17] Case 166/73 *Rheinmuhlen-Düsseldorf v. Einfuhr-und Vorratsstelle für Getreide und Füttermittel* [1974] ECR 33 at 38; [1974] 1 C.M.L.R. 523.
[18] [1983] 1 All E.R. 1042 at 1055.

tion made under them, and an intimate familiarity with the functioning of the Community market which no national judge denied the collective experience of the Court of Justice could hope to achieve. Where questions of administrative intention and practice arise the Court of Justice can receive submissions from the Community institutions, as also where relations between the Community and non-member states are in issue. Where the interests of Member States are affected they can intervene to make their views known . . . Where comparison falls to be made between Community texts in different languages, all texts being equally authentic, the multinational Court of Justice is equipped to carry out the task in a way which no national judge, whatever his linguistic skills, could rival. The interpretation of Community instruments involves very often not the process familiar to common lawyers of laboriously extracting the meaning from words used but the more creative process of supplying flesh to a spare and loosely constructed skeleton. The choice between alternative submissions may turn not on purely legal considerations, but on a broader view of what the orderly development of the Community requires. These are matters which the Court of Justice is very much better placed to assess and determine than a national court."

Indeed, if the courts of each Member State were to take it upon themselves to construe Community law, it is probably not too much of an exaggeration to say that there would soon be at least as many systems of Community law as there are national legal systems within the EC.

To avoid this, however, the interpretation provided by the Court of Justice needs to be neither too abstract nor too vague but precise. Thus, after providing an interpretation leaving a large measure of discretion to the national courts on the legality of the Sunday opening of shops in relation to Article 30 (now Article 28) EC,[19] the Court, on a further reference from the House of Lords asking for clarification, did finally settle the issue in Case C–169/91 *Council of the City of Stoke-on-Trent*.[20]

The need for uniform interpretation applies equally to other areas of Community law which do not fall within the categories listed in the founding Treaties. This is the case with two Conventions concluded pursuant to Article 220 (now Article 293) EC: the

---

[19] See Case C–145/88 *Torfaen Borough Council v. B & Q plc* [1989] ECR 3851. See also Joined Cases C–267 and C–268/91 *Keck and Mithoard* [1993] ECR I–6097.
[20] [1992] ECR I–6635. See also Case 41/84 *Pinna* [1986] ECR 1, p. 235, below.

Convention of February 29, 1968 on the Mutual Recognition of Companies, Firms and Legal Persons, and the Convention of September 27, 1968 on jurisdiction and the Enforcement of judgments in Civil and Commercial Matters (known as the Brussels Convention, ratified by the United Kingdom with effect from January 1, 1987). As these Conventions are not Community acts, but treaties requiring ratification by Member States they fall outside Article 177. However, in each case, a separate Protocol gives the Court jurisdiction to give preliminary rulings on the interpretation of the Convention upon references from those appellate courts listed in the Protocol. The detailed provisions differ in some important respects from the scheme laid down by Article 234 (ex Article 177) EC. While the Companies Convention is still not in force the Brussels Convention has given rise to a substantial and growing body of case law.

Provisions for preliminary rulings are also contained in the Community Patent Convention, concluded on December 15, 1975 under the title "Convention for the European Patent for the Common Market"; when in force, this Convention will establish a Community patent system, under which it will be possible to take out a single patent for the whole of the EC, within the framework of the Convention on the grant of European patents. A draft Protocol to the Convention, agreed in December 1985 but still to be ratified, contains a radical proposal for creating a Community Patent Appeal Court (COPAC), to which patent appeals would lie from the national courts in the Member States, but from which references for preliminary rulings would be made to the Court of Justice on the interpretation of the Convention and its annexes (including the Protocol[21]).

In 1989 the Member States concluded two Protocols giving the Court jurisdiction to interpret the Rome Convention on the Law Applicable to Contractual Obligations.[22] These Conventions are likely to be followed by others; for instance a draft Bankruptcy Convention is at an advanced stage of negotiation. Under the Agreement on a European Economic Area[23] of May 2, 1992, an EFTA State may allow its national courts or tribunals to make a preliminary reference to the Court of Justice for a ruling on the interpretation (but not the validity) of an EEA provision.[24] It is

---

[21] See Wadilow in (1986) 11 E.L.Rev. 295.
[22] The Convention itself has now entered into force in all Member States except Portugal. The Protocols (analogous to those of the Brussels Convention) have to be ratified by the number of signatory countries necessary for them to come into force.
[23] See further Chap. 11, p. 251 and Appendix, p. 263, below.
[24] Art. 107 and Protocol 34 of the EEA Agreement.

doubtful whether any of the three EFTA States party to the EEA Treaty will authorise their courts to make such references in view of the constitutional and political problems in accepting a binding interpretation from a "foreign" jurisdiction. Instead, resort will be had rather to the jurisdiction of the EFTA Court itself to give advisory opinions on the interpretation of the EEA Agreement on the request of a court or tribunal of an EFTA State.[25]

These international instruments are progressively extending the jurisdiction of the Court and the implications of this increasing work-load will be considered in the concluding chapter.[26]

## PROCEDURE FOR PRELIMINARY RULINGS

The procedure on a reference is in all cases the same; it is described in Chapter 12. Here it is necessary to mention only certain points of procedure which are relevant to the subject of this chapter. First it should be noted that a decision to refer can be taken only by the national court. In practice such a decision will usually be taken at the instance of the parties or of one of them; but the court may also take the step of its own motion, even contrary to the express wishes of the parties. When a reference is made, the proceedings before the national court are generally stayed for the period, currently about 18 months on average, until the ruling is given. The procedure before the Court of Justice is, as we have seen, an interlocutory step in the action before the national court; but the Community institutions concerned (that is, the Commission in all cases, and the Council if a Council act is involved, and occasionally the Parliament[27]) and all the Member States, as well as the parties to the action before the national court, have the opportunity of submitting observations, both in writing and at an oral hearing, before the Court of Justice. When the ruling has been given, it is sent to the national court, and the proceedings there are resumed. Valuable guidance on framing references by national courts for preliminary rulings has now been given in a note published by the Court of Justice on December 9, 1996. This note is reproduced as an Appendix to this chapter (below, p. 242).

---

[25] Art. 34 of the EFTA Surveillance Authority and EFTA Court Agreement of 1992. For the EFTA Court, see Appendix, p. 263, below.

[26] See Koopmans "La procedure préjudicielle – victime de son succes?" in F. Capotorti & others, *Du droit international au droit de l'intégration, Liber Amicorum Pierre Pescatore* (Baden-Baden, 1987), 347.

[27] See for example Case 149/85 *Wybot v. Faure* [1986] ECR 2391, a case concerning the extent of the privileges of members of the European Parliament.

The system of preliminary rulings has its origins in analogous procedures in the legal systems of some of the original Member States, such as the reference in France from the civil to the administrative courts, or in Germany and Italy to the Constitutional Court from other courts, and these analogies have been used where procedural difficulties have arisen. Thus, the analogies in French and German law were considered by Advocate General Lagrange in the *Bosch* case,[28] and by Advocate General Warner in the *Rheinmühlen* cases.[29] In English law perhaps the closest analogies are the appeal by way of case stated and the motion for the determination of a preliminary point of law. Although these analogies with national law may sometimes be helpful, the Community system is better considered as *sui generis*. Indeed the function of the preliminary ruling is best explained by the special character of Community law itself. Community law is by its nature a common internal law among the Member States rather than a law governing relations between them; and in the absence of a developed federal structure it is natural that Community policies should fall to be implemented primarily by the authorities of the Member States and Community law to be applied by their courts. So it is to be expected that, in the normal way, Community law is enforced through the national courts, which, as mentioned above, have an exclusive jurisdiction to apply it in disputes between individuals, and between the individual and the authorities of the Member States.

Conflicts of jurisdiction between a national court and the Court of Justice can therefore rarely arise, but the exact demarcation line may be a delicate one to draw. The following sections illustrate the relationship between the two courts and the limits to their respective jurisdiction. These sections show also the pains taken by the Court of Justice both to preserve its own jurisdiction and at the same time to respect what is sometimes described as the "judicial sovereignty" of the national courts.

## The Decision to Refer

It is for the national court alone to judge whether a decision on the question is necessary to enable it to give judgment. That was established in Case 6/64 *Costa v. ENEL*[30] when objections were

---

[28] Case 13/61 *De Geus v. Bosch and another* [1962] ECR 45 at 59–60; [1962] C.M.L.R. 1.
[29] Cases 146 and 166/73 *Rheinmühlen-Düsseldorf v. Einfuhr-und Vorratsstelle für Getreide und Füttermittel* [1974] ECR 33 at 44; [1974] 1 C.M.L.R. 523.
[30] [1964] ECR 585.

raised to the admissibility of the reference: it was argued that the Court could not entertain the reference (see on this concept of admissibility Chapter 12, below). The argument was that the Milan court had requested an interpretation of the Treaty which was not "necessary" for the solution of the dispute before it. The Court of Justice simply replied to these objections that, since Article 177 (now Article 234) EC is based upon a clear separation of functions between itself and the national courts, it could not investigate the facts of the case or criticise the grounds and purpose of the request for interpretation. The Court's concern was clearly to respect the exclusive competence of the national court to decide whether a reference should be made, and at the same time to obviate the risk of challenge to the admissibility of a reference. This approach is undoubtedly correct although, as we shall see below, the Court has recently clarified the national courts' responsibility to submit appropriate questions accompanied by sufficient information to enable it to give helpful answers.

It will be seen from the wording of Article 234 (ex Article 177) EC (set out above, p. 207) that it does not require that the reference should be decisive, but only that the national court should consider that it cannot give judgment without deciding the point of Community law. If that condition is satisfied, then the court, unless it is a court of last instance, has a discretion whether or not to make a reference, and the exercise of that discretion is a matter for the national court alone, subject to the possibility of an appeal: Cases 146 and 166/73, *Rheinmühlen* (below, p. 380).

Nevertheless, the Court reserves the right not to entertain a reference arising out of a collusive action brought in one Member State with the intention of challenging the law of another Member State as contrary to Community law. Case 104/79 *Foglia v. Novello*[31] was a reference by the *Pretore* of Bra where the parties before the Italian court both contested the compatibility with Community law of a tax imposed by the French customs authorities on a consignment of Italian liqueur wine. The Court of Justice held, however, that, in the absence of a genuine dispute between the parties, it had no jurisdiction to give a ruling on the questions raised by the *Pretore* touching as they did the compatibility of French fiscal measures with Community law. It would be left then for the Commission or another Member State to challenge directly the measures in question in an enforcement action under Article 169 or 170 (now Article 226 or 277).

The holding of the Court has been criticised as introducing a kind of "preliminary censorship" of the motives of the parties and

---

[31] [1980] ECR 745

the judge in the national proceedings.[32] Certainly, the previous case law seemed to be well settled that, as was said in Case 10/69 *Portelange*,[33] "Article 177 does not give the Court jurisdiction to take cognisance of the facts of the case or to criticise the reason for the reference". Nor does the Court normally object to being asked to rule at the request of a judge in one Member State upon legislative measures or administrative acts in another Member State.[34] From the laconic judgment in *Foglia v. Novello*, read in the light of the advocate-general's opinion, it seems that the Court wished to curb what it saw as a *détournement de procédure* (abuse of procedure) by the referring judge.

In a subsequent reference in the same proceedings[35] the *Pretore* sought clarification of the Court's judgment in the first reference. The Court reaffirmed its authority to question of its own motion the admissibility of any reference for a preliminary ruling: it must retain what has been well described as this "valuable long-stop against abuse of process in exceptional cases".[36] But the Court did soften its attitude somewhat by inviting the *Pretore* to resubmit a reference if he could lay before the Court any new and relevant factors not present in the original reference: Article 177 being based upon co-operation between the national court and the Court of Justice, the latter could require the former to explain, where they were not obvious, the reasons why the national judge considered an answer to the question of Community law to be necessary in order to resolve the dispute.

How exceptional was the Court's attitude in declining jurisdiction in *Foglia v. Novello* is shown by its readiness, in a subsequent case, to accept a reference in what appeared on its face a collusive action, though no clear evidence of collusion was adduced.[37]

Subsequently, however, in Case C–83/91 *Meilicke*[38] the Court refused to answer a question (or, rather, a questionnaire extending to some 4,000 words) on the ground that it was hypothetical in nature, namely, the compatibility with the Second Company Law Directive of the doctrine in German company law of "disguised non-cash subscriptions", a doctrine upon which the learned Dr Meilicke had published a critical study.[39] The questionnaire sub-

---

[32] Barav (1980) 5 E.L.Rev. 443.

[33] *Portelange v. Smith Corona Merchant International and Other* [1969] ECR 309 at 315; [1974] 1 C.M.L.R. 397.

[34] See, for example, Case 22/76 *Import Gadgets v. LAMP SpA* [1976] ECR 1371; Case 261/81 *Rau v. De Smedt* [1982] ECR 3961; [1983] 2 C.M.L.R. 496.

[35] Case 244/80 *Foglia v. Novello* [1981] ECR 3045; [1982] 1 C.M.L.R. 585.

[36] D. Wyatt in (1981) 6 E.L. Rev. 449.

[37] Case 46/80 *Vinal v. Orbat* [1981] ECR 77; [1981] 3 C.M.L.R. 524.

[38] Case C–83/91 *Meilicke v. ADVORGA, Fa. Meyer A.G.* [1992] ECR I–4873,. Noted by Kennedy in (1993) 18 E.L.Rev. 121.

[39] *"Die 'verschleierte' Sacheinlage; eine deutsche Fehlentwicklung"* (Stuttgart, 1989). See para. 6 of the judgment.

mitted by the German court closely resembled a series of questions set out in that study.

In future, the guidance issued by the Court in its note of December 9, 1996 should help national courts to frame their references in ways acceptable to the Court (see Appendix, below p. 242).

## THE QUESTION REFERRED

The formulation of the question or questions referred is a matter for the national court alone. As is pointed out in the discussion on procedure in Article 234 (ex Article 177) EC cases (below, p. 292), a reference must usually be formulated with considerable detail if it is to be properly understood. But the question or questions referred will be answered without undue formalism. Since the proceedings in the national court will often, as we have seen, involve a challenge to national law as being contrary to Community law, the national court will often ask whether the provisions challenged are indeed contrary to Community law. Strictly such a question involves the application of Community law rather than its interpretation, but the Court will usually confine its ruling to the issue of interpretation, leaving it to the national court to draw the conclusion (which may then be readily apparent), whether in the light of that interpretation the national provisions should not be applied.

Here again the Court has sought to preserve its own jurisdiction without trespassing on that of the national court. To put the point in a different way, it has sought to provide an answer helpful to the national court while remaining within the limits of its competence.

Thus in the very first Article 177 (now Article 234) EC reference, the *Bosch*[40] case, objections were made to the jurisdiction of the Court on the ground, among others, that the question related not only to the interpretation but to the application of the Treaty. The Court had been asked to rule on the question whether the prohibition on export imposed by the Bosch company on its customers was void by virtue of Article 85(2) EC as far as exports to the Netherlands were concerned. To answer that question would have involved not merely interpreting, but applying, Article 85. The Court held, however, following Advocate General Lagrange, that

---

[40] Case 13/61 *de Geus v. Bosch* [1962] ECR 45 at 50.

". . . it is permissible for the national court to formulate its request in a simple and direct way leaving to this Court the duty of rendering a decision on that request only in so far as it has jurisdiction to do so, that is to say, only in so far as the decision relates to the interpretation of the Treaty. The direct form in which the request in the present case has been drawn up enables this Court to abstract from it without difficulty the questions of interpretation which it contains."

As it has frequently done in subsequent cases, the Court proceeded to extract from the material presented to it the questions of law which it was competent to answer. Thus, in Case 16/65 *Schwarze*[41] the national judge only asked the Court to interpret a Community measure, whereas a ruling on the measure's validity was clearly required: this the Court supplied unasked.

Recently, however, a stricter attitude has been adopted by the Court. Whereas in 1961 the reference in *Bosch* was, it is said, welcomed with celebratory champagne, today the Court groans under its overload. Now, therefore, not only are hypothetical questions refused, as we saw above, but also the national judge is expected to describe the factual and legal background of the national proceedings in sufficient detail to enable the Court to reply usefully to the questions submitted: this is particularly necessary in the field of competition law.[42] If this is not done, the Court may refuse to answer the questions submitted as manifestly inadmissible.[43]

This sanction of inadmissibility of references containing inadequate factual or legal information has been criticised as threatening the spirit of Article 177, a spirit characterised by a co-operative partnership between the national and the Community judiciary. Certainly, a test of admissibility should not be used as a disguised means of docket control.[44]

Again, where Community law has no bearing on the question referred, the Court has consistently held that it cannot give an answer to the question referred. Thus in Case 93/75 *Adlerblum*,[45] the classification under French law of a pension paid under

---

[41] Case 16/65 *Firma C. Schwarze v. Einfuhr- und Vorratsstelle für Getreide und Füttermittel* [1965] ECR 877; [1966] C.M.L.R. 172.

[42] Joined Cases C–320 to C–322/90 *Telemarsicabruzzo v. Circostel* [1993] ECR I–393.

[43] Case C–157/92 *Pretore di Genova v. Banchero*, Order of March 19, 1993 [1993] ECR I–1085.

[44] D. O'Keeffe, "Is the Spirit of Art. 177 under Attack? Preliminary References and Admissibiity." (1988) 23 E.L.Rev. 509 at 535.

[45] Case 93/75 *Adlerblum v. Caisse Nationale d'Assurance Vieillesse des Travailleurs Salariés* [1975] ECR 2147; [1976] 1 C.M.L.R. 236.

German law to a victim of Nazi persecution was held to be a matter of national law alone. However, even in such cases the Court does not simply reject the reference by a preliminary decision on admissibility. Instead, the proceedings follow their normal course and result in a ruling to the effect that the Court has no jurisdiction to answer the question referred.

A difficult issue arises where national law has incorporated rules or categories derived from Community law. A simple example is provided by Case C–231/89 *Gmurzynska-Bscher*.[46] Here the Court was asked to interpret the Common Customs Tariff because the national legislation of the referring court linked liability to national turnover tax to the Tariff. The Court proceeded to rule on what, in effect, was national law on the argument (persuasively opposed by Advocate General Darmon) that the proper functioning of the Community legal order required provisions of Community law (such as the Tariff) be given a uniform interpretation, regardless of the circumstances in which they fall to be applied. A like approach was followed in Joined Cases C–297/88 & C–197/89 *Dzodzi v. Belgium*[47] where provisions of Belgian law were based on the Community rules concerning the free movement of workers.[48]

This use by national legislatures of Community law as a kind of thesaurus of legal rules and concepts has danger and is to be discouraged. For, as Advocate General Darmon persuasively pointed out,[49] what happens if a provision of Community law incorporated by reference into national legislation is subsequently declared void by the Court of Justice in a case directly involving that provision? The result would appear to destroy the uniformity of Community law. Again, the contextual and teleological approach to the interpretation of Community law is difficult to apply where that law is incorporated into national law.

In the historic *Van Gend en Loos* case,[50] where the Court for the first time held that a provision of Community law "produces direct effects and creates individual rights which national courts must protect", the plaintiff had challenged a Dutch law as contravening Article 12 of the EEC Treaty. The Dutch and Belgian Governments submitted, *inter alia*, that the Court had no jurisdiction to decide whether the provisions of the EEC Treaty prevail over the Dutch legislation, and that the solution to this question fell within

---

[46] Case C–231/89 *Gmurzynska-Bscher v. Oberfinanzdirektion Köln* [1990] ECR I–4003.
[47] Cases C–297/88 and C–197/89 *Dzodzi v. Belgium* [1990] ECR I–3763.
[48] For further commentary see Arnull (1993) 18 E.L.Rev. 129.
[49] Opinion of Mr. Darmon [1990] ECR I–3778 at 3780.
[50] Case 26/62 *Van Gend en Loos v. Nederlandes Terixfcommissie* [1943] ECR 1.

the exclusive jurisdiction of the national courts, subject to an application under Articles 169 and 170 (now Articles 226 and 227) of the Treaty. The argument was that an alleged infringement of the Treaty by a Member State could not be brought before the Court under Article 177 (now Article 234) at the instance of an individual party to proceedings before a national court, but only in proceedings instituted before the Court directly by the Commission or by another Member State under Article 169 (now Article 226) EC and Article 170 (now Article 227) EC respectively.

The Court rejected this argument as misconceived. "A restriction of the guarantees against an infringement of Article 12 by Member States to the procedures under Articles 169 and 170 would remove all direct legal protection of the individual rights of their nationals." The decision is illuminating on the relation between the Court's jurisdiction under Article 234 (ex Article 177) EC and its jurisdiction in a direct action. It is plain on reading the judgment why a remedy in the hands only of the Commission and the Member States was considered ineffective. Such an action on their part is purely discretionary and will be affected by political calculations. The notion of the direct effect of Community law, coupled with the jurisdiction of the Court to give a preliminary ruling and so to determine the scope of the individual's rights and obligations, is a more powerful weapon. The individual has no direct remedy, before the Court, against the default of a State. The remedy lies in the national court with the use of Article 177 where appropriate, and with a possible action in damages for such default.[51]

In this way the national courts enforce, if necessary against their own State, the rights conferred on the individual by the Treaty. The doctrine of direct effect, however, has its limitations.

In an unusual case the English High Court sought a preliminary ruling on the interpretation of Articles 4(d), 65 and 66(7) of the ECSC Treaty.[52] Those provisions, like Articles 3(f), 81 and 82 (ex Articles 85 and 86) EC, aim to ensure that competition is not distorted by the activities of undertakings. However the Court held that they could not be relied upon by individuals in proceedings before national courts since the Commission had sole jurisdic-

---

[51] See the momentous decision in Cases C–6 & 9/90 *Francovich v. Italian State* [1991] ECR I–5357 and see Chap. 8 above. For commentary on Francovich and its impact: see J. E. Hanft, *Member States Liability for Failure to Implement Community Directives* (1991-92) Fordham International Law Journal 1237; K. Parker, "State Liability in Damages for Breach of Community Law" (1992) L.Q.R. 181 and J. Steiner, "From Direct Effect to Francovich: shifting means of enforcement of Community Law" (1993) 18 E.L.Rev. 3.

[52] Case C–128/92 *R.J. Banks & Company v. British Coal Corporation* [1994] ECR I–1209.

tion (subject to review by the Court of First Instance and the Court of Justice) to assess the compatibility with Article 65 ECSC of any prohibited agreement and to verify whether a dominant position was being used for purposes contrary to the objectives of the Treaty.

In this respect the Court declined to follow the opinion of Advocate General van Gerven who had proposed that those provisions should have direct effect. In his earlier opinion in *Marshall II*[53] van Gerven had already espoused the cause of so-called horizontal direct effect of directives, that is to say that, in the event of non-implementation or of incorrect or incomplete implementation of a directive, it should nonetheless give rise to rights enforceable by one individual against another in national courts.

Similar views were persuasively submitted by Advocates General Jacobs in *Vaneetveld*[54] and Lenz in *Faccini Dori*.[55] In the latter case the issue of horizontal effect arose in particularly clear fashion. Miss Faccini Dori had been persuaded by a salesman at Milan Central railway station to enter into a contract to follow a language course by correspondence. Some days later she changed her mind and sought to cancel the contract invoking her rights under a Council Directive on the protection of consumers in respect of contracts negotiated away from business premises.[56] Article 5 of the Directive provides that consumers shall have the right to cancel such a contract by sending notice within a period of not less than seven days. At the time the contract was concluded the time limit for implementing the Directive had expired but it had not yet been implemented in Italy.

The factoring company, Recreb, to whom the debt had been assigned brought proceedings to recover the sum concerned before the *Giudice conciliatore di Firenze* (Mediating Judge, Florence) who referred the case to the Court of Justice for a preliminary ruling on the question whether the provisions of the Directive could be relied upon by individuals against other individuals.

Despite the urging of the three advocates general the Court gave a firmly negative reply to that question essentially on the basis of a

---

[53] Case C–271/91 *Marshall v. Southampton and South West Area Health Authority* [1993] ECR I–4367.

[54] Case C–316/93 *Vaneetveld v. SA le Foyer* [1994] ECR I–763. As the advocate general himself pointed out, the point did not need to be decided for the purposes of resolving that case since the time-limit for implementing the directive concerned had not yet expired at the time of the events giving rise to the proceedings. The Court did not therefore address the question of any possible horizontal effect.

[55] Case C–91/92 *Faccini Dori v. Recreb Srl* [1994] ECR I–3325.

[56] Directive 85/577 [1985] O.J. L372/31.

strict interpretation of Article 189 of the Treaty. Thus it stated that to extend the principle of direct effect "to the sphere of relations between individuals would be to recognise a power in the Community to enact obligations for individuals with immediate effect, whereas it has competence to do so only where it is empowered to adopt regulations". To attenuate somewhat the harsh effects of that position the Court also re-iterated the principle that national legislative provisions should, so far as possible be interpreted so as to give effect to a directive[57] and referred to the possibility of pursuing a claim in damages against the state as in *Francovich*.[58]

Although the judgment in *Faccini Dori* is consistent with the Court's previous case law, in particular in *Marshall I*,[59] it has been called "a missed opportunity".[59a]

## Questions of Community Law

The Court has taken a wide view, also, of the questions of Community law which may be the subject of a reference. It will be recalled that under the ECSC Treaty (Article 41), the Court's jurisdiction is limited by the terms of that Article, to the validity of Acts of the High Authority and of the Council, although the Court has interpreted the Article as extending also to their interpretation[60]; under the EC Treaty (Article 234, ex Article 177) and the Euratom Treaty (Article 150) its jurisdiction extends to interpretation of the acts of the institutions.[61] As well as the EC and Euratom Treaties, the Court can interpret the amending Treaties such as the Merger Treaty, the three Treaties of Accession and relevant parts of the Maastricht Treaty and the Treaty of Amsterdam. Thus the Court can deal with any questions involving interpretation of the Treaties.

What "acts" of the Community institutions are subject to interpretation? The Court, as has been said, has taken a liberal view. In Case 181/73 *Haegeman*[62] it interpreted certain provisions

---

[57] As it had stated in Case C–106/89 *Marleasing S.A. v. Comercial Internacional de Alimentacion S.A.* [1990] ECR I–4135.

[58] Joined Cases C–6&9/90 *Francovich and Bonifaci v. Italy* [1991] ECR I–5357.

[59] By T. Tridimas, "Horizontal effect of directives: a missed opportunity" (1994) 19 E.L.Rev. 621, a critical analysis of the reasoning of the Court in *Faccini*.

[59a] Case 152/84 *Marshall v. Southampton and South West Area Health Authority* [1986] ECR 737.

[60] Case C–221/88 *ECSC v. Busseni* [1990] ECR I–495 and see p. 206, above.

[61] Including even non-binding measures such as recommendations: Case C–322/88 *Grimaldi v. Fonds des Maladies Professionnelles* [1989] ECR 4407.

[62] Case 181/73 *Haegeman* [1974] ECR 449.

of the Agreement of Association between the EEC and Greece, on the ground that such an agreement, concluded by the Council under Articles 228 and 238 (now Articles 300 and 310) EC of the EEC Treaty, was an act of one of the Community institutions within the meaning of Article 177 (now Article 234) EC.[63] Although international agreements with non-Member States can thus be interpreted by the Court, questions can of course be referred only by the courts and tribunals of the Member States, and not by the judicial bodies of other States party to the agreements.

## COURTS AND TRIBUNALS OF MEMBER STATES

The general question of what constitutes "a court or tribunal of a Member State" (in the French *"une juridiction d'un des Etats membres"*) under Article 177 is a question of Community law and must be answered by reference to general criteria applicable to all Member States rather than by reference to national law. But to determine whether those criteria are satisfied in a particular case it is necessary to look at the rules of national law governing the composition, status and functions of the body in question. Thus, although the Court is normally concerned on a reference only with questions of Community law, it may have to consider questions of national law for the purposes of determining its jurisdiction.

The question first arose in *Vaassen-Göbbels*,[64] on a reference from a Dutch social security tribunal. The tribunal, in making the reference, suggested that it was competent to do so. It stated that although it could not be considered as a court or tribunal under Dutch law, nevertheless this did not exclude the possibility that it should be regarded as a "court or tribunal" within the meaning of Article 177. The defendant, a social security fund set up under private law by organisations representing employers and wage-earners in the mining industry, submitted that the tribunal gave "non-binding opinions" rather than decisions and was therefore not competent to make a reference.

The Court held that the tribunal should be considered as a court or tribunal of a Member State for the purposes of Article 177. It took account of the fact that the responsible minister had to

---

[63] See also Case 87/75 *Bresciani v. Amministrazione Italiana delle Finanze* [1976] ECR 129; [1976] 2 C.M.L.R. 62, Case 270/80 *Polydor v. Harlequin Record Shops* [1982] ECR 329; [1982] 1 C.M.L.R. 677 and Case 12/86 *Demirel v. City of Schwäbisch Gmünd* [1987] ECR 3747.

[64] Case 61/65 *Vaassen-Göbbels v. Beambtenfonds voor het Mijnbedrijf* [1966] ECR 261; [1966] C.M.L.R. 508.

appoint the members of the tribunal, to designate its chairman and to lay down its rules of procedure; the tribunal was a permanent body which heard disputes according to an adversarial procedure and was bound to apply rules of law.

This case illustrates the interaction of national law and Community law as well as the broad view taken by the Court of its Article 234 (ex Article 177) EC jurisdiction.

In another Dutch case, a reference from the Dutch Council of State (*Raad van State*), Advocate General Mayras examined at some length the question whether that body, whose functions were strictly only advisory, was to be regarded as a court or tribunal; but the Court gave its ruling without adverting to this question and presumably entertained no doubts about the answer: Case 36/73 *Nederlandse Spoorwegen*.[65]

In Case 138/80 *Borker*[66] the Court declined to give a ruling on a reference from the Paris *Chambre des Avocats* on the ground that the Chamber was not exercising a judicial function; and in Case 65/77 *Razanatsimba*[67] the *Cour d'appel* of Douai declared that the *Conseil de l'Ordre des Avocats* of Lille was not a tribunal which could refer questions to the Court of Justice, a view with which, in *Borker*, the Court appeared to concur.

A court does not cease to be a court for the purposes of Article 234 (ex Article 177) EC, even though it combines other functions which are not strictly judicial in character. The Court so held in Case 14/86 *Pretore di Salò v. Persons unknown*[68] in accepting a reference from an Italian *Pretore*, a magistrate who combines the tasks of public prosecutor and investigating judge; the *Pretore* of Salo was seised of a complaint against persons unknown regarding the pollution of a river and asked for an interpretation of a directive which he believed in point.

So far as the United Kingdom is concerned, Article 234 (ex Article 177) EC obviously applies, not only to the ordinary courts, but also to tribunals established by statute, such as a National Insurance (now Social Security) Commissioner.[69]

Likewise, the Court of Justice has readily accepted that an organ of the State which combines both executory (or administrative)

---

[65] Case 36/73 *Nederlandse Spoorwegen v. Minister van Verkeer en Waterstaat* [1973] ECR 1299; [1974] 2 C.M.L.R. 148.

[66] Case 138/80 *Borker* [1980] ECR 1975; [1980] 3 C.M.L.R. 638.

[67] Case 65/77 *Razanatsimba* [1977] ECR 2229; [1978] 1 C.M.L.R. 246.

[68] [1987] ECR 2565.

[69] Case 17/76 *Brack v. Insurance Officer* [1976] ECR 1429; [1976] 2 C.M.L.R. 592 or the Special Commissioners of Income Tax (Case 208/80 *Lord Bruce of Donington v. Aspden (H.M.I.T.)* [1981] ECR 2205; [1981] 3 C.M.L.R. 506.

functions with judicial functions may be classified as a court or tribunal in respect of its judicial acts.[70]

On the other hand, the Director of Taxation of the Grand Duchy of Luxembourg could not make a reference under Article 177 (now 234) because he was a party to the dispute between the tax-payer and the Luxembourg tax administration. The term "court or tribunal" was to be defined in a Community context and could only refer to an authority which was a third party in relation to the body or person which had made the decision that was the subject-matter of the proceedings.[71]

A problem might, however, arise in relation to what English lawyers term domestic tribunals. In the United Kingdom such tribunals are very numerous and diverse, ranging from the Judicial Committee of the Privy Council, exercising a disciplinary jurisdiction in relation to doctors, or a statutory body like the Solicitors' Disciplinary Tribunal, to membership or disciplinary committees of such voluntary associations as the Jockey Club or the Football Association. Would they all qualify as tribunals "of" a Member State, or does the preposition denote some relationship of the tribunal to state authority or what Professor Hartley terms "some measure of official recognition."[72] Nor is it far-fetched to suggest issues could arise before such tribunals upon which a reference under Article 177 (now 234) might be appropriate. Thus, if the facts of *Russell v. Duke of Norfolk*[73] had arisen after 1972, the Jockey Club might have wished to refer to Luxembourg the question whether they could continue to deny women the right to be professional jockeys.

The approach of the Court of Justice to such problems may be illustrated by comparing Case 246/80 *Broekmeulen*[74] and Case 102/81 *Nordsee*.[75] *Broekmeulen* was a Dutch citizen holding Belgian medical qualifications and duly authorised to practise medicine in Holland. The Dutch medical authorities refused to place him on the Dutch medical register of general practitioners on

---

[70] See Case C–109/90 *Giant v. Gemeente Overijse* [1991] ECR I–1385, where the reference was accepted from the so-called executive branch of a Belgian provincial council which also acted as a local tax tribunal; and Case C–67/91 *Direccion de Defensa de la Competencia v. Asociacion Española de Banca Privada and Others* [1992] ECR I–4785, where the reference was accepted from a tribunal responsible for competition matters within the Spanish Ministry of Trade which had both administrative and judicial functions.

[71] Case C–24/92 *Corbiau v. Administration des Contributions* [1993] ECR I–1277.

[72] In *The Foundations of Community Law* (2nd ed., 1988), p. 256.

[73] [1949] 1 All E.R. 109.

[74] Case 246/80 *Broekmeulen v. Huisarts Registratie Commissie* [1981] ECR 2311; [1982] 1 C.M.L.R. 91.

[75] Case 102/81 *Nordsee v. Reederei Mond* [1982] ECR 1095.

the ground of his not having had one year's experience in general practice; as a result, he was not qualified to treat patients under the Dutch social security scheme. Broekmeulen appealed to the Dutch Appeal Committee for General Practice, which body made a reference under Article 177 (now Article 234) to ascertain whether Broekmeulen could rely on the right of establishment and the freedom to provide services conferred by Community law. On the preliminary point whether the Appeal Committee was entitled to refer under Article 177 (now Article 234), the Court held that it was, despite its being a body set up under the rules of the Dutch Medical Association, a private association. The Court decided that the Appeal Committee was exercising a public or quasi-public jurisdiction which could affect the exercise of Community rights; it also had regard to the adversarial and quasi-judicial nature of proceedings before it. Moreover such cases did not, in practice, come before the ordinary courts.

In *Nordsee* a group of German companies made an agreement for the pooling between them of a Community grant for the construction of new ships. They subsequently were in dispute as to how the grant should be allocated and, under a clause in the agreement, submitted their dispute to an arbitrator appointed by the Bremen Chamber of Commerce. The Chamber appointed the President of the Bremen *Oberlandesgericht* (Higher Regional Court) who decided to make a reference under Article 177 (now Article 234) EC on points of Community law relevant to the dispute. The Court decided, however, that the arbitration tribunal, which was established pursuant to a contract between private individuals, was not a court or tribunal of a Member State: consequently the Court had no jurisdiction to rule on the substantive issues referred to it. In reaching this decision, the Court found it significant that there was no obligation on the parties to submit their dispute to arbitration; in contrast with the position in the *Broekmeulen* case, they could have taken their case to the ordinary courts, which could also review the decision of the arbitrator and, if necessary, themselves make a reference to the Court of Justice.

The requirement that the court or tribunal be one "of a Member State" was an issue in two more recent cases. In Cases C–100/89 and C–101/89 *Kaefer and Procacci v. France*[76] a reference to Luxembourg was made by the *Tribunal administratif* of Papeete (Tahiti) in French Polynesia. The British Government raised a forlorn argument that, unlike the French *départements d'outre-mer* (orDOMs) to which the provisions of the EC Treaty were made

---

[76] Cases G–100/89 and C–101/89 *Kaefer and Procacci v. France* [1990] ECR I–4647.

expressly applicable by Article 227(2) (now Article 299(2) EC), no such general application of the Treaty was provided for in Articles 131 to 136a (now Articles 182 to 188) EC relating to French overseas territories (*territoires d'outre mer*, known as TOMs). The Court was not persuaded, simply noting, as Advocate General Mischo had pointed out, that an appeal from the Papeete Tribunal lay to the *Cour administrative d'appel* in Paris or, in certain circumstances, to the *Conseil d'Etat*.[77]

The second case concerned the Deputy High Bailiff's Court in Douglas, Isle of Man. The Isle of Man is not part of the United Kingdom. Nevertheless, at the time of British accession to the Community, the Manx authorities envisaged that their courts might refer under Article 177 (now Article 234), since certain provisions of Community law were made applicable to the Isle of Man by Article 227(5)(c) EEC and Protocol No. 3 to the Act of Accession. It was on the interpretation of that Protocol that the Deputy High Bailiff's Court sought a preliminary ruling. The Court of Justice agreed with Advocate General Jacobs that the Manx court must be regarded as within the scope of Article 177 as it was situated in a territory to which Community law applied, if only in part, and the guidance of the Court was therefore essential for the uniform application of such law.[78] Finally, in the *Christian Dior* case[79] the Court held that there was no reason in principle why a court common to a number of Member States, such as, in that case, the Benelux Court, should not be able to submit questions to the Court of Justice for a preliminary ruling. Moreover as a court from whose decisions no appeal lies, the Benelux Court was obliged to make such a reference in accordance with the third paragraph of Article 177 (now Article 234). This obligation is the subject matter of the next section.

## COURTS AND TRIBUNALS OBLIGED TO REFER

Under the last paragraph of Article 234 (ex Article 177) EC, as we have seen, a court or tribunal against whose decisions there is no

---

[77] In a later case, a reference from the *Tribunal de Paix of Papeete* was accepted without question as within Art. 177 (now Art. 234) EC: Case C–260/90 *Leplat v. Territory of French Polynesia* [1992] ECR I–643; [1992] 2 C.M.L.R. 512.

[78] Case C–355/89 *Department of Health and Social Security v. Barr and Montrose Holdings* [1991] ECR I–3479, see Arnull *loc. cit.* n. 37, above. See further Case C–171/96 *Pereira Roquer v. Governor of Jersey* [1998] ECR I–4607 and, for a brief general discussion of the geographical scope of European law see Tom Kennedy, *Learning European Law* (1999), p. 99.

[79] Case C–337/95 *Parfums Christian Dior and Another v. Evora BV* [1997] ECR I–6013.

judicial remedy under national law is not merely entitled, but obliged, to refer a question, if it considers that a decision on that question is necessary to enable it to give judgment. A reference in such a case is not discretionary but mandatory. The question arises whether the obligation to refer is restricted to those courts and tribunals whose decisions are never subject to appeal, or whether it extends to any court or tribunal whose decision in the particular case is not subject to appeal. On the first (or "abstract") view (adopted *per incuriam* by Lord Denning M.R. in *Bulmer v. Bollinger* [1974] Ch. 401) only the House of Lords in England (as to Scotland, see below), and the highest courts of the other Member States, would be obliged to refer. On the second (or "concrete") view even a quite lowly tribunal would be in the same position; on this view even the Milan magistrate in *Costa v. ENEL* (above, p. 214) was obliged to refer since his judgment was not subject to appeal in Italian law because of the small amount involved in the claim. A literal interpretation might support the first view, since the text refers to "decisions" in the plural, but as the question is one of interpretation of the Treaty, such an approach was unlikely to commend itself to the Court. More pertinent is a consideration of the purposes of the provision. Here the first view might be supported by the argument that the decisions of the highest national courts carry a special authority, and should therefore be subject to a special provision to ensure the uniform application of Community law at the highest level. On the other hand it could be argued that what is important is for the individual litigant to have the opportunity of a reference before a final decision is given in his case and that the necessity of ensuring uniform interpretation of Community law required that, ultimately, such questions must, necessarily, be referred to the Court of Justice.

Here too the Court, although not expressly invited to rule on this question, has adopted the wider view, stating in *Costa v. ENEL* (at p. 592) that the magistrate was under an obligation to make a reference in that case as there was no appeal against his decision.

In relation to the United Kingdom, the view sometimes expressed that only the House of Lords would be obliged to refer is an over-simplification even if one adopts the "abstract" view (see above). For the House of Lords is the ultimate appellate jurisdiction in the United Kingdom as a whole only for civil matters. In criminal matters, there is no appeal to the House of Lords from the Scottish criminal courts of last instance, which therefore would rank as final courts for the purpose of the last paragraph of Article 234 (ex Article 177) EC.

A complication in determining which courts or tribunals fall within the third paragraph of Article 234 (ex Article 177) EC arises from the English habit of permitting an appeal, not as of right, but by leave only. Thus, an appeal from the Court of Appeal to the House of Lords requires either the leave of the former or, if it be refused, the leave of the Appeals Committee of the House of Lords. The parties therefore do not know until after the Court of Appeal has delivered judgment, and leave to appeal from that judgment has been refused, that the Court of Appeal would thereby become the court of last instance in their case. By then, it is not possible to invoke the third paragraph of Article 234 (ex Article 177) EC and to insist on a reference: the national court has become *functus officio*, and any ruling obtained would be retrospective, not preliminary.

To this dilemma, the only logical solution and one which the spirit and intendment of the third paragraph of Article 234 dictate, is to regard that court as the court of last resort from whose decisions no appeal lies as of right.[80] This view found support from Buckley L.J. in an obiter dictum in *Hagen v. Moretti*[81] and was perhaps implicit in the judgments in the Divisional Court in *S.A. Magnavision v. General Optical Council* (No. 2).[82]

Again, in English civil procedure the prerogative orders of certiorari, prohibition or mandamus, or the post-1977 application for judicial review, pose problems by reason of these remedies being discretionary in character and conducted in two stages. In the first stage, an *ex parte* application must be made for leave to apply for the order. These remedies are not therefore available as of right, and, by analogy with what was said in relation to appeals (above), a court whose judgment is final, except for possible review by way of certiorari, etc., should, logically, be considered to fall within the third paragraph of Article 234 (ex Article 177). British writers differ on this question, but a National Insurance Commissioner has held himself to be outside the third paragraph of Article 177 (now 234) and to have a discretion whether or not to refer under the second paragraph of Article 177 (now 234) because his judgment, although "final," was reviewable by way of certiorari.[83]

In practice the problem of which courts are obliged to refer will be less acute where the courts of first instance and appeal exercise correctly their discretion.

## APPROACH OF THE NATIONAL COURTS

The success of the preliminary ruling system plainly depends on a close co-operation between the Court and the national courts.

---

[80] But see the ingenious suggestion of T. C. Hartley, *The Foundations of European Community Law* (3rd ed., 1994), pp. 248–286.

[81] [1980] 3 C.M.L.R. 253.

[82] [1987] 2 C.M.L.R. 262 (above, p. 195).

[83] See *Re a Holiday in Italy* [1975] 1 C.M.L.R. 184, *per* Mr J.G. Monroe.

With a view to fostering this co-operation, the Court has for many years arranged regular meetings in Luxembourg with judges and lawyers from the Member States, and has also visited the courts of the Member States; on occasion, members of the Court have sat on the bench in the national courts. Individual members of the Court also maintain contact with the Bench and Bar of their respective countries, and regularly give talks and lectures at conferences and meetings of lawyers.

Such efforts, however, must be fully reciprocal to be effective, and it cannot be said that the readiness of the Court to receive references, and to try to give helpful answers to the questions referred, has always been met with equal enthusiasm. Judges are generally cautious and conservative by temperament, and it was not to be expected that so radical an innovation in the European legal scene would flourish very rapidly. In the earliest years of the EEC Treaty, the Court received little but an occasional reference from a Dutch court, and subsequently only the German courts have made the fullest use of the procedure. Although it is now more widely used, there have been striking differences in the approach of the courts of different Member States, as appears from Table 6 of the Judicial Statistics (below, p. 426). In view of the importance of the preliminary ruling in the Community legal system, the approach by national courts to the exercise of their discretion to refer is crucial and has received much attention.

Those courts which have been reluctant to refer have not been very successful in their attempts to rationalise that reluctance. The French courts sought in the early days to rely on the doctrine of "*acte clair*," so that even a final court such as the *Conseil d'Etat* could avoid Article 177 on the ground that no "question" of interpretation arose because the answer was clear; but this argument is open to abuse.[84] The *Conseil d'Etat*, as we shall see, has now reconciled itself to the supremacy of Community law and so has less need to resort to the doctrine.[85]

In England when Article 177 (now Article 234) EC first came before the Court of Appeal, Lord Denning M.R. in *Bulmer v. Bollinger*,[86] sought to lay down certain "guide-lines" in an apparent attempt to restrict the use of references. The attempt was marred by some confusion of thought and met a very critical reception. Broadly the chief criticism is that, while the exercise of

---

[84] See Judge Pescatore in *Legal Problems of an Enlarged European Community* (1972), p. 27, and *Cohn-Bendit* (below, n. 84) [1980] 1 C.M.L.R. 543, and contrast the more faithful approach of Lord Diplock in *Garland v. British Rail Engineering* [1982] 2 C.M.L.R. 174.

[85] See p. 231 and n. 93, below.

[86] [1974] Ch. 401.

its discretion is a matter for the national court, that discretion must be exercised in the light of the purposes of Article 234 (ex Article 177) EC; and, as the Court of Justice itself has held, its exercise cannot be limited by any considerations of national law (the *Rheinmuhlen* cases, below, p. 000). Thus the "guide-lines" have no authority as a matter of law; but emanating from so eminent a source they have had some influence in practice.[87] The guidelines have been expressly rejected by an Irish court.[88]

Proposals have been made to remedy the problem where a final court wrongly decides not to refer; for example, a direct right of appeal to the Court could be conferred in such cases. This possibility was mentioned by the Commission in a report on European Union.[89] But the answer probably lies with the national courts themselves, and the statistics show that they have progressively adjusted to the system. Theoretically an action by the Commission under Article 169 (now Article 226) would lie against a Member State whose courts were in breach of their obligation under Article 177 (now Article 234), since the courts, although constitutionally independent, are nonetheless organs of the State for the purposes of State responsibility: see to this effect the Opinion of Advocate General Warner in Case 9/75 *Meyer-Burckhardt*.[90] But such an enforcement procedure seems inappropriate except for a flagrant breach, and even then the Commission may decide not to bring the matter before the Court for fear of exacerbating a politically sensitive situation.[91]

Manifestly, the *Conseil d'Etat*, in contrast with the French civil courts,[92] was not previously imbued with that "spirit of judicial co-operation" which the Court of Justice sees as implicit in the reference procedure. Since 1989, however, there has been a change of attitude, and the *Conseil* now fully accepts the supremacy of Community law, including the principles established

---

[87] See, for example, *Concorde Express Transport v. Traffic Examiner Metropolitan Police*, Kingston Crown Court [1980] 2 C.M.L.R. 221; also their uncritical acceptance by the editors of *The Supreme Court Practice 1993* (Vol. 1, 1611–12; commentary on R.S.C. Ord. 114. For a valuable corrective, however, see the views of Bingham J. in *Samex*, cited above, p. 210), and, more recently, his succinct summary of the main principles (now as Master of the Rolls) in *R. v. Stock Exchange, ex p. Else (1982) Ltd* [1993] 1 All E.R. 420 at 426.

[88] See F. Murphy (1982) 7 E.L.Rev. 331 at 337.

[89] Bulletin of the European Communities, Supplement 5/75.

[90] [1975] ECR 1171 at 1187.

[91] As, for instance, when the French *Conseil d'Etat* refused to refer on the ground that the Community law was clear, although the *Conseil's* view of that law was directly contrary to the established case law of the Court of Justice: *Cohn-Bendit* [1980] 1 C.M.L.R. 543.

[92] *Syndicat Général des Fabricants de Semoules de France v. Société des Cafés Jacques Vabre* [1975] 2 C.M.L.R. 336 (a decision of the *Cour de Cassation*).

by the case law of the Court of Justice.[93] Confrontation will only be avoided if national courts regard themselves also, no less than the Court of Justice, as Community courts. No less encouraging in this respect is the shift of view in the German Constitutional Court (Second Chamber) between its decision in *Internationale Handelsgesellschaft* (1974) and that of October 22, 1986,[94] which now accepts the supremacy of Community law. This led the Editor of the European Law Review to remark: "This happy ending provides an object lesson for those (including ourselves) who are inclined to cry havoc whenever a national court behaves inconsistently with established wisdom as to the relationship between Community law and national law."[95]

Significantly, in what some may see as a conciliatory gesture, the Court of Justice has conceded that the obligation to refer under the third paragraph of Article 177 still leaves the national judge free not to do so where he believes the point is sufficiently clear not to require an interpretation; the Court accepted that the *acte clair* doctrine is not limited to cases where the point in question has already been the subject of interpretation at Luxembourg in a previous case: Case 283/81 *CILFIT*.[96] At the same time the national judge was warned against assuming that the point is clear in all the language versions of the text in issue; and the Court added a reminder that the national judge should not overlook the special features of Community law – its plurilingual versions, its own individual terminology and its particular methods of interpretation (for this last, see Chapter 14, below). But Advocate General Jacobs has now warned against regarding the *CILFIT* judgment as requiring the national courts to examine any Community measure in issue in every one of the official Community languages. He points out that such examination would involve in many cases a disproportionate effort on the part of the national courts; moreover, reference to all the language versions of Community provisions is a method which appears rarely to be applied by the Court of Justice itself.[97]

The national judge should also have regard to the rule change of May 16, 2000, set out at the end of this Chapter (p. 241, below).

---

[93] See *Compagnie Alitalia*, C.E. February 3, 1989; *Nicolo*, C.E. October 20, 1989; *Boisdet*, C.E. September 24, 1990; *S.A. Rothmans et S.A. Philip Morris*, C.E. February 28, 1992 (discussed Brown and Bell, *French Administrative Law*, (5th ed., 1998), pp. 284–286).

[94] *Wunsche Handelsgesellschaft* [1987] 3 C.M.L.R. 225.

[95] (1987) 12 E.L.Rev. 162.

[96] Case 283/81 *CILFIT v. Ministry of Health* [1982] ECR 3415; [1983] 1 C.M.L.R. 472.

[97] Case C–338/95 *Wiener v. Hauptzollamt Emmerich* [1997] ECR I–6516.

## EFFECTS OF PRELIMINARY RULINGS

First, we must distinguish between the effect of the ruling in the instant case and its effect in subsequent cases. The ruling is binding upon the referring court or tribunal in the sense that the interpretation or validity of the Community law in question has been authoritatively and finally determined in Luxembourg. The national judge has consulted the oracle and must accept the reply as what indeed the Treaties say it is: a ruling, not an opinion.[98] It is then for the national judge to apply the Community law to the facts of the case.

The next question is whether the ruling is binding in future cases in which the same point of Community law arises; or, as an English lawyer might ask, is it a precedent? The whole question of precedent in the Court of Justice is discussed later in Chapter 16. Here we must anticipate the conclusion there reached, namely, that the Court prefers to follow its own previous decisions (including rulings) but that it does not hesitate to depart from them where necessary. Hence, the Court has held that a national court, at whatever level, is always free to seek a new preliminary ruling instead of following an old one: in Joined Cases 28–30/62 *Da Costa*[99] the Dutch Tax Court put exactly the same question to the Court as it had already put in the previous case of *Van Gend en Loos*,[1] and the Court endorsed its freedom to do so. Nevertheless, the Court reserves the power under Article 104(3) of its Rules of Procedure,[2] where the question referred to the Court is "identical to a question on which the Court has already ruled", to give its decision by reasoned order in which reference is made to its previous judgment. Such an order avoids the need for a formal judgment, preceded by oral hearing and advocate-general's opinion. Alternatively, the Court may instruct the Registrar to write to the referring court or tribunal, drawing attention to the previous judgment and enquiring whether the referring court wishes to maintain the reference: this often leads to the reference being withdrawn.[3] In practice, without such prompting, national courts

---

[98] See Case 29/68 *Milchkontor v. Hauptzollamt Saarbrucken* [1969] ECR 165; [1969] C.M.L.R. 390. The Court firmly reiterated this principle in Opinion 1/91 on the EEA Agreement [1991] ECR I–6079. See especially paras 58–64 at I–6109 and I–6110, discussed below at pp. 255–256.

[99] Joined Cases 28, 29 & 30/62 *Da Costa en Schaake N.V. v. Nederlandse Belastingadministratie* [1963] ECR 31; [1963] C.M.L.R. 224.

[1] Case 26/62 [1963] ECR 1; [1963] C.M.L.R. 105.

[2] Article 104(3) added to the CJ Rules on May 15, 1991 [1991] O.J. L176/1, was amended on May 16, 2000 so as to relieve pressure further on the Court of Justice: see p. 241, below.

[3] See A. Arnull, "Owning up to fallibility: precedent and the Court of Justice" (1993) 30 C.M.L. Rev. 247 at 252.

frequently accept previous rulings as clarifying the question of Community law in issue now before them so as to render otiose a further reference[4] and a United Kingdom court is bound by statute to accept not only the ruling in a case which it has referred but also the principles laid down by the Court and any relevant previous decision.[5]

The doctrine of precedent is concerned with the prospective effect of a judgment (or ruling). Whether a ruling has retrospective effect is a different matter and requires us to distinguish between (1) a ruling on interpretation, and (2) a ruling on validity (or invalidity).

## 1. Rulings on Interpretation

It is the characteristic of an oracle to make plain what has always been. Thus, when in 1963 the Court of Justice ruled in *Van Gend en Loos* (above), that Article 12 (now, after amendment Article 25) EC had direct effect, it was declaring what had always been the correct interpretation of that Article since the Treaty entered into force on January 1, 1958. However, in exceptional cases where the interest of legal certainty so demands, the Court has been prepared to limit the general retrospective effect of its ruling on interpretation.[6]

## 2. Rulings on Validity

It is only common sense that provisions of Community law enjoy a presumption of validity. Rulings on invalidity, therefore, are much less frequent than rulings on interpretation: Community law is often obscure, seldom invalid.[7]

Where the Court rules that a Community measure is valid or invalid, the ruling is binding upon the referring court in the same way as we have seen a ruling on interpretation binds that court. Similarly, the ruling has force as a precedent: if, however, the Court has ruled that no factors indicating invalidity have appeared, then new factors may be suggested in a future case, while of course

---

[4] See, for example, the *Terrapin* case before the German Federal Supreme Court [1978] 3 C.M.L.R. 102.

[5] See the European Communities Act 1972, s.3(1) and below, p. 379.

[6] See Case 43/75 *Defrenne* [1976] ECR 455; [1976] 2 C.M.L.R. 98, and Case 24/86 *Blaizot v. University of Liége* [1988] ECR 379, fully discussed below, p. 242 and Case C–262/88 *Barber v. Guardian Royal Exchange* [1990] ECR I–1889 and its *sequelae*, noted at p. 342, below.

[7] For a ruling of invalidity see Case 120/86 *Mulder v. Minister van Landbouw en Visserij* [1988] ECR 2321; [1989] 2 C.M.L.R. 1, discussed in Chap. 8, p. 180, above.

if the measure has been held invalid the question cannot arise again.

When ruling a measure to be invalid, the Court has treated it as being void *erga omnes*: the ruling under Article 234 (ex Article 177) EC is therefore different from a decision under Article 241 (ex Article 184) EC which merely declares the measure to be inapplicable in the instant case.[8]

*Ratione temporis*, however, the Court may decide to limit the retrospective effect of its ruling in order to leave previous transactions unaffected. We have already seen in *Defrenne*, above, how it did this when ruling upon interpretation, but the same concern for legal certainty may operate a fortiori when it rules a Community measure to be void.

Thus, in Case 41/84 *Pinna*[9] the Court declared invalid a provision in a Council regulation which granted to France a special exemption from the obligation to pay family allowances in respect of an immigrant worker's family resident in another Member State. The Court went on to limit the retrospective effect of the ruling: only the claimant and those who had already commenced proceedings prior to the date of its judgment could claim allowances for periods prior to that date. Subsequently, the Commission, alleging failure to comply with the ruling in *Pinna*, introduced Article 169 (now Article 226) proceedings against France.[10]

Earlier, in Cases 4, 109 & 145/79 *Providence Agricole de la Champagne and Others v. ONIC* (the Maize and Starch cases),[11] the Court held a Council regulation to be void which had caused the applicants (and other processors of the same products) to receive lower payments for their products than they would otherwise have done. Nevertheless, the Court went on to hold that the applicants should not be entitled to claim against their national authorities the extra sums which would be due to them if transactions concluded prior to the date of the ruling were to be re-opened. The Court claimed jurisdiction to do this in proceedings under Article 177 (now Article 234), by analogy with the power conferred upon it by the second paragraph of Article 174 (now Article 231) whereby the Court may state which of the

---

[8] For Art. 184 and the plea of illegality, see p. 164, above.

[9] Case 41/84 *Pinna v. Caisse des Allocations Familiales de la Savoie* [1986] ECR 1; [1988] 1 C.M.L.R. 350.

[10] Case 371/88 *Commission v. France* [1991] O.J. C78/12 the case was removed from the Court register in February 1991.

[11] [1980] ECR 2823. See Brown, "Agrimonetary Byzantinism and Prospective Overruling" (1981) 18 C.M.L.R. 509.

effects of the regulation it has declared void in proceedings under Article 230 (ex Article 173) EC shall be considered as definitive.[12]

In the result, the Court evolved a doctrine of great flexibility akin to that of prospective overruling in the United States. Whereas, in *Defrenne* and *Pinna*, the applicant – but not future applicants – was able to benefit from the ruling, in the *Maize and Starch* cases not even the applicants could benefit from the ruling. In reality, of course, the applicants (and all fellow processors) would be better off in the future by reason of the offending regulation being held void.

## CONCLUSIONS

Earlier chapters have shown the narrow limits within which the individual can bring a case directly before the Court: limits which the Court itself has strictly construed. In contrast, the Court's policy, as this chapter has shown, has been to welcome references from national courts; and it has availed itself of the opportunity presented by such references to develop the law in ways which are explored in Part Four. Recently, as we have seen, the Court has shown itself increasingly ready to decline to answer a reference partly in response to its increasing workload. Nevertheless in these decisions, as in the Note for Guidance reproduced in the Appendix, the Court's concern is not simply to choke off the flow of cases referred to it but to make the procedure more effective and thereby to enable it to provide helpful answers to the questions submitted to it. The circumstances in which the Court may decline to answer a question submitted to it have been dealt with in earlier pages of this Chapter, but it may be helpful to summarize them here:

- The court will only answer questions submitted to it by a "court or tribunal of a Member State" (see above, and the *Vaassen-Göbbels, Nordsee, Broekmeulen* and *Corbiau* cases).
- It will not answer hypothetical questions or those contrived in a collusive action (see p. 215, above, and the *Foglia v. Novello* and *Meilicke* cases).
- It will not deal with a question the answer to which is not "necessary" in order for the national court to give a decision (see Case C–343/90 *Lourenço Dias v. Director da Alfandega do Porto*).[13]

---

[12] For the complex consequences of these rulings in the French courts, and the divergent attitudes of the French *Cour de Cassation* and *Conseil d'Etat*, see Hartley, *The Foundations of European Community Law* (3rd ed., 1994), pp. 252–255.

[13] [1992] 1 ECR I–4673.

- It will not deal with a case in which the national court fails to provide sufficient information on the factual and legal background to the questions which it wishes to have answered (see p. 218, above, the *Telemarsicabruzzo* and *Banchero* cases[14] and the "Note for Guidance", paras 5 and 6).

- It will not answer a question which raises only issues of national law (see p. 218, above, and the *Adlerblum* case and the "Note for Guidance", paras 3 and 7).

- It will not allow an abuse of procedure, such as attempting to circumvent the time limits under Article 230 (ex Article 173) EC (see Chapter 7 and p. 156, above, and the *TWD* case).

- Where a question is manifestly the same as one upon which the Court has already ruled it may deal with it by an order simply referring to its earlier judgment (see now amended RP104(3), below). This possibility should not however be confused with the *acte clair* doctrine explained in the *CILFIT* case (above, p. 241) under which a national court of last instance confronted by a question of Community law (which it would otherwise have been bound to refer under the terms of the third paragraph of Article 234 (ex Article 177)) may be excused from doing so if the Court has already ruled on the point or if the correct application of Community law is obvious (para. 1 of the "Note for Guidance").

Characteristically, in cases referred under Article 177 (now Article 234), what is at stake between the parties in the action before the national court may be relatively little; but the case often raises wider principles concerning the impact of the Communities on the sovereignty of the Member States and the ruling of the Court is such as to determine authoritatively, and with binding force, the conflict between Community law and national law. In addition, other principles of a constitutional character have been laid down. The two classic illustrations are the judgments in *Van Gend en Loos* in 1963 and in *Costa v. ENEL* in 1964. In the former case, as we have seen, the question concerned a tariff classification made under Dutch law which the plaintiff challenged in the Dutch court as contrary to Article 12 (now, after amendment Article 25) of the EC Treaty. The action raised the issue of conflict between national legislation and the provisions of the Treaty. The Court not only resolved this issue in favour of the primacy of Community law, but

---

[14] See too the Court's Order in Case C–167/94 *Grau Gomis and Others* [1995] ECR I–1023.

also formulated the doctrine of direct effect, thus providing for a direct guarantee of rights arising under Community law before the national courts, and ensuring, incidentally, that the future development of the law would be the responsibility of the national courts acting, where appropriate, under the guidance of the Court through the use of Article 177 (now Article 234).

In *Costa v. ENEL* the sum involved, the amount of the plaintiff's electricity bill, was trivial – little more than £1; but by challenging its legality before the Italian magistrate he put in issue the validity, under the EC Treaty, of State measures of nationalisation. While leaving the magistrate to apply its ruling as he thought fit (he, in fact, upheld the plaintiff's submission), the Court took the opportunity, in this most famous of its judgments, of elaborating its doctrine that membership of the Community limited the sovereignty of the Member States:

> "By contrast with ordinary international treaties, the EC Treaty has created its own legal system which, on the entry into force of the Treaty, became an integral part of the legal systems of the Member States and which their courts are bound to apply.
>
> By creating a Community of unlimited duration, having its own institutions, its own personality, its own legal capacity and capacity of representation on the international plane and, more particularly, real powers stemming from a limitation of sovereignty or a transfer of powers from the States to the Community, the Member States have limited their sovereign rights, albeit within limited fields, and have thus created a body of law which binds both their nationals and themselves."[15]

In another reference from Italy, Case 106/77 *Simmenthal*[16] the Court was faced with a conflict between a directly applicable Community rule and a later national law. Developing the doctrine in *Costa v. ENEL* of the Community as a new legal order and of the primacy of Community law, the Court was careful not to rule that the Community rule had made the subsequent Italian law void; rather, it precluded the valid adoption of new legislative measures to the extent to which they would be incompatible with Community provisions. The Court declared:

> "A national court which is called upon, within the limits of its jurisdiction, to apply provisions of Community law is

---

[15] [1964] ECR 585 at 593; [1964] C.M.L.R. 425.
[16] Case 106/77 *Simmenthal v. Amministrazione delle Finanze dello Stato* [1978] ECR 629; [1978] 3 C.M.L.R. 263.

under a duty to give full effect to those provisions, if necessary refusing of its own motion to apply any conflicting provision of national legislation, even if adopted subsequently, and it is not necessary for the court to request or await a prior setting aside of such provisions by legislative or other constitutional means."[17]

Further and striking application of the primacy of Community law was provided, in relation to English law, in the series of cases known as the *Factortame* affair.[18] In the outcome, the principle at common law (which has now been abandoned)[19] that an English court could not issue an interim injunction against the Crown was overridden by the obligation under Community law to safeguard potential rights under that law. Moreover, even an Act of Parliament should not be applied by the English judge if the Act were incompatible with Community law. This was dramatically confirmed when the House of Lords declared certain provisions of the Employment Protection (Consolidation) Act 1978 to be incompatible with Community law, thereby ensuring equal treatment for part-time workers who were mostly women.[20]

Quite apart from the content of its rulings, this aspect of the jurisdiction of the Court of Justice is of constitutional significance in other respects. In the first place, if a reference is made on the validity of, for example, a Council regulation, the Court may be required to consider the compatibility of the Community enactment with the founding Treaties in the same way as a constitutional court is required to consider the constitutionality of national legislation. Second, the ruling of the Court is final in a sense

---

[17] At p. 644. The late Professor Hood Phillips commented on this passage that would not prevent the British Parliament from repealing the whole or part of the European Communities Act 1972 so as to deprive British courts of the relevant jurisdiction referred to above (see (1979) L.Q.R. 167); but see *contra*, Usher, *European Community Law and National Law: The Irreversible Transfer?* (1981).

[18] *R. v. Secretary of State, ex p. Factortame*: the High Court referred on the substantive issue to Luxembourg on March 10, 1989; the Court of justice replied on July 25, 1991: C–221/89 [1991] ECR I–3905; [1991] 3 C.M.L.R. 589. Meanwhile, on the procedural issue concerning interim relief, there was appeal to the Court of Appeal and thence to the House of Lords, which referred this issue to Luxembourg on May 18, 1989; the Court replied on June 19, 1990: C–213/89 [1990] ECR I–2433; [1990] 3 C.M.L.R. 1. In addition, the Commission brought an enforcement action against the United Kingdom resulting in an interim order on October 10, 1989: C–246/89 R [1989] ECR 3125; [1991] 3 C.M.L.R. 706; and a ruling on October 4, 1991 [1991] ECR I–4585. On the issue of liability in damages, see Joined Cases C–46 & 48/93 *Brasserie du Pêcheur; Factortame III* [1996] ECR I–1929.

[19] See *M. v. Home Office and Another* (House of Lords) [1994] 1 A.C. 377.

[20] *Equal Opportunities Commission and another v. Secretary of State for Employment* [1994] 1 All E.R. 910.

*The Court's Judgment in the first* Factortame *case was widely interpreted as making a radical change to the British Constitution.*

unknown in systems which have a sovereign legislature. Thus in the United Kingdom a decision of even the highest court can, in the last resort, be reversed by an Act of Parliament. In the Communities, however a ruling on the interpretation of the Treaties could be reversed only by an amendment of them; and such an amendment, requiring the unanimous approval of the Member States in accordance with their respective constitutional provisions, is almost impossible to attain.[21] Here too therefore the Court is more comparable to a constitutional court than to an

---

* Drawing by Les Gibbard published in *The Guardian*, July 26, 1991 following the Court's judgment in Case C–213/89 *The Queen v. Secretary of State for Transport, ex p. Factortame and others.*

[21] See however the Protocol concerning Art. 141 (ex 119) EC, annexed to the Maastricht Treaty which seeks to clarify some of the uncertainties arising from the *Barber* judgment (see p. 234, n. 6, above).

ordinary court. Moreover, during periods when the normal law-making processes in the Community were partially paralysed by the lack of power and influence of the Parliament and by the unanimity rule of practice in the Council, the Court assumed a creative law-making role for which the Article 177 system has been the principal vehicle.

## EXTENSION OF USE OF REASONED ORDERS

In order to relieve pressure further on the Court of Justice, on May 16, 2000 the Rules of Procedure relating to preliminary rulings underwent important amendment. The amended Article 104(3) now extends to rulings the simplified procedure of reasoned order in the following terms:

Article 104(3) shall be replaced by the following text:

> "3. Where a question referred to the Court for a preliminary ruling is identical to a question on which the Court has already ruled, where the answer to such a question may be clearly deduced from existing case-law or where the answer to the question admits of no reasonable doubt, the Court may, after informing the court or tribunal which referred the question to it, after hearing any observations submitted by the persons referred to in Article 20 of the EC Statute, Article 21 of the Euratom Statute and Article 103(3) of these Rules and after hearing the Advocate-General, give its decision by reasoned order in which, if appropriate, reference is made to its previous judgment or to the relevant case-law."

# Appendix

# Court of Justice of the European Communities

# Note for Guidance on References by National Courts for Preliminary Rulings (published on December 9, 1996)

**The Court of Justice has issued the following guidance to national courts on the exercise of their power and duty to refer questions to it.**

The development of the Community legal order is largely the result of co-operation between the Court of Justice of the European Communities and national courts and tribunals through the preliminary ruling procedure under Article 234 (ex 177) of the EC Treaty and the corresponding provisions of the ECSC and Euratom Treaties.[22]

In order to make this co-operation more effective, and so enable the Court of Justice better to meet the requirements of national courts by providing helpful answers to preliminary questions, this Note for Guidance is addressed to all interested parties, in particular to all national courts and tribunals.

It must be emphasised that the Note is for guidance only and has no binding or interpretative effect in relation to the provisions governing the preliminary ruling procedure. It merely contains practical information which, in the light of experience in applying the preliminary ruling procedure, may help to prevent the kind of difficulties which the Court has sometimes encountered.

---

[22] A preliminary ruling procedure is also provided for by protocols to several conventions concluded by the Member States, in particular the Brussels convention on Jurisdiction and the Enforcement of Judgements in Civil and commercial Matters.

Any court or tribunal of a Member State may ask the Court of Justice to interpret a rule of Community law, whether contained in the Treaties or in acts of secondary law, if it considers that this is necessary for it to give judgment in a case pending before it. Courts or tribunals against whose decisions there is no judicial remedy under national law must refer questions of interpretation arising before them to the Court of Justice, unless the Court has already ruled on the point or unless the correct application of the rule of Community law is obvious.[23]

The Court of Justice has jurisdiction to rule on the validity of acts of the Community institutions. National courts or tribunals may reject a plea challenging the validity of such an act. But where a national court (even one whose decision is still subject to appeal) intends to question the validity of a Community act, it must refer that question to the Court of Justice.[24] Where, however, a national court or tribunal has serious doubts about the validity of a community act on which a national measure is based, it may, in exceptional cases, temporarily suspend application of the latter measure or grant other interim relief with respect to it. It must then refer the question of validity to the Court of Justice, stating the reasons for which it considers that the Community act is not valid.[25]

Questions referred for a preliminary ruling must be limited to the interpretation or validity of a provision of Community law, since the Court of Justice does not have jurisdiction to interpret national law or assess its validity. It is for the referring court or tribunal to apply the relevant rule of Community law in the specific case pending before it.

The order of the national court or tribunal referring a question to the Court of Justice for a preliminary ruling may be in any form allowed by national procedural law. Reference of a question or questions to the Court of Justice generally involves stay of the national proceedings until the Court has given its ruling, but the decision to stay proceedings is one which is for the national court alone to take in accordance with its own national law.

The order for reference containing the question or questions referred to the Court will have to be translated by the Court's translators into the other official languages of the Community. Questions concerning the interpretation or validity of Community

---

[23] Judgment in Case 283/81 *CILFIT v. Ministry of Health* [1982] ECR 3415.
[24] Judgment in Case 314/85 *Foto-Frost v. Hauptzollamt Lübeck-Ost* [1987] ECR 4199.
[25] Judgments in Joined Cases C–143/88 and C–92/89 *Zuckerfabrik Süderdithmarschen and Zuckerfabrik Soest* [1991] ECR I–415 and in Case C–465/93 *Atlanta Fruchthandelsgesellschaft* [1995] ECR I–3761.

law are frequently of general interest and the Member States and Community institutions are entitled to submit observations. It is therefore desirable that the reference should be drafted as clearly and precisely as possible.

The order for reference should contain a statement of reasons which is succinct but sufficiently complete to give the Court, and those to whom it must be notified (the Member States, the Commission and in certain cases the Council and the European Parliament), a clear understanding of the factual and legal context of the main proceedings.[26]

In particular it should include:

— a statement of the facts which are essential to a full understanding of the legal significance of the main proceedings;

— an exposition of the national law which may be applicable;

— a statement of the reasons which have prompted the national court to refer the question or questions to the Court of Justice; and

— where appropriate, a summary of the arguments of the parties.

The aim should be to put the Court of Justice in a position to give the national court an answer which will be of assistance to it.

The order for reference should also be accompanied by copies of any documents needed for a proper understanding of the case, especially the text of the applicable national provisions. However, as the case-file or documents annexed to the order for reference are not always translated in full into the other official languages of the Community, the national court should ensure that the order for reference itself includes all the relevant information.

A national court or tribunal may refer a question to the Court of Justice as soon as it finds that a ruling on the point or points of interpretation or validity is necessary to enable it to give judgment. It must be stressed, however, that it is not for the Court of Justice to decide issues of fact or to resolve disputes as to the interpretation or application of rules of national law. It is therefore desirable that a decision to refer should not be taken until the national proceedings have reached a stage where the national court is able to define, if only as a working hypothesis, the factual and legal context of the question, on any view, the administration of justice is likely to be best served if the reference is not made until both sides have been heard.[27]

---

[26] Judgment in Joined Cases C–320, 321 & 322/90 *Telemarsicabruzzo* [1993] ECR I–393.

[27] Judgment in Case 70/77 *Simmenthal v. Amministrazione delle Finanze dello Stato* [1978] ECR 1453.

The order for reference and the relevant documents should be sent by the national court directly to the Court of Justice, by registered post, addressed to:

The Registry
Court of Justice of the European Communities
L-2925 Luxembourg
Telephone (352) 43031

The Court Registry will remain in contact with the national court until judgment is given, and will send copies of the various documents (written observations, Report for the Hearing, Opinion of the Advocate General). The Court will also send its judgment to the national court. The Court would appreciate being informed about the application of its judgment in the national proceedings and being sent a copy of the national court's final decision.

Proceedings for a preliminary ruling before the Court of Justice are free of charge. The Court does not rule on costs.

# Chapter Eleven

# Opinions: External Relations

As well as the judgments which it gives in direct actions, and the rulings which it delivers on references from national courts, the Court has an advisory jurisdiction to give "Opinions" under Article 300 (ex Article 228) of the EC Treaty, although, as we shall see, these Opinions are more than merely consultative in nature.

Article 300 (ex Article 228) concerns the negotiation and conclusion of agreements between the Community and non-Member States or international organisations. Paragraph 6 provides that, where such an agreement is envisaged, the Council, the Commission or any Member State may seek the Opinion of the Court as to whether the agreement is compatible with the provisions of the Treaty. There is a corresponding, although more vague, provision under Article 103 of the Euratom Treaty, while under Article 95 ECSC proposed amendments to that Treaty must be submitted to the Court for its Opinion. Article 300 (ex Article 228) further provides that, where the Opinion of the Court is adverse, the agreement may enter into force only in accordance with the process prescribed by Article 48 (ex Article N) TEU,[1] that is to say the cumbersome procedure of an intergovernmental conference which is required to amend the EC Treaty itself.[2] Thus although this aspect of the Court's jurisdiction is advisory, and it gives only an "Opinion," it does rule definitively under Article 300 (ex Article 228) on the vital question of the treaty-making power of the Community.

Moreover, Article 107(2) of the Court of Justice's Rules of Procedure provides that the Court's Opinion may deal not only

---

[1] Art. 48 (ex Art. N) (1) TEU embodies the text of the former Art. 236 EEC which it repealed.

[2] Note that this does not necessarily mean that the Treaty itself must be amended. Four possible courses of action are open: the proposed agreement may be abandoned or it may be amended by negotiation (as in the case of the EEA Agreement discussed below), or the EC Treaty may be changed; or the agreement may be adopted by the same procedure and ratified by all the Member States.

with the question of whether the agreement concerned is compatible with the Treaty but also with the question whether the Community or any Community institution has the power to enter into that agreement.[3]

That power has been widely construed, although the provisions of the EC Treaty are rudimentary. Remarkably, the Treaty leaves the general question as to the scope of the Community's treaty-making powers unanswered; in particular, it fails to specify the dividing line between the treaty-making powers of the Community and those of the Member States. There are only three Articles which deal with the matter expressly. First, Article 133 (ex Article 113) EC provides for a "common commercial policy" governing the Community's trade with non-Member States and covering in particular "changes in tariff rates, the conclusion of tariff and trade agreements, the achievement of uniformity of liberalisation, export policy and measures to protect trade such as those to be taken in case of dumping and subsidies". By Article 133(3) (ex Article 113(3)) (which now refers explicitly to Article 300), where agreements with third countries need to be negotiated, the Commission is to conduct the negotiations under the general supervision of the Council. Secondly, Article 302 (ex Article 229) EC instructs the Commission to ensure the maintenance of "all appropriate relations" with the United Nations, and with international organisations generally. Lastly, Article 310 (ex Article 238) EC empowers the Community to conclude association agreements. Here the outstanding achievement has been the conclusion of a succession of agreements with African, Caribbean, and Pacific States, currently under the title of the Fourth Lome Convention.

In addition the Court has pointed out in its Opinion on a Draft Agreement establishing a European laying-up fund for inland waterway vessels[4] that authority to enter into international agreements may not only arise from an express attribution by the Treaty, but may also flow implicitly from its provisions. Thus whenever Community law creates, within its internal system, powers for the institutions for the purpose of attaining a specific objective, the Community has authority to enter into the international commitments necessary for the attainment of that objective – even in the absence of an express provision for that purpose.

The division of competences between the Community institutions is governed by Article 300 (ex Article 228).[5] According to

---

[3] It may seem surprising that the jurisdiction of the Court can apparently be extended by its Rules of Procedure but it must be remembered that those Rules are adopted only with the unanimous approval of the Council (Art. 245 (ex Art. 188) EC third paragraph). The principle was affirmed most recently by the Court in *Opinion 2/91* of March 19, 1993 [1993] ECR I–1061, discussed below.

[4] *Opinion 1/76* of April 26, 1977 [1977] ECR 741; [1977] 2 C.M.L.R. 278.

[5] As amended by Art. G(80) TEU.

that Article, where the Treaty provides for the conclusion of international agreements by the Community, the Commission conducts the negotiations and the Council concludes the agreements. It might be thought, from a reading of Article 300 (ex Article 228), that the treaty-making powers of the Community are limited to those enumerated in Article 133 (ex Article 113) EC (common commercial policy), Article 302 (ex Article 229) (relations with international organisations) and Article 310 (ex Article 238) (association agreements). That view has been roundly rejected by the Court of Justice, which has allowed the Community's external competence to expand progressively beyond those limits. In the *ERTA*[6] case which, as we have seen (p. 138), came before the Court under Article 173 (now Article 228) and not under Article 228 (now Article 300), the Court held that the Community had the capacity to establish treaty relations with non-Member States over the whole field of objectives specified in Part One of the Treaty.

In order to determine whether the Community had such capacity in a particular case, the Court looked to the whole scheme of the Treaty, as well as to its specific provisions. The capacity was found to arise not only where it was expressly conferred, as by Articles 113 and 238 (now Articles 133 and 310), but also from other provisions of the Treaty, or from measures taken by the Community institutions within the framework of such provisions. In particular, whenever the Community implemented a common internal policy, Member States were deprived of the right to undertake separately any obligations in their external relations which might affect the Community's common rules. As the Court said in the *ERTA* judgment (at p. 274): "As and when such common rules come into being, the Community alone is in a position to assume and carry out contractual obligations toward third countries affecting the whole sphere of application of the Community legal system."

The Court has developed this approach in a succession of cases, usually at the instigation of the Commission, and often in the face of opposition from the Member States. In this way, the external competence of the Community has been progressively expanded.

The next step in the development of the Court's case law was taken in 1975 in the *Export Credits* case: Opinion 1/75.[7] Here an agreement on export credits was being prepared within the OECD in the form of a draft "Understanding on a Local Cost Standard". The Commission recommended the Council to take a decision

---

[6] Case 22/70 *Commission v. Council* [1971] ECR 263; [1971] C.M.L.R. 335.
[7] *Opinion 1/75, Export Credits* [1975] ECR 1355.

under Article 113 (now Article 133) EC according to which the attitude of the Community would be expressed by the Commission. When doubts arose about the Community's competence in the matter, the Commission asked the Court for an Opinion pursuant to Article 228(1) EEC (now Article 300(6) EC). The Court took the view not only that the Community was competent to participate in the agreement but that its competence was exclusive: Member States had no concurrent power.

Elsewhere the Court has recognised the possibility of "mixed agreements" where the competence to negotiate and to conclude a treaty may be shared between the Community and the Member States. Most recently this was the case in respect of a convention concerning safety in the use of chemicals at work adopted by the International Labour Organisation. The Court's Opinion was sought under Article 228(1) EEC (now Article 300(6) EC) as to whether that convention (known as ILO Convention No. 170) came within the Community's sphere of competence and, if so, whether the competence was exclusive in nature. In Opinion 2/91 of March 19, 1993[8] it was held that the conclusion of that Convention was a matter which fell within the joint competence of the Member States and the Community.

On the one hand the scope of the Convention was wider than that of the Community directives in that field. Therefore since the commitments arising from the Convention which fell within the area of those directives might affect Community rules laid down in those directives, Member States could not undertake such commitments outside the framework of the Community.

However, social policy and in particular co-operation between the two sides of industry were matters which fell predominantly within the competence of the Member States. As a result it was all the more necessary that the Community and the Member States co-operate because, as international law stood at present, the Commission could not itself conclude an ILO Convention and had to do so through the medium of a Member State.

The division of competences between the Community and the Member States may come before the Court by other routes as well, in particular, by a question referred for a preliminary ruling under Article 234 (ex Article 177). It did so in Joined Cases 3, 4 & 6/76 *Kramer*.[9] Here the question arose when Dutch fishermen were prosecuted in a Dutch court for infringing Dutch conservation measures designed to conserve stocks of sole and plaice in the

---

[8] [1993] ECR I–1061. See also *Opinion 1/78* [1979] ECR 2871; [1979] 3 C.M.L.R. 639, concerning a commodity agreement, the International Agreement on Natural Rubber.

[9] [1976] ECR 1279; [1976] 2 C.M.L.R. 440.

North East Atlantic. The connection with Community law was not immediately apparent since the Dutch measures had been adopted pursuant to the North East Atlantic Fisheries Convention, which was not a Community treaty: the parties to the Convention were seven Member States and seven non-Member States. But the Dutch court asked, among other questions, whether the Member States were still competent to assume commitments on the international plane, or whether the Community alone had authority to enter into such commitments. The Court of Justice answered that, since there was not yet a fully developed Community policy on conservation, the Member States did have, at the time, the competence to assume the commitments in question, but that their competence was only temporary and would expire at the end of the transitional period laid down by Article 102 of the Act of Accession, that is at the end of 1978.

The international competence of the Community was further explored, under Article 228 (now Article 300), in Opinion 1/76 mentioned above and in Ruling 1/78,[10] concerning a draft convention on the protection of nuclear materials. The latter ruling, given under Article 103 of the Euratom Treaty, provoked an extraordinarily virulent reaction in France, where two parliamentarians introduced a Bill seeking to have the judgment declared illegal on the ground of "fraud" and seeking to provide, in terms designed to recall the re-establishment of French independence after the end of the German occupation in 1944, that any French authority submitting to the Court's ruling should be guilty of the crime of "forfeiture". The Bill did not become law; but the strength of political reactions to the judgments of the Court raises questions to which we must return in the concluding chapter.

Here it may be appropriate to consider why the Court was given this somewhat unusual advisory jurisdiction. Normally, courts do not have, and do not like exercising, advisory functions, nor jurisdiction to rule on measures which are merely proposals or other hypothetical questions. The purpose of this jurisdiction, according to the *Export Credits* case, is to forestall complications which might arise subsequently if the question of compatibility with the Treaty were raised after the Community had concluded an international agreement. It is noteworthy that, under international law, the relations between the parties to a treaty cannot normally be affected, once the treaty is concluded, by a ruling of a court of one of the parties that the treaty is, in its view, invalid.[11] As we have seen, the Court has gone well beyond the original

---

[10] *Opinion 1/76* of April 26, 1976 [1977] ECR 741; Ruling 1/78 of [1978] ECR 2151; [1979] 1 C.M.L.R. 131.
[11] See Art. 46 of the Vienna Convention on the Law of Treaties.

purpose of its jurisdiction under Article 228 in order to prevent the Member States from encroaching on the international competence of the Community.

## THE EUROPEAN ECONOMIC AREA

Although in general we have eschewed examination of the substance of cases cited in this book as opposed to dealing with aspects having a direct bearing on the Community's legal system the two Opinions delivered by the Court in connection with the creation of the European Economic Area[12] merit closer examination because they deal with important questions relating to the Court's place in the Community legal order and provide a rare insight into the Court's collective view of its own function.[13]

The purpose of the agreement was to create a so-called European Economic Area (EEA) covering the territories of the Community Member States and those of the EFTA[14] countries. The EEA is essentially intended to extend to the EFTA countries the benefits of the internal market. Thus it sought to ensure that throughout the territory of the 19 states concerned common rules on the freedom of movement of goods, workers, services and capital were applied based on common rules and equal conditions of competition. To that end adequate means of enforcement were provided for *inter alia* at a judicial level. The venture took on added importance since it was realised that several of the EFTA countries either had already or were likely shortly to become applicants for full membership of the Community and hence that the EEA might constitute a convenient half-way house, providing many of the benefits of membership of the Community without the concomitant transfer of national sovereignty. If successful the EEA might prove a model for the possible future strengthening of

---

[12] *Opinion 1/91* of December 14, 1991 [1991] ECR I–6079; and *Opinion 1/92* of April 10, 1992 [1992] ECR I–282.

[13] For further, more detailed commentary on those opinions see: N. Burrows [1992] E.L.Rev. 352 and [1993] E.L.Rev. 63; B. Brandtner [1992] Eur. J. of Int. Law 300; T. Hartley [1992] I.C.L.Q. 841; H. Schermers [1992] C.M.L.Rev. 991.

[14] European Free Trade Association then comprising Austria, Finland, Iceland, Liechtenstein, Norway, Sweden and Switzerland. It should be recalled that, prior to their accession to the European Communities, the United Kingdom, Denmark and Portugal had been members of EFTA. Switzerland's negative referendum on December 6, 1992 then kept that country outside the EEA, although it remains, with Norway, Iceland and Liechtenstein, a member of EFTA; it does not however participate in the EFTA Court, whose jurisdiction now extends only to Norway, Iceland and Liechtenstein: its seat of jurisdiction was appropriately moved in September 1996 from Geneva to Luxembourg, reinforcing its kinship with the Court of Justice.

links with the emerging democracies of the Eastern European countries with a view to their eventual membership of the Community itself.[15]

*The Court's Opinion 1/91 which held that the proposed agreement establishing a European Economic Area was incompatible with the EEC Treaty caused delay in the signing and entry into force of that agreement.*[16]

In its Opinion the Court, as it had been requested by the Commission, confined itself to examining the compatibility with the EEC Treaty of the system of judicial supervision which it was proposed to set up under the EEA Agreement.

## The Proposed System of Judicial Protection

In order to fulfil the aims of the EEA and, in particular, to ensure the homogeneous interpretation and application of the law throughout the EEA, the Agreement contained provisions which were identically worded to those of the corresponding provisions of Community law and a parallel system of courts was to be

---

[15] This role for the EEA has not materialised. In practice the Central and Eastern European countries applied for membership directly (see Ch. 17, p. 284 below) leaving the EEA as a somewhat anachronistic anomaly.

[16] Drawing by Peter Bensch, published in *Handelsblatt*, December 17, 1992. The bride and groom represent respectively EFTA and the European Community on their way towards the altar of the EEA (EWR – *Europaisches Wirtschaftsraum*) when they are halted by the Court (EuGH – *Europaisches Gerichtshof*) wielding a hook, which is a symbol commonly used in German legal texts.

established. The Agreement therefore provided for the setting up of an EEA Court to which a Court of First Instance was to be attached. The jurisdiction of the EEA Court covered the settlement of disputes between the contracting parties (*i.e.* the Community on the one hand and the EFTA Member States on the other), actions concerning the surveillance procedure regarding the EFTA States (equivalent to proceedings under Article 169 (now Article 226 EC)) and, in competition matters, appeals concerning decisions taken by the EFTA Surveillance Authority which was to have powers equivalent to those of the Commission in that field.

In order to ensure consistency of interpretation with the provisions of Community law the Agreement was to be interpreted in accordance with rulings of the Court of Justice on the corresponding provisions of the EC Treaty which had been given prior to the date of signature of the Agreement. For the same purpose it was provided that when applying or interpreting the provisions of the Agreement and the provisions of the EC and ECSC Treaties, the Court of Justice, the EEA Court, the Courts of First Instance of the Communities and of the EEA as well as the Courts of the EFTA Member States were to pay due account to the principles laid down in decisions delivered by the other Courts in order to ensure as uniform as possible an interpretation of the Agreement. Finally it was provided that the EEA Court was to be composed of eight Judges of whom five would be drawn from the Court of Justice of the European Communities while the composition of the Chambers of three or five Judges was to ensure an appropriate balance of Judges of the Court of Justice and EFTA Judges a mechanism for which was to be laid down in the Statute of the EEA Court. The EEA Court of First Instance was to be composed of five Judges with three nominated by the EFTA States and two Judges of the Court of First Instance of the European Communities. There were also provisions under which the EFTA States might authorise their courts and tribunals to ask the Court of Justice to "express itself" (*sic*) on the interpretation of the provision of the Agreement.

## THE FIRST EEA OPINION

In its Opinion 1/91 the Court first compared the aims and context of the Agreement with those of Community law. It pointed out that the mere fact that the provisions of the Agreement and the corresponding Community provisions were identically worded did not mean that they were necessarily to be interpreted identically since an international treaty had to be interpreted not only on the basis of its wording but also in the light of its objectives. Both the objectives and the context of the EEA Agreement were different from those of the Community. The EEA Agreement merely created rights and obligations as between the contracting parties and provided for no transfer of sovereign rights to the intergovernmental institutions which it established. The Court then contrasted those points with the classic definition of the Community which it had laid down in Case 26/62 *Van Gend & Loos*[17] with its principles of primacy over conflicting provisions of the laws of the Member States and direct effect of many of the provisions of Community law.

Since homogeneity could not be secured by the provisions of the Agreement and of Community law being identical in content or wording, it was necessary to examine whether there were other means for guaranteeing that homogeneity.

The Court concluded for two reasons that the stipulation that the rules of the Agreement were to be interpreted in conformity with the case law of the Court of Justice would not enable the desired legal homogeneity to be achieved. First, only rulings of the Court of Justice given prior to the date of signature of the Agreement were referred to. Since the case law would inevitably evolve, it would be difficult to distinguish the new case law from the old and hence the past from the future. Secondly, although the Agreement did not clearly specify whether it referred to the Court's case law as a whole, and in particular the case law on the direct effect and primacy of the Community law, it appeared that compliance with the case law of the Court did not extend to essential elements of that case law which were irreconcilable with the characteristics of the Agreement. It followed that the divergences between the aims and context of the Agreement and those of Community law, stood in the way of achieving homogeneity of interpretation and application of the law in the EEA.

### Autonomy of the Community Legal Order

By now the proposed Agreement was doomed since the Court went on to say that it was in the light of the contradiction which it had identified that it had to consider whether the proposed system of courts might undermine the autonomy of the Community legal order in order to pursue its own particular objectives.

It was inherent in the structure envisaged that the EEA Court might have to consider the definition of the expression "Contracting Party". Which of the various possible interpretations[18] to use

---

[17] [1963] ECR 1; [1963] C.M.L.R. 105. See para. 21 of *Opinion 1/91*.
[18] On the Community side the Court identified three possible interpretations: the Community and the Member States, or the Community, or the Member States, depending on the case.

was to be deduced in each case from the relevant provisions of the Agreement and from the respective competences in the Community and the Member States as they followed from the EC Treaty and the ECSC Treaty. Thus the EEA Court would have to rule on the respective competences of the Community and the EC Member States.

Clearly such jurisdiction might impinge upon the exclusive jurisdiction of the Court of Justice assigned to it by Article 164 (now Article 220) of the EC Treaty and confirmed by Article 219 (now Article 292) under which Member States undertake not to submit a dispute concerning the interpretation or application of the Treaty to any method of settlement other than those provided for in the Treaty itself.

Furthermore the Agreement itself was an act of one of the institutions of the Community (the Council) within the meaning of Article 177 (now Article 234) EC and therefore the Court had jurisdiction to give preliminary rulings on its interpretation. It also had jurisdiction to rule on the Agreement in the event that Member States of the Community failed to fulfil their obligations under the Agreement.

Where, however, an international agreement provided for its own system of courts, including a Court with jurisdiction to settle disputes between the contracting parties and, as a result, to interpret its provisions, the decisions of that Court would be binding on the Community institutions, including the Court of Justice.

The Court accepted that an international agreement providing for such a system of courts was in principle compatible with Community law, foreshadowing, and perhaps removing one of the obstacles to, an eventual accession of the Community to the European Convention on Human Rights and Fundamental Freedoms.[19] However, although the EEA Court was under a duty to interpret the provisions of the Agreement in the light of the relevant rulings of the Court of Justice prior to the date of signature the EEA Court would not be subject to that obligation in the case of decisions given by the Court of Justice after that date and therefore the Court of Justice would be bound by those interpretations. Since the EEA Court could thereby determine the future interpretation of the Community rules on free movement and competition, the machinery of courts provided for in the EEA Agreement was in conflict with Article 164 (now Article 220) of the EC Treaty and, as if that were not enough, the Court added "with the very foundations of the Community".

---

[19] See further Chap. 17, below. The Council later submitted a request for an Opinion pursuant to Art. 228(6) EC on this question: *Opinion 2/94*. See below p. 259.

## The Proposed Organic Links

The institutional links between the proposed two pairs of courts could not resolve this problem since, depending on whether they were sitting on the Court of Justice or on the EEA Court the Judges of the Court of Justice who were also Members of the EEA Court would have to apply and interpret the same provisions but using different approaches, methods and concepts in order to take account of the nature of each Treaty and of its particular objectives.

In those circumstances it would be very difficult, if not impossible, for those judges, when sitting in the Court of Justice, to tackle questions with completely open minds where they had previously taken part in determining those questions as members of the EEA Court.

## "Self Expression"?

The procedure whereby EFTA States might allow their national courts to ask the Court of Justice to "express itself" was also incompatible with Community law. The procedure envisaged left the EFTA States free to authorise or not to authorise their Courts to refer questions to the Court of Justice and did not make such a reference obligatory in the case of courts of last instance in those States, unlike the third paragraph of Article 177 (now Article 234) EC. Furthermore there was no guarantee that the answers given by the Court of Justice in such proceedings would be binding on the Courts making the reference. As we have seen in Chapter 10, above, that procedure is fundamentally different from that provided for in Article 234 (ex Article 177) EC.

Although the principle of such a mechanism was, in itself, unobjectionable the Court stated that it was unacceptable that the answers which the Court of Justice might give to the Courts and Tribunals in the EFTA States would be purely advisory and without any binding effect. Such a situation would change the nature of the function of the Court of Justice as defined in the EC Treaty, namely that of a court whose judgments were binding. The Court added, as we have pointed out above, that even in the very specific case of Article 228 (now Article 300) itself the Opinion given by the Court of Justice has the binding effect stipulated in that article.

## THE SECOND EEA OPINION

The thoroughness of the Court's condemnation of the Agreement caused stunned consternation in the Council and Commission and among the EC and EFTA Member States. However the contracting parties recovered with remarkable speed and reopened negotiations which concluded only two months later in a number of changes to the Agreement on which the Commission, no doubt with some trepidation, again sought the Court's opinion. On this occasion none of the Community Member States sought to submit observations; however the European Parliament, at its own request, was given leave to do so.

The main change in the revised agreement was that it no longer provided for an EEA Court of mixed composition, but for a separate EFTA Court which would have jurisdiction only within the framework of EFTA and which would have no personal or operational links with the Court of Justice.[20] Secondly the Agreement provided for two procedures, the first intended to ensure the uniform interpretation of the Agreement and the other being concerned with the settlement of disputes between contracting parties. In the context of the latter procedure the Court of Justice may be asked to give a ruling on the interpretation of the relevant rules.

Thirdly, under the Agreement[21] the EFTA States may authorise their Courts to submit questions to the Court of Justice by way of a preliminary ruling for a decision on the point of Community law and not merely inviting it "to express itself" on the interpretation of a provision of the Agreement. Given the reluctance and in some cases the constitutional impossibility of EFTA countries to submit to "foreign" Judges (which was the main reason why the initial Agreement did not simply give exclusive jurisdiction to the Court of Justice), entailing a clear transfer of sovereignty, it seems highly unlikely that any of the EFTA countries will avail themselves of this opportunity.

Finally the revised Agreement no longer contains any provision requiring the Court of Justice to pay due account to decisions of other Courts.

In its Opinion 1/92[22] the Court pointed out that the divergences between the aims and context of the Agreement on the one hand and those of Community law on the other, which had led it to hold (in its earlier Opinion) that the proposed system of Courts was liable to undermine the autonomy of the Community legal order, still remained in the new Agreement. The question was therefore whether the new provisions replacing those which the Court regarded as incompatible with the autonomy of the Community legal order were liable to raise similar objections.

---

[20] For a brief note on the organisation, jurisdiction and procedure of the EFTA Court see the Appendix to this Chapter, pp. 263–268, below.

[21] Art. 107 and Protocol 34.

[22] *Opinion 1/92* of April 10, 1992 [1992] ECR I–2821.

In that regard Article 105 of the Agreement requires the Joint Committee to keep under constant review the development of the case law of the Court of Justice and of the EFTA Court. After pointing out the risk that the Joint Committee might be led to disregard the binding nature of its decisions, the Court of Justice accepted that a minute[23] adopted by the Contracting Parties according to which decisions taken by the Joint Committee under Article 105 were not to affect the case law of the Court of Justice constituted "an essential safeguard which is indispensable for the autonomy of the Community legal order".

The Joint Committee also has the power to settle any dispute brought before it by the Community or an EFTA State on the interpretation or application of the Agreement including any disputes relating to differences in case law which the Committee has been unable to settle under the procedure mentioned above. According to the Court the link between the procedure provided for in Article 105 and that provided for in Article 111 of the Agreement implied that the principle set out in the minute would also apply where the Joint Committee tries to settle a dispute in accordance with Article 111.

It followed that the powers conferred on the Joint Committee by Article 111 did not call in question the binding nature of the Court's case law or the autonomy of the Community legal order since the minute was binding on the contracting parties.

Finally, having accepted in Opinion 1/91 that an international agreement might confer on the Court jurisdiction to interpret the provisions of such an agreement, provided that the Court's decisions had binding effect, the Court concluded that since both the contracting parties and the Joint Committee would be bound by the Court's interpretation of the rules at issue if such a question were to be raised, that power was compatible with the EC Treaty.

For those perhaps tenuous reasons the Court concluded that the provisions of the Agreement dealing with the settlement of disputes were compatible with the Treaty, as long as the principle that decisions taken by the Joint Committee were not to affect the case law of the Court of Justice was laid down in a form binding on the contracting parties. It remains to be seen how far the "proces-verbal" will be binding in practice.

Two more recent opinions must be mentioned as they demonstrate the importance of this procedure in developing the Community Legal Order within the Context of International Law.

---

[23] Referred to as a "*procès-verbal agréé ad Art. 105*".

# THE WTO OPINION

First the Court ruled in *Opinion 1/94*[24] that the scope of the Common Commercial Policy embodied in Article 113 (now Article 133) EC included only a limited amount of international trade in services and that the extent of international trade in public procurement, included within Article 113, was confined solely to the procurement of goods. Subsequently, in Case C–360/93 *European Parliament v. Council of the European Union*[25] the Court has extended the scope of Article 113 to include procurement of services based on existing international agreements for trade in services.

# THE HUMAN RIGHTS OPINION

Earlier, in an important Opinion,[26] given at the request of the Council of the European Union, the Court, while acknowledging that Community law respects fundamental rights, held that the provisions of the European Convention on Human Rights "cannot in themselves have the effect of extending the scope of the Treaty provisions beyond the competences of the Community". The Court reaffirmed that the European Union has only those powers which have been conferred upon it. It could not therefore accede to the Convention as Community law then stood, in particular having regard to the exclusive jurisdiction of the Court of Justice under Articles 164 and 219 (now Articles 220 and 292) EC.

# PROCEDURE[27]

Proceedings under Article 300 (ex Article 228) of the EC Treaty and Article 95 of the ECSC Treaty are non-contentious in nature.[28] A request under Article 300(6) (ex Article 228(6)) may be

---

[24] *Opinion 1/94* on the Agreement establishing the WTO [1994] ECR I–5267.

[25] [1996] ECR I–1195.

[26] *Opinion 2/94, Accession by Community to the European Convention on Human Rights* [1996] ECR I–1759.

[27] The account which follows of procedure under Art. 300 (ex Art. 228(6)) is drawn essentially from the commentary on CJ Rules Arts 107 and 108 in Butterworth's commentary on the *Procedure of the Court*. That commentary was drafted by one of the authors of this book and Butterworth's permission to adapt the material is gratefully acknowledged.

[28] See *Opinion 1/75* of November 11, 1975 [1975] ECR 1355 at 1361; [1976] 1 C.M.L.R. 85.

submitted by either the Council, the Commission or a Member State, although, until recently, it had invariably been the Commission which did so.[29] By contrast, in the case of amendments provided for by Article 95 ECSC, a request for the Court's Opinion is obligatory and the amendments must be jointly submitted to the Court by the Commission and the Council.[30]

As the Court pointed out in its *Opinion 1/75* of November 11, 1975 the Treaty lays down no time limit for the submission of a request under Article 228 (now Article 300) EC.[31] Nonetheless the second paragraph of Article 300(6) (ex Article 228(6)) refers to "an agreement envisaged" and therefore an agreement which had been concluded, so as to produce binding effects on the contracting parties, could be reviewed by the Court of Justice, either under Articles 169 or 173 (now Articles 226 or 230) of the EC Treaty or submitted by a national court under the preliminary ruling procedure under Article 177 (now Article 234) but not, at that stage, under Article 228 (now Article 300).[32] In *Opinion 1/78* of October 4, 1979, relating to a proposal that the Community should enter an International Agreement on natural rubber the Commission had lodged its request for an Opinion at a time when the negotiations were still at any early stage. The Council therefore raised the question whether, in those circumstances, the request was premature. The Court however found that the request was admissible since the subject matter of the agreement envisaged was already known at the time and, even though there were a number of alternatives still open with regard to the drafting of particular clauses, the documents submitted to the Court and the information that had been provided by the parties made it possible for it to form a sufficiently certain judgment on the question raised by the Commission.[33] In *Opinion 3/94*[34] the Court ruled inadmissible a German request for an Opinion on the compatibility with Community law of the 1994 Framework agreement on bananas, on the ground that a request for an Opinion on an agreement which had already been *concluded* must be rejected as inadmissible.

---

[29] Belgium submitted a request for an Opinion (*Opinion 2/92*) on the competence of the Community or of its institutions to take part in a decision of the Council of the OECD, and the Council of the European Union asked the Court for an Opinion (*Opinion 2/94*) on the compatibility with the EC Treaty of the Community's accession to the European Convention on Human Rights and Fundamental Freedoms, (see above) and see also *Opinion 3/94* below.

[30] Fourth para. of Art. 95 of the ECSC Treaty and the first paragraph of CJ Rules Art. 109.

[31] [1975] ECR 1355 at 1361.

[32] See *Opinion 1/75* of November 11, 1975 [1975] ECR 1355 at 1361.

[33] *Opinion 1/78* of October 4, 1979 [1979] ECR 2871 at para. 34 of the Opinion [1979] 3 C.M.L.R. 639.

[34] *Opinion 3/94 on Framework Agreement on Bananas* [1995] ECR I–4577.

The procedure to be followed by the Court in arriving at its Opinion is laid down only in outline in the CJ Rules. The first paragraph of Article 107 (1) provides for service of the request on the Council, the Commission and the Member States according to which of them submitted the request. It may be noted that the non-Member States or international organisations with whom the Community intends to conclude an agreement are not served with copies of the request, nor do they have the opportunity to submit written or oral observations to the Court. Following their accession to the European Union the request for an Opinion on the Accession by the Community to the European Convention on Human Rights (*Opinion 2/94*, see above) was served upon Austria, Finland and Sweden.

The procedure laid down in Article 108 is common to proceedings under both Article 95 ECSC and Article 300 (ex Article 228) EC. Although no mention is made of an oral part to the procedure it appears that the Court is free to organise a hearing of the parties if it feels it would be helpful in the circumstances of a particular case.[35] In the second EEA Opinion 1/92 no observations were submitted by the Council or the Member States; but it appears that, at its own request, the European Parliament was given leave to submit observations.[36]

Having considered the written and oral observations, if any, the Court hears the views of all of the advocates general in the deliberation room.[37] The advocates-generals' views are not made public.

Once adopted the Court's Opinion is not read out in open court, in the manner of a judgment[38]; however it is notified immediately to the Council, the Commission and the Member States and made public by the Court's Information Division once it is clear that those parties have received it.[39]

---

[35] See, for example, *Opinion 1/78* [1979] ECR 2871 at 2879 referring to oral observations made at a hearing on May 9, 1979 and *Opinion 1/91* on the EEA in which a hearing was held in camera on November 26, 1991 [1991] ECR 6079. In *Opinion C–2/91* [1993] ECR I–1061 on the compatibility with the Treaty of ILO Convention No. 170, the Court heard oral observations in open court on June 30, 1992.

[36] [1992] ECR I–2821 at 2826. The Court gave no reasons for acceding to that request.

[37] See *Opinion 1/75* of November 11, 1975 [1975] ECR 1355 at 1359; [1976] 1 C.M.L.R. 85, *Opinion 1/76* of April 26, 1977 [1977] ECR 741 at 744 and *Opinion 1/91* of December 14, 1991 [1991] ECR I–6079 at 6085.

[38] As required by Art. 64(1) of the ECJ rules.

[39] *Opinion 1/91* of December 14, 1991 was adopted on a Saturday. The Member States and Community institutions were notified during that weekend and the Opinion was made public by the information office on Monday, December 16 although the substance of the Opinion had been divulged by one or more of the parties during the weekend.

There is no provision in the Rules for determining the language of the case and the published reports of the three opinions given under Article 95 of the ECSC Treaty and *Opinions 1/75* and *1/76* given under Article 228 of the EC Treaty give no indication of the language or languages used. However the report of *Opinion 1/78* of October 4, 1979[40] makes it clear that all the then six official languages of the Community were languages of the case and the same practice has been followed by the Court (then with nine languages) in *Opinions 1/91* of December 14, 1991[41] and *1/92* of April 10, 1992.[42]

Finally, since an Opinion of this type is not a judgment, it cannot be re-submitted to the Court by way of an application for revision or interpretation or through third party proceedings, although, as in the case of the proposed Agreement on a European Economic Area, an agreement which has been amended in the light of a negative Opinion from the Court may be submitted for a fresh Opinion.

---

[40] [1979] ECR 2871; [1979] 3 C.M.L.R. 639.
[41] [1991] ECR I–6079, *The Times*, January 22, 1992.
[42] [1992] ECR I–2821, *The Times*, May 12, 1992.

# Appendix

# The EFTA Court

## INTRODUCTION

As we have seen in Chapter 11 the adverse opinion of the Court of Justice on the judicial control mechanism envisaged in the European Economic Area (EEA) Agreement led to a revision of that agreement which the Court of Justice subsequently approved.[1] However the vicissitudes of direct democracy prevented the Swiss Confederation from ratifying the agreement which could not therefore apply to Switzerland.[2] Although Liechtenstein *did* ratify the agreements, nevertheless, by virtue of its special relationship[3] with Switzerland special arrangements were required for the entry into force of the agreement so far as the Principality is concerned. These matters were dealt with in an adjusting Protocol signed in Brussels on March 17, 1993. The EEA Agreement and the Surveillance Authority and Court Agreement entered into force on January 1, 1994.[4]

The Members of the EFTA Court and of the EFTA Surveillance Authority (ESA) were sworn in at a ceremony in Geneva on January 4, 1994.

## THE ROLE OF THE EFTA COURT

The specific competence of the EFTA Court is broadly parallel to that of the Court of Justice and is dealt with below. However it is

---

[1] *Opinion* 1/92 [1992] ECR I–2821.
[2] Notwithstanding this setback the EFTA Court initially had its seat in Geneva, the seat of the EFTA secretariat. On September 1, 1996 it moved to Luxembourg, re-inforcing its kinship with the Court of Justice.
[3] Resulting in particular from its Customs Agreement of 1923 and its monetary union.
[4] For the texts of these instruments and far more detailed information about the EFTA Court, as well as the texts of its decisions, consult the website at www.efta.int.

necessary to bear in mind the scope of the Agreement and the important differences between the EEA and the EC. As mentioned in Chapter 11 the key objective of the EEA is to extend to the EFTA countries the benefits of the Single Market of the EC and in particular the rules relating to the "four freedoms"[5] and the competition rules as well as a certain number of the secondary goals in areas such as the protection of the environment, research and development, social policy and consumer protection. The principal differences between the EEA and the EC arise from the absence in the EEA Agreement of six of the EC's common policies. Thus the EEA remains a free trade area (albeit an enhanced one) but not a customs union which means that it has no common external trade policy and that border controls are retained between its Member States; nor are there common policies relating to agriculture and fisheries, taxation, monetary policy or regional aid policy.

The competition rules, including those on state aid and the rules relating to public procurement, are also extended to all EEA States. The objective of the EEA may be summarised as that of securing equal treatment and the elimination of discrimination between individuals and undertakings in all 18 EEA States in the areas covered by the EEA Agreements and the corresponding Community rules. This makes it essential to ensure homogeneity in the interpretation and application of the EEA Rules and the corresponding EC rules. As we have seen in Chapter 11, the Court of Justice pointed out in *Opinion 1/91* that the mere fact that the text of the relevant provisions is identical would not necessarily result in their being interpreted in the same manner. The EFTA Court now shares the responsibility for ensuring consistent interpretation of the two systems of law with the Court of Justice of the EC.

## JURISDICTION

Since the EFTA Court, within the context of its role outlined above, exercises jurisdiction in the fields covered by the EEA Treaty in parallel to the jurisdiction of the Court of Justice in matters covered by the EC Treaties, it is unsurprising that the various heads of jurisdiction are broadly similar to those of the Court of Justice itself. The most significant difference is that in the place of the preliminary ruling procedure established by Article 234 (ex Article 177) of the EC Treaty the EFTA Court may only

---

[5] *i.e.* the free movement of goods, persons, services and capital.

give advisory opinions on requests by national courts in the EFTA countries.[6]

The four other principal areas of jurisdiction of the EFTA Court are:

- infringement proceedings analogous to those under Article 226 (ex Article 169) EC, which may be initiated by the ESA against an EFTA Member State[7];
- the settlement of disputes between ESA States in a procedure similar to that of Article 227 (ex Article 170) EC[8];
- actions to annul a decision of the EFTA Surveillance Authority[9]; and in
- actions brought against the EFTA Surveillance Authority for its failure to act (compare Article 232 (ex Article 175) EC).[10]

Provisions corresponding to those in the EC Treaty also provide for the EFTA States to take the necessary measures to comply with the judgments of the EFTA Court,[11] although unlike Article 228 (ex Article 171) EC there is no provision for financial penalties to be imposed. Under Article 35 of the ESA/EFTA court Agreement the latter has unlimited jurisdiction with regard to penalties imposed by the ESA. Article 39 gives the EFTA Court jurisdiction in actions against the ESA relating to compensation for damage caused by it or by its servants in the performance of their duties in accordance with the general principles of law governing non-contractual liability. It is interesting to note that the EFTA Court does not have jurisdiction with regard to staff cases. The staff of the Court and the ESA must, like their colleagues in the EFTA secretariat, take any grievances before an ILO Arbitration Tribunal.

When so required the EFTA Court may prescribe any necessary interim measures or order that the application of a contested act be suspended. The relevant provisions are identically worded to those of the corresponding provisions in Articles 242 and 243 (ex Articles 185 and 186) EC.

The procedure under Article 32 ESA/EFTA differs from that provided by Article 227 (ex Article 170) EC in that the EFTA States do not need to notify the ESA before bringing the matter

---

[6] Art. 31 ESA/EFTA Court Agreement.
[7] Art. 34 ESA/EFTA Court Agreement.
[8] Art. 32 ESA/EFTA Court Agreement.
[9] Art. 36 ESA/EFTA Court Agreement.
[10] Art. 37 ESA/EFTA Court Agreement.
[11] Art. 33 ESA/EFTA Court Agreement.

before the EFTA Court. Furthermore the disputes which may be dealt with under this Article may be more wide ranging than its (rarely used) EC counterpart in that they may be brought between two or more EFTA States and may concern the interpretation or the application of the EEA Agreement itself, the ESA/EFTA Court Agreement or the Agreement on the Standing Committee of the EFTA States.

As we have seen in Chapter 11, in its *Opinion 1/91*[12] the Court of Justice categorically rejected the provisions which were to have allowed it "to express itself" on the interpretation of the EEA rules following a request from a court of an EFTA State. According to Article 107 of the Agreement as negotiated, EFTA States may permit their domestic courts or tribunals to ask the Court of Justice to decide on the interpretation of an EEA rule. None of the signatory states to the EEA has, so far, decided to avail itself of this possibility.

As a result of constitutional objections in the EFTA countries it was not possible to give the EFTA Court jurisdiction to deliver binding preliminary rulings and so Article 34 of the ESA/EFTA Court Agreement provides that where a question of interpretation of the EEA Agreement is raised before any court or tribunal in an EFTA State, that court or tribunal may, if it considers it necessary to enable it to give judgment, request the EFTA Court to give an advisory opinion.

## COMPOSITION AND ORGANISATION

There are four principal differences between the composition of the EFTA Court and that of the Court of Justice. In the first place there are only three judges.[13] Secondly, according to Article 29 of the ESA/EFTA Court Agreement the EFTA Court will sit only in plenary sessions and therefore there are no chambers. Thirdly, the EFTA Court will not be assisted by advocates general, a role which has no equivalent in any of the EFTA Countries and it was not even considered necessary to provide for *ad hoc* advocates general as in the Court of First Instance. Finally, contrary to the proposals in the first version of the EEA Agreement, no separate Court of First Instance was included in the EEA judicial control mechanism.

All of the provisions relating to the qualifications and appointment of the judges, the length of their mandate and other matters of the organisation of the Court are laid down in the Protocol on

---

[12] *Opinion 1/91* [1991] ECR I–6079.
[13] One each from Iceland, Liechtenstein and Norway.

the Statute of the EFTA Court in provisions which correspond almost identically to those of the Statute of the Court of Justice.

The quorum for a valid decision by the EFTA court is three judges so, in case one of the three permanent judes is disqualified or is otherwise unavailable for a particular case the two remaining judges select the third, *ad hoc*, judge form a list of qualified lawyers from the three States concerned.

## PROCEDURE

The rules governing the procedure in proceedings before the EFTA Court are laid down in Part 3 of the Statute contained in Protocol 5 of the ESA/EFTA Court Agreement. They reflect almost exactly the corresponding provisions in the Statute of the Court of Justice.

One of the main differences concerns rights of representation, in that Article 17 expressly provides that, as well as the EFTA States and the ESA, the Community and the Commission of the EC must be represented before the EFTA by an agent appointed in each case.[14]

Lawyers who assist agents or who represent a party must be entitled to practise before a Court in a contracting party to the EEA Agreement. Thus lawyers who are entitled to practise before a court in an EC Member State, and hence before the European Court of Justice, are also entitled to practice before the EFTA Court.

Article 20 of the Statute, providing for notification of requests for opinions, requires the Registrar of the EFTA Court to notify the governments of the EFTA States, the ESA, the Community and the EC Commission *(sic)* all of whom may submit written or oral observations to the EFTA Court. This possibility covers not only requests for advisory opinions but also other cases brought before the EFTA Court, a much more flexible procedure than the rules governing intervention, which possibility is also open to the Community and the Commission. The reason for this apparently wider openness towards participation in proceedings from the Community side is to facilitate the attainment of homogeneous interpretation of the EEA Agreement.

---

[14] It is worth noting that in accordance with the Final Act of the EEA Agreement the Community amended the Statute of the Court of Justice and the Court of First Instance of the European Communities so as to enable agents appointed for each case, on representing an EFTA State or the EFTA Surveillance Authority, to be assisted by the adviser or a lawyer entitled to practice before a court of an EFTA State. Lawyers entitled to practise before a Court of an EFTA State may represent individuals or companies before the Court of Justice and the Court of First Instance of the European Communities.

Finally the language regime of the new court should be mentioned. Although Article 16 of the Statute provides that the rules
governing the languages of the court are to be laid down in its
rules of procedure, the EFTA States decided to keep their single
working language, English – which has the advantage of not being
the language of any of the States concerned – as the only language
of the court. This has the immeasurable advantage of avoiding the
necessity for a staff of translators. Translation and interpretation
facilities however are necessary in proceedings upon requests for
advisory opinions from the national courts of the EFTA countries
which may be put in the language used by the courts concerned
and which should be in principle answered in that language,
although the answer will also be available in English. The decisions
given by the EFTA Court in response to such requests are
published in both languages.

# PART THREE:
# PROCEDURE AND PRACTICE

## INTRODUCTORY

It is a lawyer's commonplace that procedure often counts for more than substantive law. But the role of procedure in the Court of Justice is in some ways more limited than in national legal systems. The procedure has no long tradition behind it. It was devised for lawyers from the differing legal backgrounds of the six original Member States and therefore was not tied to any particular national system. When first devised and published in 1953, the Rules of Procedure[1] were based on those of the International Court of Justice at The Hague. There is also a family resemblance to the procedure of the French *Conseil d'Etat,* a resemblance developed, whether consciously or unconsciously, by the presence in Luxembourg over the years of a series of judges and advocates general drawn from the *Conseil.*

Modifications in the procedure have hitherto been few. Minor amendments were introduced after the enlargement of the Communities in 1973 and again in 1979 and 1981. A consolidated version of the Rules was published in the Official Journal in 1982. From 1989, of course, regard must be had to the procedural rules adopted for the Court of First Instance, for the division of competences between that court and the Court of Justice and for the machinery of appeals and traffic between one and the other.

A lawyer from the British Isles is likely to find the procedure very strange. The oral and adversary character of English civil procedure (and its Scottish and Irish counterparts) is in marked contrast with the written and inquisitorial features of the Luxembourg procedure, features which cause the continental lawyer little or no surprise.

---

[1] Hereafter referred to as "the Rules". Where necessary to avoid ambiguity these will be referred to as "the Court Rules" or "the Court of First Instance Rules" as the case may be. Individual Articles of either Rules will be cited as CJ Rules Article X or CFI Rules Article Y, as required.

The emphasis on written procedure is explicable on two grounds, historical and practical. In continental civil procedure there is a very long tradition of a written or documentary process, derived from Roman and canon law models; the absence of the English-type institution of the lay jury meant there was little pressure to evolve towards a more oral process. With this shared background, it was natural for the original framers of the procedure at Luxembourg to devise a process with more emphasis on written argument to persuade the legal mind than on forensic flourishes to impress a jury.

In practical terms, a mainly written procedure makes good sense. For the administration of Community justice is ultimately controlled by its single supreme court at Luxembourg which has to serve a territory stretching from the Shetlands to Sicily, from the Atlantic Ocean to the Aegean Sea. The geographical isolation of Luxembourg from the other capitals (and principal legal centres) of the Member States means that lawyers will not wish to prolong their visits to the Court and burden their clients with additional costs. By the time the oral stage is reached the main work has been done on paper by the lawyers working in the convenience of their own offices or chambers.

The Rules of Procedure binding upon the Court are drawn up by the Court itself but submitted for approval to the Council; as Article 188 (now Article 245) EC states: "The Court of Justice shall adopt its rules of procedure. These shall require the unanimous approval of the Council." The Rules themselves fill out and amplify the organisational and procedural framework set out in the Protocols on the Statute of the Court of Justice which are annexed to the three founding Treaties.

However, the Rules themselves are relatively brief and give only schematic guidance: there is much less detail than, for example, in the English Rules of the Supreme Court and although there is a handy compendium of texts, "Selected Instruments Relating to the Organisation, Jurisdiction and Procedure of the Court", published by the Court itself, there is no semi-official practitioner's manual equivalent to the English Supreme Court Practice. In recent years, however, two practice books have been published which provide valuable guidance for English-speaking lawyers: these are Usher's *European Court Practice* (1983) and Lasok's *The European Court of Justice: Practice and Procedure* (1984, 2nd ed., 1994). Butterworth's *European Court Practice* (1993) sets out the Rules of each Court Article by Article followed by a commentary on each somewhat in the manner of the Supreme Court Practice.

Within the framework of the Rules, decisions on procedural questions are taken by the Court, on the advice of the judge-rapporteur and advocate general, but often without the parties being consulted. Such decisions are taken at regular "Administrative Meetings" (now styled "General Meetings") of the Court, held in private in the Deliberation Room. The decisions are communicated to the parties but are not normally reported, so that a lawyer who needs to know the practice of the Court on a particular point can only inquire of the Registry. There is a need in this respect for some system equivalent to the Practice Notes or Directions issued by English superior courts: precedents already exist in the Notes for Guidance of counsel (reproduced in the Appendix to the next Chapter, p. 312) and the Note for Guidance on References by National Courts for Preliminary Rulings (reproduced in the Appendix to Chapter 10, pp. 242, above).

# Chapter Twelve

# Procedure and Practice

## INTRODUCTION

Within the categories of cases coming before the Court a broad distinction is drawn between direct actions and references for preliminary rulings. The latter involve a reference by a national court to Luxembourg for a preliminary ruling on a point of Community law; the procedure is distinctive and forms the subject of a separate section (below, p. 292). The account which follows is confined to direct actions, that is, those where a private individual, a company, a Member State or a Community institution is bringing proceedings directly before the Court – usually with a Member State or a Community institution as the defendant.[1] As we have seen (in Chapter 5) most cases brought by individuals and companies will now normally go to the Court of First Instance, with an appeal on points of law to the Court of Justice. The Court of First Instance has adopted its own Rules of Procedure which for the reasons previously mentioned (at p. 85) are in most respects similar to those of the Court of Justice. The main distinguishing features of the Court of First Instance Rules have already been discussed, so it may be assumed that what follows applies to actions before both Courts unless otherwise stated.

The Court of Justice has also adopted its own rules for dealing with appeals from the Court of First Instance. The procedure in such appeals is modelled, with some modifications, on the procedure governing direct actions which is considered here.

---

[1] The only direct action in which the defendant might be another person or body would be a claim based upon an arbitration clause, pursuant to Art. 181 (now Article 238) EC. See for example Case 426/85 *Commission v. Zoubek* [1986] ECR 4057; [1988] 1 C.M.L.R. 257.

## A. The Usual Stages in Procedure

The procedure has four stages, of which the second and/or the third stage may sometimes be omitted. These stages are: (1) the written proceedings; (2) the investigation or preparatory inquiry; (3) the oral proceedings including the advocate-general's opinion; (4) deliberation and judgment. The first and second stages are essentially private, in contrast to the third which takes place publicly in open court where the judgment is also delivered.

Despite the number of stages, and the heavy case-load, the procedure moves along with relative despatch; indeed, by the standards of many national courts it is still quite swift despite the steady increase in the time taken shown in Table 3 (p. 423, below). Thus, a straightforward direct action currently takes, on average, between 20 and 24 months from commencement of proceedings to judgment; a preliminary reference may take rather less, as the Court always gives priority to such cases, taking the view that time is here of the essence in order to enable the national court to resume its own adjourned proceedings as soon as possible; moreover, as we shall see, the preliminary ruling procedure has a significantly shorter written phase. In recent years (see Table 3), the average time taken has increased by several months for each type of case, but the establishment of the Court of First Instance should prevent the situation from deteriorating further and may allow it to be somewhat improved. However, the Court of First Instance itself is now grappling with considerable case overload.

### 1. Written Procedure

Proceedings are begun by the filing of an application (*requête*) with the Registrar. No set form is required for the application but under the Rules it must contain certain information.[2] Thus, the applicant must set out the subject matter of the dispute and the grounds upon which the application is based. He must also state the form of order that is being sought (for example, an order to quash an act or for damages) and the nature of the evidence being relied upon. Any claim for costs must be included in the application. These are the minimum requirements, but the successful drafting of an application requires considerable skill.[3]

---

[2] Laid down in CJ Rules, Art. 38.

[3] See the helpful guidance offered by Advocate General Sir Gordon Slynn (as he then was) in the English Bar's Journal *Counsel*, September/October 1988. The Registrar of the Court of First Instance has drawn up a note giving advice for lawyers and agents regarding the written procedure before the Court of First Instance [1994] O.J. C120.

The document is the equivalent neither of an English writ nor of a statement of claim, although it performs the function of both. It is much more, for it contains, in effect, the whole of the applicant's case. It should include a full statement of the facts, of the nature of the complaint, and of the arguments of law upon which the applicant relies; any documentary evidence must be annexed (or its exact whereabouts indicated so as to permit a subsequent court order for production). Moreover, since the form of order sought cannot normally be amended, and since the Court cannot adjudicate *ultra petita*, the contents of the application circumscribe the scope of the action. The case can be expanded in the reply to the defence or at the oral hearing, but no new plea in law may be introduced at these later stages unless it is based upon matters of law or fact which come to light in the course of the procedure.[4]

Other, more technical information required in the application includes an address for service in Luxembourg: usually, this is the office of a Luxembourg *avocat* but the address may be of any person enjoying the confidence of the applicant. In addition, the lawyer acting for the applicant must file a certificate of his entitlement to practise before the courts of a Member State. The question of the right of audience is considered in the next chapter. It should be noted that legal representation is obligatory in direct actions,[5] but a preliminary application for legal aid may be made without the services of a lawyer.[6]

The language in which an application is drafted will normally be taken to be the language of the case.[7] Where the applicant is a Member State or an individual (or company) who is proceeding against a Community institution, the general rule is that the applicant has the choice among the 12 languages allowed by the Court: Danish, Dutch, English, Finnish, French, German, Greek, Irish, Italian, Portuguese, Spanish or Swedish. But where the action is against a Member State (or, as may exceptionally arise, an individual or company in a Member State), the choice of language belongs to the defendant. As a matter of practical convenience, however, the Court has settled upon French as its working language. Accordingly, whatever language is chosen for the particular case, the necessary documents will always be translated at least into French for internal use.

The application, if in satisfactory form, is then served upon the defendant. Service of this, as of all other documents, is effected by

---

[4] CJ Rules, Art 42(2); CFI Rules, Art. 48(2).
[5] See below, p. 299.
[6] See below, p. 309, and see T. Kennedy, "Paying the Piper, Legal Aid in Proceedings before the Court of Justice" (1988) C.M.L.Rev. 559.
[7] CJ Rules, Art. 29(2); CFI Rules, Art. 35(2).

the Registrar by registered post at the address for service mentioned above.

The defendant has one month in which to file his defence. The defence is of similar scope to the application, and should set out the considerations of fact and law on which the defendant relies, an indication of the supporting evidence – again annexed to the pleading – and also any counterclaim or other relief sought. The time for filing a defence can be extended for good reason by the President of the Court.

The Court has adopted the practice, common to many legal systems, of distinguishing generally between the admissibility of the action and its merits or substance. Questions of admissibility include all questions which go to the jurisdiction of the Court: they may include, for example, the question whether the applicant has the necessary standing to challenge the measure in issue, whether the action has not been brought out of time, or whether the "*conclusion*" or form of relief sought by the applicant is one which the Court can grant.

Accordingly the defendant often sets out his submissions under two heads, admissibility and substance; or he may make a "preliminary objection" to the admissibility of the action, and ask the Court to take a decision on that alone, which may obviate the need for a decision on the substance. The Court may also consider, of its own motion and at any time, whether there is an "absolute bar" to proceeding with a case, what the French term *un moyen d'ordre public*, that is, a bar which does not require to be pleaded by the parties and cannot be waived by them.

In the absence of a defence, judgment can be given by default.[8] These are, however, extremely rare and, usually, a defence is lodged. This allows the applicant to put in a reply, to which the defendant in turn can respond by a rejoinder. Although not obligatory, both reply and rejoinder are common steps in the pleading of a case at Luxembourg; but in some cases, in order to speed up proceedings the applicant may waive his right to reply, thus depriving the defendant of the opportunity of a rejoinder. The time limits for each are usually one month, subject to any extensions which may be allowed by the President. With the rejoinder the written pleadings are closed.

## 2. Investigation or Preparatory Inquiry

Meanwhile, upon the lodging of the application, the case will have been assigned by the President to one of his colleagues to act as

---

[8] CJ Rules Art. 94, CFI Rules Art. 122. See for example Case 68/88 *Commission v. Greece* [1989] ECR 2965; [1991] 1 C.M.L.R. 31 and Case T–42/89 *Yorck von Wartenburg v. Parliament* [1990] ECR II–31.

judge-rapporteur. The three-judge Chamber to which that judge belongs will carry out any investigation or preparatory inquiry which may be necessary. At the same time the First Advocate General will designate the advocate general for the case.

All the papers relating to the case will have been distributed to all members of the Court, but at this stage, they will only have been studied closely by the judge-rapporteur and the advocate general to whom the case is assigned – and their respective legal secretaries.

The pleadings being closed, the Court now takes over the direction of the proceedings. Up to this point the procedure has been adversarial, or *"contradictoire"*; it now becomes inquisitorial, especially if the Court decides an *"instruction"* of the case is needed. This term of French procedure has become "preparatory inquiry" in the English version of the Rules.

This and other procedural decisions are based upon the preliminary report (*"rapport préalable"*) of the judge-rapporteur. The confidential report is submitted to the full Court at one of its regular General Meetings or, in the Court of First Instance, to the plenary conference of that court. Guided by this report and any views expressed by the advocate general, the Court decides what (if any) issues of fact need to be proved and what evidence is to be adduced for the purpose, including whether witnesses (and if so, which) are to be summoned to testify. This decision is made at a General Meeting (see p. 270, above) held in private in the Deliberation Room. An order setting out any measures of inquiry is served upon the parties.

The Court may also decide at this stage whether the case will be heard by the Chamber to which it was assigned, to a Chamber of five judges or whether it should be heard by a full Court consisting, in the jargon of the Court, of a *"Petit Plenum"* of nine judges or a *"Grand Plenum"* consisting of all 15 judges, a decision depending on the difficulty or importance of the case. Cases are never listed to be heard by only nine judges (the legal quorum for a full Court) because of the risk that one judge may for some reason (for example, ill health) become unavailable later in the proceedings and thus necessitate the re-opening of the proceedings before a reconstituted Court. When the Court sits with 12, 13 or 14 judges it usually means that the case has been listed for a *Grand Plenum* but that one or more of the judges is unavailable (or ineligible) to sit on the day of the hearing: a judge who does not sit during the oral hearing or during the advocate-general's opinion may not then take part in the deliberation on the case.

The Court may also decide that there should be a joinder of the case with other closely related cases (see p. 290, below).

The investigation may include all or any of the following: the personal appearance of the parties; the production of documents or the supply of information by the parties; the summoning of witnesses to appear and give evidence; the commissioning of a report by an expert; or the arranging of a visit or inspection.[9] The Rules permit these measures to be conducted either by the Court itself, by the Chamber dealing with the case, by the three judge Chamber to which the judge-rapporteur belongs or by the judge-rapporteur individually.

It should be noted that the hearing of witnesses is part of the investigation, not part of the oral proceedings; moreover, the witnesses or the expert are witnesses of the Court, not of the parties. It is possible for the parties to request the Court to hear a witness in order to prove certain specified facts; if there is good reason for this request, the Court will accede to it, and the witness then becomes the Court's witness.

The taking of evidence from a witness conforms, for the most part, with the normal practice of continental courts – practice which common lawyers generally regard as much inferior to their own for the establishment of facts where this depends on the credibility of a witness. The order sets out what facts are to be established: see the example in Case 18/63 *Wollast v. EEC.*[10] The witness is heard by the Chamber in the presence of the parties or their representatives. After the witness has given his or her evidence, questions may be put to the witness by the presiding judge, the other judges or the advocate general. Until the revision of the Rules of Procedure in 1974, the parties' lawyers could only put questions through the medium of the presiding judge, but now they may be permitted to put their questions directly, as in cross-examination – although the different context of the Luxembourg questioning makes it no more than a pale shadow of the English original.[11] The statement of the witness, attested on oath, is recorded and later transcribed.

Letters *rogatory* are an alternative method for taking evidence. These are in the form of an order for a witness to be examined, on specified facts, by a judicial authority in the Member State where

---

[9] See also the section on measures of organisation of procedure before the Court of First Instance at p. 87, above.

[10] [1964] ECR 85 at 95.

[11] For an intriguing example of the contrast between the two legal cultures see Case 145/83 *Adams v. Commission* [1985] ECR 3539; [1986] 1 C.M.L.R. 506. The parties were each represented by distinguished leading counsel from the English bar who were repeatedly admonished by the presiding judge for attempting to turn the inquisitorial hearing of witnesses into an adversarial trial. The evidence elucidated at the hearing is summarised at pp. 3572 to 3576 of the "Facts and Issues" section of the judgment and referred to in paras 20 to 25 (pp. 3582 *et seq.*) of the Decision. The information which emerged at the hearing was crucial to the resolution of the case.

he permanently resides. Their use is extremely rare: indeed, the only instance to date is that in Case 160/84 *Oryzomyli Kavallas v. Commission*[12] where it appears that the replies requested took nine months to reach the Court.

A formal investigation or preparatory inquiry is relatively rare. Thus, up to January 1, 1989 (some 36 years after the Court came into existence) the Court had heard witnesses in only 44 cases and had appointed only 16 experts; there had been only one reported instance of an inspection: this was under the ECSC Treaty, where it was necessary to ascertain conditions of production in the iron and steel industry.[13] If witnesses are to be heard, the inquiry may be fixed on the day preceding, or the same day as, the oral proceedings in order to save the lawyers a double journey to Luxembourg. This practice is also followed by the Court of First Instance.[14]

More commonly, the Court at its General Meeting may decide, at the prompting of the judge-rapporteur, to ask the parties, or the Commission, to reply, either in writing or at the oral hearing, to questions put by the Court in advance of the hearing, or to produce documents or objects for the Court's inspection.[15] Whatever material is added to the court file of the case as a result of a preparatory inquiry or the informal requests just mentioned, it must be made freely available to the parties, who have then the right to make written submissions upon its content. In this respect, the procedure conforms with the requirement that it be (as the French would say) *une procédure contradictoire*, that is one in which the arguments and evidence of each party are made available to, and can be commented upon by, the other.

---

[12] [1985] ECR 675; [1986] ECR 1633; [1986] 2 C.M.L.R. 269.

[13] See Case 14/59 *Société de Fondéries de Pont-à-Mousson* [1959] ECR 215 at 224 and 237 for a visit by the Court to the applicant's foundry at Pont-à-Mousson.

[14] See for example the *Welded Steel Trellis* case, Joined Cases T–141 to 145 and 147 to 152/89 *Tréfileurope Sales and Others v. Commission* [1995] ECR II–791 in which two witnesses were examined on a Monday morning with legal submissions beginning that afternoon and lasting all week.

[15] A selection of products has been presented to the Court in this way. See, *e.g.* the "laughing device" produced in Case 22/76 *Import Gadgets* [1976] ECR 1371, the "Monchichi" doll in Case 38/85 *Bienengraber und Co. v. Hauptzollamt Hamburg-Jonas* [1986] ECR 811; tobacco leaves in Case 141/86 *The Queen v. HM Customs and Excise ex p. Imperial Tobacco* [1988] ECR 57; [1988] 2 C.M.L.R. 403 and Case 182/84 *Miro B.V.* [1985] ECR 3731; [1986] 3 C.M.L.R. 545, in which the judges sat solemnly on the bench with a bottle of gin (unopened) in front of each of them. A similarly bibulous sight occurred at the hearing in Case C–136/96 *Scotch Whisky Association v. La Martiniquaise* [1998] ECR I–4571.

## 3. Oral Procedure

Once the pleadings have been exchanged and the preparatory inquiry (if any) has been conducted, the President of the Court fixes the earliest convenient date for the public hearing. The parties and their lawyers are given at least three weeks' notice to attend. With the current congestion of the Court's time-table, hearings are now often fixed months in advance. Once fixed, the date cannot readily be changed. In England it has been accepted that a barrister's obligation to attend a hearing before the Court of Justice takes precedence over obligations before all courts save the House of Lords.

However, notwithstanding the apparently unambiguous wording of Article 18 of the Statute, in certain cases the Court may dispense with the oral procedure. This important and, from a common lawyer's point of view, surprising innovation was first introduced into the Court's procedure by Article 52 of the Statute, one of the new provisions added as title 4 of the Statute by the Decision establishing the Court of First Instance.[16]

Although Article 52 of the Statute echoes Article 18 in stating that where an appeal is brought against a decision of the Court of First Instance, the procedure before the Court of Justice shall consist of a written part and an oral part, the second sentence goes on to provide that, in accordance with conditions laid down in the CJ Rules, the Court of Justice, having heard the advocate general and the parties, may dispense with the oral procedure.

To that end, the new Article 120 added to the CJ Rules by the 1989 revision provided that, on such an appeal, the Court might, after having heard the advocate general and the parties[17] decide to dispense with the oral procedure unless one of the parties objects on the ground that the written procedure did not enable him fully to defend his point of view.

A more radical change was made by the amendments to the rules of May 1991 which enabled the oral procedure to be dispensed with in other types of direct actions. A new provision, Article 44a of the CJ Rules, provides that the procedure before the Court shall include an oral part except in specific cases in which the Court, acting on a report from the judge-rapporteur, after hearing the advocate general and with the express consent of the parties, decides otherwise. This measure, designed to accelerate the disposal of straightforward cases, is likely to be used sparingly.[18] For

---

[16] See further Chap. 5, above.

[17] In this context the "hearing" of the parties is assumed to be carried out in writing, the advocate general gives his views, as usual, at the General Meeting.

[18] In practice it seems in nearly 10% of cases; however the cases concerned are, by definition, the more straightforward ones and the saving of court time is not commensurate.

the purposes of applying this new rule the parties are automatically asked by the Registry after the closure of the written procedure, whether they wish to have a hearing, at its general meeting the Court will decide whether, in its view, a hearing is necessary and should it be decided not to hold a hearing the advocate general will be invited to fix a date upon which to deliver his opinion.

Some time before the hearing (if not dispensed with) the judge-rapporteur issues his report for the hearing ("*rapport d'audience*") which is communicated to the parties in advance and made public on the day of the hearing. This sets out the facts of the case and summarises the respective arguments of the parties. The original purpose of the report was that it should be read aloud at the start of the oral hearing to inform the public and preserve the public character of the proceedings. But it is now always taken as read. It now serves different purposes, including the instruction of members of the Court who may be less familiar with the full contents of the file than the judge-rapporteur and advocate general. It is distributed before the hearing to the parties' lawyers so that they can make any comments either formally at the hearing or otherwise. Immediately before the hearing, copies of the report are placed on a table outside the Courtroom for interested members of the public. Until 1994, as we have seen (above, p. 30) the report in cases before the Court of Justice will be published in the Court's reports and may make it easier to understand the judgment, which will often contain a reference back to the report for fuller detail of the facts and argument. Since 1994 the report has been obtainable from the Registry, but only in the language of the case.

In the Court of First Instance the report for the hearing, although it is issued to the parties and made public on the day of the hearing, is not subsequently published. This is because of the fact-finding role of the Court of First Instance: not only does the report have a different role in the conduct of the proceedings, but also the judgment of the Court includes the findings of fact.

Immediately before the case is called, counsel for the parties and the agents for any Community institution involved are invited into the judges' retiring room where there is often informal discussion, for example, as to the order and length of speeches in the forthcoming proceedings.

The members of the Court take up their seats on the bench in their order of precedence after the usher has called out "The Court" (spoken in the language of the case) as a signal to those present to stand.

The oral proceedings are reduced in practice to the addresses by the opposing lawyers, questions put from the Bench, very brief replies to opposing speeches and the opinion submitted by the advocate general. This opinion, as we shall see below, is almost always delivered at a subsequent sitting of the Court.

So far as the lawyers' addresses are concerned, strict time limits are now imposed: normally each party is allowed 30 minutes, and only 15 minutes in cases before a Chamber of three judges.[19] Counsel cannot therefore waste the Court's time by going over again the facts and arguments already fully set out in the written proceedings and so known to the Court. Instead, they should show their skill in marshalling the salient points of their case and the weaknesses of the other side. High-flown rhetoric is eschewed. Unless the language of the case is English or French, some members of the Court will be dependent upon their earphones for simultaneous translation, a barrier which not even the oratory of a Demosthenes could surmount.

It is not customary, at least before the full Court, to interrupt the main speeches. Each side is allowed a brief right of reply to the other. In recent years the judges and the advocate general have increasingly exercised their right to put questions: usually, these questions are reserved until after the two main speeches, but before a Chamber, especially a Chamber of three judges, counsel may find himself interrupted with questions – an ordeal with which counsel from the British Isles at least are familiar.

At the end of the hearing, the advocate general will usually announce the date on which he will deliver his opinion, and the case is then adjourned. Only very rarely might the opinion be delivered forthwith, for example, where the case is already exactly covered by a previous decision of the Court to which the advocate general might then simply refer. Usually, the opinion is delivered in open court at a hearing some weeks later.

Until 1991 the opinion was read out *in extenso*, in his own language, by the advocate general concerned who would stand to address the Court as an indication that he is in no sense a member of the tribunal of judgment but rather their impartial adviser.

Since 1991 a reading of an opinion *in extenso* is extremely rare, the presentation of the advocate-general's submissions in open court (as required by Article 18 of the Statute) taking the form of a "communication" to the Court, by the advocate general assigned to whichever case is due to be heard, of the conclusion of the opinion or opinions, whether his own or those of his colleagues. The conclusion, containing the advocate-general's recommendation to the Court as to how to decide the case, is read out in French (as the Court's working language) and made available, in full, in writing in that language and, where they are different, in the advocate-general's own language and in the language of the case. This lip-service to the Statute in the Court of Justice may be

---

[19] See the Notes for the Guidance of Counsel, appended to Chap. 13.

contrasted with the freedom accorded the *ad hoc* advocate general in the Court of First Instance to deliver his opinion in writing, with no oral presentation at all.[20]

The advocate-general's opinion closes the oral proceedings, so that it is he, and not the parties, who has the last word. Exceptionally, the Court may order further investigative steps to be taken, which may mean the advocate general has to deliver a second opinion. The same situation may arise if the advocate general delivers a first opinion which urges the Court to decide the case upon a preliminary point without entering into the merits: if the Court decides against him on the preliminary point, it will ask him to deliver a second opinion on the substance.

An illustration of the re-opening of oral proceedings is provided by Case 155/79 *AM&S Europe Ltd v. Commission*,[21] which raised the question of the scope of legal professional privilege in Community law. In the course of an investigation by the Commission under the competition rules, AM&S claimed privilege for certain documents which they refused to make available to the Commission. The Commission did not accept the claim and AM&S took the matter to court. After the oral procedure had been completed, with a very full opinion by Advocate General Warner, the Court decided that the oral procedure should be re-opened: it decided itself to look at the documents for which privilege had been claimed, and for this purpose ordered the applicant to produce them under seal, and decided also to hold a further hearing, after which Advocate General Sir Gordon Slynn gave a further opinion.

## 4. Judgment

The Court always reserves its judgment. Following continental traditions, the Court preserves strictly the principle of the secrecy of its deliberations, a practice which reinforces the independence of the members of the Court. Thus, only the judges are admitted to the Deliberation Room; neither the advocate general for the case nor the Registrar is present. The principle also entails the exclusion of interpreters, so that the judges have had to settle upon a language which they all understand. In the result, the deliberations of the Court are conducted in French.

The principle of secrecy of deliberations has an additional consequence. Dissenting judgments cannot be publicly expressed.[22]

---

[20] Art. 46 of the Statute. See Chap. 5.

[21] [1982] ECR 1575; [1982] 2 C.M.L.R. 264. See also Case C–2/90 *Commission v. Belgium* [1992] ECR I–4431; [1993] 1 C.M.L.R. 365, *The Times*, July 1, 1992, in which Advocate General Jacobs delivered no less than three opinions.

[22] But addressing the Court upon his departure, Sir Gordon Slynn (as he then was) speculated that the time might soon come, with the growing maturity of the Community legal order, when dissenting opinions might be admitted (Formal Hearing March 10, February 1992).

Where the Court finds itself divided, a majority view must be determined by vote and this will then emerge as the judgment of the Court. The outside world has no way of knowing whether the judgment was unanimous or by a majority. The interesting implications of the single collegiate judgment are discussed in Part Four (below, p. 319).

Where a vote has to be taken the Rules of Procedure require votes be cast in the reverse order to the order of precedence of the judges; as Professor Schermers explains "Voting in the reverse order to the order of seniority is an old judicial custom in European courts and is designed to prevent the votes of the older and more experienced judges from influencing their younger colleagues".[23] Whether the Rules are always observed on this point, in practice, only the judges will know.

The Statute requires that judgments should state the reasons on which they are based and give the names of the judges who took part in the deliberations. When subsequently drawn up in the language of the case, the judgment is signed by all the judges who took part in the deliberations and authenticated by the signatures of the President (who may not necessarily have sat on the case) and the Registrar. The authentic version is that in the language of the case. Consequently, except where this language is French, the authentic version will be a translation of the text as agreed in the Deliberation Room; but, to ensure conformity, the translation will be checked by the judge whose native tongue is that of the language of the case. Despite this safeguard, slips may occur; for example, in Case 131/79 *Santillo*,[24] where a ruling was sought on whether lapse of time may deprive a recommendation to deport of its validity under Directive 64/221, the Court, according to the authentic English text, provided a criterion in terms of whether the lapse of time "is liable to deprive" the recommendation of its validity, whereas the more precise French text employs the words *"est de nature à priver"*. The ambiguity of the English may have misled the Divisional Court and the Court of Appeal in their application of the ruling.[25] As we have seen (p. 24, above), the French text of judgments will have had the advantage since 1980 of careful checking by the *lecteur d'arrêts*.

The operative part of the judgment (what the French term *"le dispositif"*) is read out at the next available public hearing of the Court, either by the President (or President of Chamber) or the judge-rapporteur or as linguistic convenience may dictate; thus, if

---

[23] *Judicial Protection in the European Communities* (4th ed., 1987), p. 449.
[24] *R. v. Secretary of State for Home Affairs, ex p. Santillo* [1980] ECR 1585; [1980] 2 C.M.L.R. 308.
[25] See Barav (1981) 6 E.L.Rev. 139.

the language of the case is Danish or Greek, the Danish or Greek judge, as the case may be, may read out the judgment.

The *dispositif* must then be published in the Official Journal, in all the different language series.[26] In the event of some discrepancy having legal significance between the different language versions, the version in the language of the case, being regarded as authentic, must prevail.

## B. Execution and Enforcement

The Court has no powers of its own to enforce its judgments. It has no criminal jurisdiction whatsoever, nor does it have the power to commit for contempt which is the peculiar weapon at the disposal of the English judge. This has led to certain problems, theoretical rather than practical, for dealing with perjury by witnesses at Luxembourg.

It will be appreciated from what has been said in previous chapters about the effects of judgments of the Court that questions of execution or enforcement rarely arise. The implementation of preliminary rulings is a matter for the national courts. In actions against Community institutions, the consequences of a judgment given against them are either automatic, as in the case of annulment, or at any rate unlikely to raise problems of non-compliance. A judgment against a Member State is declaratory. There is no provision for enforcement of judgments against Member States or Community institutions, although as we have seen (p. 122) the ECSC Treaty contains provisions for sanctions against Member States. The EC Treaty merely places the State or institution under an obligation to take the necessary measures to comply with the Court's judgment.

As we have seen in Chapter 6, the Maastricht Treaty added teeth to a judgment in a direct action against a Member State, by empowering the Court to impose a financial penalty on a recalcitrant Member State refusing to comply with a judgment. The procedure for enforcement of such a penalty is summarised at p. 119.

On the other hand, even prior to the Maastricht Treaty, where the judgment imposed a pecuniary obligation on a private individual or company (as distinct from a Member State) such a judgment has enforceable effect by virtue of Article 192 (now Article 256) EC. The Article goes on to provide that enforcement shall be

---

[26] The case will then be reported. For details of the different series of law reports see Chap. 2 above, pp. 32.

governed by the rules of civil procedure in the Member State where enforcement is being sought. In other words, the successful party, armed with an authenticated copy of the judgment, is left to pursue his judgment debtor in the national forum.

## C. Costs

This is a subject of great practical importance. It is linked with the subject of legal aid, to be dealt with in the next chapter.

One preliminary difference between the Luxembourg Courts and most national courts is that there are no court fees, because of the principle that procedure before the former is free of charge. A further saving follows from the principle that the service of pleadings is effected by the Registry of the Court. A minor qualification to the gratuitous principle is that the Court may order a party to pay court costs which could have been avoided or where the proceedings are deemed vexatious.

Regarding party and party costs, the Court is bound by rule to include in its judgment a decision as to costs. The general principle is that the unsuccessful party is ordered to pay the costs if they have been asked for by the successful party in his application (or defence). There are however a number of exceptions, real or apparent, to this principle.[27]

Thus, one party may be only partly successful; for example, the Court may grant his application to annul a Community decision but refuse his claim for damages. Or there may be several parties suing jointly, some of whom succeed while others fail. In such cases the Court may apportion the costs as it thinks fit or simply leave each party to bear his own costs.

If a party withdraws or discontinues proceedings, he may be ordered to pay all the costs, unless the withdrawal or discontinuance is justified by the conduct of the other party.

In practice, although the Commission and Member States claim costs in actions between each other and the Court invariably orders the losing party to pay the winner's costs they are almost never recovered. This kind of "knock-for-knock" arrangement is said to be justified on grounds of the efficiency of Court proceedings and in the interest of sound financial management.[28]

The question of costs on references for preliminary rulings is dealt with below.

---

[27] The special rules on costs in staff cases before the Court of First Instance and before the Court of Justice on appeal are dealt with in Chap. 9.

[28] See reply to a question in the European Parliament [1992] O.J. C102/39. But as the Commission is almost always the winner, one may question whether this practice constitutes a drain in the Community budget.

What items are included under costs may give rise to dispute. They appear to cover the travelling and subsistence expenses of parties and their lawyers, the fees of lawyers or other specialist advisers, and the costs involved in providing an address for service in Luxembourg. If the parties cannot agree the items, the Rules provide that one of the parties may apply for costs to be taxed by the Court. This is done by one of the Chambers, whose order is not subject to appeal. In the history of the Court there have only been 30 or so applications for taxation.

Taxation in Luxembourg is quite different from taxation in London: the Court will make a rough assessment of the appropriate level of fees, based on what it considers reasonable in the circumstances.

Decisions on taxation are not normally reported, but in an order in Case 238/78 *Ireks-Arkady v. EC*[29] the Court clarified the definition of recoverable costs mentioned in Article 73(b) of the Rules of Procedure. After emphasising that the Court was not required to have regard to any national scale fixing lawyers' fees it added that "as Community law has not laid down any provisions in the nature of a scale, the Court must undertake a free appreciation of the facts of the dispute, having regard to its object and nature, its importance from the point of view of Community law and the difficulties of the proceedings, the amount of work which the litigation may have caused the lawyer and what the dispute may have meant to the parties in financial terms."

Case 126/76 *Dietz v. Commission*[30] also established a point of principle. The Commission claimed from the unsuccessful plaintiff the sum of 75,000 Belgian Francs (rather less than £1,000 at the then rate of exchange) for the conduct of the case by its agent, a member of its Legal Service. The Court upheld the applicant's challenge to this claim and ruled that, although the Community institutions could recover fees paid to outside counsel, the position was different where they chose to be represented by one of their own officials acting as agent: they could then recover only the travel and subsistence expenses incurred in attending the hearing in Luxembourg.

# D. Some Special Matters of Procedure

## 1. Interim Measures

An applicant in a direct action may apply to the Court for interim relief (a procedure known in French as *le référé*). For example, the

---

[29] Case 238/78 *Ireks-Arkady v. EC* [1983] ECR I–723.
[30] Case 126/76 *Dietz v. Commission* [1979] ECR 2131.

party may wish to obtain a stay of execution of the decision which is being challenged in the principal suit. The circumstances must justify such a stay, and this condition has been strictly construed so as to limit it to cases where there is (a) urgency and (b) a risk of irreparable damage or serious prejudice to the applicant. This reluctance to grant stays of execution is in accordance with French practice where *le référé* is seldom successful before the administrative courts. In accordance with Article 36 of the Statute, applications for interim measures are generally adjudicated upon by the President of the Court.

As we saw in Chapter 6, the Court has even been prepared to order interim measures in proceedings brought by the Commission against Member States under Article 169 (now Article 226) EC. An example occurred in the continuing "Wine war" between France and Italy where the President made an order against France.[31] Interim relief may also be granted to a company appealing against a Commission decision in competition proceedings. Thus in Case 27/76R *United Brands Co. v. Commission*,[32] the President suspended two provisions of a Commission decision (requiring United Brands to cease to charge dissimilar and unfair prices and to cease prohibiting the resale of green bananas) until the Court had given judgment on the appeal from that decision; United Brands had pleaded that there was a threat to it of irreversible damage and financial disaster.

The application for interim relief is dealt with separately from the principal suit to which it is, in a sense, ancillary. It is made in writing, and the document must set out the grounds of fact and law so as to establish a prima facie case for the relief being sought. A copy of the application is served on the other side, which may then submit written observations within a short time limit fixed by the President. In the not infrequent event of an oral hearing, the President may be assisted by the judge-rapporteur and the advocate general, but the decision is the President's alone whether to grant or refuse the relief sought. Exceptionally, he may refer an application to the full Court.[33]

The orders granting or refusing interim relief are not always easy to reconcile, one with another: the decisions are by a single judge (usually the President) and delivered in situations of urgency

---

[31] Case 42/82R [1982] ECR 841 (as explained in Chap. 2, the letter R after the Case number denotes *référé*.

[32] Case 27/76R *United Brands Co. v. Commission* [1976] ECR 425; [1976] 2 C.M.L.R. 147.

[33] See Case C–280/93R *Germany v. Council* [1993] ECR I–3667, or, more recently, Case C–180/96R *United Kingdom v. Commission* [1996] ECR I–3903, in which the U.K. unsuccessfully sought suspension of the ban on the export of British beef during the B.S.E. epidemic.

which may curtail the full articulation of reasons; rather, there has to be a quick assessment of the facts as presented. The approach is on a case by case basis, rather than to construct a consistent body of jurisprudence.

Applications for interim relief have been on the increase and now average some 20 a year, of which only about a quarter have been successful.

## 2. Preliminary Objections to Admissibility

In a direct action the defendant, usually a Community institution, may wish to contest the admissibility of the action, without entering into the substance of the case (see p. 276, above). For example in an action for annulment brought by a natural or legal person against the Council or Commission under the second paragraph of Article 230 (ex Article 173) EC, the Council or Commission may contend that the measure at issue is a regulation which the applicant has no *locus standi* to attack (see above, pp. 146 *et seq.*). The defendant may then, without entering a full defence, make a preliminary objection to admissibility. The applicant will then reply and the hearing will be limited to the question of admissibility. Only if the Court finds the action admissible, or decides to reserve the issue of admissibility, will the action continue on the substance in the usual way.

## 3. Interventions by Third Parties

The Protocols on the Statute of the Court of Justice under both the ECSC and the EC Treaties permit the intervention in proceedings of third parties provided they have a sufficient interest in the suit between the principal parties. Notice to potential third parties (and to the world at large) of all proceedings before the Court is given by publication in the Official Journal, as required by the Rules, of every application to originate proceedings. An application to intervene must be made within three months of such publication.

Under the EEA Agreement the EFTA States and the EFTA Surveillance Authority may be permitted to intervene upon proof of sufficient interest.[34] This is to match reciprocal rights of intervention before the EFTA Court accorded to the Community and its Commission.[35]

---

[34] See the declaration included in the Final Act to the EEA Agreement. As the Court of Justice pointed out in *Opinion 1/91* (paras 66 to 68) that right to intervene could be ensured by simple amendment of the Statute of the Court.

[35] For the interaction of the two judicial systems in relation to trademark rights, see Alexander, "Exhaustion of Trade Mark Rights in the EEA" (1999) 24 E.L.Rev. 56, discussing the *Silhouette* case, in which the Court of Justice disagreed with the advisory opinion of the EFTA Court in the *Maglite* case, Case E–2/97 [1998] 1 C.M.L.R. 331; Case C–355/96 *Silhouette* [1998] 2 C.M.L.R. 593.

Under the ECSC Statute, a Community institution, a Member State, or a private individual or a company may intervene upon proof of sufficient interest, in order to argue for or against the cases put forward by the principal parties. In the EC Statute it is presumed that a Community institution or Member State has a sufficient interest to intervene: only a private individual or company is put to proof of their interest, but their intervention is never permitted in suits between Member States or between Member States and Community institutions. Where permitted, the intervention may only support the submissions of one of the principal parties and may not include claims for separate relief.

As we have seen, the intervention of the European Parliament was accepted by the Court in proceedings against the Council in the *Roquette* and *Maizena* cases (above, p. 159), despite the Council's objection that the Parliament was seeking to use the intervention procedure to circumvent its lack of a direct right of action under Article 230 (ex Article 173) EC – a right it now enjoys (as we have seen, p. 143, above) since the amendment of Article 230 by the Maastricht Treaty. The Court has sometimes been liberal in admitting interventions: for example, by a national consumers' association in the *Sugar Cartel* case[36]; and by the CCBE, a body representing the Bars and Law Societies of the Member States, in the *AM&S* case concerning the scope of legal professional privilege in Community law (above, p. 283).

## 4. Joinder of Actions

Where two or more actions are concerned with similar or closely related matters, they may be joined at any stage of the proceedings, This is done by an order of the Court, either on the initiative of the Court itself or at the request of one of the parties.

Joinder of actions is quite a frequent occurrence, as will be apparent from the number of cases cited in this book which bear more than one serial number. But even without a formal joinder, the Court may arrange administratively for suits which are proceeding concurrently and have a common subject matter to come for oral hearing on the same day, or again the advocate general may deliver a single opinion – a sensible economy in time and effort.[37]

---

[36] Joined Cases 40, etc. /73 *Suiker Unie and Others v. Commission* [1975] ECR 1663; [1976] 1 C.M.L.R. 295.

[37] See for example the series of preliminary rulings from courts in different Member States seeking clarification of the effect in time of the judgment in Case C–262 *Barber v. Guardian Royal Exchange* [1990] ECR I–1889. Thus in Cases

## 5. Can Judgments be Appealed Against?

Unlike a judgment of the Court of First Instance a judgment of the Court of Justice is final and not subject to any appeal. There are, however, five special procedures which may be invoked with reference to a judgment of either Court that has already been delivered.

The first is an application for an interpretation by the Court of its judgment. Thus, a party or a Community institution with a sufficient interest may so apply if difficulty arises in understanding the meaning or scope of a judgment of the Court. An early example was Case 5/55 *ASSIDER v. High Authority.*[38] But the Court has been severe in restricting such applications to cases where there is a real ambiguity in the judgment.

Secondly, there is a procedure for rectification of a judgment: the Court may, of its own motion or on application by a party made within two weeks after the delivery of a judgment, rectify clerical mistakes, errors in calculation and obvious slips.[39]

Thirdly, there is the application for a judgment to be reconsidered: the French term is *révision*. A party may apply for this reconsideration if the judgment was given in ignorance of facts which subsequently came to light and which would have had a decisive influence. The new facts may even be subsequent to the judgment of the Court[40]; but the procedure must not be abused as an attempt to appeal.[41] Three months are allowed for the lodging of the application from the date when the party learns of the new facts; no application can be brought after the expiration of 10 years from the date of the judgment.

Fourthly, there is the procedure known in French as *"tierce opposition"* and in the English version of the Rules of Procedure as "third party proceedings". This is an application for reconsideration of a judgment brought by a third party not involved in the

---

C–109/91 *Ten Oever v. Stichting Bedrijfspensioenfonds*; C–110/91 *Moroni v. Collo GmbH*; C–152/91, *Neath v. Hugh Steeper Ltd* and C–200/91 *Coloroll Pension Trustees Ltd v. Russel and Others* the arguments of all the parties were heard on January 26, 1993 and Advocate General Van Gerven delivered his single opinion in Dutch as his own language (whereas the cases were dealt with respectively in Dutch, Italian and English) on April 28. A similar approach was adopted by the Court of First Instance in the *Polypropylene Cartel* cases in which Judge Vesterdorf as *ad hoc* advocate general delivered a single opinion, although individual judgments were subsequently delivered (see Chap. 5 at p. 100).

[38] [1954–1956] ECR 135.
[39] See, *e.g.* Case 27/76 *United Brands v. Commission* [1976] ECR 446 and 450, and Case 158/80 *Rewe v. Hauptzollamt Kiel* [1981] ECR 1805; [1982] 1 C.M.L.R. 449 (the *"butter boats"* case (1982) 7 E.L.Rev. 316 at 322).
[40] See Case 56/75 *Elz v. Commission* [1977] ECR 1617.
[41] See Case 116/78 *Bellintani v. Commission* [1980] ECR 23.

original proceedings. The third party may be a private individual or company, a Member State or a Community institution. It must be shown that the judgment adversely affects their interests and that the proceedings had not been brought to their notice, a difficult burden given the publication of all actions in the Official Journal. The Rules of Procedure reduce the scope of this procedure by requiring the applicant to show that the judgment would occasion actual damage to the applicant. The application has to be notified to all the original parties and may include a request for a stay of execution. Two months are allowed for such applications from the date of the publication of the judgment in the Official Journal.[42]

Finally, if a judgment by default has been given against a defendant who was properly served with the application but who did not duly enter an appearance, the defendant is allowed one month from the service of the judgment in which to lodge an application for it to be set aside for cause shown.[43]

# E. PRELIMINARY RULINGS

The procedure that we have considered so far is the procedure in direct actions, which are brought directly before the Court, and which originate and terminate there. The procedure in preliminary rulings is different: here the Court is ruling, at the request of a national court, on a question of Community law in issue before the national court. The procedure is incidental to, or, in the Court's words (above, p. 206), a step in, the action before the national court. Before the Court of Justice the proceedings on such a reference are not, strictly speaking, contentious, and there are formally no parties to such proceedings. As we saw in Chapter 10, it is regarded as more in the nature of a dialogue between the national court and the Court of Justice conducted in a spirit of "judicial co-operation". This has important consequences for the character of the procedure.

When the order for reference has reached the Court from the national court, after translation into the other 10 official languages (but not into Irish), a copy is sent by the Registry to the parties to the action before the national court, to the EU and EFTA Member

---

[42] See for example Case C–147/86 *Panhellinia Omospondia Idioktiton Frontistirion Xenon Glosson and Others v. Hellenic Republic and Commission of the European Communities* [1989] ECR 4103.

[43] T–42/89 *Yorck von Wartenburg v. European Parliament* [1990] ECR II–31 and See Case T–42/89 OPPO *European Parliament v. Yorck von Wartenburg* [1990] ECR II–299.

States, to the Commission, the EFTA Surveillance Authority and, where a measure of the Council is in issue, to the Council.[44] These may all submit written observations within a single period of two months although they have no obligation to do so. They may also submit oral observations at the hearing of the case; in practice, the Commission always attends such hearings, the parties usually do so, and sometimes also one or more Governments. After the hearing, the advocate-general's opinion and the ruling of the Court follow in the usual way, as in direct actions.

The Court deals with references as expeditiously as possible. Sometimes there is a delay in the transmission of the reference to the Court but, once received, the questions were, until the early 1980s, answered within about six months, which includes the two month period for the submission of written observations. Since the 1980s the great increase in the Court's case-load has led to considerable delays, the average period rising to about 18 months; but efforts are being made to reduce these delays, notably by the transfer of whole categories of direct actions to the Court of First Instance, as discussed in Chapter 5 above and, increasingly, by being able to dispense with the necessity of having an oral hearing. As a result some preliminary rulings in cases being heard by Chambers may be dealt with in as little as 10 months. Nonetheless, taking into account certain delays inherent in the procedure (translation, notification and the time for written observations), as well as the calls upon the time of the judges and advocates general for other cases and finally the incidence of judicial vacations, it seems that the minimum "incompressible" period for dealing with a preliminary ruling before the full Court (which invariably holds an oral hearing) is about 14 months.[45] Justice, like digestion, cannot be rushed.

Although in principle the same Rules of Procedure apply to both direct actions and preliminary rulings, the various special features of procedure in direct actions which have been described under head D above are inapplicable to preliminary rulings. Thus in one case where the plaintiff before the German court asked the Court of Justice to supplement its ruling, the Court said that "Article 177 of the EC Treaty establishes a direct form of co-operation between the Court of Justice and the national courts or tribunals by means

---

[44] In rare cases the Court may invite the European Parliament to submit information or observations as in Case 149/85 *Wybot v. Faure* [1986] ECR 2391; [1987] 1 C.M.L.R. 819 which turned on the definition of the expression "session" of the Parliament for the purpose of immunity of its members.

[45] Judge Edward arrived at this conclusion in his contribution to a Conference on the preliminary ruling procedure held at King's College London on June 12, 1993.

of a non-contentious procedure, in which the parties to the main action cannot take any initiative and during the course of which they are only invited to submit their observations within the legal context outlined by the court making the reference."[46] Accordingly a further ruling could be given only if a further reference were made by the national court. Examples of such supplementary references are to be found in Cases 104/79 and 244/80 *Foglia v. Novello I* and *II*[47] and Cases 283/81 and 77/83 *CILFIT v. Ministry of Health I* and *II*[48] on the interpretation of Article 177 EC and in Case 41/84 and 359/87 *Pinna v. Caisse d'allocations familiales de la Savoie I* and *II*.[49]

Similarly an application by the Edison electricity company to intervene in Case 6/64 *Costa v. ENEL* was rejected by the Court which stated that:

> "Article 177 of the EC Treaty does not envisage contentious proceedings designed to settle a dispute but prescribes a special procedure whose aim is to ensure a uniform interpretation of Community law by co-operation between the Court of Justice and the national courts and which enables the latter to seek the interpretation of Community provisions which they have to apply in disputes brought before them."[50]

The character of the proceedings also determines many other aspects of the procedure which differ from direct actions. No address for service in Luxembourg is necessary. The language of the case is that of the national court or tribunal which made the reference, although a Member State retains the right to submit observations in its own language, and the advocate general will deliver his opinion in his own language. Again, in contrast to direct actions, the ruling will *ex hypothesi* be concerned only with an abstract question of law and based upon facts as found by the referring court. Normally therefore there will be no occasion for any preparatory inquiries.

Objections to the admissibility of a reference, or to the jurisdiction of the Court, also have a more limited scope than in a direct action. As we saw in Chapter 10, the Court will not normally allow such objections as that a decision on the question referred is

---

[46] Case 13/67 *Becker v. Hauptzollamt Munchen* [1968] ECR 187 at 197; [1968] C.M.L.R. 187.

[47] [1980] ECR 745; [1981] 1 C.M.L.R. 45 and [1981] ECR 3045; [1982] 1 C.M.L.R. 585.

[48] [1982] ECR 3415; [1983] 1 C.M.L.R. 472 and [1984] ECR 1257.

[49] [1986] ECR 1; [1988] 1 C.M.L.R. 350 and [1989] ECR 585; [1990] 2 C.M.L.R. 561.

[50] [1964] ECR 585 at 614.

not necessary to enable the national court to give judgment. Apart from special circumstances such as those of *Foglia v. Novello* and *Meilicke* (above, pp. 215–216), the Court has consistently held that its jurisdiction is dependent on the mere existence of a reference. As we have also seen it requires the national court to provide it with sufficient information on the factual and legal background to the case to enable it to provide a useful answer to the questions referred.[51] Generally however, a question of admissibility is likely to arise only if the very existence of the reference is itself in doubt, as when for example the order for reference has been set aside on appeal in the national courts. But the practice of the Court is to discontinue its proceedings only if the order for reference is withdrawn by the court making it or quashed by a higher court; otherwise the Court proceeds to judgment.[52]

The position on costs is also different. The costs of the parties are always reserved to the national court, the Court's decision on costs invariably stating, as the reason for this, that the proceedings are, insofar as the parties to the main action are concerned, in the nature of a step in the action pending before the national court, a formula first used in the *De Geus v. Bosch* case[53] and subsequently incorporated into Article 104 of the Rules of Procedure. The costs incurred by the Member States and by the Community institutions in submitting observations, whether written or oral, are not recoverable. When the national court comes to rule on the costs incurred by the parties in connection with the reference, it must do so, as the law now stands, in the context of its own national law.[54] However the Court of Justice can itself grant legal aid for the purposes of the preliminary ruling procedure. This is laid down in one of the very few provisions in the Rules of Procedure specifically concerned with preliminary rulings. Another provision in the same Article, Article 104, deals with legal representation. We revert to this and to legal aid in the next chapter.

---

[51] See Joined Cases C–320 to 322/90 *Telemarsicabruzzo v. Circostel and Others* [1993] ECR I–393; *The Times*, February 10, 1993 and C–157/92 *Banchero* [1993] ECR I–1085, *The Times*, May 20, 1993.

[52] Case 127/73 *B.R.T. v. S.A.B.A.M* [1974] ECR 51; [1974] 2 C.M.L.R. 238.

[53] Case 13/61 *De Geus v. Bosch and Another* [1962] ECR 45.

[54] Case 62/72 *Paul G. Bollmann v. Hauptzollamt Hamburg-Waltershof* [1973] ECR 269.

# Chapter Thirteen

# Lawyers in the Court

## INTRODUCTION

In this chapter we consider the role of the lawyer representing his client before the Court of Justice. For the English or Scottish lawyer, this role may seem different, in some respects, from that which he plays before the national courts.

In the first place, the nature of the procedure, as described in the previous chapter, is such as to give a different emphasis to the lawyer's task. In the written procedure, as we have seen, the drafting of the pleadings requires considerable skill; the lawyer will also have to set out in writing the substance of his arguments. In the oral procedure, which has a more limited scope, the opportunity for forensic talents is correspondingly reduced.

Second, the advocate general plays a crucial role which supplements that of being the parties' representatives. Indeed, the parties may feel that the judges will be more influenced by the advocate-general's opinion than by anything their own representatives may say. But the advocate general will himself have had a full opportunity to consider the submissions of the parties, both written and oral, and to put questions to them at the hearing since the proceedings are invariably adjourned before he delivers his opinion. By contrast, in the French *Conseil d'Etat*, the advocate-general's counterpart, the *commissaire du gouvernement*, gives his view of the case immediately after the oral submissions, if any.

Third, in the Court of Justice, the judges themselves see their own role as an active rather than a passive one. Their function is not only to adjudicate on the basis of the respective strength of the parties' submissions, but (as we shall see in Part Four) to develop the law and to give due weight to the interest of the Communities. Here the lawyer can both serve his client and assist the Court by relating his submissions to those wider interests.

Perhaps the most important limitation for the lawyer arises from the novelty of the Community legal system. In principle, as we shall see, any lawyer qualified to practise before a court of a

Member State is entitled to appear before the Court of Justice. Inevitably, the lawyer trained in his own legal system faces new problems. He will often be unfamiliar with Community law and the procedure of the Court, since even in the original six Member States those subjects are still not sufficiently widely known or taught. He may have to acquaint himself, not merely with a new branch of law, but with a fundamentally new approach to law, with what is in effect a new legal system having, for example, its own principles of interpretation which differ to a greater or lesser extent from those of his own national law, and which derive in part from the plurilingual character of Community law. Indeed, the lawyer must always appreciate that this plurilingual character adds a dimension to Community law not present in his own law: thus, the British or Irish lawyer must shed the blinkers interposed by the English language when reading a Community text, or at least be aware of their presence and effect.

Considerable efforts have been and are being made to overcome these problems. The Court for its part regularly invites, and receives visits from, groups of lawyers from the Member States, but out of the enormous total of nearly 350,000 lawyers in the Communities, only a very small proportion can be reached in this way.

Within the Member States, lawyers have set up their own organisations to encourage interest in and knowledge of Community law. A leading part has been played by the International Federation for European Law (*Fédération Internationale pour le Droit Européen* - FIDE), with its national groups such as the United Kingdom Association for European Law, which include both practising and academic lawyers. Practitioners have formed their own associations, such as the Scottish Lawyers European Group, and the Solicitors' European Group and the Bar European Group in England. A Community-wide forum for problems of mutual interest to practitioners is provided by the Council of the Bars and Law Societies of the European Community (usually referred to by its French initials CCBE).[1]

In some respects, indeed, more progress has probably been made in the United Kingdom than in other Member States, apart perhaps from the Netherlands. Since the early 1960s the British Institute of International and Comparative Law and the Europa Institute of Leiden University have organised joint annual meetings on Community law attended by academics, practitioners and judiciary. Again, long before British accession the British Institute

---

[1] For "*Comité Consultatif des Barreaux Européens*". This acronym is still used by the CCBE itself despite the changes in its title to "*Conseil des Barreaux de la Communité européenne*".

had provided extensive programmes of lectures and conferences to acquaint British lawyers with developments in Community law and, from 1962, the Common Market Law Reports made available the only English translations of the main judgments of the Court of Justice until, following accession, the ECR also appeared in an English version. Community law is now widely taught in the universities and in other law schools, and has also featured for many years in the English Bar examinations, although not, until overdue reforms in 1996, in solicitors' examinations. The Faculty of Advocates and the Law Society of Scotland have gone one stage further in requiring aspiring practitioners to pass an examination in Community law as a condition for admission to the respective professions which they represent. Degree courses have been introduced by many universities combining the study of domestic law with the law and legal system of another Member State and of the relevant European language.[2] Many British lawyers of the future will therefore be better equipped to meet the demands of Community law, but much remains to be done if the lawyer is to play the fullest part and to have a truly European perspective in the Community of the future.

The role of the lawyer in the Court of Justice is only one aspect of this wider perspective. Articles 43 to 48 (ex Articles 52 to 58) EC envisage, as part of the right of establishment, the right of nationals of Member States to practise a profession throughout the EC, while Articles 49 to 55 (ex Articles 59 to 66) EC envisage the right to provide services, including professional services (as in law), across national boundaries.[3] Case 427/84 *Commission v. Germany* concerned the Directive on Lawyers' Services (77/249) which was issued by the Council to facilitate the provision of cross-frontier services by lawyers: in the preparation of this Directive an active role was played by the CCBE.

Perhaps because of stern criticism[4] of that Directive, the Council adopted a broader brush approach in the Directive on Mutual

---

[2] The Community's "ERASMUS" programme has accelerated this trend.

[3] See on the right of establishment of lawyers Case 2/74 *Reyners v. Belgium* [1974] ECR 631; [1974] 2 C.M.L.R. 305, Case 7/76 *Thieffry v. Conseil de l'ordre des avocats à la Cour de Paris* [1977] ECR 765, Case 107/83 *Ordre des avocats au bureau de Paris v. Klopp* [1984] ECR 2971; [1985] 1 C.M.L.R. 99 and Case 292/86 *Gullung v. Conseils de l'ordre des avocats du bureau de Colmer et de Saverne* [1988] ECR 111; [1988] 2 C.M.L.R. 57; and on the provision of legal services Case 33/74 *van Binsbergen v. Bedrijfsvereiniging Metaalingverheid* [1974] ECR 1299; [1975] 1 C.M.L.R. 298, *Gullung*, above, and Case 427/85 *Commission v. Germany* [1988] ECR 1123; [1989] 2 C.M.L.R. 677. For a convenient summary of these cases see Tom Kennedy "Learning European Law" (London, 1998), pp. 312–320.

[4] See Walters (1978) 3 E.L.Rev. 256 and Edward, himself a former President of the CCBE, in *In Memoriam J.D.B. Mitchell* (1983), p. 231, who calls the directive "a conceptual dog's breakfast since it is based on the false premise that equivalence of title implies equivalence of status, function and activity".

Recognition of Higher Education Diplomas (89/48) which is intended to facilitate the right of establishment for all the liberal professions throughout the Community. This Directive introduced a general system for the recognition of higher education diplomas and professional titles awarded on the completion of professional education and training of at least three years' duration. A lawyer who has such a diploma or title in one Member State may ask to have it recognised in another Member State in order to practice law there under the professional title used in the latter State, subject to satisfying conditions such as an aptitude test.

Still more sweeping provision is contained in Directive 98/5, made by the Council after long consultation with the CCBE. This will facilitate practice of the profession of lawyer on a permanent basis in a Member State other than that in which the professional qualification was obtained. This Directive is to be implemented in each Member State by March 14, 2000. It will allow practice in the host Member State under the lawyer's home-country professional title.

In this chapter, however, we are not directly concerned with the right of establishment or cross-frontier legal services[5] but only with the practice of the lawyer before the Court of Justice. Most of what follows also applies to lawyers practising before the Court of First Instance.

## Legal Representation

Parties before the Court must normally be represented by a lawyer. This rule is laid down in the Statute of the Court.[6] So in general a litigant cannot plead his own case. The only exception is that, possibly in order to widen the rights of audience on a reference from a national court, the Rules of Procedure (Article 104) require account to be taken of the rules of procedure of the national court concerning the representation of the parties. So where a litigant appeared in person before the national court, he may also appear in person before the Court of Justice. This happened, for example, on a reference from a Dutch court in Case 39/75 *Coenen*[7] and in the *Gullung* case mentioned above. It has also been suggested that this Article imposes an obligation, on a reference from those English courts where barristers still have an exclusive right of

---

[5] Matters which, as the Court emphasised in Case C–55/94 *Gebhard v. Consiglio dell'Ordine degli Avvocati e Procuratori di Milano* [1995] ECR I–4165, are mutually exclusive.

[6] Art. 17 – see below.

[7] [1975] ECR 1547; [1976] 1 C.M.L.R. 30.

audience, that a barrister (as opposed to a solicitor) be instructed before the Court of Justice; but the Court has, as we shall see (p. 301), been prepared to accept that the proceedings in Luxembourg be conducted even by a lawyer from a different jurisdiction.

A Member State or a Community institution is represented by an agent appointed for the case, assisted, as necessary, by an adviser or lawyer. Member States appear quite frequently; apart from their role as parties in direct actions, usually as defendants in proceedings by the Commission under Article 169 EC, Member States frequently make use of their right to submit observations in references from national courts other than those from their own courts. The British, German, Italian and Spanish Governments have been particularly active in exercising this right. The practice on representation varies in the different Member States. The Italian Government has been represented by a member of the diplomatic service, the German Government by an official from a Government department who is also a lawyer. In the United Kingdom the practice has been to instruct counsel in practice at the Bar, and in this way a number of barristers have gained experience of the workings of the Court. For the purposes of the written procedure the United Kingdom Government has been represented by lawyers employed in the Treasury Solicitor's Department often assisted by a lawyer from the Government department most directly concerned.

The Council and the Commission are usually represented by a member of their respective Legal Services, although they occasionally instruct private practitioners. The role of the Legal Service of the Commission is particularly important. The Commission, apart from appearing as applicant or defendant in most contentious cases, always submits observations in references from national courts, and can assist the Court by explaining the background to the particular Community instrument in question, which it will usually have been responsible for drafting. It can also supply information on the economic context of a provision, or on the way in which it has been implemented in the Member States. Because of the Commission's special expertise it quite often happens that the Court adopts the interpretation proposed by the Commission, although at other times, of course, the Court adopts a more restrictive, or a more adventurous response. An illustration of a more restrictive approach can be found by comparing the observations of the Commission, the opinion of Advocate General Trabucchi, and the judgment of the Court in Case 118/75 *Watson and Belmann*[8]; and an illustration of a more adventurous approach can

---

[8] Case 118/75 *Watson and Belmann* [1976] ECR 1185; [1976] 2 C.M.L.R. 552.

be found by means of a similar comparison in Case 43/75 *Defrenne*.[9]

## RIGHT OF AUDIENCE

No special qualifications are required of a lawyer to appear before the Court. The only requirement is that he must be a "lawyer entitled to practise before a court of a Member State" (Article 17 of the Statute of the Court) - a category which extends to university teachers of law whose national law accords them a right of audience. A lawyer wishing to appear before the Court must lodge with the Registrar a certificate that he or she satisfies that requirement when submitting an application or defence.[10] For this purpose, the Registrar accepts a CCBE identity card issued or validated within the previous year. On a reference for a preliminary ruling, the parties will normally be represented by the lawyers who acted in the national court and who may have had no previous encounter with Community law. In a direct action, the parties are more likely to instruct a lawyer with some experience of the Court, but, perhaps because of the diversity of the Court's jurisdiction, there is little sign at present, with the exception of a few lawyers who appear regularly, of the development of a specialist Bar. As a result, there cannot be the same kind of relationship between Bench and Bar as exists in the English High Court or the Scottish Court of Session. The relations, and also the style of the proceedings, are necessarily less personal.

Moreover, the Court has apparently accepted that a lawyer entitled to practise before a court of any Member State has the right of audience in both direct actions and references for preliminary rulings; thus, a French lawyer could appear in Luxembourg on a reference from an English court. In Case 234/81 *Du Pont*,[11] a reference from the English High Court, the applicant companies were represented in Luxembourg by an advocate of the Scots Bar practising in Brussels. In Case 186/87 *Cowan*,[12] a case referred to it by the Commission *d'indemnisation des victimes d'infraction*[13] attached to the *Tribunal de grande instance de Paris* Mr Cowan was represented by three lawyers: a solicitor practising

---

[9] Case 43/75 *Defrenne v. SABENA* [1976] ECR 455; [1976] 2 C.M.L.R. 98; for an interesting analysis, see Eric Stein (1981) Am. journal of International Law 1.

[10] Art. 38(3) of the Rules of Procedure.

[11] Case 234/81 *Du Pont de Nemours v. Commissioners of Customs and Excise* [1982] ECR 3515.

[12] Case 186/87 *Cowan v. Trésor Public* [1989] ECR 195; [1990] 2 C.M.L.R. 613.

[13] Compensation board for victims of an offence.

in England, another solicitor who was a member of and in practice at the Liège bar and a Belgian *avocat* practising at the Liège bar.

However, in some cases a broadening of the right of audience could give rise to difficulties. For example, in a case referred by a German court in which questions of German law as well as Community law arose, a lawyer from outside Germany might be at a disadvantage, and might also place the Court of Justice at a disadvantage when it sought to put questions for guidance on German law. Moreover, the national court, when the case returned to it with the ruling of the Court of Justice, might be surprised to discover that proceedings which are, as we have seen (p. 206, above), a step in the proceedings before the national court, had been conducted by a lawyer who had not appeared, and might not be entitled to appear, before it. There might even be difficulties about which rules of professional conduct were applicable in respect of the Luxembourg proceedings, or how they were to be enforced. And where legal aid has been granted by the national authorities for the purpose of those proceedings, it might be doubtful whether public funds could be used to pay the fees of a lawyer from a different jurisdiction who might not be subject to the local code of discipline or whose fees were customarily fixed on a much more generous scale. The Court's liberal approach to the right of audience accords with the literal wording of the Statute which, as we have seen, refers to a lawyer entitled to practise before *a* court of *a* Member State; but it may be questioned whether it accords with the requirement of Article 104 of the Rules of Procedure, mentioned above, that, on a reference from a national court, account must be taken of the rules of procedure of that court concerning the representation of the parties.

## RIGHTS AND OBLIGATIONS OF LAWYERS

Rules governing lawyers' professional ethics (in French "*la déontologie*") vary widely between Member States.[14] Moreover, apart from the notes for the guidance of counsel for the parties at the hearing, which are intended to ensure the efficient management of court business, there are no common rules governing the conduct

---

[14] For useful comparative information see J. Lonbay and L. Spedding, *International Professional Practice* (London, 1992) and Sheridan and Cameron, *EEC Legal Systems: An Introductory Guide* (London, 1992). The CCBE has adopted a "Code of Conduct for lawyers in the European Community" based on a principle of mutual respect, but this leaves many important questions unanswered.

of lawyers before the Court of Justice and the Court of First Instance[15] and it would be invidious for the Court of Justice to attempt such a labour of Sisyphus. The Rules of Procedure in this respect[16] therefore contain only a limited number of rules designed to deal specifically with the situation of the lawyer who must travel, as the majority of them must inevitably do, to a foreign country in order to represent his or her client before an international institution.

The third paragraph of Article 17 of the EC Statute[17] provides laconically "that agents, advisers and lawyers shall, when they appear before the Court, enjoy the rights and immunities necessary to (*sic*) the independent exercise of their duties, under conditions laid down in the Rules of Procedure." From this it is clear that the privileges concerned cover only the lawyers'[18] functions while they are actually engaged in proceedings and that they may not be relied upon for any other purpose. This is reinforced by Article 34 of the CJ Rules which spells out that the privileges, immunities and facilities concerned are granted exclusively in the interests of the proper conduct of proceedings. However, since the immunity is extended to proceedings before any judicial authority to which the Court may have addressed letters rogatory, it is probable that other aspects of the preparation and conduct of a case are intended to be covered even where the activities concerned do not take place in Luxembourg.[19]

The immunities include exemption from search and seizure of papers or documents relating to the proceedings. In the event of a dispute a procedure is provided for the Court itself to determine whether the documents concerned are covered. Agents, advisers and lawyers are expressly entitled to such allocation of foreign currency as they may require for the performance of their duties and to travel for that purpose without hindrance.

---

[15] We have reproduced, at the end of this chapter, the notes for guidance issued by the Court of First Instance which, although essentially similar to those issued by the Court of Justice to lawyers appearing there, appear to be more up to date and have eliminated certain infelicities of drafting.

[16] Chap. 7 of Title 1 of the CJ Rules containing Arts 32 to 36, and Chap. 6 of Title 1 of the CFI Rules containing Arts 38 to 42, which are identically worded with each other.

[17] Worded identically to Art. 17 of the Euratom Statute and, following the Merger Treaty, to Art. 20 of the ECSC Statute. By virtue of Art. 46 of the EC Statute and the equivalent provisions in the other two Statutes those Articles also apply to procedure before the Court of First Instance.

[18] *Quaere*: whether such privileges are available to a party appearing in person in the limited circumstances permitted by CJ Rules Art. 104.

[19] For a lengthier discussion of the potential scope of the privileges and immunities see K.P.E. Lasok, *The European Court of Justice: Practice and Procedure* (London, 1984), pp. 75–88.

The necessity for such rules, which were first introduced in 1954, dates back to a time before it was clear that the EC Treaty rules on freedom of movement and freedom to provide services had direct effect, a time when exchange control regulations governing the movement of currency across borders were rigorously applied. The provisions concerned, which appear never to have been invoked in practice, may now be regarded as superseded, although the Registry of the Court still provides a certificate for lawyers, if requested, and forwards an extract from the cause list of the Court to the Ministry of Foreign Affairs of the Grand Duchy of Luxembourg as a matter of courtesy.

Of far greater practical importance is the question of legal professional privilege or confidentiality of communications between lawyers and clients which was introduced into Community law by the Court's decision in Case 155/79 *AM&S Europe Ltd v. Commission*.[20] In the context of a Commission investigation into competitive conditions in the zinc industry, Commission officials carried out an investigation at the premises of AM&S Europe Limited in Bristol in the course of which they took copies of certain documents and requested the company to produce others. The company refused to make available certain of the documents which its legal advisers considered were covered by legal privilege, that is to say, the principle of legal professional privilege or confidentiality as then understood in common law jurisdictions. The Commission therefore adopted a decision[21] under Article 14(3) of Council Regulation No. 17 requiring the company to submit to further investigation and to produce various documents including all those for which legal privilege was claimed. Further negotiations having failed to resolve the matter the company brought proceedings before the Court for the annulment of that decision.

In its judgment the Court pointed out that the protection of written communications between lawyers and clients was generally recognised in the legal systems of the Member States, although under varying conditions. Apart from such differences however the Court found that the national laws of the Member States protected, in similar circumstances, the confidentiality of those communications provided, on the one hand, that they were made for the purposes and in the interests of the client's rights of defence

---

[20] Case 155/79 *AM&S Europe Limited v. Commission* [1982] ECR 1575; [1982] 2 C.M.L.R. 264. We have had occasion to mention this case elsewhere to illustrate the possibility of the Court re-opening the procedure before it (p. 283), the possibility of intervention by an interested third party (p. 290) and the use of comparative law as an aid to interpretation (p. 338).

[21] Decision 79/670/EC of July 6, 1979 [1979] O.J. L199/31.

and, on the other hand, that they emanated from independent lawyers, that is to say, lawyers who were not bound to the client by an employment relationship.

Those two conditions were elaborated further in the judgment and the Court also adumbrated the procedure to be followed in order to establish whether particular documents were covered by any claim to confidentiality, concluding that it was for the Commission to make such a determination which, if necessary, could be subject to judicial review by the Court itself.

The "legal traditions common to the Member States" referred to in that judgment are also important in the context of the powers of the Court to deal with misconduct by lawyers. In this context the fourth paragraph of Article 17 of the Statute, without referring to disciplinary matters, provides that, in respect of advisers and lawyers appearing before it, the Court is to have the powers normally accorded to courts of law under conditions laid down in the Rules of Procedure. The omission of the word "agents" would seem to imply that the representatives of Member States or Community institutions escape the Court's disciplinary powers in this sense.

The powers concerned are laid down in CJ Rules Article 35 which provides that any adviser or lawyer whose conduct towards the Court, a Chamber, a judge, an Advocate General or the Registrar is incompatible with the dignity of the Court, or who uses his rights for purposes other than those for which they were granted, may at any time be excluded from the proceedings by an order of the Court or Chamber after the advocate general has been heard and the person concerned been given an opportunity to defend himself. Once again that somewhat draconian power appears never to have been invoked in practice and its effects are attenuated, so far as the party whose lawyer has been excluded is concerned, by the requirement that proceedings be suspended for a period fixed by the President in order to allow that party to appoint another adviser or lawyer. Furthermore such decisions may be rescinded.[22] There is no provision for any such decision excluding a lawyer from the proceedings to be published nor, unlike the rules governing perjury by a witness or expert,[23] for it to be reported to the competent authority in the Member State concerned. However it seems likely that, whether through the intermediary of a disgruntled client or informally from the Court itself, those authorities would be so informed and that they would take a serious view of any such misconduct.

---

[22] CJ Rules Art. 35(3).
[23] Governed by CJ Rules Art. 124 and Arts 6 and 7 of the Supplementary Rules.

It is a corollary of the very broad right of audience provided by Article 17 of the Statute that there is no specialist bar with exclusive rights of audience, and lawyers appearing in Luxembourg remain members of their own national legal professions. It is therefore natural that when appearing in Luxembourg lawyers wear the robes which they would don while carrying out their duties before their national courts, a tradition[24] which may have spectacular results where several Member States are involved in a hearing in which the gold or silver braid of the Italian *avvocatura dello stato* mingles with the fur trimmings of the Belgian and Luxembourg Bars and the large badge, rather like a garter star, worn by the Spanish *abogados del estado*. Although the basic colour of the robes is almost invariably a uniform black this may contrast sharply with the occasional bright crimson or blue or yellow of a German university professor.[25]

Of course British and Irish barristers and advocates wear their wigs[26] and stuff or silk gowns according to their status. The problem that the headphones necessary to follow the simultaneous interpretation of the proceedings sit uncomfortably and inelegantly on the head of a bewigged lawyer has been resolved by the introduction at counsels' tables of smaller, more discreet earphones which simply hook over one ear. As pointed out by a former judge of the Court this has the advantage not only of making common law barristers and advocates look less ridiculous when appearing before the Court, it also means that they, and of course all lawyers who appear before the Court, are equipped in the same fashion as the judges and advocate general and, like them, are able to hear both the simultaneous interpretation and the original delivery.

## SPECIAL PROBLEMS OF A DIVIDED PROFESSION

Problems may arise in countries with a divided profession. Within the Communities those countries include England and Wales, Scotland, Northern Ireland and the Republic of Ireland. But some civil law countries too have different categories of Lawyers: thus, in France a specialised bar has the monopoly of pleading before the *Cour de Cassation* and the *Conseil d'Etat*, a monopoly which Directive 98/5 (discussed above) still accepts; and generally in civil law countries *le barreau* is sharply distinguished from *le notariat*. Although the United Kingdom is a single entity as a Member State

---

[24] There appears to be no explicit rule requiring such a formality.
[25] Who has a right of audience by virtue of the final paragraph of Art. 17.
[26] In 1993 the English Bar decided, after much head scratching, to retain their wigs.

of the European Communities, for many domestic purposes England and Wales, Scotland and Northern Ireland constitute three separate jurisdictions, and the legal profession is separately regulated in each jurisdiction.

The right of audience at Luxembourg is expressed so widely as to appear to include solicitors as well as barristers and advocates. Has then a solicitor a right of audience before the Court?

In Scotland and Northern Ireland there has been no formal arrangement between the two branches of the profession regarding audience at Luxembourg, and to date very few cases, surprisingly, have come to the Court from these jurisdictions.[27]

In England and Wales a working agreement had been reached by representatives of the Bar and of the Law Society in 1971 in anticipation of the United Kingdom's entry into the Communities. The general purport of the agreement was to give solicitors almost complete equality of opportunity with barristers to play a full part in the legal professional life of the enlarged Communities. To this end, solicitors as well as barristers were to be placed on equal terms with the French *avocat* and the equivalent categories of lawyers in the other countries of the original Six, wherever reference was made to *avocats* (or their equivalents) in the Treaties or other Community instruments.

The one important exception to such equality was to reserve to barristers the right of audience before the Court of Justice in preliminary references from the English High Court, the Court of Appeal or the House of Lords. At that date (1971), these were, of course, the courts in which the Bar still enjoyed an exclusive right of audience. But since December 1993 solicitors who hold an "Advocate's certificate" have a right of audience in the High Court, a right which they have long enjoyed in the County and Magistrates' Courts. In 1998 the Lord Chancellor gave a clear indication that the barrister's monopoly even in the higher courts will not long endure. Account must also be taken of the developing rights of audience of legal executives. The 1971 agreement was never embodied into the English Practice Rules. Serious doubts were subsequently expressed as to its compatibility with Community law, and in 1981 the whole agreement was quietly

---

[27] Examples are Case 83/78 *Pigs Marketing Board (Northern Ireland) v. Redmond* [1978] ECR 2347; [1979] 1 C.M.L.R. 177, in which members of the English and Irish Bars represented the parties; Case 24/83 *Gewiese v. Mackenzie* [1984] ECR 817; [1984] 2 C.M.L.R. 409, a reference from the Court of Session which brought Edinburgh counsel to Luxembourg, in the person of the Solicitor General for Scotland; and Case 370/88 *Procurator Fiscal v. Marshall* [1990] ECR I–4071; [1991] 1 C.M.L.R. 419, Case C–78/91 *Hughes v. Chief Adjudication Officer* [1992] ECR I–4839; [1992] 3 C.M.L.R. 490.

abandoned by the Law Society, the Bar *non obstante*. And since, as we have seen, the Court of Justice may be willing to extend the right of audience to lawyers from a different jurisdiction, it cannot be supposed that the Court would be concerned to uphold purely domestic demarcations. However, from an English perspective, it might still seem curious if a solicitor were to act alone on a reference from, say, the House of Lords, but times are changing.

The first appearance by a solicitor as advocate before the Court was in a staff case, Case 175/80 *Tither v. Commission*,[28] and this precedent has occasionally been followed. *Tither* was, of course, a direct action. It seems unlikely that many solicitors will seek to specialise in advocacy at Luxembourg since (as we have seen) very real problems might arise in references for preliminary rulings from English (or Scottish) courts in which they have no right of audience.

It is accepted that an English barrister may appear on behalf of a client without being instructed by a solicitor: as the requirement for such instructions is only a rule of etiquette of the Bar, the Court will accept both his written pleadings and oral argument.[29]

Notwithstanding this flexibility, there is a popular misconception (shared by some practitioners) that lawyers representing parties before the Court of Justice or the Court of First Instance must act in conjunction with a member of the Luxembourg Bar. This erroneous idea derives from the requirement already mentioned (Chapter 12 above, at p. 275) that parties in direct actions must have an address for service in Luxembourg. Luxembourg lawyers have no special privilege in this regard; a party may designate any person with an address in the Grand Duchy and in whom he has confidence that documents and correspondence will be reliably and promptly forwarded. The address for service is really no more than a letter box enabling the Registries of the two Courts to be sure that documents have been duly served and to certify the date of such service.

In practice lawyers representing private parties from outside Luxembourg most frequently do designate Luxembourg law firms which is why the names and addresses of the latter appear at the top of the official reports, after the names of the parties' legal representatives. Some however use the address of accountants' firms, other professional advisers or even their own home

---

[28] [1981] ECR 2345.

[29] See Case 167/80 *Curtis v. Parliament and Commission* [1981] ECR 1499; *cf. Prais v. Commission* [1976] ECR 1589; [1976] 2 C.M.L.R. 708, where the applicant was herself a solicitor.

address.[30] Member States invariably give the address of their Embassy in Luxembourg for this purpose while all of the Community institutions, except the Council, have offices there, the Council relying on the good offices of the European Investment Bank.

## LEGAL AID[31]

Ligitation is an expensive pursuit, although in the Court of Justice it is probably less expensive than, for example, in the High Court in England, because hearings are generally much shorter and the preliminary proceedings generally simpler.

Where a party is wholly or in part unable to bear the costs of the proceedings the Court may grant legal aid. The decision is made by a Chamber, after considering the application and the written observations of the other party although the reason for allowing the other party to make submissions in this regard is hard to discern. The application for legal aid need not be made through a lawyer. Consequently anyone contemplating bringing an action may himself apply for legal aid, stating the subject of the proceedings which he intends to introduce. In practice, applications are a handful each year: in 1985 there were only four. Again, up to March 1988, only 30 grants of legal aid had been accorded.

In granting legal aid the Court acts on the principle of *ex aequo et bono*: it considers the justice and equity of the matter. Acting on this basis it may, therefore, grant legal aid even where the applicant would not be eligible for legal aid in his own country.[32] The Court, in practice, requires a certificate of the applicant's means from the competent authority in his own country.

Legal aid takes the form of a cash grant in aid rather than the payment of a taxed bill of costs. Indeed the Court has no such English device as a taxing master. Therefore, taxation, where necessary, is carried out by the three-judge Chamber to which the judge-rapporteur belongs. However, the rules go so far as to provide that if a person is granted legal aid he may, if he loses the

---

[30] See for example the staff case C–293/87 *Vainker v. European Parliament* [1989] ECR 23, in which the applicant, an official of the European Parliament based in Luxembourg, had appointed a member of the Scottish Bar to represent him and gave his own home address as his address for service.

[31] See generally T. Kennedy, *Paying the Piper: Legal Aid in Proceedings before the Court of Justice* (1989) 25 C.M.L.Rev. 559.

[32] *e.g.* because he falls outside the financial conditions or because his own country in fact has no system of legal aid: see *Lee v. Minister for Agriculture*, below.

case, be ordered to repay the whole or part of the funds advanced to meet his costs.[33]

This provision does not seem to apply to legal aid on a reference for a preliminary ruling. Here there is a separate provision merely empowering the Court to provide funds, in special circumstances, to assist the representation and attendance of a party. Since the reference is to be regarded as a step in the proceedings before the national court a party may also be able to obtain legal aid for this purpose under national law.

This question arose in England when a stipendiary magistrate's court made a reference in the case of *Pierre Bouchereau*. *Pierre Bouchereau* was a French national working in England who was convicted by the magistrate of unlawful possession of drugs. For these proceedings he had been granted legal aid. Before deciding whether to recommend deportation, the magistrate referred certain questions to the Court of Justice, but declined to extend the legal aid order to cover proceedings in the Court of Justice on the ground that he had no jurisdiction to do so. The Divisional Court, however, held that the existing legal aid certificate covered the proceedings before the Court of Justice, since these were a step in the proceedings before the national court.[34] But in civil proceedings the authority of the Area Committee (after 1988, the Legal Aid Board and from 2000 the Legal Services Commission) is required before a legal aid certificate may extend to proceedings in the Court of Justice.

In other cases, the parties may be unable to obtain legal aid in the particular national proceedings. In the United Kingdom, for example, this may arise in claims before social security tribunals, where legal aid is not available. A person claiming pension rights under Community law would then not be eligible for legal aid before the United Kingdom tribunals, but, if a reference were made, could apply to the Court of Justice for legal aid to meet the costs of the reference. Again, difficulty may arise where the reference is from a country which has no scheme of legal aid. Thus in Case 152/79 *Lee v. Minister for Agriculture*,[35] a reference was brought from a court in Ireland (where only limited provision existed for civil legal aid). The plaintiff in the Irish proceedings then sought, and was granted, legal aid from the Court of Justice in respect of the reference. Although the eventual ruling was

---

[33] As in Case 25/68 *Schirtzer v. European Parliament* [1977] ECR 1729, or if he succeeds, his opponent may be ordered to repay the Court, as in Case 175/80 *Tither v. Commission* [1981] ECR 2345.

[34] *R. v. Marlborough Street Stipendiary Magistrate, ex p. Bouchereau* [1977] 1 W.L.R. 414.

[35] [1980] ECR 1495; [1980] 2 C.M.L.R. 682.

unfavourable to the plaintiff and the Irish court subsequently gave judgment against him, the Court of Justice did not seek to recover the funds advanced to him to meet his costs at Luxembourg. The Court may also grant legal aid where the national authority competent in the matter refuses to extend legal aid to cover a reference.[36]

---

[36] Case 320/82 *D'Amario v. Landesversicherungsanstalt Schwäben* [1983] ECR 3811 (the report does not refer to this aspect of the case, but see K.P.E. Lasok, *The European Court of Justice: Practice and Procedure* (2nd ed., 1994), p. 149, n.41).

# Appendix:

# Notes for the Guidance of Counsel for the Parties at the Hearing (before the Court of First Instance)

These notes are designed to explain to Counsel[37] for the parties the purpose of the oral procedure before the Court of First Instance and the manner in which it is organised. They are prompted by a concern to reconcile in the best possible manner the quality of judicial protection in the Community legal order and the need for proceedings to be conducted expeditiously and efficiently.

## I. THE PURPOSE OF THE ORAL PROCEDURE

When the stage of the oral procedure is reached the members of the bench hearing the case and, as the case may be, the Member of the Court performing the function of Advocate General, already have a good knowledge of the case and have carefully studied the conclusions, submissions and arguments of the parties. There is therefore no point in repeating orally everything that has been said in writing or even in giving a commentary on the pleadings or written observations.

The purpose of the oral procedure is:

to recall, if need be, by way of a highly condensed summary, the position taken by the parties, with emphasis on the essential submissions in support of which written argument has been presented;

to clarify, if necessary, certain arguments expounded during the written procedure and to submit any new arguments

---

[37] The word "counsel" is used here in a non-technical sense so as to include all those appearing before the Courts and acting as advocate, whatever their capacity or precise professional status.

based on matters which arose after the close of the written procedure and which, for that reason, could not be set out in the pleadings;
to reply to any questions put by the Court.

## II. The Hearing of Oral Argument

### 1. The Value of Oral Argument

It is for each Counsel to judge, in the light of the purpose of the oral procedure, as defined above, whether there would really be any point in presenting oral argument or whether a simple reference to the pleadings or written observations would suffice. The hearing could then be devoted essentially to the replies to questions put by the Court. If Counsel does consider it necessary to address the Court, he may always limit himself to dealing with certain points and refer to the pleadings as regards other points.

The Court would like to stress that if a party refrains from presenting oral argument, this will never be construed as constituting acquiescence in the oral argument presented by another party if the line of argument in question has already been refuted in writing. The party who so refrains will not be prevented, by virtue of his silence, from replying to oral argument put forward by the other party.

In certain circumstances the Court may judge it preferable to begin the hearing with questions put by its Members to Counsel for the parties. In that case, Counsel are requested to take account of this if they wish subsequently to submit brief oral argument.

### 2. Presentation and Structure of Oral Argument

In the interests of clarity and for the better comprehension by the Members of the Court of the oral argument presented, it is generally preferable to speak freely on the basis of notes rather than to read a written text. The reading of a text causes difficulties for the simultaneous interpretation of the oral argument.

Counsel for the parties are also requested to simplify as far as possible their presentation of the case. A series of short sentences will always be preferable to long and convoluted periods. It would also assist the Court if Counsel were to structure their oral argument and to indicate, before presenting it, the structure they intend to adopt.

### 3. The Constraints Imposed by Simultaneous Interpretation

Counsel are reminded that, depending on the case, only certain Members of the Court may be able to follow the oral argument in the language in which it is presented and the others will listen to the simultaneous interpretation. Although the interpreters are highly qualified, their task is a difficult one and it is highly recommended to Counsel, in the interests of the better conduct of the proceedings, that they should speak slowly and into the microphone. If Counsel intend to quote passages of certain texts or documents, and in particular passages not mentioned in the documents before the Court, it would be helpful if they would indicate these to the interpreters before the hearing. Similarly, it may be helpful to draw to the interpreters' attention any terms which may be difficult to translate. If the hearing takes place in the Salle Dalsgaard or the Salle "bleue," courtrooms equipped with an automatic sound amplification system, Counsel are requested to press the button on the microphone in order to switch it on and should wait for the light to come on before starting to speak.

### 4. Duration of Oral Argument

The Court is well aware that the time involved in the presentation of oral argument may vary, depending on the complexity of the case and on whether there are any new matters of a factual nature. However, having regard to the purpose of the oral procedure, nothing useful is, as a general rule, achieved by exceeding certain limits for the duration of the procedure. It is therefore recommended that Counsel should as a rule limit oral argument on behalf of each party to about 30 minutes before the Court sitting in plenary session or before a Chamber of five Judges and to 15 minutes or thereabouts before a Chamber of three Judges. This limitation of course applies only to the oral argument properly so-called and not to the time spent in answering questions put at the hearing. In the absence of any indication to the contrary, the Court will assume, for the purposes of organising its work, that these limits will not be exceeded.

If circumstances so require, a request may be made to the Registry, at least 15 days before the date fixed for the hearing, for leave to exceed the time normally allowed. The request should be properly reasoned and should indicate the time considered necessary for addressing the Court. Counsel will be informed, following such a request, of the time which will be allowed to them for the presentation of oral argument.

Where a party is represented by more than one Counsel, no more than two of them may present oral argument and the total time entailed in so doing must not exceed the limits specified above. The other Counsel for the party may, however, answer questions put by the Court and reply to Counsel for the other party or parties.

Where a number of parties are defending the same point of view before the Court, a situation which may arise in particular where there are interventions or where cases are joined, their Counsel are requested to consult together before the hearing with a view to avoiding any repetition of oral argument.

## III. MISCELLANEOUS

### 1. Report for the Hearing

The Court will endeavour to ensure that Counsel for the parties receive the Report for the Hearing three weeks before the hearing. Before the Court, the sole purpose of this document is to prepare for the hearing. The Court will not refer to it in its judgment and it will not form part of the judgment.

If the Report for the Hearing contains mistakes of fact, Counsel are requested to inform the Registry of this in writing before the hearing and to propose the necessary amendments. Similarly, if the Report for the Hearing does not correctly convey a party's argument in all essential respects, Counsel may propose such amendments as they consider appropriate.

If Counsel submit at the hearing oral observations on the Report for the Hearing, they should subsequently submit those observations in writing to the Registry.

### 2. Quotations

Counsel are requested, if they quote a judgment of the Court of Justice or the Court of First Instance, to give all the references, including the names of the parties, and should state the number of the page of the Reports of Cases on which the passage in question appears.

### 3. Documents

The Court of First Instance would point out that under Article 43(1) of the Rules of Procedure of the Court of First Instance, the documents relied on by the parties must be annexed to a pleading. Save in exceptional circumstances, and with the consent of the parties, the Court of First Instance will not accept documents produced outside the procedural time limits; these include documents submitted at the hearing.

Since all oral argument is recorded on tape, the Court does not allow notes of oral argument to be lodged.

# PART FOUR:
# THE COURT AS LAW-MAKER


## INTRODUCTORY

In this Part we examine what is sometimes termed judicial legislation by the Court. For the Court's decisions constitute a source of Community law in a number of ways. First and foremost, the Court has formulated certain fundamental doctrines which were at most only implicit in the Treaties. Most notable have been the twin doctrines of direct effect and supremacy of Community law. We have referred already to the landmark cases of *van Gend en Loos* and *Costa v. ENEL*.[1] The development and refinement of both doctrines is still continuing. Thus, *von Colson* and *Marleasing*[2] have introduced a notion (which some have called indirect effect)[3] whereby national courts must, so far as possible, interpret their domestic law to achieve the objects of a directive, whether or not it is directly effective; and *Francovich*[4] has gone further in requiring a Member State to compensate an individual who suffers loss as a result of its failure to implement a directive which conferred rights upon him. In relation to supremacy *Simmenthal*[5] requires not only national law to be disregarded if in conflict with Community law but also, as dramatically illustrated in *Factortame I*,[6] effective remedies to be granted by the national judge to safeguard even putative Community rights.

Secondly, in relation to the Treaties and legislation made thereunder, decisions of the Court provide authoritative inter-

---

[1] Case 26/62 *van Gend en Loos v. Nederlandse administratie der belastingen* [1963] ECR 1, and Case 6/64 *Costa v. ENEL* [1964] ECR 585.

[2] Case 14/83 *von Colson and Kamann v. Land Nordrhein-Westfalen* [1984] ECR 1891; Case C–106/89 *Marleasing S.A. v. Comercial Internacional de Alimentacion S.A.* [1990] ECR I–4135; [1992] 1 C.M.L.R. 305.

[3] See J. Steiner, *Textbook of EEC Law* (3rd ed., 1992) p. 34.

[4] Joined Cases C–6 and 9/90 *Francovich and Bonifaci v. Italian Republic* [1991] ECR I–5357; [1993] 2 C.M.L.R. 66.

[5] Case 106/77 *Amministrazione delle Finanze dello Stato v. Simmenthal S.p.A.* [1978] ECR 629; [1978] 3 C.M.L.R. 263.

[6] Case C–213/89 *The Queen v. Secretary of State for Transport, ex parte Factortame and others* [1990] ECR I–2433; [1990] 3 C.M.L.R. 1.

pretations, explaining and developing the texts by reference to concrete cases: as such they supply an essential gloss upon the *corpus* of Community *lex scripta,* which must always be read in the light of the Court's rulings, much as the English statute book (or the French Civil Code) is incomplete unless annotated with references to the relevent case-law. The Court of Justice has evolved its own methods and style of interpretation, and this forms the subject of Chapter 14.

Thirdly, the Treaties refer to the general principles of law common to the Member States as a source of Community law. The elucidation of these principles is an important function of the Court and amounts (as we see in Chapter 15) to a creative act of judicial legislation. For whatever the fiction, the legal reality is that the Court largely creates, and does not merely declare, these general principles. Inevitably, a common lawyer will be reminded of the Blackstonian theory of the King's judges ("repositories of the law, the living oracles") declaring the immemorial customs of the realm as the common law of England. That a court established by, and consisting predominantly of, civil lawyers should have this creative function illustrates the increasing convergence in Europe of the common law and civil law traditions; thus, in *Kloppenburg*[7] the German Federal Constitutional Court, in support of the case-law method of developing Community law, stated that there could be no doubt:

> "that it was the intention of the Member States to provide the Community with a Court which would ascertain and apply the law by methods developed over centuries of common European legal tradition and refinement of law. In Europe the judge was never merely '*la bouche qui prononce les paroles de la loi*'. Roman law, the English common law and the German *Gemeines Recht* were to a large extent the creation of the judges in the same way as in more recent times in France, for instance, the development of general legal principles of administrative law by the *Conseil d'Etat* or, in Germany, general administrative law, a large part of the law of employment or security rights in private-law business transactions."

Fourthly, in fulfilling these interpretative and creative functions. the Court has had to come to terms with the principle of *stare decisis.* Like any court, the Court of Justice seeks to be consistent, and to the extent that consistency prevails over the competing pressure to adjust Community law to ever-changing circumstances,

---

[7] [1988] 3 C.M.L.R. 1 at 19.

the Court's decisions are "precedents" in the English sense – or (better) in the American sense, being at most persuasive and never binding upon the Court for the future. This topic forms the subject of Chapter 16.

We have seen in previous Parts the style in which the Court's judgments are drafted and the process by which they emerge. Here we consider how far their collegiate character is appropriate for the Court's law-making functions.

Undoubtedly, the great advantage of the single, collegiate judgment is to enhance its authority. Whatever the hidden reservations or concealed dissents, the judgment moves, syllogistically, to its logical conclusion, to which the appearance of single-mindedness then attaches greater legal certainty. In 1952 it was practical wisdom to adopt the rule of unanimity for the new-born Court of the Coal and Steel Community. Now that the Court has long since come of age its authority seems assured, but the single judgment has special value for reinforcing the unity of Community law. For the need to prolong deliberation to secure, if at all possible, a collegiate judgment without recourse to a vote helps to produce an agreement (or compromise) which is truly *communautaire,* that is, one in which all the judges, with their differing viewpoints, bring forward and blend together in the eventual judgment various elements from all the national legal systems. In this way, as Professor Schermers points out, the inability openly to dissent "aids the amalgamation of rules from all the national legal orders and their assimilation into Community law".[8]

The absence of individual judgments has also the advantage of not identifying a particular judge with a particular decision. To this extent it is made easier for the Court as a whole to adopt a new departure in its case-law, without fear of the charge of inconsistency being laid at the door of one judge rather than another.

In addition, the single judgment is seen as a means of strengthening judicial independence. The twin principles – of secrecy of deliberation and singleness of judgment – provide together an effective shield for the individual judge against pressure from his government or from public opinion in his own country.

---

[8] *Judicial Protection in the European Communities* (4th ed., 1987), p. 451.

# Chapter Fourteen

# Methods of Interpretation

## Introduction

The judicial process is characteristically the two-fold one of the interpretation of the law and then its application to the case in hand. As we have seen, however, the Court of Justice may find its role limited to that of interpretation only; where a preliminary ruling is sought from it, the application of the law is reserved to the national court. Under its other heads of jurisdiction the Court has both to interpret and apply the law. This chapter will survey the methods adopted by the Court in interpreting Community law. Community law includes, of course, both the Treaties and the legislation made thereunder, but the methods of interpretation do not substantially differ as between the two categories of Community law.

The methods of interpretation employed by the Court have added importance for British lawyers since they constitute the "European way" which Lord Denning was quick to recognise the courts of England (and Scotland) should follow when called upon themselves to interpret Community law. In *Bulmer v. Bollinger* Lord Denning declared:

> "The (EC) Treaty is quite unlike any of the enactments to which we have become accustomed . . . It lays down general principles. It expresses its aim and purposes. All in sentences of moderate length and commendable style. But it lacks precision. It uses words and phrases without defining what they mean. An English lawyer would look for an interpretation clause, but he would look in vain. There is none. All the way through the Treaty there are gaps and lacunae. These have to be filled in by the judges, or by regulations or directives. It is the European way . . . Seeing these differences, what are the English courts to do when they are faced with a problem of interpretation? They must follow the European pattern. No longer must they argue about the precise grammatical sense. They must look to the purpose

and intent . . . They must divine the spirit of the Treaty and gain inspiration from it. If they find a gap, they must fill it as best they can . . . These are the principles, as I understand it, on which the European Court acts."[1]

This view of Lord Denning is reinforced by the terms of section 3(1) of the European Communities Act 1972, which provides:

> "For the purposes of all legal proceedings any question as to the meaning or effect of any of the Treaties, or as to the validity, meaning or effect of any Community instrument, shall be treated as a question of law (and, if not referred to the European Court, be for determination as such in accordance with the principles laid down by and any relevant decision of the European Court *or any court attached thereto*[2])."

The reference here to "the principles laid down by the European Court" is wide enough to include its methods of interpretation.

These methods Sir Patrick Neill, Warden of All Souls, criticised in 1995 "as having liberated the European Court from the customarily accepted discipline of endeavouring by textual analysis to ascertain the meaning of the language of the relevant provision".[3] We will return later to assess whether this charge is justified.

PLURILINGUAL DIMENSION OF COMMUNITY LAW

A problem peculiar to interpreting Community law, as distinct from English law, which we must add to those mentioned by Lord Denning in the passage cited above, is the Community's "linguistic regime". This term describes the principle of linguistic equality which has been accepted in the Communities since the EC Treaty. With each enlargement of the Community the principle that the languages of all the Member States should rank equally has been steadfastly upheld, no matter at what cost or inconvenience. In the

---

[1] *Bulmer v. Bollinger* [1974] Ch. 401 at 425; [1974] 2 All E.R. 1226 at 1237, and see the extract from the judgment at Bingham J. (as he then was) cited at p. 210 above.

[2] The italicised phrase was added to take account of the creation of the Court of First Instance in 1988 and of the possible future establishment of specialised Courts or Tribunals to deal with trademarks or staff cases.

[3] See "The European Court of Justice; a case study in judicial activism", a memorandum submitted to the House of Lords Select Committee on the European Communities (HL Paper 88, Session 1994–95, 18th Report), p. 218 at p. 244.

result, Community law has a plurilingual dimension not encountered in English law nor, indeed, in most national legal systems. In particular, all the texts of Community law rank equally in the different official languages (since Finnish and Swedish accession, 11 in number), so that the Court of Justice has had to evolve methods of interpretation appropriate to plurilingual texts.

## THE COURT'S OWN STYLE OF INTERPRETATION

Generally, the Court does not discuss in its judgments the methods of interpretation being employed, although its choice of phrase may sometimes serve as a signpost of the road it has followed to reach its conclusions. Fortunately, individual members of the Court have been less laconic in their extra-judicial speeches and writings, and a considerable literature now exists on the subject of interpretation, some of which must be considered authoritative having regard to its source.[4]

Interpretation of law is in no way an exact science but rather a judicial art. In the end, it is a matter of judicial instinct, and because the judge proceeds instinctively, the process cannot be reduced to a series of mechanical rules. Writers sometimes refer to "canons of interpretation", but it is better to think in terms of varying approaches: sometimes one approach is preferred, sometimes another, sometimes a combination of several; or one approach may be followed by another as a check upon the result achieved by the first.

The Court of Justice has no special methods of its own but uses those with which national courts are familiar. But the Court's use of traditional methods should not deceive us: the distinctive nature of Community law, when compared with national laws on the one hand and international law on the other, as well as the manner in which the Treaties are drafted, have led the Court to evolve its own particular style of interpretation.

Moreover, as we have emphasised above, the plurilingual character of Community law introduces an extra dimension not normally encountered in the courts of the Member States. In addition, resort to comparative law is more common in the sense that the Court may look to the national laws of the Member States for guidance. This is especially so when the Court is venturing

---

[4] For some particularly enlightening (if sometimes contradictory) views see the papers presented at the Judicial and Academic Conference held at the Court of Justice on September 27 to 28, 1976. The Reports presented at that conference were published by the Court and still represent one of the most authoritative discussions of the subject.

beyond mere interpretation into creative law-making: of this a notable example is the Court's development of the doctrine of the general principles of law, to be discussed in the next chapter.

In the exposition which follows, four methods of interpretation are discussed *seriatim*. These are the literal, historical, contextual and teleological. Although this order has a certain logic and accords broadly with the way in which the approaches to interpretation by national courts are traditionally presented, it would be quite wrong to assume that the methods are placed in descending order of importance. As will become apparent, the dominant approaches of the Court of Justice are the contextual and teleological with increasing resort to the latter.

## LITERAL INTERPRETATION

Every court must begin from the words of the text before it. If their meaning is plain, either in their ordinary connotation or in some special sense appropriate to the particular context, then for the national judge the task of interpretation is a light one and ends there. Usually, the same can be said for the Court of Justice, but exceptionally the Court may be led to disregard the plainest of wording in order to give effect to what it deems the overriding aims and objects of the Treaties. In other words the literal interpretation is displaced by the contextual or teleological approach, although the Court may speak rather in terms of looking to "the spirit" of the text in question.

The ERTA case[5] provides a good example. The Commission sought the annulment of a Council discussion to co-ordinate the attitude to be adopted by the six Member States in certain international negotiations to revise the European Road Transport Agreement. The Council's defence included the plea that the discussion did not constitute an "act" subject to annulment within the meaning of that term in Article 230 (ex Article 173) EC: any such act was limited to the categories of regulation, directive or decision as enumerated in Article 249 (ex Article 189) EC. Despite the apparently exhaustive wording of Article 249 (ex Article 189) EC, the Court found against the Council on this plea, holding that the aim of Article 230 (ex Article 173) EC was to subject to judicial review all measures taken by the institutions designed to have legal effect and declaring that "It would be inconsistent with this objective to interpret the conditions under which the action is admissible so restrictively as to limit the availability of this

---

[5] Case 22/70 *Commission v. Council* [1971] ECR 263; [1971] C.M.L.R. 335.

procedure merely to the categories of measures referred to by Article 189."[6]

As Lord Denning has indicated, literal interpretation is made more difficult for the Court by the general absence in the Treaties of definitions of the terms used. An English or Scottish Court may often be able to resolve a question of interpretation by the help of the glossary or dictionary which the legislator has thoughtfully provided in the definition or interpretation section of the particular statute. Such definitions are rare in Community law. Rather, the Treaties adopt the opposing continental approach of preferring to leave to judicial interpretation (assisted by doctrinal opinion) the meaning of terms which have been deliberately left undefined in the texts. Examples from the EC Treaty include:

> "charges having equivalent effect" (Articles 23 (ex Article 9) and 25 (ex Article 12))[7]
> "worker" (Article 39 (ex Article 48))[8]
> "public policy" (Article 39 (ex Article 48))[9]
> "abuse of a dominant position" (Article 82 (ex Article 86))[10]
> "general principles common to the laws of the Member States" (Article 288 (ex Article 215)).[11]

By contrast, although definitions do not normally feature in the Treaties, the different technique is used of providing either an exhaustive list or a number of examples which is deliberately left open-ended: for the former, see the list of products subject to the Common Agricultural Policy set out in Annex II to the EC Treaty, and for the latter, see the five examples in Article 81(1)(c) (ex Article 85(1)) EC of prohibited agreements under that Article.

By its very nature and purpose, secondary legislation under the Treaties is much more tightly drafted. Thus the Common Customs Tariff is a detailed catalogue of nearly 3,000 items; it may still however give rise to problems of interpretation.[12] But Community legislation also often makes use of vague terms: see, for example, Council Directive 64/221 which failed to clarify sufficiently the reference in Article 39 (ex Article 48) EC to "grounds of public

---

[6] Now Art. 249 EC.
[7] See the *Gingerbread* case below, p. 335.
[8] See Case 75/63 *Hoekstra (née Unger) v. Bestuur der Bedrijfsvereniging voor Detailhandel en Ambachten* [1964] ECR 177; [1964] C.M.L.R. 319 and Case 53/81, *Levin v. Staatssecretaris van Justitie* [1982] ECR 1035; [1982] 2 C.M.L.R. 454.
[9] See *Van Duyn v. Home Office*, below n. 13.
[10] See *Continental Can* case below, p. 340.
[11] See Chap. 15.
[12] See Case 22/76 *Import Gadgets v. L.A.M.P. SpA* [1976] ECR 1371.

policy, public security or public health", a clarification which the Court had to supply in Case 41/74 *Van Duyn v. Home Office*.[13]

Faced as it often is with texts which are vague, ambiguous or incomplete, the Court has recognised the limitations for itself of the literal methods of interpretation. Particularly after 1958, when the Court was confronted with the more programmatic EC Treaty, its interpretation shifted perceptibly towards the contextual and teleological, with emphasis on the *ratio legis* and the objectives of the Treaty. Thus in Case 6/60 *Humblet* it declared: "it is not sufficient for the Court to adopt the literal interpretation and the Court considers it necessary to examine the question whether this interpretation is confirmed by other criteria concerning in particular the common intention of the High Contracting Parties and the *ratio legis*".[14] Again in Case 26/62 *Van Gend en Loos* the Court stated:

> "To ascertain whether the provisions of an international treaty [namely, Article 12 EC (now Article 25)] extend so far in their effects it is necessary to consider the spirit, the general scheme and the wording of those provisions."[15]

Significantly perhaps, the Court ranked the wording in third place, as it did in similar language in Case 6/72, Continental Can:[16] "In order to answer this question, one has to go back to the spirit, general scheme and wording of Article 86 EEC (now Article 82 EC), as well as to the system and objectives of the Treaty." But in its earlier decisions the Court gave greater emphasis to wording: thus in Case 9/56 *Meroni*[17] it re-affirmed the view it had expressed in Case 8/55 *Fédéchar*,[18] that an argument *a contrario* is only admissible if no other interpretation appears to be appropriate and compatible with the express wording, with the context and with the purpose of the provisions.

It should, however, not be assumed that literal interpretation leads inevitably to a narrow construction of the text. In *Plaumann*,[19] for example, the Court extended its jurisdiction to receive applications from individuals under the second paragraph of

---

[13] Case 41/74 *Van Duyn v. Home Office* [1974] ECR 1337; [1975] 1 C.M.L.R. 1. See also Case C–219/91 *Ter Voort* [1992] ECR I–5485 on the question whether tisane was within the term medicament as used in Council Regulation 65/65.

[14] Case 6/60 *Humblet v. Belgium* [1960] ECR 559 at 575.

[15] Case 26/62 *Van Gend en Loos v. Nederlandse administratie der belastingen* [1963] ECR 1 at 12; [1963] C.M.L.R. 105.

[16] Case 6/72 *Continental Can v. Commission* [1973] ECR 215 at 243; [1973] C.M.L.R. 199.

[17] Case 9/56 *Meroni v. High Authority* [1958] ECR 133 at 140.

[18] Case 8/55 *Fédéchar v. High Authority* [1954–56] ECR 245.

[19] Case 25/62 *Plaumann v. Commission* [1963] ECR 95; [1964] C.M.L.R. 29.

Article 173 EC (now the fourth paragraph of Article 230 EC) by holding that both the wording and the grammatical construction of that provision justified the widest interpretation.

In comparison with a national court, the task of the Court of Justice is inevitably more difficult because, as we have seen, there will seldom be a single text before it. In the event of ambiguity it may have to consider the versions in the various Community languages, all equally authentic. Very real difficulties may arise from subtle differences between the alternative texts. Thus, Article 48(3) (now Article 39(3)) EC uses, in the English text, the expression "public policy" to translate the French term "*ordre public*", a false equation with which Advocate General Warner wrestled valiantly to find the *mot juste* in Case 30/77 *Bouchereau*.[20] Likewise, the French term "*détournement de pouvoir*" as used in Article 230 (ex Article 173) EC has a more precise meaning than the vague English term "misuse of powers" employed in the English texts: the same expression in Article 33 ECSC has presented problems of interpretation for the Court because of its various shades of meaning in the original six Member States.[21] Again, in Case 29/69 *Stauder*[22] the Court had to consider the different versions of a Commission decision addressed to the Member States permitting the sale of butter at reduced prices to persons in receipt of welfare benefits. The Dutch and German texts required the beneficiaries to receive their butter in exchange for a "coupon indicating their names". A German citizen challenged this in his national courts as an infringement of fundamental rights. The Court referred to the French and Italian versions which only stipulated the production of a "coupon referring to the person concerned". It adopted this more liberal version of the decision which would enable its objective to be achieved by other and unexceptional methods of identifying the beneficiaries.[23]

In Case 100/84 *Commission v. United Kingdom*,[24] linguistic analysis having failed to resolve the problem, recourse was had to teleological interpretation. British trawlers had cast their empty fishing nets into the Baltic Sea and had passed the ends of those nets to Polish trawlers, which trawled the nets without at any time

---

[20] Case 30/77 *R. v. Bouchereau* [1977] ECR 1999; [1977] 2 C.M.L.R. 800.
[21] See Case 3/54 *ASSIDER v. High Authority* [1954–56] ECR 63.
[22] Case 29/69 *Stauder v. Stadt Ulm* [1969] ECR 419; [1970] C.M.L.R. 112.
[23] Case C–72/95 *Kraaijeveld BV* [1996] ECR I–5403 is a more recent example of the Court grappling with different language versions (now increased to 11): in the event of divergence between the versions, reference must be made to the purpose and general scheme of the rules involved.
[24] Case 100/84 *Commission v. United Kingdom* [1985] ECR 1169; [1985] 2 C.M.L.R. 199.

taking them on board their vessels or entering their territorial waters. When the trawl was completed, the British trawlers drew alongside the Polish vessels and lifted the nets, the ends of which had been passed back to them by the Polish vessels. The contents of the nets were taken on board the British trawlers, which then took the fish back to the United Kingdom. The local United Kingdom Customs Officer first considered that the fish concerned were of Polish origin and therefore required security to be furnished against any import duty that might be payable. However, on appeal H.M. Customs and Excise decided that the fish were of Community origin and thus entitled to duty-free admission. The Commission brought proceedings against the United Kingdom for failing to fulfil its obligations under the Council Regulation on the common definition of origin of goods.[25] The case turned on the interpretation of the expression in that regulation "products taken from the sea". Both Advocate General Mancini and the Court itself carried out a comparative examination of the different language versions of that provisions.[26] As Mancini put it "this dispute centers precisely on the term "*extraits de la mer*" and the corresponding terms used in the other language versions of the provision: "taken from the sea", "*estratti dal mare*", "*gefangen*", "*uit de zee gewonnen*", "*optages fra havet*", "εξαγσμενα εκ τηζ Θαλάσσηζ".

However, that comparative examination of terminology did not enable a conclusion to be reached in favour of any of the interpretations suggested. The Court therefore pointed out that, as it had previously held in *Bouchereau*,[27] in the case of divergence between the language versions the provision in question was to be interpreted by reference to the purpose and general scheme of the rules of which it formed a part. It therefore held that the "nationality" of the fish was to be determined by reference not to the flag flown by the vessel that merely raised the nets out of the water, but to the flag flown by the vessel which carried out the essential part of the operation of catching fish, that is to say, the location of the fish and netting them so that they could no longer move freely in the sea. Accordingly the fish were Polish.

In Case C–149/97 *Institute of the Motor Industry v. Customs & Excise Commissioners*,[28] the Institute claimed exemption from

---

[25] Regulation 802/68: on the common definition of concept of the origin of goods [1968] O.J. Spec. Ed. 165 Art. 4(2).

[26] In his opinion Mancini remarks that: "I doubt whether Marguerite Yourcenar or Graham Greene would be prepared to read each morning a piece or two of Community legislation our *'pour prendre le ton'* as Stendhal used to read Articles of the Code Civil. In other words I admire the wisdom of the Community legislature but not its carelessness and too often imprecise language" at p. 1173.

[27] Case 30/77 *R. v. Boucherau* [1977] ECR 199; [1977] 2 C.M.L.R. 800.

[28] Case C–149/97 *Institute of the Motor Industry v. Commissioners of Customs and Excise* [1998] ECR I–7053.

VAT as an organisation "with aims of a trade union nature", the expression used in the English version of the relevant Directive. The French text referred to "*objectifs de nature syndicale*". Faced with a divergence between these language versions, the provision had to be interpreted, declared the Court, by reference to the purpose and general scheme of the rules of which it formed a part. According to the Court, this meant that the organisation's main aim must be to defend the collective interests of its members, whether workers, employers or traders, and to represent them *vis-à-vis* appropriate third parties, including the public authorities. It left to the national tribunal to assess, in the light of these considerations and on the facts before it, whether the Institute qualified for VAT exemption.

Faced thus by a disparity of texts the Courts looks, where the context so permits, for that text which offers the most liberal solution in relation to the rights of the individual, being guided by the spirit and intention of the texts rather than by the verbal symbols in which they are expressed: this is an approach consistent with its own doctrine of proportionality whereby the Court requires a Community act to use the minimum of means to achieve the desired end (see p. 350, below).[29]

Only rarely will a national court embark on so elaborate an analysis of the different language versions of the provisions of a regulation as was attempted in the Northern Irish High Court in *Cunningham v. Milk Marketing Board for Northern Ireland*.[30] But the English Court of Appeal was emboldened to interpret a British statute by reference to the French text of the international convention on which the statute was based.[31]

At the Community level, nevertheless, literal interpretation will be the preferred approach of the Court of Justice, contrary to Sir Patrick Neill's charge against it, where the Community legislature has made its intentions clear through the use of detailed provisions. Such detailed legislative schemes occur, for example, in the fields of agriculture and social security. The Court may then feel itself bound to accept the results which the provisions were designed to achieve, even though these results are then held to be flawed as failing to respect a general principle of Community law and, consequently, must be struck down as invalid. A striking

---

[29] Other cases posing problems of textual disparity include: Case 9/79 *Koschniske v. Raad von Arbeid* [1979] ECR 2717; [1980] 1 C.M.L.R. 87, Case 814/79 *Netherlands v. Ruffer* [1980] ECR 3807; [1981] 3 C.M.L.R. 293, Case 131/79 *R. v. Secretary of State for Home Affairs, ex p. Santillo* [1980] ECR 1585; [1980] 2 C.M.L.R. 308: see generally Brown (1981) 15, Valparaiso Univ. Law Rev. 319.

[30] [1988] 3 C.M.L.R. 815 at 877–887.

[31] *James Buchanan & Co. v. Babco Forwarding & Shipping (U.K.)* [1977] 1 All E.R. 518, per Lawton L.J. at p. 530.

example is the series of so-called 'SLOM' cases in relation to milk quotas (discussed above Chapter 8, p. 180) which involved the principle of respect for legitimate expectations. Of these cases, Advocate General Jacobs remarked:

". . . the Court did not feel itself able to interpret these provisions in such a way as to bring them into conformity with Community law. It seems to me that the Court was unable to do so because the intention of the legislature, however defective, was abundantly clear, and there was accordingly no occasion to depart from the literal meaning of the provisions in which it was expressed."[32]

## HISTORICAL INTERPRETATION

By historical interpretation is usually meant the quest for the subjective intention of the author of the text. It may also mean the discovery of the objective intention of the measure in question, to be deduced from its purpose at the date of enactment. The English so-called "Mischief Rule" as laid down in *Heydon's Case*[33] confines the English judge to the objective legislative intent, whereas in most Continental countries the judge may examine the *travaux préparatoires* ("preparatory work") in pursuit of the subjective intention of the legislature. This is only a generalisation, for on both sides of the Channel there is movement towards a more intermediate position, limited access to certain *travaux préparatoires* becoming acceptable in England, while such materials are treated with increasing caution in some continental jurisdictions. Thus, in *Pepper v. Hart*,[34] the House of Lords has now accepted that resort may be had to Hansard to refer to reports of debates and proceedings in Parliament as an aid to construing legislation which was ambiguous, obscure or the literal meaning of which led to absurdity; but such reference should only be permitted if it disclosed the mischief aimed at or the legislative intention lying behind the ambiguous or obscure words.[35]

Historical interpretation in either sense is little used by the Court of Justice. In regard to the Treaties, the negotiations have remained shrouded in secrecy by common agreement of the contracting States. Professor Pescatore, later a distinguished judge

---

[32] Case C–85/90 *Dowling* [1992] ECR I–5305, 5320–5322
[33] (1584) 3 Co.Rep. 7a.
[34] [1992] 3 W.L.R. 1033; [1993] 1 All E.R. 42, HL.
[35] For a still valuable comparative survey, see Norman S. March, *Interpretation in the National and International Context* (1973).

of the Court, was himself the head of the Luxembourg team which negotiated the EC Treaty, and he has explained in a public lecture in 1963 the wisdom of excluding recourse to the records of the negotiations:

> "Treaties are not established unilaterally, they are negotiated. In order to interpret an international treaty correctly, account must therefore be taken of the actual conditions in which it was negotiated. However, it is precisely one of the rules of negotiation that one does not always reveal one's intentions. It is not, in actual fact, on the intentions of the contracting parties that agreement is reached, but on the written formulas of the treaties and only on that. It is by no means certain that agreement on a text in any way implies agreement as to intentions. On the contrary, divergent, even conflicting intentions may perfectly well underlie a given text and I would even go so far as to say . . . that the art of treaty-making is in part the art of disguising irresolvable differences between the contracting States."

A former President of the Court, Robert Lecourt, in his Geneva Lectures *Le juge devant le Marché commun* (1970), confirms the view of Judge Pescatore that it is not the function of the Luxembourg Court to rediscover the intention of the parties in the manner which is traditional for interpreting treaties in international law. He explains (at p. 64) that:

> "In the Community the judge is the repository of the will of the authors of the Treaties, who moved into the background on the day of signature, to reappear only at rare moments when they sign new agreements. They have made the judge the guardian of their common achievement, that is to say, of its objectives, institutions and law. They have carried so far the trust which they have placed in the judge as the custodian of their common will that they have even destroyed every official trace of their *travaux préparatoires*."

Somewhat greater freedom in resorting to *travaux préparatoires* is manifested by the advocates general of the Court in their opinions. In particular, they have occasionally referred to the record of proceedings in the national parliaments when the Treaties were being submitted for ratification. Thus in Case 6/54 *Netherlands v. High Authority*[36] concerning the interpretation of Article 33 ECSC Advocate General Roemer suggested, after citing the explanations given to their national legislatures by the German and French

---

[36] [1954–56] ECR 103.

Governments, that "the Court should examine the statement of reasons laid before the parliaments of the other countries". Again in Case 3/54 *ASSIDER v. High Authority*[37] Advocate General Lagrange concluded: "I can refer to a passage in the preamble to the Luxembourg ratification Law [ratifying the ECSC Treaty] which is couched in the following terms: . . . The intention of the authors of the Treaty seems therefore to be beyond doubt."

The Court itself in Case 6/60 *Humblet*[38] referred in its judgment to the fact that "the opinions of the governments put forward during the parliamentary debates on the ECSC Treaty do not touch on this question. The same is true of the parliamentary votes on the EEC and EAEC Treaties which contain a provision in substantially the same terms." In *Humblet* the Court had to determine the scope of the provision in the Protocol on the Privileges and Immunities which exempted the salaries of Community officials from national charges; having found the parliamentary debates silent on the point, the Court then resorted to a comparison of different national laws as an aid to interpretation of the Protocol.

Because of the dynamic character of the Treaties as laying down programmes for the future, such reference to *travaux préparatoires*, whether by the Court or its advocate general, tends to diminish as the dates of concluding the Treaties (or Protocols) recede into the past. The late President Kutscher declared indeed that "It is useless to look at such pointers in the more recent judgments . . . interpretations based on the original situation would in no way be in keeping with a Community law orientated towards the future."[39]

So far as Community legislation is concerned, both the Council and the Commission deliberate in secret, and especially in the Council hard bargaining is common. Accordingly, even if available, the records of deliberations in these bodies would be open to the same objections as those attached by MM. Pescatore and Lecourt to the negotiations of the Treaties. On the other hand, certain official *travaux préparatoires* are available for Community legislation. Thus the Official Journal publishes all legislative proposals by the Commission as well as formal opinions of the European Parliament and the Economic and Social Committee, which may relate to proposed legislation. Significantly, however, the Court never makes use of the debates of the European Parliament upon such legislative proposals.

---

[37] [1954–56] ECR 63 at 87.
[38] Case 6/60 *Humblet v. Belgium* [1960] ECR 559.
[39] H. Kutscher, *Methods of Interpretation as seen by a judge of the Court of Justice* (1976), pp. 21–22.

In addition, the regulations, directives and decisions of the Council and Commission are required by Article 253 (ex Article 190) EC to state the reasons on which they are based and to refer to any proposals or opinions which were required to be obtained pursuant to the Treaty. These obligatory recitals in the preamble to such legislation throw light on the intention of the Council or Commission and are frequently referred to by the Court as a guide to the interpretation of their provisions. Thus in Case 14/69 *Markus v. Hauptzollamt Hamburg-Jonas*[40] the Court held that:

> "according to the seventh recital of the preamble to the regulation in question . . . the eighth recital of the same preamble states . . . It must therefore be assumed that the authors of the first paragraph of Article 16 intended . . . The solution is confirmed by the penultimate recital of the preamble to the said regulation according to which. . . ."

Again, in Case 9/72 *Brunner*[41] the Court held that: "It is clear from the recitals of the preamble to that regulation that . . ." And in the *Import Gadgets* case[42] the Court followed its normal practice of interpreting the Common Customs Tariff by reference to the Explanatory Notes to the Brussels Nomenclature, that is, notes relating to the Convention of December 15, 1950 on nomenclature for the classification of goods in customs tariffs, this Nomenclature, which provides the historical basis for the Common Customs Tariff, being legally binding as an international obligation on all the Member States and, in the view of the Court, on the Community itself.

A recent discussion of the use of *travaux préparatoires* in relation to a regulation is to be found in Joined Cases C–68/94 & C–30/95 *France v. EC Commission ("Kali + Salz")*.[43] In this complex case, the parties disagreed whether Regulation 4064/89 on mergers should be interpreted as applying only to concentrations which created or strengthened an *individual* dominant position or could extend to those involving a collective dominant position (or "oligopoly"). *Travaux préparatoires* to the Regulation did not, in the Court's view, express clearly the intention of the authors. Hence, as the Court held:

> "Since the textual and historical interpretations of the Regulation, and in particular Article 2 thereof, do not permit its

---

[40] [1969] ECR 349; [1970] C.M.L.R. 206.
[41] Case 9/72 *Brunner v. Hauptzollamt Hof* [1972] ECR 961; [1972] C.M.L.R. 931.
[42] Case 22/76 *Import Gadgets v. L.A.M.P. S.p. A.* [1976] ECR 1371.
[43] [1998] ECR I–1375. See valuable comment by A. Arnull in Editorial (1998) 23 E.L.Rev. 199.

precise scope to be assessed as regards the type of dominant position concerned, the provision in question must be interpreted by reference to its purpose and general structure."

So interpreted, the provision, the Court concluded, did extend to oligopolies.

## CONTEXTUAL INTERPRETATION

This method is extensively used by the Court in interpreting both the Treaties and Community legislation. It involves placing the provision in issue within its context and interpreting it in relation to other provisions of Community law. The Treaties, in particular the EC Treaty, set out a grand design or programme, and it is natural to stress the interrelationship of the individual Treaties and their provisions as component parts of the total scheme. Not seeing the wood for the trees is, for the Court, a cardinal sin. Hence, its judgments abound with references such as –

"the context of all the provisions establishing a common organisation of the market": Case 190/73 *Van Haaster*[44];
"the general scheme of the Treaty as a whole": Cases 2 & 3/62 *Gingerbread* case[45];
"taking account of the fundamental nature, in the scheme of the Treaty, of the principles of freedom of movement and equality of treatment of workers": Case 152/73 *Sotgiu*[46];
"one must have regard to the whole scheme of the Treaty no less than to its specific provisions": Case 22/70 *ERTA* case[47];
"the context of the Treaty": Case 23/75 *Rey Soda*[48];
"the framework of Community law": Cases 90 & 91/63 *Dairy Products* case,[49] Case 6/64 *Costa v. ENEL*[50];
"Article 37(1) EEC must be interpreted in its context in relation to the other provisions of the article and taking account of its place in the general scheme of the Treaty": Case 59/75 *Manghera*[51];

---

[44] Case 190/73 *Officer van Justitie v. Van Haaster* [1974] ECR 1123; [1974] 2 C.M.L.R. 521.
[45] Cases 2 & 3/62 *Commission v. Luxembourg and Belgium* [1962] ECR 425; [1963] C.M.L.R. 199.
[46] Case 152/73 *Sotgiu v. Deutsche Bundespost* [1974] ECR 153.
[47] Case 22/70 *Commission v. Council* [1971] ECR 263; [1971] C.M.L.R. 335.
[48] Case 23/75 *Rey Soda v. Cassa Conguaglia Zucchero* [1975] ECR 1279; [1976] 1 C.M.L.R. 185.
[49] Cases 90 & 91/63 *Commission v. Luxembourg and Belgium* [1964] ECR 625; [1965] C.M.L.R. 58.
[50] Case 6/64 *Costa v. ENEL* [1964] ECR 585; [1964] C.M.L.R. 425.
[51] Case 59/75 *Pubblico Ministero v. Manghera* [1976] ECR 91; [1976] 1 C.M.L.R. 557.

"the provision in question must be interpreted by reference to its purpose and general structure": Joined Cases C–68/94 & C–30/95 *France v. EC Commission*.[52]

A striking example of the effect of this systematic interpretation of the Treaty can be found in the Court's treatment of customs duties and charges having equivalent effect in Article 25 (ex Article 12) EC. Article 25 provides that:

"Member States shall refrain from introducing between themselves any new customs duties on imports or exports or any charges having equivalent effect, and from increasing those which they already apply in their trade with each other."

In the *Gingerbread* case[53] the Court held that:

"The position of those Articles [Articles 9 and 12] [now Articles 23 and 25] towards the beginning of that Part of the Treaty dealing with the 'Foundations of the Community' – Article 9 being placed at the beginning of the Title relating to 'Free Movement of Goods', and Article 12 at the beginning of the section dealing with the 'Elimination of Custom Duties' – is sufficient to emphasise the essential nature of the prohibitions which they impose."

Relying on, among other things, the "general scheme" of those provisions and of the Treaty as a whole, the Court went on to argue that there was evidence of "a general intention to prohibit not only measures which obviously take the form of the classic customs duty but also all those which, presented under other names or introduced by the indirect means of other procedures, would lead to the same discriminatory or protective results as customs duties."

It is interesting to compare the approach which an English court might adopt to the expression "customs duties and charges having equivalent effect". An English court would be likely to apply the more restrictive approach, according to which, when general words are used, they are to be confined to those kinds of things with which the context deals explicitly or implicitly: the *eiusdem generis* rule is a specific instance of this approach where two examples of a category are given, followed by a general expression. An English court, therefore, would refer to the context of the

---

[52] Cases C–68/94 and C–30/95 *France v. EC Commission* [1988] 4 C.M.L.R. 829, discussed above.
[53] Cases 2 & 3/62 *Commission v. Luxembourg and Belgium* [1962] ECR 425; [1963] C.M.L.R. 199.

provision "customs duties and charges having equivalent effect", but rather with a view to limiting the general expression in the light of that context. In the *Gingerbread* case, on the contrary, the Court uses the general expression "any charges having equivalent effect" as a "catch all" concept to cover not only charges of the same kind but charges of all kinds having the same effect. Hence it takes Chapter 1 of this part of the Treaty as prohibiting all pecuniary obstacles to trade between Member States.

In other cases,[54] the same result is achieved in relation to Chapter 2, on the elimination of quantitative restrictions. All measures having equivalent effect to quotas, prohibited by Article 28 (ex Article 30) EC, are taken to exclude, in effect, all non-pecuniary trade barriers, subject only to the exceptions expressly provided (and narrowly construed) in Article 30 (ex Article 36) EC. Thus, by looking at this Title of the Treaty as a whole, and construing its very general provisions in the light of its supposed aims, the Court takes it as abolishing at a stroke, with very limited exceptions, all barriers, pecuniary or otherwise, to trade between Member States.

In a characteristic passage in Case 24/68 *Commission v. Italian Republic*,[55] the Court held (at 200–201):

> "Thus, in order to ascribe to a charge an effect equivalent to a customs duty, it is important to consider this effect in the light of the objectives of the Treaty, in the Parts, Titles and Chapters in which Articles 9, 12, 13 and 16[56] are to be found, particularly in relation to the free movement of goods. Consequently, any pecuniary charge, however small and whatever its designation and mode of application, which is imposed unilaterally on domestic or foreign goods by reason of the fact that they cross a frontier, and which is not a customs duty in the strict sense, constitutes a charge having equivalent effect within the meaning of Articles 9, 12, 13 and 16 of the Treaty, even if it is not imposed for the benefit of the State, is not discriminatory or protective in effect and if the product on which the charge is imposed is not in competition with any domestic product."

Contextual interpretation is no less important in relation to Community legislation. Typically, the Court may have to interpret

---

[54] See for example Case 120/78 *REWE-Zentral v. Bundesmonopolverwaltung fur Branntwein* ("*Cassis de Dijon*") [1979] ECR 647; [1979] 3 C.M.L.R. 494.

[55] Case 24/68 *Commission v. Italian Republic* [1969] ECR 193; [1971] C.M.L.R. 611.

[56] Arts 9 and 12 EC are now Arts 23 and 25 respectively; Arts 13 and 16 were repealed by the Treaty of Amsterdam.

a regulation of the Commission which implements a regulation of the Council which itself is issued pursuant to a provision in the Treaties: Case 64/69 *Compagnie Française Commerciale et Financière v. Commission*[57] was such a case. The Court will necessarily examine the subordinate regulation immediately in issue for its compatibility both with the enabling regulation and with the superior law of the treaty provision. Having examined the vertical context it will also consider the horizontal relationship of the regulation with other Commission regulations *in pari materia*. Again, the language of the Court's judgments is indicative of this approach, for example:

> "the Regulation (No. 3 on social security for migrant workers made pursuant to Article 51 EC) (now Article 42 EC) must he interpreted in the context and within the bounds of this article and having regard to the fundamental principles which it lays down."[58] And in Case 17/76, *Brack v. The Insurance Officer*[59] "The Regulation [No. 1408/71 which superseded No. 3 above] must be interpreted above all in the light of the spirit and of the objectives of the Treaty."

Finally, where a provision in a regulation, directive or even a Treaty provision amounts to an exception to the general purpose or scheme of the legislation, the Court will always construe the exception narrowly.[60]

## COMPARATIVE LAW AS AID TO INTERPRETATION

Part of the context in which Community law operates is interrelationship with the national laws of the Member States. The judges of the Court themselves bring to their task the conceptual background and instinctive reactions derived from previous careers in their own legal systems. Almost subconsciously, therefore, comparative law must be influencing their interpretative function.

In addition, Community law may use terms or concepts which are well known in the national laws, without itself defining them. In this case, the Community sense of the term may involve a

---

[57] Case 64/69 *Compagnie Française Commerciale et Financière v. Commission* [1970] ECR 221; [1970] C.M.L.R. 369.

[58] Case 28/68 *Torrekens* [1969] ECR 125; [1969] C.M.L.R. 377.

[59] Case 17/76 *Brack v. The Insurance Officer* [1976] ECR 1429; [1976] C.M.L.R. 592.

[60] See most recently judgment of December 15, 1993 in Case C–116/92 *Criminal Proceedings v. Charlton and Others* [1993] ECR I–6755, *The Times*, December 27, 1993.

comparison of the relevant national laws: see, for example, the opinion of Advocate General Lagrange in Case 3/54 *ASSIDER v. High Authority*[61] concerning the term *détournement de pouvoir* in the authentic French text and its Dutch, German and Italian equivalents in Article 33 ECSC. The Brussels Convention (p. 212, above) offers particular scope for the comparative method in its interpretation. To secure its uniform application in all the Member States, the Court has been persuaded to adopt autonomous Community meanings for legal terms and concepts employed in the Convention: the advocates general have demonstrated in several cases that such terms lack any consistent meaning in the various national laws.[62]

Likewise, Community law may simply be silent on questions of principle which have received solutions in the laws of the Member States. Thus, the question whether Community law admitted the revocation of measures creating subjective rights was answered by the Court in Cases 7/56 & 3-7/57 *Algera*[63] "by reference to the rules acknowledged by the legislation, the learned writing and the case law of the member countries", and there followed in the judgment "a comparative study of this problem of law".[64]

So extensive a comparative examination in an actual judgment is rare, indeed unique; but the opinions of the advocates general contain much comparative analysis. The judgment of the Court may then briefly adopt the result of such analysis, as, for example, in Case 32/62 *Alvis*,[65] which upheld in Community law the generally accepted principle of administrative law in the Member States whereby a civil servant must be allowed the opportunity to reply to allegations against him before being disciplined (see further p. 199, above). Again in Case 155/79 *AM&S*[66] both Advocate General Warner and (in the re-opened oral proceedings) Advocate General Slynn included in their opinions extensive comparative analysis of the scope of legal professional privilege in all the Member States with a view to guiding the Court how far that privilege should extend as a general principle of Community law.

More specifically, as we have seen in Chapter 8, the second paragraph of Article 288 (ex Article 215) EC bases the non-

---

[61] Case 3/54 *ASSIDER v. High Authority* [1954–56] ECR 63.
[62] See, for example Case 29/76 *LTU v. Eurocontrol* [1976] ECR 1541; [1977] 1 C.M.L.R. 88, opinion of Advocate General Reischl; Case 814/79 *Netherlands v. Ruffer* [1980] ECR 3807; [1981] 3 C.M.L.R. 293, opinion of Advocate general Warner.
[63] Cases 7/56 and 3-7/57 *Algera v. Common Assembly* [1957–1958] ECR 39.
[64] For the facts of this case, see p. 198, above.
[65] Case 32/62 *Alvis v. Council* [1963] ECR 49; [1963] C.M.L.R. 396.
[66] Case 155/79 *AM&S v. Commission* [1982] ECR 1575; [1982] 2 C.M.L.R. 264.

contractual liability of the Community for damage caused by its institutions or by its servants in the performance of their duties upon "the general principles common to the laws of the Member States". In the earlier chapter we saw how the Court had drawn, by an eclectic process, upon the national legal systems to create a uniform Community law governing tortious liability or reparation.

Resort to *jus commune Europaeum*, which is explicitly required by the second paragraph of Article 288 (ex Article 215) EC (Article 188 Euratom), is also an underlying feature of the wider doctrine of "general principles of law" which the Court has developed as an additional source of Community law. This important topic is returned to more fully in Chapter 15, but it is relevant here as a further example of the Court's use of comparative law as an aid to interpretation. Of necessity, much comparative research is constantly undertaken on behalf of the members of the Court, and we have seen in Chapter 2 what internal arrangements exist to facilitate this. In addition, the Commission's Legal Service often includes comparative material in presenting its observations to the Court, or the Commission may be expressly requested by the Court to include such material in its observations.[67]

## TELEOLOGICAL INTERPRETATION

The term teleological is applied to an interpretation which is based upon the purpose or object of the text facing the judge. This approach, which is increasingly favoured by the Court, is peculiarly appropriate in Community law where, as we have seen, the Treaties provide mainly a broad programme or design rather than a detailed blue-print. In setting forth the grand design the Treaties, both in their preambles and in certain Articles, express the objectives of the Communities in very general terms; in turn, these objectives are knit together by the underlying assumption that they will lead eventually to an economic and political union. Article 2 (ex Article 2) EC, as amended by the Maastricht and Amsterdam Treaties, is a striking example with its declaration of intent that:

> "The Community shall have as its task, by establishing a common market and an economic and monetary union and by implementing the common policies or activities referred to in Articles 3 and 4, to promote throughout the Community a harmonious and balanced development of economic

---

[67] P. Pescatore, "*Le Recours, dans la jurisprudence de la Cour de justice des Communautés Européennes, à des normes déduites de la comparaison des droits des Etats membres*" (1980) *Revue Internationale de Droit Comparé* 337.

activities, a high level of employment and of social protection, equality between men and women, sustainable and non-inflationary growth, a high degree of protection and improvement of the quality of the environment, the raising of the standard of living and quality of life, and economic and social cohesion and solidarity among Member States."

And the Treaty on European Union (Article 2 (ex Article B)) sets its objective, *inter alia*, as "the establishment of economic and monetary union, ultimately including a single currency".

Faced with a body of law whose core is couched in such terms the Court of Justice has naturally adopted the teleological method in interpreting both the Treaties and the legislation derived from them. For Judge Pescatore, as for President Kutscher, the teleological and contextual methods assume greater importance than the historical or literal methods.[68]

From the case law of the Court we have already discussed one notable example, Case 22/70 *ERTA*.[69] A further illustration is a leading case on Article 86 (now 82) EC, Case 6/72 *Continental Can*[70] Article 86 prohibits any "abuse of a dominant position within the common market or in a substantial part of it . . . in so far as it may affect trade between Member States". The *Continental Can* case raised the question whether Article 86 could apply to takeovers or mergers.

According to a decision taken by the Commission, Continental Can Company Inc. of New York, which held, through the medium of its German subsidiary, a dominant position over a substantial part of the common market in certain packaging products, had abused that dominant position by acquiring, through a Belgian subsidiary Europemballage Corporation, a Dutch company which was the only significant competitor in those products.

The Commission's decision required Continental Can to put an end to its alleged infringement of Article 86 and to submit proposals to the Commission for that purpose by a specified date. The decision was challenged before the Court by Continental Can and by Europemballage, who argued that the Commission had wrongly interpreted Article 86 and was trying to introduce merger control in the EC Treaty. The ECSC Treaty made express provision for merger control but there was no such express provision in the EC Treaty. The Court rejected comparison with the ECSC

---

[68] See above, p. 331 and p. 332.
[69] Case 22/70 *Commission v. Council* [1971] ECR 263; [1971] C.M.L.R. 335 (see p. 302, above).
[70] Case 6/72 *Europemballage Corporation and Continental Can Co. Inc. v. Commission* [1973] ECR 215; [1973] C.M.L.R. 199.

Treaty as a method of interpretation and referred instead to "the spirit, general scheme and wording of Article 86, as well as to the system and objectives of the Treaty". It went on to examine the Article in the context of the other treaty provisions on competition and in the light of the principles and objectives set out in Articles 2 and 3. Ultimately it annulled the decision on other grounds, but it upheld the Commission's extensive interpretation of Article 86.

The use of the teleological method of filling gaps in codes or statutes is a familiar one in continental legal systems. It is expressly enjoined upon the Swiss courts by the Swiss Civil Code of 1922. In Community law the original Treaties were designed to have their details filled out by legislation of the Council and Commission. The political near-paralysis which has often crippled the legislative institutions of the Communities in the past has left yawning gaps in the enacted Community law. The Court of Justice sees itself as charged by the Treaties with upholding Community law, and accordingly it must fill the gaps left in that law by the default of the other institutions or the inactivity of the Member States.

Thus, the adjustment of State monopolies of a commercial character was required of Member States under Article 37 (now Article 31) EC during the transitional period; in default of the adjustment by the Italian Government of its tobacco monopoly (albeit this default was with the tacit acquiescence of the Council), the Court, in Case 59/75 *Manghera*,[71] took upon itself to declare the incompatibility of that monopoly with the Treaty and to draw the necessary consequences.

Again, in the second *Defrenne* case,[72] the Court had to consider the application of the principle of equal pay for equal work imposed by Article 119 (now Article 141) EC, and whether that principle had become directly enforceable in the national courts at the end of the first stage of the transitional period (December 31, 1961), or whether the further period of grace granted by the Council to Member States for implementing Article 119 was valid. The Court held the Article to have come into operation on January 1, 1962 and to have direct effect. It supported this conclusion by reference to the nature of the equal pay principle and the objective of this principle and its place in the EEC Treaty. It combined the teleological with the contextual approach in emphasising not only the dual purpose (economic and social) of Article 119 but also its relationship to other provisions, particularly Article 117 (now Article 136) concerning the need to promote improved working conditions and an improved standard of living for workers.

---

[71] Case 59/75 *Pubblico Ministero v. Manghera* [1976] ECR 91; [1976] 1 C.M.L.R. 557.
[72] Case 43/75 *Defrenne v. SABENA* [1976] ECR 455; [1976] 2 C.M.L.R. 98.

That the Court consciously assumed a legislative role in this case is confirmed by the further (and controversial) component of its judgment in which, in the interest of legal certainty, it declined to give a general retrospective effect to its ruling on Article 119: only those who had already commenced legal proceedings could claim pay for periods prior to the date of judgment.[73] But the Court has emphasised that such a limitation *ratione temporis* should only be introduced where there were over-riding considerations of legal certainty.[74]

The problems which may be caused by attempting to limit the effect of a judgment in time are graphically illustrated in relation to pensions by the *Barber* case[75] and its consequences which included a series of further preliminary references[76] and an attempted clarification of the position by means of a special Protocol to the Maastricht Treaty.[77]

This teleological approach is also extensively used in interpreting Community legislation. Thus, in Case 9/67 *Colditz*[78] concerning certain social security regulations, the Court declared that:

> "the solution to this question . . . can only emerge from the interpretation of those regulations in the light of the objectives of the provisions of the Treaty (Articles 48 to 51 [now Articles 39 to 42])."

Also, as we have seen in considering contextual interpretation, regulations and directives recite in their preambles the reasons on which they are based. This enables the Court to invoke the objectives of the measure by reference to such recitals and to interpret it accordingly.[79]

---

[73] For a similar limitation on the retrospectivity of a ruling on validity, see Case 41/84 *Pinna v. Caisse d'allocations familiales de la Savoie* [1986] ECR 1; [1988] 1 C.M.L.R. 350 (discussed p. 235, above).

[74] Case 24/86 *Blaizot v. University of Liège* [1989] 1 C.M.L.R. 57.

[75] Case 262/88 *Barber v. Guardian Royal Exchange Assurance Group* [1990] ECR I–1889; [1990] 2 C.M.L.R. 513.

[76] See judgments of October 6, 1993 in Case C–109/91 *Ten Oever v. Stichting Bedrijfspensioenfonds voor bet Glazenwassers- en Schoonmaakbedrijf* [1993] ECR I–4879 of December 14, 1993 in Case C–110/91 *Moroni v. Collo GmbH* [1993] ECR I–6591 and of December 22, 1993 in Case C–152/91 *Neath v. Hugh Steeper Ltd* [1993] ECR I–6935.

[77] Protocol concerning Art. 119 of the Treaty establishing the European Community [1992] O.J. C224/104.

[78] Case 9/67 *Colditz v. Caisse d'assurance vieillesse des travailleurs salariés de Paris* [1967] ECR 229.

[79] See Case C–56/90 *Commission v. United Kingdom* [1993] ECR I–4109. The Commission brought infringement proceedings relating to the implementation of the bathing water directive in respect of beaches in Blackpool, Formby and Southport. The Court said that the expression "bathing water" "must be

As part of its teleological approach the Court not infrequently refers to the principle of effectiveness (*l'effet utile*), a concept borrowed from international law which is sometimes rendered inelegantly into English as "useful effect"; "effectiveness" is a better, though still not wholly satisfactory translation. In Community law this has come to mean that "preference should be given to the construction which gives the rule its fullest effect and maximum practical value".[80] Cases in which the Court has invoked this principle of what we would term "Community efficacy" (compare the principle of "business efficacy)",[81] extend back to the earliest days of the Court.[82]

Case C–6 & 9/90, *Francovich* (p. 317, above), perhaps the most important of the Court's recent decisions, may be seen as an illustration both of teleological interpretation in general, and of resort to the doctrine of *l'effet utile*, in particular.

Not surprisingly, after over a quarter of a century of our membership of the Community, British courts have been attracted to the teleological approach. Thus, Lord Griffiths observed in 1993 that British judges "now adopt a purposive approach which seeks to give effect to the true purpose of legislation and are prepared to look at much extraneous material that bears upon the background against which the legislation was enacted."[83]

## THE EUROPEAN WAY

The separating out in this chapter of the various methods or approaches which the Court brings to its task of interpreting Community law should not mislead the reader into concluding that the Court operates in some mechanical way. As we have said, interpretation is an art in which the judicial instinct looms large. Frequently the Court uses a combination of methods, much as the artist blends the primary colours of his palette. A characteristic example is provided (as we have seen) by Case 6/72 *Continental Can*[84] where the judgment states:

---

interpreted in the light of the directive's underlying objectives which, according to the first two recitals in the preamble thereto, include the protection of the environment and public health and the improvement of living conditions."

[80] Kutscher *op. cit.* 41.

[81] As laid down for English law in *The Moorcock* (1889) 14 P.D. 64.

[82] Case 8/55 *Fédéchar v. High Authority* [1954–56] ECR 245 and 292; Case 20/59 *Italy v. High Authority*; Case 25/59 *The Netherlands v. High Authority* [1960] ECR 325 and 355; and Case 34/62 *Germany v. Commission* [1963] ECR 131; [1963] C.M.L.R. 369.

[83] In *Pepper v. Hart* [1993] A.C. 593 at 617; see, above, p. 330.

[84] [1973] ECR 215 at 243; [1973] C.M.L.R. 199.

> "In order to answer this question [whether Art. 86 EC applies to changes in the structure of an undertaking] one has to go back to the spirit, general scheme and wording of Article 86, as well as to the system and objectives of the Treaty."

Literal, contextual and teleological approaches are here all mixed together to enable the Court to reach its landmark decision on the full scope of Article 86 (now Article 82) EC.

Finally, over the four decades of its existence the Court has changed the emphasis of its methods, especially in interpreting the founding Treaties. The earlier reliance on literal interpretation has given place increasingly to the contextual and teleological approaches, approaches which befit a jurisdiction charged with a quasi-constitutional function as the guardian of the grand objectives laid down in the Treaties.

## PITFALLS FOR THE COMMON LAWYER

Non-civilian lawyers, be they English, Irish or Scottish, should beware of approaching Community law as if it were no different from their national law: they must heed the injunction of Lord Denning with which we began this chapter. In particular, they should not strain to apply to Community law the canons of interpretation which the common law judges have evolved over the centuries. It would be a salutary exercise for the English-speaking lawyer who has some French to make a practice of looking at the French as well as the English version of the text in issue. Illustrations abound of where English courts may have gone astray in interpreting Community law.[85]

Finally, to return to Sir Patrick Neill's criticism of the Court, with which we introduced this chapter, the Court of Justice is never unmindful of the words of the text before it. But it is conscious too of the overriding duty which the EC Treaty has laid upon the Court, as well as the Parliament, the Council and the Commission, to assure *"la réalisation des tâches confiées à la Communauté"*.[86]

---

[85] See *Schorsch Meier v. Hennin* [1975] Q.B. 416 (Lord Denning M.R.); *R. v. Henn and Darby* [1980] 2 All E.R. 166 (Lord Widgery CJ), see above, p. 206; *R. v. Secchi* [1975] 1 C.M.L.R. 383 (Metropolitan Magistrate), see Plender [1976] Crim.L.R. 676; Durand (1979) 4 E.L. Rev. 3 at 9; Case 131/79 *R. v. Santillo* [1980] ECR 1585; [1980] 2 C.M.L.R. 308 (Divisional Court and Court of Appeal), see Dashwood (1981) 6 E.L. Rev. 73.

[86] The French text of EC Art 7 (ex Art. 4) makes this point clearer than the English text.

# Chapter Fifteen

# Fundamental Doctrines & General Principles of Community Law

## INTRODUCTION

We have already had occasion to refer to the "general principles of law" used by the Court to supplement the written sources of Community law set out in the Treaties and in the legislation made pursuant to those Treaties. We have also met the doctrines of direct effect and primacy of Community law developed by the Court in its case law. However, for several reasons these subjects must be dealt with in more detail here. First, they illustrate both the character of Community law as developed by the Court and its relationship with the national legal systems of the Member States. Secondly, they illustrate well the law-making function of the Court.

At the outset, we must deal with certain problems of terminology, as, in this area, there is little consistency of usage either by commentators or by the Court of Justice itself. There are three related concepts involved which are difficult to define concisely and occasionally difficult to distinguish one from the other. They are:

- fundamental doctrines of Community law;
- general principles of law; and
- general principles *of Community Law*.

By fundamental doctrines we take to mean here those basic axioms of Community law which have been developed through the case law of the Court, rather than being spelled out in the Treaties. Nonetheless, as the Court has found, they are implicit in the Treaties and Community law is characterised by them, particularly the doctrines of direct effect and supremacy already mentioned. They also form part of the *acquis communautaire* that any aspiring Member State must accept, despite the sometimes uncomfortable results which may be produced in the domestic legal systems.

General principles of law are a collection (not a closed category) of principles which underlie all legal relationships and which cannot usually be overridden by other rules of law, even when the latter are expressly laid down in Treaties, agreements or other instruments. The "general principles of Community law" are the specific expressions of those broader general principles in the Community law context. The distinction between the two is drawn out below (pp. 247 *et seq.*).

It is difficult to draw the line between fundamental doctrines as so defined and general principles of Community law. Perhaps no clear line can be drawn, it is a matter of organisation of the concepts and placing them in a hierarchy according to the relative importance one believes they should have. This is inevitably a subjective matter and one which may vary according to context.

## FUNDAMENTAL DOCTRINES

The linked doctrines of direct effect and supremacy of Community law have already been referred to, as established in the leading cases of *van Gend en Loos* and *Costa v. ENEL*. The Court reasoned that both doctrines, although not expressly mentioned, were implicit in the spirit and general context of the Treaties. Likewise, the doctrine of the uniformity of Community law was until the last decade regarded as fundamental to the whole notion of a Community legal order, embraced on equal terms by a number of different Member States. However, with the Treaties of Maastricht and Amsterdam and with a Community enlarged to include 15 States, flexibility and diversity have become accepted features of that legal order, involving in the European jargon "multi-speed" (differentiation between Member States in time), "variable geometry" (differentiation in space) and "differentiation à la carte" (increasing adoption of opt-outs).

In recent years a new fundamental doctrine has been spelled out by the Court. This is the doctrine of a Member State's liability to the individual in damages for losses caused by a breach by that State of Community law. The leading cases here are the *Francovich*[1] and *Factortame* No. 3[2] cases.

It is arguable that other doctrines might be categorised as fundamental. For example, the doctrine of precedent itself, as

---

[1] Joined Cases C–6 and C–9/90 *Francovich and Bonifaci v. Italy* [1991] ECR I–5357.

[2] Joined Cases C–46 and C–48/93 *Brasserie du Pêcheur v. Germany and The Queen v. Secretary of State, ex p. Factortame* [1996] ECR I–1029[ Non-British lawyers know this judgment as the *Brasserie du Pêcheur* case].

applied by the Court,[3] could be regarded as a basic feature of the Community legal order, just as it is so regarded (and designated as a fundamental doctrine) in the common law of England. Alternatively, precedent can be seen in Community law as only an application of the general principle of legal certainty (discussed below); or, put another way, the Court makes a virtue of consistency.

The four fundamental doctrines referred to above, being all based on the Court's case law, may be distinguished from the fundamental doctrine of the direct applicability of Community law, because this is a doctrine based on a Treaty provision, namely, Article 249 (ex Article 189) EC: "A regulation shall be . . . directly applicable in all Member States". By contrast, Articles of the Treaties, even Article 249, are not "directly applicable": they are simply "applicable" by virtue (in the case of the United Kingdom) of the Treaty of Accession 1972, as endorsed by the European Communities Act 1972.

A second fundamental doctrine that is treaty-based rather than court-elicited is the doctrine of subsidiarity. This was introduced by the Maastricht Treaty which added a new Article, Article 5 (ex Article 3b), to the EC Treaty in the following terms:

> "In areas which do not fall within its exclusive competence, the Community shall take action, in accordance with the principle of subsidiarity, only if and in so far as the objectives of the proposed action cannot be sufficiently achieved by the Member States and can therefore, by reason of the scale or effects of the proposed action, be better achieved by the Community.
>
> Any action by the Community shall not go beyond what is necessary to achieve the objectives of this Treaty.

How the new doctrine will be received and developed by the Court lies in the future.

## GENERAL PRINCIPLES

We now turn to the distinction between "general principles of law" (*tout court*) and "general principles *of Community law*".

The use of general principles of law, or something very similar in effect, is found in many legal systems. The Statute of the International Court of Justice requires that Court to apply, *inter alia*, "the general principles of law recognised by civilised nations"

---

[3] See Chap. 16 below.

(Article 38(1)). In the European Communities there is no such comprehensive direction to the Court to apply the general principles of law; and the criterion applied by the Court is less exacting, since the general principles need be found only in the legal systems of the Member States, and, in the Court's practice, need not be common to all nor even to a majority of them. As Advocate General Lagrange stated nearly 40 years ago:

> "In this way the case law of the Court, in so far as it invokes national laws (as it does to a large extent) to define the rules of law relating to the application of the Treaty, is not content to draw on more or less arithmetical 'common denominators' between the different national solutions, but chooses from each of the Member States those solutions which, having regard to the objects of the Treaty, appear to it to be the best or, if one may use the expression, the most progressive. That is the spirit, moreover, which has guided the Court hitherto."[4]

General principles of law are found, not only in international law, but also in many municipal legal systems. The principle of proportionality (below) is especially prominent in German law, where it has a status similar to that of a general principle. Although not expressly mentioned in the German Basic Law, it has been held by the German courts to be the principle underlying two fundamental Articles of the Basic Law, Articles 2 and 12. Indeed German law has made perhaps the greatest contribution to the development of the general principles of law applied by the Court, including the principle of proportionality (*Verhaltnismässigkeit*) and the principle of protection of legitimate expectations (*Vertrauensschutz*) (below, p. 353).

For the English lawyer the closest analogies are perhaps to be found in the rules of natural justice in administrative law, in the common law notion of reasonableness, and in the maxims of equity; we shall see that these also are now making their mark on Community law.

The French lawyer is familiar with the doctrine of *les principes généraux du droit*. In French administrative law, the general principles of law have restrictive effect in relation to *réglements* or governmental decrees which they do not have on legislation, that is, *lois* enacted by the French parliament. But in the last two decades the *Conseil Constitutionnel* has developed its own doctrine of general principles as constitutional norms by reference to

---

[4] Case 14/61 *Hoogovens v. High Authority* [1962] ECR 253 at 283–284; [1963] C.M.L.R. 73.

which it may veto bills (*projets de loi*), before their enactment, as unconstitutional.[5]

In Community law, general principles may be invoked to interpret the treaty provisions, but they cannot prevail over the express terms of the Treaty. In the *Sgarlata* case,[6] the applicants sought to challenge Commission regulations fixing the reference prices for lemons and other citrus fruits. Faced with the objection that the application was inadmissible under Article 173 (now Article 230) EC as being directed against regulations rather than decisions, the applicants argued that if recourse to Article 173 were to be refused by reason of a restrictive interpretation of its terms, individuals would be deprived of all judicial protection under both Community law and national law, which would be contrary to the fundamental principles prevailing in all the Member States. Advocate General Roemer considered that this argument would require the Court not to interpret but to amend the Treaty on this point and the Court agreed that the considerations invoked by the applicants could not be allowed to override the clearly restrictive wording of Article 173. Hence the application was inadmissible. The result would of course have been different if the measures challenged, although in the form of regulations, had been in substance decisions of direct and individual concern to the applicants (above, p. 146). This they also alleged, but were unable to establish.

While general principles of law, or their analogue, can be found in many legal systems, they play a special part in Community law, as will be seen when we look in turn at those principles upon which the Court has most often relied and which, when so endorsed by the Court, become general principles of Community law. This term has now received recognition in the Maastricht Treaty which expressly requires the European Union to respect fundamental rights "as general principles of Community law": Article 6 (ex Article F) TEU.

From the survey which follows it will become apparent that, whereas "general principles of law" describes a generic source or reservoir of legal rules, the selection and endorsement of these rules by the Court creates a specific category of "general principles of Community law".

---

[5] See Brown and Bell, *French Administrative Law* (5th ed., 1998), pp. 14–24, for interaction of *Conseil Constitutionnel* with *droit administratif*; also generally Bell, *French Constitutional Law* (1992).

[6] Case 40/64 *Sgarlata and Others v. Commission* [1965] ECR 215; [1966] C.M.L.R. 314.

## 1. PROPORTIONALITY

The earliest decisions of the Court under the Coal and Steel Treaty contain references to general principles of law such as the principle of proportionality. Mention has already been made of Case 8/55 *Fédéchar*,[7] where the Court held that, by a generally accepted rule of law, the reaction of the High Authority to an unlawful act must be proportional to the scale of the act. The principle of proportionality, expressed in those terms, sounds unfamiliar to the English lawyers, but they use a similar concept when they talk of what is reasonable.[8] The Court too has used the language of reasonableness. In another early case, it held that the High Authority must go no further than is reasonable and must avoid causing harm to the extent that it is, within reason, possible to do so.[9]

A graphic illustration of proportionality (or, rather, disproportionality) is afforded by Case 181/84 *R. v. Intervention Board for Agricultural Produce, ex parte Man (Sugar)*.[10] Here an export company had paid to the Board a substantial deposit (some £1,670,000) in anticipation of its application for an export licence; when the application reached the Commission four hours past the deadline, the Board declared the whole deposit to be forfeit, as it was required to do by the Commission legislation; the Court ruled, upon a reference from the English court under Article 177 EEC (now Article 234 EC), that the forfeiture of the entire deposit for so trivial a breach of the deadline was a disproportionate act: the company could recover the entire sum, with interest and costs.

These cases illustrate the characteristic role of general principles of law as limiting the power of the administration to take measures affecting the citizen, even in the absence of any written text to this effect. Such principles were typically applied in actions for annulment under Article 33 ECSC, and subsequently under Article 173 (now Article 230) EC: an administrative act could be annulled as contrary to the general principles of law. If a formal justification were required for annulling measures on this ground, it could be found in the references in those Articles to the infringement of any rule of law relating to the application of the Treaties. Further, the

---

[7] Case 8/55 *Fédéchar v. High Authority* [1954–56] ECR 245 and 292.

[8] See for example *R. v. Barnsley Metropolitan Borough Council, ex p. Hook* [1976] 1 W.L.R. 1052.

[9] Case 15/57 *Hauts Fourneaux de Chasse v. High Authority* [1958] ECR 211 at 228.

[10] Case 181/84 *R. v. International Board for Agricultural Produce, ex p. Man (Sugar)* [1985] ECR 2889; [1985] 2 All E.R. 115; [1985] 3 C.M.L.R. 739.

Court is required to ensure that, in the interpretation and application of the Treaties, "the law is observed" (Article 31 ECSC, Article 220 (ex Article 164) EC). The reference here to "the law" is manifestly to a body of law outside the Treaties themselves, and can only be to unwritten rules whose origin it is natural to seek in the legal systems of the Member States.

The general principles of law are thus one, but only one example of the contribution of national law to Community law. Whenever the Court is faced with a question of law which is not resolved by any written Community text, it is likely to be influenced by the laws of the Member States. The advocate general, in his opinion, will very often survey these laws and the Court in its judgment will apply what it sees as the most appropriate solution. Many concepts undefined in the Treaties, such as "misuse of powers" (above, p. 160), and many other legal problems, have been clarified in this way; we have seen examples of the approach in the previous chapter (p. 337).

The principle of proportionality has also played an important part in the Court's approach to the treaty provisions on the free movement of goods (Articles 28 to 30 (ex Articles 30, 34 and 36) EC, which the Court has treated as imposing far-reaching prohibitions on national measures restricting trade between Member States (see above, p. 335). While such measures may be defended by the State on public policy grounds under Article 30 (ex Article 36), a defence of this kind is subject to the important proviso that the measures do not constitute, in the words of Article 30 (ex Article 36) EC, "a means of arbitrary discrimination or a disguised restriction on trade between Member States". In applying this proviso, the Court has used the principle of proportionality so as to declare State measures unlawful if other, less restrictive measures would achieve the same purpose.[11] Here the principle is parallel to the doctrine of the "less restrictive alternative" applied by American courts to assess the compatibility of State legislation with the United States Constitution: the question there too is whether the State interest, however legitimate, could be achieved by a measure less damaging to free trade than the one adopted[12] or, in simpler language – do not use a sledgehammer to crack a nut.

## 2. Freedom of Commercial Activity

The principle of proportionality in some situations appears to reflect a broader notion, still to be fully defined, that of freedom of

---

[11] See, *e.g.* Case 104/75 *de Peijper* [1976] ECR 613; [1976] 2 C.M.L.R. 271.
[12] See T. Sandalow and E. Stein, *Courts and Free Markets*, Vol. 1, p. 28.

commercial activity – a freedom which accords with the mercantil-
ist philosophy of the EC Treaty and is found entrenched in the
Federal German Constitution. Under this freedom we have
grouped, as well as the principle of proportionality: the freedom
to pursue a trade or profession, the freedom from unfair competition, and a general freedom to act as one wishes unless the law
prohibits the act in question.

All these four principles were invoked together in Cases
133-136/85 *Walter Rau v. BALM*[13] and Case 249/85 *ALBAKO v.
BALM*.[14] A scheme of "Free Butter for Free Berlin", a brainwave
of the Commission to help increase butter consumption and
thereby to reduce intervention stocks (the so called "butter
mountain") was introduced in the summer of 1985. For 10 weeks,
up to 900 tons of butter held in store were to be offered to West
Berliners on the basis of one free 250 gram block of butter for
each 250 gram block purchased. This scheme of two blocks of
butter for the price of one naturally outraged the manufacturers of
margarine, one of whom (Rau) challenged the Commission decision both by a direct action under Article 173 (now Article 230)
EC and in proceedings in the German courts against the German
intervention agency (BALM) charged with administering the
scheme. The Court of Justice adjudged that none of the four
principles above were infringed by the scheme – a not surprising
decision in view of the Court's earlier upholding of a cheap
"Christmas Butter" scheme in Cases 279, 280, 285 & 286/84
*Walter Rau v. EC*.[15]

## 3. NON-DISCRIMINATION

Several provisions of the EC Treaty, and many provisions of
Community legislation, prohibit specific forms of discrimination.
Article 6 EC prohibits discrimination on grounds of nationality
across the whole field of the Treaty; Article 34(2) (ex Article
40(3)) EC prohibits discrimination in relation to agriculture;
Article 141 (ex Article 119) EC contains the principle that men
and women should receive equal pay for equal work. However the
Court of Justice has taken the view that, beyond those specific
provisions, the guarantee of equal treatment or the prohibition of
discrimination, is a general principle of law which must be
observed in the whole field of Community law: see, for example,

---

[13] Case 133-136/85 *Walter Rau v. BALM* (1987) 12 E.L.Rev. 451.
[14] Case 249/85 *ALBAKO v. BALM* [1987] ECR 2354.
[15] Cases 279, 280, 285 and 286/84, *Walter Rau v. EC* [1987] ECR 1069; [1988] 2
  C.M.L.R. 704.

Case 1/72 *Frilli*[16]: the rule of equality of treatment "is one of the fundamental principles of Community law".

Similarly in one of the *Isoglucose* cases the Court held that the provisions of Council Regulation 1111/77 establishing the production levy system for isoglucose "offend against the general principle of equality of which the prohibition on discrimination set out in Article 40(3) (now Article 34(2)) of the Treaty is a specific expression": Joined Cases 103 & 145/77.[17]

A different form of discrimination was at issue in a staff case. Signora Sabbatini (*née* Bertoni) was employed by the European Parliament and benefited, under the Staff Regulations, from an expatriation allowance. On her marriage she lost this allowance since the Staff Regulations provided that an official should forfeit it if, on marriage, he did not become a head of household. Under the Regulations, a married man was classified *ipso facto* as a head of household, but a married female official was so treated only if her husband was unable to work being an invalid or seriously ill. Signora Sabbatini successfully contended that the Regulations were discriminatory on grounds of sex, and therefore contrary both to a general principle of law and to Article 119 (now Article 141) EC. Accepting her plea of illegality under Article 184 (now Article 241) EC (see above, p. 164), the Court held that the Regulations were unlawful and annulled the decision withdrawing the applicant's expatriation allowance.[18] In accordance, however, with the nature of the plea of illegality, the judgment only declared the offending Regulations to be inapplicable *inter partes*: consequently, other female officials could not rely on this judgment to bring their own claims out of time.[19] The offending Regulations were subsequently amended by the Council.

## 4. PROTECTION OF LEGITIMATE EXPECTATIONS

Another rather exceptional case concerned the annual review by the Council of staff salaries.[20] Here the Court held that the discretion which the Council enjoyed, under Article 65 of the Staff Regulations, in fixing those salaries was subject to the principle of

---

[16] Case 1/72 *Frilli v. Belgium* [1972] ECR 457 at 466.
[17] Joined Cases 103 and 145/77 *Royal Scholten-Hönig (Holdings) Ltd and Tunnel Refineries Ltd v. Intervention Board for Agricultural Produce* [1978] ECR 2037 at 2081; [1979] 1 C.M.L.R. 675.
[18] Case 20/71 *Sabbatini v. European Parliament* [1972] ECR 345; [1972] C.M.L.R. 945.
[19] See Case 15-33, etc., /73 *Schots-Kortner v. Council, Commission and Parliament* [1974] ECR 177, p. 198, above.
[20] Case 81/72 *Commission v. Council* [1973] ECR 575; [1973] C.M.L.R. 639.

protection of legitimate expectations so that the staff of the Community institutions were entitled to rely on the implementation of a system which the Council had adopted experimentally for a three-year period. When the Council departed from that system, after only nine months, in adopting a new Regulation on salaries, the Commission took the Council to court, and obtained the partial annulment of the Regulation, which was promptly replaced by a Regulation made in conformity with the new system (see above, p. 142).

The judgment illustrates effectively the technique of the Court in handling the general principles of law. Although such principles were considered extensively by Advocate General Warner with full references to national law, the principle of protection of confidence, which had not been considered by the advocate general or relied upon by the Commission, at least in that form, was adopted by the Court without reference to its origins and with only limited explicit justification.

The principle of protection of confidence applied in this case is related to a number of other general principles which have featured in the reports. This family includes the protection of legitimate expectations, the principle of non-retroactivity of legislation, legal certainty, and respect for acquired rights; these principles shade into one another, and the same case may raise one or more of them.[21] All these principles had their origin in the laws of the original Member States, particularly in German administrative law; for although the system of remedies contained in the Treaties was principally based on French administrative law, the German courts have been and remain by far the most active in referring cases to the Court of Justice, with consequent opportunities for the German lawyer to draw the Court's attention to the principles of his legal system.

The principle of legal certainty, in particular, is exemplified by the second paragraph of Article 231 (ex Article 174) EC, whereby the Court is empowered to declare definitive specified effects of a regulation which it has annulled in proceedings under Article 230 (ex Article 173) EC. The Court has exercised the like power, by analogy, when ruling on the invalidity of a regulation under Article 234 (ex Article 177) EC.[22]

---

[21] See, *e.g.* Case 62/70 *Bock v. Commission* [1971] ECR 897; [1972] C.M.L.R. 160; Case 74/74 *CNTA v. Commission* [1975] ECR 533, esp. at 556; [1977] 1 C.M.L.R. 171; Case 2/75 *Einführ-und Vorratsstelle für Getreide v. Mackprang* [1975] ECR 607, esp. at 622 *et seq.*; [1977] 1 C.M.L.R. 198, and Case 98/78 *Racke v. Hauptzollamt Mainz* [1979] ECR 69.

[22] See Case 4/79 *Providence Agricole de la Champagne v. ONIC* [1980] ECR 2823, Case 109/79 *Maïseries de Beauce v. ONIC* [1980] ECR 2883 and Case 145/79 *Roquette Frères v. French Customs Administration* [1980] ECR 2917 (See p. 235, above).

The protection of legitimate expectations has affinity with the common law doctrine of estoppel. The expression itself has now even been adopted, partly through the influence of this principle in Community law, as a ground for judicial review in English law.[23]

## 5. THE RIGHT TO BE HEARD

The enlargement of the Communities in 1973 left intact the general principles derived from the legal systems of the founding Member States, but enabled the Court to extend its sources to the laws of the new Member States, as happened again on the further enlargements in 1981, 1986 and 1994. English and Scottish decisions were cited by Advocate General Warner as early as March 1973, in the *Staff Salaries* case, and later cases contain frequent references to Danish, English, Irish, and Scots law, especially in the opinions of the first advocate general from the new Member States, Mr J-P. Warner, and of his British successors, Sir Gordon Slynn and Mr Francis Jacobs. Perhaps the best illustration is the *Transocean* case, in which Advocate General Warner invoked a close analogy in English law to the general principles of law, namely the rules of natural justice.[24]

Here the applicant Association had been exempted by the Commission from the provisions of Article 85 (now Article 81) of the EC Treaty, but the exemption was subject to certain conditions, one of which the applicant considered too onerous. The condition in question was a requirement that the members of the Association, who were medium-sized firms manufacturing ship paint, should inform the Commission without delay of any links between them and any other company or firm in the paint sector. The Association, which was a loosely-knit grouping designed to enable its members to compete with the big multinational manufacturers, brought an action before the Court to annul this single condition in the decision, which it considered would be difficult if not impossible to comply with. It contended that the requirement was not mentioned in the notice of objections which the Commission had sent it and that it was never given the opportunity of

---

[23] For suggestions as to the origin of this concept see *obiter dictum* of Lord Denning M.R. in *Schmidt v. Secretary of State for Home Affairs* [1969] 2 Ch. 149: see further Foulkes, *Administrative Law* (7th ed., 1990), pp. 272–277 ("Legitimate expectation"); also Lord Mackenzie Stuart *"Recent Developments in English Administrative Law* – The Impact of Europe?" in *Du droit international au droit de l'intégration: Liber Amicorum Pierre Pescatore* (eds Capotorti *et al.*) (1987), pp. 411–420.

[24] Case 17/74 *Transocean Marine Paint Association v. Commission* [1974] ECR 1063; [1974] 2 C.M.L.R. 459.

making its views known on the subject. It relied on Regulation 99/63 which governs the procedure before the Commission and maintained that the Commission, by not giving it an opportunity to make its views known, had not followed the proper procedure.

The difficulty with that argument was that Regulation 99/63[25] was not sufficiently detailed to provide for a hearing on the particular matter to which the applicant objected. However the Court is not limited to the arguments which the parties put before it; and the advocate general took the view that the procedure had infringed, not the terms of the Regulation, but one of the rules of natural justice, the principle *audi alteram partem*, which, he said, requires an administrative authority, before wielding statutory power to the detriment of a particular person, to hear what that person has to say about the matter, even if the statute does not expressly require it. Having reviewed the scope of the principle in the laws of the Member States, the advocate general concluded that "the right to be heard forms part of those rights which 'the law' referred to in Article 164 (now Article 220) of the Treaty upholds, and of which, accordingly, it is the duty of this Court to ensure the observance".

In its judgment the Court, while following the advocate general, stated the principle in even broader terms, referring to "the general rule that a person whose interests are perceptibly affected by a decision taken by a public authority must be given the opportunity to make his point of view known". It is doubtful, however, whether the principle is to be treated as going as far as this formulation suggests. It is characteristic of the Court's jurisprudential approach to lay down a principle in broad, even absolute terms, but to leave its application to be refined by subsequent developments in the case law.

The right to a fair hearing is a principle whose fundamental character has been stressed on numerous occasions in the case law of the Court. The right requires that the applicant must be informed in advance of the case he has to meet, and this requirement must be observed not only in proceedings which may result in the imposition of penalties but also in investigative proceedings prior to the adoption of anti-dumping regulations which, despite their general scope, may directly and individually affect the undertakings concerned and entail adverse consequences for them. The Court so held in *Al-Jubail*.[26]

---

[25] Regulation 99/63 J.O. 2268/63, August 20, 1963; Spec. Ed. 1963–4, p. 47.
[26] Case C–49/88 *Al-Jubail Fertilizer Co. v. Council* [1991] ECR I–3187; [1991] 3 C.M.L.R. 377.

# 6. Fundamental Rights

Some of the cases cited in the previous section have what might be called a "human rights flavour". The Court has accepted general principles of law which serve to protect the individual or undertaking from the administration. In some cases, such as the sex equality cases, the same result was secured by the use of general principles as might have been achieved by an express catalogue of fundamental rights written into the Treaties. But the Treaties contain no such bill of rights, despite suggestions that they should be amended to include one. And the Court over a period of years rejected appeals to the fundamental rights protected by national laws such as the German Basic Law.

In a series of early cases,[27] the Court refused to recognise fundamental rights as such. Perhaps its reaction is, with hindsight, explicable; the issue may have been presented to it in the wrong way. When an applicant sought to rely directly on a fundamental right protected by his own law, even by his national constitution, the Court reacted by re-asserting the supremacy of Community law over the laws, even the constitutional laws, of the Member States. The development of Community law has often naturally responded to the way in which a question has been put to it, whether by an applicant in a direct action or by a court of a Member State on a reference.

So it was only when an administrative judge in Stuttgart asked the Court whether a particular requirement was compatible, not with the fundamental rights of national law, but with "the general principles of Community law", that the Court expressly included the protection of fundamental rights within those principles. The case, mentioned above, p. 327, arose out of an attempt by the Commission to reduce the Community "butter mountain". A decision of the Commission authorised Member States to sell butter at a reduced price to persons receiving social assistance. To ensure that the cheap butter reached only those persons for whom it was intended, provision was made in the decision for them to be issued with coupons. The wording of that provision was not precisely the same in all the official language versions, and led to doubts as to whether the beneficiary was required to disclose his name to the shop assistant. As implemented by the German authorities, he was required to do so, and one such beneficiary, Erich Stauder, challenged that requirement.

The Court interpreted the provision on the basis of all the language versions and having regard to its purpose, and held that it

---

[27] Notably Case 1/58 *Stork v. High Authority* [1959] ECR 17, Joined Cases 36–38, and 40/59 *Geitling v. High Authority* [1960] ECR 423 and Case 40/64 *Sgarlata and Others v. Commission* [1965] ECR 215; [1966] C.M.L.R. 314.

did not require – although it did not prohibit – the identification of beneficiaries by name. Then the Court ruled that, so interpreted, that provision contained nothing capable of prejudicing "the fundamental human rights enshrined in the general principles of Community law and protected by the Court".[28]

Two linguistic comments must be made on this formula which recognises for the first time the principle of protection of fundamental rights under Community law. First, the expression "general principles of Community law" – the term used by the Stuttgart court – must be taken as shorthand for the general principles of law recognised in the Community legal order. The term "general principles of law" was the preferred term used in subsequent decisions; but see now the endorsement of the expression "general principles of Community law" in the Maastricht Treaty (p. 2, above). Secondly, the original French text of the judgment refers to *"les principes généraux du droit communautaire dont la Cour assure le respect"*. These words repeat the formulation of Article 164 (now Article 220) EC requiring the Court to ensure that in the interpretation and application of the Treaty the law is observed. They show that the general principles, including fundamental rights, are part of "the law" referred to in Article 164 – a point which is lost in the English version of the judgment.

The recognition of fundamental rights was taken a step further in the *Internationale Handelsgesellschaft* case.[29] What was stated elliptically, almost parenthetically, in *Stauder v. Ulm* (that the general principles of law include the protection of fundamental rights) is here put into the forefront of the judgment. This was understandable, since the Court was here faced with a direct challenge by the German courts to the supremacy of Community law. The Frankfurt administrative court had already held certain provisions of Community law, relating to the system of agricultural export licences and the deposits attached to them, to be invalid as contrary to fundamental rights protected by the German Basic Law. A German company had forfeited a deposit equivalent to about £3,000 for not using export licences for ground maize which it had been granted. On a reference from the Frankfurt court, the Court again refused to look at German constitutional law but asked instead whether there was any analogous guarantee of fundamental rights in Community law. It held that there was. The respect for such rights formed part of the general principles of law. But, having examined the provisions in question, the Court ruled that those rights had not been infringed.

---

[28] Case 29/69 *Stauder v. Ulm* [1969] ECR 419 at 425; [1970] C.M.L.R. 112.
[29] Case 11/70 *Internationale Handelsgesellschaft v. Einführ-und Vorratsstelle Getreide* [1970] ECR 1125; [1972] C.M.L.R. 255.

The sequel is well known. The Frankfurt court, not content with this reply, referred the case to the German Federal Constitutional Court and asked whether the Community provisions were compatible with the German Basic Law. The Second Chamber of the Constitutional Court agreed with the Court of Justice on the substance. But the important question was whether the reference was admissible. Could the German courts pronounce, after a ruling of the Court of Justice, on the validity of Community law? The Constitutional Court ruled, by a five to three majority, that the German courts could. So long as Community law contained no catalogue of fundamental rights, passed by a Parliament and equivalent to the catalogue of rights contained in the Basic Law, the German courts remained competent to examine whether the acts of German authorities, although done under Community law, were compatible with the Basic Law.

The judgment of the Federal Constitutional Court was much criticised, not least by the dissenting minority in that very Court, then was qualified by a second judgment[30] and was finally over-ruled, in effect, by the same Court in *Wünsche Handel-gesellschaft*.[31] But the challenge to the supremacy of Community law at least had the merit of reinforcing concern at the Community level for the protection of fundamental rights. The Court of Justice had already gone somewhat further. After the Council of Europe's European Convention on Human Rights had finally been ratified by all the Member States, it accepted, in the second *Nold* case, that the European Convention, and also more generally "international treaties for the protection of human rights on which the Member States have collaborated or of which they are signatories, can supply guidelines which should be followed within the framework of Community law".[32]

Subsequently, in its judgment in the *Rutili* case,[33] the Court took further the applicability of the European Convention. Rutili was an Italian national resident in France whose trade union and political activities had incurred the disapproval of the French authorities. His residence permit was subjected to a restriction prohibiting him from residing in certain parts of France. On a reference from the administrative court of Paris, before which he had challenged that restriction, the Court of Justice considered the limitations imposed by Community law on the powers of Member States in respect of the control of aliens, in particular under

---

[30] See Steinike und Weinlig [1980] 2 C.M.L.R. 531.
[31] [1987] 3 C.M.L.R. 225.
[32] Case 4/73 *Nold v. Commission* [1974] ECR 491 at 507; [1974] 2 C.M.L.R. 338.
[33] Case 36/75 *Rutili v. Minister for the Interior* [1975] ECR 1219; [1976] 1 C.M.L.R. 140.

Council Directive 64/221 and Regulation 1612/68. It held that these limitations were "a specific manifestation of the more general principle", enshrined in the European Convention, to the effect that (in the words of the Convention) "no restrictions in the interests of national security or public safety shall be placed on the rights secured by Articles 8, 9, 10 and 11 of the Convention other than such as are necessary for the protection of those interests in a democratic society".

Here the Court appeared to come close to giving direct effect to the Convention, but in Case 118/75 *Watson and Belmann*,[34] Advocate General Trabucchi considered that the *Rutili* judgment "did not involve any substantive reference to the [Convention] provisions themselves, but merely a reference to the general principles of law of which, like the Community rules with which the judgment drew an analogy, they are a specific expression".

A further development in the Court's approach can be seen in the *Hauer* case.[35] A Council regulation prohibiting the new planting of vines was in issue. The German administrative court, putting questions on the interpretation of the regulation to the Court of Justice, had suggested that the regulation might not be applicable in Germany as being incompatible with fundamental rights protected by the German Basic Law, including the right of property. The Court of Justice sought to dispel those doubts by not merely repeating its earlier references to "general principles", but citing specific provisions of the Basic Law and of the Irish and Italian Constitutions, as well as the European Convention on Human Rights, in order to show that the right of property was subject to limitations in the public interest and that the regulation in issue did not go beyond the limitations generally allowed. It has been suggested[36] that the unusual course taken by the Court, in referring expressly to provisions of national law, may be explained as an attempt to reassure those courts "which fear that their fundamental principles are threatened by the primacy of Community law, that in practice these principles are taken into account at the Community level".

Where the legislation of a Member State lies, as the Court of Justice held, outside the scope of Community law, then the question of the compatibility of that legislation with the European Convention is not a matter within the jurisdiction of the Court.[37]

---

[34] Case 118/75 *Watson and Belmann* [1976] ECR 1185; [1976] 2 C.M.L.R. 552.
[35] Case 44/79 *Hauer v. Land Rheinland-Pfalz* [1979] ECR 3727; [1980] 3 C.M.L.R.
[36] By J. A. Usher (1980) 5 E.L. Rev. 209.
[37] So held by a *Grand Plenum* of 13 judges in Case C–159/90 *The Society for the Protection of Unborn Children Ireland Ltd v. Grogan and others* [1991] ECR I–4685; [1991] 3 C.M.L.R. 849.

From the point of view of the general principles of law, the recent judgments of the Court dealing with fundamental rights are of particular interest as showing the sources on which the Court will rely. In the *Internationale Handelsgesellschaft* case the Court refers to "the constitutional traditions common to the Member States" – a very wide term. In the *Nold* and *Rutili* cases it goes further and refers to international treaties as a source of such general principles. In the *Hauer* case it cites specific provisions of national constitutions, a practice hitherto avoided.

Article 8 of the European Convention was referred to by the Court in two cases subsequent to *Hauer*. In *National Panasonic*[38] it had to consider the investigative powers of the Commission in the light of the guarantee in Article 8 of respect for private and family life, but it held that the powers fell within an exception to that guarantee. And in *Dow Benelux*[39] the Court confirmed that Article 8 served in Community law to protect the private dwelling of natural persons rather than the premises of undertakings[40]; yet in exercising its investigative powers the Commission must observe the principle of proportionality.

Article 7 of the European Convention, which prohibits retroactivity of penal provisions, was held by the Court in *Kirk* to prevent a Community regulation from validating retrospectively a fine imposed by a British court for a fisheries infringement which was not punishable at the time it was committed. The Court declared that the principle against retroactivity of penal provisions, common to all the legal orders of the Member States and enshrined in Article 7 as a fundamental right, "take its place among the general principles of law whose observance is ensured by the Court of Justice".[41]

Despite the efforts which the Court had made to develop its case law, debate continued on whether the case law approach provides sufficient protection on this sensitive issue, or whether, as the Federal Constitutional Court suggested in the *Internationale Handelsgesellschaft* case, an enacted catalogue of fundamental rights was required (see below, p. 362.) The European Parliament, the Council and the Commission appeared to endorse the approach of the Court of Justice when they adopted, on April 5, 1977, a joint declaration in which they underline the paramount

---

[38] Case 136/79 *National Panasonic v. Commission* [1980] ECR 2033; [1980] 3 C.M.L.R. 169.

[39] Case 85/87 *Dow Benelux v. Commission* [1989] ECR 3137; [1991] 4 C.M.L.R. 410.

[40] But see now the judgment of December 16, 1992 of the European Court of Human Rights in *Niemietz v. Germany* (72/1991/324/396).

[41] Case 63/83 *Regina v. Kirk* [1984] ECR 2689; [1984] 3 C.M.L.R. 522.

importance which they attach to the respect for fundamental rights and especially those derived from the constitutions of the Member States, and from the European Convention on Human Rights, and declare that, in the exercise of their powers and in pursuance of the objectives of the European Communities, they respect and will continue to respect those rights.[42] This commitment was endorsed by the Heads of State and Government at the European Council of April 1978.

As we have seen (above, p. 359), by 1986 the German Federal Constitutional Court was sufficiently reassured by the developments just outlined to overrule its previous decision in the *Internationale Handelsgesellschaft* case: the German court accepted that fundamental rights were now sufficiently protected in Community law despite the absence still of any enacted catalogue.[43]

The Commission, in the past, has advocated the adoption of a Community Bill of Rights,[44] but, in recognition of the difficulties inherent in such a proposal, has suggested that, as a first step, the Community should itself accede to the European Convention on Human Rights.[45] But accession too raises a number of legal, political and institutional problems[46] and the question of the place of human rights in the Community legal order is far from resolved.

The view, however, of the European Parliament is clear. In April 1989 it adopted its own catalogue of fundamental rights which, while having no legal force, sets out the Parliament's view of those rights deserving of special protection in the European Community. The Parliament was also instrumental in securing endorsement of fundamental rights in the Preamble to the Single European Act of 1986 and again in Article 6 (ex Article F) of the Treaty on European Union signed at Maastricht in February 1992. Article 6 states:

> "The Union shall respect fundamental rights, as guaranteed by the European Convention for the Protection of Human Rights and Fundamental Freedoms signed in Rome on 4 November 1950 and as they result from the constitutional

---

[42] [1977] O.J. C103/103.

[43] See Case 126/81 *Wünsche Handelsgesellschaft v. Germany* [1982] ECR 1479; [1987] 3 C.M.L.R. 225, p. 359, above.

[44] See *The Protection of Fundamental Rights in the European Community*, Bulletin of the EC, Supplement 5/76.

[45] Bulletin of the EC, Supplement 2/79. See further Chap. 17 below, pp. 397 *et seq.*

[46] See House of Lords Select Committee on the European Communities, Session 1979/80, 71st Report, "Human Rights"; and J. McBride and L. N. Brown *Yearbook of European Law* (1981), p. 167. The compatibility of such accession with the Community Treaties has now been denied by the Court which was asked by the Council for its Opinion on the question pursuant to Art. 228(6) EC (see Chap. 11, above, p. 259, *Opinion 2/94* [1996] ECR I–1195).

traditions common to the Member States, as general principles of Community law."

The Maastricht Treaty makes no further reference to general principles of law but does introduce and define a principle (or doctrine) of subsidiarity: see Article 5 (ex Article 3b) TEU, set out above.

In its *Opinion 2/94*[47] the Court of Justice warned that accession by the Community to the European Convention would be impossible without Treaty amendment. However, the Amsterdam Treaty contains no provision to facilitate such accession. By contrast, the United Kingdom, under its New Labour Government, has fulfilled its commitment to incorporate the Convention into its national law.[48]

## 7. Effective National Remedies to Uphold Community Rights

The general principles discussed under the previous six headings have all drawn their inspiration from the legal systems or constitutional traditions of the Member States. In recent years, however, one may observe the reverse process taking place, whereby a reciprocal obligation, as it were, is imposed upon the courts of the Member States by the Community legal order.

For in its recent case law the Court of Justice has been much concerned to ensure that where a person claims a Community right they should be guaranteed an effective remedy to uphold that right in the courts of a Member State: *ubi remedium ibi jus*. For the doctrine of direct effect in itself only bestows the Community right upon the individual: it does not spell out how that right is to be enforced. Moreover, Community rights may arise outwith the doctrine of direct effect, as in *Francovich*.[49]

This is a delicate area at the interface between the Community legal order and the national legal orders. It touches the tender quick of national judicial independence and, at a deeper level, the issue of national sovereignty.

---

[47] *Opinion 2/94* of the Court of March 28, 1996 an Accession by the Community to the European Convention for the Protection of Human Rights and Fundamental Freedoms [1996] ECR I–1195.

[48] At the Cologne Council in June 1997 the Council set up a body ("the Convention") to draft a Charter of Fundamental Rights for the European Union, for submission to the European Council at Nice in December 2000. The Council's proposal has been criticised as pretentious, vague and confusing: see Editorial (2000) 25 E.L.Rev. 97 (White).

[49] Joined Cases C–6/90 *Francovich and Another v. Italian Republic* [1991] ECR I–5357; [1993] 2 C.M.L.R. 66.

The problem became more pressing after the SEA set as its goal the completion of the internal market by 1993. The hundreds of Community measures, especially directives, needed to help meet this deadline could not be allowed to be frustrated by inadequate or unequal enforcement at the national level. Article 10 (ex Article 5) EC is a constant reminder to Member States of their duty to facilitate the achievement of the Community's tasks.

In Case 68/88 *Commission v. Hellenic Republic*[50] Greece was told by the Court in no uncertain terms that it should have applied criminal or other disciplinary sanctions to deal with a massive fraud involving the cereals market. The Court, while leaving the Member State discretion to choose enforcement measures which it considered appropriate, stated the principle that infringements of Community law should be punished under substantive and procedural rules analogous to those applicable to infringements of national law of similar gravity, and which, in any event, make the penalty "effective, proportionate and dissuasive". In brief, remedies to enforce Community rights should match those to enforce national rights.

National remedies must above all be effective. Thus, in Case C–213/89 *Factortame I*[51] this meant the British court being empowered by Community law to provide a remedy which it was unable to give in a purely domestic case: in *Factortame* an interim injunction was issued against the Crown to suspend a statute which appeared *prima facie* to deprive certain companies of their rights under Community law, thereby causing them irreparable harm. By this case was established the principle that national courts must ensure provisional protection of putative Community rights.

Then, in Joined Cases C–143/88 & C–92/89 *Zuckerfabrik Süderdithmarschen*[52] the Court ruled that, where a national judge orders the provisional suspension of a domestic measure as based on a possibly invalid Community act, he is obliged to refer such act to the Court for a ruling on its validity.

Finally, in *Francovich* the principle of effectiveness (in French "*effet utile*") was invoked to justify imposing on Italy a duty to provide a remedy in damages to make good loss sustained by

---

[50] Case 68/88 *Commission v. Hellenic Republic* [1989] ECR 2965; [1991] 1 C.M.L.R. 817, a unique example of a judgment by default given against a Member State in accordance with Art. 94 of the Court of Justice Rules (see para. 9 of the judgment at p. 2982).

[51] Case C–213/89 *The Queen, ex p. Factortame Ltd and Others v. Secretary of State for Transport* [1990] ECR I–2433; [1990] 3 C.M.L.R. 1.

[52] Joined Cases C–143/88 and C–92/89 *Zuckerfabrik Suderdithmarschen AG v. Hauptzollamt Itzehoe and Zuckerfabrik Soest v. Hauptzollamt Paderborn* [1991] ECR I–415; [1993] 3 C.M.L.R. 1.

employees of two Italian firms as a result of the non-implementation of a directive, a failure for which Italy had already been held guilty in an enforcement action under Article 169 EC. The extent of this duty of reparation (to adopt the Scots term) has now been defined in subsequent cases, notably Joined Cases C–46 & 48/93 *Brasserie du Pêcheur* and *Factortame III*, Case C–5/94 *Hedley Lomas*, Case C–392/93 *R. v. British Telecommunications plc* and Joined Cases C–178, 179, 188 & 190/94 *Dillenkofer and Others*.[53]

The State's duty of reparation has been given wide scope so as to encompass any breach of Community law conferring rights on individuals; the rights have to be clear, and there must be a causal link between the breach by the State and the loss sustained by the individual. Nevertheless, not every infringement of Community law affecting an individual should give an automatic entitlement to damages. To found an action for damages the infringement must be "manifest and serious". The Court has made clear that State liability may arise from national legislation contrary to Community law, that is, it is not confined to administrative action. An infringement will be sufficiently serious where the State has manifestly and gravely disregarded the limits on its discretion. Given a manifest and serious breach, no finding of fault is required: the liability is strict, no-fault liability. The damages awarded must amount to full compensation including, where appropriate, loss of profit, and may extend to exemplary damages where the latter are payable for a comparable breach of the State's domestic law.

This represents a major advance in the Court's case law, prompted by the policy aim of ensuring equal compliance by all Member States with their Community obligations – a policy seen also in Article 228 (ex Article 171) EC to allow the imposition of penalty payments for non-compliance with the Court's judgments. The case law is also in the spirit of the Declaration on the Implementation of Community law, in the Final Act annexed to the Maastricht Treaty, which declares (*inter alia*) that:

> "it is essential for the proper functioning of the Community that the measures taken by the different Member States should result in Community law being applied with the same effectiveness and vigour as in the application of their national law."

---

[53] Joined C46/93 and C48/93 *Brasserie du Pêcheur* and *Factortame III* [1996] ECR I–1029; Case C–5/94 *Hedley Lomas* [1996] ECR I–2553; Case C–392/93 *R. v. British Telecommunications plc* [1996] ECR I–1631; Joined Cases C–178/94, 179/94, 188/94, 189/94 and 190/94 *Dillenkofer and Others* [1996] ECR I–4845.

Although treated here as another general principle of Community law, the principle of State liability for breach of Community law is of such amplitude and importance as to justify its being categorised, as we indicated in the introduction to this chapter, as a fundamental doctrine of Community law to be set alongside the doctrines of direct applicability, direct effect and supremacy of that law.

The spirit of the Declaration on the implementation of Community law had been anticipated in a long series of judgments of the Court of Justice. The Court's basic approach was formulated in *Rewe* back in 1976.[54] The Court there acknowledged the procedural autonomy of Member States to determine the conditions governing legal actions to uphold Community rights in a national court, but such autonomy is subject to the important proviso that such conditions cannot be less favourable than those relating to similar actions in respect of rights under national law. Specifically, the Court will adjudge inapplicable as contrary to Community law any national rules making it virtually impossible or excessively difficult to exercise Community rights.

In Joined Cases C–430 & 431/93 *van Schijndel*, the question arose whether a Dutch procedural rule precluding a Dutch court from considering of its own motion a point of Community law, which had not been raised timeously by the parties, was itself compatible with Community law. The Court of Justice agreed with Advocate General Jacobs that, while in general Community law did not require national courts to abandon their traditionally passive role in civil litigation nor to go beyond the ambit of the dispute as defined by the parties, yet in proceedings concerning civil rights protected by the EC Treaty the national judge should apply the Treaty provisions even though not relied on by a party, but only where the national judge would be required to apply of his own motion a corresponding provision of national law. On this basis, in *van Schijndel* the Court adjudged the Dutch rule of procedure to be compatible with Community law.

In some areas, specific Community legislation has intervened in relation to national remedies. An early example is Directive 69/221 where adoption by a Member State of a restriction on a worker's free movement on the ground of public policy has been

---

[54] Joined Cases C–430 & 431/93 *van Schijndel* and *van Veen* [1995] ECR I–4705; [1996] 1 C.M.L.R. 801, discussed by C.M.G. Himsworth (1997) 22 E.L.Rev. 291, at pp. 296–301; contrast Case C–312/93 *Peterbroeck v. Van Campenhout SCS & Cie* [1995] ECR I–4599; [1996] 1 C.M.L.R. 793, where the Court differed from its advocate general in holding the national rule to be contrary to Community law. See generally F. Jacobs "Enforcing Community Rights & Obligations in National Courts" in J. Lonbay & A. Biondi (eds.) *Remedies for Breach of EC Law* (Wiley, 1996) 25.

made subject to a procedure of prior consultation with an independent authority. In recent years the field of public procurement has become of such importance that a special regime of remedies at both the national and the Community levels has been provided in 1980 by two Council directives.

Generally, however, where no specific Community legislation applies, it is the Court of Justice which has filled the gap with an expanding framework of general principles governing national remedies. As well as the principles derived from the cases discussed above, mention may be made of:

(a) the right to effective judicial protection[55];
(b) the right to non-discrimination by reason of nationality[56];
(c) the right to a fair hearing[57];
(d) the remedy must be proportionate and adequate[58]; and
(e) the prohibition of procedural conditions which make virtually impossible the repayment of national charges levied contrary to Community law.[59]

These developments in the Court's case law, complemented by Community legislation, are helping ensure effective protection of Community rights in the courts of the Member States.

---

[55] Case 224/84 *Johnston v. Royal Ulster Constabulary* [1986] ECR 1451, Case 222/86 *UNECTEF v. Heylens* [1987] ECR 4097.
[56] Case 98/79 *Pecastaing v. Belgium* [1980] ECR 691; [1980] 3 C.M.L.R. 685.
[57] Case C–49/88 *Al-Jubail Fertilizer Company v. Council* [1991] ECR I–3187.
[58] Case 157/89 *R. v. Pieck* [1980] 2171; Case C–271/91 *Marshall v. Southampton & South West Hampshire Area Health Authority (No. 2)* [1993] ECR 1.
[59] Case 199/82 *Amministrazione delle Finanze dello Stato v. San Giorgio* [1983] ECR 3595; *cf.* Case C–208/90 *Emmott v. Minister for Social Welfare and the Attorney General* [1991] ECR I–4269; [1991] 3 C.M.L.R. 894.

# Chapter Sixteen

# Precedent

It is a fundamental principle of the administration of justice that like cases should be decided alike. Inconsistency in judicial decisions affronts even the most elementary sense of justice. In this sense the principle of *stare decisis*, of abiding by previous decisions, figures prominently in most legal systems, including those of all the Member States of the Communities. In England, whose law, at least in some important areas, is still based largely on case law, the principle of *stare decisis* has been elaborated and extended into a complex doctrine of precedent, to which whole books have been devoted.[1] Strict rules have developed, based on the practice of the courts, as to the circumstances in which one court must follow its own decision, or the decision of another court, in a previous case. Much depends on the respective positions of the courts within the hierarchy of the legal system. According to Professor Cross's "preliminary statement" of the English doctrine of precedent (*op. cit.* p. 7), every court is bound to follow any case decided by a court above it in the hierarchy, and appellate courts (except, since 1966, the House of Lords) are bound by their own previous decisions. But a decision of the High Court, for example, is a persuasive precedent, although not of course binding, even for courts above it in the hierarchy.

In France, at any rate in theory, such a doctrine of precedent has no place; indeed, it is expressly prohibited by Article 5 of the Civil Code. In France, as in other countries sharing the civil law tradition, the predominant view is that judicial decisions are not a formal source of law at all. The reasons for this contrast between England and France throw much light not only on the law and constitution, but also on the politics and history of the two countries.[2] Here it must suffice to note that the French judge does

---

[1] *e.g.* Rupert Cross, *Precedent in English Law* (3rd ed., 1977).
[2] See Kahn-Freund, Levy and Rudden, *A Source-book on French Law* (3rd ed., 1991), Pt. I; also Bell, Boyron & Whittaker, *Principles of French Law* (1998), Ch. 1, "Sources of Law".

not regard himself as bound by a single decision of any court; instead, he tries, with the aid of the writings of legal scholars ("*la doctrine*"), to discern the general trend of decisions on a particular point. Unlike the common law judge he does not feel compelled to analyse or to reconcile earlier judgments, or to explain his own judgments in those terms.

A former member of the Court, Judge Koopmans, has well observed that "although the Court's way of formulating principles, or general propositions of law, is closely akin to methods used by the French *Conseil d'Etat*, its techniques of relying on previous cases, of invoking the authority of its own case law and of determining the *ratio decidendi* of earlier judgments are not dissimilar to those used by the English common law courts".[3]

Judicial decisions are of great importance in Community law, where many fundamental doctrines, as well as much of the elaboration of the texts, are the creation of the Court. However, it is a feature of the Community legal system that Community law is applied not only by the Court of Justice and the Court of First Instance but also by the courts of the Member States, although it can only be authoritatively interpreted by the Court of Justice. Accordingly this chapter is divided into three parts: the first two consider precedent in the Court of Justice and the Court of First Instance respectively, while the third considers precedent in the national courts.

## A. Precedent in the Court of Justice

The Court's decisions are of course authoritative. But what does this mean? Certainly the English rules for ascertaining the principle upon which the case was decided, the *ratio decidendi*, have no automatic application to the Court's judgments. These judgments, as has already been remarked, have been strongly influenced by the model of the higher French courts. They are abstract and syllogistic, rather than concrete and discursive like the typical English or Scottish judgment: Judge Pescatore speaks of their "lapidary serenity". From the earliest days, the Court has referred to its previous case law: the first example can be found in the very first volume of its reports.[4] Although they frequently refer

---

[3] T. Koopmans, "Stare decisis in European Law", in *Essays in European Law and Integration* (ed. D. O'Keeffe and H. Schermers) (Kluwer, 1982), p. 27.

[4] Case 4/52 *ISA v. High Authority* [1954–56] ECR 91, referred to by Koopmans, *ibid.*, 17.

to previous decisions which they are following, they rarely allude to any earlier decisions from which they may be departing.[5]

Their character has a decisive impact on the question of precedent. First, it means that the judgments often start from broad propositions of law which may not be intended to be taken at face value, in absolute terms, but rather to be refined by subsequent decisions. If taken literally, these propositions are sometimes strikingly broad: we have seen an example in the general principle stated in the *Transocean* case.[6] Secondly, judgments of this kind do not easily lend themselves to the characteristic technique of distinguishing earlier judgments in the way of an English lawyer. But in Case 112/76[7] Advocate General Warner did use the language of *stare decisis* and *ratio decidendi* in his opinion.

Like any other court, the Court prefers to follow its own previous decisions. Thus the Court frequently introduces a statement of the law with the phrase "it is well established case law that . . ." or "as the Court has consistently held . . ." (in French "*il est de jurisprudence constante . . .*"). For example, in *Matisa*,[8] it cited its previous decision (Case 14/70 *Bakels*)[9] on the authority of the Brussels Nomenclature in interpreting the Common Customs Tariff and continued: "Since there is nothing in the present case capable of leading to a different conclusion, it is proper to reply to the same effect". And in the *Import Gadgets*[10] case the Court followed, but without citing, both the earlier cases on this point.

The Court of Justice has not hesitated however to depart from its own previous decisions where it thought it necessary. Such departures may take different forms. Sometimes it is a matter of developing a particular doctrine, such as the doctrine of the direct effect of provisions of Community law. Here the Court started from rather narrow criteria in deciding whether a Treaty provision had direct effect, as in Case 26/62 *Van Gend en Loos* (above, p. 219). Subsequently it has taken a progressively broader view of the circumstances in which the Treaty has direct effect in cases such as the second *Defrenne* case (above, p. 241); and the doctrine was extended to directives in cases such as *Van Duyn* (above, p. 326)

---

[5] For such explicit overruling of a previous decision, see Case C–10/89 *CNL Sucal SA v. Hag GF A.G.* [1990] ECR I–3711; [1990] 3 C.M.L.R. 571, and the judgment of November 24, 1993 in Joined Cases C–267 and C–268/91 *Keck and Mithouard* [1993] ECR I–6097.

[6] Above, p. 355.

[7] Case 112/76 *Manzoni v. FNROM* [1977] ECR 1647 at 1662; [1978] 2 C.M.L.R. 416.

[8] Case 35/75 *Matisa v. Hauptzollamt Berlin Packhof* [1975] ECR 1205 at 1210.

[9] Case 14/70 *Bakels v. Oberfinanzdirektion München* [1970] ECR 1001; [1971] C.M.L.R. 188.

[10] Case 22/76, *Import Gadgets, S.à.r.l., Paris v. L.A.M.P. S.p.A.* [1976] ECR 1371.

and *Becker* (above, p. 57). In this way the Court has been able to give direct effect to a far wider range of Community provisions than would have been possible if the narrower criteria had been retained. At other times the Court has appeared to overrule directly, if not explicitly, an earlier decision. An example of the Court changing its mind was on the question whether an act had to be annulled before a claim for damages for the injury caused by that act could be successful. As we have already seen (p. 182, above), the Court's original view was that prior annulment was a condition precedent to the action for damages. This was so decided in Case 25/62,[11] which discouraged for several years the bringing of such actions. Then, in *Lütticke*,[12] the Court adopted the view that the action for damages was established by the EC Treaty as an independent form of action and could, in consequence, be brought in respect of an act that had not already been annulled. After a return to the *Plaumann* approach in Case 96/71 *Haegeman*,[13] the Court finally confirmed the *Lütticke* view in Case 43/72 *Merkur*.[14] The *Hag II* case[15] is a recent example of explicit overruling, the Court making clear its abandonment of the heavily criticised doctrine of common origin laid down in *Hag I*. More recently still, in *Keck*[16] the Court, qualifying its case law on the free movement of goods, gave as its reason for its departure from previous authority "the increasing tendency of traders to invoke Article 30 as a means of challenging any rules whose effect is to limit their commercial freedom". It then categorically stated that "contrary to what has previously been decided", the application to products from other Member States of national provisions restricting or prohibiting certain selling arrangements (such as type of shop, shop hours and various promotion techniques), was not such as to hinder trade between Member States within the meaning of the *Dassonville* principle,[17] provided that they applied to all affected traders operating in the State concerned and that they affected equally the marketing of domestic products and those from other Member States. A still more forthright rejection of an earlier decision as confined to its facts and not to be followed occurred in Case C–308/93 *Cabanis-Issarte*, a social security

---

[11] Case 25/62 *Plaumann v. Commission* [1963] ECR 95; [1964] C.M.L.R. 29.

[12] Case 4/69 *Lutticke v. Commission* [1971] ECR 325.

[13] Case 96/71 *Haegemann v. Commission* [1972] ECR 1005; [1973] C.M.L.R. 365.

[14] Case 43/72 *Merkur v. Commission* [1973] ECR 1055.

[15] Above, n. 5: *Hag* II overruling *Hag I* (Case 192/73 *Van Zuylen v. HAG* [1974] ECR 731).

[16] Judgment of November 24, 1993 in joined Cases C–267 and C–268/91 *Keck and Mithouard* [1993] ECR I–6097, *The Times*, November 25, 1993.

[17] Case 8/74 *Dassonville v. Commission* [1974] ECR 837; [1974] 2 C.M.L.R. 494.

decision which overruled Case 40/76 *Kermaschek v. Bundesanstalt für Arbeit*.[18]

The Court has thus shown that it does not regard itself as bound by its previous decisions. Although the English lawyers may find it strange that the Court should not always expressly recognise that it is departing from precedent let alone give no reasons for doing so, the fact that it should have this freedom can be readily understood. A final court can only be bound by its previous decisions if the law established by those decisions can, in the last resort, be amended by legislation. Since reversal of the decisions of the Court of Justice could be affected only by an amendment of the Treaties, in effect a practical impossibility, it is inevitable that it should be flexible in its approach to precedent. Like a constitutional court, its freedom can be explained by the finality of its decisions. But such departures from precedent are very much the exception. Difficulties do arise, however, where the Court does not make clear whether it is reversing itself.[19]

The problem arises in a different form in decisions of the Chambers. The Chambers may disagree *inter se* on a question of law, so that, again very exceptionally, there are conflicting precedents. This has occasionally happened in staff cases,[20] but in future the wider use of a Chamber as the normal organ of judgment (see p. 40, above) will increase the danger of conflicting precedents unless care is taken to channel difficult cases to the full Court. Experience in other divided courts shows that it is often difficult to foresee such a potential conflict; fortunately, the Rules (Article 95(4)) permit a Chamber at any time to refer to the Court a case assigned to it.

As we saw when discussing preliminary rulings in Chapter 10 (pp. 233–234, above), the Court's flexible attitude to precedent applies no less to its preliminary rulings, where it has made clear its general readiness to accept a new reference on a point which it has already determined: the Court acknowledges that it may

---

[18] Case 308/93 *Cabanis-Issarte* [1996] 2 C.M.L.R. 729; Case 40/76 *Kermaschek v. Bundesanstalt fur Arbeit* [1976] ECR 1669.

[19] *e.g.* Joined Cases 115 & 116/81 *Adouai and Cornuaille v. Belgium* [1982] ECR 1665; [1982] 3 C.M.L.R. 631, in relation to Case 41/74 *Van Duyn v. Home Office* [1974] ECR 1337; [1975] 1 C.M.L.R. 1; Case 104/79 *Foglia v. Novello (No. 1)* [1980] ECR 745; [1981] 1 C.M.L.R. 45 in relation to Case 244/80 *Foglia v. Novello (No. 2)* [1981] ECR 3045; [1982] 1 C.M.L.R. 585 (see p. 215, above); Case 121/85 *Conegate v. H.M. Customs & Excise* [1986] ECR 1007; [1986] 1 C.M.L.R. 739 in relation to Case 34/79 *R. v. Henn & Darby* [1979] ECR 3795; [1980] 1 C.M.L.R. 246: see the subsequent struggle of the Divisional Court in *Noncyp* [1988] 3 C.M.L.R. 84.

[20] See for example Case 266/83 *Samara v. Commission* [1985] ECR 189 and Case 273/83 *Michel v. Commission* [1985] ECR 347.

sometimes be persuaded by counsel or by the advocate general to think differently today from what it thought yesterday.

On the other hand, where the validity of a Community act has been upheld by a preliminary ruling, a national court is not then entitled, in a subsequent case, to suspend a national measure adopted to give effect to that act: Case C–465/95 *Atlanta Fruchthandelsgesellschaft II*.[21]

So far we have considered the authority of judgments of the Court and of the Chambers. A separate question is that of the authority of opinions of the advocates general. These may be, and frequently are, cited in subsequent cases, both by counsel and by advocates general themselves but not by the Court. In this context four separate situations must be considered.

First, they may be the only authority available on a particular point: this will be the case if the judgment has not dealt with a point on which the advocate general has expressed a view. Since the opinions are often more wide-ranging than the judgments, this situation arises very frequently; there are many unsettled areas of Community law where only the dicta of the advocate general can be cited as directly in point. Such dicta might be compared with the statements of a single judge in the English Court of Appeal on an issue on which the other judges have not pronounced.

Secondly, the Court may have dealt with the point considered by the advocate general, but have differed from him. Should one then treat the opinion as having been, in effect, overruled; or should one treat it rather as a dissenting judgment? The answer would seem to be that, since the Court is not bound by its own decisions, it should be treated as a dissenting judgment; and here too the advocate general is, in practice, cited by counsel, although they must then of course seek to show that the judges were wrong and the advocate general was right.

Thirdly, and perhaps most commonly, where the Court has followed the advocate general on the point in question, it may be unnecessary to refer to the opinion at all, except perhaps to strengthen the authority of, or clarify the reasoning behind, the judgment. But, whether the Court has followed it or not, the opinion may help to show for precisely what proposition the case is indeed authority.

Finally, the practice of the Court, in certain straightforward cases,[22] of simply adopting the reasoning of the advocate general

---

[21] [1995] ECR I–3799.

[22] See for example the judgments in Case C–284/91 *Suiker Export v. Belgium* (Opinion of Advocate General Gulmann) [1992] ECR I–5473; and Case C–377/92 *Felix Koch Offenbach Couleur und Karamel GmbH v. Oberfinanzdirektion Munchen* (Opinion of Advocate General Jacobs of September 16, 1993) [1993] ECR I–4795.

by direct reference: "For the reasons given by the advocate general . . ." means that, in those cases, the opinions, rather like the *conclusions* of the *Commissaire du gouvernement* in the French *Conseil d'Etat*, become the only source for the reasoning of the Court. To that extent the opinion will thus become an authoritative precedent for the point concerned.

So far we have considered the significance for the Court of its own decisions. What then is the significance for the Court of national court decisions? These are not, of course, authoritative for the Court on questions of Community law; they are most frequently cited as evidence of the existence of one or more general principles of law (considered in the previous chapter). Often, as we have seen, fundamental concepts have been elucidated with the aid of comparative law. But decisions of national courts are rarely cited directly on questions of Community law, unless for purposes of comparison; and for these purposes even decisions from non-Member States have occasionally been cited, as in the American cases on extra-territorial jurisdiction cited by Advocate General Mayras in the Dyestuffs cases[23] and by Advocate General Darmon in the Woodpulp cases.[24]

Decisions of national courts may also be relevant where questions of national law have to be decided by the Court. Such cases are infrequent but three examples may be given. First, in Case 18/57, *Nold v. High Authority*[25] the Court had to consider questions of German law in order to decide whether Nold himself had the necessary capacity to bring proceedings before the Court in the name of his company, then in liquidation. Secondly, just as the question may arise, in a direct action, whether the applicant has the capacity to bring proceedings, so on a reference for a preliminary ruling the question may arise whether the body making the reference is competent to do so, that is, whether it is a "court or tribunal of a Member State"; and the answer to this question may, as we have seen,[26] depend partly on national law. Finally, national law may be in issue, not as a preliminary question but on the substance of the case, in direct actions against Member States,[27] if it is alleged that the law of that State is contrary to the

---

[23] Cases 48, 49 and 50–57/69 *ICI and Others v. Commission* [1972] ECR 619. These cases were not joined; however Mr Mayras gave a single Opinion, reported at p. 665. The judgments in the other cases are reported from p. 713 to p. 958.

[24] Joined Cases 90, 104, 114, 116, 117 and 125 to 129/85 *Åhlström Osakeyhtiö and Others v. Commission* [1988] ECR 5193, at p. 5214, Opinion of May 25 1988.

[25] Case 18/57 *Nold v. High Authority* [1957] ECR 121.

[26] p. 209.

[27] Chap. 6.

Treaty.[28] Here the question whether a provision of national law infringes Community law is a two-part one: first, the Court must determine the rule of Community law which is allegedly infringed, and this is a question of law; secondly, the Court must determine the rule of national law under attack as infringing that Community rule, and this for the Court is a question of fact.[29] It is significant of the relationship between the Court of Justice and the national courts that, in all these cases, the questions of national law are, for the Court of Justice, merely questions of fact, which require to be proved, just as questions of national law are questions of fact for international courts and questions of foreign law are questions of fact for national courts. In contrast, it is a fundamental principle of the Community legal order that questions of Community law are questions of law, not questions of fact, for the courts of the Member States, which must take judicial notice of the provisions of Community law. In the United Kingdom this is expressly recognised by section 3 of the European Communities Act 1972 (below, p. 379), but this is merely declaratory, and the principle is valid for all Member States.

## B. Precedent in the Court of First Instance

As we have explained in Chapter 5 the Court of First Instance is "attached" to the Court of Justice. The approach of the lower court reflects this subordination to the higher court.

Precedent apart, in the event of a successful appeal to the Court of Justice and a reference back to the Court of First Instance, the Statute of the Court expressly provides that it shall be bound, in the specific case, by the decision of the Court of Justice on points of law.[30]

Although the Court of First Instance, like the Court of Justice, does not regard itself as bound by its own previous decisions, it will not lightly depart from them, out of due regard for the principle of legal certainty. This is especially likely to be so where a decision has been that of the Court of First Instance sitting *in pleno* and not the subject of an appeal: this occurred, as we saw in Chapter 5, in the *Tetra Pak* case,[31] which established an important

---

[28] See, *e.g.* Case 167/73 *Commission v. French Republic* [1974] ECR 359; [1974] 2 C.M.L.R. 216 (above, p. 124).

[29] See Audretsch, *Supervision in European Community Law* (2nd ed., 1986), p. 73.

[30] Art. 54, second paragraph, added by the Decision establishing the Court of First Instance.

[31] Case T–51/89 *Tetra Pak Rausing v. Commission* [1990] ECR II–309; [1991] 4 C.M.L.R. 334; see p. 99, above.

point in competition law and is generally accepted as a precedent on that point unless and until the Court of Justice rules otherwise.

Furthermore, the Court of First Instance will regard itself as bound by precedents set by the Court of Justice for two reasons. First, as in the court systems of the Member States, the lower court in the hierarchy accepts, as a general rule, the authority of precedents set by the higher court. Secondly, the decision establishing the Court of First Instance prescribes as one of the grounds of appeal to the Court of Justice "the infringement of Community law". The precedents set by the Court are, of course, part of Community law, so that where these are clear and consistent the lower court would regard itself as bound to follow them at risk of its decision being set aside on appeal. Only in the presence of unclear or conflicting decisions of the higher court would it feel free to decide the matter as it thought fit.

As the Court of First Instance has gained in experience and confidence, it has become bolder and more ready to depart from decisions of the Court of Justice in which passage of time or changing social or economic conditions have revealed flaws. Here the lower court may venture to disregard the precedent of the higher court and, if there be an appeal, provide an occasion for the higher court to reconsider its previous stance.

Moreover, in an early case, when it was faced with a decision of the Court of Justice which it felt was too far-reaching, the Court of First Instance showed itself ready to indulge in the well known common-law technique of distinguishing an awkward precedent. Thus in Cases T–79/87 etc., *BASF v. Commission*[32] the applicants sought to annul a Commission decision, taken in competition proceedings under Article 85 (now Article 81) EC, on the ground *inter alia* that the Commission had infringed its own rules of procedure. The Commission invoked Case C–69/89 *Nakajima All Precision v. Council*,[33] in which the Court of Justice held an individual could not invoke an alleged breach of the internal rules of a Community institution: their purpose, declared the Court, was not to protect individuals but to ensure the proper internal functioning of the institution. The Court of First Instance interpreted the *Nakajima* judgment as drawing a distinction between procedural rules concerned solely with the internal working arrangements of the institution and those which create rights for individuals and are a factor contributing to legal certainty for such persons. It then proceeded to classify in this latter category the rule of procedure put in issue by BASF.[34]

---

[32] Cases T–79/89, etc. *BASF and Others v. Commission* [1992] ECR II–315.
[33] Case C–69/89 *Nakajima All Precision v. Council* [1991] ECR I–2069.
[34] See further A. Arnull, "Owning up to fallibility: precedent and the Court of Justice" (1993) 30 C.M.L.Rev. 247.

In Case T–30/91 *Solvay v. Commission* and Case T–36/91 *ICI v. Commission*[34a] the Court of First Instance plainly disagreed with the decision of the Court of Justice in Joined Cases 43 & 63/82 *VBVB and VBBB v. Commission* to the effect that the Commission was not required to divulge the contents of its files to the parties in competition cases. Rather the Court of First Instance declared access to the file as "one of the procedural safeguards intended to protect the rights of the defence", respect for the rights of the defence in all proceedings in which sanctions may be imposed being "a fundamental principle of Community law which must be respected in all circumstances". In Case T–586/93 *Kotzonis v. ESC* [1995] ECR I–665 the Court of First Instance bluntly stated that the case law of the Court of Justice on the effect of a provision of the Staff Regulations "ought to be reconsidered" and proceeded not to follow it. Again, the Court of First Instance in several subsequent cases has been loath to follow the Court's cryptic decision in Case C–309/89 *Codorniu v. Council* [1994] ECR I–1853 which sought to relax the strict requirements of *locus standi* for natural and legal persons seeking to annul a Community measure under Article 173 EC.

Nevertheless the guiding philosophy of the Court of First Instance remains that which was declared by its first President J.L. da Cruz Vilaça in his inaugural address[35]:

> "And if we are now 'being born', we are not being born without a past. Our collective memory is in the case law of the Court of Justice; we shall remain loyal to the fundamental values which have inspired it and we shall continue to add to it the contribution of our own experience."

## C. PRECEDENT IN THE NATIONAL COURTS

Apart from the role of precedent in the Court itself, the authority of judicial decisions on Community law must also be considered from the point of view of the courts of the Member States, since, as we have seen, they too are Community courts. Three questions arise. Firstly, what is the authority, for them, of decisions of the Court of Justice? Second, what is the authority, within the national hierarchy of the courts, of the decisions on Community law of

---

[34a] *Solvay v. Commission* [1995] ECR II–1775; *ICI v. Commission* [1995] ECR II–1847; VBVB and VBBB [1984] ECR 19.

[35] Formal sitting of the Court of Justice of September 25, 1989, address by Mr. J.L. da Cruz Vilaca, President of the Court of First Instance (Luxembourg, 1990), reprinted in [1990] 15 E.L.Rev. 4.

their supreme courts, for example, the House of Lords in the United Kingdom, the *Cour de Cassation* and *Conseil d'Etat* in France, or the various federal supreme courts in Germany? And finally, what is the authority, within the courts of one Member State, of the decisions of the courts of other Member States?

Two overriding principles may be of guidance in attempting to answer these questions. Firstly, there is no Community hierarchy of courts. The judicial systems of the Member States remain autonomous. In the absence of any federal structure, the Community system respects the judicial independence of the Member States, subject always of course to the principle that the courts, like all other State organs, are bound by the obligations of the Community Treaties.

Secondly, while the courts of the Member States remain sovereign, subject to that principle, in the application of Community law, only the Court of Justice can pronounce authoritatively on its interpretation. So much indeed is apparent from the last paragraph of Article 177 (now 234) EC, which obliges the national courts of last instance to refer questions of Community law to the Court.

What then, in the light of these principles, is the status for national courts of decisions of the Court of Justice?

Plainly, in a case where it has given a ruling on a question referred to it, that ruling is binding on the referring court. But is the ruling also binding on other courts in subsequent cases raising the same question? The Court itself has taken the view that, where it has already answered the question in a previous case, there is no need for even a court of last instance, which would otherwise be obliged to refer under the third paragraph of Article 177, to do so, since, in *Da Costa en Schaake* it said "the authority of an interpretation under Article 177 already given by the Court may deprive the obligation of its purpose and thus empty it of its substance".[36] On the other hand, the Court held in the same case that a national court may always, if it considers it desirable, refer questions of interpretation to the Court again. Even where the same question has already been answered, it may do so if it considers for some reason that a different answer might be appropriate in the case before it. Since the Court of Justice does not regard itself as strictly bound by its previous decisions, it will be able to modify its previous ruling if necessary. Thus the conclusion would seem to be that, in a case raising a question on which the Court has already ruled, the national court has a choice: it can either apply the ruling, or seek a new ruling. But it is bound by the ruling in the sense that it cannot simply disregard it.

---

[36] Joined Cases 28, 29 and 30/62 *Da Costa en Schaake v. Nederlandse Belasting administratie* [1963] ECR 31 at 38; [1963] C.M.L.R. 224.

Cases in the Court of Justice have even gone so far as to lay down a principle of construction that national courts should follow in the interpretation and application of national legislation. Where this legislation was passed to implement a directive, the national courts must interpret the national measure (at least where it is ambiguous) so as to give effect to the directive.[37] And in *Marleasing*[38] the Court went further by expecting national judges, in interpreting and applying their national law, to take account of the terms and purpose of a directive, even where the national law in question pre-dates the directive. Lord Slynn has difficulty however in accepting "that a statute of 1870 must be interpreted in the light of a 1991 directive".[39] This accords with the approach of the House of Lords in *Duke v. GEC Reliance*[40] where the House of Lords refused "to distort the meaning" of an Act of Parliament in order to give effect to a directive which (in their view) the Act was not passed to implement.[41]

So far as the courts in the United Kingdom are concerned, the binding force of decisions of the Court is recognised and given effect (albeit parenthetically) by the European Communities Act 1972. Section 3(1) of the Act provides that:

> "For the purposes of all legal proceedings any question as to the meaning or effect of any of the Treaties, or as to the validity, meaning or effect of any Community instrument, shall be treated as a question of law (and, if not referred to the European Court, be for determination as such in accordance with the principles laid down by and any relevant decision of the European Court or any court attached thereto)."[42]

It would seem to follow also, from what has been said, that, no matter what the national rules of precedent may provide, the lower courts of a Member State cannot be bound by any decision of a higher court in that State on a question of Community law. It could only be so bound if the higher court had obtained a ruling from the Court of Justice on the point in issue; and even then the

---

[37] Case 14/83 *von Colson and Kamann v. Land Nordrhein-Westfalen* [1984] ECR 1891; [1986] 2 C.M.L.R. 430, reaffirmed in Case 80/86 *Kolpinghuis Nijmegen* [1987] ECR 3639; [1989] 2 C.M.L.R. 18.

[38] Case C–106/89 *Marleasing SA v. Comercial Internacional de Alimentacion SA* [1990] ECR I–4135.

[39] Gordon Slynn, *Introducing a European Legal Order* (1992), p. 124.

[40] [1988] 1 All E.R. 626.

[41] But see the persuasive criticism of this case by Anthony Arnull in (1988) P.L. 313.

[42] The last phrase was added to take account of the establishment of the Court of First Instance in 1989.

lower court would be bound by that ruling rather than by the higher court's decision. And it would remain free to refer any new question of Community law.

This point was established by the Court in the *Rheinmuhlen* cases,[43] which were episodes in a long legal battle between a German cereal exporter, Rheinmuhlen-Dusseldorf, and the German intervention agency for cereals. The *Hessisches Finanzgericht* (Finance Court, Hesse) had decided that Rheinmuhlen was not entitled, under Community law, to any refunds on the export of certain consignments of barley. On appeal the *Bundesfinanzhof* (Federal Finance Court), having obtained a preliminary ruling on certain questions of Community law (Case 6/71), quashed this judgment and ruled that Rheinmuhlen was at least entitled to a refund at a lower rate. The case was accordingly sent back to the Hessian court to decide certain questions of fact.

Under German law the Hessian court was bound by the federal court's ruling on the point of law. However, the Hessian court considered that that ruling raised a new question of Community law, which it accordingly referred to the Court of Justice (Case 146/73). It also asked whether it was permissible for a lower court to make a reference only when the case came before it for the first time or whether it might do so also when reconsidering the case after the judgment of a lower court had been quashed by a higher court.

This reference by the Hessian court was challenged by Rheinmuhlen in the federal court, which then itself made a further reference (Case 166/73). It asked whether a lower court had a completely unfettered right to make a reference or whether Article 177 left unaffected rules of national law under which a lower court was bound on points of law by the judgment of a higher court.

On this question the Court of Justice ruled that the power of a lower court to make a reference could not be abrogated by such a rule of national law; and it gave the same answer to the Hessian court. Advocate General Warner went further, arguing that the discretion of a lower court to make a reference could not be fettered by any rule of national law, and he concluded from this that the Treaty did not allow appeals against a decision to refer. The Court held, however, that Article 177 did not preclude an appeal of a type normally available under national law. But the

---

[43] *Rheinmuhlen-Dusseldorf v. Einführ-und Vorratsstelle für Getreide und Füttermittel*: Case 6/71: (reference by the *Bundesfinanzhof*) [1971] ECR 823; [1972] C.M.L.R. 401; Case 166/73 (reference by the *Bundesfinanzhof*) [1974] ECR 33; [1974] 1 C.M.L.R. 523; and Case 146/73: (reference by the *Hessisches Finanzgericht*) [1974] ECR 139; [1974] 1 C.M.L.R. 523.

Court's judgments on the two references do establish that, although a lower court may be bound under national law to follow the ruling of a higher national court, it remains free to refer a new question under Article 177 (now Article 234) EC, and to follow the ruling given by the Court in reply. To that extent any national rule concerning the binding force of a higher court's decision upon a lower court, whether in the same litigation (as in *Rheinmuhlen*) or *a fortiori* under the doctrine of precedent, is displaced by Community law.

Finally, what is the authority in one Member State of decisions of courts of other Member States on questions of Community law? Again, it seems clear that such decisions can in no sense be regarded as binding, although any rulings given by the Court of Justice on references in such cases will be followed unless a new reference is considered necessary. In the absence of a reference, the authority of the national decision will be at best persuasive.

The need to avoid divergence of interpretation by national courts is recognised in the Lugano Convention[44] and in the EEA agreement (see Chapter 11 and Appendix). Those two instruments, to which both the Member States of the Community and EFTA countries are parties, lacking as they do a single court to provide uniform and authoritative interpretations, have established a system of central recording of all relevant decisions. This record is held at the Registry of the Court of Justice. In declarations annexed to the Lugano Convention the Member States call upon the Court of Justice to "pay due account" to rulings under the Lugano Convention while the EFTA states call upon their own courts to "pay due account" to rulings of the Court of Justice and of national Courts of EC Member States on provisions of the Brussels Convention which are substantially reproduced in the Lugano Convention.

---

[44] Convention of September 16, 1998 on Jurisdiction and the Enforcement of Judgments in Civil and Commercial Matters (O.J. L319, 25.11.88, p. 9). That convention signed at Lugano on September 16, 1988, between the 12 Community Member States and the then EFTA countries Austria, Finland, Iceland, Norway, Sweden and Switzerland, aims to extend the principles of the Brussels Convention to all of those countries.

# Chapter Seventeen

# Conclusions: Future of the Court

## INTRODUCTORY

We have seen in previous chapters the ways in which the Court of Justice (assisted since 1989 by the Court of First Instance) has carried out its task, under Article 120 (ex Article 164) EC, of ensuring that, in the interpretation and application of the Treaty, the law is observed. The Communities themselves are creatures of law, and are governed by law in every aspect of their operations. Readers may be left to judge for themselves the extent to which the Court has succeeded in preserving the rule of law, and in ensuring that on the judicial level, at least, European integration is being progressively realised.

Here we shall attempt, instead of a retrospective survey of the nearly five decades since the setting up of the Coal and Steel Community in 1952, a brief look forward into the future as well as a critique of the present.

As observed in previous editions of this book, it would of course be rash to venture firm predictions on the future of the Court, which must largely depend on the unpredictable future of the Communities themselves. The Communities (now under the umbrella of the European Union) are volatile structures which, if they do not progress, are liable to slip backwards: like a man walking a tight-rope, they need momentum if they are not to fall. Being relatively young and artificial creations, they cannot be left to fend for themselves but need constantly to be nurtured in order to survive. Yet, plagued as they have been both by economic difficulties and by political differences, their future development must remain a matter of conjecture. At best we can only base ourselves on a number of hypotheses.

The increasing workload of the Court of Justice.
Drawing by Nik Baker, published in the *Financial Times*.

## ENLARGEMENT OF THE COMMUNITIES: IMPACT ON THE JUDICIAL SYSTEM

Since the first edition of this book, the Communities have been successively enlarged from nine to 15 Member States by the accession of Greece (1981), Portugal and Spain (1986) and Austria, Finland and Sweden (1995). These enlargements have already had a practical impact on the working of the institutions, and especially of the Court of Justice, an impact likely to be repeated in even greater measure by the various accessions now in train.[1]

The Intergovernmental Conference, which opened in February 2000, does not have the reform of the Community judicial system on its agenda, despite the pressing need to resolve problems facing the two Community Courts, problems which will be exacerbated if, as is expected, the Conference will recommend the early admission to the Community of at least six new Member States – the Czech Republic, Estonia, Hungary, Poland, Slovenia and Cyprus. Also in February 2000 accession negotiations were opened by seven more countries – Latvia, Lithuania, Malta, Bulgaria, Romania, Slovakia and Turkey, as agreed at the Helsinki Summit of December 1999.[2] In the present Community of fifteen, some vestiges have survived of the homogeneity of the original six members with regard to their legal systems, politics and economics. In the next phase, of the Community of twenty-one, very little will be left of this homogeneity.

Moreover, Community law is no longer mainly concerned with trade and commerce, but, in Douglas Hurd's memorable phrase, it penetrates now into "the nooks and crannies of national life". In addition, the geopolitical background is totally transformed from the decade of the founding Treaties: the Iron Curtain and the Cold War have become matters of history.

Furthermore, as the resignation of the whole Commission in March 1999 demonstrated, the Community institutions are now expected to observe the principles of accountability and transparency and to meet exacting standards of probity.

---

[1] 1 For a valuable discussion of the problems raised by further accessions, see A.Arnull,"Judicial architecture or judicial folly? The challenge facing the European Union" (1999) 24 E.L. Rev. 516. What follows is heavily indebted to this Article.

[2] Turkey was granted candidate status at the Helsinki Summit of December 1999. The *Financial Times* of December 13, 1999, commented in its editorial (p.14) "By throwing open its doors to seven new candidates for membership, including Turkey, the EU is preparing to become a pan-European group, not just a club of the rich. And by including Turkey, it would accept a frontier well beyond the borders of what used to be called Christendom".

## Proposals for the future of the Communities' Judicial System[3]

Two important reports have recently emanated from the Court of Justice itself concerning the future of the judicial system of the European Communities.

First, a discussion paper on "The Future of the Judicial System of the European Union" was presented by the President of the Court to the Council, in May 1999. It gives the thinking of the Community Courts on the future of the judicial system of the Union.[4]

More recently still, in January 2000 a "Reflection Group", presided over by the former President of the Court of Justice Ole Due,[5] presented its report to the Commission on the future of the judicial system of the European Communities. This greatly expanded the earlier discussion paper of May 1999 from the Court. Only the main proposals of the Reflection Group's report will be mentioned here.

The necessity to change the existing structures was seen by the Reflection Group to arise from three developments. First, the continued increase in the number of cases brought to the Court of Justice and the Court of First Instance. Secondly, the increasing gap between the number of cases brought and those decided. Thirdly, the lengthening time taken to decide cases. Together these developments created a serious crisis and the risk of a breakdown of the Community judicial system, especially with the likely accession of new Member States as well as the impact of expansion into new areas of jurisdiction under Treaty changes. New Member States would also aggravate the problem of the multilingual regime of the Courts. The Group accepts that the changes it proposes may have to be implemented over a period as long as 15 years.

In relation to preliminary references under Article 234 (ex Article 177) EC, which it sees as the "key-stone" of the Com-

---

[3] The tensions and pressures referred to above are reflected in the burgeoning of such proposals by government bodies, academic institutions and in Law Reviews. A research note by the Court's Library, Research & Documentation Centre summarising the available writings in July 1998 referred to 20 such reports of official or semi-official bodies and over 100 law review Articles. These no doubt contributed to the Courts' thinking in their discussion paper below.

[4] "The Future of the Judicial System of the European Union: Proposals and Reflections", May 1999 : available on the Europa website http://europa.eu.int/cj/en/pres/aveng.pdf.

[5] As well as Due, the Group included Galmot, Everling and Slynn (three former judges of the Court of Justice) and Da Cruz Vilaça (former Advocate General of the Court of Justice and past President of the Court of First Instance): hence the authority of the Group's Report. The Group was instituted pursuant to a Commission Decision of April 20 and May 4, 1999.

munity judicial system, the Report rejects restricting the right to make a reference only to courts of last resort. Instead, it favours encouraging all national judges to be less shy in deciding for themselves questions of Community law[6]: only if there is a reasonable doubt as to the answer on an important question of Community law should a reference be sought. And the same criteria moreover should be applied by courts of last instance.

The Court of Justice should have an express power to reject "useless, premature or ill-prepared" references or ones which concern only the *application* of Community law, not its interpretation.

If this encouragement to national courts to interpret for themselves Community law were to lead to national case law contrary to Community law, then the Group suggests the Commission should be empowered to bring to the Court of Justice an "application in the interest of the law" (*un recours dans l'intérêt de la loi*) to ensure the future uniform application of Community law. Such an action would not however affect existing national decisions, which would be considered as *res iudicata*

In addition, for avoidance of doubt, the principle in the *Foto-Frost* case-law, namely, that national Courts have no jurisdiction to declare a Community act invalid[7] should be explicitly approved by incorporation in the Treaty.

The Report rejects a system of regional courts in the Member States with jurisdiction over preliminary references.[8] It also rejects any system of selection by the Court of Justice of which references it would accept. It similarly rejects any wholesale transfer of preliminary references to the Court of First Instance. Nevertheless, a strictly limited category of disputes could be referred for preliminary rulings to the Court of First Instance. Into this group of "*contentieux spéciaux*" would fall, for example, intellectual property disputes such as Community Trade-mark decisions based upon the Community Trade-mark Office in Alicante.

The Report aims to lighten the burden of the Court of Justice by making the Court of First Instance the normal jurisdiction to

---

[6] The Commission has now proposed, in a submission of February 2000, to the Intergovernmental Conference on institutional reform, that an introductory provision be inserted in Art. 234 (ex Art. 177) EC in these terms: "Subject to the provisions of this Article, the courts and tribunals of the Member States shall rule on the questions of Community law which they encounter in exercise of their national jurisdiction."

[7] Case 314/85 *Foto-Frost v. Hauptzollant Lübeck-Ost* [1987] ECR 4199, see p. 209 above.

[8] A tier of regional Courts was mooted a decade ago by Professors Jacqué and Weiler, "On the Road to European Union – A New Judicial Architecture: An Agenda for the Intergovernmental Conference" (1990) 27 C.M.L. Rev. 185. It was this article which coined the useful phrase "judicial architecture".

which direct actions are brought,[9] including those where the applicant is a Member State or Community institution. A proposal to this effect is currently before the Council.

Some limited categories of direct actions, however, would remain within the exclusive jurisdiction of the Court of Justice; the guiding principle would be their urgency and importance. In this category would fall the growing number of infringement actions against Member States. But here relief for the Court's burden could be secured by shifting to the Commission the responsibility to make the initial decision on the State's infringement and leaving it to the State, if it is dissatisfied, to seek the annulment of that decision before the Court. This follows the model of the procedure under Article 88 of the ECSC Treaty.[10] Member States, it is believed, would often accept the Commission's decision and not appeal to the Court.

It would also remain in the exclusive jurisdiction of the Court of Justice to impose a pecuniary penalty upon a Member State for non-compliance with a decision of the Court of Justice or of the Court of First Instance that it had infringed Community law (Article 228 (ex Article 171) EC).

With the aim of reducing the growing burden of the Court of Justice arising from appeals to it from decisions of the Court of First Instance, the Report proposes a filtering system for such appeals. The Treaty already limits such appeals to questions of law. The Report would now add a requirement that the case is of great importance for the development of Community law or the protection of individual rights. The request for leave to appeal on these grounds would be examined by a special three-judge Chamber of the Court; the procedure would be rapid and in writing; the Chamber must deliver a reasoned opinion (*avis*) without an advocate-general's opinion. In the light of the Chamber's opinion the President of the Court would grant or refuse permission to pursue the appeal.

The danger of overloading the Court of First Instance by the various changes proposed prompts the Reflection Group to suggest the creation of several new courts of first instance of specialized jurisdiction.

Thus, staff cases should be dealt with by a new independent Tribunal of three members: a lawyer, an assessor chosen by the

---

[9] In French parlance, "*la juridiction de droit commun*".

[10] The ECSC Treaty of April 18, 1951 is due to expire 50 years after its entry into force on July 25, 1952 (see Art. 97 ECSC). The specific powers and institutional arrangements for the Coal & Steel industries will probably be absorbed into the general scheme of the EC Treaty. The retention of the Art. 88 ECSC procedure for general purposes would be a fitting legal memorial to the first Community Treaty.

Community institutions, and an assessor chosen by representatives of Community civil servants. An appeal, but only in law, would lie to the Court of First Instance as the court of last resort. However, the Court of Justice could be asked by the Commission in an "application" in the interest of the law to quash prospectively erroneous case law but without retrospective effect upon decisions already reached.

Similarly, if the work-load demands, one or more specialised courts of first instance may be needed in relation to intellectual property disputes in connection with Community trade-marks, patents and designs, or registered plant varieties. These Courts too would be linked by appeal on points of law to the Court of First Instance and subject to the overall control of the Court of Justice through Commission applications "in the interest of the law".

Again, a specialised court of first instance may prove necessary in respect of "measures in the field of judicial co-operation in civil matters" as provided for in Article 65 (ex Article 73m) EC. These measures raising questions of private international law may require either a specialised Chamber of the Court of First Instance or a new Community Tribunal whose members would be specialists in private international law. Similarly, Title VI of the TEU relating to co-operation in the fields of justice and home affairs and Title IV EC relating to visa, asylum and immigration may in the future call for one or more specialised courts of first instance. The Commission White Paper on Competition published in May 1999 may also justify in due course granting to the Court of First Instance jurisdiction to receive preliminary references in this field.

The Report of January 2000 also suggests a number of reforms of procedure aimed to smooth and speed the processes of the two Courts.

## NUMBER OF JUDGES & ADVOCATES GENERAL AND THEIR APPOINTMENT

The Report accepts the need for there to be one judge from each Member State on each Court. Otherwise the Courts of the Community might lose their legitimacy in the State without a judge on that Court. Also, the judge brings to Community law the benefit of his or her national legal tradition. While these are important considerations, they might also be satisfied by considering the Community judicial system as *a whole* and therefore having at least one judge of eventually as many as 28 Member States in the corps of the Community judiciary. The number of those judges serving on the Court of Justice could remain fixed and thereby avoid overstepping "the invisible boundary between a collegiate judicial body and a deliberative assembly" referred to in the Court's report to the 1996 IGC.

With new enlargements being planned, first of six countries, then of up to a further seven, changes are proposed in the composition of the future Court of Justice of 21 (or 28) judges when sitting as a plenary Court. The Report proposes that the *plenum* should consist of half of the total number of judges (plus an extra judge to ensure an odd number). This would permit, eventually, two plenary formations to sit simultaneously, a situation familiar to German lawyers whose Supreme Court, the *Bundesgerichtshof*, sits in two formations know as the First and Second Senates. The Reflection Group is of opinion, whatever the future number of Member States, the plenary Court should never sit with more than 13 judges.[10a]

The Report considers that it is not necessary that each case should require the opinion of an advocate general, but only cases of importance involving new points of law, ones changing the existing case law, or ones of great complexity: the President of the Court would decide where to appoint an advocate general. This reform might permit a reduction in the number of advocates general. The Court of First Instance, on the other hand, should change to having a limited number of permanent advocates general; this would replace the present system, which has not worked well, of an *ad hoc* advocate general chosen for a particular case from among the judges.

The Court of First Instance would also see an increase in the number of its judges (to include, say, two from each Member State), not only because of the accession of new States, but also to cope with its increasing case-load, as it becomes the general Community Court of First Instance[11] as well as handling the influx of cases under its proposed new jurisdiction to receive certain preliminary references discussed above.

The present system for nominating judges and advocates general lacks transparency[12] and is open to the charge of political influence. It has been suggested that there should be a judicial appointments panel consisting of senior national judges and present and past members of the Courts, which would then make the choice from a shortlist drawn up by the Member States. The choice should not, however, require the assent of the European Parliament.

---

[10a] It may be noted that under the revised enforcement mechanism of the European Convention on Human Rights the largest judicial formation of the Human Rights Court will be the Grand Plenum of 17 judges, notwithstanding the 42 Member States of the Council of Europe.

[11] See n. 8 above.

[12] This applies no less strongly to the nomination of Legal Secretaries.

This runs directly counter to the proposal of Committee of the European Parliament[13] which in 1993 had recommended that the judges and advocates general of the Court of Justice should cease to be appointed by the Member States. Instead, they should be elected (*sic*) by the Parliament and the Council. Although the Parliament's report expressly excluded any American-style public hearings, it is hard to see how the names of the candidates could be kept from public knowledge, with resultant exposure in the media of their past foibles and idiosyncrasies. In the event, the report appears to have been quietly dropped. Certainly, the Reflection Report only goes so far as to propose a consultative committee of highly qualified and independent jurists to verify the legal competence of candidates being presented to the Member States for appointment.

The Reflection Group Report makes the radical proposal that the term of appointment of both judges and advocates general in both Courts be lengthened from six to 12 years, without possibility of renewal.

## THE PROBLEM OF LANGUAGES

Alongside delay because of case overload, another question of great practical importance is the problem of languages, which the enlargement of the Community has aggravated and will aggravate further. The Community principle of linguistic equality may be in danger of becoming its sacred cow impeding the path of justice.

Yet within the Court of Justice it seems an inescapable requirement, at least in preliminary rulings, that it should be able to receive and deal with a case submitted in any of the national languages of all the Member States, even if it became necessary to restrict the choice of language for other purposes. It would not be practicable to require of courts in some Member States that they should submit their references other than in their own language.

Both the Courts, in their paper, and the Reflection Group accept that important judgments should continue to be published in all Community languages simultaneously, even though the next enlargement being considered will take the number of languages from 11 to 16. However, all recognise that there is, at the present time, a crisis because of the lack of resources for the Courts' translation service.

One learned commentator[14] suggests how the courts might be more selective in the decisions they publish. Already, staff cases are

---

[13] Report of the Parliament's Committee on Institutional Affairs on the role of the Court of Justice in the development of the EC's constitutional system (Rapporteur: Mr Willi Rothley, July 6, 1993) E.P. session document A3-0228/93.

[14] A. Arnull, *op.cit.* p. 522.

no longer systematically published in full in all of the official languages. One possibility might be for publication in all the languages to be confined to cases which are considered sufficiently significant, as decided by the formation of judgment, again following the current practise in respect of staff cases.

The translation burden might also be somewhat eased if Member States, who are at present entitled to use their official language when intervening in a direct action or submitting observations in a reference for a preliminary ruling, were required to supply translations of their written pleadings into the language of the case or into the Courts' working language.

Nevertheless, the possible combinations of languages for translation and interpretation would rise, on the next enlargement, say, to 21 Member States, to a mind-boggling 240.

On a positive note, however, the addition of new legal systems, although adding to the language problems, will, if past experiences are a guide, further encourage the Court of Justice to resort extensively to the rich thesaurus of national laws in developing the general principles of Community law, the role of which we have explored in Chapter 15.

## DEVELOPMENTS IN THE COURT'S JURISDICTION AND PROCEDURE

Other developments, apart from the enlargement of the Communities, may affect the Courts' work-load. There are likely to be developments in their jurisdiction. Some of these have been mentioned in previous chapters; for example the jurisdiction to give advisory opinions (Chapter 11) and to interpret Conventions concluded between Member States (Chapter 10). The latter jurisdiction might be further extended to include other international agreements in the economic field which have not been entered into pursuant to the Treaties but which may nonetheless require uniform interpretation in the different Member States. The EEA Agreement makes provision for binding interpretations to be sought from the Court in order to preserve the principle of homogeneity between Community law and the EEA legal system.[15] However this possibility has not been and seems unlikely to be, used by the three remaining EFTA States which are members of the EEA.

Conversely, the work-load in staff cases and competition cases has been lightened as a result of the creation of the Court of First

---

[15] See T. Hartley, *The European Court and EEA* (1992) 41 I.C.L.Q. 841.

Instance and, from 1993, there has been further relief by the transfer to the lower Court of all direct actions brought by individuals.[16] Then too the Maastricht Treaty[17] allowed the Council to transfer all direct actions including those brought by Member States or the Commission; this is now being implemented, as we saw in Chapter 5, above. Nevertheless, the principle of "unity of jurisdiction" has been preserved by the right of appeal (on law) from the lower Court to the Court of Justice.

To assist it in its formidable task the Court has made annual pleas for budgetary provision for more generous staffing and we have seen (Chapter 3, above) the complement of legal secretaries has been more than doubled since 1980, and the total number of staff increased from 244 in 1977 to 825 in January 1993. The staff complement authorised in the Budget for the year 2000 is 1006, itself an increase of 45 posts over 1999.[18] More than half of that increase is in Lawyer Linguist posts for the hard-pressed translation directorate and related clerical support. The establishment of the Court of First Instance necessitated a considerable increase in the staff of the Court of Justice, including both staff permanently assigned to the new Court and additional staff in the existing departments of the Court.

Such growth in personnel, however, has its dangers. Professor Vining of Michigan warned 20 years ago that the American federal court system was becoming a "depersonalized bureaucracy" as judges increasingly rely on the growing cadre of law clerks to write a major share of their opinions, which then cease to be authoritative reflections of the workings of a single legal mind or the joint efforts of judges accurately to reflect the dialogue that produced the collegiate decision.[19]

Another similar danger, if the Court becomes overloaded, has been stressed by Professor Cappelletti of Florence. He points out that "constitutional decision-making demands that kind of careful consideration which it is unrealistic to expect from courts which are submerged under thousands of cases they are obliged to decide; it requires a high degree of creativity and of policy-oriented balancing of interests and values which bureaucratic and routine-oriented judges can hardly provide".[20]

Comparisons, however, with a fully fledged federal legal system are not entirely apt when describing the Court as the Community's

---

[16] Decision 93/350 (Euratom, ECSC, EC) [1993] O.J. L144/1. This decision entered into force, so far as anti-dumping cases are concerned, on March 11, 1994 [1994] O.J. L66/29.

[17] Art. 168a EC, as amended by the Maastricht Treaty.

[18] This total is made up of 765 permanent and 241 temporary posts.

[19] (1981) 26 Law Quadrangle Notes, Ann Arbor, No. 1, p. 5.

[20] *Festschrift fur Konrad Zweigert* (1981), p. 391.

supreme constitutional court. For the Community legal system is one in which any national court or tribunal may rule upon constitutionality of its national law in relation to Community law: if the national (*i.e.* State) judge elects to decide such a "federal" question instead of referring it to Luxembourg under Article 177 (now Article 234) EC, he is usually free to do so (only a final court must refer). To this extent, the burden of adjudicating upon constitutional issues is shared by the Court with the national judiciary.

Another common device for easing congestion and one very familiar in common law systems is the filter provided by leave to appeal (or the application for judicial review made subject to leave). As we have seen above, the Reflection Group does canvas the possibility of such a filter for appeals from the Court of First Instance to the Court of Justice, but not for preliminary references. Indeed, without Treaty revision such a filter would be incompatible with the terms of Article 234 (ex Article 177) EC and the unfettered right of, or even obligation on, national courts to refer cases to the Court of Justice where a decision on the point of Community law concerned is "necessary" to enable them to reach a decision. Faced however with its increasing overload of cases, the Court has long recognised that it would not be in the interests of expeditious justice, either within the Member States or before the Court of Justice itself, for every question of Community law which arises to be referred. Thus as early as 1963 in Joined Cases 28-30/62 *Da Costa v. Nederlandse Belastingadministratie*[21] the Court qualified the obligation on courts of last instance in the Member States to refer every question of interpretation raised before them, especially in cases when the question raised was materially identical with a question which already had been the subject of a preliminary ruling in a similar case. Building on that argument the Court gave further scope for national supreme courts not to make references in Case 283/81 *CILFIT v. Ministry of Health*[22] which added to that exception the possibility for a national court not to refer if the correct application of Community law was so obvious as to leave no scope for any reasonable doubt as to the manner in which the question raised was to be resolved. As we have seen in Chapter 10 above, the Court attached warnings of the risks for a national judge inherent in such reliance upon the doctrine of *acte clair*.

In respect of other courts too, the Court has now signalled its intention to take a stricter line on admissibility of preliminary

---

[21] [1963] ECR 31; [1963] C.M.L.R. 224.
[22] [1982] ECR 3415.

rulings and in doing so has given clear guidance to national courts as to what it expects from them on their side of the dialogue. Thus a run of recent decisions discloses the Court's new willingness to review the status of the referring court,[23] to review the grounds of the order of reference,[24] and, finally, to review the relevance of the questions referred.[25]

Those developments have taken place within the context of the Court's power to interpret Article 177 (now Article 234) EC as well as its own Rules of Procedure. More radical solutions but certainly more effective in reducing the number of cases referred to the Court are canvassed, as we have seen, by the Reflection Group, including introducing a filter procedure requiring leave to appeal from the Court of First Instance to the Court of Justice; but it rejects any such filter for applications for preliminary references. Nor does the paper support any restriction in which national courts should have a discretion to make preliminary references.

Nevertheless, a restriction on which national courts may refer under Article 234 (ex Article 177) has respectable precedents in the form of the Protocols on the interpretation by the Court of Justice of the Brussels Convention of September 27, 1968 on jurisdiction and the enforcement of judgments in civil and commercial matters and the Protocol on the interpretation by the Court of the Rome Convention on the law applicable to contractual obligations. Article 2 of each Protocol first lists the Supreme Courts of the Member States as being entitled to request the Court of Justice to give a preliminary ruling on questions of interpretation of the Convention concerned and adds that other courts in the contracting states may make such a reference when they are sitting in an appellate capacity.[26]

---

[23] See Case C–24/92 *Corbiau v. Directeur de l'Administration Fiscale* [1993] ECR I–1277.

[24] See joined Cases C–320-322/90 *Telemarsicabruzzo v. Circostel and Others* [1993] ECR I–393; and Case C–157/92 *Banchero* [1993] ECR I–1085. In the latter case the Court simply made an order under Art. 92(1) of the Rules of Procedure declaring the request manifestly inadmissible and repeated the requirement for the national court to define the factual and legislative background to the questions to which it sought an answer or at least to explain the factual circumstances on which those questions were based.

[25] See Case C–343/90 *Lourenço Dias v. Director da Alfândega do Porto* [1992] ECR I–4673 in which the Court refused to answer six out of eight questions referred to it by the Oporto Tax Tribunal on the ground that they bore no relation to the actual circumstances of the case; and Case C–83/91 *Meilicke v. ADV/ORGA F.A. Meyer AG* [1992] ECR I–4871 in which the Court repeated its refusal to give opinions on general or hypothetical questions which it had first formulated in Case 244/80 *Foglia v. Novello II* [1981] ECR 3045.

[26] In the case of the Brussels Convention it is further provided that the court referred to in Art. 37 may make references in the context of an appeal against a decision authorising enforcement of a judgment.

However, while a general restriction on which courts may refer under Article 234 (ex Article 177) would have a certain logic and would undoubtedly reduce the number of cases referred to the Court and hopefully lead to an increase in the quality of the cases which were referred, such a restriction would represent a fundamental shift in the judicial protection of individual interests in the Member States. Thus individuals and companies faced with a misapplication of Community law by national administrative authorities, and whose rights to bring proceedings directly before the Court are already severely limited under Article 230 (ex Article 173) EC, would be unable to obtain the benefit of a definitive ruling on their Community rights without pursuing their case through various additional steps in the national legal system; a process which would be inevitably costly and in many cases would take longer than a reference. Furthermore the case law of the Court of Justice from *Costa* to *Francovich* is littered with cases in which important points of principle were identified and referred to the Court of Justice by national judges sitting at first instance or in specialised and administrative tribunals. The choking off of such a fertile source of development of Community law would inevitably slow down that development and could contribute to confusion and uncertainty within the Member States.

A less disturbing alternative would be to allow the Court of Justice to select, from the questions referred to it, those to which it felt a reply was needed. Such a procedure would he analogous to the certiorari system of docket control in the U.S. Supreme Court whereby of the many hundreds of cases submitted to it the Supreme Court only certifies as requiring a decision a number corresponding to its capacity of disposal in a given judicial year.[26a] Similar filtering systems exist in several Community Member States: for example in the United Kingdom an appeal may be made to the House of Lords only by leave of the Court of Appeal or by that of the Appeals Committee of the House itself. A filter as regards both admissibility and substance was, until October 1998, operated by the Commission of Human Rights in Strasbourg with regard to cases submitted to the Court of Human Rights. It should be remembered that cases may only be referred to that Court after exhaustion of national remedies, which doctrine has no place in Community law. In May 1994 the Member States of the Council of Europe decided that the Commission and the Court of Human

---

[26a] Around 200 cases each year – a number comparable to the total of judgments given by the Court of Justice.

Rights should be merged, with the filtering function carried out by special three-judge panels of the Court.[27]

Clearly a similar system could be devised in the Community context. However the possibility of leave being refused might itself discourage references from being made in appropriate cases and, by emphasising a procedure analogous to an appeal, might undermine the spirit of judicial co-operation between the national courts and the Court of Justice which is so characteristic of the preliminary ruling procedure. For such reasons the Refletion Group rejects any filter upon preliminary references.

Overload on the Court might lead to the Court and its Chambers sitting on more days of the week although this would eat into the time available for preparation and deliberation of cases. Increasing the number of judges, even ahead of the natural increase by admission of new Member States, would permit the creation not only of more Chambers but also, if the quorum remained at nine, of the apparently paradoxical situation of holding two "plenary" sittings of the Full Court simultaneously, although, as we saw above, such arrangements are not unheard of in national jurisdictions.

Another solution is to offload more of the Court's jurisdiction upon the Court of First Instance.

As we have seen,[28] the cases which have been switched from the Court to the lower Court already include all applications for judicial review under Article 230 (ex Article 173) EC begun by natural or legal persons or actions by such persons for failure to act under Article 232 (ex Article 175) EC as well as claims for damages under Article 235 (ex Article 178) EC. Such changes did not require any further Treaty amendment.

The Maastricht Treaty by its amendment to Article 225 (ex Article 168a) EC allowed the Council to transfer all direct actions, not only those brought by individuals but also those brought by Member States and Community institutions - including infringement proceedings brought by the Commission against Member States under Article 226 (ex Article 169) EC. That Article as amended, however, still expressly excludes references under Article 234 (ex Article 177) EC (and by implication under the Judgments Convention and other similar instruments) from the competence of the Court of First Instance.

---

[27] For further details of this important development see the "Explanatory Report to the 11th Protocol" Council of Europe 1994, published in (1994) 17 E.H.R.R. 514 and (1994) 15 M.R.L.J. 86. For a flow chart of the working of the re-shaped control mechanism of the Human Rights Convention, see T. Kennedy, *Learning European Law* (London, 1999), p. 190.

[28] Chap. 5 above, p. 78.

Accordingly, further Treaty amendment would be needed to permit a transfer to the lower court, even of a limited category of Article 234 (ex Article 177) references, such as those *contentieux spéciaux* discussed above in the Report of the Reflection Group.

Another possibility is the establishing of more courts of first instance, each with a specialised jurisdiction. We have seen above the suggestions of the Reflection Group on such new courts.

## THE PROTECTION OF FUNDAMENTAL RIGHTS

As we have seen in Chapter 15 above, since the Court's landmark judgment in the *Stauder* case[29] it has been clearly recognised that "fundamental rights form an integral part of the general principles of law, the observance of which [the Court] ensures".[30] The Court's jurisprudential lead in this regard was followed by the other institutions in the joint declaration by the European Parliament, the Council and the Commission on fundamental rights of April 5, 1977[31] and subsequently in the preamble to the SEA in which the Member States declared that they were "determined to work together to promote democracy on the basis of the fundamental rights recognised in the constitutions and laws of the Member States (and) in the Convention for the protection of human rights and fundamental freedoms". The continuing importance of human rights and fundamental freedoms for the Communities was further underlined in the preamble to the Maastricht Treaty as well as in Article F(2) TEU which uses terms clearly based upon the Court's judgments in the *International Handelsgesellschaft* and *Nold* cases[32] (discussed in Chap. 15, above) where it states:

> "The Union shall respect fundamental rights, as guaranteed by the European Convention for the Protection of Human Rights and Fundamental Freedoms signed in Rome on 5 November 1950 and as they result from the constitutional traditions common to the Member States, as general principles of Community law."

However, the express reference to the Convention in the SEA, the TEU and in the case law of the Court raises the problem of the

---

[29] Case 29/69 *Stauder v. Stadt Ulm* [1969] ECR 419; [1970] C.M.L.R. 112.

[30] See Case 4/73 *Old v. Commission* [1974] ECR 491 at 507; [1974] 2 C.M.L.R. 338.

[31] [1977] O.J. C103/103.

[32] Case 11/70 *International Handelsgesellschaft v. Einfuhr- und vorratsstelle Getreide* [1970] ECR 1125 at 1134; and *Nold v. Commission* [1974] ECR 491 at 507.

relationship between the Community legal system and the system set up by the Convention under the aegis of the Council of Europe. For at present the acts of Member States as contracting parties to the Convention are subject to review by the Convention bodies in Strasbourg and the acts of the Community institutions by the Court of Justice in Luxembourg. Thus the possibility cannot be excluded that measures taken by Member States in implementation of their Community obligations, while valid under Community law, might by open to challenge in both Strasbourg and Luxembourg with possibly conflicting results. For, although the Court of Justice has the power to ensure that Community action respects fundamental rights, its paramount concern may be promotion of integration, and the standards which it applies may not he the same as those of bodies whose main function is to preserve the rights of the individual.[33] Thus it appears necessary to review the division of responsibilities in the field of protection of fundamental rights as between the Court of Justice on the one hand and the Court of Human Rights on the other.

Two principal questions arise in this context. First the possibility of accession by the Community as such to the Convention (each of the Member States is of course already a signatory) and secondly, the possibility of some mechanism to ensure the consistent development of the law in this field, perhaps enabling the Court of Justice to ask the Human Rights Court for preliminary rulings on points of law within its competence. While such ideas are appealing in that they would reinforce legal protection within the Community as well as the constitutional nature of the Community legal system, both measures are subject to serious practical objections as well as difficulties of principle.[34]

However, these matters reached the political agenda and were discussed at a meeting of Justice Ministers of Community Member States on September 28, 1993.[35] At the meeting the Ministers decided to constitute a group of experts who would be invited to prepare a catalogue of the benefits and problems to which such

---

[33] For an example of such potential conflict see the judgment of Court of Justice in Joined Cases 47/87 and 227/88, *Hoechst v. Commission* [1989] ECR 2859; [1991] 4 C.M.L.R. 410 where the Court stated that Art. 8(1) of the Convention was concerned with the development of man's personal freedom and might not therefore be extended to business premises (at p. 2924). At that time, the Court pointed out, there was no case law of the European Court of Human Rights on the subject. Subsequently however, the Court of Human Rights has ruled otherwise: judgment of December 16, 1992, *Niemietz v. Germany* (72/1991/324/396).

[34] For an earlier discussion of the problems raised by Community accession to the Convention see McBride and Brown, *Yearbook of European Law* (1981), p. 167.

[35] See [1993] 6076 *Agence Europe* of Friday, October 1, 1993.

direct action might give rise. According to the Belgian President in office there were two orders of problems. First, at the political level, accession by the Community to the Convention would be a natural development, given the commitment of the Community to the protection of fundamental rights and the use by the Court of Justice of the Convention as a source for developing those principles. Furthermore, it might be seen as anomalous were the Community not to be a signatory while constantly encouraging non-Member countries, especially the emerging democracies of Eastern Europe and among the ACP States, to respect those same principles. However, it might also be argued that a simple accession to the Convention would not have any significant effect at the judicial level, given that the Convention was already a source of Community law and that all the Member States are already signatories and therefore bound by it.

Secondly, even if a political consensus on such an accession were to be achieved (both within the Community and the other Member States of the Council of Europe – now numbering 47 in total) serious legal problems would still remain. These would include the matter of representation of the Community within the Strasbourg bodies – some non-Community Member States might take objection to an apparent "double representation" of the Community, both through the individual Member States and through the Community as a whole; the problem of avoiding conflicts of jurisdiction between the Court of Justice and the Court of Human Rights while ensuring that judicial protection was consistently ensured, and finally how would the uniformity of interpretation of Community law, at present ensured solely by the Court of Justice, be maintained in the light of such accession. In practice the Court of Justice itself has now removed the issue from the political agenda by holding, in *Opinion 2/94*[36] that, as Community law now stands that the Community has no competence to accede to the Convention. In other words to effect such accession the Member States would have to make an explicit amendment to the TEU and the EC Treaties.

So far as references to the Strasbourg Court in the context of disputes on Community law are concerned, there are two possibilities. Either a preliminary ruling procedure might be instituted in the scheme of the Convention or alternatively the Court of Justice itself might have the possibility of submitting questions to the Strasbourg Court on matters of interpretation of the Convention. The desirability of the latter possibility was suggested by

---

[36] *Opinion 2/94* of 28 March 1996 on *Accession by the Community to the European Convention on Human Rights*; [1996] ECR I–1759 (see Chap. 11, p. 259, above).

Advocate General Warner as long ago as 1976 in his opinion in *Prais v. Council*.[37]

The first objection might be that parties to proceedings before a court of a Member State who had referred questions for resolution in Luxembourg, would be dismayed to find that their case required the further intervention of the Strasbourg Court, whose reply presumably would have to be given to the Court of Justice in order to enable it to give its preliminary ruling which would then in turn be referred back to the national court with all of the consequent risks of delay entailed in such a circuitous procedure. Furthermore the scheme of the Convention is to create a series of minimum rules and not to harmonise rules on the protection of fundamental rights. At present therefore Member States and the Community itself may adopt higher standards upon which the Strasbourg Court would not be able to adjudicate. Finally, if national courts were able to submit questions for preliminary rulings to Strasbourg, although this might save a great deal of time, by-passing the rule of exhaustion of remedies, the question would arise as to whether or not, in cases with a Community element, the replies given by the Strasbourg Court on matters within its competence would ultimately bind the Court of Justice or not.

## DEFIANCE OF THE COURT AND OTHER CRITICISMS

The plea made by President Giscard d'Estaing at the Dublin Summit in 1975 "to do something about the Court and its illegal decisions" did not fall on deaf ears in his own country. As we have seen (above, p. 231), the *Conseil d'Etat* later went out of its way, in Cohn-Bendit (1978), to confront the Court with an uncompromising rejection of its case law on the doctrine of direct effect of directives. It is to be expected that governments in the Member States may sometimes, under political pressure, be slow to comply with Community law. But defiance by the national judiciary is a more alarming phenomenon which, if it were to spread, would be the death-knell of that doctrine of judicial co-operation which is the hallmark of the procedure under Article 177 (now Article 234) EC. Happily, the German *Bundesverfassungsgericht* (Federal Constitutional Court) has moderated its earlier attitude (see p. 231, above), and by 1992 the *Conseil d'Etat* had showed itself willing to accept that a directive must prevail over a subsequent conflicting French statute.[38]

---

[37] Case 130/75 *Prais v. Council* [1976] ECR 1589 at 1607; [1976] 2 C.M.L.R. 708.
[38] See *Nicolo* C.E. October 20, 1989 and *Société Anonyme Rothmans and Société Philip Morris* C.E. February 28, 1992. See also Brown and Bell, *French Administrative Law* (5th ed., 1998), p. 283.

The reaction of the Court has been deliberately restrained and low-key apparently preferring to regard such incidents as temporary misunderstandings rather than as head to head conflicts. Its recent judgments have defined more clearly the limits upon the direct effect doctrine and the responsibilities of national courts in the context of the Article 177 procedure; judicial conferences have continued to bring national judiciary to Luxembourg to become better informed about the Court and to improve mutual understanding under the mellowing influence of wine and good cheer; and the great majority of national judges have loyally accepted the supremacy of Community law and its concomitant, the authority of the Court's rulings and decisions.

It appears that problems similar to those encountered in France and Germany earlier in the history of the development of Community law have arisen in Spain. In two cases, the Spanish Constitutional Court has declined to make references to the Court of Justice[39] where, on the face of it, it would have been appropriate to do so, there being little doubt that the court falls within the third paragraph of Article 177 (now Article 234) EC. Those two decisions were severely criticised by Spanish academic writers,[40] and it is to be hoped that they will prove only temporary aberrations attributable to the teething troubles of a Member State coming to grips with new and unfamiliar legal concepts.

More disturbing however was the attack on the Court led by former Chancellor Kohl of Germany who has not only sternly criticised certain developments in the Court's case law relating to social legislation,[41] but has suggested that the Court had exceeded its jurisdiction and that at some future intergovernmental conference the powers of the Court should be reduced. As is pointed out in a percipient editorial comment in the Common Market Law

---

[39] Judgment No. 28/1991 of the Constitutional Court of February 14, 1991 (1991) *Boletin Oficial del Estado* March 15, 1991; (*Asociacion Profesional de Empresarios de Pesca Comunitarios*) Case 207/86 *Apesco v. Commission* [1988] ECR 2151; [1989] 3 C.M.L.R. 687. Judgment No. 64/1991 of the Constitutional Court of March 22, 1991, *Boletin oficial del Estado* (April 24, 1991).

[40] See for example Araceli Mangas Martin, *La Constitucion y la Ley ante el Derecho Comunitario* (1991) La Ley, 587; Jose Julian Izquierdo Peris, "*El Tribunal Constitucional como organo de garantia del Derecho Comunitario en Espania*" Gaceta Juridica de la C.E., (September) [1993] 15; Jose Palacio Gonzalez, "*Jurisprudencia Constiticional en sede comunitaria y proteccion de los particulares*" Servicio Central de Publicaciones del Gobierno Vasco.

[41] Particular opprobrium attached to the judgment in Case C–45/90 *Paletta v. Brennet A.G.* [1992] ECR I–3423, in which the Court held that an employer was bound, both in fact and in law, by a medical diagnosis carried out at the place of residence of an employee so far as the intervention and duration of incapacity were concerned as long as the employer had not exercised his rights to have the person concerned examined by a doctor of his choice.

Review,[42] while criticism of individual Court decisions is perfectly legitimate, a more general attack on the functioning of the Court, its methods of interpretation and the manner in which it finds the law, is quite a different matter. "The political level is not the most appropriate one for such debate. Governments have much to lose and little to gain from an exercise that risks undermining the authority of the Court and puts into question its role in European integration." Kohl's outburst may be put down to political bluster since neither Germany nor any other Member State submitted any such proposals to the Intergovernmental conferences which have since been held.

Falling far short of defiance of the Court, there has been informed criticism of its procedures and decisions in the Member States, notably by the House of Lords Select Committee on the European Communities, which reviewed the Court's procedures and recommended that there should be formal collaboration between the Court and practitioners on questions of procedure, with consideration being given to the establishment of a joint Committee.[43] Such a joint Committee has not yet been established.

Certainly, the Court has shown itself responsive to criticism, some of it, indeed, self-criticism. Thus, in the *Sugar Cartel* cases,[44] it reformed its procedure for taking evidence of witnesses so as to expedite consideration of the factual issues before it; in one of its longest judgments (to date) the Court demonstrated its ability to deal with complicated facts, every point of fact and every argument of the parties being given due consideration in the decision. Nevertheless, this was only achieved after prodigious expenditure of effort and time. So too in the *Pioneer* case,[45] where even more voluminous evidence fell to be examined.

The Court of First Instance, for matters falling within its jurisdiction, has improved judicial protection by its careful scrutiny of the factual basis of its decisions and, according to one of its judges, by the improved quality of legal reasoning in its decisions.[46]

A criticism of the Court that has not been met is that it frequently adjudicates on points (usually of law but sometimes of fact) which have not been argued before it. This inspires more objection in common lawyers, accustomed as they are to an

---

[42] [1993] C.M.L. Rev. 899.

[43] House of Lords Select Committee, Session 1979–80, 23rd report, p. 18.

[44] Cases 40 to 48 etc./73 *Suiker Unie and Others v. Commission* [1975] ECR 1663; [1976] 1 C.M.L.R. 295.

[45] Cases 100-103/80 *Pioneer v. Commission* [1983] ECR 1825; [1983] 3 C.M.L.R. 221.

[46] See K. Lenaerts, "The European Court of First Instance: ten years of interaction with the Court of Justice" in *Essays in honour of Lord Slynn of Hadley* (Kluwer, 2000).

adversarial process of trial in which the court makes up its mind according to the ebb and flow of argument by counsel: the judge who engages in his own research is hardly playing the game. The civil lawyers, by contrast, have been conditioned to accept that the judge may turn inquisitor – a change of role not unfamiliar to those dispensing justice in British administrative tribunals.

A particular aspect of this problem is the lack of provision in the Rules of Procedure to permit counsel to comment upon the advocate-general's opinion, even in cases where it raises new issues upon which no argument has been presented. Only exceptionally will the Court order the re-opening of the oral proceedings[47] and even then, counsel are in no better position in relation to the second opinion. The House of Lords Select Committee proposed that the Court should give parties a right to submit, within a limited period, written comments on statements of fact in an advocate-general's opinion, and should be willing to re-open the oral procedure where it is alleged that the advocate general has introduced a new point of law.[48]

## JUDICIAL ACTIVISM

A new mood of confidence in the Community, born of the SEA, proved short-lived, dissipated by the difficult debate and referenda on the Maastricht Treaty and the Community's inability to act decisively in the Yugoslav debacle. In the 20 years or so before the SEA the Community's decision-making process was often faced with a political impasse. The Court of Justice then felt itself constrained to promote legal integration by judicial decision.

But the line between legal and political integration is a fine one and, if crossed, may produce conflicts with the political organs of government both in the Community and the Member States. Post-Maastricht the Court may find itself once again called to renew its pro-active role.

What Professor Rasmussen has called "uncontrolled pro-Community activism" may now, in his view, have dangers for the Court, not least a perception of it in the Member States as a not

---

[47] See Case 155/79 *AM & S v. Commission* [1982] ECR 1575; [1982] 2 C.M.L.R. 264; and Case C–2/90 *Commission v. Belgium* [1992] ECR I–4431; [1993] 1 C.M.L.R. 365, in which the oral procedure was reopened twice, thus requiring Advocate General Jacobs to deliver three Opinions.

[48] In Case C–17/98 *Aruba*, *The Times*, February 29, 2000, the Court of Justice rejected the argument that it was a breach of Art. 6.1 of the European Convention on Human Rights not to allow parties to submit written observations in response to the advocate-general's opinion: see Chap. 4, p. 74, n. 17a, *ante*.

fully trustworthy neutral arbiter.[49] Such concerns have been voiced at a worrying level by former Chancellor Kohl (see above, p. 401). From the Court itself Judge Koopmans (as he then was) has reflected whether it should not go back to a minimal role, stripping its case law of its more daring and activist sidelines.[50]

How far such arguments for judicial restraint will convince the Court is a question made more difficult by its changing composition and the diversity of its membership to which we have already referred. Past history, however, suggests that the Court does not easily succumb to faint hearts or cold feet and that, because of the principle of collegiality of its judgments, the pronouncements for or against closer integration made by members of the Court prior to their appointment to the Court may have little bearing on the work of the institution during their tenure: the whole is greater than the sum of the parts.

## THE OMBUDSMAN

It is appropriate briefly[51] to mention here a development, which although not directly connected with the Court of Justice, will no doubt contribute to increasing protection of the individual interests of Community citizens. The "Ombudsman" is an institution of Swedish origin which has already been introduced into the national legal systems of several Member States: thus in the United Kingdom his official title is "Parliamentary Commissioner for Administration" and in France he is styled *le Médiateur*.[52] The creation of the office in the Community context by the Maastricht

---

[49] H. Rasmussen, *On Law and Policy in the European Court of Justice* (1986); Professor Cappelletti has cogently refuted this suggestion in "Is the European Court of Justice 'Running Wild'?" in (1987) 12 E.L. Rev. p. 3. See also Sir Patrick Neill "The European Court of Justice: A Case Study in Judicial Activism" (1994-5 H.L. Paper 88, p. 218), replied to by Judge David Edward "Judicial Activism – Myth or Reality?" in *Legal Reasoning and Judicial Interpretation in European Law – Essays in honour of Lord Mackenzie Stuart* (1996); and T.C. Hartley, "The European Court, Judicial Objectivity and the Constitution of the European Union" (1996) 112 L.Q.R. 95, replied to by A. Arnull in (1996) 112 L.Q.R. 411.

[50] Koopmans, "The Role of Law in the Next Stage of European Integration" (1986) 35 I.C.L.Q. 925, and now see Koopmans "The Future of the Court of Justice of the European Communities" (1991) 11 Y.E.L. 15.

[51] For a more detailed study see M. Hedemann-Robinson "The individual and the EC Ombudsman" (1994) 144 New L.J. 609; also, P. Gjerlaeff Bonner, "The European Ombudsman: a novel source of soft law in the European Union" (2000) 25 E.L.Rev. 39.

[52] See Brown and Lavirotte, "The Mediator: A French Ombudsman?" (1974) 90 L.Q.R. 212.

Treaty may be regarded as the first example of the influence of Nordic legal traditions to which we refer below.

The Maastricht Treaty added a new Article 138e (now Article 195) to the EC Treaty which requires the European Parliament to appoint an Ombudsman who will be empowered to receive complaints from any citizen of the European Union or any natural or legal person relating to instances of maladministration in the activities of the Community institutions or bodies. Only the Court of Justice and the Court of First Instance, while acting in their judicial capacity, are expressly excluded from the purview of the Ombudsman.

The Ombudsman may conduct inquiries for which he finds ground, either on his own initiative or on the basis of complaints submitted to him either directly or through a Member of the European Parliament. He may not investigate matters that either are or have been the subject of legal proceedings. The only remedy open to the Ombudsman, following such inquiries is, having heard the view of the institution concerned, to prepare a report to the European Parliament and that institution. The complainant is also to be informed of the outcome of the inquiries.

The detailed rules relating to the appointment of the Ombudsman and the general conditions governing the performance of his duties have been laid down by the European Parliament,[53] subject to the approval of the Council. However, like the members of the Courts and the Commission, he is to be completely independent in the performance of his duties. He may neither seek nor take instructions from any body, nor engage in any other occupation during his term of office. The Ombudsman is to be appointed after each election to the European Parliament for the duration of its term of office and he may only be dismissed by the Court of Justice at the request of the European Parliament if he no longer fulfils the conditions required for the performance of his duties or if he is guilty of serious misconduct.

It is too early to say what impact this new office may have on the Community and it does not at present seem that the Ombudsman will himself have any *locus standi* to bring matters before the Court of his own initiative, nor will his actions be open to challenge by way of judicial review proceedings before the Court. The appointment of the first Ombudsman, a critical choice for the future of the office, was embarrassingly delayed by an arcane and arguably unnecessary debate over voting procedure during 1994. In the event Mr Jacob Söderman of Finland was appointed in 1995.

---

[53] [1994] O.J. L113/15, E.P. Decision 94262 of March 9, 1994.

## CROSS-FERTILISATION OF NATIONAL AND COMMUNITY LEGAL SYSTEMS

In the United Kingdom there is a long tradition of cross-fertilisation between the distinct legal systems of England and Scotland. On matters of law reform this has been encouraged by the two Law Commissions set up north and south of the border in 1965. In the result English and Scottish lawyers may be more receptive to the transplanting of legal concepts and institutions than lawyers of neighbouring Member States on the continent whose national laws do not enjoy the same diversity. Since British accession English and Scottish lawyers have been exposed to an additional model, the law of the European Communities and the legal order upon which it is based.

Cross-fertilisation between Community law and the national legal systems is a two-way process. First, in previous chapters, and especially in Chapter 15, we have seen examples of the impact of national law upon Community law. Until 1973 Community law was largely a product of the relatively homogeneous laws of the Six: only competition law reflected outside influence, that of the United States. But, since the first enlargement, the distinctive legal families of the British Isles and of Scandinavia have added their important contribution, to be joined in succession by the laws of Greece, Portugal, Spain, Austria, Sweden and Finland. The scope for comparative legal research at Luxembourg is now obviously immense, and we have seen how well equipped are the various services of the Court for this purpose. The fruits of this research emerge in the opinions of the advocate general and more indirectly in the Court's decisions. Moreover, by a kind of process of osmosis, common law concepts and modes of thought now permeate the Court by the mere presence there of British and Irish lawyers, whether as judge, advocate general, member of the Commission's Legal Service, or counsel for the parties.

Secondly, Community law, as it becomes more widely known, is having an increasing influence upon national law. So far as the United Kingdom is concerned, several developments may already be remarked in this direction.

The first relates to the principles of interpretation (which we have examined in Chapter 14) applied by the Court and applied also now by United Kingdom courts to provisions of Community law. These principles, as they become increasingly familiar, are having some impact in our own courts' approach to domestic legislation. Examples are the judgments of Lord Denning M.R. in *Macarthys v. Smith*[54] and of the Court of Appeal in *James*

---

[54] *Macarthys v. Smith* [1979] 1 W.L.R. 1189, C.A.

*Buchanan & Co. v. Babco.*[55] The House of Lords pointedly disagreed with the latter judgment in favour of the traditional English methods of construction but some 14 years later the House took the radical step of permitting recourse by judges to reports in Hansard of statements by a Minister or other promoter of a bill where the resulting legislation was ambiguous or obscure, or at least led to an absurdity.[56] It will be interesting to see whether the presence in the House of Lords of Lord Slynn of Hadley, sometime advocate general and judge at the Court of Justice, may lead to greater use of the Community methods and style of interpretation. In the longer term, Community methods of interpretation may influence the style of our own legislative drafting as may closer acquaintance with the practices of our Community neighbours.[57]

A matter of concern, we are told[58] is the practice of grafting EC directives on to British law by simply "copying out" verbatim such directive with no attempt to adapt their style and language to the domestic tradition of drafting. The practice stems in part from the fear of punitive damages under the principle of *Francovich*, should a Member State fail fully to implement a directive. The interpretation however of texts copied out, in time may create confusion in the courts, resulting in an increased number of references to the Court of Justice.

The wider basis of judicial review in the Community legal order (discussed in particular in Chapter 7) throws into relief the more restrictive approach of our own law, although in recent years English administrative law has been revitalised through the twin principles of reasonableness, akin to proportionality, and fairness. Judicial review as effected at Luxembourg for constitutionality has also prompted the reform of our law by the enactment of the Human Rights Act 1998 which, when fully implemented, will mean the incorporation into British domestic law of the European Convention on Human Rights (as well as the *acquis* of the case law of the Strasbourg Court) and will subject the entire legal system in the United Kingdom to a fundamental process of judicial review and, where necessary, reform by the judiciary.

British administrative law is also likely to be affected by the decision of the Court of Justice in *Francovich*.[59] If failure to

---

[55] *James Buchanan & Co. v. Babco* [1978] A.C. 141.
[56] See *Pepper v. Hart* [1993] 1 All E.R. 42, HL.
[57] See Sir William Dale (ed.), *British and French Statutory Drafting* (1987) reviewed in (1988) 37 I.C.L.Q. 696 (Brown).
[58] Michael Dynes, Whitehall Correspondent, writing in *The Times*, November 15, 1993, p. 2: see also "Copying Europe: British law needs better draftmanship" *ibid.* leading article, p. 15.
[59] Joined Cases C–6 and C–9/90 *Francovich and Bonifaci v. Italian State* [1990] ECR I–5357; [1993] 2 C.M.L.R. 66.

implement a Community directive may now found a claim for damages against the offending Member State, provided direct loss can be proved, it will be difficult to sustain the principle in domestic law that no remedy lies in damages for breach of a public law duty by the administration. Lord Goff[60] has already thrown doubt upon the decision of the Court of Appeal in *Bourgoin*[61] by suggesting a Sunday trader might rely upon *Francovich* to seek damages against central or local government where the Shops Act 1950 had been enforced against him if that Act was then held to be contrary to Article 30 EC.[62]

Again the immunity at common law of the Crown in respect of orders for interim relief[63] was rejected by the House of Lords in *Factortame*, at least where that immunity would prevent the effective protection of an individual's Community rights. The House loyally applied in this respect the ruling of the Court of Justice. Nor could that immunity survive where no Community rights, but only domestic rights, were at risk: in *M. v. Home Office*[64] the Court of Appeal held that compulsory orders might be made against the Minister of the Crown who then, if he disobeyed such an order, might be guilty of contempt of court; and this decision was upheld by the House of Lords.[65]

In another case in the House of Lords, concerning the right of the tax payer to recover from the state a payment made in respect of tax which was not due,[66] Lord Goff noted that an analogous payment under Community law could be recovered and added:

"At the time when Community law was becoming increasingly important, it would be strange if the right of the citizen to recover overpaid charges was to be more restricted under domestic law than it was under European law."

Parallel developments may occur in the field of procedure, a subject to which we have adverted in Chapter 12. The simplicity, flexibility, and relative speed of the Court's procedures may in the course of time have some effect on the reform of national court procedure, at least in the higher courts and in cases concerned

---

[60] In *Kirklees Borough Council v. Wickes Building Supplies* [1992] 7 C.L. 390, HL.

[61] *Bourgoin v. Ministry of Agriculture, Fisheries and Food* [1986] Q.B. 716.

[62] But see now Case C–169/91 *Stoke-upon-Trent City Council and Another v. B&Q plc* [1992] ECR I–6635; [1993] 1 C.M.L.R. 426, judgment of December 16, 1992, and joined Cases C–267 & 268/91 *Keck and Mithouard* [1993] ECR I–6097.

[63] Such as an interim injunction.

[64] *M. v. Home Office* [1992] 2 W.L.R. 73, CA.

[65] *M. v. Home Office* [1993] 3 W.L.R. 433, HL.

[66] *Woolwich Building Society v. Inland Revenue Commissioners* [1992] 3 W.L.R. 366, HL.

primarily with questions of law. Already in the Commercial Court and in the House of Lords judgments are handed down in writing as in Luxembourg, and not read out *in extenso*. For the determination of questions of law, the Court's methods have proved themselves effective and have made savings in time and in costs which are hard to quantify but must be very great. Conversely, the practitioner accustomed to English methods may find cause for concern in the Court's methods for resolving issues of fact. Here English lawyers will feel that there is scope for contributions from their own practices to the working of the Court: since 1973 there have already been changes in the hearing of witnesses. And since 1990, as we have seen in Chapter 5, the Court of First Instance, with its measures of organisation of procedure, has further reinforced the fact-finding capacity of the European judiciary.

Again, the recent suggestion that British judges should have the help in complex cases of a "judicial assistant" to research and investigate the law may be prompted as much by the Luxembourg model of the legal secretary as by the older American institution of the law clerk.[67]

Improvements can obviously be made in both directions; in any event, the greater exposure of judges, practitioners and students (the practitioners of tomorrow) from the Member States to the Luxembourg method can only be salutary.

An increasing convergence of ways of thinking and of practices, both in law and procedure, would thus be of mutual benefit. Beyond the development of Community law itself, this may lead to a wider integration within the Community. For as Mr Roy Jenkins reminded the European Parliament in his inaugural address as President of the Commission on January 11, 1977: "In all our activities, we must remember our underlying political purposes. Our means are largely economic, but our end is and always has been political. It is to make a European Union."

## Conclusion: Whither European Union

Since those words were spoken the fulfilment of such a Union has been advanced in two important respects. First, a single internal market has come into effect from January 1993 pursuant to the SEA 1986. Secondly, at Maastricht on February 7, 1992, the

---

[67] The suggestion is made by the Lord Chancellor, Lord Mackay of Clashfern, in his series of Hamlyn Lectures (delivered in November–December 1993). A judicial assistant was appointed in the marathon Sellafield enquiry presided over by Mr Justice French: see Philip Nicol-Gent, "Why a Judge Needs a Right-Hand Man", *The Times*, December 7, 1993.

Treaty was signed which proclaimed itself as the Treaty on European Union. Deliberately, however, the Union was not described in terms of federalism and had within it significant concessions to the sensitivities of Member State governments and their citizens such as the principle of subsidiarity and the opt-out provisions for Denmark and the United Kingdom (provisions which were further clarified at the European Council in Edinburgh in December 1992). Economic and monetary union also received a setback from the partial collapse of the exchange rate mechanism amid the turmoil of the international money markets after September 1992 and was further weakened in July 1993 when the Council had to modify radically its operation even for those countries still within the system. On the other hand, the introduction of the single currency, the Euro, in 11[68] of the Member States with effect from January 1999, was a big step in the progress towards economic and monetary union.

Jacques Delors, the long-serving President of the Commission, during his tenure strongly upheld a vision of the ever closer Union being fulfilled. But the then British Prime Minister, Margaret Thatcher, in her Bruges speech in September 1988, put a different view: for her "willing and active co-operation between independent sovereign states is the best way to build a successful European Community. To try to suppress nationhood and concentrate power at the centre of a European conglomerate would be highly damaging and would jeopardise the objectives we seek to achieve." That the Thatcherite view of the aims and methods of the Community still strikes a chord with many was confirmed by the Danish and French referenda of 1992 on ratification of the Maastricht Treaty.

France, in its post-Mitterand era, continues to show signs of a reluctance to accept the sharing of sovereignty implicit in the scheme of the Community, and now of the European Union, which it first manifested during the 1960s and which resulted in the infamous "Luxembourg compromise". In 1999 the French Parliament, by an overwhelming majority, adopted legislation on hunting wild birds flagrantly contrary to the terms of a directive,[69] which had been adopted unanimously (*i.e.* including France itself) by the Council. More recently the same Member State refused to accept the recommendation of the Community's Scientific Steering Committee to allow the resumption of imports of British beef. The legal consequences of such unwillingness to comply with Treaty obligations remain to be seen, but the Commission formally

---

[68] *i.e.* without the U.K., Denmark, Sweden and Greece.
[69] Directive 79/409 on the conservation of wild birds [1979] O.J. L103/1; C–96/98 *Commission v. France*, C–166/97 *Commission v. France*.

launched its court case against France, in respect of the beef ban, on January 4, 2000, France having disregarded the Commission's reasoned opinion issued under Article 226 (ex Article 169) EC on December 14, 1999.

The Community in its history has lived with, and survived, such tensions between the whole and the parts. In the future, as in the past, the Court of Justice has a vital role to play in helping to relieve the tensions inherent in the very concept of the Community, whilst remaining constant to the ultimate objective, however shadowy its nature and however distant its achievement, of an ever closer union of the peoples of Europe.

# Appendix I

# Select Bibliography

This bibliography is confined to a selection of mostly recent English-language publications which give special emphasis to the Court of Justice and all its activities. More complete bibliographical information may be obtained from *Bibliographie juridique de l'intégration européenne* and *Notes* published by the Court's own library, both accessible on the Internet at www.curio.eu.int.

CHAPTER ONE – GENERAL INTRODUCTION

Anthony Arnull, *The European Union and its Court of Justice* (Oxford University Press, 1999).
Ellis & Tridimas, *Public Law of the European Community: Text, Materials & Commentary* (Sweet & Maxwell, 1995).
D. A. Wyatt and A. Dashwood, *Wyatt and Dashwood's European Community Law* (3rd ed., Sweet & Maxwell, 1993).
T. C. Hartley, *The Foundations of European Community Law* (4th ed., Oxford University Press, 1998).
T. Kennedy, *Learning European Law* (Sweet & Maxwell, 1998).
A. J. Mackenzie Stuart, *The European Communities and the Rule of Law* (Hamlyn Lectures, Sweet & Maxwell, London, 1977).
Curtin and O'Keeffe (eds.), *Constitutional Adjudication in European Community and National Law* (Butterworths, 1992).
Schermers & Waelbroeck, *Judicial Protection in the European Communities* (5th ed., Kluwer, Deventer, Netherlands, 1992).
Gerhard Bebr, *Development of Judicial Control of the European Communities* (Martinus Nijhoff, 1981).
T. C. Hartley, "Constitutional and Institutional Aspects of the Maastricht Agreement" (1993) 42 I.C.L.Q. 213.
T. C. Hartley, *Constitutional Problems of the European Union* (Hart, 1999)
N. M. Hunnings, *The European Courts* (Cartermill, 1996).

CHAPTER TWO – COURT ORGANISATION

Court of Justice, *Annual Report* (prior to 1991 called *Synopsis of the Work of the Court of Justice and the Court of First Instance of the European Communities*).

CHAPTERS THREE AND FOUR – JUDGES AND ADVOCATES GENERAL

Francis G. Jacobs, "The Judicial Process in the European Court and the Role of the Advocate General" (1990) University of Exeter, Centre for European Legal Studies.
Lord Slynn of Hadley, "What is a European Community Law judge?" (1993) 52 Camb.L.J. 234.
A. A. Dashwood, "The advocate general in the Court of Justice of the European Communities" (1982) 2 L.S. 202.
Court of Justice, *Annual Report,* certain biographical information on members of the Court of Justice and the Court of First Instance.
Kirsten Borgsmidt, "The advocate general at the European Court of Justice: A Comparative Study" (1988) 13 E.L. Rev. 106.


CHAPTER FIVE – THE COURT OF FIRST INSTANCE

Fifth Report of the Select Committee on the European Communities, *A European Court of First Instance, with Evidence* (1987/88, H.L.).
F. Hubeau "Changement des Règles de Procédure devant les Juridictions Communautaires de Luxembourg" [1991] C.D.E. 499.
R. Joliet and W. Vogel, "Le Tribunal de Première Instance des Communautés Européenes" [1989] R.M.C. 423.
T. Kennedy, "The Essential Minimum: the Establishment of the Court of First Instance" [1989] 14 E.L. Rev. 7 and "The Essential Minimum: a Postscript" [1990] 15 E.L. Rev. 54.
T. Millett, *The Court of First Instance of the European Communities* (Butterworths, London, 1990).
O. Due and J.C. da Cruz Vilaça, "Formal Sitting of the European Court on September 25, 1989" [1990] 15 E.L. Rev. 3.
Bo Vesterdorf, "The Court of First Instance of the European Communities after Two Full Years in Operation" (1992) 29 C.M.L. Rev. 897.
Ole Due, "The Court of First Instance" (1988) 9 Y.E.L. 1.
A. Oldland, "Rules of procedure of the Court of First Instance" (1991) 12 Eur.Comp.L.Rev. 101.
L. N. Brown, "The First Five Years of the Court of First Instance and Appeals to the Court of Justice: Assessment & Statistics" (1995) 32 C.M.L. Rev. 743.
Koenraad Lenaerts, "The European Court of First Instance: ten years of interaction with the Court of Justice" in *Essays in honour of Lord Slynn of Hadley* (Kluwer, 2000).


CHAPTER SIX – ACTIONS AGAINST MEMBER STATES

European Commission, *Annual Reports to the European Parliament on Commission Monitoring of the Application of Community Law.*


CHAPTER SEVEN – JUDICIAL REVIEW OF COMMUNITY ACTS

Anthony Arnull, "Pirate applicants and the action for annulment under Article 173 of the EC Treaty" (1995) 32 C.M.L. Rev. 7.
C. Harding, "Who goes to Court in Europe? An analysis of litigation against the European Community" (1992) 17 E.L. Rev. 105.
A. M. Burley, "Democracy and judicial review in the European Community" [1992] Univ. of Chicago Legal Forum p. 81.

G. Ress and J. Ukrow, "Direct actions before the Court of Justice – the case of EEC anti-dumping law" in *Adjudication of international trade disputes in international and national economic law* Vol. 7, p. 159, Fribourg University Press, 1992.

Ole Due, "Legal Remedies for the failure of European Community institutions to act in conformity with Treaty obligations" (1991) 14 Fordham Int.L.J. 341.

## CHAPTER EIGHT – PLENARY JURISDICTION

H. G. Schermers & Others, *Non-Contractual Liability of the European Communities* (Kluwer, 1989).

N. M. Hunnings, "The Stanley Adams Affair or the Biter Bit" (1987) 24 C.M.L. Rev. 65.

W. Wils, "Concurrent Liability of the Community and a Member State" (1992) 17 E.L. Rev. 191.

G. E. Zur Hausen, "Non-contractual liability under European Community Law" in *Governmental Liability* (U.K. National Committee for Comparative Law, London 1991).

## CHAPTER NINE – STAFF CASES

Jeanne Penaud, "La fonction publique des Communautés Européennes", *Problèmes Politiques et Sociaux,* Paris, La Documentation Française No. 617 (1989).

## CHAPTER TEN – PRELIMINARY RULINGS

Andenas (ed.) *Article 177 References to the European Court: Policy & Practice* (1994).

Anthony Arnull, "References to the European Court" (1990) 15 E.L. Rev. 375.

Alan Dashwood and Anthony Arnull, "English Courts and Article 177 of the EEC Treaty" (1984) 4 Y.E.L. 255.

Ami Barav, "Preliminary Censorship? The Judgments of the European Court in *Foglia v. Novello*" (1980) 5 E.L. Rev. 443.

Gerhard Bebr, "Preliminary rulings of the Court of Justice, their Authority and Temporal Effect" (1981) 18 C.M.L. Rev. 475.

H. G. Schermers & Others, *Article 177 EEC: Experience and Problems* (North Holland, 1987).

Dermot Walsh, "The Appeal of an article 177 EEC referral", (1993) 56 Mod.L.Rev. p. 881.

## CHAPTER ELEVEN – OPINIONS: EXTERNAL RELATIONS

Barbara Brandtner "The 'drama' of the EEA: comments on *Opinions 1/91 and 1/92*" (1992) 3 Eur.J.Int.L. p. 300.

T. C. Hartley, "*The European Court and the EEA*" (1992) 41 I.C.L.Q. 841.

## CHAPTER TWELVE – PROCEDURE AND PRACTICE

K. P. E. Lasok, *The European Court of Justice: Practice and Procedure* (Butterworths, London, 2nd ed., 1994).

Christine Gray, "Interim Measures of Protection in the European Court" (1979) 4 E.L. Rev. 80.

John A. Usher, *European Court Practice* (Sweet & Maxwell, London, 1983).

David Vaughan and Paul Lasok (eds.), *Butterworths European Court Practice* (London, 1993).

Court of Justice, *Selected Instruments relating to the Organisation, Jurisdiction and Procedure of the Court* (Luxembourg, 1993).

Peter Oliver, "Interim measures, some recent developments" (1992) 29 C.M.L. Rev. 7.


CHAPTER THIRTEEN – LAWYERS IN THE COURT

Francis G. Jacobs, "Preparing English Lawyers for Europe" (1992) 17 E.L. Rev. 232.

Tom Kennedy, "Paying the Piper: Legal Aid in Proceedings before the European Court of Justice" (1988) 25 C.M.L. Rev. 559.

Jules Lonbay, *Training Lawyers in the European Community* (The Law Society, London, 1990).

Zahd Yaqub "Lawyers in the European Community Courts" in *The Legal Professions in the new Europe,* p. 36, Blackwell, Oxford 1993.


CHAPTER FOURTEEN – METHODS OF INTERPRETATION

Hjalte Rasmussen, *On Law and Policy in the European Court of Justice* (Nijhoff, 1986).

T. Millett, "Rules of Interpretation of EEC Legislation" (1989) 10 Stat.L.R. 163.

Richard Plender, "The Interpretation of Community Acts by Reference to the Intentions of the Authors" (1982) 2 *Yearbook of European Law* 57.

*Reports presented to a Judicial and Academic Conference,* Court of Justice of the European Communities (Luxembourg, 1976).

Hjalte Rasmussen, "Between Self-Restraint and Activism: A Judicial Policy for the European Court" (1988) 13 E.L. Rev. 28.

Mauro Cappelletti, "Is the European Court Running Wild?" (1987) 12 E.L. Rev. 3.

Bastiaan van der Esch, "The principles of interpretation applied by the Court of Justice of the European Communities and their relevance for the scope of the EEC competition rules" (1992) 15 Fordham Int.L.J. 366.

Bengoetxea, *The Legal Reasoning of the European Court of Justice* (1993).


CHAPTER FIFTEEN – GENERAL PRINCIPLES OF LAW

Anthony Arnull, *The General Principles of EEC Law and the Individual* (Pinter, London, 1989).

L. N. Brown, "State liability & damages: an emerging doctrine of European Union Law" in *Festschrift Geoffrey J. Hand* (1996) 31 Irish Jurist 7.

Lonbay & Biondi (eds.) *Remedies for Breach of EC Law* (Wiley, 1997).

Andenas & Jacobs (eds.) *European Community Law in the English Courts* (Oxford University Press, 1998).

Josephine Steiner, "How to Make the Action Suit the Case: Domestic Remedies for Breach of EEC Law" (1987) 12 E.L. Rev. 102.

CHAPTER SIXTEEN – PRECEDENT AND THE COURT

Anthony Arnull, "Interpretation and precedent in English and Community Law: evidence of cross-fertilisation?" in Andenas (ed.) *English Public Law & the Common Law of Europe* (1998) Ch. 6.
Anthony Arnull, "Owning up to Fallibility: Precedent and the Court of Justice" (1993) 30 C.M.L. Rev. 247.
T. Koopmans, "Stare Decisis in European Law" in *Essays in European Law and Integration* (eds. O'Keeffe and Schermers) (Kluwer, Deventer, Netherlands, 1982), p. 11.


CHAPTER SEVENTEEN – CONCLUSIONS: FUTURE OF THE COURT

T. Koopmans, *"The Role of Law in the Next Stage of European Integration"* (1986) 35 I.C.L.Q. 925.
J. H. H. Weiler, "Journey to an unknown destination: a retrospective and a prospective of the European Court of Justice in the arena of political integration." (1993) 31 Journal of Common Market Studies 417.
Koen Lenaerts, "Some thoughts about the interaction between judges and politicians" in *"Europe and America in 1992 and beyond. Common problems . . . common solutions?"* (University of Chicago, 1993).
William Robinson, "The Court of Justice after Maastricht" in *"Legal Issues of the Maastricht Treaty,"* Eds. D. O'Keeffe a.o. Chancery, London 1994.
Jeremy Mcbride and L. Neville Brown, "The United Kingdom, the European Community and the European Convention on Human Rights" (1981) 1 *Yearbook of European Law* 167.
M. H. Mendelson, "The European Court of Justice and Human Rights" (1981) 1 *Yearbook of European Law* 125.
Jean-Paul Jacqué and Joseph H. H. Weiler, "On the Road to European Union: A New Judicial Architecture" (1990) 27 C.M.L.Rev. 185.
Anthony Arnull, "Judging the New Europe" (1994) 19 E.L. Rev. 3.
Gordon Slynn, *Introducing a European Legal Order* (43rd Hamlyn Lectures, Sweet & Maxwell, 1992).
Anthony Arnull, "Refurbishing the judicial architecture of the European Community" (1994) 43 I.C.L.Q. 296.
British Institute of the International & Comparative Law, *The Role and Future of the European Court of Justice* (1996).

# Appendix II

# Judicial Statistics

## The work of the Court of Justice

## The work of the Court of First Instance

CAUTIONARY NOTE

It is axiomatic that "there are lies, damned lies and statistics". That jibe refers to the uses made of them rather than to the accuracy of the statistics themselves which are (usually) compiled carefully and in good faith. The statistics compiled by the Registries of the Court of Justice and the Court of First Instance upon which the following tables are based are no exception. However, one must be wary as to the conclusions to be drawn from those tables.

To take but one example, the table showing numbers of cases brought against Member States for failure to fulfil their Community obligations might be taken to indicate which Member States fulfil those obligations most and least conscientiously. However, such a conclusion would not take account of the different periods for which Member States had been members of the Community, differing political circumstances and economic conditions within each Member State, different constitutional arrangements or the varying success rates of the Commission's proceedings.

In certain years statistics may be distorted by cases arising from specific sets of circumstances. Thus in 1979, 1,112 staff cases were brought as a result of legislation changing pension entitlements and during the period 1990–92 nearly 400 claims were brought for compensation for damages caused by the "SLOM" milk quota regime (see p. 180, above). Some 380 of the latter group of cases were transferred from the jurisdiction of the Court of Justice to that of the Court of First Instance in 1993.

Some apparent discrepencies arise because information is not always dealt with consistently. Thus for example staff cases, which are direct actions, are treated as such in certain tables while in others they are enumerated separately. Again, some tables take no account of joinder of cases and show a gross figure whereas others show a net number.

Finally care must be exercised in analysing figures relating to cases transferred to the Court of First Instance (see Chapter 5).

The tables are based on those published in the Annual Report of the Court of Justice[1]. The introduction of a new, computerised case mangement system in 1996 resulted in changes to the statistics in the Annual Report. In some cases this makes comparison with the years prior to 1995 difficult. Where necessary we have supplemented the tables with additional information provided by the Registries of the two Courts, for whose assistance we are most grateful.

---

[1] Formerly known as "*Synopsis of the work of the Court of Justice and the Court of First Instance of the European Communities.*"

TABLE 1

## GENERAL TREND

Cases brought from 1953 to December 31, 1999

| Year | Direct Actions[1] | References for Preliminary Ruling | Appeals (from 1990) | Total | Applications for Interim Measures | Judgments |
|------|------|------|------|------|------|------|
| 1953 | 4 | | | 4 | | 2 |
| 1954 | 10 | | | 10 | | 4 |
| 1955 | 9 (2) | | | 9 | 2 | 6 |
| 1956 | 11 (2) | | | 11 | 2 | 4 |
| 1957 | 19 (5) | | | 19 | 2 | 10 |
| 1958 | 43 (0) | | | 43 | 0 | 13 |
| 1959 | 47 (9) | | | 47 | 5 | 18 |
| 1960 | 23 (4) | | | 23 | 2 | 11 |
| 1961 | 25 (3) | 1 | | 26 | 1 | 20 |
| 1962 | 30 (2) | 5 | | 35 | 2 | 17 |
| 1963 | 99 (36) | 6 | | 105 | 7 | 31 |
| 1964 | 49 (3) | 6 | | 55 | 4 | 52 |
| 1965 | 55 (35) | 7 | | 62 | 4 | 24 |
| 1966 | 30 (6) | 1 | | 31 | 2 | 24 |
| 1967 | 14 (9) | 23 | | 37 | 0 | 27 |
| 1968 | 24 (17) | 9 | | 33 | 1 | 30 |
| 1969 | 60 (25) | 17 | | 77 | 2 | 64 |
| 1970 | 47 (35) | 32 | | 79 | 0 | 60 |
| 1971 | 59 (46) | 37 | | 96 | 1 | 61 |
| 1972 | 42 (23) | 40 | | 82 | 2 | 80 |
| 1973 | 131 (100) | 61 | | 192 | 6 | 63 |
| 1974 | 63 (41) | 39 | | 102 | 8 | 78 |
| 1975 | 61 (26) | 69 | | 130 | 5 | |

| Year | Direct Actions[1] | | References for Preliminary Ruling | Appeals | Total | Applications for Interim Measures | Judgments |
|---|---|---|---|---|---|---|---|
| 1976 | 51 | (19) | 75 | | 126 | 6 | 88 |
| 1977 | 74 | (24) | 84 | | 158 | 6 | 100 |
| 1978 | 145 | (22) | 123 | | 268 | 7 | 97 |
| 1979 | 1216 | (1163) | 106 | | 1322 | 6 | 138 |
| 1980 | 180 | (116) | 99 | | 279 | 14 | 132 |
| 1981 | 214 | (94) | 108 | | 322 | 17 | 128 |
| 1982 | 216 | (85) | 129 | | 345 | 16 | 185 |
| 1983 | 199 | (68) | 98 | | 297 | 11 | 151 |
| 1984 | 183 | (43) | 129 | | 312 | 17 | 165 |
| 1985 | 294 | (65) | 139 | | 433 | 22 | 211 |
| 1986 | 238 | (57) | 91 | | 329 | 23 | 174 |
| 1987 | 251 | (77) | 144 | | 395 | 21 | 208 |
| 1988 | 194 | (58) | 179 | | 373 | 17 | 238 |
| 1989 | 246 | (41) | 139 | | 385 | 20 | 188 |
| 1990 | 222 | | 141 | 16 | 379 | 12 | 193 |
| 1991 | 142 | | 186 | 14 | 342 | 9 | 204 |
| 1992 | 253 | | 162 | 25 | 440 | 4 | 210 |
| 1993 | 265 | | 204 | 17 | 486 | 13 | 203 |
| 1994 | 128 | | 203 | 13 | 344 | 4 | 188 |
| 1995 | 109 | | 251 | 48 | 408 | 3 | 172 |
| 1996 | 132 | | 256 | 28 | 416 | 4 | 193 |
| 1997 | 169 | | 239 | 35 | 443 | 1 | 242 |
| 1998 | 147 | | 264 | 70 | 481 | 2 | 254 |
| 1999 | 214 | | 255 | 72 | 541 | 4 | 235 |
| **TOTAL** | **6437** | | **4157** | **338** | **10932** | **317** | **4996** |

[1] Figures in brackets and italic show the number of staff cases brought before the Court of Justice prior to the transfer of jurisdiction in such cases to the Court of First Instance.

TABLE 2

CASES DEALT WITH AND CASES PENDING 1980–1999

| Year | Cases Lodged | Judgments Delivered | Total Cases Concluded[3] | Cases Pending on December 31[3] |
|------|------|------|------|------|
| 1980 | 279 | 132 | 206 | 328 |
| 1981 | 323 | 128 | 210 | 441 |
| 1982 | 345 | 185 | 329 | 465 |
| 1983 | 297 | 151 | 275 | 489 |
| 1984 | 312 | 165 | 340 | 465 |
| 1985 | 433 | 211 | 331 | 574 |
| 1986 | 329 | 174 | 324 | 626 |
| 1987 | 395 | 208 | 380 | 603 |
| 1988 | 373 | 238 | 386 | 605 |
| 1989 | 385 | 188 | 489[1] | 501 |
| 1990 | 379 | 193 | 302 | 583 |
| 1991 | 342 | 204 | 289 | 639 |
| 1992 | 440 | 210 | 345 | 736 |
| 1993 | 486 | 203 | 793[2] | 433 |
| 1994 | 344 | 188 | 293 | 429 |
| 1995 | 408 | 172 | 289 | 620 |
| 1996 | 416 | 193 | 349 | 694 |
| 1997 | 443 | 242 | 377 | 683 |
| 1998 | 481 | 254 | 420 | 748 |
| 1999 | 541 | 235 | 395 | 896 |

[1] 153 cases were transferred to the Court of First Instance on November 15, 1989.

[2] 451 cases, including 380 relating to milk quotas were transferred to the Court of First Instance on September 27, 1993.

[3] Gross figure (*i.e.* not taking account of joined cases).

TABLE 3

TIME TAKEN TO DEAL WITH CASES[1] 1986–1999

| Year | Direct Actions | Preliminary Rulings | Appeals |
|------|---------------|--------------------|---------|
| 1986 | 20.7 | 15.5 | — |
| 1987 | 23.0 | 17.6 | — |
| 1988 | 23.7 | 17.5 | — |
| 1989 | 22.4 | 16.6 | — |
| 1990 | 24.9 | 17.5 | — |
| 1991 | 24.0 | 18.2 | 15.4 |
| 1992 | 25.8 | 18.8 | 17.5 |
| 1993 | 22.9 | 20.4 | 19.2 |
| 1994 | 20.8 | 18.0 | 21.2 |
| 1995 | 17.1 | 20.5 | 18.5 |
| 1996 | 19.6 | 20.8 | 14.0 |
| 1997 | 19.7 | 21.4 | 17.4 |
| 1998 | 21.0 | 21.4 | 20.3 |
| 1999 | 23.0 | 21.2 | 23.0 |

[1] Time taken is shown in months and tenths of a month. Cases in which proceedings have been suspended or an interlocutory judgment given are not included.

TABLE 4

INFRINGEMENT PROCEEDINGS1

| Direct Actions brought against | 1990 | 1991 | 1992 | 1993 | 1994 | 1995 | 1996 | 1997 | 1998 | 1999 | 1953/1999 |
|---|---|---|---|---|---|---|---|---|---|---|---|
| Belgium | 11 | 7 | 6 | 6 | 10 | 6 | 20 | 19 | 22 | 13 | 238 |
| Denmark | 3 | 1 | — | — | — | — | — | — | 1 | 1 | 22 |
| Germany | 5 | 1 | 5 | 3 | 5 | 10 | 9 | 20 | 5 | 9 | 131 |
| Greece | 8 | 9 | 3 | 3 | 18 | 12 | 17 | 10 | 17 | 12 | 172 |
| Spain | 3 | 2 | 5 | 5 | 9 | 7[2] | 9 | 7 | 6 | 7 | 67[2] |
| France | 6 | 4 | 1 | 2 | 8 | 6 | 11 | 15 | 22 | 35 | 220[3] |
| Ireland | 2 | 3 | 4 | — | 12 | 6 | 4 | 6 | 10 | 13 | 97 |
| Italy | 19 | 19 | 9 | 9 | 12 | 17 | 9 | 20 | 12 | 29 | 384 |
| Luxembourg | 3 | 3 | 11 | 6 | 6 | 3 | 4 | 8 | 8 | 14 | 100 |
| Netherlands | 2 | 7 | 1 | 5 | 4 | — | 2 | 3 | 3 | 1 | 60 |
| Austria | — | — | — | — | — | — | 1 | — | 5 | 8 | 13 |
| Portugal | 2 | 2 | 1 | — | 5 | 4 | 6 | 15 | 4 | 13 | 54 |
| Finland | — | — | — | — | — | — | — | — | 1 | — | 1 |
| Sweden | — | — | — | — | — | — | — | — | 1 | 1 | 2 |
| United Kingdom | 2 | - | 4 | — | 1 | 2 | 1 | 1 | 1 | 6 | 47[4] |
| Total | 66 | 58 | 50 | 39 | 90 | 73 | 93 | 124 | 118 | 162 | 1608 |

[1] Arts 169, 170, 171, 225 EC now Arts 226 EC, 227 EC, 228 EC and 229 EC, Arts 141, 142, 143 EA and Art.88 CS.
[2] Including one case based on Art. 170 EC (now Art. 227 EC) brought by Belgium.
[3] Including one case based on Art. 170 EC (now Art. 227 EC) brought by Ireland.
[4] Including one case based on Art. 170 EC (now Art. 227 EC) brought by France and Spain.

TABLE 5

CASES LODGED FOR FAILURE TO GIVE EFFECT TO A JUDGMENT OF THE COURT

(Article 228 EC (ex Article 171))

| Member States | Cases Brought | Judgments | Cases Withdrawn | Cases Pending on 31.12.99 |
|---|---|---|---|---|
| Belgium | 10 | 9 | 1 | 0 |
| Germany | 3 | 1 | 2 | 0 |
| Greece | 3 | 1 | 0 | 2[1] |
| France | 6 | 2 | 2 | 2 |
| Italy | 22 | 11 | 11 | 0 |
| Netherlands | 1 | 1 | 0 | 0 |
| TOTAL | 45 | 25 | 16 | 4 |

[1] On July 4, 2000 Greece was ordered to pay a penalty payment of £20,000 per day for failing to comply with a judgment on disposal of toxic waste dating from 1992 (Case C–387/97 *Commission v. Greece* (not yet reported).

## TABLE 6

## REFERENCES FOR A PRELIMINARY RULING
## MADE UP TO DECEMBER 31, 1993

| Belgium | | Luxembourg | |
|---|---|---|---|
| Cour de cassation | 50 | Cour supérieure de justice | 10 |
| Cour d'arbitrage | 1 | Conseil d'État | 13 |
| Conseil d'État | 20 | Cour administrative | 1 |
| Other Courts | 339 | Other Courts | 22 |
| **Total** | **410** | **Total** | **46** |
| **Denmark** | | | |
| Højesteret | 15 | **Netherlands** | |
| Other Courts | 66 | Raad van State | 35 |
| | | Hoge Raad der Nederlanden | 94 |
| **Total** | **81** | Centrale Raad van Beroep | 41 |
| **Germany** | | College van Beroep voor het Bedrijfsleven | 98 |
| Bundesgerichtshof | 68 | Tariefcommissie | 34 |
| Bundesarbeitsgericht | 4 | Other Courts | 214 |
| Bundesverwaltungsgericht | 46 | | |
| Bundesfinanzhof | 171 | **Total** | **516** |
| Bundessozialgericht | 61 | | |
| Staatsgerichtsthof | 1 | **Austria** | |
| Other Courts | 811 | Oberster Gerichtshof | 20 |
| | | Bundesvergabeamt | 8 |
| **Total** | **1162** | Verwaltungsgerichtshof | 19 |
| **Greece** | | Vergabekontrollsenat | 1 |
| Cour de cassation | 2 | Other Courts | 67 |
| Conseil d'État | 7 | | |
| Other Courts | 47 | **Total** | **115** |
| **Total** | **56** | **Portugal** | |
| **Spain** | | Supremo Tribunal Administrativo | 22 |
| Tribunal Supremo | 4 | Other Courts | 16 |
| Audiencia Nacional | 1 | | |
| Juzgado Central de lo Penal | 7 | **Total** | **38** |
| Other Courts | 113 | | |
| | | **Finland** | |
| **Total** | **125** | Korkein hallinto-oikeus | 3 |
| **France** | | Korkein oikeus | 1 |
| Cour de cassation | 58 | Other Courts | 11 |
| Conseil d'État | 19 | | |
| Other Courts | 534 | **Total** | **15** |
| **Total** | **611** | **Sweden** | |
| **Ireland** | | Högsta Domstolen | 2 |
| Supreme Court | 11 | Marknadsdomstolen | 3 |
| High Court | 15 | Regeringsrätten | 6 |
| Other Courts | 13 | Other Courts | 17 |
| **Total** | **39** | **Total** | **28** |
| **Italy** | | **United Kingdom** | |
| Corte suprema di Cassazione | 63 | House of Lords | 24 |
| Consiglio di Stato | 30 | Court of Appeal | 12 |
| Other Courts | 531 | Other Courts | 255 |
| **Total** | **624** | **Total** | **291** |
| **Grand Total** | | | **4157** |

TABLE 7

## THE WORK OF THE COURT OF FIRST INSTANCE

### General Trend

| Year | Cases lodged | Pending cases on 31 December | Cases concluded | Judgments delivered[1] | Decisions having given rise to an appeal[2] |
|---|---|---|---|---|---|
| 1989 | 169 | 164 (168) | 1 (1) | — (—) | — (—) |
| 1990 | 59 | 123 (145) | 79 (82) | 59 (61) | 16 (46) |
| 1991 | 95 | 152 (173) | 64 (67) | 41 (43) | 13 (62) |
| 1992 | 123 | 152 (171) | 104 (125) | 60 (77) | 24 (86) |
| 1993 | 596 | 638 (661) | 95 (106) | 47 (54) | 16 (66) |
| 1994 | 409 | 432 (628) | 412 (442) | 60 (70) | 12 (105) |
| 1995 | 253 | 427 (616) | 197 (265) | 98 (128) | 47 (142) |
| 1996 | 229 | 476 (659) | 172 (186) | 107 (118) | 27 (133) |
| 1997 | 644 | 640 (1117) | 179 (186) | 95 (99) | 35 (139) |
| 1998 | 238 | 569 (1007) | 279 (348) | 130 (151) | 67 (214) |
| 1999 | 384 | 663 (732) | 322 (659) | 115 (150) | 60 (177) |
| Total | 3199 | | 1904 (2467) | 812 (951) | 317 (1170) |

[1] Figures in brackets show the number of cases concluded by a judgment.
[2] Figures in brackets and in italic show the number of appealable decisions (judgments, orders, interim measures, no need to give a judgment, refusal of leave to intervene) in which the time limit to appeal has expired or an appeal has been lodged.

TABLE 8

## DURATION OF THE PROCEEDINGS[1]

|  | 1997 | | 1998 | 1999 |
|---|---|---|---|---|
| **Other actions** | 29.3 | 11.2 | 20.0 | 12.6 |
| **Intellectual Property** | — | — | — | 8.6 |
| **Staff cases** | 18.7 | 10.7 | 16.7 | 17.0 |

---

[1] In this table, the length of proceedings is expressed in months and tenths of a month. In 1998 the separate presentation of cases concluded by a judgment and those concluded by order was dropped from the statistics, published in the Annual Report.

TABLE 9

## RESULTS OF DECIDED APPEALS (1997–1999)

| Result | 1997 | 1998 | 1999 | Total | % |
|---|---|---|---|---|---|
| Unfounded | 15 | 15 | 22 | 52 | 41.6 |
| Manifestly Unfounded | 3 | 1 | 6 | 10 | 8.0 |
| Manifestly Inadmissible | 2 | 1 | 3 | 6 | 4.8 |
| Manifestly Inadmissible and Unfounded | 6 | 9 | 15 | 30 | 24.0 |
| Decision quashed and referred back | 4 | 7 | 2 | 13 | 10.4 |
| Decision quashed and not referred back | — | — | 4 | 4 | 3.2 |
| Decision partially quashed and referred back | — | 1 | — | 1 | 0.8 |
| Decision parttially quashed and not referred back | 2 | 1 | 2 | 5 | 4.0 |
| Removed from the Register | — | 1 | 3 | 4 | 3.2 |
| Total | 32 | 36 | 57 | 125 | 100.0 |

# Appendix III

# Members of the Court of Justice

(Up to December 31, 1999)

| Name [1]<br>*Date of birth<br>+ Date of death | Nationality | Sworn in | Mandates | President | Left Office<br>(Expiry of<br>current<br>mandate) |
|---|---|---|---|---|---|
| PILOTTI Massimo (J)<br>*01.08.1879<br>+ 29.04.1962 | Italian | 10.12.52 | 1 | 10.12.52 to 06.10.58 | 06.10.58 |
| SERRARENS Petrus Joséphus Servatius (J)<br>*12.11.1888<br>+ 26.08.1963 | Netherlands | 10.12.52 | 1 | | 06.10.58 |
| RIESE Otto (J)<br>*27.10.1894<br>+ 04.06.1977 | German | 10.12.52 | 2 | | 06.02.63 |

| | | | | | |
|---|---|---|---|---|---|
| DELVAUX Louis (J) *21.10.1895 +24.08.1976 | Belgian | 10.12.52 | 3 | | 09.10.67 |
| RUEFF Jacques (J) *23.08.1896 +24.04.1978 | French | 10.12.52 | 2 | | 18.05.62 |
| HAMMES Charles Léon (J) *21.05.1898 +09.12.1967 | Luxembourgish | 10.12.52 | 3 | 08.10.64 to 09.10.67 | 09.10.67 |
| VAN KLEFFENS Adrianus (J) *14.10.1899 +02.08.1973 | Netherlands | 10.12.52 | 1 | | 06.10.58 |
| LAGRANGE Maurice (AG) *14.05.1900 +05.09.1986 | French | 10.12.52 | 2 | | 08.10.64 |
| ROEMER Karl (AG) *30.12.1899 +21.12.1894 | German | 02.02.53 | 4 | | 09.10.73 |
| VAN HOUTTE Albert (Registrar) *12.11.1914 | Belgian | 26.03.53 | 5 | | 09.02.82 |
| ROSSI Rino (J) *14.08.1889 +06.02.1974 | Italian | 07.10.58 | 1 | | 08.10.64 |

[1] (AG) Advocate General
(J) Judge

| Name [1]<br>*Date of birth<br>+Date of death | Nationality | Sworn in | Mandates | President | Left Office<br>(Expiry of<br>current<br>mandate) |
|---|---|---|---|---|---|
| DONNER Andreas Matthias (J)<br>*15.01.1918<br>+24.08.1992 | Netherlands | 07.10.58 | | 07.10.58 to 07.10.64 | 29.03.79 |
| CATALANO Nicola (J)<br>*17.02.1910<br>+05.08.1984 | Italian | 07.10.58 | 2 | | 08.03.62 |
| TRABUCCHI Alberto (J & AG)<br>*26.07.1907<br>+18.04.1998 | Italian | (Judge) 08.03.62<br>(Advocate General) 09.01.73 | 4 | | 07.10.76 |
| LECOURT Robert (J)<br>*19.09.1908 | French | 18.05.62 | 4 | 10.10.67 to 06.10.76 | 25.10.76 |
| STRAUSS Walter (J)<br>*15.06.1900<br>+01.01.1976 | German | 06.02.63 | 2 | | 28.10.70 |
| MONACO Riccardo (J)<br>*02.01.1909 | Italian | 08.10.64 | 2 | | 03.02.76 |
| GAND Joseph (AG)<br>*28.02.1913<br>+04.10.1974 | French | 08.10.64 | 1 | | 06.10.70 |

| | | | | | |
|---|---|---|---|---|---|
| MERTENS DE WILMARS Joseph Marie Honoré Charles (J) *22.06.1912 | Belgian | 09.10.67 | 3 | 30.10.80 to 10.04.84 | 10.04.84 |
| PESCATORE Pierre (J) *20.11.1919 | Luxembourgish | 09.10.67 | 3 | | 07.10.85 |
| KUTSCHER Hans (J) *14.12.1911 +24.08.1993 | German | 28.10.70 | 2 | 07.10.76 to 30.10.80 | 30.10.80 |
| DUTHEILLET DE LAMOTHE Alain Louis Georges (AG) *25.08.1919 +02.01.1972 | French | 07.10.70 | 1 | | (died) 02.01.72 |
| MAYRAS Henri (AG) *29.03.1920 +09.07.1995 | French | 22.03.72 | 2 | | 18.03.81 |
| O'DALAIGH Cearbhall (J) *12.02.1911 +21.03.1978 | Irish | 09.01.73 | 2 | | 12.12.74 |
| SØRENSEN Max (J) *19.02.1913 +11.10.1981 | Danish | 09.01.73 | 1 | | 08.10.79 |

[1] (AG) Advocate General
(J) Judge

| Name [1] *Date of birth +Date of death | Nationality | Sworn in | Mandates | President | Left Office (Expiry of current mandate) |
|---|---|---|---|---|---|
| MACKENZIE STUART Alexander John (J) *18.11.1924 | British | 09.01.73 | 3 | 10.04.84 to 06.10.88 | 06.10.88 |
| WARNER Jan-Pierre (AG) *24.09.1924 | British | 09.01.73 | 2 | | 26.02.81 |
| REISCHL Gerhard (AG) *17.07.1918 +16.04.1998 | German | 09.10.73 | 2 | | 11.01.84 |
| O'COAIMH Aindrias (J) *04.10.1912 +29.12.1994 | Irish | 12.12.74 | 2 | | 16.01.85 |
| CAPOTORTI Francesco (J & AG) *09.02.1925 | Italian | (Judge) 03.02.76 (Advocate General) 07.10.76 | 2 | | 06.10.82 |
| BOSCO Giacinto (J) *25.01.1905 +11.10.1997 | Italian | 07.10.76 | 2 | | 06.10.88 |
| TOUFFAIT Adolphe (J) *26.03.1907 +12.03.1990 | French | 26.10.76 | 1 | | 06.10.82 |
| KOOPMANS Thymen (J) *11.08.1929 | Netherlands | 29.03.79 | 3 | | 29.03.90 |

| | | | | 07.10.88 to 06.10.94 | |
|---|---|---|---|---|---|
| DUE Ole (J) *10.02.1931 | Danish | 08.10.79 | 3 | 07.10.88 to 06.10.94 | 06.10.94 |
| EVERLING Ulrich (J) *02.06.1925 | German | 30.10.80 | 2 | | 06.10.88 |
| CHLOROS Alexandros (J) *15.08.1926 +15.11.1982 | Greek | 12.01.81 | 1 | | (died) 15.11.82 |
| SLYNN Sir Gordon (AG & J) *17.02.1930 | British | (Advocate General) 26.02.81 (Judge) 07.10.88 | 3 | | 10.03.92 |
| ROZES Simone (AG) *29.03.1920 | French | 18.03.81 | 2 | | 13.02.84 |
| VERLOREN VAN THEMAAT Pieter (AG) *16.03.1916 | Netherlands | 04.06.81 | 1 | | 13.01.86 |
| GREVISSE Fernand (J) *28.07.1924 | French | 04.06.81 | 1 | | 06.10.82 |
| HEIM Paul (Registrar) *23.05.1932 | British | 10.02.82 | 1 | | 09.02.88 |
| BAHLMANN Kai (J) *29.01.1927 | German | 07.10.82 | 1 | | 06.10.88 |
| MANCINI Giuseppe Federico (AG & J) *23.12.1927 +21.07.1999 | Italian | (Advocate General) 07.10.82 (Judge) 07.10.88 | 3 | | (died) 21.07.99 |

[1] (AG) Advocate General
(J) Judge

| Name [1]<br>*Date of birth<br>+Date of death | Nationality | Sworn in | Mandates | President | Left Office<br>(Expiry of<br>current<br>mandate) |
|---|---|---|---|---|---|
| GALMOT Yves (J)<br>*05.01.1931 | French | 07.10.82 | 1 | | 06.10.88 |
| KAKOURIS Constantinos (J)<br>*16.03.1919 | Greek | 14.03.83 | 3 | | 06.10.97 |
| LENZ Carl Otto (AG)<br>*05.06.1930 | German | 11.01.84 | 3 | | 06.10.97 |
| DARMON Marco (AG)<br>*26.01.1930 | French | 13.02.84 | 2 | | 06.10.94 |
| JOLIET René (J)<br>*17.01.1938<br>+15.07.1995 | Belgian | 10.04.84 | 3 | | (died)<br>15.07.95 |
| O'HIGGINS Thomas Francis (J)<br>*23.07.1916 | Irish | 16.01.85 | 2 | | 06.10.91 |
| SCHOCKWEILER Fernand (J)<br>*15.06.1935<br>+01.06.1996 | Luxembourgish | 07.10.85 | 2 | | (died)<br>01.06.96 |
| MISCHO Jean (AG)<br>*07.09.1938 | Luxembourgish | 13.01.86 | 1 | | 06.10.91 |
| DE CARVALHO MOITINHO DE ALMEIDA<br>José Carlos (J)<br>*17.03.1936 | Portuguese | 31.01.86 | 3 | | (06.10.00) |

| | Nationality | | | | |
|---|---|---|---|---|---|
| DA CRUZ VILAÇA José Luis (AG) *20.09.1944 | Portuguese | 31.01.86 | 1 | | 06.10.88 |
| RODRIGUEZ IGLESIAS Gil Carlos (J) *26.05.1946 | Spanish | 31.01.86 | 3 | 07.10.94 to 6.10.2000) | (06.10.03) |
| GIRAUD Jean-Guy (Registrar) *12.04.1944 | French | 12.02.88 | 1 | | 09.02.94 |
| GREVISSE Fernand (J) *28.07.1924 | French | 07.10.88 (Second appointment) | 1 | | 06.10.94 |
| DIEZ DE VELASCO Manuel (J) *22.05.1926 | Spanish | 07.10.88 | 1 | | 06.10.94 |
| ZULEEG Manfred (J) *21.03.1935 | German | 07.10.88 | 1 | | 06.10.94 |
| VAN GERVEN Walter (AG) *11.05.1935 | Belgian | 07.10.88 | 1 | | 06.10.94 |
| JACOBS Francis (AG) *08.06.1939 | British | 07.10.88 | 3 | | (06.10.03) |
| TESAURO Giuseppe (AG) *15.11.1942 | Italian | 07.10.88 | 2 | | 04.03.98 |
| KAPTEYN Paul Joan Georges (J) *31.01.1928 | Netherlands | 29.03.90 | 2 | | (06.10.00) |

[1] (AG) Advocate General
(J) Judge

| Name [1] *Date of birth +Date of death | Nationality | Sworn in | Mandates | President | Left Office (Expiry of current mandate) |
|---|---|---|---|---|---|
| GULMANN Claus (AG & J) *22.04.1942 | Danish | (Advocate General) 07.10.91 (Judge) 07.10.94 | 3 | | (06.10.03) |
| MURRAY John L. (J) *27.06.1943 | Irish | 07.10.91 | 2 | | 05.10.99 |
| EDWARD David A.O. (J) *14.11.1934 | British | 10.03.92 | 2 | | (06.10.00) |
| GRASS Roger (Registrar) *23.04.1948 | French | 10.02.94 | 1 | | (09.02.06) |
| LA PERGOLA Antonio (J & AG) *13.11.1931 | Italian | (Judge) 07.10.94 (Advocate General) 01.01.95 | 1 | | (06.10.00) |
| COSMAS Georgios (AG) *14.07.1932 | Greek | 07.10.94 | 1 | | (06.10.00) |
| PUISSOCHET Jean-Pierre (J) *03.05.1936 | French | 07.10.94 | 1 | | (06.10.00) |
| LEGER Philippe (AG) *10.12.1938 | French | 07.10.94 | 1 | | (06.10.00) |
| HIRSCH Günter (J) *30.01.1943 | German | 07.10.94 | 1 | | (06.10.00) |
| ELMER Michael Bendik (AG) *26.02.1949 | Danish | 07.10.94 | 1 | | 18.12.97 |

| | Nationality | | [1] | |
|---|---|---|---|---|
| JANN Peter (J) *20.01.1935 | Austrian | 19.01.95 | 1 | (06.10.00) |
| RAGNEMALM Hans (J) *30.03.1940 | Swedish | 19.01.95 | 1 | (06.10.00) |
| SEVÓN Leif (J) *31.10.1941 | Finnish | 19.01.95 | 2 | (06.10.03) |
| FENNELLY Nial (AG) *03.05.1942 | Irish | 19.01.95 | 1 | (06.10.00) |
| RUIZ-JARABO COLOMER Dámaso (AG) *20.06.1949 | Spanish | 19.01.95 | 2 | (06.10.03) |
| WATHELET Melchior (J) *06.03.1949 | Belgian | 19.09.95 | 2 | (06.10.03) |
| SCHINTGEN Romain (J) *22.03.1939 | Luxembourgish | 12.07.96 | 2 | (06.10.03) |
| IOANNOU M. Krateros (J) *03.06.1935 + 10.03.99 | Greek | 07.10.97 | 1 | (died) 10.03.99 |
| ALBER Siegbert (AG) *27.07.1936 | German | 07.10.97 | 1 | (06.10.03) |
| MISCHO Jean (AG) *07.09.1938 | Luxembourgish | 19.12.97 (Second appointment) | 1 | (06.10.03) |

[1] (AG) Advocate General
(J) Judge

| Name [1]<br>*Date of birth<br>+ Date of death | Nationality | Sworn in | Mandates | President | Left Office<br>(Expiry of<br>current<br>mandate) |
|---|---|---|---|---|---|
| SAGGIO Antonio (AG)<br>*19.02.1934 | Italian | 05.03.98 | 1 | | (06.10.00) |
| SKOURIS Vassilios (J)<br>*06.03.1948 | Greek | 08.06.99 | 1 | | (06.10.03) |
| MACKEN Fidelma (J)<br>*28.02.1945 | Irish | 06.10.99 | 1 | | (06.10.03) |

[1] (AG) Advocate General
(J) Judge

# Appendix IV

# Members of the Court of First Instance

(UP TO DECEMBER 31, 1999)

| Name<br>Date of birth (–)<br>Date of death (+)<br>Nationality | Previous career | Sworn in | Mandates (including partial mandates) |
|---|---|---|---|
| José Luis DA CRUZ VILAÇA<br>–20.09.44<br><br>Portuguese | Practising lawyer; Secretary of State for European Affairs; Advocate General at ECJ January 1986 to October 1988 | 25.09.89 | 2 |
| Donal Patrick Michael BARRINGTON<br>–28.02.28<br><br>Irish | High Court Judge, Ireland | 25.09.89 | 2 |
| Antonio SAGGIO<br>–19.02.34<br><br>Italian | Judge of the Italian Corte Suprema di Cassazione(*) | 25.09.89 | 2 |
| David Alexander Ogilvy EDWARD<br>–14.11.34<br><br>United Kingdom | Scottish Q.C. and Salvesen Professor of Law, Edinburgh; President of CCBE | 25.09.89 | 1 |
| Heinrich KIRSCHNER<br>–07.01.38<br>+06.02.97<br><br>German | Judge and senior official of German Ministry of Justice | 25.09.89 | 2 |
| Christos G. YERARIS<br>–13.09.38<br><br>Greek | Member of the Greek council of State | 25.09.89 | 1 |

| | | | |
|---|---|---|---|
| Romain Alphonse **SCHINTGEN** –22.03.39 Luxembourgish | Avocat-avoué; Specialist in Labour Law; Senior official in Ministry of Labour | 25.09.89 | 2 |
| Cornelis Paulus **BRIËT** –23.02.44 Netherlands | Vice-President of Arrondisse-mentsrechtbank, Rotterdam | 25.09.89 | 2 |
| Bo **VESTERDORF** –11.10.45 Danish | Lawyer-linguist at ECJ; Official of Danish Ministry of Justice; Judge on Østre Landsret | 25.09.89 | 3 |
| Rafael GARCIA-VALDECASAS Y FERNANDEZ –09.01.46 Spanish | Abogado del Estado; Registrar of Administrative Courts of Jaén and Cordoba; Head of legal section of Ministry of Foreign Affairs | 25.09.89 | 2 |
| Jacques **BIANCARELLI** –18.10.48 French | Auditeur at French Conseil d'Etat(*) | 25.09.89 | 1 |
| Koenraad Maria Jan Suzanna **LENAERTS** –20.12.54 Belgian | Professor at Katholieke Univer-siteit Leuven; member of Brussels bar (*) | 25.09.89 | 3 |
| Hans **JUNG** –29.10.44 (Registrar) German | Member of Frankfurt Bar; Assistant Professor, Berlin; Deputy Registrar of the Court of Justice (*) | 10.10.89 | 2 |
| Christopher William **BELLAMY** –25.04.46 United Kingdom | Barrister; Q.C.; co-author of "Bellamy Child, Competition Law" | 10.03.92 | 2 |
| Andreas **KALOGERO-POULOS** –22.04.44 Greek | Member of the Athens Bar; Pro-fessor of Public Law and European Law Athens; Legal adviser at the Court of Auditors of the EC (*) | 18.09.92 | 1 |
| Virpi Eija **TIILI** –18.06.42 Finland | Director of Legal Affairs of Chamber of Commerce of Fin-land; Director General of Finnish Consumer Protection Service | 18.01.95 | 2 |

| | | | |
|---|---|---|---|
| Pernilla LINDH<br>–08.10.45<br><br>Swedish | Judge on Stockholm Court of Appeal; Director-General of Legal Service of commercial section of Ministry of Foreign Affairs | 18.01.95 | 2 |
| Joseph AZIZI<br>–14.04.48<br><br>Austrian | Lecturer in economics and law, Vienna; Ministerial adviser and head of division of Federal Chancellory | 18.01.95 | 2 |
| André POTOCKI<br>–21.06.50<br><br>French | Head of European and international affairs. Ministry of Justice; Vice-President of Tribunal de Grande Instance, Paris; Secretary General of the Cour de Cassation | 18.09.95 | 1 |
| Rui Manuel GENS DE MOURA RAMOS<br>–30.06.50<br><br>Portuguese | Professor of Law, Coimbra and Porto; visiting Professor, The Hague, Paris | 18.09.95 | 2 |
| John D. COOKE<br>–07.05.44<br><br>Irish | Senior Counsel of the Irish Bar; President of CCBE | 10.01.96 | 1 |
| Marc JAEGER<br>–04.10.54<br><br>Luxembourgish | Avocat; Vice-President of the Tribunal d'arrondissement, Luxembourg; Lecturer at Centre universitaire du Luxembourg (*) | 11.07.96 | 2 |
| Jörg PIRRUNG<br>–27.03.40<br><br>German | Head of private international Law section and later of civil law directorate of Federal Ministry of Justice | 11.06.97 | 1 |
| Paolo MENGOZZI<br>–16.06.38<br><br>Italian | Professor of international and European law, Bologna; visiting Professor New York, Georgetown, Georgia, Paris II, Under-secretary of State for Trade and Industry | 04.03.98 | 1 |
| Arjen W. H. MEIJ<br>–01.12.44<br><br>Netherlands | Counsellor at Supreme Court of Netherlands; Vice-President of College Van Beroep voor het bedrijfsleven (*) | 17.09.98 | 1 |
| Michalis VILARAS<br>–07.12.50<br><br>Greek | Advocate of Athens Bar; Auditor and *Maître des requêtes* Greek Council of State; Director of Legal service of the secretariat general of the Greek Government | 17.09.98 | 1 |
| Nicholas James FORWOOD<br>–22.06.48<br><br>United Kingdom | Barrister; Q.C.; Head of delegation of CCBE to ECJ | 15.12.99 | 1 |

* Former Legal Secretary at ECJ.

# Appendix V

# Tables of Equivalences referred to in Article 12 of the Treaty of Amsterdam

Article 12 of the Treaty of Amsterdam provides for the renumbering of the Articles, titles and sections of the Treaty on European Union and the EC Treaty. Although this step is welcome in principle as a contribution to improving and in Community jargon, the transparency of the TEU and the EC Treaty the simplistic and unimaginative way in which it has been carried out will cause problems for all users of the Treaty for many years to come. As a result, in writing about or discussing cases or other subjects involving provisions of the Treaties, it will be necessary to exercise great care to ensure that the correct article has in fact been cited. Lawyers, students and anyone else needing to use the Treaties – other than those who wish to attempt prodigious feats of memory – will need to refer to the table of equivalences annexed to the Treaty and reproduced below.

The method chosen for the renumbering was first to add to the Treaties all of the new provisions and amendments made, both to the TEU and the EC Treaty by the Treaty of Amsterdam, then to delete all redundant articles and, finally, without reordering or restructuring the Treaty in any way, simply to renumber them from Articles 1 to 53 in the case of the TEU and 1 to 314 in the case of the EC Treaty. In the consolidated version of the Treaties published by the Office for Official Publications of the Communities, each article is referred to by its new number first with the old one in brackets. In this book we have adopted the usage:

"Article 85 EC (now Article 81)"

*or* "Article 234 EC (formerly Article 177)"

*or* "Article 234 EC (ex Article 177)"

*or* "Article 230 (formerly Aricle 173)".

TABLE OF EQUIVALENCES

## A. TREATY ON EUROPEAN UNION

(\*) indicates new Article introduced by the Treaty of Amsterdam
(\*\*) indicates new Title introduced by the Treaty of Amsterdam
(\*\*\*) indicates Title restructured by the Treaty of Amsterdam

| Previous numbering | New numbering |
|---|---|
| Title I | Title I |
| Article A | Article 1 |
| Article B | Article 2 |
| Article C | Article 3 |
| Article D | Article 4 |
| Article E | Article 5 |
| Article F | Article 6 |
| Article F.1 (*) | Article 7 |
| Title II | Title II |
| Article G | Article 8 |
| Title III | Title III |
| Article H | Article 9 |
| Title IV | Title IV |
| Article I | Article 10 |
| Title V (***) | Title V |
| Article J.1 | Article 11 |
| Article J.2 | Article 12 |
| Article J.3 | Article 13 |
| Article J.4 | Article 14 |
| Article J.5 | Article 15 |
| Article J.6 | Article 16 |
| Article J.7 | Article 17 |
| Article J.8 | Article 18 |
| Article J.9 | Article 19 |
| Article J.10 | Article 20 |
| Article J.11 | Article 21 |
| Article J.12 | Article 22 |
| Article J.13 | Article 23 |
| Article J.14 | Article 24 |
| Article J.15 | Article 25 |
| Article J.16 | Article 26 |
| Article J.17 | Article 27 |
| Article J.18 | Article 28 |
| Title VI (***) | Title VI |
| Article K.1 | Article 29 |
| Article K.2 | Article 30 |
| Article K.3 | Article 31 |
| Article K.4 | Article 32 |
| Article K.5 | Article 33 |
| Article K.6 | Article 34 |
| Article K.7 | Article 35 |

| Previous numbering | New numbering |
|---|---|
| Title VI (***)—*cont.* | Title VI—*cont.* |
| Article K.8 | Article 36 |
| Article K.9 | Article 37 |
| Article K.10 | Article 38 |
| Article K.11 | Article 39 |
| Article K.12 | Article 40 |
| Article K.13 | Article 41 |
| Article K.14 | Article 42 |
| Title VIa (**) | Title VII |
| Article K.15 (*) | Article 43 |
| Article K.16 (*) | Article 44 |
| Article K.17 (*) | Article 45 |
| Title VII | Title VIII |
| Article L | Article 46 |
| Article M | Article 47 |
| Article N | Article 48 |
| Article O | Article 49 |
| Article P | Article 50 |
| Article Q | Article 51 |
| Article R | Article 52 |
| Article S | Article 53 |

# B. TREATY ESTABLISHING THE EUROPEAN COMMUNITY

(*) indicates new Article introduced by the Treaty of Amsterdam
(**) indicates new Title introduced by the Treaty of Amsterdam
(***) indicates Chapter 1 restructured by the Treaty of Amsterdam

| Previous numbering | New numbering |
|---|---|
| Part One | Part One |
| Article 1 | Article 1 |
| Article 2 | Article 2 |
| Article 3 | Article 3 |
| Article 3a | Article 4 |
| Article 3b | Article 5 |
| Article 3c (*) | Article 6 |
| Article 4 | Article 7 |
| Article 4a | Article 8 |
| Article 4b | Article 9 |
| Article 5 | Article 10 |
| Article 5a (*) | Article 11 |
| Article 6 | Article 12 |
| Article 6a (*) | Article 13 |
| Article 7 (repealed) | - |
| Article 7a | Article 14 |
| Article 7b (repealed) | - |
| Article 7c | Article 15 |
| Article 7d (*) | Article 16 |
| Part Two | Part Two |
| Article 8 | Article 17 |
| Article 8a | Article 18 |
| Article 8b | Article 19 |
| Article 8c | Article 20 |
| Article 8d | Article 21 |
| Article 8e | Article 22 |
| Part Three Title I | Part Three Title I |
| Article 9 | Article 23 |
| Article 10 | Article 24 |
| Article 11 (repealed) | - |
| Chapter 1 Section 1 (deleted) | Chapter 1 - |
| Article 12 | Article 25 |
| Article 13 (repealed) | - |
| Article 14 (repealed) | - |
| Article 15 (repealed) | - |
| Article 16 (repealed) | - |
| Article 17 (repealed) | - |
| Section 2 (deleted) | - |
| Article 18 (repealed) | - |
| Article 19 (repealed) | - |
| Article 20 (repealed) | - |
| Article 21 (repealed) | - |
| Article 22 (repealed) | - |
| Article 23 (repealed) | - |

| Previous numbering | New numbering |
|---|---|
| Chapter 1—*cont.*<br>Section 2 (deleted)—*cont.* | Chapter 1—*cont.*<br>- |
| Article 24 (repealed) | - |
| Article 25 (repealed) | - |
| Article 26 (repealed) | - |
| Article 27 (repealed) | - |
| Article 28 | Article 26 |
| Article 29 | Article 27 |
| Chapter 2 | Chapter 2 |
| Article 30 | Article 28 |
| Article 31 (repealed) | - |
| Article 32 (repealed) | - |
| Article 33 (repealed) | - |
| Article 34 | Article 29 |
| Article 35 (repealed) | - |
| Article 36 | Article 30 |
| Article 37 | Article 31 |
| Title II | Title II |
| Article 38 | Article 32 |
| Article 39 | Article 33 |
| Article 40 | Article 34 |
| Article 41 | Article 35 |
| Article 42 | Article 36 |
| Article 43 | Article 37 |
| Article 44 (repealed) | - |
| Article 45 (repealed) | - |
| Article 46 | Article 38 |
| Article 47 (repealed) | - |
| Title III<br>Chapter 1 | Title III<br>Chapter 1 |
| Article 48 | Article 39 |
| Article 49 | Article 40 |
| Article 50 | Article 41 |
| Article 51 | Article 42 |
| Chapter 2 | Chapter 2 |
| Article 52 | Article 43 |
| Article 53 (repealed) | - |
| Article 54 | Article 44 |
| Article 55 | Article 45 |
| Article 56 | Article 46 |
| Article 57 | Article 47 |
| Article 58 | Article 48 |
| Chapter 3 | Chapter 3 |
| Article 59 | Article 49 |
| Article 60 | Article 50 |
| Article 61 | Article 51 |
| Article 62 (repealed) | - |
| Article 63 | Article 52 |
| Article 64 | Article 53 |

| Previous numbering | New numbering |
|---|---|
| Chapter 3—*cont.* | Chapter 3—*cont.* |
| Article 65 | Article 54 |
| Article 66 | Article 55 |
| Chapter 4 | Chapter 4 |
| Article 67 (repealed) | - |
| Article 68 (repealed) | - |
| Article 69 (repealed) | - |
| Article 70 (repealed) | - |
| Article 71 (repealed) | - |
| Article 72 (repealed) | - |
| Article 73 (repealed) | - |
| Article 73a (repealed) | - |
| Article 73b | Article 56 |
| Article 73c | Article 57 |
| Article 73d | Article 58 |
| Article 73e (repealed) | - |
| Article 73f | Article 59 |
| Article 73g | Article 60 |
| Article 73h (repealed) | - |
| Title IIIa (**) | Title IV |
| Article 73i (*) | Article 61 |
| Article 73j (*) | Article 62 |
| Article 73k (*) | Article 63 |
| Article 73l (*) | Article 64 |
| Article 73m (*) | Article 65 |
| Article 73n (*) | Article 66 |
| Article 73o (*) | Article 67 |
| Article 73p (*) | Article 68 |
| Article 73q (*) | Article 69 |
| Title IV | Title V |
| Article 74 | Article 70 |
| Article 75 | Article 71 |
| Article 76 | Article 72 |
| Article 77 | Article 73 |
| Article 78 | Article 74 |
| Article 79 | Article 75 |
| Article 80 | Article 76 |
| Article 81 | Article 77 |
| Article 82 | Article 78 |
| Article 83 | Article 79 |
| Article 84 | Article 80 |
| Title V<br>Chapter 1<br>Section 1 | Title VI<br>Chapter 1<br>Section 1 |
| Article 85 | Article 81 |
| Article 86 | Article 82 |
| Article 87 | Article 83 |
| Article 88 | Article 84 |
| Article 89 | Article 85 |
| Article 90 | Article 86 |

| Previous numbering | New numbering |
|---|---|
| Chapter 1—*cont.* | Chapter 1—*cont.* |
| Section 2 (deleted) | - |
| Article 91 (repealed) | - |
| Section 3 | Section 2 |
| Article 92 | Article 87 |
| Article 93 | Article 88 |
| Article 94 | Article 89 |
| Chapter 2 | Chapter 2 |
| Article 95 | Article 90 |
| Article 96 | Article 91 |
| Article 97 (repealed) | - |
| Article 98 | Article 92 |
| Article 99 | Article 93 |
| Chapter 3 | Chapter 3 |
| Article 100 | Article 94 |
| Article 100a | Article 95 |
| Article 100b (repealed) | - |
| Article 100c (repealed) | - |
| Article 100d (repealed) | - |
| Article 101 | Article 96 |
| Article 102 | Article 97 |
| Title VI | Title VII |
| Chapter 1 | Chapter 1 |
| Article 102a | Article 98 |
| Article 103 | Article 99 |
| Article 103a | Article 100 |
| Article 104 | Article 101 |
| Article 104a | Article 102 |
| Article 104b | Article 103 |
| Article 104c | Article 104 |
| Chapter 2 | Chapter 2 |
| Article 105 | Article 105 |
| Article 105a | Article 106 |
| Article 106 | Article 107 |
| Article 107 | Article 108 |
| Article 108 | Article 109 |
| Article 108a | Article 110 |
| Article 109 | Article 111 |
| Chapter 3 | Chapter 3 |
| Article 109a | Article 112 |
| Article 109b | Article 113 |
| Article 109c | Article 114 |
| Article 109d | Article 115 |

| Previous numbering | New numbering |
|---|---|
| Chapter 4 | Chapter 4 |
| Article 109e | Article 116 |
| Article 109f | Article 117 |
| Article 109g | Article 118 |
| Article 109h | Article 119 |
| Article 109i | Article 120 |
| Article 109j | Article 121 |
| Article 109k | Article 122 |
| Article 109l | Article 123 |
| Article 109m | Article 124 |
| Title VIa (**) | Title VIII |
| Article 109n (*) | Article 125 |
| Article 109o (*) | Article 126 |
| Article 109p (*) | Article 127 |
| Article 109q (*) | Article 128 |
| Article 109r (*) | Article 129 |
| Article 109s (*) | Article 130 |
| Title VII | Title IX |
| Article 110 | Article 131 |
| Article 111 (repealed) | - |
| Article 112 | Article 132 |
| Article 113 | Article 133 |
| Article 114 (repealed) | - |
| Article 115 | Article 134 |
| Title VIIa (**) | Title X |
| Article 116(*) | Article 135 |
| Title VIII Chapter 1 (***) | Title XI Chapter 1 |
| Article 117 | Article 136 |
| Article 118 | Article 137 |
| Article 118a | Article 138 |
| Article 118b | Article 139 |
| Article 118c | Article 140 |
| Article 119 | Article 141 |
| Article 119a | Article 142 |
| Article 120 | Article 143 |
| Article 121 | Article 144 |
| Article 122 | Article 145 |
| Chapter 2 | Chapter 2 |
| Article 123 | Article 146 |
| Article 124 | Article 147 |
| Article 125 | Article 148 |

| Previous numbering | New numbering |
|---|---|
| Chapter 3 | Chapter 3 |
| Article 126 | Article 149 |
| Article 127 | Article 150 |
| Title IX | Title XII |
| Article 128 | Article 151 |
| Title X | Title XIII |
| Article 129 | Article 152 |
| Title XI | Title XIV |
| Article 129a | Article 153 |
| Title XII | Title XV |
| Article 129b | Article 154 |
| Article 129c | Article 155 |
| Article 129d | Article 156 |
| Title XIII | Title XVI |
| Article 130 | Article 157 |
| Title XIV | Title XVII |
| Article 130a | Article 158 |
| Article 130b | Article 159 |
| Article 130c | Article 160 |
| Article 130d | Article 161 |
| Article 130e | Article 162 |
| Title XV | Title XVIII |
| Article 130f | Article 163 |
| Article 130g | Article 164 |
| Article 130h | Article 165 |
| Article 130i | Article 166 |
| Article 130j | Article 167 |
| Article 130k | Article 168 |
| Article 130l | Article 169 |
| Article 103m | Article 170 |
| Article 130n | Article 171 |
| Article 130o | Article 172 |
| Article 130p | Article 173 |
| Article 130q (repealed) | - |
| Title XVI | Title XIX |
| Article 130r | Article 174 |
| Article 130s | Article 175 |
| Article 130t | Article 176 |
| Title XVII | Title XX |
| Article 130u | Article 177 |
| Article 130v | Article 178 |
| Article 130w | Article 179 |
| Article 130x | Article 180 |
| Article 130y | Article 181 |

| Previous numbering | New numbering |
|---|---|
| Part Four | Part Four |
| Article 131 | Article 182 |
| Article 132 | Article 183 |
| Article 133 | Article 184 |
| Article 134 | Article 185 |
| Article 135 | Article 186 |
| Article 136 | Article 187 |
| Article 136a | Article 188 |
| Part Five<br>Title I<br>Chapter 1<br>Section 1 | Part Five<br>Title I<br>Chapter 1<br>Section 1 |
| Article 137 | Article 189 |
| Article 138 | Article 190 |
| Article 138a | Article 191 |
| Article 138b | Article 192 |
| Article 138c | Article 193 |
| Article 138d | Article 194 |
| Article 138e | Article 195 |
| Article 139 | Article 196 |
| Article 140 | Article 197 |
| Article 141 | Article 198 |
| Article 142 | Article 199 |
| Article 143 | Article 200 |
| Article 144 | Article 201 |
| Section 2 | Section 2 |
| Article 145 | Article 202 |
| Article 146 | Article 203 |
| Article 147 | Article 204 |
| Article 148 | Article 205 |
| Article 149 (repealed) | - |
| Article 150 | Article 206 |
| Article 151 | Article 207 |
| Article 152 | Article 208 |
| Article 153 | Article 209 |
| Article 154 | Article 210 |
| Section 3 | Section 3 |
| Article 155 | Article 211 |
| Article 156 | Article 212 |
| Article 157 | Article 213 |
| Article 158 | Article 214 |
| Article 159 | Article 215 |
| Article 160 | Article 216 |
| Article 161 | Article 217 |
| Article 162 | Article 218 |
| Article 163 | Article 219 |

| Previous numbering | New numbering |
|---|---|
| Section 4 | Section 4 |
| Article 164 | Article 220 |
| Article 165 | Article 221 |
| Article 166 | Article 222 |
| Article 167 | Article 223 |
| Article 168 | Article 224 |
| Article 168a | Article 225 |
| Article 169 | Article 226 |
| Article 170 | Article 227 |
| Article 171 | Article 228 |
| Article 172 | Article 229 |
| Article 173 | Article 230 |
| Article 174 | Article 231 |
| Article 175 | Article 232 |
| Article 176 | Article 233 |
| Article 177 | Article 234 |
| Article 178 | Article 235 |
| Article 179 | Article 236 |
| Article 180 | Article 237 |
| Article 181 | Article 238 |
| Article 182 | Article 239 |
| Article 183 | Article 240 |
| Article 184 | Article 241 |
| Article 185 | Article 242 |
| Article 186 | Article 243 |
| Article 187 | Article 244 |
| Article 188 | Article 245 |
| Section 5 | Section 5 |
| Article 188a | Article 246 |
| Article 188b | Article 247 |
| Article 188c | Article 248 |
| Chapter 2 | Chapter 2 |
| Article 189 | Article 249 |
| Article 189a | Article 250 |
| Article 189b | Article 251 |
| Article 189c | Article 252 |
| Article 190 | Article 253 |
| Article 191 | Article 254 |
| Article 191a (*) | Article 255 |
| Article 192 | Article 256 |
| Chapter 3 | Chapter 3 |
| Article 193 | Article 257 |
| Article 194 | Article 258 |
| Article 195 | Article 259 |
| Article 196 | Article 260 |
| Article 197 | Article 261 |
| Article 198 | Article 262 |

| Previous numbering | New numbering |
|---|---|
| Chapter 4 | Chapter 4 |
| Article 198a | Article 263 |
| Article 198b | Article 264 |
| Article 198c | Article 265 |
| Chapter 5 | Chapter 5 |
| Article 198d | Article 266 |
| Article 198e | Article 267 |
| Title II | Title II |
| Article 199 | Article 268 |
| Article 200 (repealed) | - |
| Article 201 | Article 269 |
| Article 201a | Article 270 |
| Article 202 | Article 271 |
| Article 203 | Article 272 |
| Article 204 | Article 273 |
| Article 205 | Article 274 |
| Article 205a | Article 275 |
| Article 206 | Article 276 |
| Article 206a (repealed) | - |
| Article 207 | Article 277 |
| Article 208 | Article 278 |
| Article 209 | Article 279 |
| Article 209a | Article 280 |
| Part Six | Part Six |
| Article 210 | Article 281 |
| Article 211 | Article 282 |
| Article 212 (*) | Article 283 |
| Article 213 | Article 284 |
| Article 213a (*) | Article 285 |
| Article 213b (*) | Article 286 |
| Article 214 | Article 287 |
| Article 215 | Article 288 |
| Article 216 | Article 289 |
| Article 217 | Article 290 |
| Article 218 (*) | Article 291 |
| Article 219 | Article 292 |
| Article 220 | Article 293 |
| Article 221 | Article 294 |
| Article 222 | Article 295 |
| Article 223 | Article 296 |
| Article 224 | Article 297 |
| Article 225 | Article 298 |
| Article 226 (repealed) | - |
| Article 227 | Article 299 |
| Article 228 | Article 300 |
| Article 228a | Article 301 |
| Article 229 | Article 302 |
| Article 230 | Article 303 |
| Article 231 | Article 304 |
| Article 232 | Article 305 |

| Previous numbering | New numbering |
|---|---|
| Part Six—*cont.* | Part Six—*cont.* |
| Article 233 | Article 306 |
| Article 234 | Article 307 |
| Article 235 | Article 308 |
| Article 236 (*) | Article 309 |
| Article 237 (repealed) | - |
| Article 238 | Article 310 |
| Article 239 | Article 311 |
| Article 240 | Article 312 |
| Article 241 (repealed) | - |
| Article 242 (repealed) | - |
| Article 243 (repealed) | - |
| Article 244 (repealed) | - |
| Article 245 (repealed) | - |
| Article 246 (repealed) | - |
| Final Provisions | Final Provisions |
| Article 247 | Article 313 |
| Article 248 | Article 314 |

# Index